Database Design and Development

A Visual Approach

Raymond Frost
Ohio University

John Day
Ohio University

Craig Van Slyke
University of Central Florida

PEARSON

Prentice Hall

Upper Saddle River, New Jersey 07458

Library of Congress Cataloging-in-Publication Data

Frost, Raymond, [date]
    Database design and development: a visual approach / Raymond D. Frost, John Day,
Craig Van Slyke.
       p.   cm.
    Includes index.
    ISBN 0-13-035122-9
     1. Electronic commerce—Databases.   2. Business—Databases.   3. Database
design.   4. Database management.   5. Management information systems.
I. Day, John C. (John Charles), [date]   II. Van Slyke, Craig.   III. Title.
    HF5548.32.F76 2005
    005.74—dc22

2005047182

Executive Editor: Robert Horan
VP/Publisher: Jeff Shelstad
Senior Project Manager: Jeannine Ciliotta
Editorial Assistant: Ana Cordero
Manager, Product Development: Pamela Hersperger
Media Project Development Manager: Nancy Welcher
AVP/Executive Marketing Manager: Debbie Clare
Marketing Assistant: Joanna Sabella
Associate Director, Production Editorial: Judy Leale
Managing Editor: Renata Butera
Production Editor: Kelly Warsak
Permissions Supervisor: Charles Morris
Manufacturing Buyer: Michelle Klein
Design Manager: Christy Mahon
Designer: Kevin Kall
Interior Design: Karen Quigley
Cover Design: Anthony Gemmellaro
Cover Illustration: Image Bank
Illustrator (Interior): BookMasters, Inc.
Formatter, Print Production: Suzanne Duda
Composition: Integra Software Services
Full-Service Project Management: Jennifer Welsch/BookMasters, Inc.
Printer/Binder: Courier-Kendallville
Typeface: 10/12 Simoncini Garamond

Credits and acknowledgments borrowed from other sources and reproduced, with
permission, in this textbook appear on appropriate page within text.

Microsoft® and Windows® are registered trademarks of the Microsoft Corporation in the
U.S.A. and other countries. Screen shots and icons reprinted with permission from the
Microsoft Corporation. This book is not sponsored or endorsed by or affiliated with
the Microsoft Corporation.

Pearson Education LTD.
Pearson Education Singapore, Pte. Ltd
Pearson Education, Canada, Ltd
Pearson Education–Japan

Pearson Education Australia PTY, Limited
Pearson Education North Asia Ltd
Pearson Educación de Mexico, S.A. de C.V.
Pearson Education Malaysia, Pte. Ltd

10 9 8 7 6 5 4 3 2 1
ISBN 0-13-035122-9

To my sons, Raymond and Luke, who remind me that

books are more fun when they have pictures.

—Raymond Frost

To Ruth, for all your love and support, without

which none of what I do would be possible.

—John Day

To Debbie, your courage and quiet grace inspire

and strengthen me. I am truly a lucky man.

—Craig Van Slyke

BRIEF CONTENTS

CONTENTS

Chapter 5: Advanced Database Designs 89

Chapter 6: Creating Databases with Oracle Using SQL 119

Chapter 7: Retrieving Data with Oracle 145

Chapter 8: Creating Databases with Microsoft Access 203

Chapter 9: Retrieving Data with Microsoft Access 231

Chapter 10: Creating Databases with Microsoft SQL Server 297

Chapter 11: Retrieving Data with SQL Server   333

You are about to take a database course—a fascinating subject at the heart of every business system today. Dozens of books offer approaches to the course. How do you choose? The wrong book can lead to a mind-numbing course, low retention, and poor preparation for the rest of the curriculum. You need a book with a crystal-clear presentation of theory as well as an equally straightforward development methodology. You want a book that uses realistic business examples. You would like a book that is interesting and fun. This is that book.

What This Book Can Do for You

Many books teach one or more methodologies for design, another for development, and a procedure for translating between them. It's somewhat like enrolling in a Spanish course that asks you to outline in Esperanto but then write in Spanish. Esperanto, you are told, is language-independent and therefore does not influence your thinking about any one modern language. That's great, but wouldn't it be a lot less confusing to outline *and* write in Spanish?

This scenario would never happen in a modern language course, but it happens all the time in database courses—with predictable results. Students are usually asked to design in some variation of a Chen Entity Relationship Diagram (ERD) and then translate their design into a relational database. Why not just make a relational database design from the start? What's more, relational diagrams have a higher resolution than Chen ERDs. You can fit a more complex design on the same size page. Not surprisingly, many in industry have moved toward relational designs. It's time for academia to catch up.

This book simplifies the design process, but not the end result. Our design methodology is step by step, intuitive, and requires no additional translation for the development process.

Every design must be carefully matched to business requirements. To make the business examples as realistic as possible, we use examples from the Web. Designs derived from Web sites are more realistic; things don't fit quite so neatly as they do in a carefully crafted textbook example. Thus, your learning experience becomes that much more valuable, and marketable.

When you finish a database course, you should be able to progress through the systems development life cycle to design and develop a database that solves a business problem. We know employers routinely lament that MIS graduates enter the workforce unable to apply their knowledge to solve business problems. So we aimed to bridge the gaps between theory, business problem solving, and hands-on practice.

This book is also about having fun. Why can't database be the most exciting course in the curriculum? We think it can, and we'll show you how.

What You WILL Find Here

- **Relational theory:** Thorough mastery of relational theory is necessary to produce solid designs.
- **Conceptual design:** We present a step-by-step procedure for completing a conceptual database design that also meets business needs.
- **Advanced database design:** Many business problems require inheritance or recursion in their solutions. We tackle these designs head on.
- **Verification of design:** Normalization is one of the best tools to verify a design. We cover five normal forms—1NF, 2NF, 3NF, BCNF, 4NF—and give business examples of each.

- **Database development:** Practice reinforces theory. The acid test of development helps verify the accuracy of the design.
- **Data manipulation:** Multi-table joins, subqueries, grouping, and functions can all be tricky, but they are essential concepts for business reporting.
- **Application development in a three-tier architecture:** The best way to understand where a database belongs in a system is to build the system. We show you how to build a Web-enabled system using the .NET framework. It's fun and it's definitely cool.
- **Diagrams, diagrams, and more diagrams:** We use diagrams to explain design examples step by step. It isn't obvious how to get from A to Z when designing a database. Seeing all the steps along the way helps tremendously. The text's visual approach to database design is like no other book on the market. Although every database book has diagrams, the break-through development in this text is the use of multi-frame diagrams. Each frame advances one conceptual step at a time. Multi-frame diagrams are an enormous help to learning because they allow for visual comparisons between each step in the design or query.

What You WON'T Find Here

- **Multiple design methodologies:** We pick one methodology and stick with it. Think relational, design relational. We even encountered one book that shows Chen, Crow's foot, IDEF1X, Rein85, and relational diagrams all in the same book! Sound confusing? It is.
- **Legacy database models:** It is beyond the scope of an introductory course to introduce hierarchical, network, and object-oriented models—especially when that discussion will just leave students hanging as to how those models are really different, and how one would translate among them. Face it: It's a relational world.
- **Emerging topics:** Star schemas, data warehousing, data mining, and so forth are fascinating, but ultimately not topics for an introductory book.

 # To the Instructor

This book may be used as a text for the introductory database course. It will also appeal to professionals who want to learn this topic one step at a time in an integrated framework. No familiarity with a programming language is required.

The book is targeted to students and practitioners who want to learn how to design rather than just manipulate relational databases. Several popular books shed light on the problems, opportunities, and techniques of database design, and we have used them in our classes with some success. This textbook is different in many important ways.

1. **Its visual approach to database design is unique.** Students are taught to visualize the output *prior* to designing a database. Examples are all illustrated with multiple diagrams. The diagrams appeal to the visual learner and help reinforce the text.
2. **The text makes extensive use of e-commerce examples.**

   - The Web builds interest, because it is a natural attention draw.
   - Students can *experience* real business problems rather than the sanitized examples often found in textbooks.
   - Businesses don't put their databases online—students see only the front-end application for the database. This challenges them to reverse engineer the underlying database by looking at the requirements of the front-end application—a true exercise in critical thinking.

3. **The text progresses at a comfortable pace.** Although the examples become progressively difficult, they do so in logical sequence.
4. **Students are taught to present their designs.** The are taught not only how to design, but also how to present the results of their designs in a format that makes it easy for them to spot their own errors and for the professor to critique their work.
5. **Each example follows a complete cycle,** from design through to the acid test of development.

Pedagogical Features

We included many features to enhance learning in *Database Design and Development: A Visual Approach*. Based on years of teaching experience, we've identified the best practices in university teaching and integrated items that work well for us.

- **Conceptual focus:** In each chapter we review several database concepts and then show how to design and implement using those concepts.
- **Learning objectives:** Each chapter begins with a list of objectives that, after studying the chapter, students should be able to accomplish. Given our active learning preference, the objectives are behavioral in nature.
- **Multiple diagrams in each chapter:** Wherever possible we show actual database tables to provide an example of the concept under review. The diagrams' captions provide a useful visual review.
- **Chapter summaries:** Each chapter ends with a summary. While these summaries capture the major points, they were not created so that students can read them instead of the chapter.
- **Key concepts and terms**: Also at the end of each chapter is a list of important terms and concepts in the chapter to assist the student in checking for understanding.
- **Review questions, discussion questions, and design exercises:** The review questions at the end of the chapter aim to facilitate recall of chapter concepts. The discussion questions are geared toward higher levels of learning, such as synthesis and evaluation. The design questions integrate all levels of learning in a problem-based format.

Book Organization

The book begins with an introduction to the role of database in business. Almost all businesses today use relational databases. Chapter 2 covers relational database theory. A strong understanding of database theory leads to sound database designs. In Chapter 3, students are taught a step-by-step methodology to create good designs. Chapter 4 discusses normalization as a way to verify the accuracy of a database design. But this is not your daddy's normalization. The explanations are clearly presented with plenty of examples. Chapter 5 looks at advanced design topics commonly encountered in business. These include inheritance and recursion, which are presented with informative and sometimes entertaining examples.

The next six chapters are dedicated to mastering SQL on your particular platform; they cover, in turn, Oracle, MS Access, and MS SQL Server. Chapter 6 creates Oracle databases; Chapter 7 shows how to query those databases. Chapter 8 creates MS Access databases; Chapter 9 shows how to query those databases. Chapter 10 creates MS SQL Server databases; Chapter 11 shows how to query those databases.

The last two chapters show how to design Web-enabled applications using .NET. The applications are built using a three-tier architecture—client, application, and database. Chapter 12 covers reporting from a database via the Web. Chapter 13 shows how to create Web forms for data input and manipulation.

Supplements

All support materials for the text are available online at **www.prenhall.com/frost**.

Instructor's Manual

The Instructor's Manual not only features answers to questions and exercises in the text, but also contains teaching objectives and suggestions, plus additional pedagogical materials.

Test Item File and TestGen

The Test Item File is a comprehensive collection of true-false, multiple-choice, fill-in-the-blank, and essay questions arranged by chapter. TestGen, a computerized test bank, is available on the Web site with downloadable conversions for WebCT, BlackBoard, and Course Compass courses.

PowerPoint Slides

Electronic color slides illustrate and build upon key concepts in the text. We are very excited about the slides for the course. They make use of animation, step-by-step sequencing, and even a little humor to step students through the design process.

Image Library

The Image Library is an impressive resource for instructors: Nearly every figure in the text is provided, organized by chapter. Images can be easily imported into Microsoft PowerPoint to create new presentations or add to existing ones.

Companion Web Site (www.prenhall.com/frost)

A dedicated Web site for the text provides a dynamic complement to text material. The site includes all supplements (Instructor's Manual, Test Item File and TestGen, PowerPoint slides, Image Library) plus Glossary, updates, errata, and additional projects. Instructor supplements can be downloaded from the secure faculty section of the Web site. On the student section, students can access such resources as PowerPoint slides, Glossary, and additional projects and updates.

Acknowledgments

We would like to first and foremost thank our students, whose patience and feedback has lead to the refinement of this text. One student in particular, Ms. Jacqueline Pike, was incredibly instrumental in helping to conceptualize the course and the text. Ms. Pike is a graduate of the Honors Tutorial College at Ohio University. She is currently a graduate student at the University of Pittsburgh. Jacqueline is also a Microsoft Most Valuable Professional, and in our view, a most valuable student and colleague.

Although we'd like to acknowledge all our other students by name, we'll limit ourselves to some special ones over the years—Mike Hajoway, Amanda Hannah, and Kelly Stypula. We also thank our colleagues Sean McGann, Vic Matta, and Wayne Huang, who taught the course and provided us with valuable feedback

Last but not least we thank the many faculty members who took valuable time out of their schedules to review the text:

Barbara Abdul-Karim, *Prince George's Community College*
Reza Barkhi, *Virginia Polytechnic Institute and State University*
David Chao, *San Francisco State*
Elizabeth Falcone, *George Mason University*
Edward J. Garrity, *Canisius College*
Mike Godfrey, *California State University, Long Beach*
Tim Hilboldt, *DeVry University, Kansas City*
Gail Kaiser, *Columbia University*
Gigi Kelly, *College of William and Mary*
Rashmi Malhotra, *St. Joseph's University*
Rick Mathieu, *St. Louis University*
Margaret McCoey, *LaSalle University*
C. Dallas McGee, *Wor-Wic Community College*
Claire McInerney, *Rutgers University, New Brunswick*
Michelle Moore, *Texas A&M*
Bruce Myers, *Austin Peay State University*
Linda Preece, *Southern Illinois University, Carbondale*
Jerry Ross, *Linfield College*
Kenneth Rowe, *Purdue University*
Tim Shea, *University of Massachusetts, Dartmouth*
Diane Walz, *University of Texas at San Antonio*
Virginia Werner, *Lansing Community College*

Raymond Frost is a Professor of Management Information Systems at Ohio University. He has published scholarly papers in the information systems and marketing fields. Frost is co-author of *E-Marketing* and *Building Effective Web Sites.* Dr. Frost teaches database, systems analysis and design, and information analysis and design courses. He has received numerous teaching awards, including the University Professor and Presidential Teaching awards from Ohio University. Dr. Frost is currently working on publications in data modeling, pedagogy, and information analysis and design. He earned a doctorate in business administration and an M.S. in computer science at the University of Miami (Florida), and received his B.A. in philosophy at Swarthmore College.

John Day is the O'Bleness Professor and Chair of the MIS department at Ohio University. He has published articles in the *Journal of Computer Information Systems* and the *Information Resource Management Journal.* Dr. Day has also published five textbooks in MIS, including *Implementing Databases in Oracle 9i.* He teaches courses in database management, local area networking, systems analysis and design, and programming. He has extensive experience with problem-based group projects and has implemented several technological platforms to support that learning approach. He is a charter member of the Association for Information Systems and a founding member of AIS, SIG on IS in Asia Pacific. Dr. Day holds a B.A., M.S., and Ph.D. from Ohio University.

Craig Van Slyke is an Assistant Professor of Management Information Systems at the University of Central Florida, where he teaches courses in database, managing information technology, and electronic commerce. Dr. Van Slyke holds a Ph.D. in Information Systems from the University of South Florida, an M.B.A. from Appalachian State University, and a B.S.B.A. from the University of Central Florida. In addition to his academic experience, he spent ten years in the information technology industry. His current research interests focus on perceptual issues related to business-to-consumer electronic commerce, and information systems education.

The Role of Databases in Electronic Business

Introduction

Learning Objectives

After completing this chapter, you will be able to:

- Describe the basic network, hardware, software, and content components commonly found in organizational systems.
- Explain the concepts of client/server and three-tier architectures.
- Define the terms *database* and *database management system.*
- Define the terms *record, field,* and *primary key.*
- Explain why databases are important to business.

For decades, organizations have been using information and communications technologies to enhance their operations. Today, most organizations are heavily dependent on their computer systems; without them, the organizations would not be able to operate effectively. Many different technologies must work together to implement a successful organizational system. One of the most important of these technologies is the **database** that sits at the core of the system. Any interactive organizational system uses some sort of database. When you check the price of a textbook online, you are accessing a database. If you register for classes electronically, you are using a database-enabled system. Buying tickets to a concert also requires a database.

The goal of this book is to teach you how to design, build, and use databases. The principles you learn can be applied to computer applications in almost any organization. In this chapter, we set the stage by giving you a short overview of organizational systems and the various components that come together to enable these systems. This overview will help you understand where databases fit into the picture. Chapter 1 also introduces the concept of a database and defines some important database-related terms. Then, the chapter explains the importance of databases to organizational systems and provides some examples of how databases are used in traditional and electronic business (e-business) systems.

Components of an Organizational System

When we talk about organizational systems in this book, we are primarily concerned with computer applications that help the organization with its processes. Examples of such systems range from automatic teller machines to payroll systems to the online catalogs of Web merchants. Most of these systems share a number of components, all of which must work together for an organizational system to work properly. A complete, detailed discussion of all of these components is beyond the scope of this text. Rather, we provide an overview of the key components in a typical organizational system. Keep in mind that the exact components included vary from system to system. However, the components discussed in this section are included in most organizational applications. We break down our discussion of organizational system components into the network, the hardware, the software, and the content. Understanding how these components fit together helps you understand the role of databases in organizational systems. Also, this knowledge will be helpful when we discuss Web-enabled databases in later chapters.

Network

Organizational systems typically make use of some sort of communications network. Many systems today use the Internet, but organizations also use other types of networks. For example, many large organizations use private networks to engage in *electronic data interchange (EDI)*.

There are many different components to a network, including bridges, routers, and the transmission media, among others. One important aspect of a network is the communications protocols used. For example, the Internet uses a set of protocols called *Transmission Control Protocol/Internet Protocol (TCP/IP)*. Using TCP/IP ensures that all computers on the Internet can interact (assuming they follow the protocols correctly). It does not matter who manufactured the computer or what operating system it is running. As long as it "speaks" TCP/IP and has the proper connection to the Internet, the computer can access information from any server on the Internet (of course, the user must have authorization to access some servers).

Hardware

An organizational system typically includes different types of hardware. Among the most important hardware components of an organizational system are the computers. Some computers act as *servers,* which means that they provide services to other computers. The computers that request services are called clients. Most organizational systems follow multitier architectures. What is a multitier architecture? Perhaps you have heard of the most basic multitier architecture, which is the client/server architecture. Let's go over a brief explanation of client/server, then move on to the more complex three-tier architecture.

Exhibit 1-1 illustrates a **client/server architecture.** The client has two jobs, presentation and requests. Presentation is also known as the interface; it simply gives the user a way to interact with the computer and also formats data received from the server in a way that is useful to the user. The client also makes requests of the server and the server simply responds to requests made by clients. Of course, although this process sounds simple, in practice it can be quite complicated.

To help you better understand how a client/server system works, we will use a well-known example, the Web. You may not have known this, but when you use the Web, you are using a multitier architecture. We will keep things simple for now, and just have two tiers (a client and a single server), as shown in Exhibit 1-1.

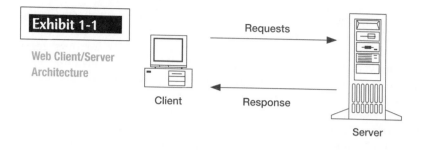

Exhibit 1-1

Web Client/Server
Architecture

Suppose you want to use your favorite Web search engine. We will use Google.com in our example. You are already connected to the Internet and you have your Web browser running. So, you simply type Google's address in the proper place in your browser and hit Enter or click Go. This is an example of the client performing its presentation task. The browser gives you a place to enter a Web address and a way to instruct the browser to "go to" that address. What actually happens when you click Go is that the browser sends a request to Google's Web server for the Google home page. The home page is actually a file in a special language called Hypertext Markup Language *(HTML)*. The Web server responds to your browser's request by sending the data that makes up the home page across the Internet to your computer (the client). Your Web browser then takes the data (in the form of an HTML file) and converts all the codes to make the Google home page look the way you expect it to. This is another part of the presentation function: making data appear in a useful form. To summarize, the client (your computer running the Web browser software) gives you a reasonable way to make a request from the server, then sends that request across the Internet to the Google Web server. The server then sends the requested data back across the Internet to your computer, where the Web browser formats the Web page for you. This process is shown graphically in Exhibit 1-2.

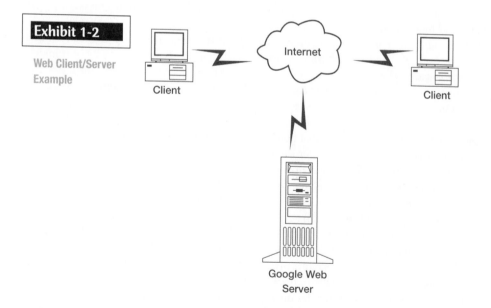

Exhibit 1-2

Web Client/Server
Example

Now that you understand the basic client/server setup, let's make things a bit more complex. Suppose that you are doing some online shopping. Your Web browser still makes requests the same way and formats the response data just as it did in the last example. This time, however, there is more than one server involved.

Just as in the last example, you enter the Web address for your favorite online music store. Your browser sends the request to the store's Web server, and the store's home page appears on your computer's screen. One of the CDs shown on the home page is by an artist you like, but you are not sure which songs are on the CD. You know that you can see the track listing of the CD. So you click the title of the CD, which you recognize is also a hyperlink to the CD's details. Your Web browser recognizes your click as a request for a particular resource, and your browser sends a request to the Web server. This time, however, the Web server recognizes the request as something that needs to access data from a database. The Web server takes your request and passes it along to a database server. The database server looks at the request, accesses the data required to service your request (the track listing and other details about the CD), and sends it to the Web server. The Web server uses the data to build an HTML file that is then sent across the network to your computer. Your Web browser formats the HTML into a Web page containing the requested track listing.

One additional point must be made regarding clients and servers. Although we often talk about clients and servers in terms of computers, in actuality, they are *processes* rather than separate computers. It is possible for both client and server processes to run on the same computer, although this situation is not common for large-scale applications. The important point to remember is that the various tiers in a multitier computing architecture refer to processes, rather than individual computers.

Software

If you read the previous section carefully, and if you already know a bit about client/server systems, you may recognize that several software components are implicitly mentioned. For example, *your Web browser* is more correctly referred to as your Web browser client software. The term *client software* refers to computer programs that perform client processes. Another good example is your electronic mail software. Unless you are using a Web-based email system, such as Hotmail, when you view email messages, you are using email client software. There is also email server software running on a computer at your email service provider. Other common client software you may have used includes instant messaging, chat software, and media players (such as RealPlayer).

As you might have imagined, a variety of server software is also used in organizational systems. For each of the client software examples in the previous paragraph, there is matching server software. There is Web server software, email server software, instant messaging server software, and media server software, to mention just a few. Remember that client processes make requests of server processes, and server processes satisfy those requests. Put in terms of software, your Web browser software requests data from Web servers, which satisfy those requests. The same basic idea holds for email and the other examples.

There are two other types of server software that are critical to most organizational systems. Application servers hold application software that implements the business logic of an organization. **Business logic** is simply the set of rules that govern an organization's processes. For example, when you order a CD from a Web site, business logic dictates that your order should not be accepted unless the particular CD you ordered is in stock. Of course, most organizations have a huge number of these rules, which can also be very complex. Computer programs called *application software* are used to implement many of these rules.

Database servers are also very important to organizational systems. As you will see throughout this book, data is crucial to organizational systems. Database servers are used to provide data to the software that resides on application servers. Two major goals of this book are to help you understand how to design databases that can properly satisfy application requests, and to help you learn to write code that can access the data.

In combination, application and database servers represent an extension of the basic client/server model we discussed earlier. The client/server model is extended by dividing up the server tasks into two tiers, the application and data tiers. Sometimes the application tier is called the *logic tier*. So now, instead of two tiers (client and server), we have three tiers (client, application server, and data server), a situation that is called **three-tier architecture.** Exhibit 1-3 illustrates the three-tier architecture graphically.

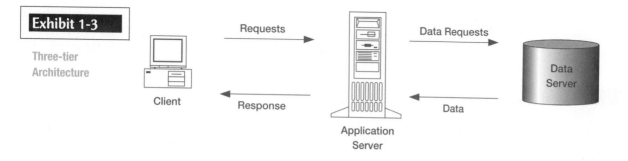

Exhibit 1-3

Three-tier
Architecture

Client — Requests → Application Server — Data Requests → Data Server
Data Server — Data → Application Server — Response → Client

Content

Content is important to organizational systems. Consider the systems of a Web merchant. Content attracts users and helps retain visitors. It is really not that different from what happens in the offline world. Think about the following two situations.

A new music store opens in your neighborhood. You are into music, so, of course, you check it out. Walking into the store, you notice that the store does not seem to have many CDs. Amazingly, as you're browsing through the meager contents of the store, you realize that the few CDs the store does have are not displayed in any organized way, as far as you can tell. The CDs also seem to be of poor quality; most of the jewel cases are cracked. You spend a few minutes browsing through the randomly organized store and finally give up all hope of finding anything worthwhile, so you leave the store.

In the second situation, a new bookstore opens in your area. You read a lot, so you decide to visit the store to see what it has to offer. Walking into the store, you are stunned by the number of books displayed in the store. There are literally thousands of them! Picking a few random books off the shelves, you notice that all of the books are in excellent condition; they have no bent pages or scuffed covers. You are getting ready to take a summer trip to the coast near Barcelona, Spain, so you decide to see what sort of travel books the store has. A prominently displayed store directory points you to the travel book section. When you arrive in the proper section, you are happy to see that the books are logically organized by country, then by city or region. This organization allows you to quickly find the Spain section, then to locate a book on Barcelona. After flipping through the book, you buy it, and you leave the store happy.

Which of the two stores are you more likely to visit again? Most people are much more likely to return to the bookstore. Why? First, the bookstore simply has more to offer in the way of products. Second, the overall quality of the books is much better than that of the CDs. Finally, the books in the bookstore are much better organized, which makes finding something of interest much easier.

Now let's state these three advantages of the bookstore a little differently. The bookstore has more content (the first factor), the content is of higher quality (the second factor), and the content is easier to locate (the third factor). Business Web sites are affected by similar factors. An e-business site that has more high-quality, easy-to-locate content is much more likely to retain visitors. Visitors are also likely to spread the word about the site, which helps attract more visitors.

How is content related to databases? On most e-business Web sites, much of the site's content is stored in a variety of databases. Database management systems are used to organize and retrieve the content. A large online merchant such as Amazon.com uses databases to store product information, customer recommendations, order data, customer information, and the like. When properly designed and built, these databases work together smoothly, making it easy for visitors to quickly and easily locate the desired information.

To summarize, content is an important component of organizational systems, and most organizational systems have a large volume of content that must be organized and retrieved. Databases store the content, and database management systems help retrieve the content. Therefore, databases and database management systems are critical components of organizational systems.

Now that you have some understanding of why databases are important to organizational systems, let's get more specific about exactly what a database is. In the following section, we provide a definition of the term *database* and describe some different types of databases.

What Is a Database?

Put simply, a database is a collection of data that is used by a system. Traditionally, *data* referred to the values stored in databases. But today, the data might be a song, a picture, or a video clip in addition to a value. A **database management system** is a collection of programs that help store, manage, and use the collections of data, regardless of the form. More formally, a database management system is software that creates, maintains, and uses databases. Popular large-scale database management systems include Oracle, Microsoft SQL Server, and IBM DB2. You may have used a smaller-scale database management system such as Microsoft Access.

Most databases used today fall into a category called **relational databases,** which organize data in a set of overlapping tables. Although relational databases are the focus of this book, there are other types of databases. For example, many older systems use *flat-file* databases, which organize data as one big table. There are also *object-oriented, hierarchical,* and *network* databases.

To learn about relational databases, it is helpful to understand some key terms and concepts. To help you understand these terms and concepts, it is useful to picture a table of data, as illustrated in Exhibit 1-4, which shows a table of customer data.

Exhibit 1-4

Table of Data

CustomerID	FirstName	LastName	Email
1	Joe	Cary	joe@isp.com
2	Sally	Reid	sally@school.edu
3	Fred	Wilson	fred@nfp.org
4	Juan	Ramerez	juan@isp.com
5	Ram	Kumar	ram@isp.com
6	Natasha	Karamazov	natasha@uni.edu.ru
7	Debbie	Harry	harry@music.org
8	Chet	Vance	chet@army.mil
9	Mary	Johnson	mary@pcfb.org
10	Jean	Smith	jean@bowling.com

Field — Primary Key — Record/Row

A table is organized into rows and columns. Each row contains data about a single customer, with the columns containing a specific item of data. Each cell in table contains a **data item** or single piece of data. Rows are also called **records,** and columns are sometimes called **fields.** Each row in the table is identified by a column or set of columns that we know will be unique. In database terms, a unique identifier is called a **key.** A table can have more than one key, but only one is selected to be the **primary key,** which serves as the identifier for that table. Each of these concepts is identified in the table shown in Exhibit 1-4.

Relational databases follow a set of very specific rules that ensure the data contained in the databases will be consistent. Note that we did not say "correct." The rules just make sure that you will not have inconsistent data. We will discuss these rules in detail in Chapters 2 and 4.

Why Are Databases Important to Business?

Data is at the core of most business computer applications. In fact, in the early days of computerization, the department in charge of computer applications was often called *data processing*. Even though the applications of today are much more sophisticated and capable, data still sits at the center of most business software. Because data is central to business applications, and databases are used to store businesses' data, by extension, databases are critical to business applications. In this section, we provide two examples that illustrate the importance of databases to businesses.

Both of our examples fall into the category of *transaction processing applications,* which simply means that they focus on processing groups of operations that are all related to a business event, such as a sale or an order. Even though our examples focus on transaction processing, databases are also a critical element to other types of organizational systems, such as decision support systems. Also, for each of our examples, it is necessary to limit the scope of the example. To keep the discussion manageable, we will only discuss a few of the business transactions that might be supported by a database. Hopefully, this limited discussion will be sufficient to illustrate the importance of databases to businesses.

General Business Example

The first example comes from a small bookstore, which we will call the Reading Fool bookstore. We will look at just a single transaction, ordering books from a supplier. The form Reading Fool uses to organize the data about each order is shown in Exhibit 1-5.

Exhibit 1-5

Reading Fool
Bookstore
Purchase Order
Form

Order No.:	12548		Date:	11/3/2002
Supplier ID:	87459		Contact:	Sally Jones
Name:	Bithlo Books			
Address:	27 E. SR 50		Acct. No.:	707-113
	Bithlo, FL 32158		Placed by:	Alex Smith

ISBN	Title	Quantity	Cost	Extended
1-55860-294-1	Database Modeling & Design	5	10.00	50.00
3-12368-998-2	Pinky & The Brain Guide to the Outback	7	12.00	84.00
2-78912-437-5	Sports Heroes of the 1700s	2	16.25	32.50
	TOTAL COST			166.50

Now let's extract the individual data items shown in the form. Exhibit 1-6 shows the data contained in the order form from Exhibit 1-5.

Exhibit 1-6

Data Items for
Orders to
Suppliers

Category	Data Items
Supplier	Supplier ID, supplier name, street, city, state, postal code, phone number, Reading Fool account number
Supplier contact	Contact ID, first name, last name, phone number
Book	ISBN (a unique ID for books), title
Order	Order number, order date, order total
Employee	First name, last name (of the employee placing the order)
Order details	ISBN, quantity ordered, cost, extended price (quantity times cost)

Notice how many different data items are involved in this relatively simple transaction. Even though we did not include payment and account data (other than account number), there is still quite a bit of data that is required to carry out the transaction. We must include data about the supplier, the book, and the order. Additional information is required about the supplier (the specific person we contact to place the order) and the order (the details of each line item included in the order).

Also, notice that each item of data can be placed in a category according to the thing described by the data. In database terms, each of these things is referred to as an *entity*. An **entity** is simply something we want to store data about. Identifying entities and the data that goes along with them is the subject of Chapters 3 and 5. Eventually, each of these entities becomes a table in the database. We discuss how to translate the entities and relationships among them into tables in Chapter 3, whereas creating and putting data into the actual tables are covered in later chapters.

Even a relatively simple form, such as Reading Fool's order form, contains data about several different entities. In this single form, there is data about six different entities. A typical business may have dozens of such forms, each of which contains data about one or more entities. Although there is often overlap among the data represented on various forms, an organization may have thousands of different items of data. For example, the University of Central Florida has over six thousand data items stored in its databases. Although this sounds like a large number, it is actually quite typical.

All of this data must be stored in a way that makes it easy to retrieve and use. If errors are to be avoided, the data must also be stored consistently. For example, we do not want to store three different addresses for the same supplier. Following the rules of relational databases ensures that we do not have these kinds of inconsistencies. Designing a database (or databases) that supports all of the operations and decision making that occur in an organization is a complex, time-consuming, and difficult task. Even when the design is completed, the database must be implemented and maintained, both of which are also complex tasks. Throughout this book, we will show you how to complete various tasks associated with designing and building a database.

Now let's look at another example. This one has two differences from the first example. First, it is a "real life" example. Second, it is an example that comes from the online world.

E-business Example

For the e-business example, we use the shopping cart of Amazon.com, the online retailer. An example of this shopping cart is shown in Exhibit 1-7. Note that some information about the customer and credit cards has been intentionally changed for privacy reasons.

Exhibit 1-7

Amazon.com
Customer Order
Form

Source: ©2005
Amazon.com, Inc. All
Rights Reserved.

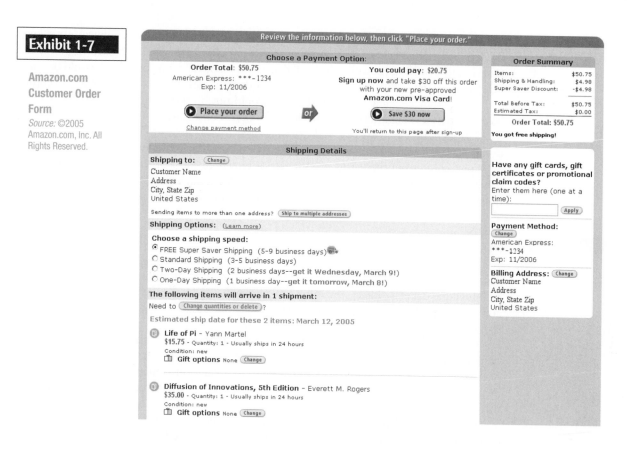

If you compare the Reading Fool purchase order form and the Amazon.com shopping cart, you may note some similarities and differences. Both forms contain data about several entities. However, the entities differ between the two forms, despite the fact that there are some common entities (order details and order, for example). The Amazon.com form also seems more complex, especially in terms of the order data items. Exhibit 1-8 shows some of the data items from the Amazon.com form. Note that there are some items in the table that are not on the form. These items are included because there are data items that are used by various applications that do not need to be viewed by the customer at the time the order is placed. Examples include order number, item number, and order date. From personal experience, we can tell you that Amazon.com does, in fact, keep track of these data items.

Exhibit 1-8

Data Items for
Customer Orders

Category	Data Items
Customer	Customer ID, first name, last name
Shipping address	Street, city, state, postal code, country
Billing address	Street, city, state, postal code, country
Order	Order number, date, shipping speed, shipping method, shipping charge, pre-tax subtotal, tax amount, total, promotion code, estimated ship date, payment method, type, account number, expiration date
Item	Item number, title, author
Order detail	Item number, quantity, price, shipping time, gift option

As was the case with the Reading Fool example, Amazon.com's databases must keep track of and make available all of the data shown in Exhibit 1-8. Again, the data shown in the table is only a small portion of the overall data required by Amazon.com; there would be many other items of data concerning other types of products, suppliers, business partners, inventory, facilities, employees, and other entities. We would not be surprised if Amazon.com's databases contained thousands of data items and millions of records.

Throughout this book, we will use a number of similar examples to illustrate how to design, implement, and use databases. To make things more concrete for you, many of our examples come from the world of e-business. However, most of the skills and knowledge gained through the e-business examples will transfer quite well to non-e-business applications. In the next section, we provide a brief overview of the organization of the book.

 ## Organization of the Text

This book is organized around three major activities that occur in the life cycle of a database. Although the database life cycle can be broken down into smaller parts, there are three main activities that take place: design, implementation, and use. We organized the book around these three activities.

Chapters 2 through 5 discuss database design. Before getting too deeply into database design, however, it is useful to understand the database development environment and some of the theory behind relational database design. Chapter 2 introduces the database environment, defines a number of important terms, and provides an overview of relational database theory.

We can break database design into two broad categories, conceptual design and logical design. When engaging in conceptual design, you do not need to worry about the rules of relational databases we mentioned earlier. Conceptual design is implementation free, meaning that the exact means of implementation is not a concern. All that you are worried about during conceptual design are the entities about which the database must store data, what data must be stored, and how the entities are related to each other. Conceptual design is covered in Chapters 3 and 5. Chapter 4 discusses the important topic of normalization, which is the process of ensuring that a database design meets the relational rules. Violating these rules can result in data inconsistencies.

Database implementation and use are covered in pairs of chapters that are organized according to the database management system used to implement the database design. Chapter 6 discusses how to create database tables using Oracle. Inserting, deleting, and updating the data in Oracle tables are also covered in Chapter 6. Chapter 7 describes how to retrieve data from a database using Oracle's version of *structured query language (SQL)*. Chapters 8 and 9 parallel this content but use Microsoft Access as the target database management system. Using Microsoft SQL Server for creating and using a database is covered in Chapters 10 and 11. It is likely that your instructor will only assign one of these chapter pairs, but you may wish to explore the other database management systems on your own using the other chapter pairs.

Increasingly, databases are accessed through *Web front ends*. In other words, more organizations are allowing users to retrieve and manipulate data through Web pages, rather than through direct interaction with the database management system using SQL. Chapter 12 describes using a Web page to access data, and Chapter 13 discusses updating the data in a database through a Web page.

From Chapter 2 on, each chapter provides a number of useful learning aids. First, each chapter has a glossary of key terms introduced in that chapter. Second, review and discussion questions and practice exercises are provided. By completing the review and discussion questions, you perform a self-check of your understanding of the conceptual material covered in the chapter. Finally, most chapters also include hands-on design and implementation exercises. These practice exercises allow you to put the concepts of the chapter into practice.

SUMMARY

- Most organizational computer systems have elements in common, including communications networks, various types of hardware, a variety of software, and content that must be organized and retrieved.
- Today, most organizational systems use a multitier architecture, which means that computing tasks are divided among different processes.
- A client/server architecture is a multitier architecture with two tiers. The client tier is responsible for the interface and making requests from the server. The server tier responds to requests from the client.
- The Web is a good example of a multitier architecture.
- A three-tier architecture includes clients, an application server, and a data server.
- The application server holds application software that embodies the business logic of the organization. The application server interacts with clients and requests data from a data server.
- Organizing various types of content is a key challenge for most organizations.
- Databases help with the organization and use of content.
- A database is a collection of data.
- Relational databases store data in sets of overlapping tables, which organize data into rows and columns.

KEY TERMS

Business logic. Rules that govern an organization's processes.

Client/server architecture. A computing arrangement where tasks are divided between clients, and which handles presentation (interface) tasks and makes requests from servers, which then respond to those requests.

Data item. A single piece of data.

Database. An organized collection of data.

Database management system. Collection of programs that help store, manage, and use the collections of data.

Entity. Something about which we want to store data.

Field. A single piece of data.

Key. A field or set of fields that uniquely identifies a record.

Primary key. The key used to uniquely identify a record in a table.

Record. A collection of related data items that are specific to an instance of an entity.

Relational database. A database that organizes data into overlapping tables.

Three-tier architecture. A computing architecture that consists of clients; application servers, which enable business logic; and data servers, which provide data to the application servers.

EXERCISES

Review

1. What is a database?
2. What are the four components of an organizational system?
3. Briefly describe the functions performed by each tier of the client/server architecture.
4. What is the function of the client and the server in client/server architecture?
5. Name the tiers of three-tier architecture. Briefly describe the functions performed by each tier.
6. What is an entity?
7. What is business logic?
8. What is a relational database?
9. How do the following terms relate to one another: record, table, field, primary key?
10. What purpose does a primary key serve in a table?

Discuss

1. Think about a time when you interacted with an organizational system. Describe how you used the system. List the items of data that were used by the system.
2. Why is content important to organizations?
3. Why are databases critical to organizational systems?
4. Describe a situation where poorly organized content, or a lack of content, hindered you when completing some task.
5. Suppose you wanted to order a compact disc from a Web merchant. Describe how this process illustrates the concept of three-tier architecture.

Practice

1. Organize the following list of fields into the given entities.

   ■ Fields: first name, title, room, day, time, credit hours, last name
   ■ Entities: student, course, section

2. Look at your latest grade report. Identify the fields and entities represented in the report. Match each field with the appropriate entity.
3. Consider a table of data about employees. Which of the following fields are keys? Which one would you choose as the primary key? Why?

   Employees: First name, last name, phone number, social security number, employee ID, date of birth, date hired, middle name

4. Identify the fields and entities represented in the invoice form shown in Exhibit 1-9. Match each field with the appropriate entity.

Invoice Form

Invoice No.:	0001	Order Date:	September 26, 2005
Customer No.:	1058		
Name:	Sally Tooloud	Sales Rep ID:	005
Address:	828 East SR 50	Rep. Name:	Bart Terwillinger
	Bithlo, FL 32815		

ItemID	Description	Price	Qty	Ext
0001	SuperLoud Speakers	225.00	2	450.00
0052	SuperClearReceiver w/CD	400.00	1	400.00
0795	SuperLoud Powered Subwoofer	250.00	1	250.00
	ORDER TOTAL			1100.00

5. Identify the fields and entities represented in the tutoring client activity report shown in Exhibit 1-10. Match each field with the appropriate entity.

Tutoring Client Activity Report

Client:	Jane Doe	Type:	Monthly
Address:	123 West First Ave.	Phone:	407-000-0000
	Christmas, FL 32709	Email:	doejane@isp.net

Date	CourseID	Course Name	Tutor	Hours	Comments
09/07/05	317	Database	Jane Smith	1.5	Still not getting normalization
09/16/05	317	Database	Larry Johnson	2.0	Seems to understand normalization now
09/25/05	221	Acct 1	Ram Kumar	1.5	Understands debit/credit idea
10/11/05	305	Finance 1	Sam Cary	1.0	Needs more work on PV

Relational Theory

Introduction

This chapter introduces the theory behind the relational database. Many concepts are introduced that will be referred to throughout the text.

Relational databases are only one piece of an information system that includes people, policies, computers, and application software. The goal is to make the system appear very simple and easy to use.

It is very unusual to give end users direct access to a database, because many end users would find the database too difficult to use. Additionally, the end user could actually do some damage, either by retrieving incorrect information or by corrupting existing information. Most businesses write programs that intercede between the end user and the database. These programs produce forms and reports.

Forms are used for data input. In today's world, the forms are increasingly written in HTML. For example, upon checkout from an e-commerce site, the user supplies billing and shipping information. The user completes the form on the browser and clicks the Submit button. The user then receives an order confirmation screen.

Learning Objectives

After completing this chapter, you will be able to:

- Describe the relational model.
- Identify the symbols used in an entity relationship diagram (ERD).
- Define and select a primary key.
- Explain the role of foreign keys.
- Identify and apply integrity rules.
- Explain the advantages of relational databases.

Relational Model

The relational model is perhaps the simplest and most intuitive data model ever developed; that is part of its appeal. The entire model is based upon tables with rows and columns. In mathematics, tables are called *relations,* and hence the term *relational model* is used. Other equivalent terms are shown in Exhibit 2-1.

Exhibit 2-1

Relational
Model–Equivalent
Terms

Table = Relation   Column = Field = Attribute

ORDER

id	date	customer
001	010188	1111 ←——— Row = Record = Tuple
002	020389	2222
003	030389	1111

Relational Database Management System (RDBMS)

The **relational database management system (RDBMS)** is the software that runs on the database server. This software allows for creation and maintenance of databases. The RDBMS protects the data both against unauthorized access and against authorized access that inadvertently tries to corrupt the data. The command language used to communicate with the RDBMS is **structured query language (SQL).**

This command language has a simple syntax and is compact. However, it is deceptively powerful. Most RDBMSs also enable you to use a graphical interface to communicate with the RDBMS. The graphical interface is sometimes called *query by example (QBE),* although queries represent just a piece of the interface's functionality. Personal computer products, such as Microsoft Access, feature the graphical interface because it is easy to use. Professionals prefer using SQL.

Database Administrator (DBA)

The **database administrator (DBA)** is the person who runs the RDBMS. The DBA creates and maintains the databases using the RDBMS. The DBA may also grant access to users to create and maintain their own databases, such as the databases that you might create for your class. On a single-user system, the end user is also the DBA.

Entity Relationship Diagrams

Databases must be carefully designed to ensure reliable and valid data storage. The most common way to design a database is by creating a model of the data items and their interrelationships. A **conceptual model** is a generic description of the data that is not tied to any specific database software product (Access, Oracle, SQL Server, SYBASE, DB2, etc.). The most common method of representing a conceptual model is through the creation of a diagram, which is a pictorial representation of the database. Diagrams make it much easier to comprehend the relationships among items in the database.

Databases are designed as a group of related entities. **Entities** are like nouns—they are the persons, places, or things being modeled in the world (e.g., employees, orders, or books). **Relationships** are like verbs—they show action or possession (e.g., a customer *places* orders; an employee *has* dependents; a doctor *treats* patients; and a patient can *visit* multiple doctors). **Attributes** are like adjectives that describe an entity. Examples of attributes are identification numbers, names, phone numbers, and so forth. A visual model of the entities and their relationships is called an **entity relationship diagram (ERD, or ER diagram).**

Entity relationship diagrams use symbols to represent entities, attributes of those entities, and relationships among entities. There are many varieties of ERDs, and unfortunately, there is no clear standard of ERD design (Song, Evans, Park, 1995).[1] Years ago, it was thought to be a virtue to use an ERD unrelated to any particular database product, whether it be hierarchical, network, relational, or object oriented (see the discussion later in this chapter). At the time, there were competing standards for database systems, and designers might not, at the outset, know in which system their design would be implemented. The predominant diagramming technique was the Chen ERD. Over the past 15 years, the relational model has dominated the marketplace. Most professionals now use ERDs that look very much like relational databases.[2] Many relational database products even provide built-in design tools. Following this trend, we will feature a diagram similar to that used by relational database products. Entities in these diagrams are modeled as tables (boxes), relationships are modeled with connecting lines, and attributes are modeled as field lists in the boxes. In fact, we will use the terms *entity* and *table* interchangeably, and the terms *attribute* and *field* interchangeably. Strictly speaking, however, the entity is the person, place, or thing being modeled in the real world; a table is the device used to model that person, place, or thing.

The ER notation uses lines terminated by crow's feet to model relationships. Every relationship joins a parent to a child table. The crow's foot always points toward the child table. The diagrams in Exhibit 2-2 show one-to-many relationships—for example, one customer places many orders; one employee has many dependents. Thus, "customer" is the parent and "order" is the child, and "employee" is the parent and "dependent" is the child. The terms *parent* and *child* are very useful when describing relationships in a database.

Exhibit 2-2

One-to-Many
Relationships

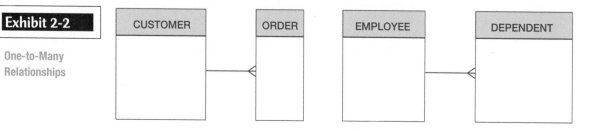

Many-to-many relationships are represented by a third table. A doctor treats many patients, and a patient can visit many doctors. One is tempted to draw a crow's foot in both directions, but doing so would be incorrect, because it would create tremendous data duplication. Rather, a new associative table must be created between the two tables to represent the many-to-many relationship, as shown in Exhibit 2-3. Any other representation would result in duplicate data. For further discussion of problems with duplicate data, refer to Chapter 4.

---

[1]Dozens of varieties of ER diagrams are in circulation. The number continues to grow as DBMS vendors introduce new diagramming tools with their products.

[2]Chen diagrams, and their extensions, continue to be popular in the academic community, though not with industry. The tide is beginning to shift as some textbooks, including this one, model directly in a more relational ERD. Even Microsoft has dropped support for Chen ERDs in its 2002 release of Visio. Die-hard proponents of the Chen model claim that it is more intuitive for students to learn. These proponents claim that students have difficulty modeling a many-to-many relationship as a separate table. We have seen no published evidence to support this position. On the contrary, our experience is that students are able to model as easily in a relational ERD. Furthermore, these students do not face the often tricky decision of whether to model certain information as an entity or as a relationship. Modeling in a relational ERD also saves the multistep process required to convert a Chen ERD to the relational model for implementation.

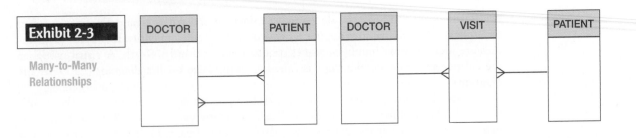

Exhibit 2-3

Many-to-Many
Relationships

In a table, attributes are modeled as fields. For people, the fields often show demographic information—name, social security number, birth date, address, and so forth. Fields are listed inside each table, as shown in Exhibit 2-4.

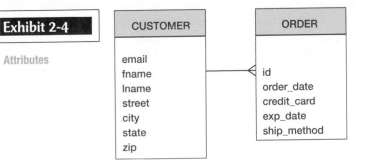

Exhibit 2-4

Attributes

Primary Keys

Keys are the foundation and glue of the relational model. A **primary key** uniquely identifies each record in a table. For example, email is a primary key that uniquely identifies each customer; id is a primary key that uniquely identifies each order. Ideally, a primary key is formed of only one field. However, sometimes more than one field might be required to form a primary key. For example, longitude and latitude might both be required to specify a location. Primary keys are underlined and boldfaced in the ER diagram.

Primary keys must be carefully chosen. Every primary key should support the following properties:

- **Unique:** The value of the primary key uniquely identifies each record in the table. In the United States, social security numbers uniquely identify each person. Vehicle identification numbers (VINs) uniquely identify each car.
- **Minimal:** If social security numbers are unique, there is no need to form a primary key from social security number plus birth date. Similarly, the make and model of a car does not further help to identify the vehicle if we already have the VIN. Nonetheless, there will be circumstances under which more than one field will be required to form a primary key.
- **Not null:** Because the primary key is a unique identifier, its value cannot be left blank. Every record in a table must have a value for the primary key.
- **Nonupdateable:** A unique identifier should not change over time. Social security numbers last a lifetime. Vehicle identification numbers last the life of a vehicle. However, phone numbers change as people move. Therefore, phone numbers are not an ideal primary key. However, in many business settings, an updateable primary key must be used for the convenience of customers. For example, many e-commerce sites use email as a primary key, in spite of the fact that a person's email might change as that person switches jobs or Internet service providers (ISPs).

There is a tension between the unique and minimal properties of a primary key. The more fields included in the primary key, the greater the chance that it will be unique. However, the minimal property requires the designer to find the smallest group of fields that combine to form a unique key. Exhibit 2-5 shows a series of choices for primary key that are unique but *not* minimal. Exhibit 2-6 shows the correct choice for primary key that is both unique and minimal.

Exhibit 2-5

Unique But NOT
Minimal Primary
Keys

MEMBER

email	fname	lname	phone	jumps	equip	level
dayj@ohio.edu	John	Day	592-0646	5	Y	B
compton@ohio.edu	Ted	Compton	592-1111	12	N	I
mcgann@ohio.edu	Sean	McGann	592-2222	20	Y	A

MEMBER

email	fname	lname	phone	jumps	equip	level
dayj@ohio.edu	John	Day	592-0646	5	Y	B
compton@ohio.edu	Ted	Compton	592-1111	12	N	I
mcgann@ohio.edu	Sean	McGann	592-2222	20	Y	A

MEMBER

email	fname	lname	phone	jumps	equip	level
dayj@ohio.edu	John	Day	592-0646	5	Y	B
compton@ohio.edu	Ted	Compton	592-1111	12	N	I
mcgann@ohio.edu	Sean	McGann	592-2222	20	Y	A

Exhibit 2-6

Email Is a Unique
AND Minimal
Primary Key

MEMBER

email	fname	lname	phone	jumps	equip	level
dayj@ohio.edu	John	Day	592-0646	5	Y	B
compton@ohio.edu	Ted	Compton	592-1111	12	N	I
mcgann@ohio.edu	Sean	McGann	592-2222	20	Y	A

In practice, finding a primary key that supports all the above mentioned properties can be challenging. We will look at four common scenarios for choosing a primary key: using existing fields, having the computer generate a field, modeling a dependent table, and modeling an associative table.

Primary keys are most often formed from one or more existing fields in a table. For example, social security number might be a good primary key for employees; vehicle identification number might be a good primary key for automobiles. Primary keys consisting of a single field are preferred because of their simplicity. However, on occasion, more than one field may be required to form the primary key, such as longitude and latitude together forming the primary key for topography. A primary key formed of more than one field is still referred to in the singular. Primary keys formed from existing fields are shown in Exhibit 2-7.

Exhibit 2-7

Primary Keys
Formed from
Existing Fields

CUSTOMER
email
fname
lname
street
city
state
zip

TOPOGRAPHY
longitude
latitude
elevation

In many cases, businesses invent numbers for quick reference to unique records. Reservation numbers, order numbers, and customer numbers all serve to provide unambiguous identifiers for records. These computer-generated fields are often formed by adding one to the last number assigned. Primary keys might also be computer generated to establish a single-field primary key, as opposed to one formed of multiple fields. A computer-generated primary key is shown in Exhibit 2-8.

Exhibit 2-8

Computer-
Generated
Primary Keys

ORDER
id
CUSTOMER$email
order_date
credit_card
exp_date

Creating Relationships: Foreign Keys

A parent table reproduces its primary key values in every child table to which it connects. Because these reproduced values originate outside of the child table, they are called foreign keys. **Foreign keys** link the related records between parent and child tables. A foreign key is placed in the child table (following the crow's foot). Foreign keys are boldfaced and follow the naming convention of PARENT_TABLENAME$parent_fieldname (Fleming and van Holle, 1988). For example, CUSTOMER$email is a foreign key that refers to the email field in the CUSTOMER table. The importance of foreign keys cannot be overstated. Foreign keys are the only way to represent relationships in a relational database. The database system sees only the foreign keys, not the connecting lines. Primary and foreign keys are shown in Exhibit 2-9.

Exhibit 2-9

Foreign Keys
Create
Relationships

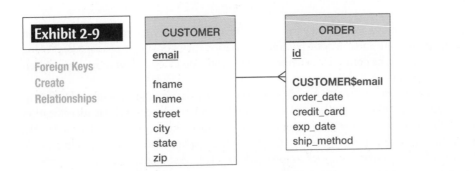

A **dependent table** (also called a **weak entity**) is a child table that requires a parent table for identification. For example, a player's jersey identifies both his number AND his team, such as player 19 on the Bobcats. Numbers are only unique within a team, because every team uses the same set of numbers. Exhibit 2-10 shows the team and player tables. Team is the parent, and player is the child table. However, player is also a dependent table, because a player must also be identified by team name. Dependent tables cannot exist in the database without their parents. The existence dependence is illustrated by including TEAM$name as part of the primary key of the player table. As in this example, dependent tables often incorporate the foreign key from the parent table as part of the primary key.

Exhibit 2-10

Weak Entity

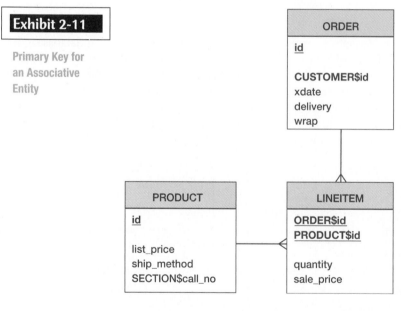

An **associative table** is a child of two parent tables that are in a many-to-many relationship. For example, an order may list many products. However, a given product may also appear on multiple orders. Therefore, there is a many-to-many relationship between order and product that is represented by the associative table LINEITEM. An associative table uses the foreign keys from both parents as part of its own primary key. To form its primary key, LINEITEM uses both ORDER$id and PRODUCT$id, as shown in Exhibit 2-11.

Exhibit 2-11

Primary Key for
an Associative
Entity

Data Integrity

Because the relational model relies on primary keys to identify entities and on foreign keys to create relationships, the integrity (validity) of the keys must be preserved. Two rules ensure the integrity of keys.

- **Entity integrity:** Every table must have a valid primary key. Entity integrity requires that the designer specify a primary key at the time that the table is created. Sadly, most database products do *not* enforce entity integrity—it is up to the designer to remember to specify a primary key.
- **Referential integrity:** No unmatched foreign key values. Referential integrity requires that foreign key values match existing primary key values in the table to which they refer.

In Exhibit 2-12, this requirement would mean that every INSTRUCTOR$id listed in the course table must match an instructor listed in the INSTRUCTOR table. Note that the opposite is not true—it is acceptable to have instructors that do not teach a course. Try to find the two entity integrity and three referential integrity violations in Exhibit 2-12.

Exhibit 2-12

Find Two Entity Integrity and Three Referential Integrity Violations

INSTRUCTOR

id	first	last	office	phone
11	JOE	SMITH	101	593-2736
22	SAM	SLICK	102	594-4657
22	SALLY	SLY	115	593-9875
44	SUE	SLIM	123	593-4756

COURSE

code	title	hour	INSTRUCTOR$id
MIS380	DATABASE I	4	45
MIS225	VISUAL BASIC	4	11
MIS420	SYSTEMS II	4	11

ENROLL

COURSE$code	STUDENT$id	grade
MIS380	1111	A-
MIS225	1111	B+
MIS225	1111	B
MIS333	2222	A
MIS225	2222	C
MIS380	3444	A

STUDENT

id	first	last	dorm	phone
1111	JIM	GREEN	450A	593-2456
2222	STEVE	BLACK	326B	594-4623
3333	LINDA	BROWN	144A	593-5575
4444	EMMA	WHITE	133B	593-4676

Answer: Entity integrity violations: (1) two instructors with id = 22, (2) two enrollment records with MIS225 and 1111. Referential integrity violations: (1) INSTRUCTOR$id = 45 in the COURSE table, (2) COURSE$code = MIS333 in the ENROLL table, (3) STUDENT$id = 3444 in the ENROLL table.

First Normal Form

One goal of database design is to create normal (properly designed) tables. A database is normalized when each field holds just one value, and each table has the correct set of fields. A table is said to be in **first normal form (1NF)** when each field in that table contains single values only. In the same way that two numbers cannot be typed into an electronic spreadsheet cell, two or more values cannot be stored in the same database field (cell), as shown in Exhibit 2-13. The higher normal forms—two through five—deal with placing fields in the wrong tables. These normal forms will be covered in Chapter 4.

Exhibit 2-13

First Normal Form (1NF)

Not in 1NF

INSTRUCTOR

id	name	course
1111	JOE	MIS380, MIS225
2222	SAM	MIS202, MIS420
3333	SALLY	MIS380

Cannot have multiple values in a single cell

In 1NF

INSTRUCTOR

id	course
1111	MIS380
1111	MIS225
2222	MIS202
2222	MIS420
3333	MIS380

Types of Database Systems

Some database systems predate the relational model, and others were developed after it. However, the relational model dominates the marketplace. One reason for this dominance is that this model has been able, over the years, to adopt the best features of all of the other models, while preserving its unique advantages. Some of the other types of database systems include:

- **Hierarchical:** The hierarchical database is the grandfather of all databases. The name comes from its representation of a database as a tree-structured hierarchy, similar to the folder system on a computer. The most famous hierarchical product, called Information Management System (IMS), was created by IBM. IMS completely dominated the large-scale database market from the 1960s through the early 1990s. One problem with IMS is that it is quite difficult to use. It requires a professional programmer to interact with the database. Despite efforts by IBM to phase it out in favor of relational products, IMS is still used today in some legacy systems for large databases, such as those used by insurance companies. Companies keep IMS for four reasons. First, it provides very quick access to millions of records. Second, migrating to a relational system might result in temporary service outages. Third, there would be a significant cost incurred in the migration. Fourth, it is difficult to effect change in an MIS shop when jobs and egos are on the line.

- **Network:** The network database, which targeted midsize systems, was an improvement on the hierarchical model. The name comes from its representation of a database as a network of connected tables. Actually, a network diagram looks very similar to the ERDs that we use in this text. The major difference between a network and a relational database is that the relational database has foreign keys to make connections between tables, whereas the network database uses physical pointers to connect tables. That seemingly small difference creates enormous differences in implementation. The most famous network product, called IDMS, was developed by Computer Associates. Like IMS, IDMS is difficult to use and requires a professional programmer to interact with the database.[3] Most shops use hierarchical and network products primarily for legacy (old) systems. New system development is almost exclusively done on relational systems.

- **Relational:** A relational database is the easiest system in which to develop and maintain a database. As a result, professionals can be much more productive using a relational system, which saves enormous costs. Furthermore, much less training is required to use the system. Ease of use is one reason why relational systems were the first to make an appearance on personal computers. The primary criticism of early relational products was for their slow speed. However, three developments over the years overcame the speed limitation. First, computers increased significantly in processing power, effectively doubling in speed every 18 months. Second, computers dropped in price. Today's thousand-dollar computer has more processing power than a multimillion-dollar mainframe in service 20 years ago. Third, relational software is much more efficient today. Sophisticated file storage and query optimization result in very fast response times.

  Within the relational world, there are many choices. Vendors such as Oracle, IBM, and Microsoft all provide competing relational products. Oracle and IBM compete in the high-end market for large servers such as those used by big businesses, whether brick-and-mortar or on the Web. Microsoft focuses on small and midrange systems. Fortunately, all of these systems are based on the same relational model and use the same structured query language (SQL).

- **Object oriented:** The object-oriented database was originally predicted to supercede the relational model. However, like IMS and IDMS, object-oriented products are difficult to use. Nonetheless, they were the first databases to allow programs (methods), and not just data, to be stored in the database. They were also the first databases to allow data objects to inherit structures from other data objects. Over time, relational products have become more object oriented—incorporating both stored procedures (programs) and inheritance—thereby eliminating the competitive advantage of object-oriented systems.

---

[3]Both IMS and IDMS developed relational-like interfaces on top of their models. Many *ad hoc* queries could be handled with these user-friendly interfaces. However, most programs written for the application server still require following the physical pointers.

Relational Advantages

Industry adopted the relational database model because it significantly improves productivity. The following advantages of the relational model will be examined in turn:

- Reliance on logical, rather than physical, links between related records
- Use of a fourth-generation language (4GL)
- Allowance for a high degree of data independence

Logical Rather Than Physical Links

Only the relational model does not rely on physical pointers to link data items together. Pointers link related records, for example, a player and a team. In physical pointer-based systems, the programmer must write procedures to follow the links to retrieve information. By contrast, the relational model uses logical pointers. To link a player with a team in a relational system, simply match foreign key records with the corresponding primary key.

Fourth-Generation Language (4GL)

Structured query language (SQL) is the language used by relational database management systems to manipulate data. As computer languages go, SQL is very concise. A ten-line SQL query can accomplish what would take hundreds of lines in another language.

Structured query language is a fourth-generation language. The first generation of computer languages was binary code. Binary code was followed in the second generation by assembly language, which was text abbreviations for binary code. The third generation includes programming languages such as COBOL, C, Fortran, Pascal, Java, JavaScript, and VBScript. These languages package multiple assembly language instructions in a single command.

Third-generation languages (3GLs) have two limitations that make them difficult to use for database manipulation—they are *procedural* and *record oriented. Procedural* means that the programmer has to specify every step of the program execution. This requirement leads to fairly long programs. *Record oriented* means that the language can only operate on one record at a time. Therefore, cycling through a group of records requires the use of a loop.

Structured query language overcomes both limitations of 3GLs. It is *nonprocedural* and *table oriented. Nonprocedural* means that the programmer specifies the desired result without having to specify each step of program execution. This process leads to very compact programs. *Table oriented* means that SQL is able to operate on an entire table at one time. The input to an SQL program is a table or tables, and the output is a table. Therefore, SQL does not require any loops. By contrast, with 3GLs, a single operation normally affects just one field in one record. Cycling through the remaining fields and records requires the use of loops. Loops add many lines of code, thus making 3GLs quite verbose by comparison.

Data Independence

Relational systems enjoy a high degree of data independence.[4] Data independence allows the DBA to reorganize the underlying structure of the data without causing programs on the application server to crash. The DBA should be able to change column names and move columns among tables without affecting the application. When these changes are possible, they are said to be transparent to the application. This data independence is achieved with the use of views.

When developers create tables in a database, they are called **base tables.** These are the tables that we have worked with all along. A **view,** by contrast, is a subset derived from the base tables. Views enable the DBA to restrict the portion of the database visible to each user. Exhibit 2-14 shows two distinct views of the same base table, MEMBER. The member_email_view contains only the address, first_name, and last_name fields, whereas the

---

[4]We refer here to logical, rather than physical, data independence. Physical data independence would avoid problems such as the two-digit date issue that engendered the Y2K hysteria.

member_phone_view contains only the first_name, last_name, and telephone fields. Note that the columns are renamed in the creation of the view. Email is renamed address, fname is renamed first_name, lname is renamed last_name, and phone is renamed telephone. There are obvious security benefits in giving end users limited views of the database.[5] However, from a data independence standpoint, the advantage of views is that they allow the DBA to change the underlying structure of the base tables while preserving each user's view.

Exhibit 2-14

Views Used to
Restrict Access
and Rename
Columns

MEMBER_EMAIL_VIEW

address	first_name	last_name
dayj@ohio.edu	John	Day
compton@ohio.edu	Ted	Compton
mcgann@ohio.edu	Sean	McGann

MEMBER_PHONE_VIEW

first_name	last_name	telephone
John	Day	592-0646
Ted	Compton	592-1111
Sean	McGann	592-2222

MEMBER

email	fname	lname	phone	jumps	equip	level
dayj@ohio.edu	John	Day	592-0646	5	Y	B
compton@ohio.edu	Ted	Compton	592-1111	12	N	I
mcgann@ohio.edu	Sean	McGann	592-2222	20	Y	A

SUMMARY

- The relational model is based upon tables with rows and columns.
- The relational database management system (RDBMS) is the software that runs on the database server and allows for creation and maintenance of databases.
- The most common way of designing a database is to create a conceptual model of the data items and their interrelationships.
- Entity relationship diagrams use symbols to represent entities, attributes of those entities, and relationships among entities.
- An entity is the person, place, or thing being modeled in the real world; a table is the device used to model that person, place, or thing.
- Lines terminated by crow's feet are used to model relationships. Every relationship joins a parent to a child table.
- Many-to-many relationships are represented by a third, associative table.
- Attributes are modeled as fields in a table.
- A primary key uniquely identifies each record in a table.
- Primary keys are underlined and boldfaced in the ER diagram.
- Primary keys should be unique, minimal, not null, and nonupdateable.

---

[5]Even application programs may be given a limited view of the database, because the application programs are also users of the database.

- A parent table reproduces its primary key values in every child table to which it connects. Foreign keys link the related records between parent and child tables.
- Foreign keys are boldfaced and follow the naming convention of PARENT_TABLE-NAME$parent_fieldname.
- A dependent table (also called a weak entity) is a child table that requires a parent table for identification.
- An associative table is a child of two parent tables that are in a many-to-many relationship.
- Entity integrity requires that the designer specify a primary key at the time that the table is created.
- Referential integrity requires that foreign key values match existing primary key values in the table to which they refer.
- A table is said to be in first normal form (1NF) when each field in that table contains single values only.
- A hierarchical database represents a database as a tree-structured hierarchy.
- A network database represents a database as a network of tables connected using physical pointers.
- An object-oriented database stores data as objects with associated methods (programs). Object-oriented databases were also the first to allow data objects to inherit structures from other data objects.
- The advantages of the relational model include:

  - Reliance on logical, rather than physical, links between related records
  - Use of a fourth-generation language (4GL)
  - Allowance for a high degree of data independence

- A view is a subset derived from the base tables. Views enable the DBA to restrict the portion of the database visible to each user.

KEY TERMS

Associative table. A child of two parent tables that are in a many-to-many relationship.

Attribute. A property of an entity or a relationship. For example, employee id is an attribute of the employee entity.

Base tables. The core set of tables in a database.

Conceptual model. A generic description of the data that is not tied to any specific database software product.

Database administrator (DBA). The person who runs the RDBMS.

Dependent table (weak entity). A child table that requires a parent table for identification.

Entity. A person, place, or thing that is being modeled. For example, employees and work locations are both entities. Entities are represented by rectangles.

Entity integrity. Requires that the designer specify a primary key at the time that the table is created.

Entity relationship diagram (ERD). A diagram containing entities, relationships, and cardinality constraints.

First normal form (1NF). A table in which each field in that table contains single values only.

Foreign keys. Duplicate primary key fields that link the related records between parent and child tables.

Primary key. A field or group of fields whose values uniquely identify each record in a table.

Referential integrity. Requires that foreign key values must match existing primary key values in the table to which they refer.

Relationship. A logical connection between records from two or more tables. All relationships can be categorized as one-to-one, one-to-many, or many-to-many.

Relational database management system (RDBMS). A software application used to implement a relational database.

Structured query language (SQL). The language used by relational database management systems to manipulate data.

View. A subset derived from the base tables. Views enable the DBA to restrict the portion of the database visible to each user.

EXERCISES

Review

1. What is an entity? Give some examples.
2. What is a relationship? Give some examples.
3. What is an attribute? Give some examples.
4. What symbols are used in an ER diagram for entities, relationships, and attributes?
5. What is a primary key?
6. What is a foreign key?
7. What is entity integrity?
8. What is referential integrity?
9. What is first normal form?
10. What is a view?

Discuss

1. Explain the rules for selecting a primary key.
2. Explain the role of a foreign key in creating a relationship between tables.
3. Explain the connection between foreign keys and referential integrity.
4. Explain the equivalence among the following terms: table, relation, row, record, column, attribute, field.
5. What is a view, and what is its role in achieving data independence?

Practice

1. In Exhibit 2-15, draw a line with a crow's foot to show the relationship that a consultant does many projects.

Exhibit 2-15

ER Diagram for
Practice Exercise 1

| CONSULTANT | | PROJECT |

2. Draw a new version of the ER diagram in Exhibit 2-16 that includes an associative table called ENROLLMENT to represent the many-to-many relationship between students and courses.

Exhibit 2-16

ER Diagram for
Practice Exercise 2

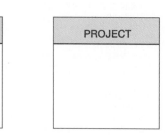

3. In the example table in Exhibit 2-17, indicate what column or columns should be selected as the primary key to best meet the desired properties for a primary key.

Exhibit 2-17

Table for Practice
Exercise 3

fname	lname	phone	birthday	Student id	Email
John	Day	592-0646	7/25/88	555667777	jd@email.com
Ted	Compton	592-1111	8/05/86	444889999	tc@email.com
Sean	McGann	592-2222	2/04/86	111446666	sm@email.com

4. In the ER diagram in Exhibit 2-18, identify the foreign key.

Exhibit 2-18

ER Diagram for
Practice Exercise 4

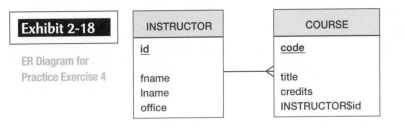

5. In the two tables in Exhibit 2-19, identify an entity integrity violation and a referential integrity violation.

Exhibit 2-19

Tables for Practice
Exercise 5

STUDENT

id	fname	lname	phone
333	John	Day	592-0646
222	Ted	Compton	592-1111
333	Sean	McGann	592-2222

ENROLLMENT

STUDENT$id	COURSE$code	grade
333	MIS100	A
222	ACCT200	C
666	MGT202	B

REFERENCES

Fleming, C. C. and van Holle, B. (1988), *Handbook of Relational Database Design,* Reading, MA: Addison-Wesley.

Song, I.-Y., Evans, M., and Park, E. K. (1995), "A Comparative Analysis of Entity-Relationship Diagrams," *Journal of Computer & Software Engineering,* 3(4), 427–59.

3

Conceptual Design

Introduction

The last chapter introduced ER diagrams. In this chapter, we will explore how to use those diagrams to create a conceptual model of a database.

ER diagrams should be constructed using a systematic process. Design should begin with a big-picture view, and detail should be progressively added to prepare for implementation. A design tool such as Microsoft Visio helps to refine the design in a systematic fashion. Unfortunately, most database products encourage exactly the opposite by prompting the user for all field names, data types, and keys at the time that the table is created. A five-step process for ERD construction is described below and will be used in the examples throughout the rest of the chapter.

Step 1: Represent Entities as Tables

■ Entities are persons, places, things, and events about which you will collect and store information. Information about those entities is recorded in tables.

Learning Objectives

After completing this chapter, you will be able to:

- Design an ERD in a systematic fashion.
- Determine cardinality between tables.
- Correctly select a primary key for a table.
- Identify foreign keys for a child table.
- Correctly determine data types for attributes.

- To identify entities, try asking two questions:

    1. *Is there more than one?* Can you envision more than one instance of the entity? More than one member? More than one visit? More than one account? If so, then you probably need a separate table to hold the information.

    2. *Is there a variation over time?* Does the number of instances vary over time? Does the number of members grow and shrink? Does the number of visits change over time? Are accounts added and removed over the years? Again, a positive answer likely indicates the need for a separate table.

- Represent each entity as a table by drawing a box and recording a unique name for the table.

- In the beginning, model all potential entities as tables—it is always easier to eliminate tables than to create new ones.

Step 2: Determine Relationships

- Relationships connect the tables together. Show the relationships by connecting the tables with lines. Every table must connect to at least one other table in the database—unless, of course, the entire database consists of only one table.

- In most cases, a record in one table will correspond to multiple records in another table. For example, one customer places multiple orders. Show this relationship by placing a crow's foot along the line pointing to the orders table. The end of the line without the crow's foot represents one; the end with the crow's foot represents many—e.g., one customer places many orders. **Cardinality** is the technical term used to describe the number of records in the relationship. Cardinality will almost always be shown as one-to-many, though there are certain designs requiring a one-to-one cardinality.[1]

- For many-to-many relationships, create a new **associative table.** By design rules, two tables may *not* point a crow's foot at each other. In such a case, a new associative table must be created between the two tables. The new table literally associates records between its two parent tables. In the database diagram, both parent tables must point to the new associative table.

Step 3: List Fields

- In business situations, entities often have many attributes.
- Model the attributes as fields listed inside each table.
- If a table from step 1 has only one field, then it might simply be a field of another table, rather than a table in its own right. If so, then merge it into the corresponding table.

Step 4: Identify Keys

- All tables must have a primary key to uniquely identify each record.
- Either select a field from step 3 that meets the requirements of a primary key (unique, minimal, not null, and nonupdateable), or create a new field that does.
- All child tables must also have a foreign key field to connect each child record with its corresponding parent.

---

[1]Microsoft Access uses the infinity symbol ∞ in place of a crow's foot to designate a cardinality of many.

■ The primary key of the parent must be defined *before* the foreign key in the child—because the foreign key is effectively a duplicate of the parent's primary key.

■ Furthermore, the primary key of the parent must be defined *before* the primary key in the child—because a child table sometimes uses a foreign key from the parent as part of its own primary key.

■ Therefore, keys are defined from the outside in—choosing parent keys and working inward to define child keys by choosing a primary key for a parent table, and then reproducing the primary key as a foreign key in each child table related to that parent. Then move on to the next parent table.

Step 5: Determining Data Types

■ Determine the data type and size of each attribute as a final design step.

■ Every attribute must have a **data type** describing the kind of information that may be stored in that attribute.

■ Most data types also include a size dimension to indicate the maximum size value that may be stored in the attribute—e.g., up to 20 characters long.

■ Primary and foreign keys must match in data type and size, because they refer to the same set of values. In technical terms, we say that the primary and foreign keys are defined on the same **domain,** where domain means a set of values.

In the following sections, we will illustrate these steps in the context of designing three databases: a single-table database, a database with a one-to-many relationship, and a database with a many-to-many relationship.

Designing a Single-Table Database

To better understand the process of creating an ER diagram, we will go through the process described above several times, starting with a very simple single-table database and working up to more complex multitable databases. In each example, we will begin with a general description of the need or problem that requires the creation of a database; we will then go through the process of creating the ER diagram for the database that solves that need or problem.

Problem Statement

Joe Garcia wants to keep track of data about the members in his skydiving club. Contact information (name, email, and phone number) should be recorded about each member, along with his or her experience level (beginner, intermediate, or advanced), whether the skydiver owns the necessary equipment, and the number of jumps the skydiver has completed.

Process

This is a straightforward problem, because it requires only one table—MEMBER. The design progresses in the following sequence: tables, relationships, fields, keys, and data types, as shown visually in Exhibit 3-1.

Exhibit 3-1

Skydiving
Membership Data
Step-by-Step
Design

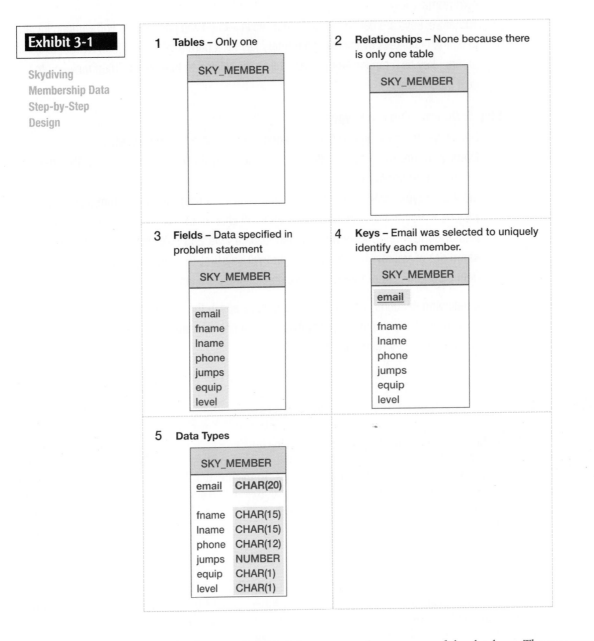

1 **Tables** – Only one

SKY_MEMBER

2 **Relationships** – None because there is only one table

SKY_MEMBER

3 **Fields** – Data specified in problem statement

SKY_MEMBER

email
fname
lname
phone
jumps
equip
level

4 **Keys** – Email was selected to uniquely identify each member.

SKY_MEMBER

email

fname
lname
phone
jumps
equip
level

5 **Data Types**

SKY_MEMBER

email	CHAR(20)
fname	CHAR(15)
lname	CHAR(15)
phone	CHAR(12)
jumps	NUMBER
equip	CHAR(1)
level	CHAR(1)

The design in Exhibit 3-1 represents the structure of the database. The structure specifies the type of data that may be placed in the database. Sample data for the skydiving database is shown in Exhibit 3-2.

Skydiving
Database Sample
Data (Vertical
Representation)

SKY_MEMBER	
email	CHAR(20)
fname	CHAR(15)
lname	CHAR(15)
phone	CHAR(12)
jumps	NUMBER
equip	CHAR(1)
level	CHAR(1)

mcgann@

Sean
McGann
592-2222
20
Y
A

luce@ohio.e

Thom
Luce
529-1111
12
N
I

dayj@ohio.edu

John
Day
592-0646
5
Y
B

Although Exhibit 3-2 has intuitive appeal because it links the visual structure of the ER diagram directly with the sample data, in practice it is an inefficient way to represent data. It is far more common to present data in the form of a table with horizontal rows, as shown in Exhibit 3-3.

Skydiving
Database Sample
Data (Horizontal
Representation)

MEMBER						
email	fname	lname	phone	jumps	equip	level
dayj@ohio.edu	John	Day	592-0646	5	Y	B
compton@ohio.edu	Ted	Compton	592-1111	12	N	I
mcgann@ohio.edu	Sean	McGann	592-2222	20	Y	A

Designing a Database with a One-to-Many Relationship

The skydiving membership example needed only a single table to solve the problem. Fortunately, some business problems require the creation of a database containing only a single table. However, many problems require multiple tables. When there are multiple tables, the design includes relationships among the tables. The next section will show how to design a database with a one-to-many relationship.

Problem Statement

Imagine the design of a database for an online video arcade to track the billable time spent by each of its members. The arcade needs to keep track of basic information about its members, including their email addresses, the passwords they use to access the online arcade, their names, and their phone numbers. In addition, each time the member accesses the arcade, a session id number is created, and the times the session started and ended need to be captured. We can thus determine how much time was spent on the site and therefore how much the member should be charged.

Process

Two entities can be identified for this application. First, we have information about the members, which means we should have a MEMBER table. Second, the visit information requires a new table, because members make multiple visits to the arcade. Whenever a database contains more than one table—for example, MEMBER and VISIT—relationships exist among the tables. In this case, the relationship between members and visits is one-to-many because a member can make many visits, but a particular visit is associated with one member. Thus, a **one-to-many relationship** means that a row in one table is matched to multiple rows in the second table, and a row in the second table is matched back to one row in the first table. Exhibit 3-4 shows the systematic construction of the ERD for the online video arcade.

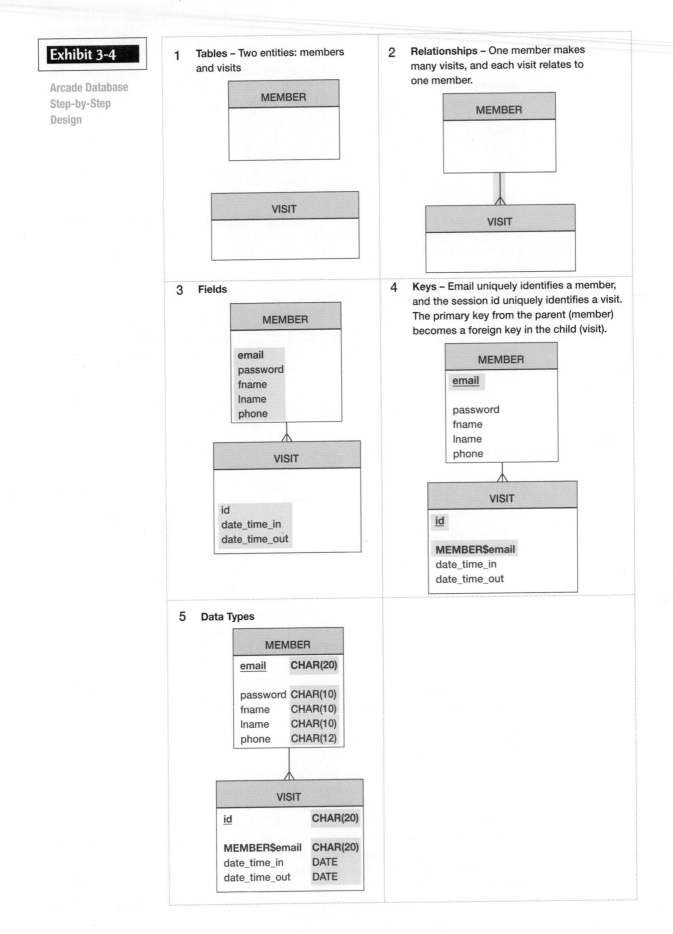

Exhibit 3-4

Arcade Database
Step-by-Step
Design

The problem describes members and their visits to the arcade. One member makes many visits—hence the one-to-many relationship. Note the crow's foot symbol pointing to the VISIT table. The crow's foot indicates *many.* Each visit receives a unique session id, generated automatically by the computer system. For each visit, the time in and time out is recorded. The difference between those times will be calculated to measure usage. Exhibit 3-5 and Exhibit 3-6 show the Arcade design with some sample data. The foreign keys reveal which member made which visit. Note that every foreign key value matches a primary key value in the member table. Remember from the last chapter that the requirement that foreign key values match (refer to) primary key values is called *referential integrity.* The converse is not necessarily true. It would be possible to have a member in the database who had not yet made a first visit. In fact, from a business standpoint, it would be critical to have the capacity to enter information about a member prior to that first visit. So every foreign key value must match a primary key value, but every primary key value does not have to have a matching foreign key value.

Exhibit 3-5

Arcade Database
Sample Data
(Vertical
Representation)

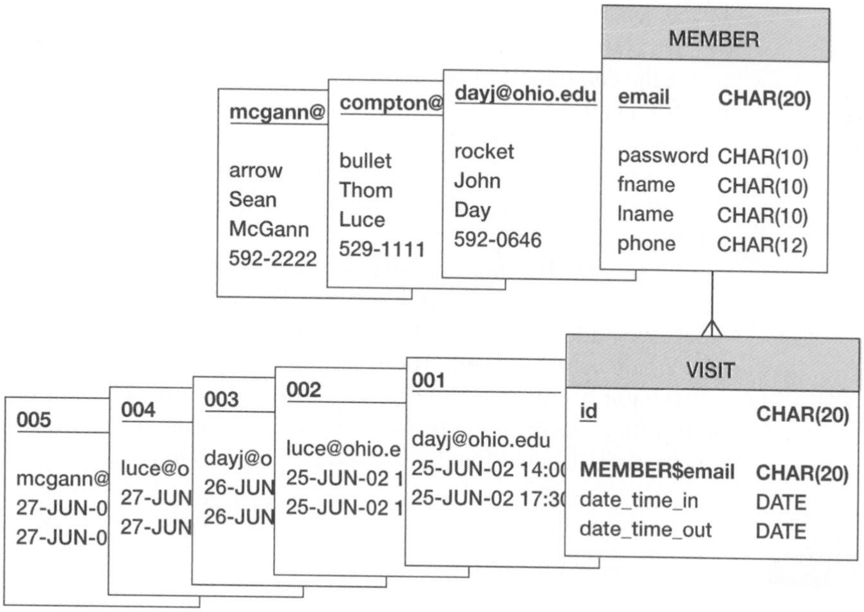

Exhibit 3-6

Arcade Database
Sample Data
(Horizontal
Representation)

MEMBER

email	password	fname	lname	phone
dayj@ohio.edu	rocket	John	Day	592-0646
luce@ohio.edu	bullet	Ted	Compton	592-1111
mcgann@ohio.edu	arrow	Sean	McGann	592-2222

VISIT

id	MEMBER$email	date_time_in	date_time_out
001	dayj@ohio.edu	25-JUN-02 14:00	25-JUN-02 17:30
002	luce@ohio.edu	25-JUN-02 18:00	25-JUN-02 20:00
003	dayj@ohio.edu	26-JUN-02 10:00	26-JUN-02 11:30
004	luce@ohio.edu	27-JUN-02 09:00	27-JUN-02 10:00
005	mcgann@ohio.edu	27-JUN-02 16:00	27-JUN-02 18:00

Database with Many-to-Many Relationships

The previous section looked at a database containing a one-to-many relationship. One-to-many relationships are a very powerful construct to model a wide range of business problems. There are other problems, however, that involve more complex relationships among tables. These relationships are called **many-to-many relationships.** In a many-to-many relationship, rows in one table are associated with many rows in the second table, and a row in the second table is associated with many rows in the first table. The next problem requires a many-to-many relationship in its solution.

Problem Statement

Dr. Phil Harmonic is the chairman of the music department at the local university. He recently purchased a computer, and he wants to use it to keep track of all the courses offered by the department.

Dr. Harmonic currently has five instructors who work in the department. He would like to use the computer to keep track of each instructor's basic contact information, such as id number, name, office location, and phone number.

For each course, the department needs to keep track of the course code, title, and the number of credit hours it is worth. When courses are offered, the section of the course receives a call number, and with that number the department keeps track of which instructor is teaching the course.

Finally, Dr. Harmonic would also like to be able to keep track of his students and to know which courses a student has taken. The information he would like to know about each student includes id number, name, dorm room, and phone number. He also needs to know what grade the student receives in each course.

Exhibit 3-7 shows the systematic development of the ERD to solve the problem. The most difficult steps in the problem are steps 2 (relationships) and 4 (keys). These steps are developed in detail in Exhibit 3-8 and Exhibit 3-9, respectively.

Exhibit 3-7   Enrollment Database Step-by-Step Design

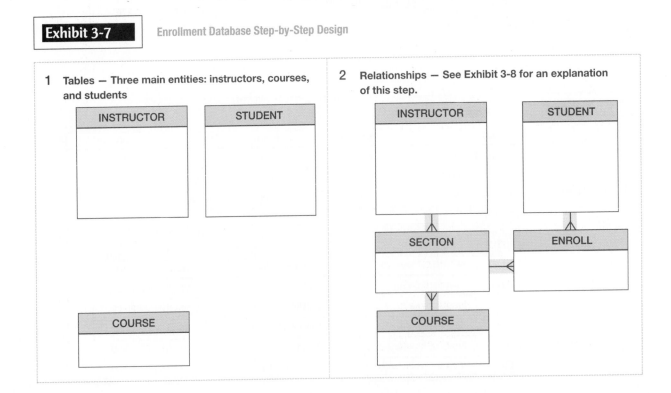

Exhibit 3-7   Continued

3   **Fields** — Note how call_no is best put in the new
     SECTION table and grade belongs in ENROLL.

4   **Keys** — See Exhibit 3-9 for an explanation of this step.

5   **Data Types**

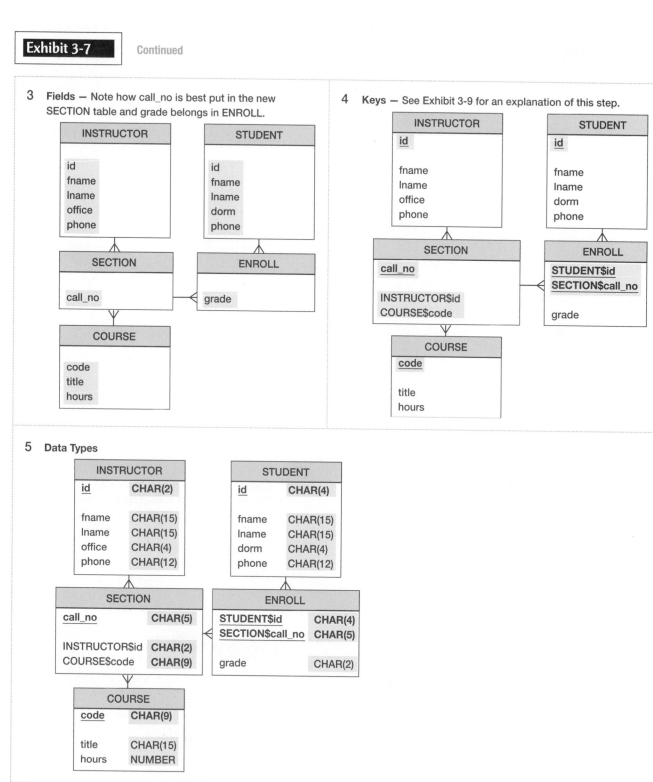

Exhibit 3-8   Enrollment Database Relationships

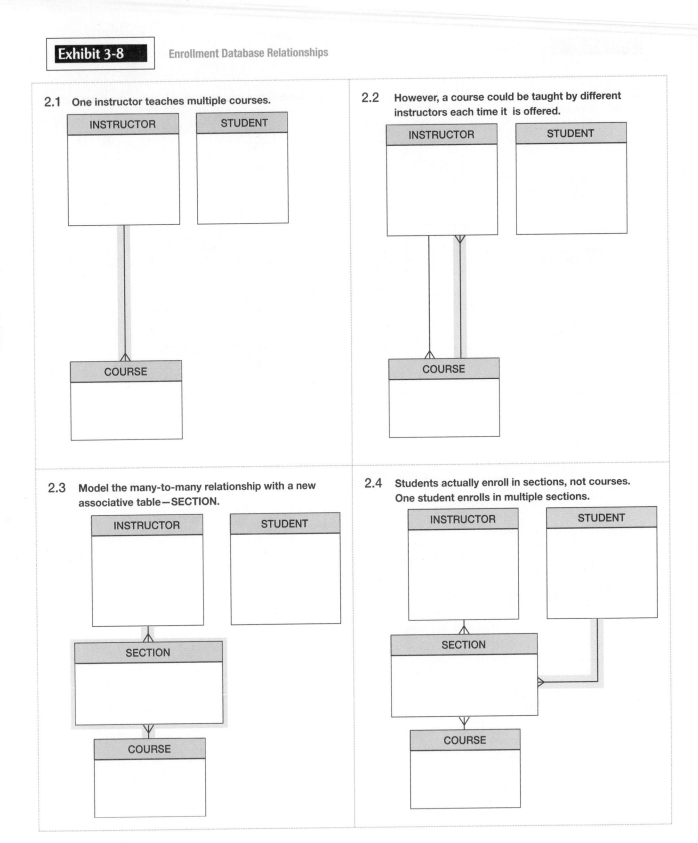

2.1 One instructor teaches multiple courses.

2.2 However, a course could be taught by different instructors each time it is offered.

2.3 Model the many-to-many relationship with a new associative table—SECTION.

2.4 Students actually enroll in sections, not courses. One student enrolls in multiple sections.

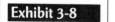

Exhibit 3-8 Continued

2.5 However, one section may also have multiple students enrolled.

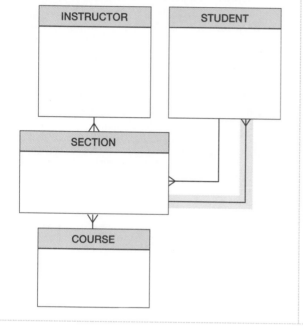

2.6 Model the many-to-many relationship with a new associative table—ENROLL.

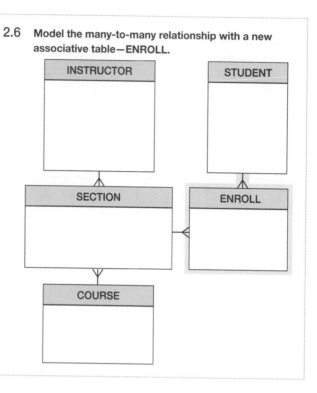

Exhibit 3-9   Enrollment Database Primary and Foreign Keys

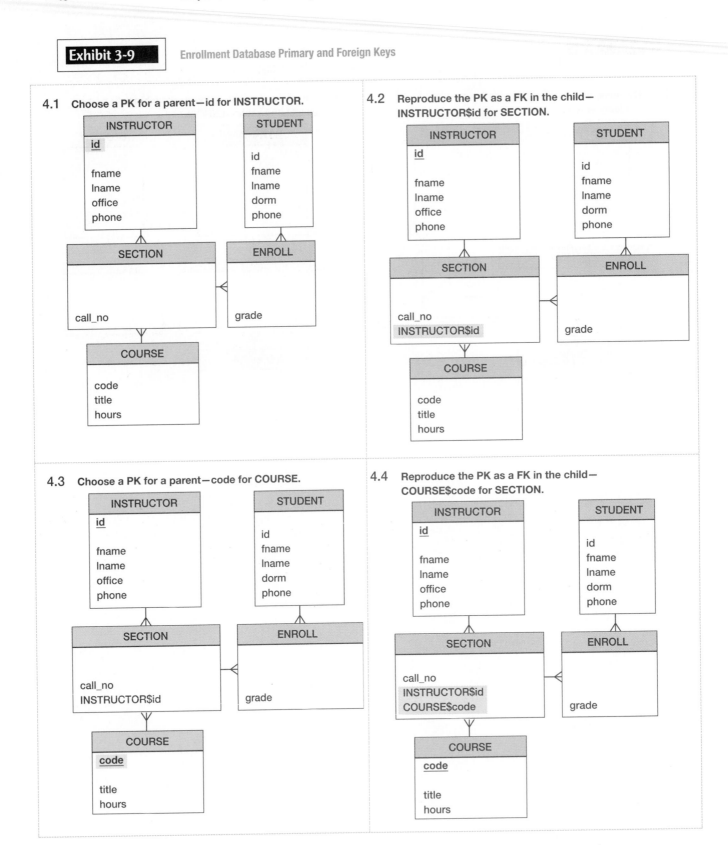

Exhibit 3-9   Continued

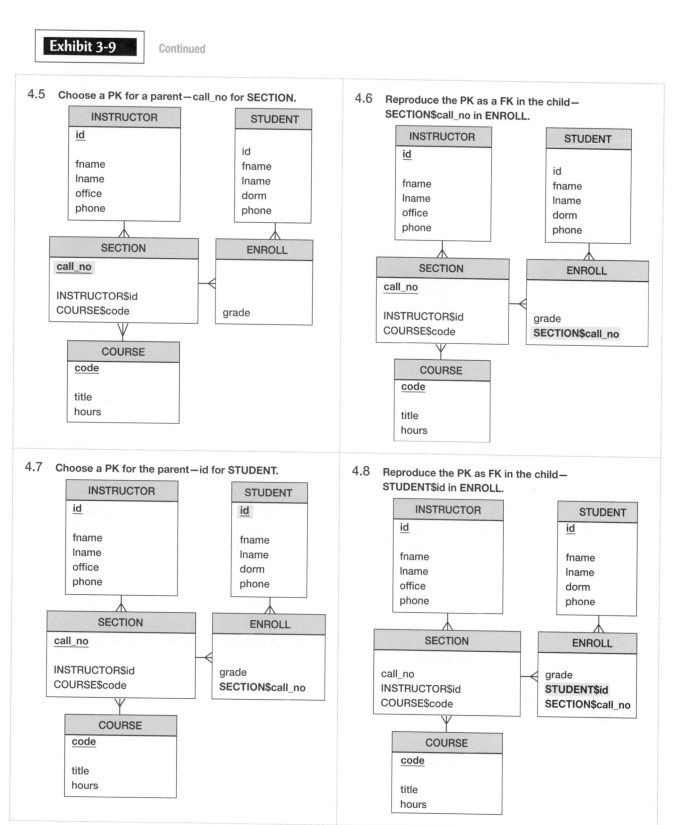

Exhibit 3-9   Continued

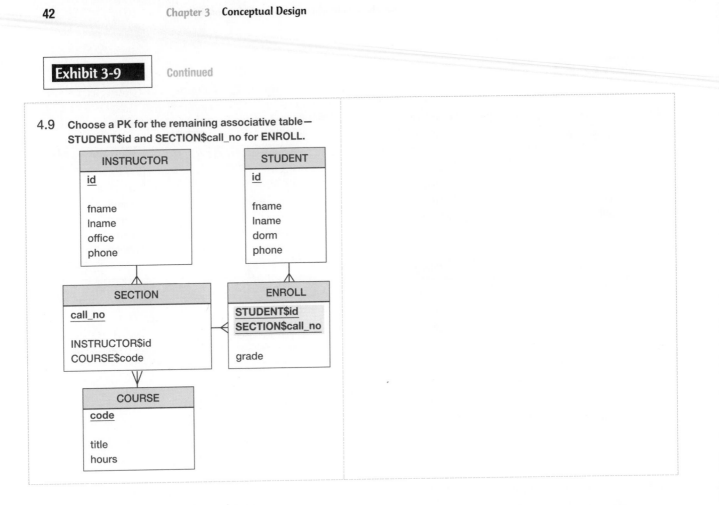

4.9 Choose a PK for the remaining associative table—
     STUDENT$id and SECTION$call_no for ENROLL.

Note that in step 4.9, the selected primary key consists of two fields, STUDENT$id and SECTION$call_no. In the ENROLL table, the rows of data will be pairs of student numbers and call numbers. Each time a student takes a section of a course, a row will appear in this table. Because a student will take many sections, the student's id will appear in the ENROLL table multiple times. Thus the values in the STUDENT$id column will not be unique, because a given student's id will appear multiple times. The same is true for call numbers, because each student who takes the section will require a row in this table, so the value in the SECTION$call_no column will also not be unique. The combination of a particular student's id and the call_no for a particular section will, however, be unique, because a student can take a section only once. Because this pair of student id and call number is unique, the combination of STUDENT$id and SECTION$call_no is selected as the primary key for the ENROLL table.

 Other Multitable Database Examples

Because these multitable design concepts are so critical, we will continue with three more problem statements and their solutions. For each problem, we will analyze the information needs and then develop a systematic solution.

The Hospital Database

Dr. U. R. Sick is the administrator of General Hospital. He is interested in creating a database for the hospital's outpatient clinic, where patients come for emergency treatment. As a patient arrives for the first time, we need to record some basic information, such as name, address, and phone number, about each patient. In addition, we need to know by which insurance companies the patient is covered. It is common for patients coming to this clinic to be covered by more than one insurance company. To assist with billing, we need to keep a list of the insurance companies our patients use, so that we have the company name, phone number, and contact name for each insurance company. Because the clinic is really for emergencies, we need to keep track of the patients' family doctors so we can send information to them. Each patient is associated with one family doctor. To assist with the contact process, we maintain a doctor list that includes the doctor's name, beeper number, and office phone number.

The entities mentioned in this scenario are patient, insurance company, and family doctor. Each of these entities is modeled as a table. Insurance coverage forms a relationship between patient and insurance company. Exhibit 3-10 shows that the relationship between patient and insurance company is many-to-many. One patient can have multiple insurance companies, and an insurance company can cover multiple patients. The problem specifies that patients have only one family doctor. However, a doctor can obviously treat multiple patients. Therefore, the relationship between doctor and patient is one-to-many. Exhibit 3-10 shows the systematic design for the Hospital database. Note how names are broken into first and last names, even though this was not explicitly required by the problem. Similarly, address information is stored as street, city, state, and zip. Dividing information into separate fields serves two purposes. First, it helps eliminate data entry errors such as those caused by inverting the order of first and last names. Second, the divisions assist in data retrieval to produce reports, such as a list of all patients living in the state of Ohio.

Exhibit 3-10   Hospital Database Step-by-Step Design

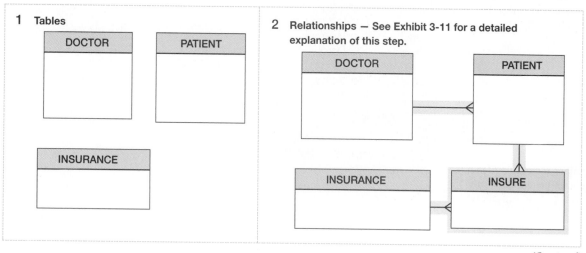

(Continued)

Exhibit 3-10   Continued

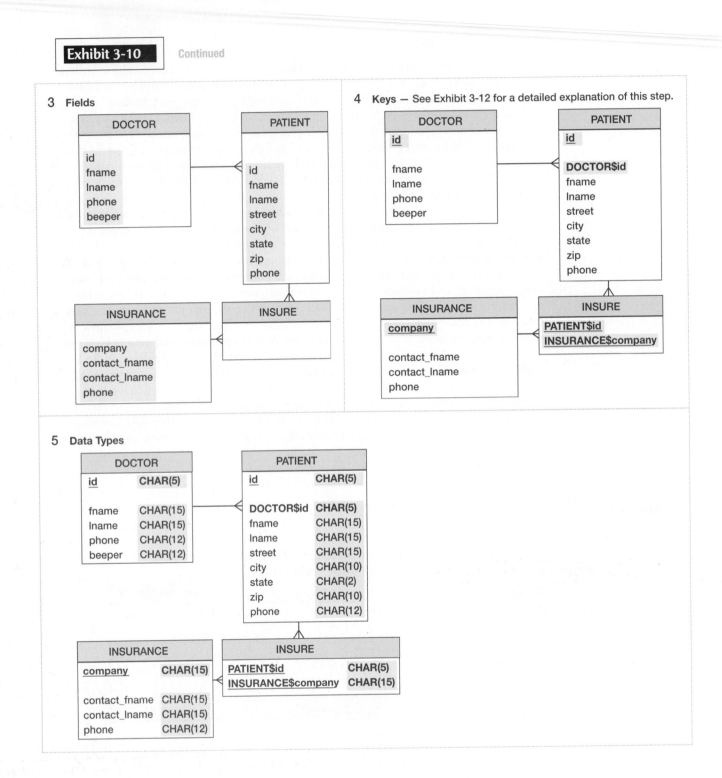

3   Fields

DOCTOR
- id
- fname
- lname
- phone
- beeper

PATIENT
- id
- fname
- lname
- street
- city
- state
- zip
- phone

INSURANCE
- company
- contact_fname
- contact_lname
- phone

INSURE

4   Keys — See Exhibit 3-12 for a detailed explanation of this step.

DOCTOR
- <u>id</u>
- fname
- lname
- phone
- beeper

PATIENT
- <u>id</u>
- **DOCTOR$id**
- fname
- lname
- street
- city
- state
- zip
- phone

INSURANCE
- <u>company</u>
- contact_fname
- contact_lname
- phone

INSURE
- **<u>PATIENT$id</u>**
- **<u>INSURANCE$company</u>**

5   Data Types

DOCTOR	
<u>id</u>	CHAR(5)
fname	CHAR(15)
lname	CHAR(15)
phone	CHAR(12)
beeper	CHAR(12)

PATIENT	
<u>id</u>	CHAR(5)
DOCTOR$id	CHAR(5)
fname	CHAR(15)
lname	CHAR(15)
street	CHAR(15)
city	CHAR(10)
state	CHAR(2)
zip	CHAR(10)
phone	CHAR(12)

INSURANCE	
<u>company</u>	CHAR(15)
contact_fname	CHAR(15)
contact_lname	CHAR(15)
phone	CHAR(12)

INSURE	
<u>PATIENT$id</u>	CHAR(5)
<u>INSURANCE$company</u>	CHAR(15)

Exhibit 3-11   Hospital Database Relationships

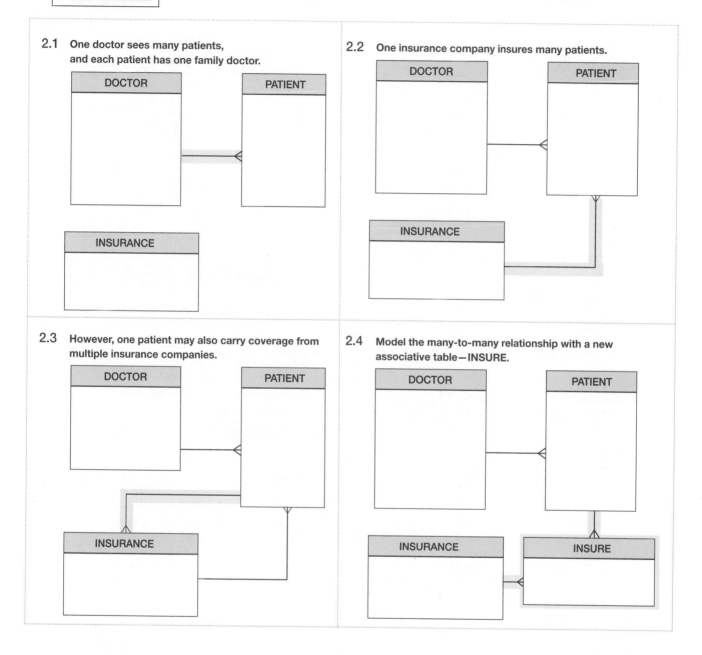

2.1 One doctor sees many patients, and each patient has one family doctor.

DOCTOR   PATIENT

INSURANCE

2.2 One insurance company insures many patients.

DOCTOR   PATIENT

INSURANCE

2.3 However, one patient may also carry coverage from multiple insurance companies.

DOCTOR   PATIENT

INSURANCE

2.4 Model the many-to-many relationship with a new associative table—INSURE.

DOCTOR   PATIENT

INSURANCE   INSURE

Exhibit 3-12 Hospital Database Keys

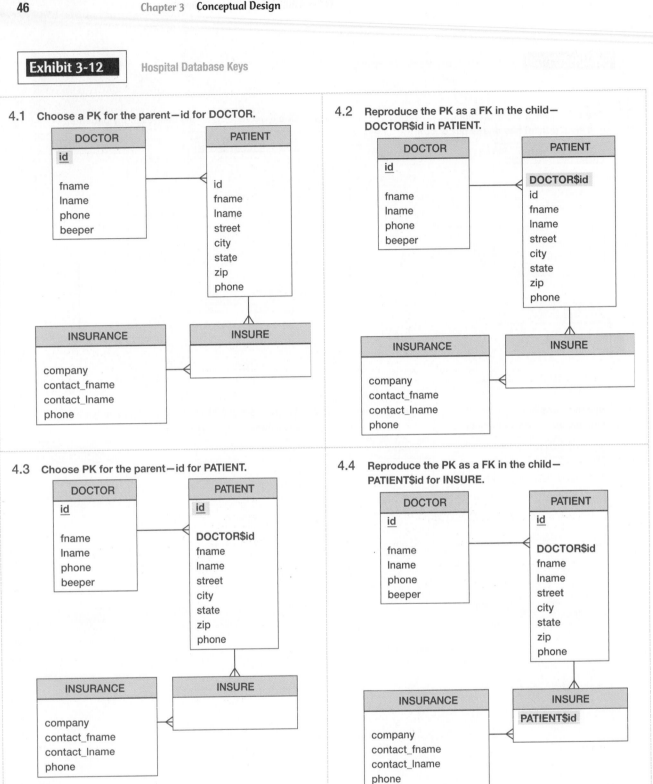

4.1 Choose a PK for the parent—id for DOCTOR.

4.2 Reproduce the PK as a FK in the child—DOCTOR$id in PATIENT.

4.3 Choose PK for the parent—id for PATIENT.

4.4 Reproduce the PK as a FK in the child—PATIENT$id for INSURE.

Exhibit 3-12 Continued

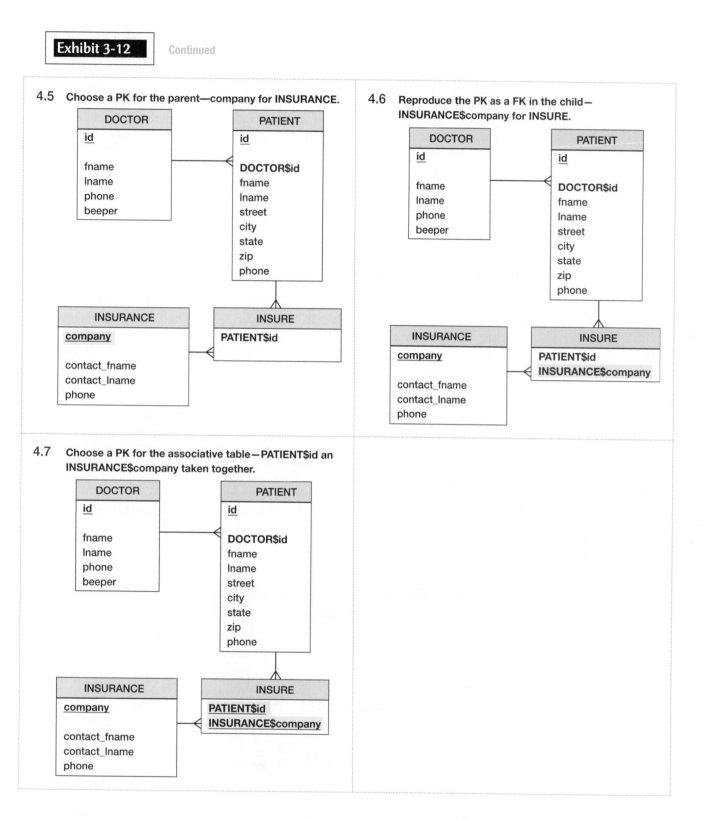

4.5 Choose a PK for the parent—company for INSURANCE.

4.6 Reproduce the PK as a FK in the child— INSURANCE$company for INSURE.

4.7 Choose a PK for the associative table—PATIENT$id an INSURANCE$company taken together.

As with the ENROLL table in the previous example, the INSURE table requires the combination of two fields to create the primary key. In this case, a patient's id will appear many times in the INSURE table—once for each insurance company that insures the patient. The same is true for the insurance company name. It will appear multiple times in the INSURE table, once for every patient that company insures. The combination of patient id and insurance company, however, will be unique, because you only need to record the association of a particular patient with a particular insurance company once.

From these two examples, you can begin to see the following pattern: An associative table that contains the primary keys from two other tables duplicated as foreign keys will usually need a primary key that is created through the combination of the two foreign keys.

The ACME Database

Often a designer faces the problem of redesigning the database for an existing system. In such a case, the existing forms (input) and reports (output) create a starting point for the database design. The designer can reverse engineer the database for a system if the input and output specifications are known. We will emphasize reverse engineering in this text—especially with regard to e-commerce sites.

Exhibit 3-13 shows the input form for the ACME Beer Company, with boxes indicating the customer, order, and lineitem information. Product information is conspicuously absent from the form. Nonetheless, we must assume that it exists somewhere in the system and model it accordingly.

Although calculated information appears on the form, that information is *not* stored in a database. Calculated information depends on other attributes, such as price and quantity, that could be updated over time. In such a case, the calculation must be updated, as well. The danger is that when implemented, the system will not automatically force the update, thereby leaving open the possibility of erroneous data. Database designers are taught to assume Murphy's Law—if something can go wrong, it will. Therefore, calculated information is not stored. The calculations will be performed on the fly, when the data is retrieved from the database.

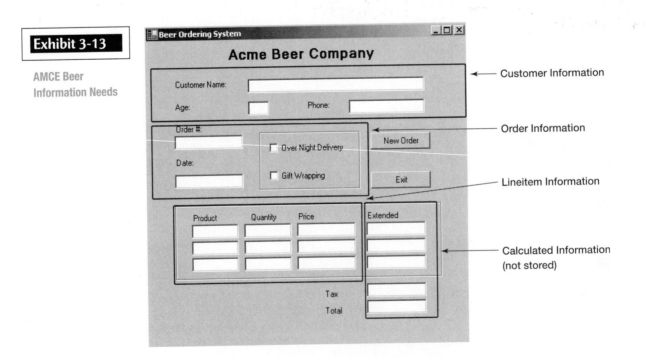

Exhibit 3-13

AMCE Beer
Information Needs

Exhibit 3-14 shows the systematic design of the ACME database. The many-to-many relationship between order and product is implemented with the lineitem associative table. Each lineitem represents a particular product on a particular order. Note that price is stored twice in this example—list price and sale price. The reason for the duplicate storage is that list prices change. However, customers need to be locked in to the price current at the time of the sale. Otherwise, they might buy at one price and later be billed at another price—not a good business tactic. Exhibit 3-15 shows how the relationships were derived, and Exhibit 3-16 shows how the keys were chosen.

Exhibit 3-14   ACME Database Step-by-Step Design

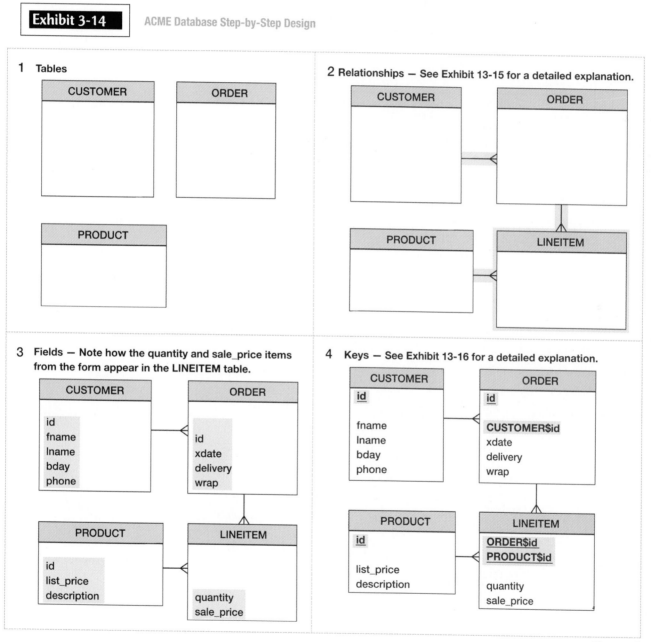

(Continued)

Exhibit 3-14   Continued

5   **Data Types**

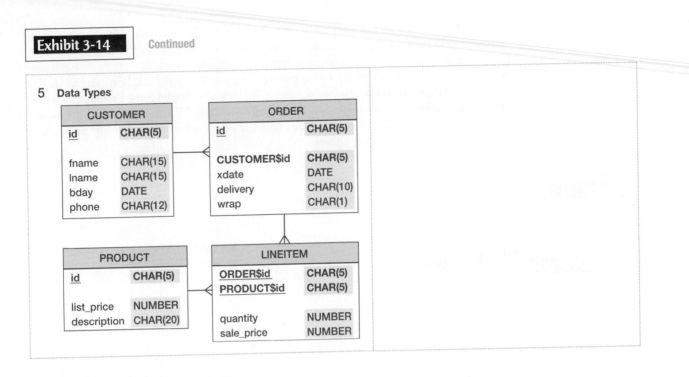

Exhibit 3-15 ACME Database Relationships

2.1 One customer places many orders, and each order belongs to one customer.

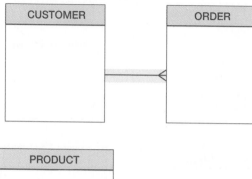

2.2 Many products may be listed on an order.

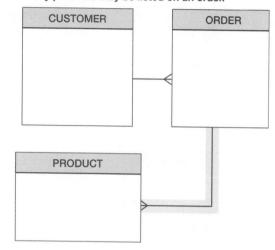

2.3 However, a given product may appear on multiple orders.

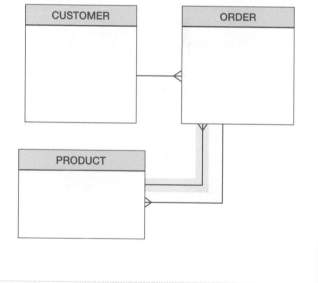

2.4 Model the many-to-many relationship with a new associative entity—LINEITEM.

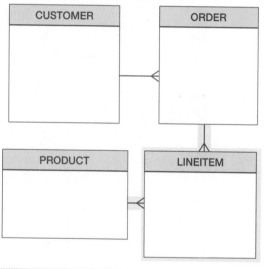

Exhibit 3-16   ACME Database Keys

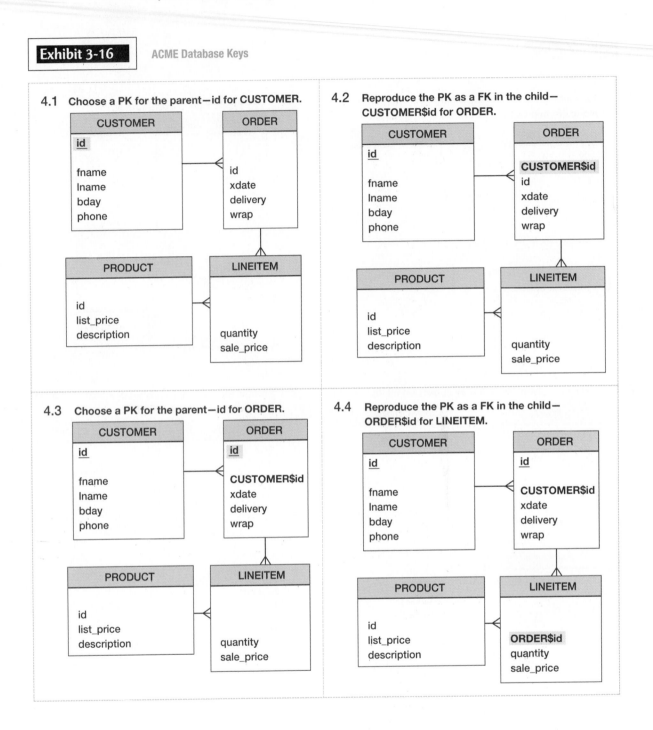

4.1   Choose a PK for the parent—id for CUSTOMER.

4.2   Reproduce the PK as a FK in the child—CUSTOMER$id for ORDER.

4.3   Choose a PK for the parent—id for ORDER.

4.4   Reproduce the PK as a FK in the child—ORDER$id for LINEITEM.

Exhibit 3-16   Continued

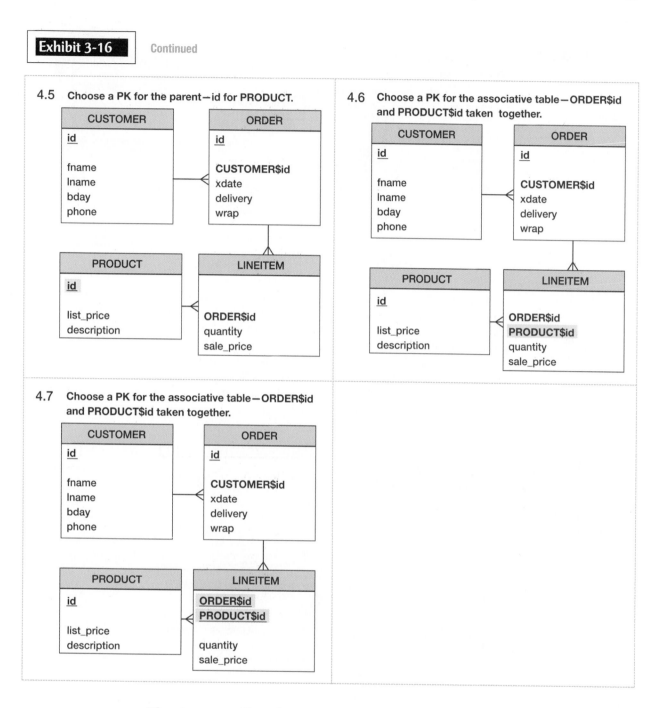

4.5   Choose a PK for the parent—id for PRODUCT.

4.6   Choose a PK for the associative table—ORDER$id and PRODUCT$id taken together.

4.7   Choose a PK for the associative table—ORDER$id and PRODUCT$id taken together.

The Amazon Database

For years, students could only study corporate information systems without any firsthand experience of using one. The Web has changed that situation completely. We now have direct access to a least a part of many corporate systems. Those Web sites may be reverse engineered to discover their underlying database design. We will begin with the largest e-commerce site in the world—Amazon.com.

Exhibit 3-17 shows a product detail page for a book listed on Amazon. There are many different pieces of data about the book, as well as links to other things like the reviews, delivery options, shopping cart, and others. To keep this application simple, we will focus on the items shown in the boxes. On this area of the screen, we can see that a book has a title, an author, and a price. Although not displayed to the user, every book has an ISBN number to uniquely identify the book.

Exhibit 3-17

Amazon Database
Product Detail
Screen
Source: ©2005
Amazon.com, Inc.
All Rights Reserved.

Exhibit 3-18 shows the order screen from an Amazon order. From the areas in the boxes, we can see that there is basic information about the order, including the order number, the date the order was placed, shipping information, and the method of payment. There is also information about the client placing the order, including name and address information. Information about each book ordered is shown in the largest box. These are often referred to as *lines* on the order. These line items show that we need to record the number of books ordered and the price of each book that was ordered. As in the ACME problem, the calculated information is *not* stored in the database.

Exhibit 3-18

Amazon Database
Order Confirmation
Screen
Source: ©2005
Amazon.com, Inc.
All Rights Reserved.

Your Account > **Where's My Stuff?** > Order Summary #104-6593028-4041515

Order Placed: September 1, 2005   Order Total: **$26.46**

When will your items arrive?

Shipment #1: 2 items - delivery estimate: December 14, 2004 - December 15, 2005

✓ **Shipment #1: Shipped on December 7, 2005**

Delivery estimate: Dec 14, 2005 - Dec 15, 2005 (More about estimates)
1 package via USPS

Shipping Address:

FirstName LastName
Street Address
City, State Zip

Shipping Speed:
FREE Super Saver Shipping

Items Ordered	Price
1 of: Welder's Handbook: A Complete Guide to Mig, Tig, Arc & Oxyacetylene Welding [Paperback] By: Richard Finch - 1 item(s) Gift options: None	$12.89
1 of: Ultimate Sheet Metal Fabrication [Paperback] By: Tim Remus - 1 item(s) Gift options: None	$13.57

Item(s) Subtotal: $26.46
Shipping & Handling: $4.98
Super Saver Discount: -$4.98

Total Before Tax: $26.46

Total for This Shipment: $26.46

Payment Information   (Need to print an invoice?)

Payment Method:
MasterCard | Last 5 digits: 77777

Billing Address:

FirstName LastName
Street Address
City, State Zip

Item(s) Subtotal: $26.46
Shipping & Handling: $4.98
Super Saver Discount: -$4.98

Total Before Tax: $26.46
Estimated Tax: $0.00

Grand Total: $26.46

Exhibit 3-19 shows the systematic design of the Amazon database. Lineitem forms the relationship between order and product. Notice that the list and sale prices are stored separately. The list price was shown as part of the book information. The sale price is the price shown with the line items. This price changes over time, and clients need to be locked in to a sale price. We have eliminated a number of attributes from the problem to keep the design relatively simple for demonstration purposes. In a business setting, the missing attributes would be included. In addition, there have been several small alterations to the fields in several tables, as follows:

- For the order, the order summary number that appears in Exhibit 3-18 has been renamed id. The order table has been renamed xorder, because some database systems reserve the word order as a built-in function of SQL. In addition to the credit card number, the expiration date is also recorded.
- In the client table, email has been added because that is how Amazon identifies a user; it is also the item a user specifies to sign in to the user's account on the site. As with the previous database example, the name and address information was broken into separate fields.
- In the BOOK table, the ISBN number was added as described earlier. In addition, a field called qoh was added. This acronym stands for *Quantity On Hand* and is basically the number of copies of the book in stock. This information would be needed to determine if an order for the book could be placed.

Exhibit 3-20 shows how the relationships were derived, and Exhibit 3-21 shows how the keys were chosen. Finally, Exhibit 3-22 shows sample data for the Amazon database.

Exhibit 3-19	Amazon Database Step-by-Step Design

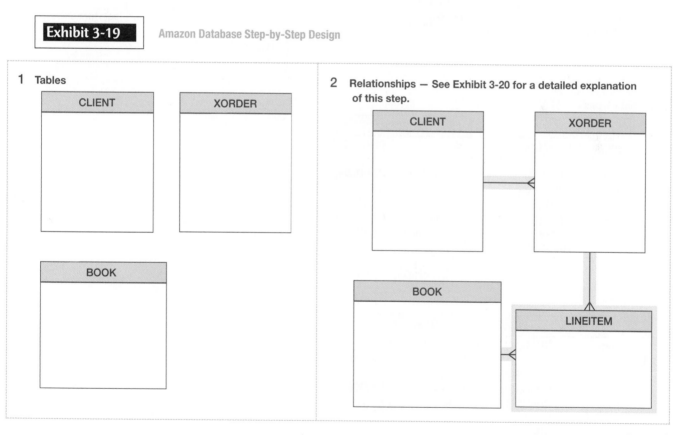

(Continued)

Exhibit 3-19   Continued

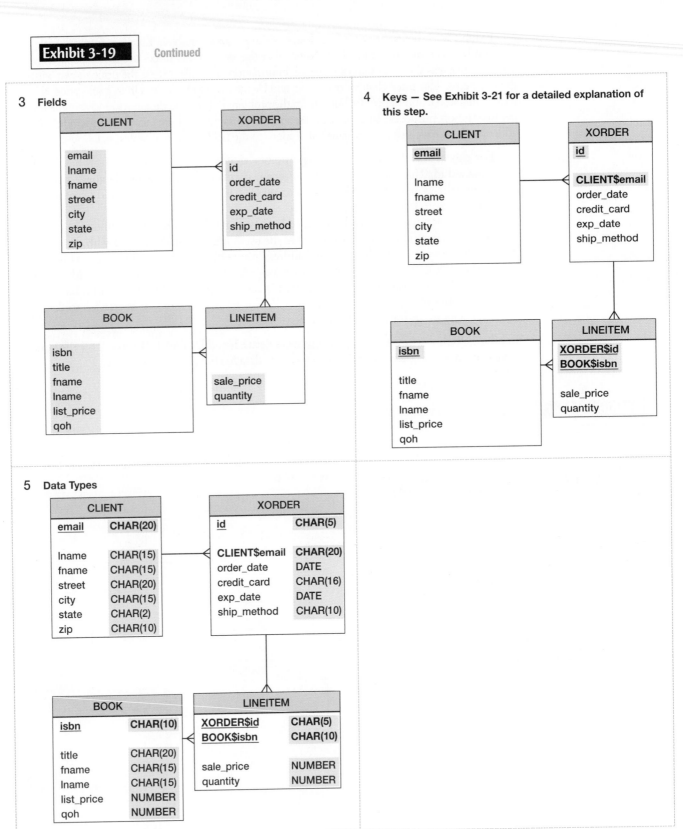

3 **Fields**

4 **Keys — See Exhibit 3-21 for a detailed explanation of this step.**

5 **Data Types**

Exhibit 3-20　Amazon Database Relationships

2.1　One client can place multiple orders, and each order belongs to one client.

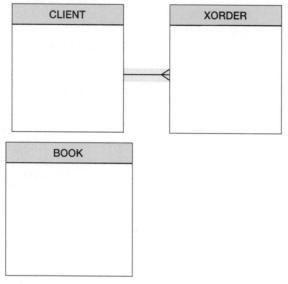

2.2　Many books may be listed on an order.

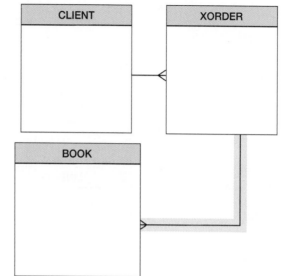

2.3　However, a given book may appear on multiple orders.

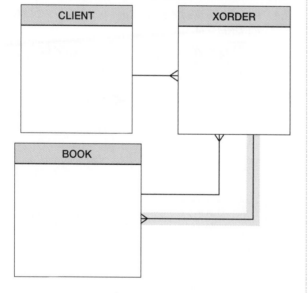

2.4　Model the many-to-many relationship as a new associative entity—LINEITEM.

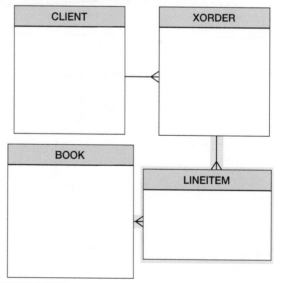

Exhibit 3-21   Amazon Database Keys

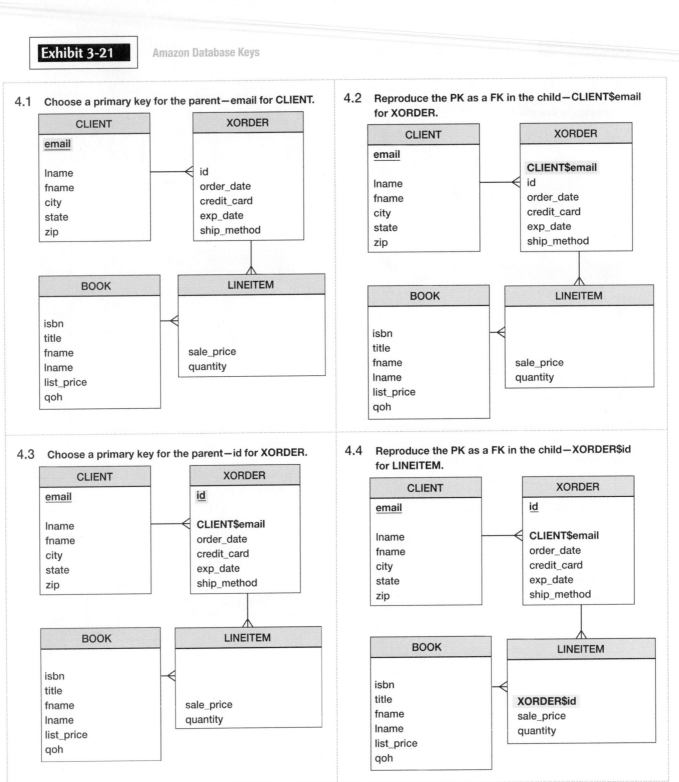

4.1   Choose a primary key for the parent—email for CLIENT.

4.2   Reproduce the PK as a FK in the child—CLIENT$email for XORDER.

4.3   Choose a primary key for the parent—id for XORDER.

4.4   Reproduce the PK as a FK in the child—XORDER$id for LINEITEM.

Exhibit 3-21 Continued

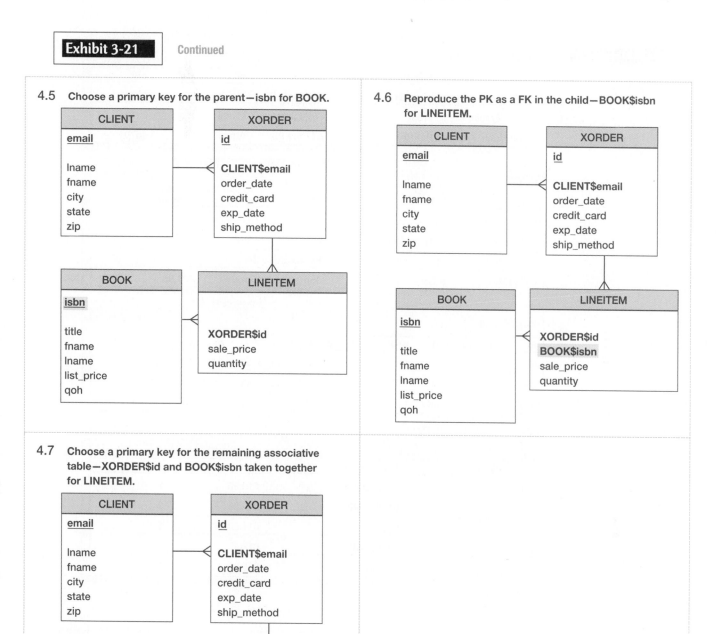

4.5 Choose a primary key for the parent—isbn for BOOK.

CLIENT

email

lname
fname
city
state
zip

XORDER

id

CLIENT$email
order_date
credit_card
exp_date
ship_method

BOOK

isbn

title
fname
lname
list_price
qoh

LINEITEM

XORDER$id
sale_price
quantity

4.6 Reproduce the PK as a FK in the child—BOOK$isbn for LINEITEM.

CLIENT

email

lname
fname
city
state
zip

XORDER

id

CLIENT$email
order_date
credit_card
exp_date
ship_method

BOOK

isbn

title
fname
lname
list_price
qoh

LINEITEM

XORDER$id
BOOK$isbn
sale_price
quantity

4.7 Choose a primary key for the remaining associative table—XORDER$id and BOOK$isbn taken together for LINEITEM.

CLIENT

email

lname
fname
city
state
zip

XORDER

id

CLIENT$email
order_date
credit_card
exp_date
ship_method

BOOK

isbn

title
fname
lname
list_price
qoh

LINEITEM

XORDER$id
BOOK$isbn

sale_price
quantity

Exhibit 3-22

Amazon Database
Sample Data

CLIENT

email	lname	fname	street	city	state	zip
thacker@ohio.edu	Thacker	Rebecca	93 Maple Dr.	Athens	OH	45701
mtfrost@yahoo.com	Frost	Tere	75 Algaringo	Miami	FL	33134
perotti@ohio.edu	Perotti	Jim	54 Pine Pl.	Athens	OH	45701

BOOK

isbn	title	fname	lname	list_price	qoh
0312099436	Women of the Silk	Gail	Tsukiyama	012.95	1
014025448X	At Home in Mitford	Jan	Karon	012.95	1
0345423097	Joy School	Elizabeth	Berg	011.95	7
0670894370	A Common Life	Jan	Karon	024.95	3

XORDER

id	CLIENT$email	order_date	credit_card	exp_date	ship_method
001	thacker@ohio.edu	11/15/2002	9999888877776666	07/31/2003	FedEx
002	perotti@ohio.edu	11/23/2002	3333444455556666	04/30/2005	USPS
003	thacker@ohio.edu	12/02/2002	4444111122223333	10/31/2004	USPS

LINEITEM

XORDER$id	BOOK$isbn	sale_price	quantity
001	0312099436	010.36	2
001	014025448X	010.36	3
002	0312099436	011.50	1
002	0670894370	017.46	2
003	0670894370	018.00	1

SUMMARY

- ER diagrams should be constructed using a systematic process. Design should begin with a big-picture view, and detail should be progressively added to prepare for implementation.
- There are five steps to the process of creating an ER diagram:

  Step 1: Represent Entities as Tables

  - Entities are persons, places, things, and events about which you will collect and store information. Information about those entities is recorded in tables.
  - Represent each entity as a table by drawing a box and recording a unique name for the table.

  Step 2: Determine Relationships

  - Show the relationships by connecting the tables with lines. Every table must connect to at least one other table in the database—unless, of course, the entire database consists of only one table.

- In most cases, a record in one table will correspond to multiple records in another table. Show this relationship by placing a crow's foot along the line pointing to the table on the many side of the relationship.
- For many-to-many relationships, create a new associative table.

Step 3: List Fields

- Model the attributes as fields listed inside each table.

Step 4: Identify Keys

- All tables must have a primary key to uniquely identify each record.
- All child tables must additionally have a foreign key field to connect each child record with its corresponding parent.

Step 5: Data Types

- Determine the data type and size of each attribute as a final design step.
- Primary and foreign keys must match in data type and size.

- A one-to-many relationship means that a row in one table is matched to multiple rows in the second table, and a row in the second table is matched back to one row in the first table.
- In a many-to-many relationship, rows in one table are associated with many rows in the second table, and a row in the second table is associated with many rows in the first table.
- Although calculated information appears on the form, that information is *not* stored in a database.

KEY TERMS

Associative table. A new table created to implement a many-to-many relationship. It literally associates records between its two parent tables.

Cardinality. The technical term used to describe the number of records in the relationship.

Data type. The kind of information that may be stored in that attribute.

Domain. A set of values.

Many-to-many relationship. Rows in one table are associated with many rows in the second table, and a row in the second table is associated with many rows in the first table.

One-to-many relationship. A row in one table is matched to multiple rows in the second table, and a row in the second table is matched back to one row in the first table.

EXERCISES

Review

1. What is an entity?
2. How is an entity modeled in an ER diagram?
3. What is an associative table?
4. Define one-to-many relationship.
5. How is a one-to-many relationship modeled in an ER diagram?
6. Define many-to-many relationship.
7. How is a many-to-many relationship modeled in an ER diagram?
8. Define cardinality.
9. What is a data type?
10. Define domain.

Discuss

1. What questions can help identify an entity?
2. Give an example of a one-to-many relationship not found in the text.
3. Why must the primary key of a parent table be determined before the foreign key in the child table?
4. Why do you suppose that determining relationships comes before establishing primary keys in the design sequence?
5. Give an example of a many-to-many relationship not found in the text.

Practice

For each of these problems, produce an ERD in accordance with the specifications of this text. These diagrams may be drawn with any design tool—even pencil and paper. However, many universities have access to Microsoft Visio as part of their site license agreement. A Visio template supporting the diagrams found in this text may be downloaded from the accompanying Web site.

1. Reel.com sells videos online. They provide the additional service of rating the movies along dimensions such as action, drama, humor, sex, violence, suspense, and offbeat energy. Exhibit 3-23 and Exhibit 3-24 show the Reel.com overview and Anatomy of a Movie. Visit Reel.com at **www.reel.com** and reverse engineer the portion of their database that holds information about films.

Exhibit 3-23

Reel.com
Overview
of a Movie
Source: ©Hollywood
Management Company
2005.

Exhibit 3-24

Reel.com
Anatomy of
a Movie
Source: ©Hollywood
Management Company
2005.

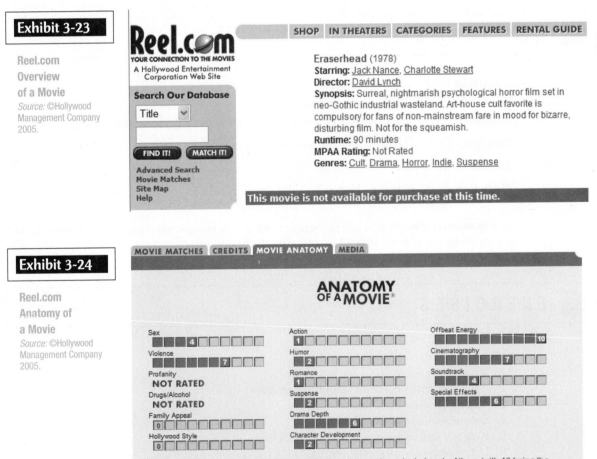

2. Soapscum Window Washing wants to keep track of its employees and the projects to which they are assigned. They need to keep track of some basic employee contact information, such as name, email address, and phone number. They use job classifications to group employees and determine salary. A classification has a code, description, and salary. Each employee is assigned to a single classification, and there can be multiple employees within the company assigned to a classification. In addition, they would like to keep track of all the projects to which each employee is assigned. For each project, there is an id number, a start date, an end date, and a cost. Each project can have multiple employees assigned to it, and an employee can be assigned to multiple projects.

3. Lame Events puts on athletic events for local athletes. They would like to have a database, including things like the sponsor for the event and where it was located, that can keep track of these events. For each event, they need a description, date, and cost. Separate costs are negotiated for each event. They would also like to have a list of potential sponsors that includes each sponsor's contact information such as the name, phone number, and address. Each event will have a single sponsor, but a particular sponsor may sponsor more than one event over time. They also need a master list of locations such as running tracks and stadiums that can be used for the events. For each location, we need to know the id, contact person, and phone number. A particular event will use only one location, but a location may be used for multiple events.

4. Cindy, owner of Cindy's Parties, wants a database to keep track of information related to the parties that she sets up. She wants to keep a list of all the clients who do business with her. She wants to track the name, address, and phone number of each client. For each party, Cindy needs to know the date and cost for the party. Cindy has a list of potential locations for parties that she can recommend to her clients. She would like the database to store the name, address, phone number, cost, and name of the manager at each location that she uses. When a party is set up, she would like to know which location was used for that party, because a party occurs at only one location. In addition to arranging the location for the party, Cindy sets up the entertainment for the client. She wants to maintain a list of bands and DJs that are used for the various parties. For each band or DJ, she needs a name, address, and phone number, as well as the normal fee they will charge for a party. Each party uses only one band or DJ. Finally, Cindy has a group of employees who work at the parties. She needs to know which employees have worked at which party, including the number of hours each employee puts in at each party. A given employee can work at several parties, and each party typically needs more than one employee to staff it. Cindy wants to know each employee's social security number, name, address, phone number, and hourly pay rate.

5. J. Crew is a leading retailer of fashion clothing. Exhibit 3-25, Exhibit 3-26, and Exhibit 3-27 show screenshots from their popular Web site. Visit their Web site at **www.jcrew.com**, and reverse engineer the portion of their database corresponding to the indicated areas in these exhibits.

J.CREW

HELP   ORDER STATUS   YOUR ACCOUNT   STORE LOCATOR   GIFT CARD   SHOPPING BAG

men   women   accessories   shoes   sale   order by item #

registration

1. Personal information

First *   M   Last *

Email (Login) *

☑ Email me promotions?

Gender ▾

Password *

Re-confirm password *

Clothing Gender Preference ▾

Clothing Type Preference ▾

* required field

2. Billing information

(Credit Card Mailing Address)

Care of (optional)

Address *

City *

State *   Zip *

USA ▾   =

Day Phone *

Evening Phone

Credit Card #

Expiration Date

Jan ▾   2005 ▾

Credit Card Type

------------------------------- ▾

Preferred shipping method:

Regular Shipping ▾

For the J.Crew Credit Card, set expiration date as Jan. 2005.

3. Shipping information

(if different from billing address)

Care of (optional)

Address

City

State   Zip

USA ▾

SUBMIT

Questions about registration?
Click here
For assistance in entering a
Japanese address, click here.

J.CREW

HELP   ORDER STATUS   YOUR ACCOUNT   STORE LOCATOR   GIFT CARD   SHOPPING BAG

men   women   accessories   shoes   sale   order by item #

previous 1 2 3 4 5 6 next

m

new arrivals

see all
sportcoats
pants & shorts
shirts •
knits & tees
swim
underwear & sleepwear
shoes
accessories

dressed up ›
suiting & blazers ›
pants ›
shorts ›
shirts ›
knits & tees ›
sweaters ›
swim ›
outerwear ›
ties ›
sweats & sleepwear ›
underwear ›
shoes ›
accessories ›

click to see larger image ›
e-mail this style to a friend ◣◢ ›

Striped linen shirt
Linen. Point collar. Standard placket. No back pleats.
Shirttail hem. Import. Machine wash.

◉ Regular $68.00 item 63832

feature color:
BLUE
CLICK TO VIEW ANOTHER COLOR

* Please select a size.
* Please select a color.

Color ▾

Size ▾   size charts

1   Qty

ADD TO SHOPPING BAG

Ship to

My Shipping ▾

Exhibit 3-27

J. Crew Lineitem Information
Source: Used by Permission of J. Crew.

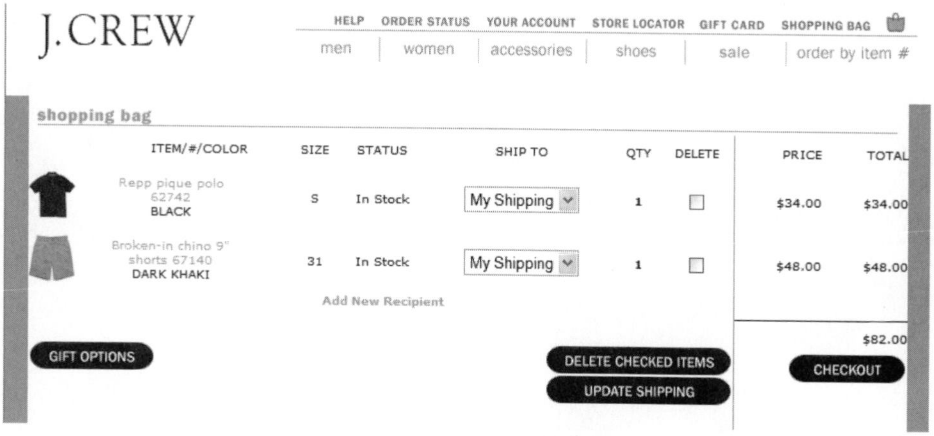

J.CREW

shopping bag

ITEM/#/COLOR	SIZE	STATUS	SHIP TO	QTY	DELETE	PRICE	TOTAL
Repp pique polo 627-42 BLACK	S	In Stock	My Shipping ▾	1	☐	$34.00	$34.00
Broken-in chino 9" shorts 67140 DARK KHAKI	31	In Stock	My Shipping ▾	1	☐	$48.00	$48.00
			Add New Recipient				
							$82.00

GIFT OPTIONS

DELETE CHECKED ITEMS

UPDATE SHIPPING

CHECKOUT

Normalization

Introduction

Chapter 2 explored the theory of the relational database. Chapter 3 applied that theory to database design. This chapter discusses how to check your work—how to verify the accuracy of a database design.

Perhaps you have had the experience of having two different phone numbers stored for your friend or associate. Perhaps one number is in your Rolodex at the office, and a different number is in your PDA. Which is the most current? Most of the time, you can figure it out. However, would a stranger who looked at both entries know which one was correct? Duplicate entries often result in uncertain information.

Similarly, a database design opens itself to errors whenever it stores the same data more than once. The repeated data is called duplicate data. Duplicate data invites errors every time records are inserted, updated, or deleted. Duplicate data can also lead to some very undesirable side effects, such as the inability to insert information into the database.

Duplicate data is created when fields from two or more tables are mistakenly combined into a single table. By contrast, tables designed to be free of duplicate data are called *normalized tables*. Normalization involves splitting the combined table into separate tables. However, detecting and solving the problem is not always obvious. Which are the right tables? Which fields belong to which table? Fortunately, normalization provides a rigorous methodology for detecting and correcting these errors.

Learning Objectives

After completing this chapter, you will be able to:

- Explain the proper function of a primary key.
- Explain the relationship between primary keys and normalization.
- Detect a denormalized design.
- Use a step-by-step process to normalize a design through fourth normal form (4NF).

Normal Forms

A database is normalized when each field holds just one value and each table has the correct set of fields. There are six **normal forms (NFs): 1NF, 2NF, 3NF, BCNF, 4NF,** and **5NF.**[1] The normal forms build upon each other. Each normal form encompasses all the lower numbered normal forms. For example, a table verified to be in 3NF is also in 1NF and 2NF. We will cover through 4NF in this chapter. Violations of 5NF are rare and beyond the scope of this text.

The normal forms may be summarized as follows:

- 1NF: All fields must contain single values only. For example, storing two phone numbers in a single phone number field is disallowed in 1NF.
- 2NF: Part of the primary key may not determine a non-key field.
- 3NF: A non-key field may not determine another non-key field
- BCNF: Every determinant is a key.
- 4NF: In an all-key table, part of the key can determine multiple values of, at most, one other field.

We will expand upon each of these definitions with visual examples throughout the chapter. Our first task, however, is to show just how serious the problem can be by looking at a denormalized design.

Denormalized Designs

Normalized designs place entities in separate tables. To this point, our designs have all been normalized. Normalized designs avoid duplicate data, or storing the same information more than once. Denormalized designs, by contrast, *do* contain duplicate data. If denormalized designs are created by merging two or more tables together into a single table, the resulting duplicate data creates insert, update, and delete problems. We will highlight the problems, and then we will discuss how to identify and fix normalization violations.

Normalizing the Arcade Database

Exhibit 4-1 shows the comparison of normalized and denormalized designs for the Arcade database. Note that in the denormalized design, the foreign key MEMBER$email disappears, because there is no relationship. The lack of foreign keys is actually an advantage of denormalized designs and probably the greatest reason that these one-table designs are favored so highly by amateurs. Exhibit 4-2 shows duplicate sample data in the denormalized design. Note that the password, name, and phone number are repeated for both John Day and Thom Luce.

---

[1]BCNF was discovered after 4NF had already been developed. BCNF is a refinement of 3NF to handle a special case that 3NF does not cover.

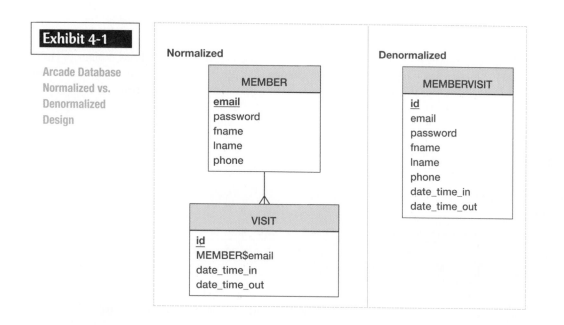

Exhibit 4-1

Arcade Database
Normalized vs.
Denormalized
Design

Normalized

MEMBER

<u>email</u>
password
fname
lname
phone

VISIT

<u>id</u>
MEMBER$email
date_time_in
date_time_out

Denormalized

MEMBERVISIT

<u>id</u>
email
password
fname
lname
phone
date_time_in
date_time_out

Exhibit 4-2   Arcade Database Denormalized Sample Data

MEMBERVISIT

<u>id</u>	email	password	fname	lname	phone	date_time_in	date_time_out
001	dayj@ohio.edu	rocket	John	Day	592-0646	25-JUN-02 14:00	25-JUN-02 17:30
002	luce@ohio.edu	bullet	Thom	Luce	592-1111	25-JUN-02 18:00	25-JUN-02 20:00
003	dayj@ohio.edu	rocket	John	Day	592-0646	26-JUN-02 10:00	26-JUN-02 11:30
004	luce@ohio.edu	bullet	Thom	Luce	592-1111	27-JUN-02 09:00	27-JUN-02 10:00
005	mcgann@ohio.edu	arrow	Sean	McGann	592-2222	27-JUN-02 16:00	27-JUN-02 18:00

Update Problem

Exhibit 4-3 shows a potential update problem caused by the denormalized design. If Thom Luce changes his password, there is a chance that the update will be made to one of his records but not to the other. The result is inconsistent data; the system really does not know for sure which password is correct.

Exhibit 4-3   Arcade Database Update Problems Due to Duplicate Data

MEMBERVISIT

id	email	password	fname	lname	phone	date_time_in	date_time_out
001	dayj@ohio.edu	rocket	John	Day	592-0646	25-JUN-02 14:00	25-JUN-02 17:30
002	luce@ohio.edu	bullet	Thom	Luce	592-1111	25-JUN-02 18:00	25-JUN-02 20:00
003	dayj@ohio.edu	rocket	John	Day	592-0646	26-JUN-02 10:00	26-JUN-02 11:30
004	luce@ohio.edu	cannon	Thom	Luce	592-1111	27-JUN-02 09:00	27-JUN-02 10:00
005	mcgann@ohio.edu	arrow	Sean	McGann	592-2222	27-JUN-02 16:00	27-JUN-02 18:00

Exhibit 4-4 demonstrates that the normalized design avoids the update problem by storing Thom's password only once. In the normalized design, a password change affects one record, and one record only. The normalized design thereby does a better job of protecting data integrity.

Exhibit 4-4

Arcade Database
No Update
Problem in
Normalized Data

MEMBER

email	password	fname	lname	phone
dayj@ohio.edu	rocket	John	Day	592-0646
luce@ohio.edu	cannon	Thom	Luce	592-1111
mcgann@ohio.edu	arrow	Sean	McGann	592-2222

VISIT

id	MEMBER$email	date_time_in	date_time_out
001	dayj@ohio.edu	25-JUN-02 14:00	25-JUN-02 17:30
002	luce@ohio.edu	25-JUN-02 18:00	25-JUN-02 20:00
003	dayj@ohio.edu	26-JUN-02 10:00	26-JUN-02 11:30
004	luce@ohio.edu	27-JUN-02 09:00	27-JUN-02 10:00
005	mcgann@ohio.edu	27-JUN-02 16:00	27-JUN-02 18:00

Insert Problem

Exhibit 4-5 shows an insert problem caused by the denormalized design. A member cannot be added to the database unless visit_id, the primary key field, receives a unique value. By definition, the primary key field may not be left blank, either. Therefore, the denormalized design prohibits inserting a member's record in advance of his first visit. From a business standpoint, this is a burdensome and impractical restriction.

Exhibit 4-5   Arcade Database Insert Problem Due to Duplicate Data

MEMBERVISIT

visit_id	email	password	fname	lname	phone	date_time_in	date_time_out
001	dayj@ohio.edu	rocket	John	Day	592-0646	25-JUN-02 14:00	25-JUN-02 17:30
002	luce@ohio.edu	bullet	Thom	Luce	592-1111	25-JUN-02 18:00	25-JUN-02 20:00
003	dayj@ohio.edu	rocket	John	Day	592-0646	26-JUN-02 10:00	26-JUN-02 11:30
004	luce@ohio.edu	bullet	Thom	Luce	592-1111	27-JUN-02 09:00	27-JUN-02 10:00
005	mcgann@ohio.edu	arrow	Sean	McGann	592-2222	27-JUN-02 16:00	27-JUN-02 18:00
	frostr@ohio.edu	turtle	Raymond	Frost	597-2902		

Exhibit 4-6 demonstrates that inserting a new member is not problematic in the normalized design, because the member information is stored in a separate table. The design is in no way compromised if a new member has not yet made a visit to the arcade. Yet, the design does allow for multiple future visits, each one of which becomes a record in the VISIT table.

Exhibit 4-6

Arcade Database No Insert Problem in Normalized Design

MEMBER

email	password	fname	lname	phone
dayj@ohio.edu	rocket	John	Day	592-0646
luce@ohio.edu	cannon	Thom	Luce	592-1111
mcgann@ohio.edu	arrow	Sean	McGann	592-2222
frostr@ohio.edu	turtle	Raymond	Frost	597-2902

VISIT

id	MEMBER$email	date_time_in	date_time_out
001	dayj@ohio.edu	25-JUN-02 14:00	25-JUN-02 17:30
002	luce@ohio.edu	25-JUN-02 18:00	25-JUN-02 20:00
003	dayj@ohio.edu	26-JUN-02 10:00	26-JUN-02 11:30
004	luce@ohio.edu	27-JUN-02 09:00	27-JUN-02 10:00
005	mcgann@ohio.edu	27-JUN-02 16:00	27-JUN-02 18:00

Exhibit 4-7 demonstrates a delete problem caused by duplicate data. Removing visit 005 eliminates all the information about Sean McGann. The member information cannot remain in the table without a value completed for visit_id, the primary key field. This case is clearly *not* what we want in a business situation.

Exhibit 4-7   Arcade Database Delete Problem Due to Duplicate Data

MEMBERVISIT

visit_id	email	password	fname	lname	phone	date_time_in	date_time_out
001	dayj@ohio.edu	rocket	John	Day	592-0646	25-JUN-02 14:00	25-JUN-02 17:30
002	luce@ohio.edu	bullet	Thom	Luce	592-1111	25-JUN-02 18:00	25-JUN-02 20:00
003	dayj@ohio.edu	rocket	John	Day	592-0646	26-JUN-02 10:00	26-JUN-02 11:30
004	luce@ohio.edu	bullet	Thom	Luce	592-1111	27-JUN-02 09:00	27-JUN-02 10:00
005	mcgann@ohio.edu	arrow	Sean	McGann	592-2222	27-JUN-02 16:00	27-JUN-02 18:00

Exhibit 4-8 shows that the normalized design avoids the delete problem by storing the member information separate from the visit information. Sean McGann's member information is not compromised if we remove his visit from the database.

Exhibit 4-8

Arcade Database
No Delete Problem
in Normalized
Design

MEMBER

email	password	fname	lname	phone
dayj@ohio.edu	rocket	John	Day	592-0646
luce@ohio.edu	cannon	Thom	Luce	592-1111
mcgann@ohio.edu	arrow	Sean	McGann	592-2222

VISIT

id	MEMBER$email	date_time_in	date_time_out
001	dayj@ohio.edu	25-JUN-02 14:00	25-JUN-02 17:30
002	luce@ohio.edu	25-JUN-02 18:00	25-JUN-02 20:00
003	dayj@ohio.edu	26-JUN-02 10:00	26-JUN-02 11:30
004	luce@ohio.edu	27-JUN-02 09:00	27-JUN-02 10:00
005	mcgann@ohio.edu	27-JUN-02 16:00	27-JUN-02 18:00

The Normal Forms

The denormalized example above was problematic because of duplicate data. How do you systematically detect duplicate data? Normal forms allow us to detect and correct duplicate data.

First Normal Form (1NF)

Definition: A table in which all fields contain single values only.

A simple way to diagnose a 1NF violation is to look for fields that contain more than a single value. Each of the fields in violation must be moved to a separate table. The phone field in Exhibit 4-9 should be moved to a new table.

Exhibit 4-9

1NF Violation

MEMBER

email	password	fname	lname	phone
dayj@ohio.edu	rocket	John	Day	592-0646
luce@ohio.edu	cannon	Thom	Luce	592-1111, 593-0212
mcgann@ohio.edu	arrow	Sean	McGann	592-2222

Fixing a normalization violation requires a redesign of the database. Use the same design technique covered in previous chapters.

1. Tables
   - Create new table(s)
   - Rename original table if necessary
2. Relationships
   - Establish relationships between original and new table(s)
3. Fields
   - Transfer fields and rename as needed
4. Keys
   - Choose PK and FK for all tables.

Exhibit 4-10 shows the four-step method in action to correct the 1NF violation shown in Exhibit 4-9. Exhibit 4-11 shows the revised design with sample data.

Exhibit 4-10

Arcade Database Solving the 1NF Violation

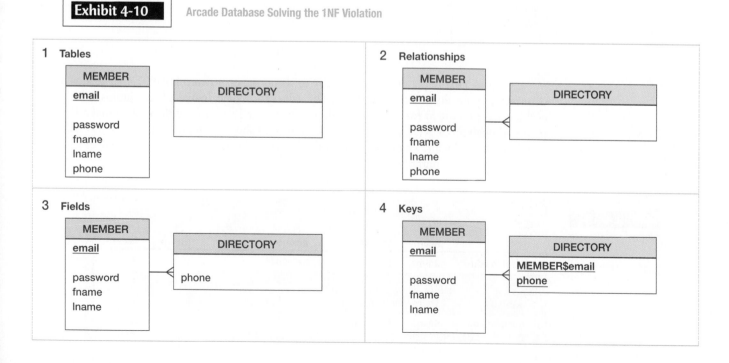

Exhibit 4-11

1NF Solution with
Sample Data

MEMBER

email	password	fname	lname
dayj@ohio.edu	rocket	John	Day
luce@ohio.edu	cannon	Thom	Luce
mcgann@ohio.edu	arrow	Sean	McGann

PHONE_LIST

MEMBER$email	phone
dayj@ohio.edu	592-0646
luce@ohio.edu	592-1111
luce@ohio.edu	593-0212
mcgann@ohio.edu	592-2222

Determinants

The higher normal forms—2 through 5—rely on the concept of a determinant. A **determinant** is a field or group of fields that controls, or *determines,* the values of another field. Field X determines field Y if any given value of X is always paired with the same value of Y. A primary key should always determine the non-key fields. Determinants can be shown using arrows (see Exhibit 4-12).

Exhibit 4-12

Primary Key
Determines
Non-key Fields

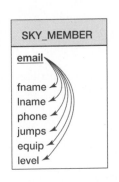

Exhibit 4-13 is badly designed in order to demonstrate a determinant. Email acts as a determinant for every record in the table. The values for fname, lname, phone, jumps, equip, and level are identical for a given email. The rows for Luce are duplicated to make the point—though this is NOT good practice. Exhibit 4-14 shows a situation in which email fails to act as a determinant. The same email address is paired with two different first names and two different phone numbers.

Exhibit 4-13

Email Acts as a
Determinant

MEMBER

email	fname	lname	phone	jumps	equip	level
dayj@ohio.edu	John	Day	529-0646	5	Y	B
luce@ohio.edu	Thom	Luce	529-1111	12	N	I
luce@ohio.edu	Thom	Luce	529-1111	12	N	I
mcgann@ohio.edu	Sean	McGann	592-2222	20	Y	A

Exhibit 4-14

Email Fails to Act
as a Determinant

MEMBER

email	fname	lname	phone	jumps	equip	level
dayj@ohio.edu	John	Day	529-0646	5	Y	B
luce@ohio.edu	Thom	Luce	529-1111	12	N	I
luce@ohio.edu	Thomas	Luce	597-8822	12	N	I
mcgann@ohio.edu	Sean	McGann	592-2222	20	Y	A

Second Normal Form (2NF)

Definition: A table in which each non-key field is determined by the whole primary key and not part of the primary key by itself.

Violations of 2NF can only occur on tables that have primary keys formed by more than one field. Exhibit 4-15 shows a design that contains a 2NF violation. The primary key of STUDENT_ENROLL is id and SECTION$call_no taken together. The primary key should determine all of the non-key fields. The 2NF violation occurs because id, which is just a part of the primary key, determines fname, lname, dorm, and phone. Exhibit 4-16 shows an update problem that could be created by the bad design. According to the data, Jim Green has two different phone numbers. It is not clear from the data which phone number is correct.

Exhibit 4-15

2NF Violation

STUDENT_ENROLL

id
SECTION$call_no

fname
lname
dorm
phone
grade

Exhibit 4-16

2NF Violation
Creates Update
Problem

STUDENT_ENROLL

id	SECTION$call_no	fname	lname	dorm	phone	grade
1111	001	Jim	Green	450A	593-2333	A
2222	001	Steve	Black	326B	594-4623	B
3333	003	Linda	Brown	144A	593-5575	A
1111	004	Jim	Green	450A	593-2456	C

The step-by-step procedure to correct the 2NF violation is shown in Exhibit 4-17. A new ENROLL table is created. The grade and call_no fields are transferred to the new table. A foreign key, STUDENT$id, establishes the one-to-many relationship between the tables—one student has many grades.

Exhibit 4-17 Enrollment Database Solving the 2NF Violation

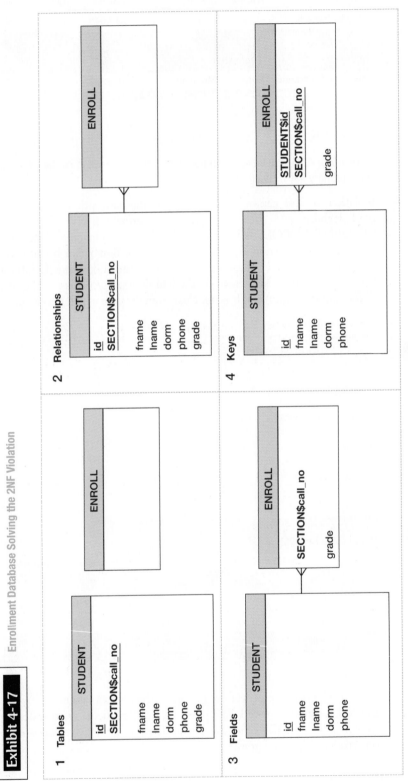

Exhibit 4-18 shows that in the revised design, only the key fields act as determinants. When only the key fields act as determinants, duplicate data is eliminated. Exhibit 4-19 stores the phone number only once for each student, thereby avoiding the update problem introduced earlier.

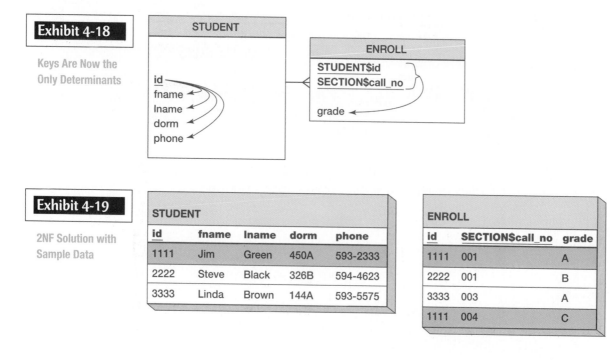

Exhibit 4-18

Keys Are Now the Only Determinants

Exhibit 4-19

2NF Solution with Sample Data

Look for 2NF violations in tables that have concatenated keys. Examine each of the non-key fields to see if it is dependent on only part of the primary key.

Third Normal Form (3NF)

Definition: A table in which none of the non-key fields determine another non-key field.

Violations of 3NF can occur in any table having more than one non-key field. To spot these violations, you need to consider any possible relationships that might exist between the non-key fields. Exhibit 4-20 shows a 3NF violation. Email, which is a non-key field, determines password, fname, lname, and phone—all of which are also non-key fields. The 3NF violation creates the potential update problem shown in Exhibit 4-21. The table stores two different passwords for Luce, and it is not clear which one is correct.

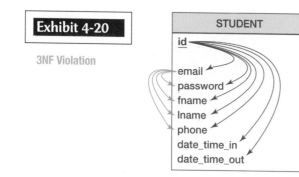

Exhibit 4-20

3NF Violation

Exhibit 4-21 3NF Violation Creates Update Problem

MEMBERVISIT

id	email	password	fname	lname	phone	date_time_in	date_time_out
001	dayj@ohio.edu	rocket	John	Day	592-0646	25-JUN-02 14:00	25-JUN-02 17:30
002	luce@ohio.edu	bullet	Thom	Luce	592-1111	25-JUN-02 18:00	25-JUN-02 20:00
003	dayj@ohio.edu	rocket	John	Day	592-0646	26-JUN-02 10:00	26-JUN-02 11:30
004	luce@ohio.edu	cannon	Thom	Luce	592-1111	27-JUN-02 09:00	27-JUN-0210:00
005	mcgann@ohio.edu	arrow	Sean	McGann	592-2222	27-JUN-02 16:00	27-JUN-02 18:00

The solution to the 3NF violation is shown in Exhibit 4-22. A VISIT table is created to hold the visit information. One member makes many visits.

Exhibit 4-22

3NF Solution

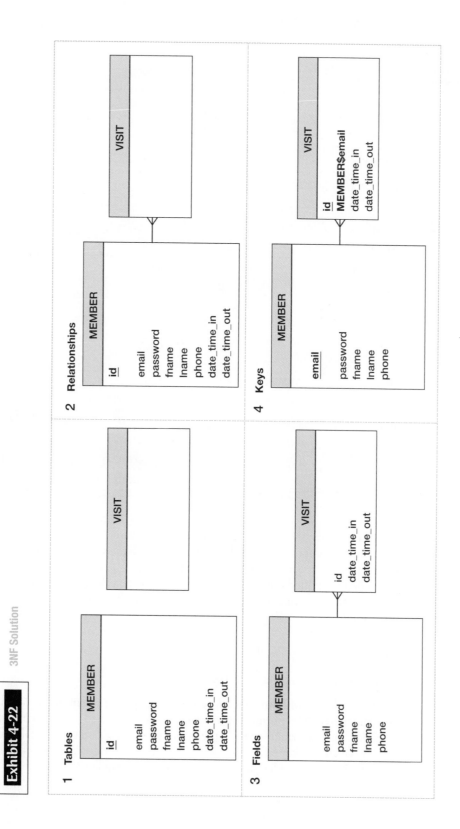

1 Tables

2 Relationships

3 Fields

4 Keys

Exhibit 4-23 shows that, in the revised design, keys are the only determinants. Exhibit 4-24 shows the 3NF solution with sample data. The password is stored only once for each member, thereby eliminating the update problem introduced earlier.

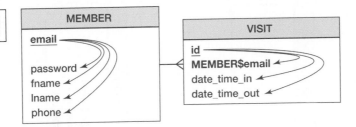

Exhibit 4-23

3NF Solution—
Keys Are Now the
Only Determinants

Exhibit 4-24

3NF Solution with
Sample Data

MEMBER

email	password	fname	lname	phone
dayj@ohio.edu	rocket	John	Day	592-0646
luce@ohio.edu	bullet	Thom	Luce	592-1111
mcgann@ohio.edu	arrow	Sean	McGann	592-2222

VISIT

id	MEMBER$email	date_time_in	date_time_out
001	dayj@ohio.edu	25-JUN-02 14:00	25-JUN-02 17:30
002	luce@ohio.edu	25-JUN-02 18:00	25-JUN-02 20:00
003	dayj@ohio.edu	26-JUN-02 10:00	26-JUN-02 11:30
004	luce@ohio.edu	27-JUN-02 09:00	27-JUN-02 10:00
005	mcgann@ohio.edu	27-JUN-02 16:00	27-JUN-02 18:00

Always be on the lookout for 3NF violations in any tables having more than one non-key field—which, unfortunately, includes most tables. Examine each combination of the non-key fields to see if there are any hidden dependencies.

A design verified through 3NF is usually a correct design. However, there are two cases in which higher normal forms must be employed. These situations are covered in the next two sections.

Boyce-Codd Normal Form (BCNF)

Definition: Every determinant is a key.

Boyce-Codd Normal Form (BCNF) was developed after the other normal forms had already been numbered. This normal form was specifically designed to cover circumstances in which a non-key field determines part of the primary key. As you may recall, 3NF only covers situations in which non-key fields determine each other. Therefore, BCNF is slightly more powerful than 3NF. As an added bonus, BCNF also has a simpler definition.

Exhibit 4-25 shows a BCNF violation. A non-key field, ssn, determines employee_id, which is part of the key. Actually, ssn and employee_id determine each other, hence the two-headed arrow. The violation leads to a potential update problem, as shown in Exhibit 4-26. Employee 8857 is shown with two different ssns—999-44-8857 and 999-44-8175. It is not clear from the table which is correct. If you knew that employee_id was derived from the last four digits of ssn, then we could deduce that 999-44-8857 is the correct ssn. However, we should not have to go through this exercise.

Exhibit 4-25

BCNF Violation

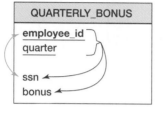

Exhibit 4-26

BCNF Violation
Creates Update
Problem

QUARTERLY_BONUS

employee_id	quarter	ssn	bonus
8857	q1	999-44-8857	1000
9216	q1	999-23-9216	500
8857	q2	999-44-8175	750

Exhibit 4-27 shows a step-by-step solution for the BCNF violation. The fields ssn and employee_id are moved to the EMPLOYEE table. One employee receives multiple quarterly bonuses.

Exhibit 4-27 BCNF Solution

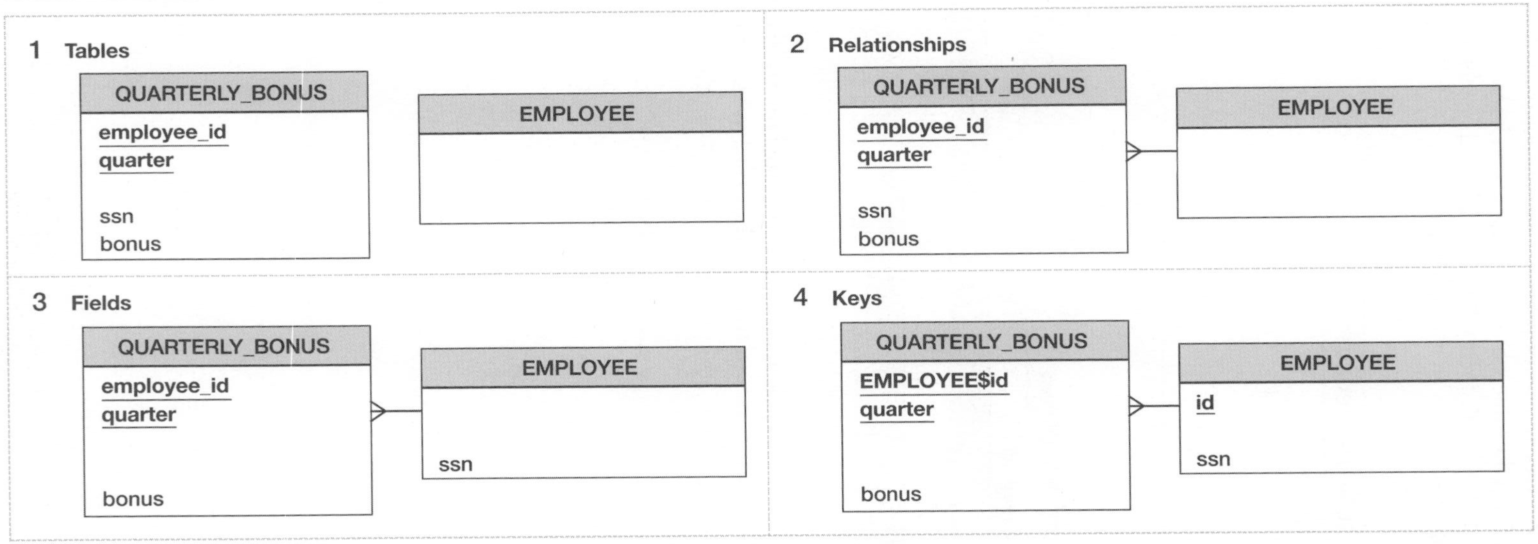

1 Tables

2 Relationships

3 Fields

4 Keys

The revised design in Exhibit 4-28 shows that only keys are determinants. Exhibit 4-29 shows that the revised design eliminates duplicate data. The update problem introduced previously is thereby eliminated by storing ssns only once for each employee.

Exhibit 4-28

BCNF Solution—
Keys Are Now the
Only Determinants

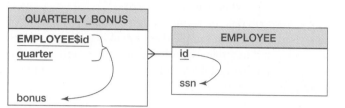

Exhibit 4-29

BCNF Solution
with Data

QUARTERLY_BONUS

EMPLOYEE$id	quarter	bonus
8857	q1	1000
9216	q1	500
8857	q2	750

EMPLOYEE

id	ssn
8857	999-44-8857
9216	999-23-9216

Fourth Normal Form (4NF)

Definition: In an all-key table, part of the key can determine multiple values of at most one other field.

In two respects, 4NF is different from the normal forms covered earlier. First, 4NF applies only to *all-key tables.* An all-key table is one without any non-key fields. Second, in 4NF one of the key fields determines multiple values of another of the key fields.

To understand fourth normal form requires introducing the concept of a **multivalued dependency (MVD).** Recall that a determinant is a field or group of fields that controls, or determines, the values of another field. A multivalued determinant is a field or group of fields that controls, or determines, *multiple* values of another field. Field X multidetermines field Y if any given value of X is always paired with the same *set* of values of Y.

The double-headed arrow in Exhibit 4-30 indicates a multivalued determinant. Exhibit 4-31 shows an update problem caused by the 4NF violation. If we drop Luce's German certification, we also lose the information that he plays tennis.

Exhibit 4-30

4NF Violation

SKILL

email
language
sport

Exhibit 4-31

4NF Violation
Creates Update
Problem

SKILL

email	language	sport
dayj@ohio.edu	Hungarian	soccer
dayj@ohio.edu	German	soccer
dayj@ohio.edu	Spanish	soccer
luce@ohio.edu	German	tennis
mcgann@ohio.edu	French	mountain climbing
mcgann@ohio.edu	French	sky diving
mcgann@ohio.edu	French	kayaking

Exhibit 4-32 shows the step-by-step redesign to solve the 4NF violation. Language information moves to the LANGUAGE table; sports information moves to the SPORT table. Surprisingly, there is no relationship between the two tables. If a new MEMBER table were created, both language and sport would have a relationship with that table. One member speaks many languages; one member plays many sports.

Exhibit 4-33 shows that the revised design contains only one MVD per table. Exhibit 4-34 shows the revised design with sample data. Email determines multiple values for language in the language table and multiple values for sport in the sport table. Luce's language and sports records are stored in separate tables. In the revised design, dropping Luce's German certification does not affect his sports records.

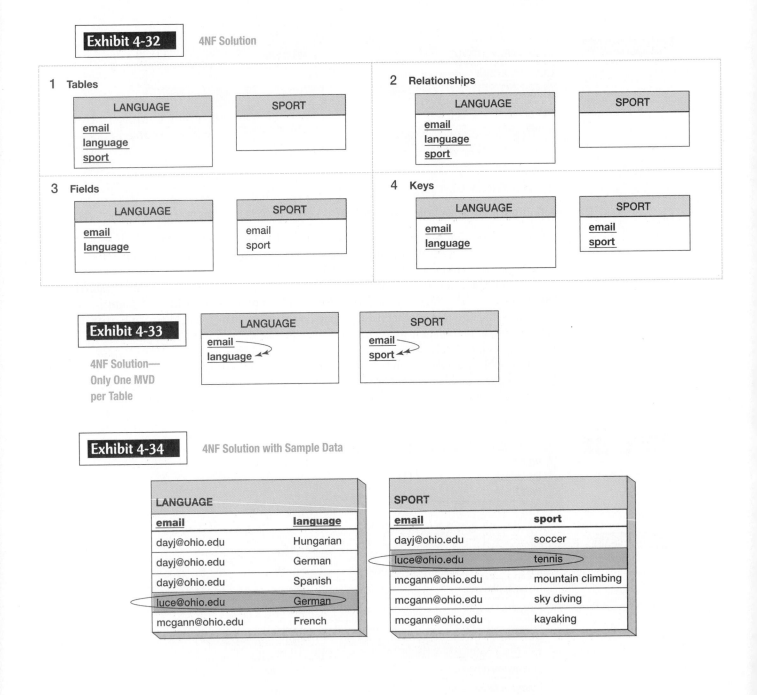

Exhibit 4-32   4NF Solution

Exhibit 4-33

4NF Solution—
Only One MVD
per Table

Exhibit 4-34   4NF Solution with Sample Data

Detecting Normalization Violations

Exhibit 4-35 shows the necessary conditions for each normalization violation. Read down each column to see all the conditions under which the violation may take place.

- A 1NF violation occurs when multiple values are stored in a single cell. First normal form is very easy to spot if you have access to the data. The table may have a key of any size.
- A 2NF violation can only occur when the table has a concatenated key *and* a non-key field that depends upon only part of the primary key.
- A 3NF violation occurs when a non-key field determines another non-key field. The table may have a key of any size. A simple heuristic used by designers to detect 2NF and 3NF violations is to take each non-key field in turn and ask whether that field depends upon the whole key (2NF) and nothing but the key (3NF). 3NF violations may also occur when a non-key field determines part of the primary key in a concatenated key table.
- A BCNF violation occurs when a non-key field determines part of the primary key. These violations can only occur in tables with a concatenated key.
- A 4NF violation occurs when the table has a concatenated key of at least three fields and there are no non-key fields. In addition, part of the key determines multiple values of another part of the key.

Exhibit 4-35

Necessary
Conditions for
Normal Form
Violations

	1NF	2NF	3NF	BCNF	4NF
Multiple values in a cell	X				
Table has any size key	X		X		
Table has concatenated key		X		X	X
Non-key field determined by part of the key		X			
Non-key field determined by another non-key field			X		
Non-key field determines part of the key				X	
Table is all key					X
Part of key determines multiple values of another part of the key					X

Let's put some of these ideas into practice with one of the examples in this chapter. Exhibit 4-1 and Exhibit 4-2 show a denormalized design that violates a normal form—but which one? It cannot be a 1NF violation, because each cell contains a single value. It cannot be a 2NF or 4NF violation, because the key is not concatenated. That leaves only 3NF. The table violates 3NF because a non-key field—email—determines four other non-key fields—password, fname, lname, and phone.

SUMMARY

- Denormalized designs are caused by mistakenly combining multiple entities into a single table. Duplicate data is the undesirable consequence of the denormalized designs. Duplicate data invites data integrity errors. It can also prevent records from being inserted under certain conditions.
- The normal forms are a systematic way to detect and correct denormalized designs. There are six normal forms—five of which were covered in the chapter.
  - 1NF: All fields must contain single values only.
  - 2NF: Part of the primary key may not determine a non-key field all by itself.
  - 3NF: A non-key field may not determine another non-key field.
  - BCNF: Every determinant is a key.
  - 4NF: In an all-key table, part of the key may determine multiple values of at most one other field.

KEY TERMS

1NF. All fields must contain single values only.

2NF. Part of the primary key may not determine a non-key field all by itself.

3NF. A non-key field may not determine another non-key field.

BCNF. Every determinant is a key.

4NF. In an all-key table, part of the key may determine multiple values of at most one other field.

Determinant. A determinant is a field, or group of fields, that determines the value of another field.

Multivalued dependency (MVD). Multivalued dependencies exist only in all-key tables. For one subset of the key, there are multiple instances of another subset of the key. For example, one employee (identified by employee id) may speak multiple languages.

Normal Form (NF). Normal forms are rules that allow designers to check for and eliminate data redundancy.

EXERCISES

Review

1. Explain the insert problem caused by a denormalized design.
2. Explain the update problem caused by a denormalized design.
3. Explain the delete problem caused by a denormalized design.
4. Define 1NF.
5. Define 2NF.
6. Define 3NF.
7. Define BCNF
8. Define 4NF.
9. What is a determinant?
10. Define multivalued dependency.

Discuss

1. Why are normal forms important? Give an example of an error that could occur in a denormalized relation.
2. Produce an example, not in the text, of a 2NF violation.
3. Produce an example, not in the text, of a 3NF violation.
4. Produce an example, not in the text, of a BCNF violation.
5. Produce an example, not in the text, of a 4NF violation.

Practice

1. Describe the normal forms violated in the following design and fix them. There may be multiple normal form violations in the design.

Exhibit 4-36

ER Diagram for
Exercise 1

PATIENT
patient_id
patient_fname
patient_lname
patient_street
patient_city
patient_state
patient_zip
patient_phone
doctor_id
doc_fname
doc_lname
doc_phone
doc_beeper

2. Describe the normal forms violated in the following design, and fix them. There may be multiple normal form violations in the design.

Exhibit 4-37

ER Diagram for
Exercise 2

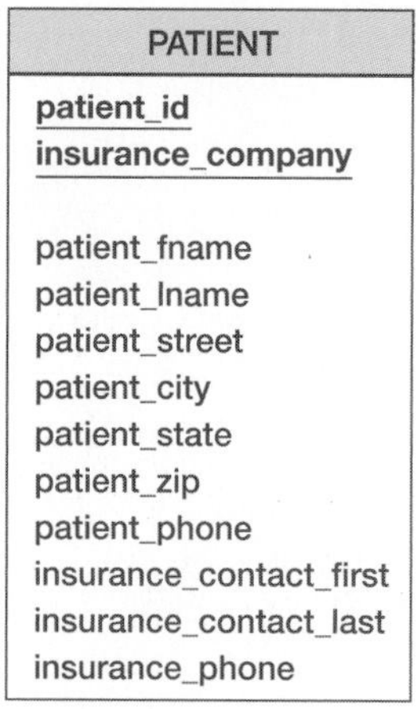

PATIENT
patient_id
insurance_company
patient_fname
patient_lname
patient_street
patient_city
patient_state
patient_zip
patient_phone
insurance_contact_first
insurance_contact_last
insurance_phone

3. Describe the normal forms violated in the following design, and fix them. There may be multiple normal form violations in the design.

Exhibit 4-38

ER Diagram for
Exercise 3

PATIENT
patient_id
symptoms
language
patient_fname
patient_lname
patient_street
patient_city
patient_state
patient_zip
patient_phone

Advanced Database Designs

Learning Objectives

After completing this chapter, you will be able to:

- Recognize when a database model requires a recursive relationship.
- Model one-to-many and many-to-many recursive relationships.
- Recognize when it is appropriate to use generalization/specialization hierarchies.
- Model generalization/specialization hierarchies.
- Recognize when the overlap and disjoint rules should be applied to generalization/specialization hierarchies.
- Recognize whether a generalization/specialization hierarchy represents partial and total specializations.
- Create complex data models that include recursive relationships and/or generalization/specialization hierarchies.

Introduction

In Chapter 3 you learned the basics of creating database designs that meet information needs. In this chapter, we extend this knowledge by introducing two special types of relationships and by providing examples of complex designs that use the newly introduced structures.

The two new structures are *recursive relationships* (sometimes called *unary relationships*) and *generalization/specialization hierarchies,* which are also known as *supertype/subtype hierarchies.* Recursive relationships are sometimes required; they may be the only way to model a situation accurately. In contrast, hierarchies are rarely required, but they often improve the design of a database.

Recursive Relationships

Typically, we think of a relationship as being between two (or more) different entity types. However, sometimes it is necessary to relate instances of an entity to other instances *of that same entity.* You are probably familiar with a classic example of a **recursive relationship,** course prerequisites. As you know, many courses require students to complete prerequisite courses. For example, systems analysis and design sometimes has database as a prerequisite. Modeling this relationship requires relating one instance (essentially a row in a table) of the course entity type (system analysis and design) to another instance (database) of the same entity type.

Another example of a recursive relationship is the supervisor relationship. In most organizations, supervisory relationships exist. For example, Jane Doe might be the supervisor for Joe Smith. Modeling this relationship requires a recursive relationship in which one instance of the employee entity type is related to another instance of the employee entity type.

How do we represent recursive relationships in a data model? The answer to this question depends on the cardinality of the relationship. Let's look at a problem to see how we model a recursive relationship.

An Example of a Recursive Relationship

Recall the Enrollment database from Chapter 3. For your reference, the data model for the Enrollment database is shown in Exhibit 5-1.

Exhibit 5-1

Enrollment
Database Design

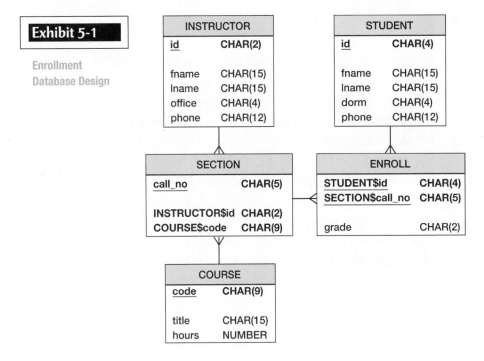

We are going to expand this model by adding two requirements. The first requirement concerns instructors. When a new instructor joins the organization, he or she is assigned to an experienced instructor, who acts as a mentor to the new instructor. To capture this relationship, we must modify the design of this database. Let's work through this modification before we discuss the second new requirement.

Creating the Mentor Recursive Relationship

Exhibit 5-2 shows the mentor relationships in the Enrollment database. Joe Smith (id = 11) is mentor to Sam Slick (id = 22) and Sally Sly (id = 33). Sally Sly mentors Sue Slim (id = 44).

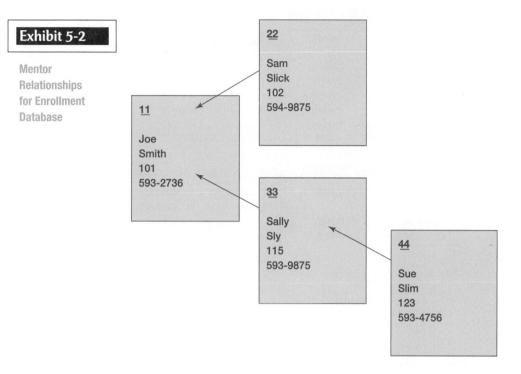

Exhibit 5-2

Mentor
Relationships
for Enrollment
Database

To capture the mentor relationship, we need to indicate that one instance of the INSTRUCTOR entity type may be related to another instance of this same entity. In other words, "mentors" is a recursive relationship. There are two ways to model recursive relationships, depending upon the cardinalities involved. In the mentor example, assume that there is a business rule in place such that each instructor may have, at most, one mentor. However, it is possible for a single instructor to act as mentor for several other instructors. In other words, the mentor relationship has a one-to-many cardinality. In Chapter 3, you learned that to represent a one-to-many cardinality, you repeat the parent entity's primary key on the one side as a foreign key in the child entity on the many side. For a recursive relationship, the same entity is both the parent and the child. So all we have to do is repeat the primary key (id in this case) as a foreign key (INSTRUCTOR$mentor), with both columns being in the INSTRUCTOR entity. The INSTRUCTOR entity with the foreign key representing the recursive relationship is illustrated in Exhibit 5-3. The data is included in the exhibit to show you how the foreign key references work.

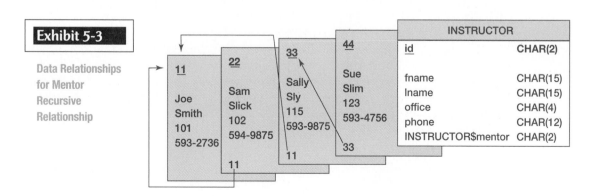

Exhibit 5-3

Data Relationships
for Mentor
Recursive
Relationship

Drawing the relationship in the ER diagram is similar to the way you draw other relationships. The only difference is that both ends of the relationship line go to the same entity. The ER diagram for the revised Enrollment database is shown in Exhibit 5-4.

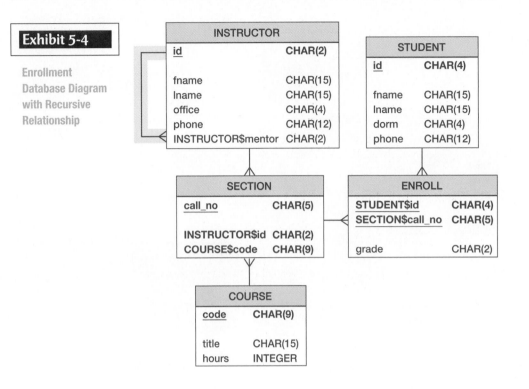

Exhibit 5-4

Enrollment
Database Diagram
with Recursive
Relationship

A Many-to-Many Recursive Relationship

The mentor relationship is an example of a one-to-many recursive relationship. Recursive relationships may also have many-to-many cardinalities. A bill-of-materials relationship is a classic example of a many-to-many recursive relationship. Basically, a bill of materials lists products that make up other products. For example, a computer may be made up of a CPU, monitor, keyboard, and mouse. A computer may also be part of a larger product. A complete system may include a computer, printer, and scanner.

Exhibit 5-5 gives another example, a home theater system. The home theater is made up of a console, remote, amplifier (amp), and speakers. A DVD/CD player and an AM/FM tuner combine to make up a console. Speakers are even more complicated. Each set of speakers is made up of a satellite, subwoofer, and center speaker. The subwoofer has components: an amp, a woofer, and a subwoofer. As you can see, bill-of-materials relationships can become quite complex. Imagine all of the product-to-product relationships that exist in an automobile!

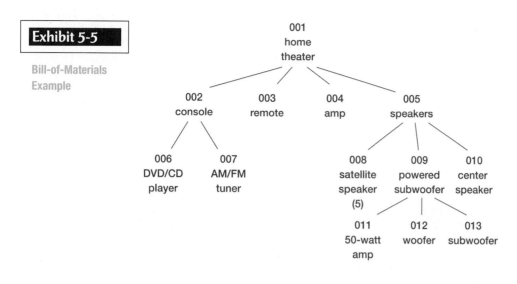

Exhibit 5-5

Bill-of-Materials
Example

Exhibit 5-6 shows the bill-of-materials data in table form. The table also includes quantity data, which is not shown in Exhibit 5-5. Notice that there are two problems with the table. First, there are many empty cells in the table. This situation translates into wasted space in a database. The second problem is more critical. We do not have any way to know what the maximum number of components might be. Therefore, we do not know how many columns we may need for products. For now, four is enough, but in the future we may have products with many more components.

Exhibit 5-6   Bill-of-Materials Table

PRODUCT

code	description	comp_1	qty_1	comp_2	qty_2	comp_3	qty_3	comp_4	qty_4
001	home theater	002	1	003	1	004	1	005	1
002	console	006	1	007	1				
003	remote								
004	amp								
005	speakers	008	5	009	1	010	1		
008	satellite speaker								
009	powered subwoofer	011	1	012	1	013	1		
011	50-watt amp								
012	woofer								
013	subwoofer								

Fortunately, these problems are easy to solve by using a recursive relationship. Although a bill-of-materials relationship might seem complex, when you think about it, it is just a relationship between products; it is a recursive relationship. There is a critical difference between this recursive relationship and the mentor relationship we examined earlier. The mentor relationship has a one-to-many cardinality. In contrast, a product may have multiple components, and that product may also be a component for several other products. For example, each of the speakers (code = 005) has three components, and the speakers may also be components of products other than the home theater system.

Representing a many-to-many recursive relationship is very similar to representing a many-to-many relationship between two different entities. Both require creating a new associative table to represent the relationship. Both typically have a primary key constructed of the foreign keys from both parent tables. For the recursive relationship, only one entity is involved in both sides of the relationship. To model the bill-of-materials relationship, we still create two foreign keys, both from the PRODUCT table, with one referring to the main product and the other to one of its components. Because of this situation, we include PRODUCT$code, which refers to the main product, along with PRODUCT$component, which refers to a component of the main product. We also include qty (quantity) as a non-key attribute. Exhibit 5-7 shows the ER diagram for the bill-of-materials relationship.

Exhibit 5-7

Bill-of-Materials
ER Diagram

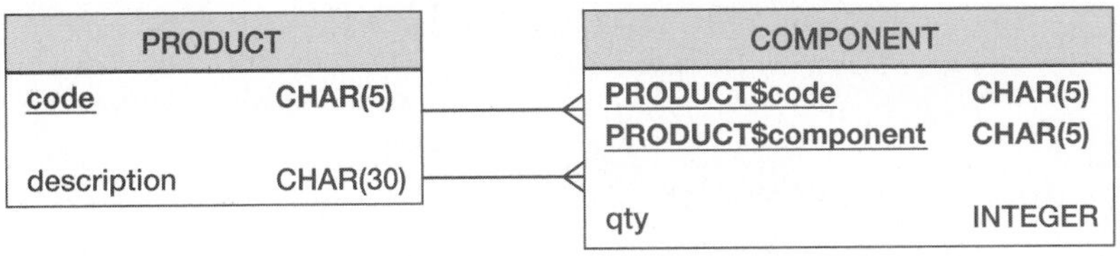

PRODUCT	
code	CHAR(5)
description	CHAR(30)

COMPONENT	
PRODUCT$code	CHAR(5)
PRODUCT$component	CHAR(5)
qty	INTEGER

Exhibit 5-8 shows how the data from the bill-of-materials table in Exhibit 5-6 would be represented in the database that results from the ER diagram above. The arrows illustrate the references from the COMPONENT table on the left to the PRODUCT table on the right. Not only do PRODUCT$code and PRODUCT$component together make up the primary key of COMPONENT, but each one individually also acts as a foreign key referencing PRODUCT.

Exhibit 5-8   Bill-of-Materials Database Tables

PRODUCT

code	description
001	home theater
002	console
003	remote
004	amp
005	speakers
006	DVD/CD player
007	AM/FM tuner
008	satellite speaker
009	powered subwoofer
010	center speaker
011	50-watt amp
012	woofer
013	subwoofer

COMPONENT

PRODUCT$code	PRODUCT$component	qty
001	002	
001	003	1
001	004	1
001	005	1
002	006	1
002	007	1
005	008	1
005	009	1
005	010	1
009	011	1
009	012	1
009	013	1

It is also possible to have recursive relationships with one-to-one cardinalities. Either of the two approaches we describe may be used to model these relationships. If there is any data associated with the relationship, it is best to model a one-to-one recursive relationship following the method we used for the many-to-many recursive relationship.

Hierarchies: Supertypes and Subtypes

In this section, we introduce the idea of *generalization/specialization hierarchies,* which are also called *supertype/subtype hierarchies.* To understand the need for these structures, consider the EQUIPMENT entity shown in Exhibit 5-9. Both the entity and a table of example data are provided. The shaded cells in the table do not currently contain data, nor will they contain data in the future.

Exhibit 5-9

Equipment Entity and Data

EQUIPMENT	
id	INTEGER
description	CHAR(30)
cost	CURRENCY
location	CHAR(10)
o_s	CHAR(10)
RAM	CHAR(10)
speed	INTEGER
cartridge	CHAR(15)

id	description	cost	location	o_s	RAM	speed	cartridge
1111	GoodPrint IJ24	125.50	BA101			10	GP204J
2222	FastPC X101	1750.00	BA221	Win XP	256MB		
3333	FastPC X220	2774.95	HP092	Win 2000	1GB		
4444	HP L223	695.59	BIO110			25	HP384X
5555	Lexmark Z52	175.80	MUS201			12	12A1970

As you can see, there are quite a few empty cells in the table. These empty cells are not much of a problem with a very small table, but when a table has hundreds of thousands of rows, having cells that will never contain data wastes valuable storage space and may degrade performance. If you look carefully at the table, you might notice that it actually contains data about two different types of hardware, computers and printers. We need to store some common data about both types, including the id, description, cost, and location. However, we need to store data about the operating system (o_s) and memory (RAM) only for computers. Speed and cartridge data are stored only for printers.

One potential solution for this problem might be to create two tables, one for all data about computers and one for all data about printers. This procedure might work in this case, but it would make certain data retrieval operations more complex. Also, because we would likely have types of equipment other than printers and computers, we would still need an EQUIPMENT entity.

A better solution is to use something called a **generalization/specialization hierarchy.** This structure consists of a general entity that includes all common attributes along with specialized entities that have the attributes common only to certain instances of the entity.

The general entity is often called a **supertype entity,** and specialized entities are commonly known as **subtype entities.** Thus, some people call the hierarchy a *supertype/subtype hierarchy.* Exhibit 5-10 shows the supertype/subtype hierarchy for the EQUIPMENT entity.

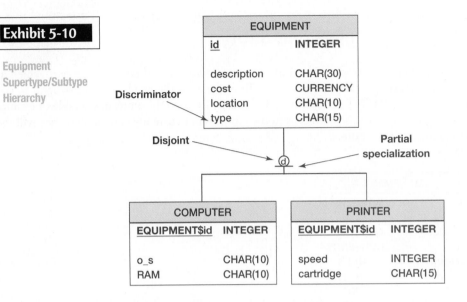

Several things about the exhibit are important to notice. First, a circle with one line below it is used to indicate that this is a supertype/subtype structure (later, we'll see an example that has two lines). Second, there is a letter in the circle; in this case it is a *d.* Also, notice that the supertype is above the subtypes. Keep in mind that you can have more than two subtypes. Another important point is that the subtypes have copies of the primary key in the supertype. Thus, we have an easy way to associate instances of the supertype to instances of the subtype. Finally, notice that we added a field called "type" to the supertype entity (EQUIPMENT). This field is called the discriminator. Such fields enable us to retrieve data more efficiently based on equipment type.

The fact that we have one line below the circle in our ER diagram indicates that this is a **partial specialization,** which means that there are some instances of the supertype that do not belong in any of the subtype categories. For example, we might have a scanner, which is neither a computer nor a printer. The alternative is a **total specialization,** which means that all instances of the supertype must belong to at least one subtype category. We will see an example of this case later.

The letter *d* inside the circle is also important. The *d* indicates that the **disjoint rule** is in effect for this hierarchy. When the disjoint rule is in effect, it simply means that an instance of the supertype may belong to *at most* one subtype category. In this example, that rule means that an instance of equipment is not allowed to be both a printer and a computer. The alternative is the **overlap rule,** which is indicated by the letter *o* in the circle. This rule means that a supertype instance may belong to more than one subtype category. Note that the disjoint/overlap and total/partial specialization decisions are independent of each other. You can have any combination of any two in a hierarchy.

In a supertype/subtype hierarchy, the concept of **inheritance** is important to understand. Basically, inheritance means that any instance of a subtype entity inherits all properties of the supertype, including its attributes and any relationships in which the supertype is involved. So, each instance of the subtype COMPUTER inherits all of the attributes of the related instance of equipment. Now let's try a little different situation.

A Supertype/Subtype Hierarchy Example

Suppose you need to create an ER diagram to store data for a small school. For now, the school's administration is interested only in storing data about people who are involved with the school. Some sample data is given in Exhibit 5-11. We need to make some simplifying assumptions. First, a student may have only one major. Second, we need to store only the highest degree earned by a faculty member. Third, the database will not store data about any other categories of people. Finally, the status column for staff members refers to whether they are part-time or full-time. Assume that all faculty members are full-time.

Exhibit 5-11

STUDENT
FACULTY, and
STAFF Tables

STUDENT

id	fname	lname	phone	major	gpa
4561	Sally	Smith	855-7748	MIS	3.75
6591	Ram	Ramesh	784-5496	ACCT	3.80
4875	Jerry	McReynolds	784-7785	MIS	2.50
7749	Robert	Johnson	859-4448	MUS	3.65
7890	Jim	Williams	616-8849	MAR	2.15
1123	Dana	Hewitt	855-4659	MGT	3.75

FACULTY

id	fname	lname	phone	department	degree
1247	Ross	Luce	855-8949	MIS	PhD
3587	France	Green	859-8849	MIS	PhD
7498	Paul	Trimmer	888-7474	ACCT	Masters
5497	Jennifer	Wilson	855-1149	MUS	Masters

STAFF

id	fname	lname	phone	status
1123	Dana	Hewitt	855-4659	Full time
1234	Cathy	Askew	859-2597	Part time
5413	Jerry	Jewel	855-2587	Full time

We could create three different entities with one entity representing each table. However, we recognize that the three tables have several columns in common. All three of the tables have columns for id, first name, last name, and phone. This situation should alert us to the possibility of using a supertype/subtype hierarchy. We need to be sure that all of the columns actually mean the same thing for all of the tables. Sometimes different tables use the same column names to store very different types of data. Fortunately, this is not the case here. So, we can take the common columns and put them into a supertype entity that we call "person." Then, we create three subtype entities, one for each of the three types of people. Another point to recognize is that Dana Hewitt (id = 1123) is in both the STUDENT and STAFF tables. This fact will be important to know later. Exhibit 5-12 shows the steps used in designing this database.

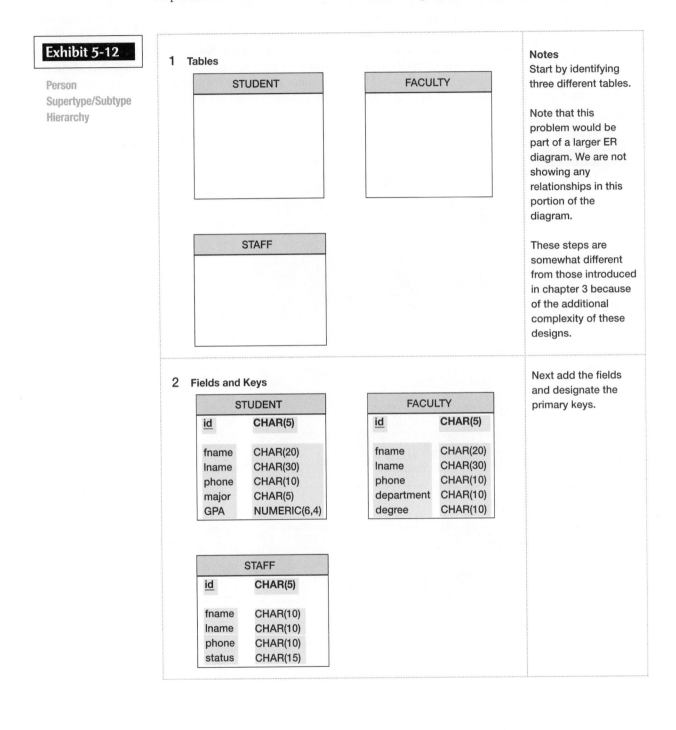

Exhibit 5-12

Person
Supertype/Subtype
Hierarchy

1 Tables

STUDENT

FACULTY

STAFF

Notes
Start by identifying three different tables.

Note that this problem would be part of a larger ER diagram. We are not showing any relationships in this portion of the diagram.

These steps are somewhat different from those introduced in chapter 3 because of the additional complexity of these designs.

2 Fields and Keys

Next add the fields and designate the primary keys.

STUDENT

id	CHAR(5)
fname	CHAR(20)
lname	CHAR(30)
phone	CHAR(10)
major	CHAR(5)
GPA	NUMERIC(6,4)

FACULTY

id	CHAR(5)
fname	CHAR(20)
lname	CHAR(30)
phone	CHAR(10)
department	CHAR(10)
degree	CHAR(10)

STAFF

id	CHAR(5)
fname	CHAR(10)
lname	CHAR(10)
phone	CHAR(10)
status	CHAR(15)

Exhibit 5-12 Continued

3 Recognize Common Fields

STUDENT

id	CHAR(5)
fname	CHAR(20)
lname	CHAR(30)
phone	CHAR(10)
major	CHAR(5)
GPA	NUMERIC(6,4)

FACULTY

id	CHAR(5)
fname	CHAR(20)
lname	CHAR(30)
phone	CHAR(10)
department	CHAR(10)
degree	CHAR(10)

STAFF

id	CHAR(5)
fname	CHAR(10)
lname	CHAR(10)
phone	CHAR(10)
status	CHAR(15)

Make sure that the fields actually store the same data for each entity. Sometimes different tables use the same name for fields storing different data.

4 Create Supertype/Subtype Hierarchy

PERSON

id	CHAR(5)
fname	CHAR(20)
lname	CHAR(30)
phone	CHAR(10)
student?	CHAR(1)
instructor?	CHAR(1)
staff?	CHAR(1)

The common fields are put into a newly created entity called "person."

Because the overlap rule should be used, we add three discriminating fields, one for each subtype.

Any fields specific to a category are put into the appropriate subtype.

The primary key of the supertype is copied into the subtypes and shown as a foreign key.

STUDENT

PERSON$id	CHAR(5)
major	CHAR(5)
GPA	NUMERIC(6,3)

FACULTY

PERSON$id	CHAR(5)
department	CHAR(5)
degree	CHAR(10)

STAFF

PERSON$id	CHAR(5)
status	CHAR(15)

(Continued)

Exhibit 5-12   Continued

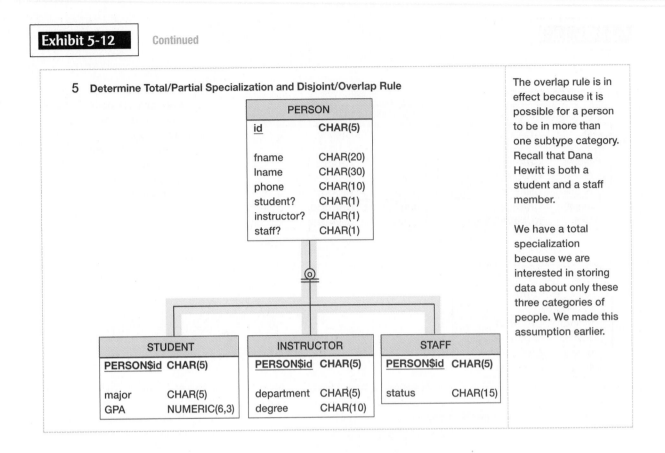

5   **Determine Total/Partial Specialization and Disjoint/Overlap Rule**

The overlap rule is in effect because it is possible for a person to be in more than one subtype category. Recall that Dana Hewitt is both a student and a staff member.

We have a total specialization because we are interested in storing data about only these three categories of people. We made this assumption earlier.

Notice that for this hierarchy, we use the overlap rule rather than the disjoint rule, because it is possible for one instance of the supertype to be an instance of more than one subtype. We know this is the case because the record for Dana Hewitt (id = 1123) is listed as both a student and a staff member. Therefore, we should use the overlap rule. Also, this hierarchy is an example of a total specialization. You might remember that in the problem statement, we said that these were the only categories of people we wanted to store in our database. Put differently, there are only three subtypes, STUDENT, INSTRUCTOR, and STAFF; each person belongs to at least one of these three categories.

There is one final item we must discuss regarding supertype/subtype hierarchies. Both of our examples illustrate situations where some instances of an entity contain fields that other instances do not. This is the reason that we used the hierarchies. There is another reason to use a hierarchy. Sometimes certain instances of an entity are involved in relationships that other instances are not involved in. Here is an example of such a situation.

A Second Supertype/Subtype Hierarchy Example

Suppose you are designing a database that must store information about student athletes and members of the student government association (SGA). For both types of students, the database must store an id, each student's first and last names, phone number, major, and current GPA. Note that only one major is stored for each student. For athletes, the database must also track which team(s) the athlete has been on and what position he or she played on each team. Also, you must track the date on which the athlete's eligibility expires. For SGA members, you need to store their current office. Exhibit 5-13 shows the ER diagram that satisfies these requirements.

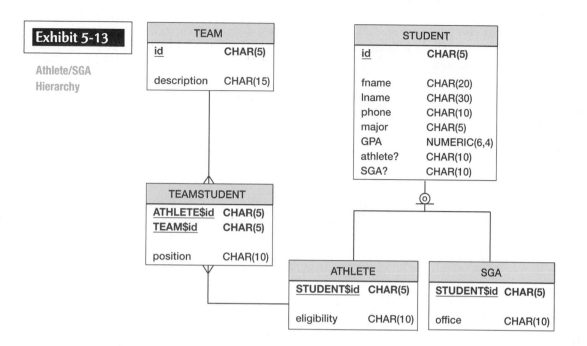

Exhibit 5-13

Athlete/SGA
Hierarchy

Notice that not only does the ATHLETE subtype have a special field, but it also participates in a many-to-many relationship with TEAM. Other instances of STUDENT do not participate in this relationship. The overlap rule is used because it is possible for a student to be both an athlete and an SGA member. The hierarchy is a partial specialization because some students may not be athletes or SGA members.

Complex Designs

Now that you know about recursive relationships and supertype/subtype hierarchies, we can solve some more complex database design problems. In this section, we present two new database problems that enable you to practice using your new knowledge.

Problem Statement: Summer Reading Fun

The Summer Reading Fun program is an educational program intended to help children improve their reading skills over the summer. You are helping the program directors design a database that will improve their program management.

To make the program seem less like school, there are no tests. Students improve their skills by reading books rather than taking tests. Books are selected according to the reading skills they will help students improve. For example, the Dr. Seuss books help students develop their phonic and rhyming skills. The Harry Potter books are good for developing comprehension skills. For each skill, the database must store an identifier and a description. Some skills have prerequisites. For example, letter recognition is a prerequisite skill for word recognition. These prerequisite relationships must be tracked. The title of each book and the author's first and last names must be stored. For books with several authors, only the first author's information is stored. Books need to be classified as either fiction or nonfiction. For fiction books, the style must be stored. For nonfiction books, the topic is stored. The skills addressed by each book need to be stored in the database. A book may address several skills. Certain information about each student must be tracked, including first and last names, grade (e.g., fourth grade), and school. It is also important to keep track of what books each student has read. The date on which the student completes the book also must be stored. Finally, the program directors want to be able to track information about which skills each student has gained. Exhibit 5-14 shows the steps for creating this database.

Exhibit 5-14   Summer Reading Fun Step-by-Step Design

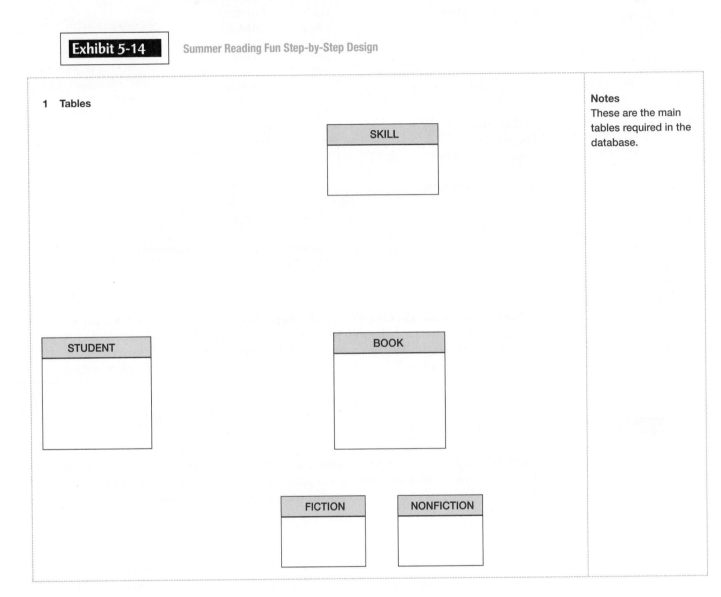

1 Tables

SKILL

STUDENT

BOOK

FICTION

NONFICTION

Notes
These are the main tables required in the database.

Exhibit 5-14   Continued

2   Relationships

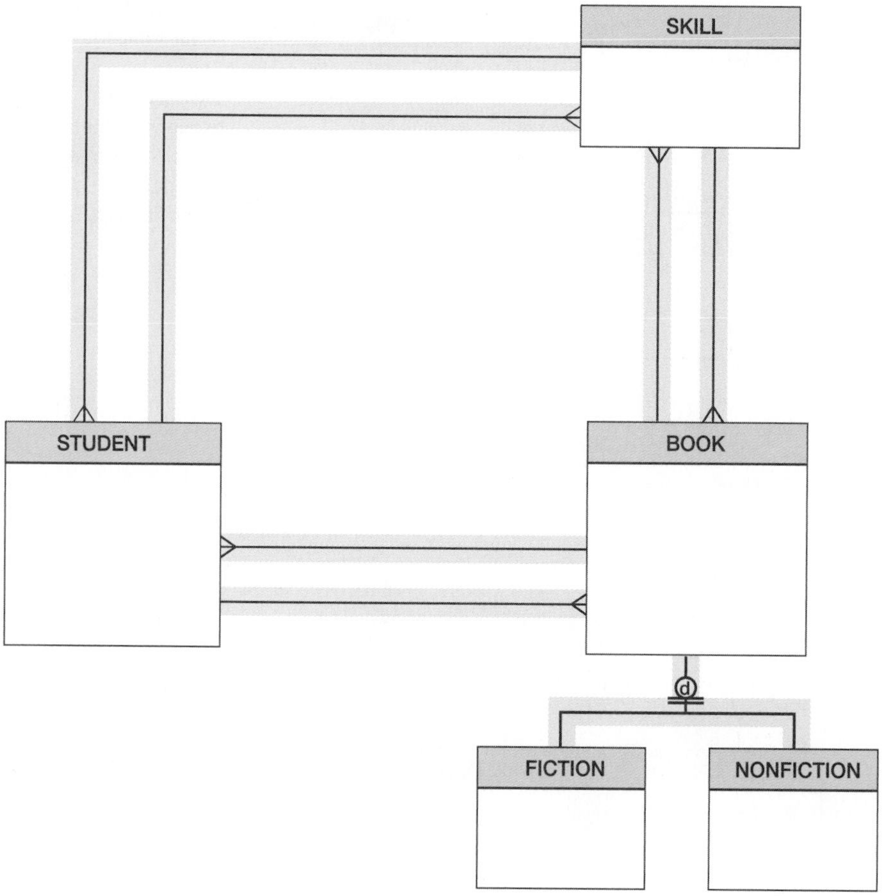

We identified fiction and nonfiction as subtypes of book. Because there are no other types of books, we have a total specialization. A book cannot be both fiction and nonfiction, so the disjoint rule is used.

There is a recursive relationship for skill prerequisite. We show this in the next step.

(*Continued*)

Exhibit 5-14   Continued

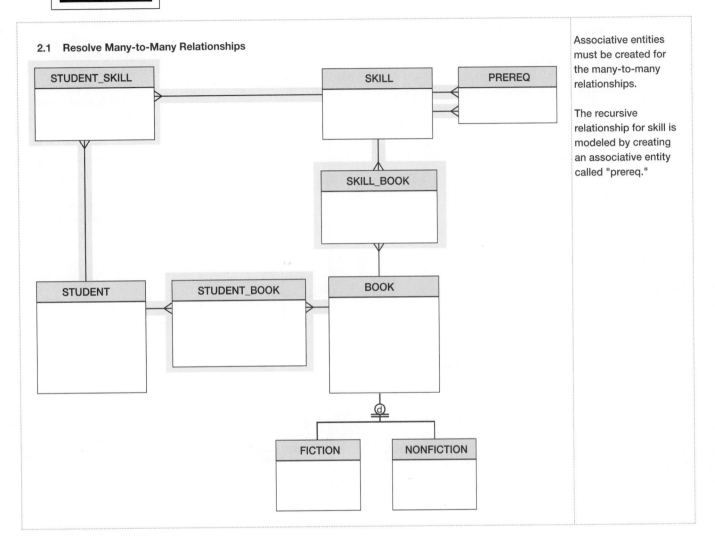

2.1   Resolve Many-to-Many Relationships

Associative entities must be created for the many-to-many relationships.

The recursive relationship for skill is modeled by creating an associative entity called "prereq."

Exhibit 5-14 Continued

4 Fields

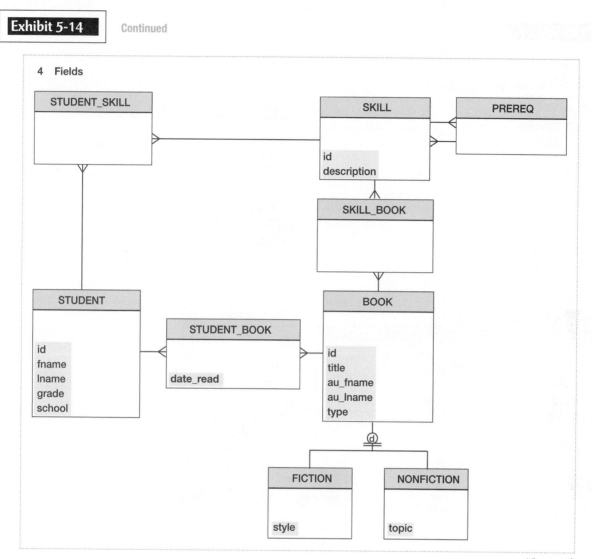

(Continued)

Exhibit 5-14 Continued

5 Keys

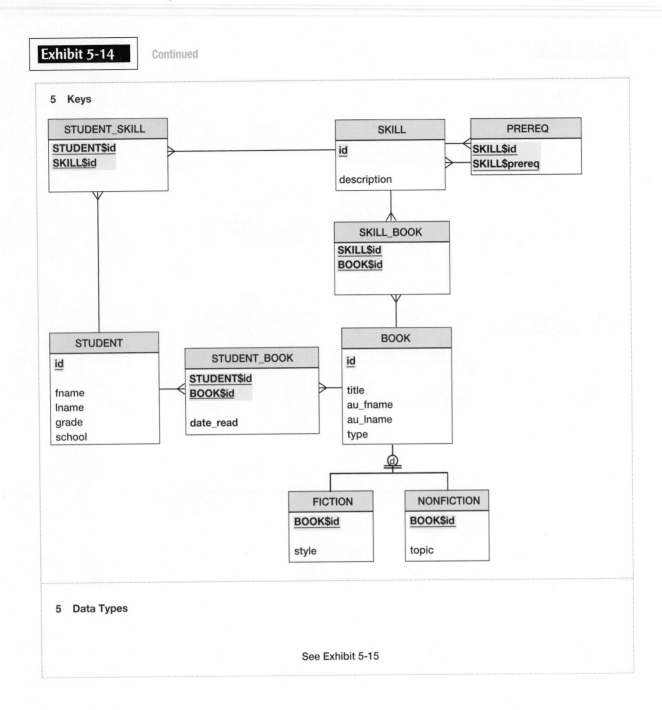

5 Data Types

See Exhibit 5-15

Exhibit 5-15   Summer Reading Fun ER Diagram with Data Types

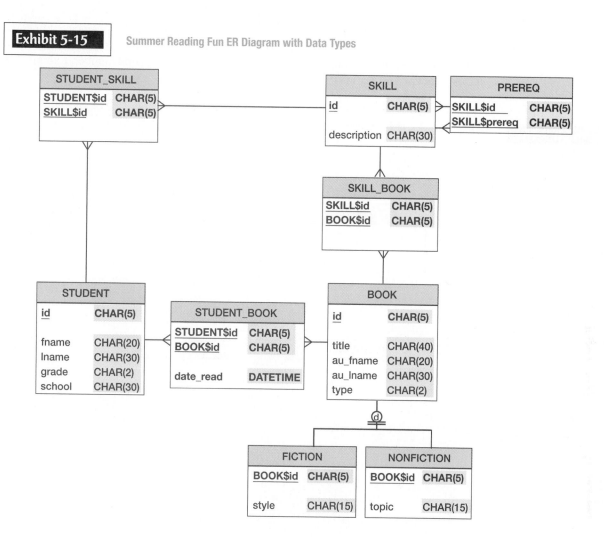

Problem Statement: Swampland Real Estate

Swampland Real Estate is a very small real estate agency owned by Jimmy Goodeal. In fact, the agency is so small that Jimmy is the only agent in the company. He wants to have a database that keeps track of key information for his company. Of course, property information is very important. Jimmy wants to be able to store the address (street, city, state, and postal code) for each property. He also wants to track the number of bedrooms and bathrooms and the listing price for each property. Some properties are single-family homes. For these properties, he wants to store the lot size. For condominiums, he wants to know the monthly association fee. Information about the area in which each property is located is also important. Jimmy wants to track the name of the area, along with the names of the schools, including the high school, elementary school, and middle school. He also wants to store general comments about the area. Jimmy uses a variety of advertising outlets, such as newspapers, magazines, and Web sites, to advertise the properties he is selling. He wants to track which outlets are used to advertise each property. Keep in mind that a property may be advertised several times in the same outlet. Jimmy also wants to know when each ad was placed and how much the ad cost. The database must also store the name and main phone number of the outlet.

Information about each client must also be stored, including first and last names, main contact phone number, and email address. Jimmy wants the database to track which client sells each property and which client buys each property. Remember that different clients sell and buy each property. Jimmy pays past clients for referring others to his agency. When such referrals result in a sale, he pays the referring client a small fee. Although a client may earn many fees, Jimmy will only pay once for a referred client.

Finally, Jimmy sometimes sells properties that are listed by other agencies. For these properties, he wants the database to track which agency listed the property. He also wants to store basic information about each agency, including name and phone number. Exhibit 5-16 shows the steps for creating this database.

Exhibit 5-16   Swampland Real Estate Step-by-Step Design

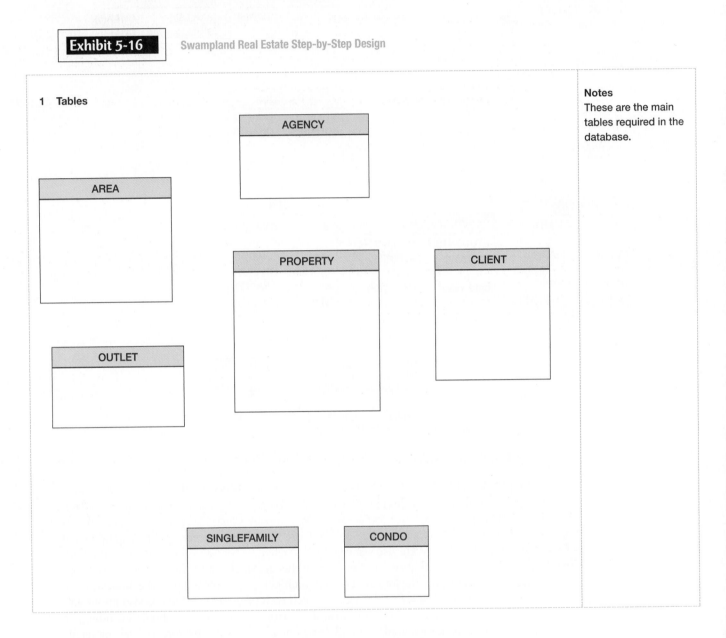

1   Tables

Notes
These are the main tables required in the database.

Exhibit 5-16 Continued

2 Relationships

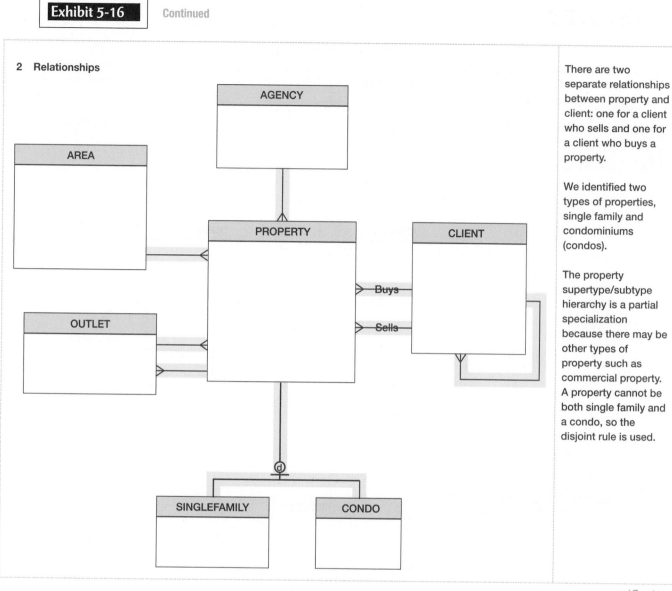

There are two separate relationships between property and client: one for a client who sells and one for a client who buys a property.

We identified two types of properties, single family and condominiums (condos).

The property supertype/subtype hierarchy is a partial specialization because there may be other types of property such as commercial property. A property cannot be both single family and a condo, so the disjoint rule is used.

(Continued)

Exhibit 5-16   Continued

2.1   Resolve Many-to-Many Relationships

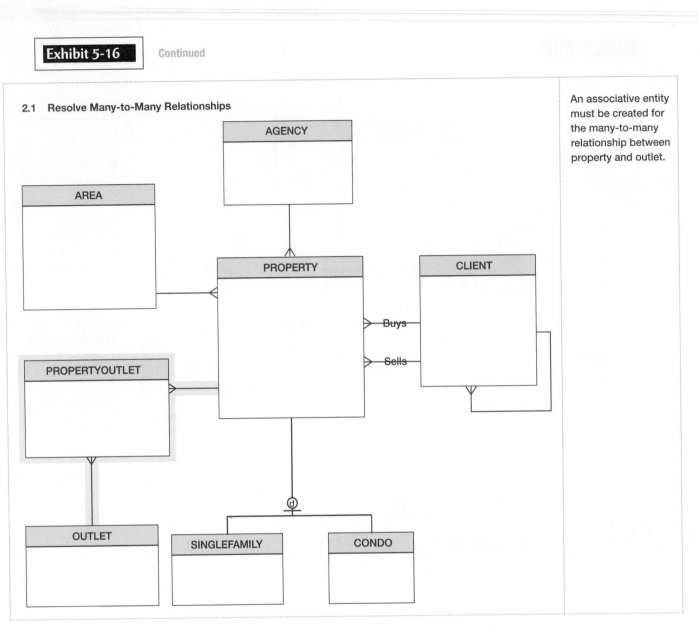

An associative entity must be created for the many-to-many relationship between property and outlet.

Exhibit 5-16 Continued

4 Fields

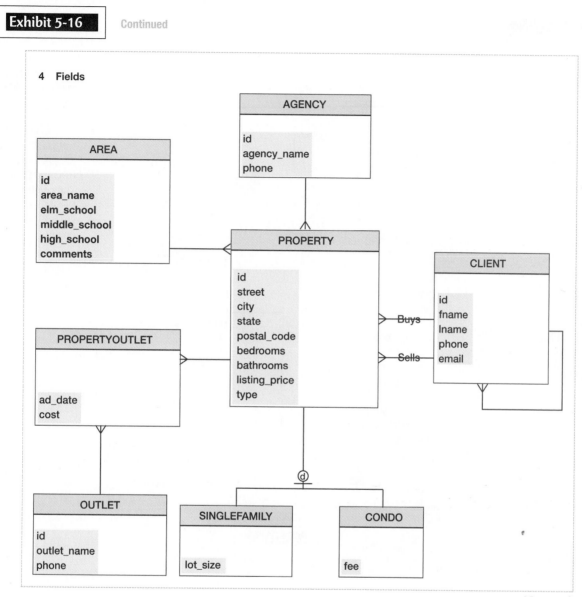

(Continued)

Exhibit 5-16   Continued

5   Keys

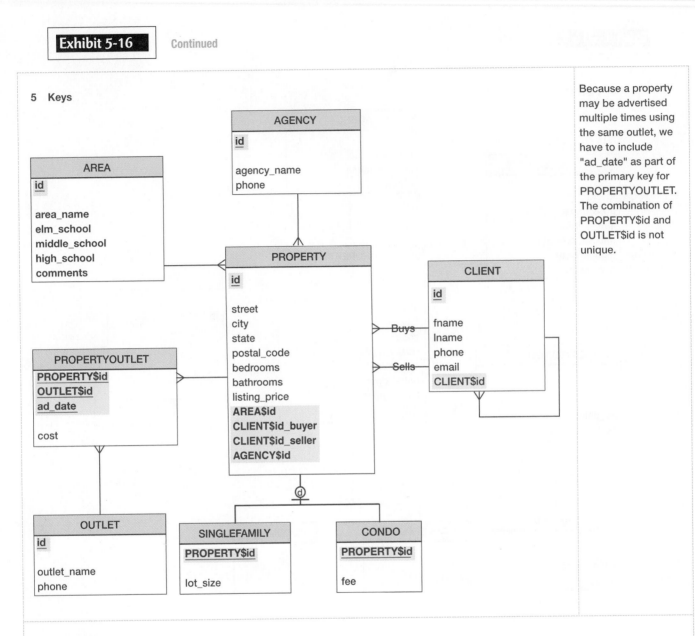

Because a property may be advertised multiple times using the same outlet, we have to include "ad_date" as part of the primary key for PROPERTYOUTLET. The combination of PROPERTY$id and OUTLET$id is not unique.

6   Data Types

See Exhibit 5-17

Exhibit 5-17 Swampland Real Estate ER Diagram

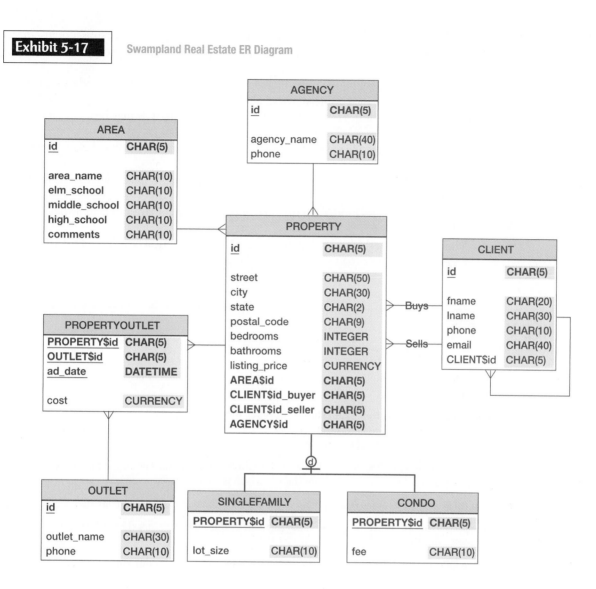

SUMMARY

- Recursive relationships (also known as unary relationships) are used in situations where an instance of one entity references another instance of that same entity.
- Model one-to-many recursive relationships by adding a foreign key to the table involved in the relationship. This foreign key references the table's primary key.
- Model many-to-many recursive relationships by creating an associative entity (linking table) that contains a concatenated primary key, with both components of the primary key acting as foreign keys referencing the table involved in the relationship. Be sure that this concatenated primary key is unique.
- Use generalization/specialization hierarchies (also known as supertype/subtype hierarchies) when some instances of an entity have columns that other instances do not, or when some instances are involved in relationships that other instances are not involved in.
- The supertype entity includes all columns that are common to all instances of the original entity.
- The supertype entity is involved in any relationships that are common to all instances of the original entity.

■ Each subtype entity includes columns that are unique to a particular subset of instances.

■ Each subtype entity is involved in any relationships that are unique to a particular subset of instances.

■ A discriminating column is often included in the supertype entity to indicate to which subtypes each instance of the supertype belongs.

■ When the disjoint rule is in effect, an instance of the supertype may be an instance of, at most, one subtype.

■ When the overlap rule is in effect, an instance of the supertype may be an instance of multiple subtypes.

■ In a total specialization, each instance of the supertype is an instance of at least one subtype.

■ In a partial specialization, each instance of the supertype may not be an instance of any subtype.

■ The disjoint/overlap rule and total/partial specialization are independent of one another.

KEY TERMS

Disjoint rule. This term simply means that an instance of the supertype may belong to *at most* one subtype category.

Generalization/specialization (supertype/subtype) hierarchy. A structure that consists of a general entity that includes all common attributes along with specialized entities that have the attributes common only to certain instances of the entity.

Inheritance. This term means that any instance of a subtype entity inherits all properties of the supertype, including its attributes and any relationships in which the supertype is involved.

Overlap rule. This term means that a supertype instance may belong to more than one subtype category.

Partial specialization. When there are some instances of the supertype that do not belong in any of the subtype categories.

Recursive relationship. Relationship that associates two instances of the same entity (also known as unary relationship).

Subtype entity. Specialized entities that have the attributes common only to certain instances of the entity in a supertype/subtype hierarchy.

Supertype entity. The general entity that includes all common attributes in a supertype/subtype hierarchy.

Total specialization. When all instances of the supertype must belong to at least one subtype category.

EXERCISES

Review

1. What is a recursive relationship?
2. Give another name for "recursive relationship."
3. What is a bill of materials?
4. How is a bill of materials represented in a data model?
5. What is a generalization/specialization hierarchy?
6. Define the term "supertype."
7. Define the term "subtype."

8. Contrast the disjoint rule with the overlap rule.

9. Contrast total and partial specializations.

10. What is inheritance?

Discuss

1. Give an example of a one-to-many recursive relationship.

2. Give an example of a many-to-many recursive relationship.

3. Describe how a one-to-many recursive relationship is represented in a data model.

4. Describe how a many-to-many recursive relationship is represented in a data model.

5. Give an example of a generalization/specialization hierarchy where the disjoint rule should be used.

6. Give an example of a generalization/specialization hierarchy where the overlap rule should be used.

7. Give an example of a generalization/specialization hierarchy that uses a total specialization.

8. Give an example of a generalization/specialization hierarchy that uses a partial specialization.

Practice

For each of these problems, produce an ERD in accordance with the specifications of this text. These diagrams may be drawn with any design tool—even pencil and paper. However, many universities have access to Microsoft Visio as part of their site license agreement. A Visio template supporting the diagrams found in this text may be downloaded from the accompanying Web site.

1. Design a database to store information for Larry's Landscaping Service. Larry needs to track the common and Latin names for each plant. Also, he wants to store standard wholesale and retail prices for each plant. For trees, the database should track the tree's height and caliper (trunk diameter). Some plants are classified as shrubs. For these plants, Larry wants the database to store the size (in gallons), the planting distance between plants (in inches), and whether the shrub is flowering or nonflowering. The database will include other types of plants (such as turfs and other ground covers), but no special data needs to be stored about these plants.

2. Billy Bob's Boats wants to use a database to track information about the boats they sell. The name, cost, selling price, length, beam (width), and manufacturer of all boats must be stored. Billy Bob also wants to track the mast height and keel type (fixed or retractable) of all sailboats. The database must also store the engine size (in horsepower) and engine type (inboard, outboard, or in-out) for all powerboats.

3. The manager of Olive's Office Supplies has asked you to design a customer information database for her company. For retail customers, the database should store the customer's first and last names, address, phone number, and sales tax rate. For wholesale customers, the database must store the company name, address, phone number, and tax identification number.

4. Hip Threads, a clothing retailer, wants to use a database to track their products. The name and retail price must be stored for all products. Hip Threads also offers special prices on clothing ensembles, which are made up of individual clothing items. For example, a men's casual ensemble might be made up of a shirt, trousers, and belt. Theses ensembles are considered items. A particular clothing item (such as a shirt) may be included in more than one ensemble.

5. Modify the Lame Events database design from Chapter 3 to include the following new requirements. Lame Events puts on many different types of events. For all events, they want to keep track of a description, date, and cost. For running events, they also want to store the distance of the run and whether or not the race course is certified by the U.S. Track and Field Association. For bicycle events, they want to know the distance and whether the event is a race or a recreational ride. For triathlons, the swim, bike, and run distances must be stored. Lame Events occasionally puts on other types of events. Finally, athletes who refer others to an event receive a credit toward future registration fees. An athlete may refer several others, but Lame Events will only provide one credit for any particular athlete being referred.

6. Cary's Casual Catering provides catering services for a variety of events. Cary wants you to design a database to store information about events and the foods (called recipes) served at each event. The database must store which recipes are served at each event. Cary currently uses an event planning sheet to track the information about what is served at each event. An example is shown in Exhibit 5-18.

Exhibit 5-18

The Event
Planning Sheet

Event Name:	Smith Wedding	Client:	Sally Smith
Date:	August 14, 2005	Location:	Memorial Hall
Head count:	100	Budget:	$2,500

Recipes:

Tapenade appetizer	5 units
Wedding soup	10 units
Summer salad	10 units
Blackened catfish	50 units
Cheese grits	10 units
Black-eyed peas	10 units
Summer fruit combo	10 units

Cary also wants to store some basic information about each client, including name, "address," and phone number. For private customers, the first and last names of the client should be stored. For corporate customers, the company name must be tracked.

Currently, Cary uses a recipe information card to track the necessary information. An example of a card is shown in Exhibit 5-19. Note that directions for making the recipe do not need to be stored.

Exhibit 5-19

A Recipe Card

Name:	Tapenade	Cost per serving:	$1.50
Prep time:	20 minutes	Number of servings:	15
Description:	Tangy spread with a strong flavor of olives. Served with crackers or toast points.		

Ingredients:

Kalamata olives	6 oz.
Capers	1 tablespoon
Olive oil	3 tablespoons
Garlic	1 clove
Lemon juice	1 tablespoon
Pepper	1/4 teaspoon

Another recipe information card is shown in Exhibit 5-20. Notice that this recipe uses Tapenade, which is the recipe from the other example, as one of its ingredients.

Exhibit 5-20

A Second Recipe
Card

Name:	Tapenade appetizer	Cost per serving:	$2.00
Prep time:	20 minutes	Number of servings:	15
Description:	Tangy spread with a strong flavor of olives, served on garlic toast points.		

Ingredients:

Tapenade	1 teaspoon
Garlic toast points	30 points

7. A local school system wants to build a database to track certain information about students and teachers. For each teacher, the database must store the first and last names, the highest degree earned, and the date on which he or she became certified. The database must also track the first and last names of each student, along with each student's date of birth. Students are assigned to teachers. These assignments must be tracked. Students are reassigned at the end of each school year, so a student may be related to multiple teachers. The assignment beginning and ending dates should be stored. Information about parents also should be stored. The database must also keep track of relationships between parents and students. For some students, special information must be stored. Some students have special language needs; these students are classified as being "ESOL" (English for speakers of other languages). For ESOL students, the database must track the native language of the child and the language spoken at home (these may be different). Exceptional education students have special educational needs. For these students, the database should store the category of special needs, such as speech, hearing, or emotional disabilities. In addition, each exceptional education student is assigned to a specialist who monitors the student's progress and works with teachers to address special needs. These assignments must be stored. It is possible for a student to work with several specialists, so it is important to store the beginning and ending dates of each assignment. The exceptional education specialists are not regular teachers. The names, phone numbers, and email addresses of these specialists must be stored in the database. In addition, the expertise (speech, hearing, or emotional disabilities) of each specialist must be stored. Note that a specialist may have multiple areas of expertise. Finally, the state subsidizes the lunch costs for some students. For these students, the database must store whether the student receives a free or half-price lunch.

Creating Databases with Oracle Using SQL

Introduction

In this chapter, you will learn how to use Oracle's structured query language (SQL) interface, iSQL*Plus, to create the databases that were designed in Chapter 3. Most relational database products (Oracle, DB2, SQL Server, Access, etc.) support SQL, even if they also support a graphical user interface. Computer professionals tend to prefer SQL over the graphical interface. Additionally, SQL must be used when embedding a query in a programming language such as Active Server Pages (ASP) or Java.

The *i* in Oracle's iSQL*Plus refers to the Internet, because the interface may be accessed through a Web browser. The *Plus* indicates that Oracle's version of SQL is enhanced with additional features.

There are other client tools to interact with an Oracle database. The advantage of iSQL*Plus is that it works through your browser. You do not have to install any additional software. Because there is no client software to install, you can complete your work from any computer with an internet connection!

Learning Objectives

After completing this chapter, you will be able to:

- Create tables in an Oracle database using iSQL.
- Define columns and data types for a table.
- Create a primary key for a table.
- Create foreign keys and use them to establish relationships between tables.
- Enter data into a table using an insert statement.
- Display data in a table using a select query.
- Delete records from a table.
- Identify reserved words that cannot be used for field names.

Physical Table Design

As you learned in Chapter 3, a conceptual model of a database provides the basic design of the database, including the tables and relationships between those tables. The model also specifies the names for the tables and the columns within those tables, including the specification of primary and foreign keys.

In addition to the general conceptual design, Chapter 3 also specified additional physical details, including data types and widths for each column in the database. Before implementing a database in a particular database management system such as Oracle, you will need to determine the data types available in that system and any restrictions on the widths of columns.

Data Types and Column Widths

Every field in a database table must have a data type and a column width. In Oracle, there are many possible data types, some of which are outlined in Exhibit 6-1. You indicate the column width after the data type in parentheses—for example, varchar(200) for a variable-length character string up to 200 characters in length. For number data types, you may also indicate decimal places—for example, *number(5,2)* for a number five digits in length, two of which appear to the right of the decimal place. The numbers 842.57 and 2.25 would fit this definition, but 9875 would not.

Exhibit 6-1 Data Types Available in Oracle	**Data Type**		**Sample Syntax**	**Legal Values**	**Illegal Values**
	Varchar	Stores character data such as text and numbers, including numbers that are not involved in calculations, such as zip codes and phone numbers.	varchar(8)	happy hopeless	incredible 305-555-1212
	Char	Similar to varchar but for fixed length fields.	char(8)	happy hopeless	incredible 305-555-1212
	Number	Numbers that will be used in calculations.	number(4,2)	22.57 8.75 8.7	9.432 (will round) 889.21 (rejected)
	Date	Contains date and time in a single field.	date	08-jun-04 21-jul-05 14:34	January 28, 2007

The Sky_Member Database

To illustrate how a database is created in Oracle, we will create the database for the skydiving club. This process will include creating the table and populating it with data. Oracle databases are created on the database server under a specific account. Once created, they remain on the server, even after shutdown. In fact, they remain on the server until you explicitly delete them.

Exhibit 6-2 shows the design, physical details, and data for the skydiving member table. The physical details, including the name and data type for each column, show how the table is created in Oracle. The design area shows the original conceptual design from chapter 3. The primary key (email) is bold and underlined. The data area shows the data and the commands to enter that data into the table.

Exhibit 6-2

Design and Data
for the Skydiving
Club Member
Database

Physical Details

```
create table sky_member
(
email      char(20) primary key,
fname      char(15),
lname      char(15),
phone      char(12),
jumps      number,
equip      char(1),
skill      char(1)
);
```

Design

SKY_MEMBER	
email	CHAR(20)
fname	CHAR(15)
lname	CHAR(15)
phone	CHAR(12)
jumps	NUMBER
equip	CHAR(1)
level	CHAR(1)

Data

```
insert into sky_member (email, fname, lname, phone, jumps, equip, skill) values
( 'bucky@ohio.edu',  'Teri',  'Bucky',  '555-5555',  22,  'Y',  'A' );
insert into sky_member (email, fname, lname, phone, jumps, equip, skill) values
( 'dayj@ohio.edu',  'John',  'Day',  '592-0646',  5,  'Y',  'B' );
AND SO FORTH...
```

email	fname	lname	phone	jumps	equip	level
bucky@ohio.edu	Teri	Bucky	555-5555	22	Y	A
dayj@ohio.edu	John	Day	592-0646	5	Y	B
johnson@bobcat.edu	Jeremy	Johnson	555-3333	15	Y	I
luce@ohio.edu	Thom	Luce	592-1111	12	N	I
mcgann@ohio.edu	Sean	McGann	592-2222	20	Y	A
mcgrath@bobcat.edu	Billie	McGrath	555-6666	3	N	B
wilson@bobcat.edu	Sally	Wilson	555-4444	6	N	B

Reserved Words

This design is slightly different from the SKY_MEMBER table introduced in the chapter on conceptual design. The name for the member skill level column has been changed from *level* to *skill*. This name change is because some database software restricts the words that can be used to name database elements such as tables and columns. These are known as **reserved words.** Common reserved words in SQL databases are *table, column, select, number, order, date,* and other words that have a meaning in SQL. Therefore, *level* has been changed to *skill* in the implementation in Exhibit 6-2. For more discussion about the error messages created by improper use of reserved words, please see the troubleshooting section later in this chapter.

The physical details area shows the **create table** command needed to create the table in the database. All fields in the *create table* statement are separated by commas. Omit the comma after the last field, because there is nothing from which to separate it. The primary key is identified by typing the words *primary key* after the data type of the email field. The data type of all but the jumps field is character. The jumps field is numeric, because it could be used in a calculation—for instance, to determine the average number of jumps for all members. Furthermore, the data type for the jumps field is an integer, because jumps always occur in whole numbers. The phone number field is a character string, because phone numbers include dashes or periods as special characters.[1]

The data panel provides the information necessary to add data to the table. The SQL statement that adds a row to a table is the **insert** statement. You must use a *separate* insert statement for each record. Yes, this is a pain, and we will show later in the ASP chapter how to make a nice, form-based interface to enter data. As with the create table statement, you must separate each element with a comma in the insert statement. Again, omit the comma after the last field, because there is nothing from which to separate it. The data for all character string fields must be enclosed in *single* quotes. The data for jumps, a numeric field, does not need to be contained in quotes.

Implementation

Oracle has a very nice SQL interface, called iSQL*Plus, that is accessible using a Web browser. The interface provides a work area to type SQL commands, as well as the ability to save and retrieve a series of commands—called a **script.**

Think of the script file as a way to automate tasks, such as those necessary to create database tables and then populate them with data. A well-designed script file has some significant advantages:

1. Errors that occur during development can be quickly located and corrected.
2. A corrupted database can be easily re-created using the script file.
3. The script file documents the creation process.

Scripts should plan for the inevitable errors that occur during implementation. The best solution after detecting an error is to start over from scratch—which means destroy the database using the **drop table** command, and then create it anew. With this idea in mind, all the script files shown below begin by dropping the database tables. The *first* time each of these scripts runs, it will generate an error, because there are no tables to drop. This error will disappear on subsequent executions.

The sections of a script file are:

1. *Set* echo on to display results.
2. *Drop* the tables in the database (if they exist).
3. *Create* the database tables.
4. *Describe* the tables that were created to verify they were properly created.
5. *Insert* data into the tables.
6. *Select* data from the tables to verify that all data was properly inserted.
7. *Commit* the changes made.

The script file also enables the developer to document the creation process by adding comments, as illustrated here:

```
/* This is the format for a comment in Oracle. Note that there must be spaces
    between the text */
/* and the leading and trailing asterisks. */
```

---

[1]The varchar data type could also be used in place of char for all examples in this chapter. Varchar is a bit more efficient since it stores a variable number of characters whereas the char data type adds blanks at the end of data that is shorter than the length of the field.

A script file for the Sky_Member database is shown in Exhibit 6-3. If you run this file, add the missing insert statements where it specifies /* AND SO FORTH */ to add all the data shown before in Exhibit 6-2.

Exhibit 6-3

Script File for the
Sky_Member
Database

```
/* Echo feedback to the screen to see each command execute or fail */
set echo on ;

/*   Drop any prior versions of the table  */
drop table sky_member;

create table sky_member
(
email      char(20) primary key,
fname      char(15),
lname      char(15),
phone      char(12),
jumps      number,
equip      char(1),
skill      char(1)
) ;

/*  Check your work by showing that the tables created in your Oracle account   */
select table_name from user_tables ;

/*  Further check your work by describing the fields in the table   */
describe sky_member ;

insert into sky_member (email, fname, lname, phone, jumps, equip, skill) values
( 'bucky@ohio.edu',  'Teri',  'Bucky',  '555-5555',  22, 'Y', 'A' ) ;
insert into sky_member (email, fname, lname, phone, jumps, equip, skill) values
( 'dayj@ohio.edu',  'John',  'Day',  '592-0646', 5, 'Y', 'B' ) ;
/* AND SO FORTH... */

/*   Check your work by showing the data in the table */
select    *
from  sky_member ;

/*   Save all changes using the commit command    */
/*   commit ;
```

Some commands buried in the script file deserve further mention:

- **Set echo on:** *Set echo on* causes Oracle to show each of your commands as they run. Otherwise, all you would see is a list of confirmation or error messages. Your system administrator can also make *set echo on* a default option for all users—thereby eliminating the need to include this command in each script.
- **Select table_name from user_tables:** *Select* is the SQL command you will use most frequently. In fact, it appears twice in this script. This version of the *select* command queries the system catalog to list the names of all of the tables that you have created under your Oracle account—not just the ones from this session.
- **Describe sky_member:** The *describe* command causes Oracle to list all fields in a particular table, as well as their data types and column widths.
- **Select * from sky_member:** *Select ** is used to retrieve data from tables. The * option selects all fields in the table and is the easiest version of the *select* command.
- **Commit:** *Commit* saves all the work that has been entered to this point. Normally, the system executes an additional *commit* when you log off of your session. The opposite of *commit* is **rollback,** which undoes any work up to the previous *commit* command.[2]

To create a script file, first sign on to iSQL*Plus using a Web browser, as shown in Exhibit 6-4. Your system administrator will be able to give you the URL of your university's Oracle server, as well as a username, password, and connection identifier (if required).

---

[2]**Commit** and **rollback** are very important commands for database implementation. Think of a banking transaction that withdraws money from one account and deposits it to another. A very bad scenario would be to make the first withdrawal and then have the system fail before the deposit. In such a case, your program would need to detect the system failure and then roll back the transaction when the system restarts.

Exhibit 6-4

iSQL*Plus Login
Screen
Source: Used by
permission of Oracle.

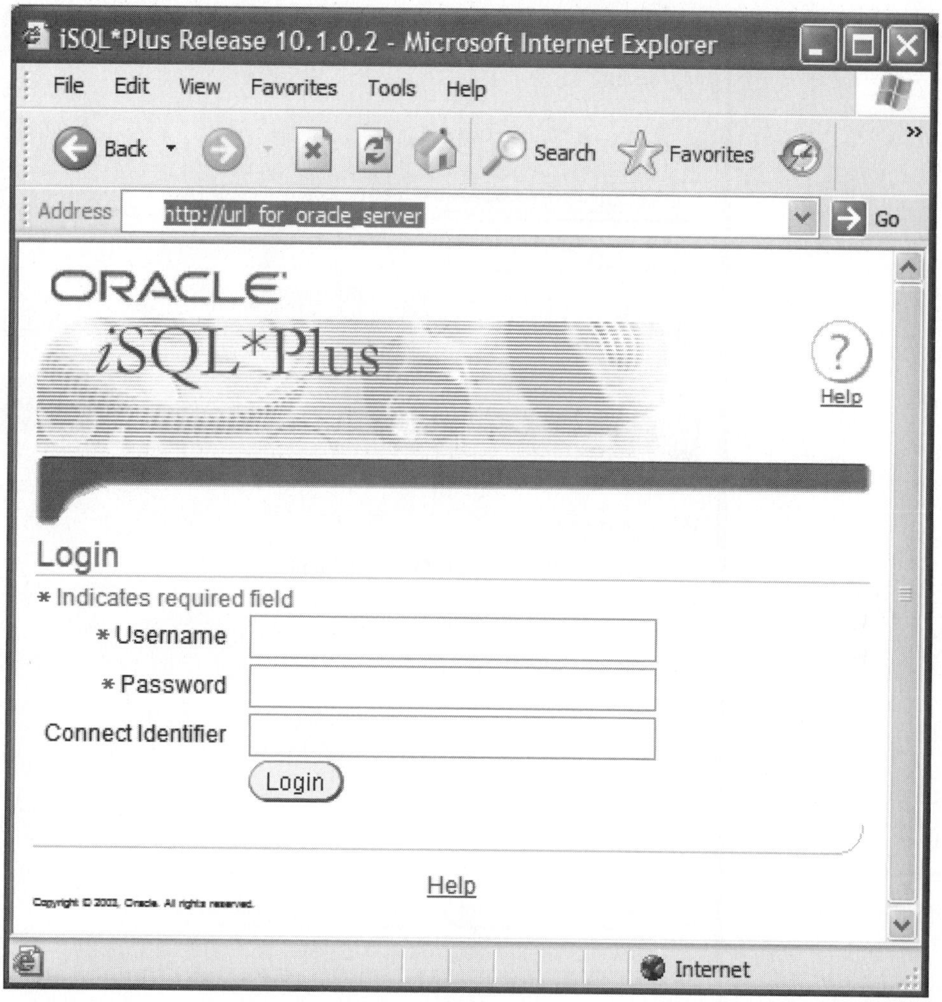

After signing on successfully, you will see the iSQL*Plus workspace shown in Exhibit 6-5. The **workspace** is the user interface where SQL commands are typed into the window and then run by clicking the *execute* button. The results of the run appear below the window.

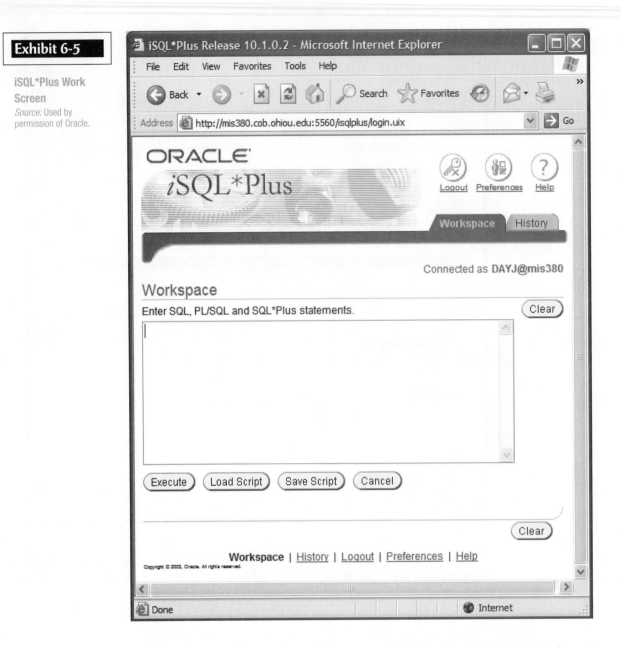

Type the script file into the work screen, and click the *Save Script* button *before* executing the code. Save it so you have a copy of the script for future use, in case there is an error with the script or you have to re-create the database. Script files are saved on your local computer, *not* the Oracle server. In a lab situation, it is probably best to save script files on a network drive or removable media (floppy or pen drive), so that your files will be available to you when you move to another computer. Once a script is saved, it can be retrieved later using the *Load Script* button.[3] The *Clear* button enables you to blank out the workspace.

The iSQL*Plus work screen is customizable using the *Preferences* link. This link enables you to configure the iSQL*Plus environment, including options for the size of the input area, whether the output is displayed below the workspace or saved in an HTML file, and how output is paginated. Other links include a *History* of scripts previously executed during this session, an option for logging out of your Oracle session, and a link to the Help system.

---

[3]Scripts may also be typed in Notepad or any other text editor and then pasted into this window.

Next, execute the script by clicking the *Execute* button. The results of the execution appear below the work screen, as shown in Exhibit 6-6.

Workspace

Enter SQL, PL/SQL and SQL*Plus statements.   (Clear)

```
(
email        char(20) primary key,
fname        char(15),
lname        char(15),
phone        char(12),
jumps        number,
equip        char(1),
skill        char(1)
) ;
```

(Execute) (Load Script) (Save Script) (Cancel)

```
drop table sky_member;
Table dropped.


create table sky_member
(
email char(20) primary key,
fname char(15),
lname char(15),
phone char(12),
jumps number,
equip char(1),
skill char(1)
) ;
Table created.
```

If the script has been entered correctly, the table will be created, and the data will be inserted and displayed. It is possible that you will make mistakes typing the script file, and error messages will be displayed. The section on troubleshooting later in this chapter will provide information for interpreting some of the more common mistakes.

The Arcade Database

Exhibit 6-7 shows the design for the Arcade database. There are several differences between this database and the Sky_Member database. The most obvious difference is that this database includes two tables rather than one. In addition, the VISIT table contains columns with a date data type.

To create the relationship between the MEMBER and VISIT tables, the member *email* field is repeated in the VISIT table as the foreign key *MEMBER$email*. MEMBER$email references its parent table (MEMBER) and corresponding column (email). The foreign key *must* have the same data type and column width as the primary key that it references.

Parent tables are always created before their children. Therefore, the MEMBER table must be created before the VISIT table. Parent tables are also loaded before the child tables. Therefore, records must be inserted first into the MEMBER table and then into the VISIT table. Loading the VISIT table first will result in a referential integrity violation; the visit records would "refer" to members who do not yet exist.

The VISIT table introduces the date data type. In the insert statements, the date fields are enclosed in single quotes as though they were character strings. Note the format for date fields in the VISIT table—DD-MON-YY HH24:MM. The hours are based on a 24-hour clock. The default format for the date field varies according to the default data format on the Oracle server, but it can be modified by a set command, as we will see later.

Exhibit 6-7

Create the Arcade
Database

Physical Details

```
create table member
(
email              char(20) primary key,
password           char(10),
fname              char(10),
lname              char(10),
phone              char(12)
) ;

create table visit
(
id                 char(20)   primary key,
member$email   char(20)   references member(email),
date_time_in     date,
date_time_out    date
) ;
```

Design

MEMBER	
email	TEXT(20)
password	TEXT(10)
fname	TEXT(10)
lname	TEXT(10)
phone	TEXT(12)

VISIT	
id	TEXT(20)
MEMBER$email	TEXT(20)
date_time_in	DATE
date_time_out	DATE

Data

```
insert into member (email, password, fname, lname, phone) values
( 'dayj@ohio.edu',  'rocket',  'John',  'Day',  '592-5910') ;
/*  AND SO FORTH  */

insert into visit (id, member$email, date_time_in, date_time_out) values
( '001',  'dayj@ohio.edu',  '25-JUN-02 14:00',  '25-JUN-02 17:30' ) ;
/*  AND SO FORTH  */
```

MEMBER

email	password	fname	lname	phone
dayj@ohio.edu	rocket	John	Day	592-0646
luce@ohio.edu	bullet	Thom	Luce	592-1111
mcgann@ohio.edu	arrow	Sean	McGann	592-2222

VISIT

id	MEMBER$email	date_time_in	date_time_out
001	dayj@ohio.edu	6/25/2002 02:00:00 PM	6/25/2002 05:30:00 PM
002	luce@ohio.edu	6/25/2002 06:00:00 PM	6/25/2002 08:00:00 PM
003	dayj@ohio.edu	6/26/2002 10:00:00 AM	6/26/2002 11:30:00 AM
004	luce@ohio.edu	6/27/2002 09:00:00 AM	6/27/2002 10:00:00 AM
005	mcgann@ohio.edu	6/27/2002 04:00:00 PM	6/27/2002 06:00:00 PM

Exhibit 6-8 shows a script file for creation of the Arcade database. The script file introduces Oracle's natural language system (NLS), which is used to change the format in which dates will be entered and displayed during the current session. This is a very useful command when dealing with dates—especially when you want to eliminate time from the display. For example, to show the date in a more common U.S. format without the time, simply type:

alter session set nls_date_format = 'dd-mm-yy' ;

This command would display dates such as 10-25-86 or 05-24-87.

Exhibit 6-8

Script File for the
ARCADE Database

```
set echo on;
alter session set nls_date_format = 'dd-mon-yy hh24:mi' ;

drop table visit ;
drop table member ;

create table member
(
email           char(20) primary key,
password        char(10),
fname           char(10),
lname           char(10),
phone           char(12)
) ;

create table visit
(
id              char(20)  primary key,
member$email    char(20) references member(email),
date_time_in    date,
date_time_out   date
) ;

select table_name from user_tables ;
describe member ;
describe visit ;

insert into member (email, password, fname, lname, phone) values
( 'dayj@ohio.edu', 'rocket', 'John', 'Day', '592-5910' ) ;
/*  AND SO FORTH */

insert into visit (id, member$email, date_time_in, date_time_out) values
( '001', 'dayj@ohio.edu', '25-JUN-02 14:00', '25-JUN-02 17:30' ) ;
/*  AND SO FORTH */

select   *
from     member ;

select   *
from     visit ;

commit ;
```

In this script, you can also see how a foreign key is defined in the create table statement. To ensure that the values inserted in the foreign key field MEMBER$email actually duplicate values in the email primary key of the MEMBER table, you add a constraint clause when the MEMBER$email column is created. The word *references* establishes the referential integrity relationship between this column and the email column in the MEMBER table. This

Missing or Invalid Option

Omitting a comma between fields in a create table statement will generate a *Missing or Invalid Option* error message. Unfortunately, Oracle may identify the wrong line in the error message, as shown in Exhibit 6-14. The comma is missing after line 8, *equip char(1)*. However, Oracle identifies line 2, the open parenthesis, as the problem. The reason for the error message is that Oracle assumes that *equip char(1)* and *skill char(1)* is all one line. Therefore, *skill* is an invalid option after *char(1)*. In cases like this one, where the line that Oracle flags is clearly correct, you will need to continue scanning the command until you find the real source of the error.

Exhibit 6-14

Omitting Commas
in the Create
Table Statement

```
create table sky_member
(
email      char(20) primary key,
fname      char(15),
lname      char(15),
phone      char(12),
jumps      number,
equip      char(1)
skill      char(1)
);
(
*
ERROR at line 2:
ORA-00922: missing or invalid option
```

Invalid User.table.column, Table.column, or Column Specification

An extra comma at the end of the column list in an insert statement will generate an *Invalid User.table.column, Table.column, or Column Specification* error. Exhibit 6-15 shows an insert statement with an extra comma after the skill field. Oracle flags the next thing it sees, the right parenthesis, as the problem, because it was expecting another field to be listed there.

Exhibit 6-15

Extra Comma in
Column List

```
insert into sky_member (email, fname, lname, phone, jumps, equip, skill, )
values
( 'dayj@ohio.edu', 'John', 'Day', '592-0646', 5, 'Y', 'B' );
insert into sky_member (email, fname, lname, phone, jumps, equip, skill, )
values
                                                                 *
ERROR at line 1:
ORA-01747: invalid user.table.column, table.column, or column specification
```

Missing Expression

An extra comma at the end of a value list in an insert statement will generate a *Missing Expression* error. Exhibit 6-16 shows an insert statement with an extra comma after the value '*B*' is entered for the skill field. Oracle flags the next thing it sees, the right parenthesis, as the problem, because it was expecting another data value to be listed there.

Exhibit 6-16

Extra Comma in
Value List

```
insert into sky_member (email, fname, lname, phone, jumps, equip, skill)
values
( 'dayj@ohio.edu',  'John',  'Day',  '592-0646',  5,  'Y',  'B', ) ;

( 'dayj@ohio.edu',  'John',  'Day',  '592-0646',  5,  'Y',  'B', )
                                                                *
ERROR at line 2:
ORA-00936: missing expression
```

Integrity Constraint Violated – Parent Key Not Found

Inserting a child record that does not have a matching parent record will generate an *Integrity Constraint Violated – Parent Key Not Found* error. This may be one of the clearest error messages that Oracle provides. Oracle is pointing out a referential integrity violation, as shown in Exhibit 6-17.

Exhibit 6-17

Referential
Integrity Violation

```
insert into visit (id, member$email, date_time_in, date_time_out) values
( '001',  'daze@ohio.edu',  '25-JUN-02 14:00',  '25-JUN-02 17:30'  ) ;


insert into visit (id, member$email, date_time_in, date_time_out) values
*
ERROR at line 1:
ORA-02291: integrity constraint (ORA1.SYS_C0042235) violated - parent key not found
```

SUMMARY

- An Oracle database consists of a collection of related tables that are stored online under the user's account.
- Every field in a database table must have a data type and column width. Four important Oracle data types are varchar, char, number, and date. The column width is specified in parentheses immediately after the data type—for example, varchar(100).
- To create a new database, simply execute a script file containing the create table statements for the database.
- The workspace is the area in iSQL*Plus used to enter and run SQL commands.
- For a single-field primary key, include *primary key* after the data type.
- Foreign keys are defined using the references keyword to associate the foreign key column with the primary key it duplicates.
- Multifield (concatenated) primary keys must be defined on a separate line.
- The describe statement can be used to display the column names and data types for a table.

■ Once the structure of a table is created, data is entered using insert statements.
■ A select * query can be used to display all the data entered into a table.
■ Oracle tries to identify the location of errors by placing an asterisk under the first item it suspects of having generated the error. Sometimes that item is fine, and you must continue scanning down to find the error.

KEY TERMS

Commit. Structured query language statement used to save all the changes made during the current session.

Create table. Structured query language statement used to create a table.

Describe table. Structured used to display the column and field names for an existing database.

Drop table. Structured query language statement used to remove a table from the database.

Insert. Structured query language statement used to add a row of data to a table.

Reserved words. Words that cannot be used to name database elements such as tables and columns.

Rollback. Structured query language command used to undo changes made since the last commit.

Script. A series of SQL commands that can be saved and executed in iSQL*Plus.

Select * from table. Select is the SQL command used to display data in a database. The * option indicates that all fields should be displayed.

Select table_name from user_tables. Structured query language command used to show all the tables you have created using your Oracle account.

Set echo on. Turns on the display of all information processed in the script when it is executed.

Workspace. The interface in Oracle iSQL*Plus for typing all SQL commands and viewing their results.

EXERCISES

Review

1. What is a script?
2. List four important data types in Oracle.
3. What is a reserved word?
4. How is a primary key specified in a create table statement?
5. How is a foreign key specified in a create table statement?
6. How is a concatenated primary key specified in a create table statement?
7. What statement adds a row to a table?
8. What command is used to remove a table?
9. What is the command to see a listing of all of the tables that you have created?
10. What is the command to see all of the field names in a particular table?

Discuss

1. List the commands that normally appear in a script to create a database in Oracle.
2. Explain how referential integrity is set up in Oracle.
3. Explain how referential integrity influences the order in which tables can be dropped and created.
4. Explain the purpose of commit and rollback.
5. Explain the three aspects to how Oracle communicates errors.

Practice

1. Create the Hospital database using the design in Exhibit 6-18 and the data in Exhibit 6-19.

Exhibit 6-18

Hospital Database
Design

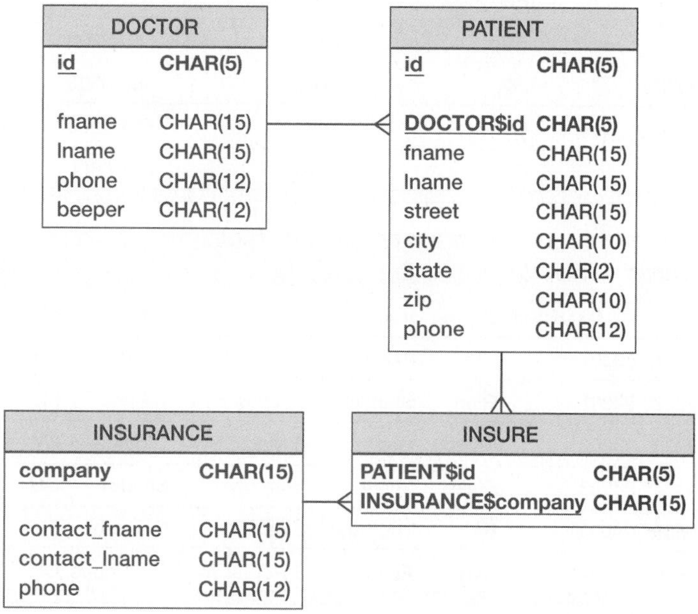

DOCTOR	
id	CHAR(5)
fname	CHAR(15)
lname	CHAR(15)
phone	CHAR(12)
beeper	CHAR(12)

PATIENT	
id	CHAR(5)
DOCTOR$id	CHAR(5)
fname	CHAR(15)
lname	CHAR(15)
street	CHAR(15)
city	CHAR(10)
state	CHAR(2)
zip	CHAR(10)
phone	CHAR(12)

INSURANCE	
company	CHAR(15)
contact_fname	CHAR(15)
contact_lname	CHAR(15)
phone	CHAR(12)

INSURE	
PATIENT$id	CHAR(5)
INSURANCE$company	CHAR(15)

Exhibit 6-19

Hospital Database
Data

DOCTOR

id	fname	lname	phone	beeper
00001	Perry	Cox	555-1111	555-1212
00002	Elliot	Reid	555-2222	555-2323
00003	JD	Dorian	555-3333	555-3434
00004	Chris	Turk	555-5555	555-4545
00005	Bob	Kelso	555-6666	555-5656

PATIENT

id	DOCTOR$id	fname	lname	street	city	state	zip	phone
11111	00001	Jim	Perotti	12 Oak St	Shade	OH	45701	555-1234
22222	00001	Glen	Stamler	1 Walnut Ave	Athens	FL	58475	555-2345
33333	00002	Maddy	Gray	45 Maple St	Glouster	KY	73674	555-3456
44444	00003	Blake	Shelton	3 Elm Blvd	Shade	OH	45701	555-4567
55555	00003	EJ	Thornton	92 Ash St	Orlando	FL	85744	555-5678
66666	00004	Dyrk	Ashton	33 Poplar Ave	Columbus	OH	47837	555-6789

INSURANCE

company	contact_fname	contact_lname	phone
Prudential	Jan	Johnson	555-9876
State Farm	Sam	Smith	555-8765
Nationwide	Randy	Buck	555-7654

INSURE

PATIENT$id	INSURANCE$company
11111	Prudential
22222	Prudential
33333	State Farm
44444	Nationwide
55555	Nationwide
66666	State Farm

2. Create the Acme database using the design in Exhibit 6-20 and the data in Exhibit 6-21.

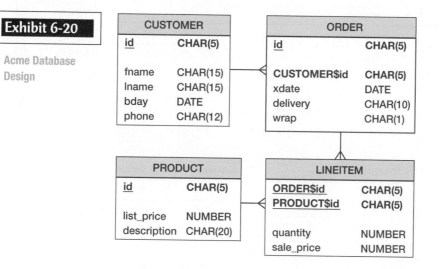

Exhibit 6-20

Acme Database Design

Exhibit 6-21

Acme Database
Design

CUSTOMER

id	fname	lname	bday	phone
11111	Glen	Stamler	9/13/1974	555-3232
22222	Maddy	Gray	8/05/1984	555-8475
33333	Blake	Shelton	7/25/1975	555-4875
44444	EJ	Thornton	2/04/1988	555-9845

ORDER

id	CUSTOMER$id	date	delivery	wrap
10000	11111	2/04/2003	N	N
10001	22222	2/05/2003	Y	Y
10002	11111	2/05/2003	N	N
10003	33333	2/06/2003	Y	N

PRODUCT

id	list_price	description
00001	15.95	lager
00002	25.24	stout
00003	13.95	light
00004	19.98	pilsner
00005	18.75	microbrew
00006	18.57	ale
00007	15.95	bock
00008	19.95	portor

LINEITEM

ORDER$id	PRODUCT$id	quantity	sale_price
10000	00001	1	15.75
10000	00003	2	13.95
10001	00002	1	23.95
10001	00005	1	18.50
10002	00008	3	21.75
10003	00006	1	18.35
10003	00001	2	15.95
10003	00003	1	12.95
10003	00004	1	19.98

3. Create the Amazon database using the design in Exhibit 6-22 and the data in Exhibit 6-23.

Exhibit 6-22

Amazon Database
Design

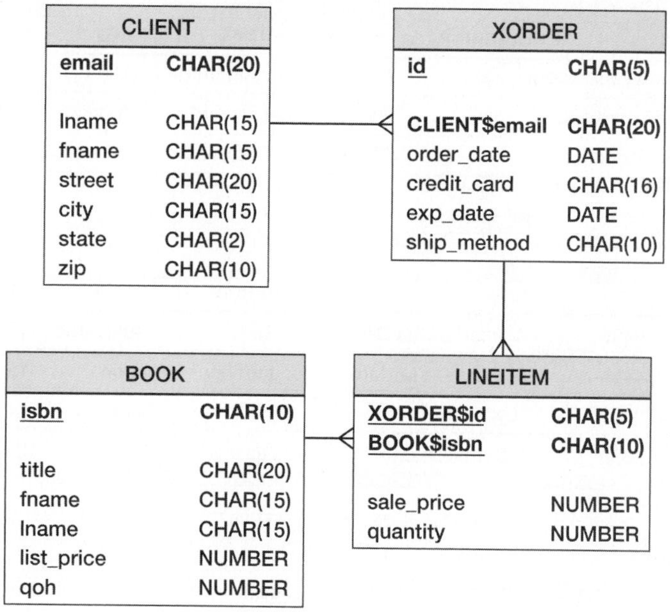

CLIENT

email	CHAR(20)
lname	CHAR(15)
fname	CHAR(15)
street	CHAR(20)
city	CHAR(15)
state	CHAR(2)
zip	CHAR(10)

XORDER

id	CHAR(5)
CLIENT$email	CHAR(20)
order_date	DATE
credit_card	CHAR(16)
exp_date	DATE
ship_method	CHAR(10)

BOOK

isbn	CHAR(10)
title	CHAR(20)
fname	CHAR(15)
lname	CHAR(15)
list_price	NUMBER
qoh	NUMBER

LINEITEM

XORDER$id	CHAR(5)
BOOK$isbn	CHAR(10)
sale_price	NUMBER
quantity	NUMBER

Exhibit 6-23

Amazon Database
Data

CLIENT

email	fname	lname	street	city	state	zip
mtfrost@yahoo.com	Tere	Frost	75 Algaringo	Miami	FL	33134
perotti@ohio.edu	Jim	Perotti	54 Pine Pl.	Athens	OH	45701
thacker@ohio.edu	Rebecca	Thacker	93 Maple Dr.	Athens	OH	45701

BOOK

isbn	title	fname	lname	list_price	qoh
0312099436	Women of the Silk	Gail	Tsukiyama	12.95	150
014025448X	At Home in Mitford	Jan	Karon	12.95	97
0345423097	Joy School	Elizabeth	Berg	11.95	129
0670894370	A Common Life	Jan	Karon	24.95	45

XORDER

id	CLIENT$email	order_date	credit_card	exp_date	ship_method
001	thacker@ohio.edu	11/15/2002	9999888877776666	07/31/2003	FedEx
002	perotti@ohio.edu	11/23/2002	3333444455556666	04/30/2005	USPS
003	thacker@ohio.edu	12/02/2002	4444111122223333	10/31/2004	USPS

LINEITEM

XORDER$id	BOOK$isbn	sale_price	quantity
001	0312099436	10.36	2
001	014025448X	10.36	3
002	0312099436	11.50	1
002	0670894370	17.46	2
003	0670894370	18.00	1

Learning Objectives

After completing this chapter, you will be able to:

- Describe the three basic relational database retrieval operations.
- Use the SQL Select statement to retrieve all data in a table.
- Specify a specific column list in a Select statement.
- Sort the results of a Select statement by one or more columns in ascending or descending order.
- Use one or more conditions in a where clause to limit the rows included in the results of a Select statement.
- Identify and properly use conditional operators in Select statements.
- Properly use AND and OR operators to express multiple conditions in a Select statement.
- Use aggregate functions in Select statements.
- Use the group by clause to create subaggregations in Select statements.
- Use the having clause to limit the results of queries involving aggregate functions.
- Properly use Distinct in a Select statement.
- Create join conditions for Select statements that involve multiple tables.
- Use column and table name aliases.
- Use subqueries.

Retrieving Data with Oracle

Introduction

One of the major advantages of the relational database approach is that it enables very flexible data retrieval. Basically, you can view the data in the database just about any way you desire. The trick is in knowing how to write the code required to retrieve the proper rows and columns. The good news is that for many retrieval operations, the code is quite simple. The bad news is that sometimes the code is very complex. As shown in Chapter 6, Oracle includes the iSQL*Plus interface to execute SQL (structured query language) statements.

In this chapter, we introduce you to data retrieval using SQL. We begin the chapter by providing an overview of the most basic retrieval operations in SQL, then we provide a number of examples of retrieving data from a single table. After you are familiar with single-table retrieval, we show you how to retrieve data from multiple tables.

Basic Retrieval Operations in SQL

There are three core data retrieval operations for relational databases: selection, projection, and joining:

- **Selection** retrieves a subset of rows.
- **Projection** retrieves a subset of columns.
- **Joining** combines data from two tables (you can use more than one join operation to combine data from more than two tables).

SQL implements all three of these operations through a single statement called the **Select** statement. The most basic form of the Select statement is shown below.

Select   [column list]

From   [table name] ;

As you can see, an SQL Select statement can be quite simple. The only required elements are (1) the word *Select* followed by a list of columns, and (2) the word *From* followed by the name of the table(s) that holds the requested data. The Projection operation we described earlier is implemented through the column list in the Select statement. Joining will be described later. The semicolon at the end marks the end of the Select statement.

Let's look at a specific example. Recall that in Chapter 6 we built the Sky_Member database in Oracle. We will use that database for the examples in this section. The Sky_Member database has only one table, called SKY_MEMBER. For your reference, the data model for the database is shown in Exhibit 7-1.

Exhibit 7-1	SKY_MEMBER	
	email	CHAR(20)
Sky_Member Database Data Model		
	fname	CHAR(15)
	lname	CHAR(15)
	phone	CHAR(12)
	jumps	NUMBER
	equip	CHAR(1)
	level	CHAR(1)

Displaying All Columns and Rows

Suppose you want a complete list of members showing all data about all members. This is the most simple SQL query (SQL Select statements are often called *queries*). Although we could list all of the column names included in the table, we can use a shortcut. If you use an asterisk (*) as the column list in a Select statement, you are indicating that you want all columns included in the query results. The Select statement used to retrieve all the data from the SKY_MEMBER table would be:

Select   *

From   Sky_Member ;

Recall from Chapter 6 that queries are created using Oracle's iSQL*Plus interface, which is accessible over the Web from any browser. First, sign on to iSQL*Plus using a Web browser. After signing on successfully, you will see the iSQL*Plus workspace. As you learned in the last chapter, SQL commands are typed into the window and then run by clicking the Execute button. The results of the run appear below the window. Each of the examples shown below can be run individually, or they may be combined in a script, as described in Chapter 6. Exhibit 7-2 shows this Select statement and the resulting display.

```
select *
from sky_member ;
```

EMAIL	FNAME	LNAME	PHONE	JUMPS	E	S
bucky@ohio.edu	Teri	Bucky	555-5555	22	Y	A
dayj@ohio.edu	John	Day	592-0646	5	Y	B
johnson@bobcat.edu	Jeremy	Johnson	555-3333	15	Y	I
luce@ohio.edu	Thom	Luce	592-1111	12	N	I
mcgann@ohio.edu	Sean	McGann	592-2222	20	Y	A
mcgrath@bobcat.edu	Billie	McGrath	555-6666	3	N	B
wilson@bobcat.edu	Sally	Wilson	555-4444	6	N	B

To understand how an SQL statement works, the diagram in Exhibit 7-3 shows a breakdown of each part of the SQL statement and how it relates to the table involved in the query. We will use this type of diagram throughout this chapter when analyzing the SQL statements introduced in each part of the chapter.

Exhibit 7-3   Analysis of the Select Statement Retrieving All Columns and Rows

SELECT ALL ROWS AND COLUMNS
List all information about all members

SELECT *
From sky_member;

The * specifies that all columns appear in the result.

email	fname	lname	phone	jumps	equip	skill
bucky@ohio.edu	Teri	Bucky	555-5555	22	Y	A
dayj@ohio.edu	John	Day	592-0646	5	Y	B
johnson@bobcat.edu	Jeremy	Johnson	555-3333	15	Y	I
luce@ohio.edu	Thom	Luce	592-1111	12	N	I
mcgann@ohio.edu	Sean	McGann	592-2222	20	Y	A
mcgrath@bobcat.edu	Billie	McGrath	555-6666	3	N	B

RESULT

email	fname	lname	phone	jumps	equip	skill
bucky@ohio.edu	Teri	Bucky	555-5555	22	Y	A
dayj@ohio.edu	John	Day	592-0646	5	Y	B
johnson@bobcat.edu	Jeremy	Johnson	555-3333	15	Y	I
luce@ohio.edu	Thom	Luce	592-1111	12	N	I
mcgann@ohio.edu	Sean	McGann	592-2222	20	Y	A
mcgrath@bobcat.edu	Billie	McGrath	555-6666	3	N	B

In this diagram, the Select statement is shown on the left, with a particular part of the statement in bold. In the table of data on the right, the aspect of the table affected by the boldfaced portion of the Select statement is indicated with shading.

In the first panel of the diagram, the Select * in the SQL statement is bold, and the diagram indicates the columns that will be selected for the query. In this case the asterisk causes all the columns to be selected, so the names of all the columns have been shaded. The second panel shows the result of the query. In this case, all the columns and all the rows will be displayed.

Using a Column List

Now let's say that you do not need all the columns, and you only want to include the first and last names and email addresses of all members, in that order. This is the basic projection operation in a relational database, as described earlier. To do this operation, use *Select* together with a comma-separated list of columns, as shown in Exhibit 7-4. Exhibit 7-5 shows the analysis for this query.

Exhibit 7-4

Query with an
Explicit Column
List (Projection
Operation)

```
select fname, lname, email
from sky_member;
```

FNAME	LNAME	EMAIL
Teri	Bucky	bucky@ohio.edu
John	Day	dayj@ohio.edu
Jeremy	Johnson	johnson@bobcat.edu
Thom	Luce	luce@ohio.edu
Sean	McGann	mcgann@ohio.edu
Billie	McGrath	mcgrath@bobcat.edu
Sally	Wilson	wilson@bobcat.edu

Exhibit 7-5   Analysis of the Select Statement with an Explicit Column List

SELECT SPECIFIC COLUMNS
List all information about all members

SELECT fname,
    lname,
    email
From sky_member;

email	fname	lname	phone	jumps	equip	skill
bucky@ohio.edu	Teri	Bucky	555-5555	22	Y	A
dayj@ohio.edu	John	Day	592-0646	5	Y	B
johnson@bobcat.edu	Jeremy	Johnson	555-3333	15	Y	I
luce@ohio.edu	Thom	Luce	592-1111	12	N	I
mcgann@ohio.edu	Sean	McGann	592-2222	20	Y	A
mcgrath@bobcat.edu	Billie	McGrath	555-6666	3	N	B

RESULT

fname	lname	email
Teri	Bucky	bucky@ohio.edu
John	Day	dayj@ohio.edu
Jeremy	Johnson	johnson@bobcat.edu
Thom	Luce	luce@ohio.edu
Sean	McGann	mcgann@ohio.edu
Billie	McGrath	mcgrath@bobcat.edu

When you use a column list in a Select statement that includes more than one column, you must separate the column names in the list by commas. Some people like to put each column on a separate line and tab over to line up the columns. This procedure is done simply to improve readability. You can actually put the entire Select statement on a single line, but the query is then much harder to read. Clear coding becomes more important as your queries become more complex.

As you can see from the result of the query above, the order of the columns in the column list dictates the order in which the columns are shown in the results. This order has no effect on the order in which the columns are actually stored in the table; it simply determines how the data will be displayed.

Sorting with Order By

Typically, the display of data can be improved by showing the results in some logical order. For example, you might want the results in order of the member's last name, which is stored in the lname column. Exhibit 7-6 shows the design of a query with this sorting.

Exhibit 7-6	Select email,
Designing a Query with Sorting	fname,
	lname
	From sky_member
	Order by lname

EMAIL	FNAME	LNAME
bucky@ohio.edu	Teri	Bucky
dayj@ohio.edu	John	Day
johnson@bobcat.edu	Jeremy	Johnson
luce@ohio.edu	Thom	Luce
mcgann@ohio.edu	Sean	McGann
mcgrath@bobcat.edu	Billie	McGrath
wilson@bobcat.edu	Sally	Wilson

In this query, the columns to be displayed will be email, fname, and lname, in that order. To sort the rows based on the data in a particular column, simply use the **order by** clause with that column. The data will appear alphabetically or numerically, from smallest to largest. The query analysis is shown in Exhibit 7-7.

 Exhibit 7-7   Select Statement with Order by Clause

SORTING
List the email, fname, and lname in alphabetical order by lname

SELECT email
      fname,
      lname,
From sky_member
Order by lname;

email	fname	lname	phone	jumps	equip	skill
mcgann@ohio.edu	Sean	McGann	592-2222	20	Y	A
dayj@ohio.edu	John	Day	592-0646	5	Y	B
bucky@ohio.edu	Teri	Bucky	555-5555	22	Y	A
johnson@bobcat.edu	Jeremy	Johnson	555-3333	15	Y	I
luce@ohio.edu	Thom	Luce	592-1111	12	N	I
mcgrath@bobcat.edu	Billie	McGrath	555-6666	3	N	B

SELECT email
      fname,
      lname,
From sky_member
Order by lname;

email	fname	lname	phone	jumps	equip	skill
mcgann@ohio.edu	Sean	McGann	592-2222	20	Y	A
dayj@ohio.edu	John	Day	592-0646	5	Y	B
bucky@ohio.edu	Teri	Buck	555-5555	22	Y	A
johnson@bobcat.edu	Jeremy	John h	555-3333	15	Y	I
luce@ohio.edu	Thom	Luce	592-1111	12	N	I
mcgrath@bobcat.edu	Billie	McG	555-6666	3	N	B
wilson@bobcat.edu	Sally	Wilson	555-4444	6	N	B

RESULT

email	fname	lname
bucky@ohio.edu	Teri	Bucky
dayj@ohio.edu	John	Day
johnson@bobcat.edu	Jeremy	Johnson
luce@ohio.edu	Thom	Luce
mcgann@ohio.edu	Sean	McGann
mcgrath@bobcat.edu	Billie	McGrath

The arrow in the lname column indicates that a sort will occur on the values in that column by moving the row for Teri Bucky to the top and moving the row for Sean McGann down. Also notice that the order of columns (email, fname, lname) is independent of the order of rows. Columns used in the order by clause will usually be included in the column list, because in most cases it would not make sense to sort by a column that is not displayed.

You should also notice that the last names appear in *A to Z* order, which is called *ascending order*. This is the default. If you want the rows to be in *descending order* (Z to A), you would add *desc* to the order by clause after the column name, as shown in Exhibit 7-8.

Exhibit 7-8

Descending Order
Sort

```
Select email,
fname,
lname
From Sky_Member
Order by lname desc ;
```

EMAIL	FNAME	LNAME
wilson@bobcat.edu	Sally	Wilson
mcgrath@bobcat.edu	Billie	McGrath
mcgann@ohio.edu	Sean	McGann
luce@ohio.edu	Thom	Luce
johnson@bobcat.edu	Jeremy	Johnson
dayj@ohio.edu	John	Day
bucky@ohio.edu	Teri	Bucky

Sorting on Multiple Columns

Sometimes a column used for sorting contains duplicate values. In this situation, there is no basis for determining the order of rows containing the same value in the sorted column. In this case, you have the option of including a secondary sort on additional columns. The secondary sort serves as a tiebreaker for duplicate values on the primary sort. Let's look at another example to illustrate this process. For this example, the skill level of each member will be displayed, followed by the number of jumps and last name. The results should be in ascending (alphabetic) order of skill. For any members with the same skill level, their order should be determined by the number of jumps (fewest to most). Exhibit 7-9 shows the design for this query.

Exhibit 7-9

Design of Query
with Multiple
Sort Columns

```
Select skill,
jumps,
lname
From sky_member
Order by skill, jumps ;
```

S	JUMPS	LNAME
A	20	McGann
A	22	Bucky
B	3	McGrath
B	5	Day
B	6	Wilson
I	12	Luce
I	15	Johnson

When sorting is specified in multiple columns, the sort order should be selected for the primary sort column (skill, in this case) first, and then for the secondary sort column (jumps, in this case). In SQL, all you have to do is list both sort columns in the order by clause with the primary sort column first, followed by the name of the secondary sort column. The column names must be separated by a comma. Exhibit 7-10 shows the analysis of the query.

Exhibit 7-10   Analysis of Sorting by Multiple Columns

SORTING ON MULTIPLE COLUMNS
List the skills, jumps, and lname in alphabetical order by skill and jumps with skill

SELECT skill,
       jumps,
       lname
From sky_member
Order by skill, jumps;

email	fname	lname	phone	jumps	equip	skill
mcgann@ohio.edu	Sean	McGann	592-2222	20	Y	A
dayj@ohio.edu	John	Day	592-0646	5	Y	B
bucky@ohio.edu	Teri	Bucky	555-5555	22	Y	A
johnson@bobcat.edu	Jeremy	Johnson	555-3333	15	Y	I
luce@ohio.edu	Thom	Luce	592-1111	12	N	I
mcgrath@bobcat.edu	Billie	McGrath	555-6666	3	N	B

SELECT skill,
       jumps,
       lname
From sky_member
Order by skill, jumps;

email	fname	lname	phone	jumps	equip	skill
mcgann@ohio.edu	Sean	McGann	592-2222	2	Y	A 1
dayj@ohio.edu	John	Day	592-0646	5	Y	B
bucky@ohio.edu	Teri	Bucky	555-5555	22	Y	A
johnson@bobcat.edu	Jeremy	Johnson	555-3333	15	Y	I
luce@ohio.edu	Thom	Luce	592-1111	12	N	I
mcgrath@bobcat.edu	Billie	McGrath	555-6666	3	N	B
wilson@bobcat.edu	Sally	Wilson	555-4444	6	N	B

RESULT

skill	jumps	lname
A	20	McGann
A	22	Bucky
B	3	McGrath
B	5	Day
B	6	Wilson
I	15	Johnson
I	12	Luce

The analysis first indicates that the skill, jumps, and lname columns are included in the query. The arrows in the second panel show that the rows will be first sorted by values in the skill column, and then by values in the jumps column. In the result panel, you can see that two members have a skill level of A (advanced). The first sort, on skill level, cannot determine which of these two rows should be displayed first. When this situation occurs, the secondary sort is used to determine that McGann should be shown before Bucky, because he has fewer jumps. The same thing happens for the members in skill level B. The primary sort cannot determine the order of the three members in this skill level, so the secondary sort is used to make that determination.

When using multiple columns in sorting, there is no requirement that both sorts be done in ascending or descending order. If you wanted the sort by skill level to be in *descending* and the secondary sort on the number of jumps to be in *ascending* order, simply insert *desc* after the skill column in the order by clause, as shown in Exhibit 7-11. Note that there is *not* a comma between *skill* and *desc.*

Exhibit 7-11

Mixing Ascending
and Descending
Order

```
Select skill,
jumps,
lname
From sky_Member
Order by skill desc, jumps ;
```

S	JUMPS	LNAME
I	12	Luce
I	15	Johnson
B	3	McGrath
B	5	Day
B	6	Wilson
A	20	McGann
A	22	Bucky

Selecting Rows with Where

Recall from the beginning of the chapter that the selection operation in a relational database is the display of a subset of rows from a table. To do this operation in SQL, we need to add another element to our simple Select statement. Rows are chosen through conditions specified in a **where clause** in the Select statement. If you wanted to see the lname and jumps columns for rows corresponding to members with more than 20 jumps, you would use the Select statement shown in Exhibit 7-12. The analysis of the query is shown in Exhibit 7-13.

Exhibit 7-12

SQL Where Clause

```
Select lname, jumps
From Sky_Member
Where jumps > 20 ;
```

LNAME	JUMPS
Bucky	22

Exhibit 7-13 Analysis of Query with a Where Clause

JUMPS > 20
List the lname and jumps for members with more than 20 jumps

SELECT lname,
       jumps
From sky_member
where jumps > 20;

email	fname	lname	phone	jumps	equip	skill
mcgann@ohio.edu	Sean	McGann	592-2222	20	Y	A
dayj@ohio.edu	John	Day	592-0646	5	Y	B
bucky@ohio.edu	Teri	Bucky	555-5555	22	Y	A
johnson@bobcat.edu	Jeremy	Johnson	555-3333	15	Y	I
luce@ohio.edu	Thom	Luce	592-1111	12	N	I
mcgrath@bobcat.edu	Billie	McGrath	555-6666	3	N	B

SELECT lname,
       jumps
From sky_member
where jumps > 20;

email	fname	lname	phone	jumps	equip	skill
mcgann@ohio.edu	Sean	McGann	592-2222	20	Y	A
dayj@ohio.edu	John	Day	592-0646	5	Y	B
bucky@ohio.edu	Teri	Bucky	555-5555	22	Y	A
johnson@bobcat.edu	Jeremy	Johnson	555-3333	15	Y	I
luce@ohio.edu	Thom	Luce	592-1111	12	N	I
mcgrath@bobcat.edu	Billie	McGrath	555-6666	3	N	B

RESULT

lname	jumps
Bucky	22

A where clause always includes at least one true/false condition, such as "jumps > 20" in the example. If a row meets the condition specified, it is included in the results. Rows that do not meet the condition are not included. Note that you can have more than one condition, but we will get to that later. If you are familiar with a programming language such as Visual Basic or Java, you already know about conditional operators. But in case you are not, the commonly used operators are shown in Exhibit 7-14. We will add to this list later.

Exhibit 7-14

Conditional Operators

Operator	Explanation	Example
=	Equal to	equip = 'N'
>	Greater than	jumps > 10
<	Less than	jumps < 20
>=	Greater than or equal to	jumps >= 10
<=	Less than or equal to	jumps <= 20
!=	Not equal to	ability != 'A'

Where Clauses Involving Text Data

When you want to use columns containing text data in a where clause, you must put any character values used as part of the condition inside *single* quotes. For example, if you wanted to see the first and last names of all members who own their own equipment, you would use the SQL statement shown in Exhibit 7-15.

Exhibit 7-15

A Condition
Involving a
Text Column

```
Select fname,
lname
From Sky_Member
Where equip = 'Y' ;
```

FNAME	LNAME
Teri	Bucky
John	Day
Jeremy	Johnson
Sean	McGann

The LIKE Operator

In SQL, there is an additional conditional operator that is useful when dealing with character-based data. The **LIKE operator** enables you to choose rows that share some common characters but are not exactly the same. For example, suppose you want to show the first names, last names, and phone numbers of all members who have phone numbers that start with "555." In SQL, the query would look like the one in Exhibit 7-16.

Exhibit 7-16

Use of the LIKE
Operator

```
Select fname,
lname,
email,
phone
From Sky_Member
Where phone like '555%' ;
```

FNAME	LNAME	EMAIL	PHONE
Teri	Bucky	bucky@ohio.edu	555-5555
Jeremy	Johnson	johnson@bobcat.edu	555-3333
Billie	McGrath	mcgrath@bobcat.edu	555-6666
Sally	Wilson	wilson@bobcat.edu	555-4444

The percent sign (%) is used as a "wildcard" representing any combination of characters (other database software sometimes use the asterisk). Any row that has a phone value starting with "555" is included in the results, regardless of what or how many characters follow.

You can also use LIKE to return rows according to characters at the end of a field value. Let's say that you want to execute the same basic query, but this time you want to limit the list to members who have ".edu" email addresses (email addresses that end in ".edu"). The SQL statement to accomplish this query is shown in Exhibit 7-17. You may be surprised to see a percent sign both before and *after* edu. The second % sign is required because the data type is char, and therefore the remainder of the field is padded with blank spaces. In other words, for Oracle, each email address ends with blanks, *not* with "edu."

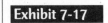

Exhibit 7-17

Find Strings
Ending in 'edu'

```
Select fname,
lname,
email,
phone
From Sky_Member
Where email like '%edu%';
```

FNAME	LNAME	EMAIL	PHONE
Teri	Bucky	bucky@ohio.edu	555-5555
John	Day	dayj@ohio.edu	592-0646
Jeremy	Johnson	johnson@bobcat.edu	555-3333
Thom	Luce	luce@ohio.edu	592-1111
Sean	McGann	mcgann@ohio.edu	592-2222
Billie	McGrath	mcgrath@bobcat.edu	555-6666
Sally	Wilson	wilson@bobcat.edu	555-4444

Complex Where Clauses

Sometimes you need to select rows according to more than one condition. With SQL, you do this operation in a single where clause. Each condition is separated by a logical operator. When conditions are separated by the **AND logical operator,** a row must meet *both* conditions to be selected. When the conditions are separated by the **OR logical operator,** a row is selected if *either* condition is met.

Let's look at some examples to illustrate how to use each logical condition. For the first example, we want to list the first and last names, number of jumps, and ability for all members who have more than 10 jumps and are at the intermediate ability level. The two conditions we want to satisfy are:

jumps > 10   AND   skill = 'I'

Which rows will be selected using these criteria? Remember that with the AND operator, *both* conditions must be satisfied. Exhibit 7-18 shows how rows will be selected for display.

Exhibit 7-18

Multiple Conditions Linked with an AND

email	fname	lname	phone	jumps	equip	skill	selected?
mcgann@ohio.edu	Sean	McGann	592-2222	20	Y	A	NO
dayj@ohio.edu	John	Day	592-0646	5	Y	B	NO
bucky@ohio.edu	Teri	Bucky	555-5555	22	Y	A	NO
johnson@bobcat.edu	Jeremy	Johnson	555-3333	15	Y	I	YES
luce@ohio.edu	Thom	Luce	592-1111	12	N	I	YES
mcgrath@bobcat.edu	Billie	McGrath	555-6666	3	N	B	NO
wilson@bobcat.edu	Sally	Wilson	555-4444	6	N	B	NO

As the exhibit indicates in the final column, only Johnson and Luce will be selected. Now let's change our condition by substituting an OR logical operator for the AND. This time, we want to list the members who either have more than 14 jumps or are at the intermediate ability level. In this case, the two conditions we want to satisfy are:

jumps > 14   OR   skill = 'I'

Can you tell which rows are selected this time? When using the OR operator, any row that meets *either* condition is selected. Exhibit 7-19 shows how rows will be selected for display.

Exhibit 7-19   Multiple Conditions Linked with an OR

email	fname	lname	phone	jumps	equip	skill	selected?
mcgann@ohio.edu	Sean	McGann	592-2222	20	Y	A	YES
dayj@ohio.edu	John	Day	592-0646	5	Y	B	NO
bucky@ohio.edu	Teri	Bucky	555-5555	22	Y	A	YES
johnson@bobcat.edu	Jeremy	Johnson	555-3333	15	Y	I	YES
luce@ohio.edu	Thom	Luce	592-1111	12	N	I	YES
mcgrath@bobcat.edu	Billie	McGrath	555-6666	3	N	B	NO
wilson@bobcat.edu	Sally	Wilson	555-4444	6	N	B	NO

As before, Johnson is selected because he meets both conditions. McGann and Bucky are also selected, because they have more than 15 jumps, even though they do not have the correct skill level. In addition, Luce is selected because he meets the skill condition, even though he does not have more than 14 jumps.

Now we will put each example in the form of a query. An example SQL statement that has two conditions joined with an AND logical operator is shown in Exhibit 7-20.

Exhibit 7-20

SQL AND Operator

```
Select fname,
lname,
jumps,
skill
From Sky_Member
Where jumps > 10
And skill = 'I' ;
```

FNAME	LNAME	JUMPS	S
Jeremy	Johnson	15	I
Thom	Luce	12	I

Notice that we have only one where clause. That is a rule; you can have only one where clause in any single Select statement. This single where clause combines two conditions with the AND logical operator. Exhibit 7-21 shows the analysis for this query.

Exhibit 7-21   Analysis of the Query Using an AND Relationship

JUMP >10 AND Skill = 'I'

List the fname, lname, jumps, and skill for members with more than 10 jumps and an intermediate skill level.

SELECT fname
        lname,
        jumps,
        skill
From sky_member
where jumps > 10
and skill= 'I';

email	fname	lname	phone	jumps	equip	skill
mcgann@ohio.edu	Sean	McGann	592-2222	20	Y	A
dayj@ohio.edu	John	Day	592-0646	5	Y	B
bucky@ohio.edu	Teri	Bucky	555-5555	22	Y	A
johnson@bobcat.edu	Jeremy	Johnson	555-3333	15	Y	I
luce@ohio.edu	Thom	Luce	592-1111	12	N	I
mcgrath@bobcat.edu	Billie	McGrath	555-6666	3	N	B
wilson@bobcat.edu	Sally	Wilson	555-4444	6	N	B

SELECT fname
        lname,
        jumps,
        skill
From sky_member
where jumps > 10
and skill= 'I';

email	fname	lname	phone	jumps	equip	skill
mcgann@ohio.edu	Sean	McGann	592-2222	20	Y	A
dayj@ohio.edu	John	Day	592-0646	5	Y	B
bucky@ohio.edu	Teri	Bucky	555-5555	22	Y	A
johnson@bobcat.edu	Jeremy	Johnson	555-3333	15	Y	I
luce@ohio.edu	Thom	Luce	592-1111	12	N	I
mcgrath@bobcat.edu	Billie	McGrath	555-6666	3	N	B
wilson@bobcat.edu	Sally	Wilson	555-4444	6	N	B

SELECT fname
        lname,
        jumps,
        skill
From sky_member
where jumps > 10
and skill= 'I';

email	fname	lname	phone	jumps	equip	skill
mcgann@ohio.edu	Sean	McGann	592-2222	20	Y	A
dayj@ohio.edu	John	Day	592-0646	5	Y	B
bucky@ohio.edu	Teri	Bucky	555-5555	22	Y	A
johnson@bobcat.edu	Jeremy	Johnson	555-3333	15	Y	I
luce@ohio.edu	Thom	Luce	592-1111	12	N	I
mcgrath@bobcat.edu	Billie	McGrath	555-6666	3	N	B
wilson@bobcat.edu	Sally	Wilson	555-4444	6	N	B

RESULT

fname	lname	jumps	skill
Jeremy	Johnson	15	I
Thom	Luce	12	I

To illustrate the use of an OR logical operator, consider the SQL statement in Exhibit 7-22 that displays members with more than 14 jumps or with an intermediate skill level. Exhibit 7-23 shows an analysis of the query.

Exhibit 7-22

OR Operator

```
Select fname,
lname,
jumps,
skill
From Sky_Member
Where jumps > 14
Or skill = 1';
```

FNAME	LNAME	JUMPS	S
Teri	Bucky	22	A
Jeremy	Johnson	15	I
Thom	Luce	12	I
Sean	McGann	20	A

Exhibit 7-23

Analysis of the Query Using an OR Relationship

JUMP >14 AND Skill = 'I'
List the fname, lname, jumps, and skill for members with more than 14 jumps or an intermediate skill level.

```
SELECT fname
       lname,
       jumps,
       skill
From sky_member
where jumps > 14
or skill = 'I';
```

email	fname	lname	phone	jumps	equip	skill
mcgann@ohio.edu	Sean	McGann	592-2222	20	Y	A
dayj@ohio.edu	John	Day	592-0646	5	Y	B
bucky@ohio.edu	Teri	Bucky	555-5555	22	Y	A
johnson@bobcat.edu	Jeremy	Johnson	555-3333	15	Y	I
luce@ohio.edu	Thom	Luce	592-1111	12	N	I
mcgrath@bobcat.edu	Billie	McGrath	555-6666	3	N	B
wilson@bobcat.edu	Sally	Wilson	555-4444	6	N	B

```
SELECT fname
       lname,
       jumps,
       skill
From sky_member
where jumps > 14
or skill = 'I';
```

email	fname	lname	phone	jumps	equip	skill
mcgann@ohio.edu	Sean	McGann	592-2222	20	Y	A
dayj@ohio.edu	John	Day	592-0646	5	Y	B
bucky@ohio.edu	Teri	Bucky	555-5555	22	Y	A
johnson@bobcat.edu	Jeremy	Johnson	555-3333	15	Y	I
luce@ohio.edu	Thom	Luce	592-1111	12	N	I
mcgrath@bobcat.edu	Billie	McGrath	555-6666	3	N	B
wilson@bobcat.edu	Sally	Wilson	555-4444	6	N	B

(*Continued*)

Exhibit 7-23   Continued

```
SELECT  fname
        lname,
        jumps,
        skill
From sky_member
where jumps > 14
or skill = 'I';
```

email	fname	lname	phone	jumps	equip	skill
mcgann@ohio.edu	Sean	McGann	592-2222	20	Y	A
dayj@ohio.edu	John	Day	592-0646	5	Y	B
bucky@ohio.edu	Teri	Bucky	555-5555	22	Y	A
johnson@bobcat.edu	Jeremy	Johnson	555-3333	15	Y	I
luce@ohio.edu	Thom	Luce	592-1111	12	N	I
mcgrath@bobcat.edu	Billie	McGrath	555-6666	3	N	B
wilson@bobcat.edu	Sally	Wilson	555-4444	6	N	B

RESULT

fname	lname	jumps	skill
Sean	McGann	20	A
Teri	Bucky	22	A
Jeremy	Johnson	15	I
Thom	Luce	12	I

You can have a virtually unlimited number of conditions joined with a combination of AND and OR operators in a single where clause. Later in this chapter, we will show you how to use both AND and OR in the same where clause.

Multiple Conditions on the Same Column

You can use AND to separate conditions that deal with the same column. This is one way in which you can select rows based on a range of values. For example, if you want to select rows representing members who have more than 10 but fewer than 20 jumps, you could use the SQL Select statement shown in Exhibit 7-24.

Exhibit 7-24

Multiple
Conditions on the
Same Column

```
Select fname,
lname,
jumps,
skill
From sky_member
where jumps > 10
and jumps < 20;
```

FNAME	LNAME	JUMPS	S
Jeremy	Johnson	15	I
Thom	Luce	12	I

In the analysis shown in Exhibit 7-25, you can see that the first half of the condition (jumps > 10) will select McGann, Bucky, Johnson, and Luce, but then the second half of the condition (jumps < 20) eliminates McGann and Bucky. Thus, the combined condition will result in the display of Johnson and Luce.

Exhibit 7-25	The Analysis of the Query Jumps > 10 and Jumps < 20

JUMP >10 AND JUMPS < 20

List the fname, lname, jumps, and skill for members with more than 10 jumps but fewer than 20 jumps.

SELECT fname
     lname,
     jumps,
     skill
From sky_member
where jumps > 10
and jumps < 20;

email	fname	lname	phone	jumps	equip	skill
mcgann@ohio.edu	Sean	McGann	592-2222	20	Y	A
dayj@ohio.edu	John	Day	592-0646	5	Y	B
bucky@ohio.edu	Teri	Bucky	555-5555	22	Y	A
johnson@bobcat.edu	Jeremy	Johnson	555-3333	15	Y	I
luce@ohio.edu	Thom	Luce	592-1111	12	N	I
mcgrath@bobcat.edu	Billie	McGrath	555-6666	3	N	B

SELECT fname
     lname,
     jumps,
     skill
From sky_member
where jumps > 10
and jumps < 20;

email	fname	lname	phone	jumps	equip	skill
mcgann@ohio.edu	Sean	McGann	592-2222	20	Y	A
dayj@ohio.edu	John	Day	592-0646	5	Y	B
bucky@ohio.edu	Teri	Bucky	555-5555	22	Y	A
johnson@bobcat.edu	Jeremy	Johnson	555-3333	15	Y	I
luce@ohio.edu	Thom	Luce	592-1111	12	N	I
mcgrath@bobcat.edu	Billie	McGrath	555-6666	3	N	B

SELECT fname
     lname,
     jumps,
     skill
From sky_member
where jumps > 10
and jumps < 20;

email	fname	lname	phone	jumps	equip	skill
mcgann@ohio.edu	Sean	McGann	592-2222	20	Y	A
dayj@ohio.edu	John	Day	592-0646	5	Y	B
bucky@ohio.edu	Teri	Bucky	555-5555	22	Y	A
johnson@bobcat.edu	Jeremy	Johnson	555-3333	15	Y	I
luce@ohio.edu	Thom	Luce	592-1111	12	N	I
mcgrath@bobcat.edu	Billie	McGrath	555-6666	3	N	B

RESULT

fname	lname	jumps	skill
Jeremy	Johnson	15	I
Thom	Luce	12	I

It is also possible to use OR where each condition includes the same column. You can use OR to select rows where a particular column has any one of several values. Suppose you want to list all members who are of beginner (B) or intermediate (I) ability. The SQL Select statement that can be used to produce this list is shown in Exhibit 7-26.

Exhibit 7-26

Using OR to Enter
Multiple Criteria
on the Same
Column

```
Select fname,
lname,
jumps,
skill
From Sky_Member
Where skill = 'B'
Or skill = 'I';
```

FNAME	LNAME	JUMPS	S
John	Day	5	B
Jeremy	Johnson	15	I
Thom	Luce	12	I
Billie	McGrath	3	B
Sally	Wilson	6	B

This kind of query sometimes causes confusion as to whether you should use AND or OR. When you want to select rows based on multiple values for the same column, using AND can cause problems. If you tried to use AND in the SQL Select statement above, the result would be an empty list. When you think about it, this result makes sense. Using AND requires that *both* conditions be met for a row to be included in the results. We know that each member has one ability level, so it is impossible for any single member to match both conditions. In other words, a particular member could not be both an Intermediate and Beginner at the same time. Thus, we get an empty list.

Using the IN Operator

If you find this information confusing, you may wish to use an alternate way to compare a column value to a list. The **IN operator** allows you to select rows based on multiple values for a particular column. Essentially, this procedure is the same as having one or more OR conditions. The SQL Select statement using IN rather than OR is shown in Exhibit 7-27.

Exhibit 7-27

Using the IN
Operator

```
Select fname,
lname,
jumps,
skill
From Sky_Member
Where skill In ('B', 'I');
```

FNAME	LNAME	JUMPS	S
John	Day	5	B
Jeremy	Johnson	15	I
Thom	Luce	12	I
Billie	McGrath	3	B
Sally	Wilson	6	B

This method is especially useful when you have many values in the value list. If you use OR conditions, you need to use a whole series of ORs to join all the values together. With IN, you simply have to add to the value list inside the parentheses. In general, IN is simpler to type, and you are less likely to make errors than when entering a series of OR conditions.

Using the BETWEEN Operator

Another useful conditional operator is *BETWEEN*. The **BETWEEN operator** enables you to choose rows based on a range of values. Recall our earlier example that listed members with between 10 and 20 jumps. We could write this query using between, as shown in the SQL Select statement in Exhibit 7-28.

Exhibit 7-28

Using the
Between Operator

```
Select fname,
lname,
jumps,
skill
From Sky_Member
Where jumps Between 10 and 20 ;
```

FNAME	LNAME	JUMPS	S
Jeremy	Johnson	15	I
Thom	Luce	12	I
Sean	McGann	20	A

In this query, each jump value is evaluated to see if it is between 10 and 20, inclusive (including 10 and 20). If so, the row is included in the results. Note that this condition is slightly different from the previous condition of jumps > 10 AND jumps < 20, which excluded McGann, who had 20 jumps. In the condition using AND, a member with jumps equal to

10 or equal to 20 would not be included. Because between includes the two numbers specified in the condition, it is actually the same as writing jumps >= 10 AND jumps <= 20. The analysis for this query is shown in Exhibit 7-29.

Exhibit 7-29   Analysis of the BETWEEN Operator

JUMPS BETWEEN 10 AND 20
List the fname, lname, jumps, and skill for members with jumps between 10 and 20.

SELECT fname,
       lname,
       jumps,
       skill
From sky_member
where jumps between
10 and 20;

email	fname	lname	phone	jumps	equip	skill
mcgann@ohio.edu	Sean	McGann	592-2222	20	Y	A
dayj@ohio.edu	John	Day	592-0646	5	Y	B
bucky@ohio.edu	Teri	Bucky	555-5555	22	Y	A
johnson@bobcat.edu	Jeremy	Johnson	555-3333	15	Y	I
luce@ohio.edu	Thom	Luce	592-1111	12	N	I
mcgrath@bobcat.edu	Billie	McGrath	555-6666	3	N	B

SELECT fname,
       lname,
       jumps,
       skill
From sky_member
where jumps between
10 and 20;

email	fname	lname	phone	jumps	equip	skill
mcgann@ohio.edu	Sean	McGann	592-2222	20	Y	A
dayj@ohio.edu	John	Day	592-0646	5	Y	B
bucky@ohio.edu	Teri	Bucky	555-5555	22	Y	A
johnson@bobcat.edu	Jeremy	Johnson	555-3333	15	Y	I
luce@ohio.edu	Thom	Luce	592-1111	12	N	I
mcgrath@bobcat.edu	Billie	McGrath	555-6666	3	N	B

RESULT

fname	lname	jumps	skill
Sean	McGann	20	A
Jeremy	Johnson	15	I
Thom	Luce	12	I

As this analysis shows, the jumps value for McGann is equal to 20, so he is included in the result. The between operator includes any rows with either of the two values specified. In addition to being able to use between on numeric data, you can also do alphabetic comparisons by using between with character-based data.

The NOT Operator

Any of the operators that we have described can be combined with the **NOT operator** to reverse the condition, by preceding the conditional operator with the word NOT. Using NOT reverses what would normally happen. The previously excluded rows become the chosen rows with the NOT operator. To illustrate, let's look at the SQL statement that selected rows representing members who were at the beginner or intermediate level. If we precede the IN operator with NOT, we get all members except those at the beginner or intermediate levels, as shown in the SQL Select statement of Exhibit 7-30.

NOT Operator

```
Select fname,
lname,
jumps,
skill
From Sky_Member
Where skill Not In ('B', 'I');
```

FNAME	LNAME	JUMPS	S
Teri	Bucky	22	A
Sean	McGann	20	A

Combining AND and OR

It is also possible to mix AND and OR operators in a single where clause. Unfortunately, this procedure can get a bit tricky. Suppose you want to get a list of all members who have their own equipment and are in either the B or I skill levels. An inexperienced SQL coder might try the SQL Select statement shown in Exhibit 7-31.

Improper Combination of AND and OR

```
Select fname,
lname,
equip,
skill
From Sky_Member
Where equip = 'Y'
And skill = 'I'
Or skill = 'B';
```

FNAME	LNAME	E	S
John	Day	Y	B
Jeremy	Johnson	Y	I
Billie	McGrath	N	B
Sally	Wilson	N	B

In an SQL Select statement, any conditions combined with an AND are evaluated first, and additional conditions combined with an OR are evaluated second. This query will show

Exhibit 7-57

Missing Join
Condition

```
Select Call_no,
code,
title,
hours
From Section, Course ;
```

CALL_	CODE	TITLE	HOURS
001	MIS380	Database I	4
002	MIS380	Database I	4
003	MIS380	Database I	4
004	MIS380	Database I	4
001	MIS225	Visual Basic	4
002	MIS225	Visual Basic	4
003	MIS225	Visual Basic	4
004	MIS225	Visual Basic	4
001	MIS420	Systems II	4
002	MIS420	Systems II	4
003	MIS420	Systems II	4
004	MIS420	Systems II	4

When you examine the results, you might notice that the results closely resemble the Cartesian product. The only difference is that the query result does not include all columns from both tables. However, there are 12 rows in the results, just as there are 12 rows in the Cartesian product.

When performing multitable queries, it is useful to check the number of rows against the maximum expected. If you have too many rows in your query results, you are missing a join. The results of such an omission are sometimes quite spectacular. For example, if you have two 1000-row tables in a query and you forget the join condition, the query result will have one million rows!

Combining Joins with Other Where Conditions

When other where conditions are combined with join conditions, it is useful to put the join conditions first, followed by whatever other conditions are required. This is not a rule, but it is helpful in reading and debugging multitable queries. Let's examine an example of adding another condition to a join. The SQL Select statement in Exhibit 7-58 produces a list of sections for MIS380. To follow the logic of this query, consider the query analysis shown in Exhibit 7-59.

Exhibit 7-58

Join Combined
with an Additional
Condition

```
Select Call_no,
code,
title,
hours
From Section, Course
Where COURSE$code = code
And Code = 'MIS380' ;
```

CALL_	CODE	TITLE	HOURS
001	MIS380	Database I	4
002	MIS380	Database I	4

Exhibit 7-59	**TWO TABLE JOIN WITH ADDITIONAL CONDITION**

List the instructor's fname, lname, and course title for MIS380.

Analysis of a
Query with a Join
Combined with a
Where Condition

```
SELECT  Call_no,
        code,
        title,
        hours
From    Section, Course
Where   Code = 'MIS380'
  And   COURSE$code = code;
```

COURSE

code	title	hours
MIS380	Database I	4
MIS225	Visual Basic	4
MIS420	Systems II	4

SECTION

call_no	INSTRUCTOR$id	COURSE$code
001	11	MIS380
002	33	MIS380
003	11	MIS225
004	44	MIS420

```
SELECT  Call_no,
        code,
        title,
        hours
From    Section, Course
Where   Code = 'MIS380'
  And   COURSE$code = code;
```

COURSE

code	title	hours
MIS380	Database I	4
MIS225	Visual Basic	4
MIS420	Systems II	4

SECTION

call_no	INSTRUCTOR$id	COURSE$code
001	11	MIS380
002	33	MIS380
003	11	MIS225
004	44	MIS420

(Continued)

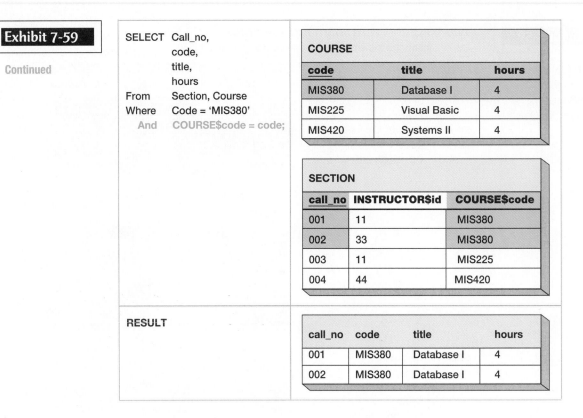

Exhibit 7-59

Continued

```
SELECT   Call_no,
         code,
         title,
         hours
From     Section, Course
Where    Code = 'MIS380'
  And    COURSE$code = code;
```

COURSE

code	title	hours
MIS380	Database I	4
MIS225	Visual Basic	4
MIS420	Systems II	4

SECTION

call_no	INSTRUCTOR$id	COURSE$code
001	11	MIS380
002	33	MIS380
003	11	MIS225
004	44	MIS420

RESULT

call_no	code	title	hours
001	MIS380	Database I	4
002	MIS380	Database I	4

In this case, the rows in the Course table are limited to MIS380, so this is the only row that will be joined to the rows in the Section table. Because there are two rows in the Section table involving MIS380, the number of rows in the result is two.

There is no practical limit to the number or type of conditions that can be included with a join. When all of your conditions are combined with AND rather than OR, the queries are typically not difficult to construct (once you understand SQL!). However, combining a join with other conditions separated by OR can be problematic for the same reasons there are problems with combining OR and AND, as discussed previously. When combining a join condition with another condition involving an OR in a single where clause, you should use parentheses to prevent the join from being combined with only part of the condition, as shown in Exhibit 7-60.

Exhibit 7-60

Use Parentheses
When Including
the OR Operator

```
Select Call_no,
code,
title,
hours
From Section, Course
Where COURSE$code = code
And (Code = 'MIS380'
Or Code = 'MIS420');
```

CALL_	CODE	TITLE	HOURS
004	MIS420	Systems II	4
001	MIS380	Database I	4
002	MIS380	Database I	4

Joining More than Two Tables

Sometimes producing the results you want requires data from more than two tables. Fortunately, writing queries that can produce such results is just an extension of what we did for two-table queries. All you have to do is add another condition for each join you want to perform. For example, suppose you wanted a grade list for each section. The list must include the section's call number, the student's id, first and last names, and the grade, and the list should be in order of the call number, then last name, then first name. The first step in writing this query is to understand which tables contain the required data. The Enrollment database data model is provided in Exhibit 7-61. A box is drawn around the required tables.

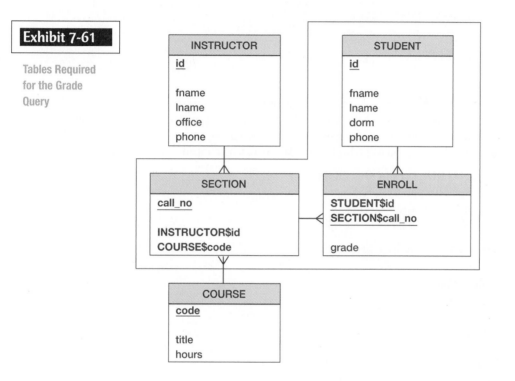

Exhibit 7-61

Tables Required
for the Grade
Query

As you can see, we need data from three tables. Combining data from these three tables requires two joins, one joining SECTION and ENROLL, and one joining ENROLL and STUDENT. This example illustrates an important point. When combining data from multiple tables, *you must have one fewer joins than the number of tables used in the query.* This is an important rule to remember. You can do a quick check of your multitable queries to see if you have the right number of joins. Just count the number of tables in your from clause, subtract one, and the result is how many join conditions you must have. The SQL Select statement to produce the grade results is shown in Exhibit 7-62. Notice how this query involving three tables has two conditions to accomplish the joins.

Exhibit 7-62

Three-Table Join

```
Select call_no,
id,
fname,
lname,
grade
From Section, Enroll, Student
Where call_no = SECTION$call_no
And id = STUDENT$id
Order by call_no, lname, fname ;
```

CALL_	ID	FNAME	LNAME	GR
001	2222	Steve	Black	B
001	1111	Jim	Green	A
003	3333	Linda	Brown	A
004	1111	Jim	Green	C

Adding data from more tables is just more of the same; simply add a join condition for each table added to the from clause. To illustrate this process, suppose we want to add the instructor's full name, the course code, and the course title to our grade report. This query includes data from all five tables in the database, which means that we need four joins (5 − 1):

- INSTRUCTOR to SECTION
- SECTION to COURSE
- SECTION to ENROLL
- ENROLL to STUDENT

Based on what we have discussed so far, you might try the query shown in Exhibit 7-63.

Exhibit 7-63

Ambiguous
Column Naming

```
Select call_no,
id,
fname,
lname,
grade,
fname,
lname,
code,
title
From Instructor, Course,
Section, Enroll, Student
Where id = INSTRUCTOR$id
And code = COURSE$code
And call_no = SECTION$call_no
And id = STUDENT$id
Order by call_no, lname, fname ;


Order by        call_no, lname, fname
                            *


ERROR at line 16:
ORA-00960: ambiguous column naming in select list
```

Using this SQL statement would generate multiple error messages, one of which is shown in the exhibit above. When two tables in a query have the same column name, you must precede the column name with the table name. The table and column names are separated by a period, as in Instructor.lname or Student.lname. The table name helps qualify the column name. Exhibit 7-64 shows a query in which every column name is fully qualified.

Exhibit 7-64

Qualifying Column
Names with Table
Names

```
Select section.call_no,
instructor.id,
instructor.fname,
instructor.lname,
enroll.grade,
student.fname,
student.lname,
course.code,
course.title
From Instructor, Course,
Section, Enroll, Student
Where instructor.id = INSTRUCTOR$id
And course.code = COURSE$code
And section.call_no = SECTION$call_no
And student.id = STUDENT$id
Order by section.call_no, student.lname, student.fname ;
```

CALL_	ID	FNAME	LNAME	GR	FNAME	LNAME	CODE	TITLE
001	11	Joe	Smith	B	Steve	Black	MIS380	Database I
001	11	Joe	Smith	A	Jim	Green	MIS380	Database I
003	11	Joe	Smith	A	Linda	Brown	MIS225	Visual Basic
004	44	Sue	Slim	C	Jim	Green	MIS420	Systems II

Subqueries

Subqueries are queries contained inside other queries. Problems such as comparing an average value with a group of records can best be solved using a subquery. Another application is finding all records in one table that do not have a match in another table—for example, all students not enrolled in a section.

The **inner query** always executes first, and then the results of this query are compared with those of the **outer query.** This is a key to understanding subqueries. Think of the results of the inner query as being fed to the outer query.

To illustrate, we will use the Sky_Members database. Suppose you want to produce a list of all members who have more than the average number of jumps. If you were producing this list manually, the first thing you would do is to compute the average. Then you would compare the number of jumps for each member to the average, and write down the information for each member who has more than the average number of jumps. We could do the same thing using two SQL queries. The first one would calculate the average. Then we could take that average and put it into a where clause that selected members with jumps greater than that average. This method would work initially, but as time would go on, members would make more jumps, and the average would change. When this process happens, the query that retrieved members with jumps higher than the average would no longer work. Because SQL can be used to determine the average number of jumps, there should be a way to write a query that determines the average and then selects members whose jumps exceed that average. This result can be obtained using the SQL Select statement containing a subquery, as shown in Exhibit 7-65.

Subquery Comparing Individual Records with an Average

```
Select fname,
lname
From Sky_Member
Where jumps >
(Select Avg(jumps)
From Sky_Member) ;
```

FNAME	LNAME
Teri	Bucky
Jeremy	Johnson
Thom	Luce
Sean	McGann

Here, the two queries are combined into a single query. The subquery, which is enclosed in parentheses, calculates the average number of jumps for all members. The subquery returns a single number. We can see this process if we run just the subquery portion all by itself, as shown in Exhibit 7-66.

Exhibit 7-66

Subqueries Can Run All by Themselves

```
(Select avg(jumps)
from Sky_Member);
```

AVG(JUMPS)
11.8571429

This trick is especially useful when trying to debug statements involving subqueries. The result of this subquery, approximately 11.86, is then used as part of the where clause in the outer query to retrieve members that have a number of jumps greater than the average. The complete analysis is shown in Exhibit 7-67.

Exhibit 7-67   The Analysis for the Subquery Returning One Value

SUBQUERY RETURNING A SINGLE VALUE

Show the email address, number of jumps, and skill for all members with more than the average number of jumps.

```
SELECT  fname,
        lname
From    sky_member
Where   jumps >
        (Select Avg(jumps)
         From Sky_Member);
```

email	fname	lname	phone	jumps	equip	skill
mcgann@ohio.edu	Sean	McGann	592-2222	20	Y	A
bucky@ohio.edu	Teri	Bucky	555-5555	22	Y	A
dayj@ohio.edu	John	Day	592-0646	5	Y	B
mcgrath@bobcat.edu	Billie	McGrath	555-6666	3	N	B
wilson@bobcat.edu	Sally	Wilson	555-4444	6	N	B
johnson@bobcat.edu	Jeremy	Johnson	555-3333	15	Y	I
luce@ohio.edu	Thom	Luce	592-1111	12	N	I
			Avg	11		

```
SELECT  fname,
        lname
From    sky_member
Where   jumps >
        (Select Avg(jumps)
         From Sky_Member);
```

email	fname	lname	phone	jumps	equip	skill
mcgann@ohio.edu	Sean	McGann	592-2222	20	Y	A
bucky@ohio.edu	Teri	Bucky	555-5555	22	Y	A
dayj@ohio.edu	John	Day	592-0646	5	Y	B
mcgrath@bobcat.edu	Billie	McGrath	555-6666	3	N	B
wilson@bobcat.edu	Sally	Wilson	555-4444	6	N	B
johnson@bobcat.edu	Jeremy	Johnson	555-3333	15	Y	I
luce@ohio.edu	Thom	Luce	592-1111	12	N	I

```
SELECT  fname
        lname
From    sky_member
Where   jumps >
        (Select Avg(jumps)
         From Sky_Member);
```

email	fname	lname	phone	jumps	equip	skill
mcgann@ohio.edu	Sean	McGann	592-2222	20	Y	A
bucky@ohio.edu	Teri	Bucky	555-5555	22	Y	A
dayj@ohio.edu	John	Day	592-0646	5	Y	B
mcgrath@bobcat.edu	Billie	McGrath	555-6666	3	N	B
wilson@bobcat.edu	Sally	Wilson	555-4444	6	N	B
johnson@bobcat.edu	Jeremy	Johnson	555-3333	15	Y	I
luce@ohio.edu	Thom	Luce	592-1111	12	N	I
			Avg	11		

RESULT

fname	lname
Sean	McGann
Teri	Bucky
Jeremy	Johnson
Thom	Luce

The subquery in the exhibit above returns a single value for the average. For this reason, we use arithmetic operators (=, <, >, <>, >=, <=) for the comparison in the where clause. However, some subqueries return multiple values; therefore, arithmetic operators may *not* be used. For example, it would not make sense to write "jumps > 11.86, 12.24, 5.13." If the subquery returns multiple values (e.g., select id), then use IN or NOT IN for the comparison in the where clause. The next example illustrates this concept.

In the Enrollment database, suppose you want to list the id, first name, and last name of all students who are *not* enrolled in a course. An easy way to compile this list is to produce in the subquery a list of all students who *are* enrolled, then in the outer query look for each student *not in* the subquery list. We use the NOT IN operator, as shown in Exhibit 7-68.

Exhibit 7-68 Subquery to Show Differences Between Tables	Select id, fname, lname From student Where id Not In (Select distinct student$id From enroll) ;

ID	FNAME	LNAME
4444	Emma	White

The subquery produces a list of student id values from the ENROLLMENT table. This is a list of all students who *are* enrolled in at least one course. The word *distinct* tells SQL not to repeat any id values, because particular student ids will appear multiple times in the ENROLL table (once for every course in which the student is enrolled). The results of running just the subquery are shown in Exhibit 7-69.

Exhibit 7-69 Subquery that Returns Multiple Values	(Select distinct student$id From enroll) ;

STUD
1111
2222
3333

The result of the subquery (1111, 2222, 3333) is used as the value list for the NOT IN expression. The outer query will return all students not in the value list. The only student not in the ENROLL table is Emma White (id = 4444). The complete analysis for this query is shown in Exhibit 7-70.

Exhibit 7-70 The Analysis for the Subquery Returning Multiple Values

SUBQUERY RETURNING MULTIPLE VALUES

List the student's id, fname, and lname for all students **not** enrolled in any course.

```
SELECT  id, fname, lname
From    student
Where   id not in
        (
        Select distinct student$id
        from enroll
        );
```

STUDENT

id	fname	lname	dorm	phone
1111	Jim	Green	450A	593-2456
2222	Steve	Black	326B	593-4623
3333	Linda	Brown	144A	593-5575
4444	Emma	White	133B	593-4676

ENROLL

STUDENT$id	COURSE$code	semester	grade
1111	MIS380A01	F01	A
2222	MIS225A02	F02	B
3333	MIS225A02	F02	A
1111	MIS420A01	S02	C

STUDENT$id
1111
2222
3333

The subquery result eliminates duplicate student$ids from the Enroll table.

```
SELECT  id, fname, lname
From    student
Where   id not in
        (
        Select distinct student$id
        from enroll
        );
```

STUDENT

id	fname	lname	dorm	phone
1111	Jim	Green	450A	593-2456
2222	Steve	Black	326B	593-4623
3333	Linda	Brown	144A	593-5575
4444	Emma	White	133B	593-4676

ENROLL

STUDENT$id	COURSE$code	semester	grade
1111	MIS380A01	F01	A
2222	MIS225A02	F02	B
3333	MIS225A02	F02	A
1111	MIS420A01	S02	C

STUDENT$id
1111
2222
3333

(Continued)

Exhibit 7-70   Continued

```
SELECT  id, fname, lname
From    student
Where   id not in
        (
        Select distinct student$id
        from enroll
        );
```

STUDENT

id	fname	lname	dorm	phone
1111	Jim	Green	450A	593-2456
2222	Steve	Black	326B	593-4623
3333	Linda	Brown	144A	593-5575
4444	Emma	White	133B	593-4676

ENROLL

STUDENT$id	COURSE$code	semester	grade
1111	MIS380A01	F01	A
2222	MIS225A02	F02	B
3333	MIS225A02	F02	A
1111	MIS420A01	S02	C

STUDENT$id
1111
2222
3333

Emma White is the only student in the student list who does not have a matching record in the subquery list.

RESULT

id	fname	lname
4444	Emma	White

SUMMARY

- Three basic retrieval operations for relational databases are selection, projection, and joining.
- These operations are implemented in SQL through the Select statement.
- Each Select statement must have, at a minimum, the word *Select,* a column list, the word *From,* and a table list.
- Using the asterisk (*) as the column list indicates that all columns in the table(s) should be included in the query results.
- The column list may also include an explicit list of column names.
- The order by clause is used to determine the order in which rows appear in the query results.
- The where clause is used to limit the rows included in the query results.
- Each where clause must include one or more conditions.
- Multiple conditions in a where clause are separated by AND and/or OR.
- SQL has a number of aggregate functions, including Count, Sum, and Avg (average), among others.
- *Distinct* is used to limit results to eliminate duplicate values in query results.
- *Group by* is used to create subaggregations in query results.
- The having clause specifies one or more conditions involving aggregate functions.
- Data from multiple tables is combined by specifying one or more equality conditions in a where clause. Each of these *join* conditions involves a primary key being equal to a corresponding foreign key.
- A query should typically have one fewer join conditions than the number of tables included in the from clause.
- Join conditions can be combined with other conditions.
- One or more queries may be nested within another query. These are known as subqueries.

KEY TERMS

Aggregate functions. Built-in functions (Sum, Avg, etc.) that can be calculated for groups (aggregations) of rows, rather than single rows.

AND logical operator. Operator used in a where clause that allows you to combine two conditions; rows must meet both conditions to be selected.

Between operator. Lets you choose rows based on a range of values.

Cartesian product. A temporary "table" that combines all rows in one table with all rows in another table.

Distinct. Option that tells SQL that you want to display each value only once.

Equi-join (or inner joins). Matching rows between tables based on equality between primary and foreign key values.

Group by. Clause that groups rows based on values in a column.

Having clause. Used to select particular groups (aggregations), rather than single rows, based on a condition.

IN operator. Allows you to select rows based on multiple values for a particular column. Similar to a series of OR conditions.

Inner query. Always executes first, and then the results of this query are used as input to the outer query.

Joining. Relational database operation that combines data from two tables.

LIKE operator. Operator used in a where clause that allows you to choose rows that share some common characters but are not exactly the same.

NOT operator. Operator used in a where clause that allows you to reverse the condition.

OR logical operator. Operator used in a where clause that allows you to combine two conditions; rows can meet either condition to be selected.

Order by. SQL clause for a SELECT statement used to sort results.

Outer query. Query containing the inner query and using the results of that inner query as input.

Projection. Relational database operation that retrieves a subset of columns.

Select. SQL statement that is used to implement all three relational database operations.

Selection. Relational database operation that retrieves a subset of rows.

Subqueries. Queries contained inside other queries.

Where clause. SQL clause for a Select statement used to choose particular rows based on a condition.

EXERCISES

Review

1. Describe the three retrieval operations for relational databases.
2. Describe the simplest form of the Select statement.
3. How can you display a subset of columns in SQL?
4. How can you sort the results from an SQL statement?
5. How do you perform a descending sort?
6. How do you sort on multiple columns?
7. How do you retrieve only some of the rows from a table?
8. Explain how the LIKE operator is used.
9. How can multiple conditions be included in the same where clause?
10. Explain the difference between the AND and OR logical operators.
11. What does the NOT operator do?

12. What are aggregate functions?

13. What is the purpose of the group by clause?

14. What does the Distinct option do?

15. How is the having clause used with group by?

16. Explain how a join is accomplished in a Select statement.

17. When you retrieve data from five tables, how many joins will you need? Why?

18. When must you be careful when combining a join with a where condition?

19. Explain what a subquery is.

20. What operators would you normally use when the inner query produces a single value? Multiple values?

Discuss

1. If you wanted to retrieve members whose email address contained "ohio," what where condition would you use?

2. If you wanted to list members that are not from Ohio, what where condition would you use?

3. If you wanted to list members that have their own equipment and have a skill level of either B or I, what where condition would you use?

4. Explain how AND and OR conditions interact in a query and how to use parentheses to ensure the result will be correct.

5. Explain the different effects that where and having can have on a query.

Practice

Exercises 1 through 20 use the Amazon database, which you created in the exercises for Chapter 6. The design of this database is shown in Exhibit 7-71, and the data is shown in Exhibit 7-72.

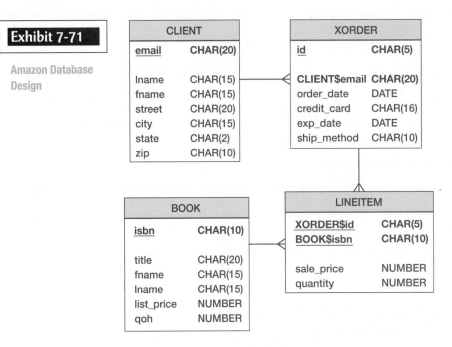

Exhibit 7-71

Amazon Database Design

Exhibit 7-72

Amazon Database
Data

CLIENT

email	fname	lname	street	city	state	zip
mtfrost@yahoo.com	Tere	Frost	75 Algaringo	Miami	FL	33134
perotti@ohio.edu	Jim	Perotti	54 Pine Pl.	Athens	OH	45701
thacker@ohio.edu	Rebecca	Thacker	93 Maple Dr.	Athens	OH	45701

BOOK

isbn	title	fname	lname	list_price	qoh
0312099436	Women of the Silk	Gail	Tsukiyama	12.95	150
014025448X	At Home in Mitford	Jan	Karon	12.95	97
0345423097	Joy School	Elizabeth	Berg	11.95	129
0670894370	A Common Life	Jan	Karon	24.95	45

ORDER

id	CLIENT$email	order_date	credit_card	exp_date	ship_method
001	thacker@ohio.edu	11/15/2002	9999888877776666	07/31/2003	FedEx
002	perotti@ohio.edu	11/23/2002	3333444455556666	04/30/2005	USPS
003	thacker@ohio.edu	12/02/2002	4444111122223333	10/31/2004	USPS

LINEITEM

ORDER$id	BOOK$isbn	sale_price	quantity
001	0312099436	10.36	2
001	014025448X	10.36	3
002	0312099436	11.50	1
002	0670894370	17.46	2
003	0670894370	18.00	1

Write and execute a query that produces the required results.

1. List all of the data in the Client table in order of email address.
2. List the email address, first name, last name, state, and zip code for all clients. Put the list in order of state, then email address.
3. List the ISBN, title, list price, and quantity on hand for all books. Put the list in *descending* order of quantity on hand.
4. List the email address, first name, last name, city, state, and zip code for all clients in Ohio (OH). Put the list in order of state, then city, then last name.
5. List the ISBN, title, list price, and quantity on hand for all books that have a quantity on hand of 90 or more. Put the list in *descending* order of quantity on hand, then title.
6. List the ISBN, title, list price, and quantity on hand for all books that have a quantity on hand of 90 or more *and* have a list price of more than $12. Put the list in *descending* order of quantity on hand, then title.
7. List the ISBN, title, list price, and quantity on hand for all books that have a quantity on hand of 90 or more *or* have a list price of more than $12. Put the list in *descending* order of quantity on hand, then title.
8. List the email addresses, first names, and last names for all clients who have email addresses ending in "edu." Put the list in order of email address.

9. List the ISBN, title, list price, and quantity on hand for all books that have a list price between $12 and $20. Put the list in *descending* order of list price.

10. List the total (sum) quantity on hand for all books. Use the column alias "Total On Hand."

11. How many orders were shipped via USPS? Use the column alias "Shipped by USPS."

12. How many *different* shipping methods were used to ship orders?

13. List the order id and total quantity for each order. Put the list in order of total quantity. (Hint: Use the Lineitem table.)

14. List the order id and total quantity for each order that has a total quantity of four or more. Put the list in order of total quantity. (Hint: Use the Lineitem table.)

15. List the order id, ISBN, sale price, quantity and extended price (sale price multiplied by quantity) for all lineitems. Use the column alias "Total" for the extended price column. Put the list in order of order id.

16. List the order id, order date, client email, first name, and last name for each order. Put the list in order of email, then order date.

17. For each order, list the order id, order date, ISBN, title, sale price, and quantity of each book included in the order. Put the list in order of order date, then title. (Hint: You must include the LINEITEM table.)

18. For each order, list the order id, order date, client email, first name, and last name, along with the ISBN, title, sale price, and quantity of each book included in the order. Put the list in order of order id, then title. (Hint: You must include the LINEITEM table.)

19. For each order placed by a customer in Ohio (OH), list the order id, order date, client email, first name, and last name, along with the ISBN, title, sale price, and quantity of each book included in the order. Put the list in order of order date, then title. (Hint: You must include the LINEITEM table.)

20. For each order that includes the books with the ISBN 014025448X or 0670894370, list the order id, order date, client email, first name, and last name, along with the ISBN, title, sale price, and quantity of each book included in the order. Put the list in order of order date, then title. (Hint: You must include the LINEITEM table.)

Exercises 21 through 38 use the Hospital database. The design of this database is shown in Exhibit 7-73, and the data is shown in Exhibit 7-74.

Exhibit 7-73

Hospital Database
Design

DOCTOR	
<u>id</u>	CHAR(5)
fname	CHAR(15)
lname	CHAR(15)
phone	CHAR(12)
beeper	CHAR(12)

PATIENT	
<u>id</u>	CHAR(5)
DOCTOR$id	CHAR(5)
fname	CHAR(15)
lname	CHAR(15)
street	CHAR(15)
city	CHAR(10)
state	CHAR(2)
zip	CHAR(10)
phone	CHAR(12)

INSURANCE	
<u>company</u>	CHAR(15)
contact_fname	CHAR(15)
contact_lname	CHAR(15)
phone	CHAR(12)

INSURE	
<u>PATIENT$id</u>	CHAR(5)
<u>INSURANCE$company</u>	CHAR(15)

Exhibit 7-74	**DOCTOR**				

Hospital Database Data

DOCTOR

id	fname	lname	phone	beeper
00001	Perry	Cox	555-1111	555-1212
00002	Elliot	Reid	555-2222	555-2323
00003	JD	Dorian	555-3333	555-3434
00004	Chris	Turk	555-5555	555-4545
00005	Bob	Kelso	555-6666	555-5656

PATIENT

id	DOCTOR$id	fname	lname	street	city	state	zip	phone
11111	00001	Jim	Perotti	12 Oak St	Shade	OH	45701	555-1234
22222	00001	Glen	Stamler	1 Walnut Ave	Athens	FL	58475	555-2345
33333	00002	Maddy	Gray	45 Maple St	Glouster	KY	73674	555-3456
44444	00003	Blake	Shelton	3 Elm Blvd	Shade	OH	45701	555-4567
55555	00003	EJ	Thornton	92 Ash St	Orlando	FL	85744	555-5678
66666	00004	Dyrk	Ashton	33 Poplar Ave	Columbus	OH	47837	555-6789

INSURANCE

company	contact_fname	contact_lname	phone
Prudential	Jan	Johnson	555-9876
State Farm	Sam	Smith	555-8765
Nationwide	Randy	Buck	555-7654

INSURE

PATIENT$id	INSURANCE$company
11111	Prudential
22222	Prudential
33333	State Farm
44444	Nationwide
55555	Nationwide
66666	State Farm

Write and execute a query that produces the required results.

21. List all of the data in the Patient table. Put the list in order of state, then last name.

22. List the first name, last name, and beeper number for each doctor. Put the list in order of last name, then first name.

23. List first name, last name, city, state, and zip code of all patients who live in Florida (FL). Put the list in order of city, then last name.

24. List first name, last name, city, state, and zip code of all patients who live in Florida (FL) or Ohio (OH). Put the list in order of city, then last name.

25. List first name, last name, city, state, and zip code of all patients who have a zip code that begins with the numeral 4. Put the list in *descending* order of city, then *ascending* order of last name.

26. List the first name, last name, phone number, and doctor id for all patients who are assigned to doctors with id 00001, 00002, or 00004. Put the list in order of doctor id, then last name.

27. List the first name, last name, phone number, and doctor id for all patients who live in Ohio (OH) and are assigned to doctors with id 00001, 00002, or 00004. Put the list in order of doctor id, then last name.

28. How many *different* doctors have patients assigned to them? (Hint: You must use the Patient table.) Use the column alias "Doctors with patients."

29. How many patients live in Florida (FL)? Use the column alias "Patients in Florida."

30. For each state that has more than one patient residing in it, list the state and the number of patients living in the state. Use the column alias "Number of patients." Put the list in *descending* order of number of patients.

31. For each patient, list the patient's first name, last name, and zip code, along with the name of the insurance company used by the patient. Put the list in order of last name.

32. For each patient, list the patient's first name, last name, and zip code, along with the name and phone number of the insurance company used by the patient. Put the list in order of the patient's last name.

33. For each patient insured by Nationwide, list the patient's first name, last name, and zip code. Put the list in order of last name.

34. For each patient living in Ohio (OH) or Kentucky (KY), list the patient's first name, last name, state, and zip code, along with the name and phone number of the insurance company used by the patient. Put the list in order of last name.

35. For each insurance company, list the company name; the contact's first name and last name; and the id, first name, and last name of all patients using that insurance company. Put the list in order of insurance company, then patient last name.

36. For each patient, list the patient's first and last names, the first and last names of the patient's doctor, and the patient's insurance company and phone number. Put the list in order of insurance company, then doctor's last name, then patient's last name.

37. For patients with the id 11111, 33333, or 55555, list the patient's first and last names, the first and last names of the patient's doctor, and the patient's insurance company and phone number. Put the list in order of insurance company, then doctor's last name, then patient's last name.

38. List the id number, first name, and last name of all doctors who do *not* have any patients assigned to him or her. Put the list in order of doctor's last name.

Exercises 39 through 46 use the Acme database. The design of this database is shown in Exhibit 7-75, and the data is shown in Exhibit 7-76.

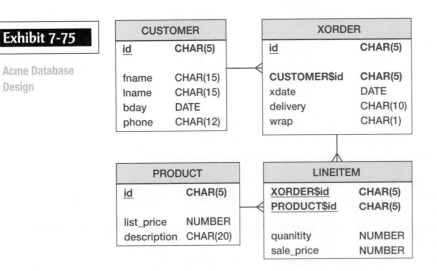

Exhibit 7-75

Acme Database Design

Exhibit 7-76

Acme Database
Data

CUSTOMER

id	fname	lname	bday	phone
11111	Glen	Stamler	9/13/1974	555-3232
22222	Maddy	Gray	8/05/1984	555-8475
33333	Blake	Shelton	7/25/1975	555-4875
44444	EJ	Thornton	2/04/1988	555-9845

XORDER

id	CUSTOMER$id	date	delivery	wrap
10000	11111	2/04/2003	N	N
10001	22222	2/05/2003	Y	Y
10002	11111	2/05/2003	N	N
10003	33333	2/06/2003	Y	N

PRODUCT

id	list_price	description
00001	15.95	lager
00002	25.24	stout
00003	13.95	light
00004	19.98	pilsner
00005	18.75	microbrew
00006	18.57	ale
00007	15.95	bock
00008	19.95	portor

LINEITEM

XORDER$id	PRODUCT$id	quantity	sale_price
10000	00001	1	15.75
10000	00003	2	13.95
10001	00002	1	23.95
10001	00005	1	18.50
10002	00008	3	21.75
10003	00006	1	18.35
10003	00001	2	15.95
10003	00003	1	12.95
10003	00004	1	19.98

Write and execute a query that produces the required results.[1]

39. How many *different* customers have placed orders?

40. List the first and last names of all customers who have placed more than one order. (Note: This is quite challenging.)

41. List the product id and number of orders that include the product for all products that have been included on more than one order. Put the list in *descending* order of product id.

42. How many orders have been wrapped?

43. List the first and last name of all customers who have *not* placed orders. Put the list in order of last name.

44. List the id, list price, and description of all products that *are* included in orders. Put the list in *descending* order of list price.

45. List the id, list price, and description of all products that *are not* included in orders. Put the list in *descending* order of list price.

46. List the product id, description, and list price for all products that have a list price greater than the average list price for all products. Put the list in order of description.

---

[1]In Oracle "order" is a reserved word. Therefore, the design above was changed from the earlier chapters to rename the ORDER table to XORDER.

Creating Databases with Microsoft Access

Introduction

In this chapter, you will learn how to use Microsoft Access to create the databases that were designed in Chapter 3. In Microsoft Access, databases consist of a collection of related tables stored in a single file with the extension mbd. In Access, this file is used to store the database tables, plus queries, forms, and reports that interact with the data stored in those tables.

Learning Objectives

After completing this chapter, you will be able to:

- Create a database in Access.
- Create one or more tables within the database.
- Define columns and data types for a table.
- Create a primary key for a table.
- Create foreign keys and use them to establish relationships between tables.
- Enter data into a table using a datasheet.
- Display data in a table using a query.

Physical Table Design

As you learned in Chapter 3, the conceptual model of a database provides the basic design of the database, including the tables and the relationships between those tables. The model also specifies the names for the tables and the columns within those tables, including the specification of primary and foreign keys.

In addition to the general conceptual design, Chapter 3 also specified additional physical details, including data types and widths for each column in the database. Before implementing a database in a particular database management system such as Microsoft Access, you will need to determine the data types available in that system and any restrictions on the widths of columns.

Data Types and Column Widths

Every field in a database table must have a data type and column width. In Access, there are 10 possible data types, as outlined in Exhibit 8-1.

Exhibit 8-1

Data Types
Available in
Microsoft Access

Text	This is the default data type for a column. Stores character data such as text and numbers, including numbers that are not involved in calculations, such as zip codes and phone numbers. Can hold up to 255 characters.
Memo	Large blocks of text up to 65,535 characters.
Number	Numbers that will be used in calculations. Size can be further specified as a long integer (+/– 2,147,483,647), integer (+/– 32,767), byte (0–255), single (+/– 3.4^{38}), double (+/– 3.4^{308}), or decimal (+/– 10^{28}).
Date/Time	Date and time values.
Currency	Numbers that will be used in calculations with one to four decimal places and up to 15 digits to the left side of the decimal.
AutoNumber	Puts a unique number (either in series or random) into the column whenever a new record is added to the table.
Yes/No	Stores a 1 (Yes) or 0 (No) in the column.
OLE Object	Allows an object such as an Excel spreadsheet, a Word document, or graphics to be stored, up to 1 GB.
Hyperlink	A string of text and numbers used as a hyperlink.
Lookup Wizard	Sets up the column to allow the user to choose a value from a list of values or data from another table.

The Sky_Member Database

To illustrate how a database is created in Access, we will create the member database for the sky-diving club. This task will include creating the table and populating it with data. Exhibit 8-2 shows the design, physical details, and data for the skydiving club member table. The physical details show how the design of the table will appear in Access when the table is completed. This design includes the name and data type for each column. The design area shows additional details, including the widths of text columns and specific numeric data types. For example, the jumps column is numeric, because it could be used in a calculation—for example, a calculation to find the average number of jumps for all members. Furthermore, it is an integer numeric data type, because jumps always occur in whole numbers.

In the design area, the primary key (email) is bold and underlined. This fact is also indicated under the physical details with the graphic of a key in front of the column name. This design is slightly different from the SKY_MEMBER table introduced in the chapter on conceptual design. The name for the column for the member's skill level has been changed from *level* to *skill,* because some database software restricts the words that can be used to name database elements like tables and columns. These words are known as *reserved words.* Common reserved words in SQL (structured query language) databases include the words *table, column, select, number,* and other words that have a meaning in SQL. *Level* is not a reserved word in Access, but it is in Oracle. To make the databases created in Access consistent with those created in the chapters on Oracle and SQL Server, the level column has been renamed skill here, as well.

Exhibit 8-2

Design and Data for the Skydiving Club Member Database

Physical Details

sky_member : Table

Field Name	Data Type
email	Text
fname	Text
lname	Text
phone	Text
jumps	Number
equip	Text
skill	Text

Design

SKY_MEMBER	
email	TEXT(20)
fname	TEXT(15)
lname	TEXT(15)
phone	TEXT(12)
jumps	INTEGER
equip	TEXT(1)
skill	TEXT(1)

Data

email	fname	lname	phone	jumps	equip	skill
bucky@ohio.edu	Teri	Bucky	555-5555	22	Y	A
dayj@ohio.edu	John	Day	529-0646	5	Y	B
johnson@bobcat.edu	Jeremy	Johnson	555-3333	15	Y	I
luce@ohio.edu	Thom	Luce	592-1111	12	N	I
mcgann@ohio.edu	Sean	McGann	592-2222	20	Y	A
mcgrath@bobcat.edu	Billie	McGrath	555-6666	3	N	B
wilson@bobcat.edu	Sally	Wilson	555-4444	6	N	B

Creating an Access Database with a Single Table

The process of creating a database in Access involves the following steps:

1. Specify the database file.
2. Create a table.
3. Create columns by
   - Entering a column name.
   - Selecting a data type.
   - Specifying a field size, when applicable.
4. Indicate the primary key.
5. Enter data.

To illustrate this process, these steps will be used to create the Sky_Member database.

Step 1: Specify the Database File

To begin creating the database, start Microsoft Access. The screen should look something like Exhibit 8-3.

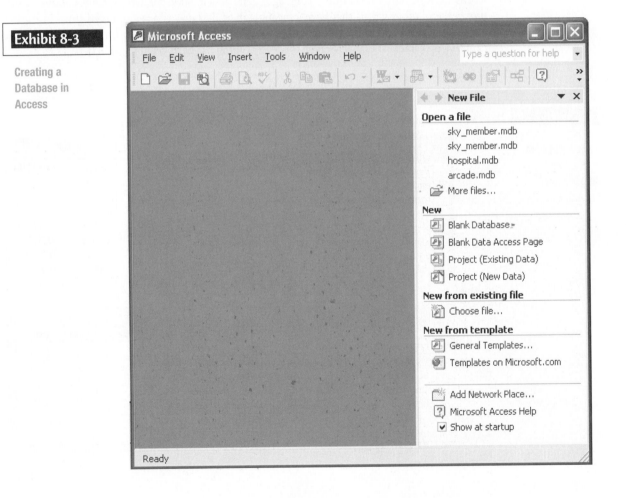

Exhibit 8-3

Creating a
Database in
Access

The Microsoft Access interface is a typical Windows application, with menus and a shortcut toolbar at the top. To the right is a pane listing options for creating or opening an Access database. If this pane does not appear, use the File, New menu option, or click the first button on the toolbar.

To create a new database, select the Blank Database option and the File New Database dialog box will appear. There, you can name the file that will be used to store the database, and you can specify the location where the file will be stored, as shown in Exhibit 8-4.

File New Database

| Save in: | My Documents |

History

My Documents

Desktop

Favorites

| File name: | sky_member.mdb | Create |
| Save as type: | Microsoft Access Databases (*.mdb) | Cancel |

For the Sky_Member database, the file should be named sky_member.mdb. The mdb extension is the standard file type for a Microsoft Access database. When a new, blank database is created or an existing database is opened, the database window is displayed, as shown in Exhibit 8-5.

sky_member : Database (Access 2000 file format)

Open Design New

Objects
- Tables
- Queries
- Forms
- Reports
- Pages
- Macros
- Modules

Groups
- Favorites

Create table in Design view
Create table by using wizard
Create table by entering data

Step 2: Create a Table

The **database window** displays the various components of an Access database and provides options for creating additional components. These components include:

- **Tables:** the basic storage units in the database.
- **Queries:** saved sets of instructions for retrieving database data.
- **Forms:** interactive screens that allow you to work with database data.
- **Reports:** display and print reports based on database data.
- **Pages:** Web pages published from Access that allow you to view and manipulate data stored in the database.
- **Macros:** lists of Access functions that can be used to automate tasks.
- **Modules:** stored procedures written in Visual Basic used to automate tasks.

The panel of options at the left lets you display existing components and create new ones of that type. This exhibit shows the options related to creating tables. You can create tables using the design view or the wizard, or by entering data and having Access determine the columns and data types based on the data you enter.

Because we already know the physical details for the SKY_MEMBER table, the design view is the most straightforward method for creating the table. Once you select this option, the design of the table is displayed as shown in Exhibit 8-6.

Exhibit 8-6

Creating a Table
in Design View

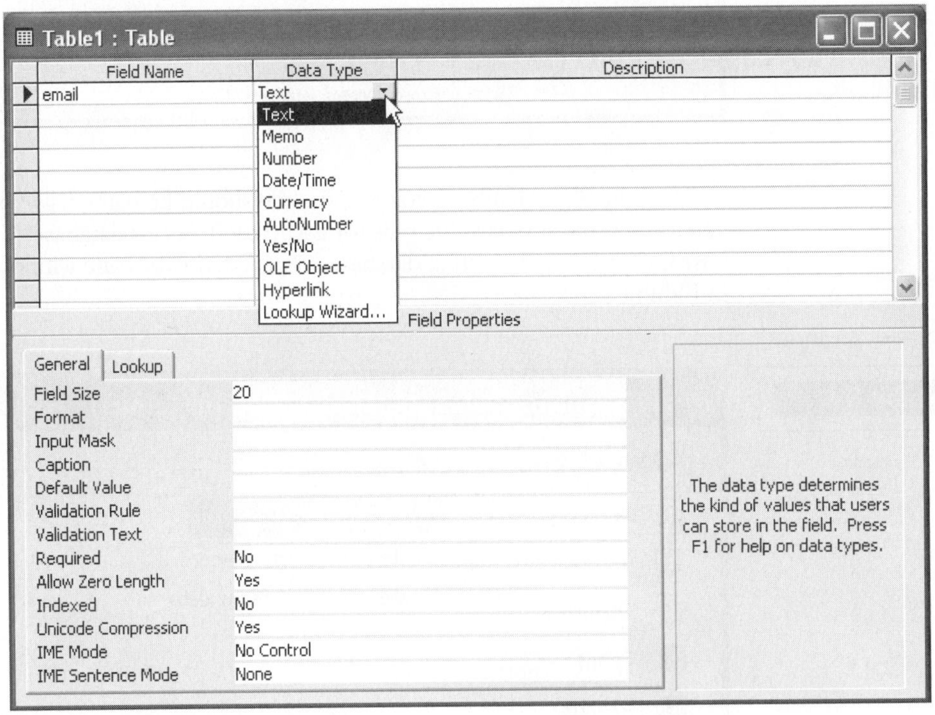

Step 3: Create Columns

In the **design view,** columns are defined by entering the name of the column under the Field Name heading and selecting the data type using the drop-down list. At the bottom of the screen, additional options related to the table columns are available. With text columns, the field size option can be used to set a maximum size for the column. The default is 50.

In the SKY_MEMBER table, the email column requires a text data type and a maximum field size of 20. When a column requires a number data type, such as the jumps column in the

SKY_MEMBER table, the field size setting provides options for the different numeric data types, as shown in Exhibit 8-7.

Exhibit 8-7

Creating a Column
with a Number
Data Type

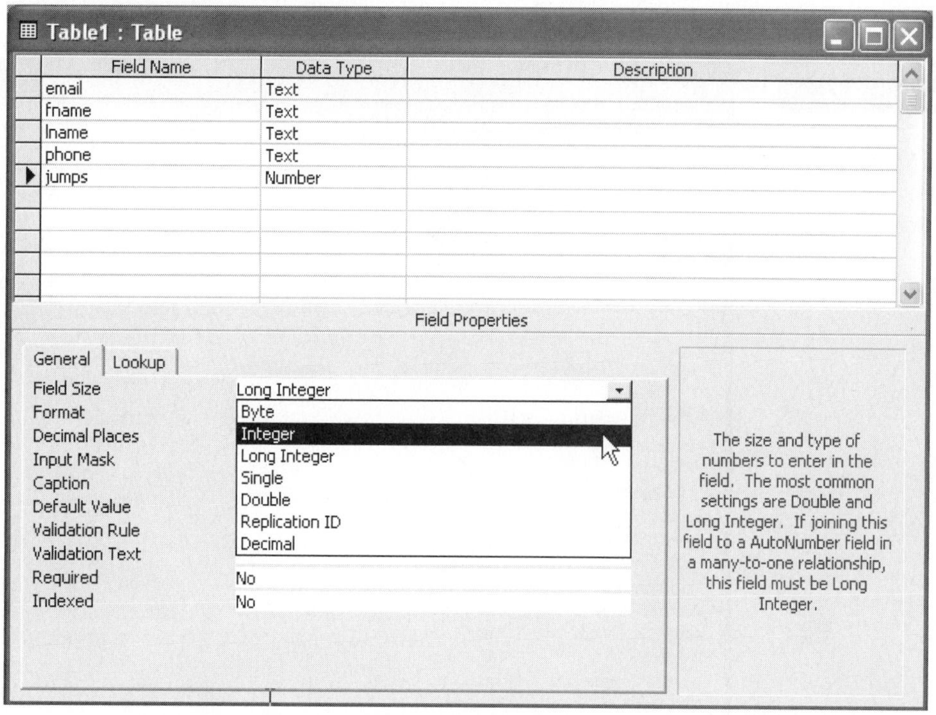

Another useful column setting is the option related to setting up a **validation rule** for a column. In the SKY_MEMBER table, the equip and skill columns have specific data values that need to be stored in them. For example, the equip column is supposed to indicate if the skydiver has his or her own equipment. The column should either contain a Y for yes or an N for No. In the skill column, the value should be either B for beginner, I for intermediate, or A for advanced. The data allowed in a column can be controlled by setting up a validation rule. When you click in the Validation Rule row, the **Expression Builder** will appear, where you can enter the rule that will restrict the values that are allowed in the column, as illustrated in Exhibit 8-8.

Exhibit 8-8

Creating a
Validation Rule

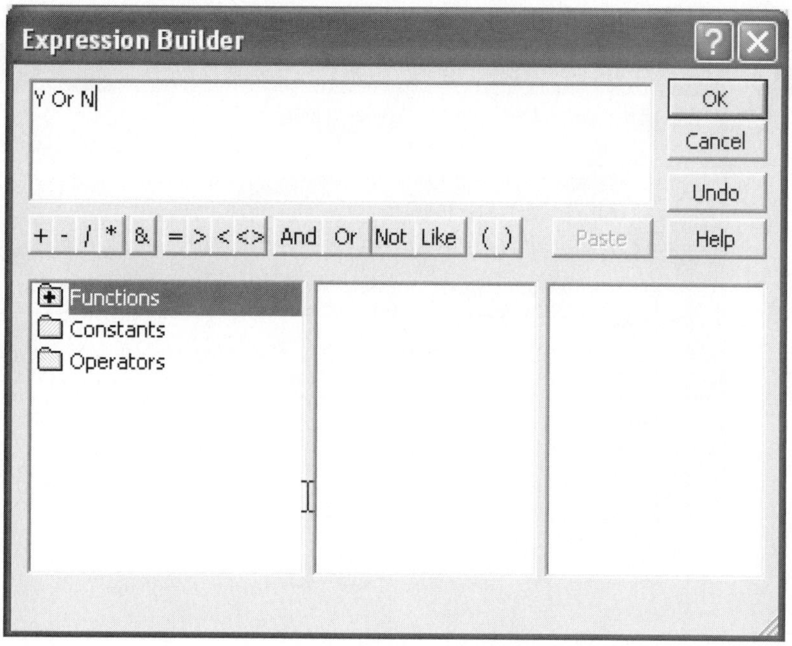

In the Expression Builder, you can type the Y, click the Or button to have the word Or inserted in the expression, and then type the N. Once the expression is complete, click OK, and you will return to the design view, with the rule displayed as shown in Exhibit 8-9.

Exhibit 8-9

The SKY_MEMBER
Table with a
Validation Rule

Field Name	Data Type	Description
email	Text	
fname	Text	
lname	Text	
phone	Text	
jumps	Number	
equip	Text	

Field Properties

General	Lookup

Field Size	1
Format	
Input Mask	
Caption	
Default Value	
Validation Rule	"Y" Or "N"
Validation Text	
Required	No
Allow Zero Length	Yes
Indexed	No
Unicode Compression	Yes
IME Mode	No Control
IME Sentence Mode	None

An expression that limits the values that can be entered in the field. Press F1 for help on validation rules.

For the skill column, you would create a validation rule that required the column to contain B, I, or A.

Step 4: Specify the Primary Key

Once the columns are defined, the final task in creating the table is to specify the primary key column for the table. Exhibit 8-10 shows how this task is accomplished.

Exhibit 8-10

Specifying the
Primary Key

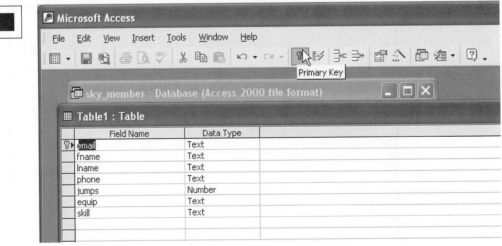

To create a primary key, click on the row containing the column that will be the primary key. You can then use the **primary key button** on the toolbar. A small key icon is then displayed in the box in front of the column name to indicate which column has been set as the primary key. Once the columns and primary key have been defined, the table design should be saved by using the Save icon on the toolbar, or by using the File, Save menu option. A dialog box where you can enter the name of the table will then be displayed. For the SKY_MEMBER table, enter sky_member as the name of the table.

Step 5: Entering Data into the Table

At this point, the structure of the table has been saved, and the empty table has been created. To enter data into the table, Access provides a **datasheet view** of the table. This view can be accessed using the View, Datasheet View menu option, or by clicking the first icon on the toolbar. The datasheet view displays the columns of the table in a form similar to a spreadsheet. Because the table is currently empty, a blank row where you can enter values for each column is displayed. Exhibit 8-11 shows the datasheet view for the SKY_MEMBER table with the first row of data entered.

sky_member : Table

email	fname	lname	phone	jumps	equip	skill
dayj@ohio.edu	John	Day	593-0646	5	Y	B
				0		

Record: 2 of 2

Once a row is entered, you simply tab to the next row, and the completed row is saved. If you enter a value in the equip or skill column that violates the validation rule, an error message will appear when Access tries to save the row, as shown in Exhibit 8-12.

Microsoft Access

One or more values are prohibited by the validation rule "Y" Or "N" set for 'Member.equip'. Enter a value that the expression for this field can accept.

OK   Help

Once all the data for the SKY_MEMBER table is entered, the status bar at the bottom of the screen should indicate that there is a total of eight rows in the table. A blank row is always displayed at the bottom to allow you to add additional rows to the table whenever you want. Exhibit 8-13 shows the completed SKY_MEMBER table.

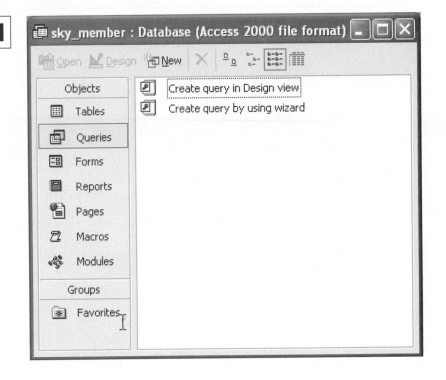

Exhibit 8-13

The Completed
SKY_MEMBER
Table

email	fname	lname	phone	jumps	equip	skill
bucky@ohio.edu	Teri	Bucky	555-5555	22	Y	A
dayj@ohio.edu	John	Day	592-0646	5	Y	B
johnson@bobcat.edu	Jeremy	Johnson	555-3333	15	Y	I
luce@ohio.edu	Thom	Luce	592-1111	12	N	I
mcgann@ohio.edu	Sean	McGann	592-2222	20	Y	A
mcgrath@bobcat.edu	Billie	McGrath	555-6666	3	N	B
wilson@bobcat.edu	Sally	Wilson	555-4444	6	N	B
				0		

Using a Query to Display Table Data

After a table is created and the data has been entered, you can display the data using a query. **Queries** provide a complex set of options to display table data. Queries will be covered in greater detail in the next chapter. For now, we will create a simple query to display all the data in a table for the purpose of verifying that all the data has been entered correctly.

To create a query, return to the database window, and select the query component from the panel at the left to display the options related to creating queries, as shown in Exhibit 8-14.

Exhibit 8-14

Creating a Query

Use the Create Query in Design View option to design a query. A dialog box will appear listing the tables in the database on which you can base the query. At this point, the SKY_MEMBER table will be the only table listed. Select this table, and add it to the query. The Query Design view will then be displayed as shown in Exhibit 8-15.

Exhibit 8-15

Designing
the Query

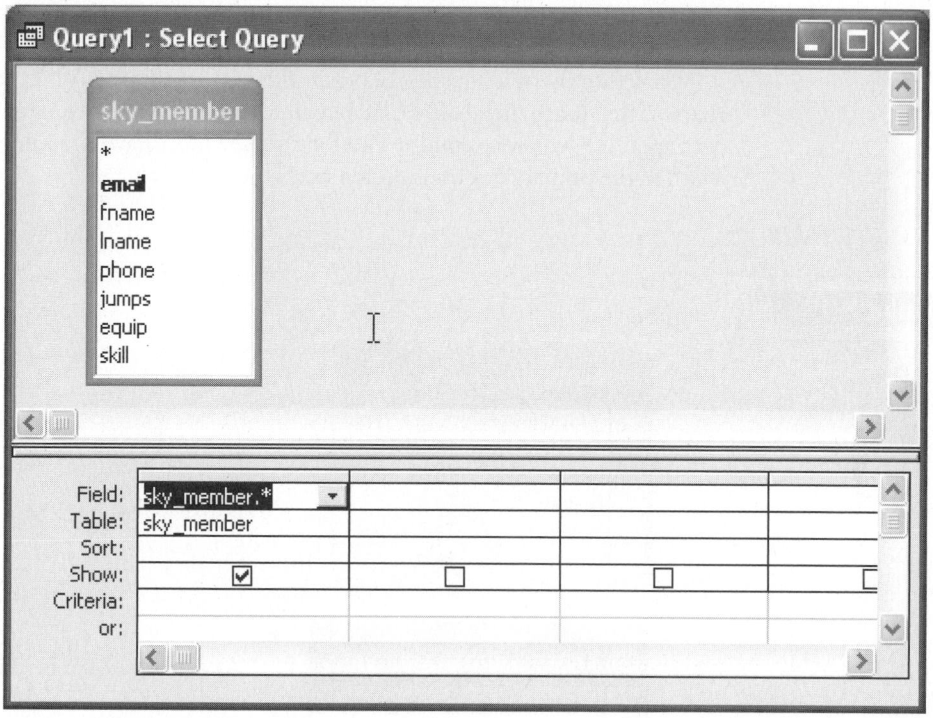

In the design view, the design of the table is displayed in the top panel, and a grid of options related to building a query is displayed in the bottom panel. These options will be covered in more detail in the next chapter. To display all the information in a table, simply double-click the asterisk (*) in the table design in the top panel. The grid will then list the query as sky_member.*, which is an instruction to Access to display all the columns in the table. To execute this query, select the Query, Run menu option, and the data in the table will be displayed as shown in Exhibit 8-16.

Exhibit 8-16

The Results
of the Query

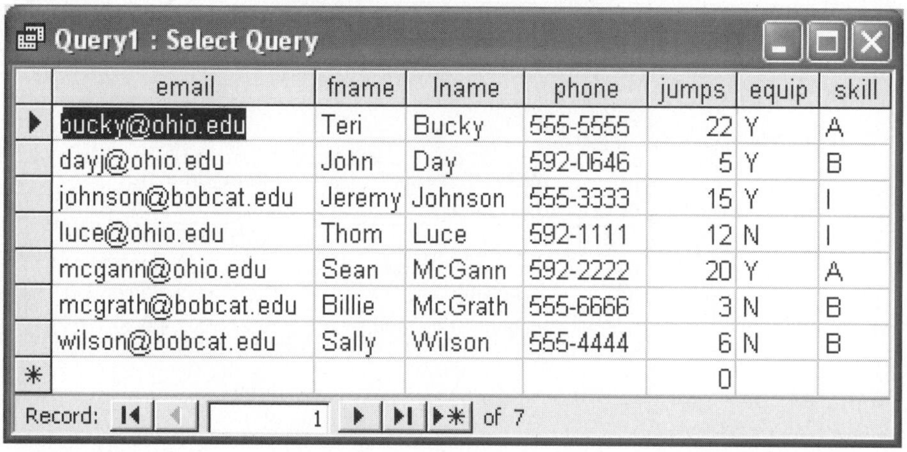

email	fname	lname	phone	jumps	equip	skill
bucky@ohio.edu	Teri	Bucky	555-5555	22	Y	A
dayj@ohio.edu	John	Day	592-0646	5	Y	B
johnson@bobcat.edu	Jeremy	Johnson	555-3333	15	Y	I
luce@ohio.edu	Thom	Luce	592-1111	12	N	I
mcgann@ohio.edu	Sean	McGann	592-2222	20	Y	A
mcgrath@bobcat.edu	Billie	McGrath	555-6666	3	N	B
wilson@bobcat.edu	Sally	Wilson	555-4444	6	N	B
*				0		

Record: 14 ◄ | 1 | ► ►I ►* | of 7

This step completes the creation of the Sky_Member database. This description illustrates the basic process of creating a single-table database in Access. Now that you are familiar with the process, we will look at how some of the more complex databases from Chapter 3 would be created using Microsoft Access.

The Arcade Database

Exhibit 8-17 shows the design for the Arcade database. There are several differences between this database and the Sky_Member database. The most obvious difference is that this database includes two tables rather than one. In addition, the VISIT table contains columns with a Date/Time data type.

To create the relationship between the MEMBER and VISIT tables, the VISIT table contains the foreign key, MEMBER$email, which references its parent table (MEMBER) and corresponding column (email). The foreign key must have the same data type and column width as the primary key that it references.

Exhibit 8-17

The Design for the
Arcade Database

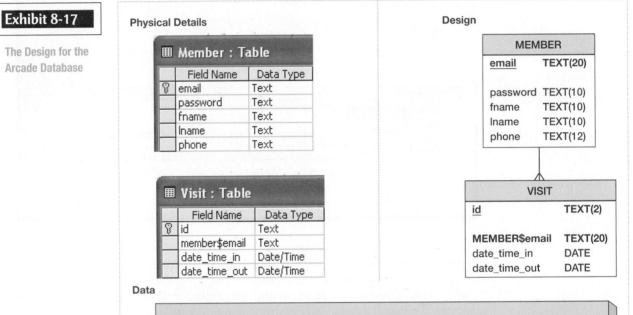

Physical Details

Member : Table

	Field Name	Data Type
🔑	email	Text
	password	Text
	fname	Text
	lname	Text
	phone	Text

Visit : Table

	Field Name	Data Type
🔑	id	Text
	member$email	Text
	date_time_in	Date/Time
	date_time_out	Date/Time

Design

MEMBER

email	TEXT(20)
password	TEXT(10)
fname	TEXT(10)
lname	TEXT(10)
phone	TEXT(12)

VISIT

id	TEXT(2)
MEMBER$email	TEXT(20)
date_time_in	DATE
date_time_out	DATE

Data

MEMBER

email	password	fname	lname	phone
dayj@ohio.edu	rocket	John	Day	529-0646
luce@ohio.edu	bullet	Thom	Luce	592-1111
mcgann@ohio.edu	arrow	Sean	McGann	592-2222

VISIT

id	MEMBER$email	date_time_in	date_time_out
001	dayj@ohio.edu	6/25/2002 2:00:00 PM	6/25/2002 5:30:00 PM
002	luce@ohio.edu	6/25/2002 6:00:00 PM	6/25/2002 8:00:00 PM
003	mcgann@ohio.edu	6/26/2002 10:00:00 AM	6/26/2002 11:30:00 AM
004	luce@ohio.edu	6/27/2002 9:00:00 AM	6/27/2002 10:00:00 AM
005	mcgann@ohio.edu	6/27/2002 4:00:00 PM	6/27/2002 6:00:00 PM

Create the Database and Tables

To create the Arcade database, use the Blank Database option to create a new database file called arcade.mdb. Then, use the design view to create a new table and define the columns for the MEMBER table. Make the email column the primary key, and then name the table when it is saved. The completed design for the MEMBER table is shown in Exhibit 8-18.

🖾 Member : Table			
Field Name	**Data Type**	**Description**	
🔑 email	Text		
password	Text		
fname	Text		
lname	Text		
phone	Text		

After the MEMBER table is finished, create another table using the design view. Set up the columns for the VISIT table as defined above. For the date_time_in and date_time_out columns, select the Date/Time data type. The completed design for the VISIT table is shown in Exhibit 8-19.

🖾 Visit : Table			
Field Name	**Data Type**	**Description**	
🔑 id	Text		
member$email	Text		
date_time_in	Date/Time		
date_time_out	Date/Time		

Create the Relationship Between the Tables

Once the tables have been defined, a relationship should be created to link the foreign key (MEMBER$email) in the VISIT table to the primary key (email) in the MEMBER table. Relationships are created from the Database view where the tables are displayed. When the tables are visible, use the Tools, Relationships menu option, or click the corresponding button on the toolbar, and the tables in the database will be displayed in the Show Table dialog box, as shown in Exhibit 8-20.

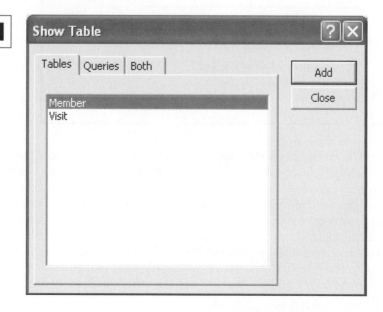

This dialog box allows you to determine which tables in the database will appear in the **Relationships view.** In most circumstances, you will want to include all the tables, because every table will be related to at least one other table in the database. In the Arcade database, you would add both the MEMBER and the VISIT tables to the Relationships view, as shown in Exhibit 8-21.

Exhibit 8-21

The Relationships View

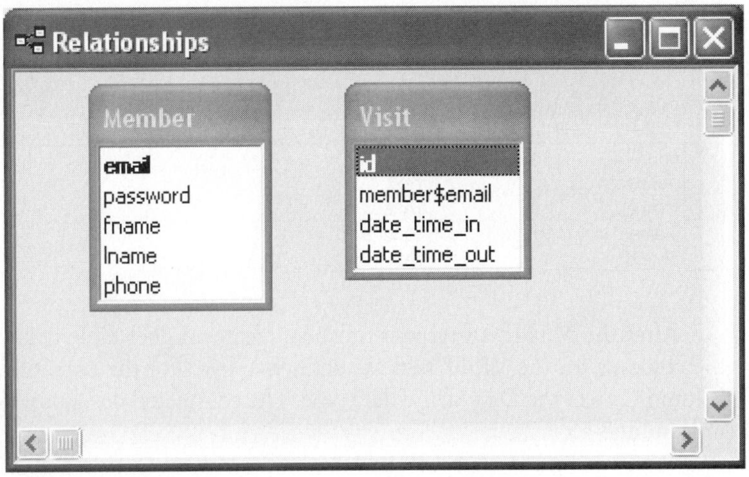

In the Relationships view, we want to indicate to Access that the email column in the MEMBER table needs to be matched to the MEMBER$email foreign key in the VISIT table. To accomplish this task, you simply click on the email column in the MEMBER table and drag it over top of the MEMBER$email column in the VISIT table. When you release the mouse button, the Edit Relationships dialog box will be displayed, as shown in Exhibit 8-22.

Exhibit 8-22

The Edit Relationships Dialog Box

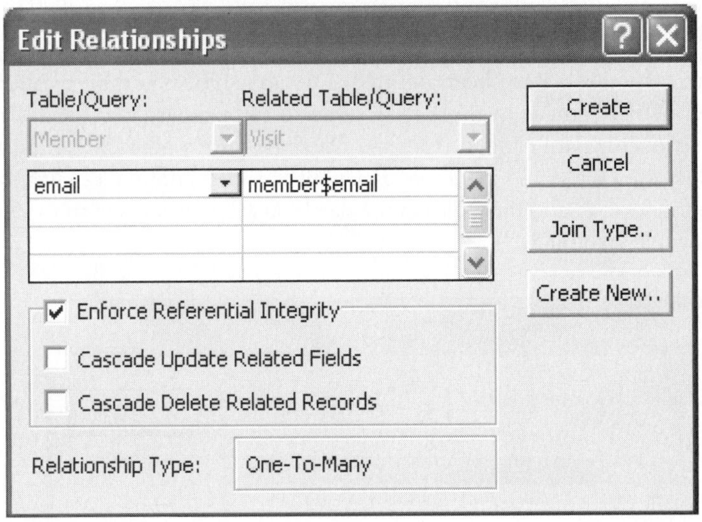

This dialog box displays the two columns involved in the relationship. For a foreign key relationship, you should check the Enforce Referential Integrity box to have Access make sure that the values in the foreign key match values in the primary key.

The two other check boxes deal with the issue of what to do with the duplicate values in the foreign key column when changes occur in the primary key column. For example, when an email address is placed in the MEMBER$email column of the VISIT table, it is a duplicate of one of the email addresses in the MEMBER table. If you now try to change the value in the email primary key column, Access will not allow the change because of the duplicate of that key in the VISIT table. The two options on the Edit Relationships dialog box related to cascading allow Access to alter the duplicate values in the foreign key column when values in the primary key column are updated or deleted. In this case, there is no need to cascade changes in the primary key to the duplicates in the foreign key column.

Once you have checked the option to enforce referential integrity, click the Create button to finish the relationship. The relationship diagram will be updated to display the relationship, as shown in Exhibit 8-23.

Exhibit 8-23

The Completed
Relationship

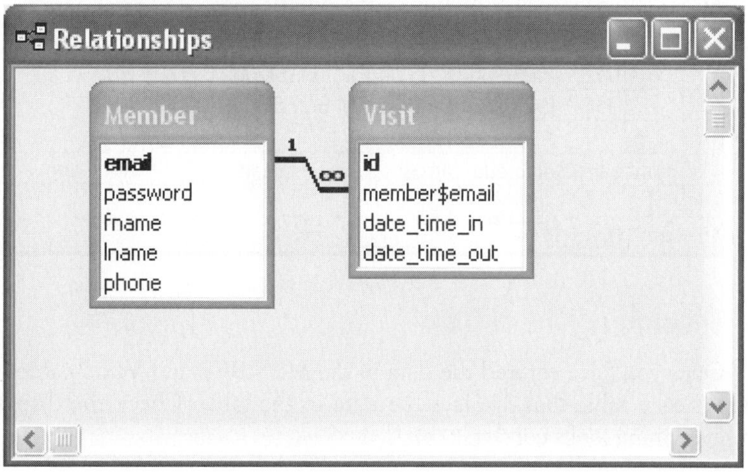

This diagram indicates that there is a one-to-many relationship established between the email column in the MEMBER table and the MEMBER$email column of the VISIT table. The infinity symbol (∞) is used to mark the many side of the relationship.

Entering the Data for the Arcade Database

Once the tables are created and the relationship is established, the data can be entered. In general, data can be placed in tables containing foreign keys only after the data is entered into the tables that they reference. This condition means that data must be inserted first into the MEMBER table. If not, then the data for the VISIT table will be rejected for referential integrity violations—the email address in the MEMBER$email column would reference data that does not yet exist in the MEMBER table.

Once the data is entered in the MEMBER table, referential integrity also means that when values are entered in the MEMBER$email column, they must match the values already in the MEMBER table. If you make a mistake entering a duplicate email address, you will receive an error message as shown in Exhibit 8-24.

Exhibit 8-24

The Error Generated
When Violating
Referential Integrity

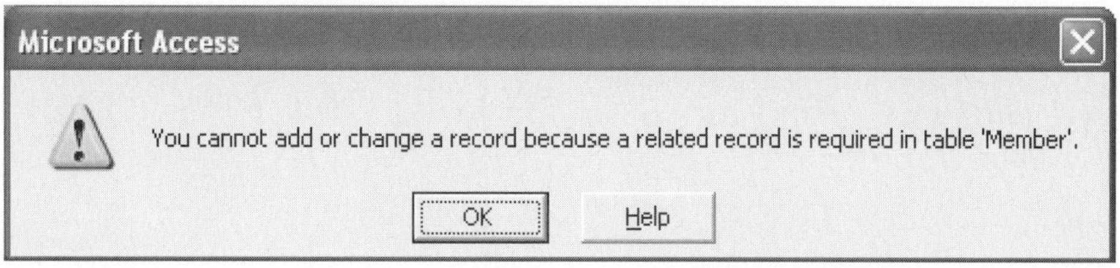

When a relationship exists between tables through a foreign key, the datasheet includes an additional feature that lets you display rows in another table that contain foreign key values that duplicate the primary key in the rows of the displayed table. In the Arcade database, rows in the MEMBER table have related rows in the VISIT table. Each row in the MEMBER table has a plus sign in the beginning, indicating that there are rows in another table with the same member email address in the MEMBER$email column. If you click the plus sign, you can see the related rows in the VISIT table for that member. Exhibit 8-25 shows the data in the MEMBER table with the associated VISIT rows displayed.

Exhibit 8-25

Displaying Related
Rows on the
Datasheet

	email	password	fname	lname	phone
+	dayj@ohio.edu	rocket	John	Day	592-0646
−	luce@ohio.edu	bullet	Thom	Luce	592-1111

	id	date_time_in	date_time_out
	002	6/25/2002 6:00:00 PM	6/25/2002 8:00:00 PM
	004	6/27/2002 9:00:00 AM	6/27/2002 10:00:00 AM
*			

	email	password	fname	lname	phone
+	mcgann@ohio.edu	arrow	Sean	McGann	592-2222
▶					

Record: ◄◄ ◄ 4 ► ►► ►* of 4

Displaying the Data

Once you have entered the data in the MEMBER and VISIT tables, create and run a query for each table that displays the data in the table. Check the displayed data to make sure everything looks correct.

The Enrollment Database

Now that you have a basic understanding of how to create a single-table database and a database involving two tables with a relationship, let's look at a more complex, multitable database. In Chapter 3, the conceptual design for the Enrollment database was presented. Now, we will look at how that database can be created in Microsoft Access.

This database requires the creation of five tables and four relationships. The new feature involved in this database is the concatenated key in the ENROLL table that requires that the STUDENT$id and SECTION$call_no combine to form the primary key of the table. The design of the Enrollment database is shown in Exhibit 8-26.

Exhibit 8-26 The Design of the Enrollment Database

Physical Details

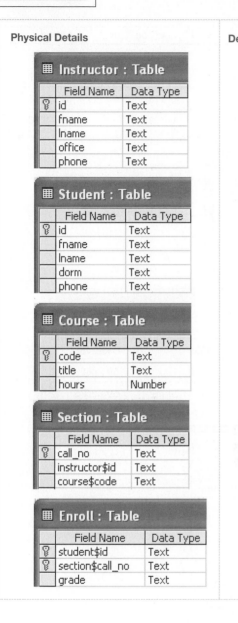

Design

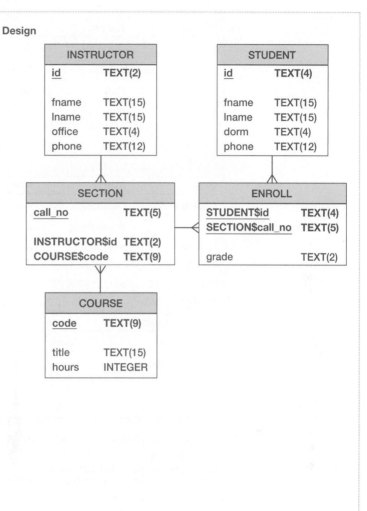

(Continued)

Exhibit 8-26

Continued

Data

INSTRUCTOR

id	fname	lname	office	phone
11	Joe	Smith	101	593-2736
22	Sam	Slick	102	594-4657
33	Sally	Sly	115	593-9875
44	Sue	Slim	123	593-4756

COURSE

code	title	hours
MIS380	Database I	4
MIS225	Visual Basic	4
MIS420	System II	4

STUDENT

id	fname	lname	dorm	phone
1111	Jim	Green	450A	593-2456
2222	Steve	Black	326B	594-4623
3333	Linda	Brown	144A	593-5575
4444	Emma	White	133B	593-4676

SECTION

call_no	INSTRUCTOR$id	COURSE$code
001	11	MIS380
002	33	MIS380
003	11	MIS225
004	44	MIS420

ENROLL

STUDENT$id	SECTION$call_no	grade
1111	001	A
2222	001	B
3333	003	A
1111	004	C

Creating the Enroll Database

Create a file for the database called enroll.mdb, and design the five tables, as shown in the database design.

Creating a Concatenated Key

The only aspect of this database that has not been introduced is the need to create a concatenated key in the ENROLL table. In this table, the primary key is the combination of the STUDENT$id and SECTION$call_no. These pairs of student ids and call numbers indicate in which sections a student is enrolled. To create a primary key using multiple columns, simply highlight all the columns when designing the table, and set them as the primary key, as shown in Exhibit 8-27.

Exhibit 8-27

Creating a
Concatenated
Primary Key

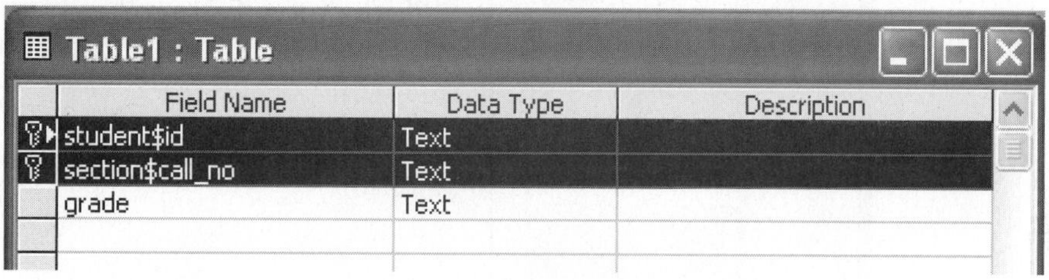

Field Name	Data Type	Description
student$id	Text	
section$call_no	Text	
grade	Text	

Relationships for the Enroll Database

The other aspect of this database that is a bit different from the previously described Sky_Member and Arcade databases is that the Enroll database requires multiple relationships. There are four foreign keys in this database, and each foreign key will require the creation of a relationship linking it to its corresponding primary key. The INSTRUCTOR$id and COURSE$code columns in the SECTION table must be linked to the primary keys in the INSTRUCTOR and COURSE tables, respectively. The STUDENT$id and SECTION$call_no columns in the ENROLL table must be linked to the primary keys in the STUDENT and SECTION tables, respectively. Use the Tools, Relationships menu option and add all the tables to the Relationships view. Exhibit 8-28 shows the relationships for the Enroll database.

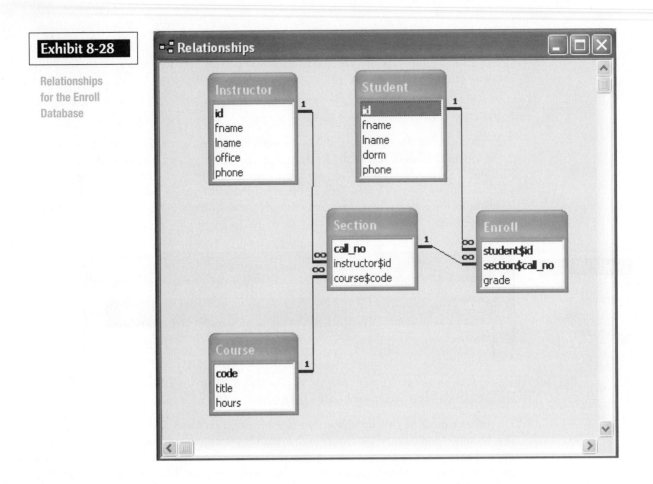

Exhibit 8-28

Relationships
for the Enroll
Database

SUMMARY

- A Microsoft Access database consists of a collection of related tables stored in a single file with an extension of mbd.
- Every field in a database table must have a data type and column width. In Access, there are 10 possible data types.
- To create a new database, select the Blank Database option, and the File New Database dialog box will appear, where you can name the file that will be used to store the database.
- The design view is the most straightforward method for creating a table.
- In the design view, columns are defined by entering the name of the column under the Field Name heading and selecting the data type using the drop-down list.
- With text columns, the field size option can be used to set a maximum size for the column.
- Another useful column setting is the option related to setting up a validation rule for a column. This validation rule limits the data that can be entered into the column.
- Primary keys can be specified by selecting the column and clicking the primary key button.
- The table is named when the design is saved.
- Once the structure of the table is created, the datasheet view can be used to enter data.
- If a validation rule is violated during data entry, a dialog box will appear indicating the error.
- A query can be used to display all the data entered into a table.
- With a multitable database, the referential integrity between the foreign and primary keys can be created in the Relationships view.
- A relationship is created by dragging the foreign key onto the matching primary key.
- Concatenated primary keys are created by selecting both columns and then clicking the primary key button.

KEY TERMS

Database window. Interface in Access in which all the components of a database (tables, queries, forms, reports, etc.) can be created and displayed.

Datasheet view. A view of a table in which data can be entered, changed, and displayed.

Design view. Part of Access where a table or other database component can be designed.

Expression Builder. An Access component where a validation rule can be specified.

Primary key button. Toolbar button that can be used to indicate that a column should be treated as a primary key for the table.

Query. A component of an Access database that is used to display data.

Relationships view. View of a database where you can display database tables and create relationships between foreign and primary keys.

Validation rule. A setting for a column where you can specify a condition that data values must conform to when being inserted into the column.

EXERCISES

Review

1. What is the file extension for an Access database file?
2. What are the data types available in Access?
3. What can be done in the database window?
4. What are some of the field size options for a number data type?
5. What is a reserved word?
6. What is the purpose of a validation rule for a column?
7. How is a primary key specified?
8. What is the datasheet view used for?
9. How is a relationship created in Access?
10. How is a concatenated primary key created?

Discuss

1. List and explain the steps for creating a database in Access.
2. What are some of the components of an Access database that appear in the database window?
3. Explain how the Expression Builder would be used to create a validation rule that required a column to contain either the word Yes or No.
4. Explain how referential integrity is set up in Access.
5. What restrictions does referential integrity place on the way data is entered into tables?

Practice

1. Create the Hospital database using the specifications shown in Exhibit 8-29.

Exhibit 8-29   Design and Data for the Hospital Database

Physical Details

Doctor : Table

	Field Name	Data Type
🔑	id	Text
	fname	Text
	lname	Text
	phone	Text
	beeper	Text

Patient : Table

	Field Name	Data Type
🔑	id	Text
	doctor$id	Text
	fname	Text
	lname	Text
	street	Text
	city	Text
	state	Text
	zip	Text
	phone	Text

Insurance : Table

	Field Name	Data Type
🔑	company	Text
	contact_fname	Text
	contact_lname	Text
	phone	Text

Insure : Table

	Field Name	Data Type
🔑	patient$id	Text
🔑	insurance$company	Text

Design

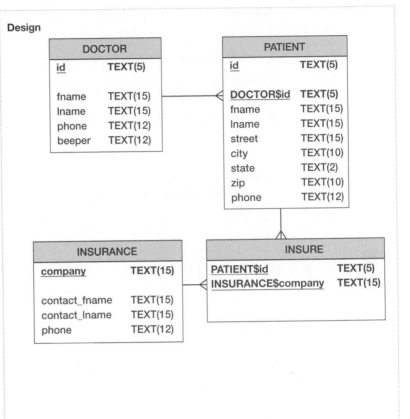

Exhibit 8-29

Continued

DOCTOR

id	fname	lname	phone	beeper
00001	Perry	Cox	555-1111	555-1212
00002	Elliot	Reid	555-2222	555-2323
00003	JD	Dorian	555-3333	555-3434
00004	Chris	Turk	555-5555	555-4545
00005	Bob	Kelso	555-6666	555-5656

PATIENT

id	DOCTOR$id	fname	lname	street	city	state	zip	phone
11111	00001	Jim	Perotti	12 Oak St	Shade	OH	45701	555-1234
22222	00001	Glen	Stamler	1 Walnut Ave	Athens	FL	58475	555-2345
33333	00002	Maddy	Gray	45 Maple St	Glouster	KY	73674	555-3456
44444	00003	Blake	Shelton	3 Elm Blvd	Shade	OH	45701	555-4567
55555	00003	EJ	Thornton	92 Ash St	Orlando	FL	85744	555-5678
66666	00004	Dyrk	Ashton	33 Poplar Ave	Columbus	OH	47837	555-6789

INSURANCE

company	contact_fname	contact_lname	phone
Prudential	Jan	Johnson	555-9876
State Farm	Sam	Smith	555-8765
Nationwide	Randy	Buck	555-7654

INSURE

PATIENT$id	INSURANCE$company
11111	Prudential
22222	Prudential
33333	State Farm
44444	Nationwide
55555	Nationwide
66666	State Farm

2. Create the Acme database using the specifications shown in Exhibit 8-30.

Exhibit 8-30 Design and Data for the Acme Database

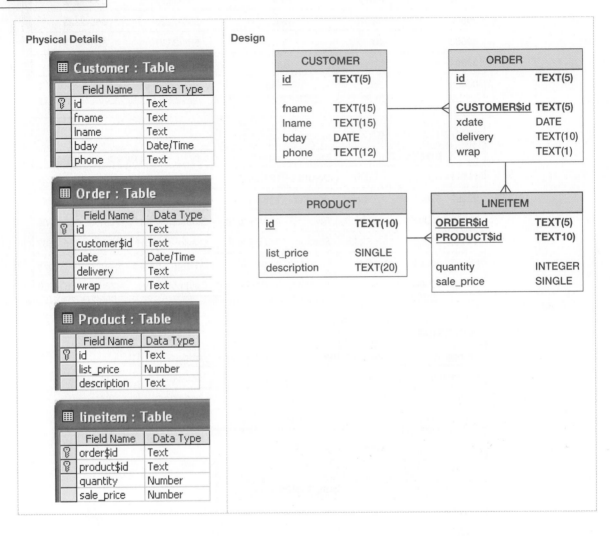

Exhibit 8-30

Continued

CUSTOMER

id	fname	lname	bday	phone
11111	Glen	Stamler	9/13/1974	555-3232
22222	Maddy	Gray	8/05/1984	555-8475
33333	Blake	Shelton	7/25/1975	555-4875
44444	EJ	Thornton	2/04/1988	555-9845

ORDER

id	CUSTOMER$id	date	delivery	wrap
10000	11111	2/04/2003	N	N
10001	22222	2/05/2003	Y	Y
10002	11111	2/05/2003	N	N
10003	33333	2/06/2003	Y	N

PRODUCT

id	list_price	description
00001	15.95	lager
00002	25.24	stout
00003	13.95	light
00004	19.98	pilsner
00005	18.75	microbrew
00006	18.57	ale
00007	15.95	bock
00008	19.95	portor

LINEITEM

ORDER$id	PRODUCT$id	quantity	sale_price
10000	00001	1	15.75
10000	00003	2	13.95
10001	00002	1	23.95
10001	00005	1	18.50
10002	00008	3	21.75
10003	00006	1	18.35
10003	00001	2	15.95
10003	00003	1	12.95
10003	00004	1	19.98

3. Create the Amazon database using the specifications shown in Exhibit 8-31.

Exhibit 8-31	Design and Data for the Amazon Database

Physical Details

Client : Table

	Field Name	Data Type
🔑	email	Text
	fname	Text
	lname	Text
	street	Text
	city	Text
	state	Text
	zip	Text

Order : Table

	Field Name	Data Type
🔑	id	Text
	client$email	Text
	order_date	Date/Time
	credit_card	Text
	exp_date	Date/Time
	ship_method	Text

Book : Table

	Field Name	Data Type
🔑	isbn	Text
	title	Text
	fname	Text
	lname	Text
	list_price	Number
	qoh	Number

Lineitem : Table

	Field Name	Data Type
🔑	order$id	Text
🔑	book$isbn	Text
	sale_price	Number
	quantity	Number

Design

CLIENT

email	TEXT(20)
lname	TEXT(15)
fname	TEXT(15)
street	TEXT(20)
city	TEXT(15)
state	TEXT(2)
zip	TEXT(10)

ORDER

id	TEXT(5)
CLIENT$email	TEXT(20)
order_date	DATE
credit_card	TEXT(16)
exp_date	DATE
ship_method	TEXT(10)

BOOK

isbn	TEXT(10)
title	TEXT(20)
fname	TEXT(15)
lname	TEXT(15)
list_price	SINGLE
qoh	INTEGER

LINEITEM

ORDER$id	TEXT(5)
BOOK$isbn	TEXT(10)
sale_price	SINGLE
quantity	INTEGER

Exhibit 8-31

Continued

CLIENT

email	fname	lname	street	city	state	zip
mtfrost@yahoo.com	Tere	Frost	75 Algaringo	Miami	FL	33134
perotti@ohio.edu	Jim	Perotti	54 Pine Pl.	Athens	OH	45701
thacker@ohio.edu	Rebecca	Thacker	93 Maple Dr.	Athens	OH	45701

BOOK

isbn	title	fname	lname	list_price	qoh
0312099436	Women of the Silk	Gail	Tsukiyama	12.95	150
014025448X	At Home in Mitford	Jan	Karon	12.95	97
0345423097	Joy School	Elizabeth	Berg	11.95	129
0670894370	A Common Life	Jan	Karon	24.95	45

XORDER

id	CLIENT$email	order_date	credit_card	exp_date	ship_method
001	thacker@ohio.edu	11/15/2002	9999888877776666	07/31/2003	FedEx
002	perotti@ohio.edu	11/23/2002	3333444455556666	04/30/2005	USPS
003	thacker@ohio.edu	12/02/2002	4444111122223333	10/31/2004	USPS

LINEITEM

XORDER$id	BOOK$isbn	sale_price	quantity
001	0312099436	10.36	2
001	014025448X	10.36	3
002	0312099436	11.50	1
002	0670894370	17.46	2
003	0670894370	18.00	1

Retrieving Data with Microsoft Access

Learning Objectives

After completing this chapter, you will be able to:

- Describe the three basic relational database retrieval operations.
- Use the SQL Select statement to retrieve all data in a table.
- Specify a column list in a Select statement.
- Sort the results of a Select statement by one or more columns in ascending or descending order.
- Use one or more conditions in a Where clause to limit the rows included in the results of a Select statement.
- Identify and properly use conditional operators in Select statements.
- Properly use AND and OR operators to express multiple conditions in a Select statement.
- Use aggregate functions in Select statements.
- Use group by to create subaggregations in Select statements.
- Use having to limit the results of queries involving aggregate functions.
- Properly use distinct in a Select statement.
- Create join conditions for Select statements that involve multiple tables.
- Use column and table name aliases.
- Use subqueries.

Introduction

One of the major advantages of the relational database approach is that it enables very flexible data retrieval. Basically, you can view the data in the database just about any way you desire. The trick is in knowing how to write the code required to retrieve the proper rows and columns. The good news is that for many retrieval operations, the code is quite simple. The bad news is that sometimes the code is very complex. As shown in Chapter 8, Microsoft Access includes a visual query-by-example interface that can be used to design queries. In addition, Access includes an SQL view for a query, in which you can view the code that is actually used to carry out the query.

SQL (structured query language) is a standard language for creating and using databases. It is used by all major database software products such as Microsoft Access, Oracle, and SQL Server. Although you do not need to understand SQL to create simple queries in Microsoft Access, there are several reasons why an understanding of SQL can be important. First, some complex queries require knowledge of SQL. Second, to be able to interact with an Access database from other applications such as a Web page, you need to send SQL commands to Access. Finally, knowledge of how SQL can be used to work with a database will allow you to create and use other database products such as Oracle and SQL Server, which make more use of SQL.

In this chapter, we introduce you to data retrieval using SQL through examples using Microsoft Access. We begin the chapter by providing an overview of the most basic operations of SQL, then we provide a number of examples of retrieving data from a single table. After you are familiar with single-table retrieval, we show you how to retrieve data from multiple tables. We encourage you to follow along with our examples and practice problems. From our years of teaching SQL, we can tell you that when you are learning SQL, there is no substitute for hands-on experience. To really understand SQL, you have to write a lot of queries. By making errors and figuring out how to fix them, you will gain a deeper understanding of the language.

Basic Retrieval Operations in SQL

There are three core data retrieval operations for relational databases, selection, projection, and join. (There are additional operations, but these three are the most important for learning SQL.)

- **Selection** retrieves a subset of rows.
- **Projection** retrieves a subset of columns.
- **Joining** combines data from two tables (you can use more than one join operation to combine data from more than two tables).

SQL implements all three of these operations through a single statement called the **Select** statement. We know that this information is a bit confusing at first, but you will get used to it quickly. The most basic form of the Select statement is shown below.

Select   [column list]

From   [table name]

As you can see, an SQL Select statement can be quite simple. The only required elements are (1) the word *Select* followed by a list of columns, and (2) the word *From* followed by the name of the table(s) that hold the requested data. The Projection operation we described earlier is implemented through the column list in the Select statement.

Displaying All Columns and Rows

Let's look at a specific example. Recall that in Chapter 8, we built the Sky_Member database in Microsoft Access. We will use that database for the examples in this section. The Sky_Member database has only one table, called SKY_MEMBER. For your reference, the data model for the database is shown in Exhibit 9-1.

Exhibit 9-1

Sky_Member
Database Data
Model

SKY_MEMBER	
email	TEXT(20)
fname	TEXT(15)
lname	TEXT(15)
phone	TEXT(12)
jumps	INTEGER
equip	TEXT(1)
skill	TEXT(1)

Suppose you want a complete list of members showing all data about all members. This is the simplest SQL query (SQL Select statements are often called *queries*). Although we could list all of the column names included in the table, we can use a shortcut. If you use an asterisk (*) as the column list in a Select statement, you indicate that you want all columns included in the query results. The Select statement used to retrieve all the data from the SKY_MEMBER table would be:

Select   *

From   **Sky_Member**

Before going any further, it is a good idea to go over how queries are constructed in Microsoft Access and how you can run SQL commands in Access. This explanation will help you if you want to try out the examples.

Recall from Chapter 8 that when a query is created in Access, the design view allows you to create the query. When the Queries object is selected in the Database view, the first option allows you to create a query in design view, as shown in Exhibit 9-2.

Exhibit 9-2

Creating a Query

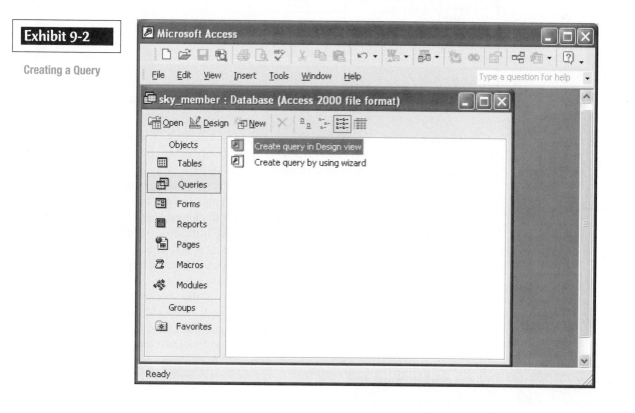

A dialog box will be displayed where you can select tables to be used in the query. In this Sky_Member database, there is only one table, so the SKY_MEMBER table should be selected, and the Add button is then used to add that table to the queries design, as shown in Exhibit 9-3.

In the **design view**, the table in the top pane is available for the query. In the Field row, you can select the columns to be included in the query using the drop-down list. In this example, the asterisk is being used to select all the columns in the table, as indicated in the query described above. In this case, the table name is specified in front of the asterisk, with a period separating the two elements. When specifying columns in SQL, the table name is sometimes placed in front of the name of a column to eliminate any ambiguity as to which table contains the column. In this case, the asterisk indicates that all the columns in the SKY_MEMBER table should be displayed. Because there is only one table in the query, preceding the asterisk with the name of the table is not necessary, but that is the default that Access uses.

This design interface can be used to create many of the queries that will be discussed in this chapter. When a query is created in this design view, Access is actually using the specifications to create an SQL statement to be used to execute the query. You can display this SQL statement at any time using the SQL view, as shown in Exhibit 9-4.

When the **SQL view** is selected, Access will display a window with the SQL statement that is used by Access to execute the query. In this window, you can modify the SQL statement for the query, or if you know how to write SQL statements, you can go immediately to this view and enter the SQL statement rather than using the design view. Exhibit 9-5 shows the window containing the SQL statement for the above query.

Exhibit 9-5

The SQL View
for a Query

```
🔳 Select All : Select Query   [ _ ][ □ ][ ✕ ]

SELECT sky_member.*
FROM sky_member;
|
```

To understand how an SQL statement works, the diagram in Exhibit 9-6 shows a breakdown of each part of the SQL statement and how each part relates to the table involved in the query. We will use this type of diagram throughout this chapter when analyzing the SQL statements introduced in each part of the chapter.

Exhibit 9-6   The Analysis of the Select Statement Retrieving All Columns and Rows

SELECT ALL ROWS AND COLUMNS
List all information about all members.

SELECT *
From sky_member;

*The * specifies that all columns appear in the result.*

email	fname	lname	phone	jumps	equip	skill
bucky@ohio.edu	Teri	Bucky	555-5555	22	Y	A
dayj@ohio.edu	John	Day	592-0646	5	Y	B
johnson@bobcat.edu	Jeremy	Johnson	555-3333	15	Y	I
luce@ohio.edu	Thom	Luce	592-1111	12	N	I
mcgann@ohio.edu	Sean	McGann	592-2222	20	Y	A
mcgrath@bobcat.edu	Billie	McGrath	555-6666	3	N	B
wilson@bobcat.edu	Sally	Wilson	555-4444	6	N	B

RESULT

email	fname	lname	phone	jumps	equip	skill
bucky@ohio.edu	Teri	Bucky	555-5555	22	Y	A
dayj@ohio.edu	John	Day	592-0646	5	Y	B
johnson@bobcat.edu	Jeremy	Johnson	555-3333	15	Y	I
luce@ohio.edu	Thom	Luce	592-1111	12	N	I
mcgann@ohio.edu	Sean	McGann	592-2222	20	Y	A
mcgrath@bobcat.edu	Billie	McGrath	555-6666	3	N	B
wilson@bobcat.edu	Sally	Wilson	555-4444	6	N	B

In this diagram, the Select statement is shown on the left, with a particular part of the statement in bold. In the table of data at the right, the aspect of the table affected by the highlighted portion of the Select statement is indicated with shading.

In the first part of the diagram, the Select* in the SQL statement is bold, and the diagram indicates the columns that will be selected for the query. In this case, the asterisk causes all the columns to be selected, so the names of all of the columns have been shaded. The second panel shows the result of the query. In this case, all of the columns and all of the rows will be displayed.

Using a Column List

Now let's say that you do not need all of the columns, and you only want to include the first names, last names, and email addresses of all members, in that order. This is the basic projection operation in a relational database, as described earlier. To perform this operation, we will use three panels in the query design, one for each column, as shown in Exhibit 9-7.

Exhibit 9-7

Query with an Explicit Column List

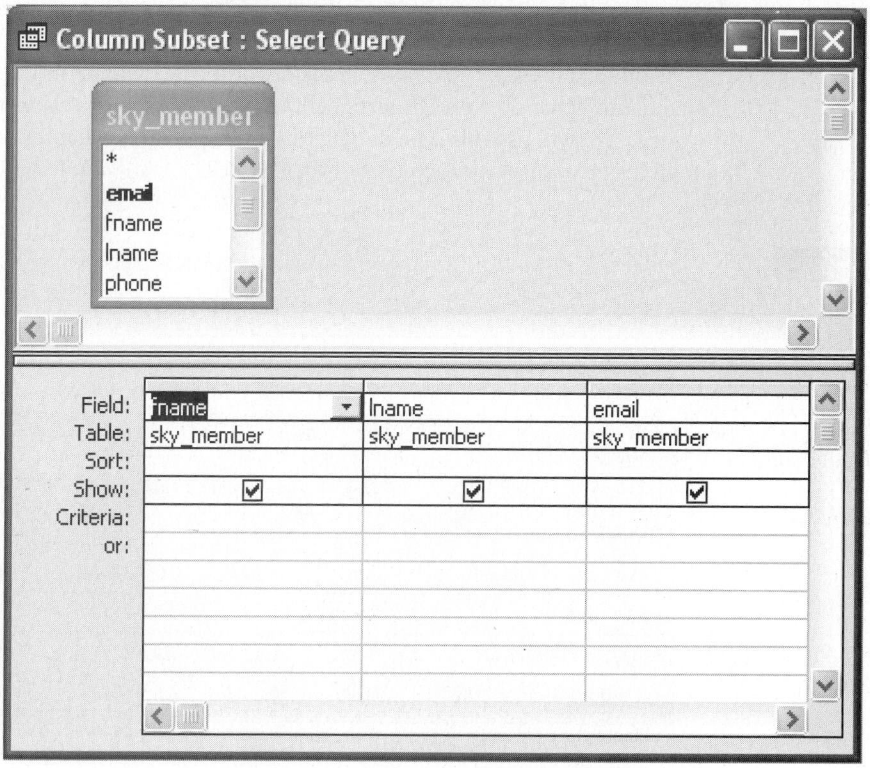

Because the Field row in each pane includes a drop-down list of all of the columns in the query table, you can select any column in each panel. The order in which the columns are selected across the panels determines the order in which the columns will be displayed. Exhibit 9-8 shows the Select statement generated for this query and the corresponding analysis.

Exhibit 9-8   The Analysis of the Select Statement with an Explicit Column List

SELECT SPECIFIC COLUMNS
List first name, last name, and email for all members.

SELECT fname,
        lname,
        email
From sky_member;

email	fname	lname	phone	jumps	equip	skill
bucky@ohio.edu	Teri	Bucky	555-5555	22	Y	A
dayj@ohio.edu	John	Day	592-0646	5	Y	B
johnson@bobcat.edu	Jeremy	Johnson	555-3333	15	Y	I
luce@ohio.edu	Thom	Luce	592-1111	12	N	I
mcgann@ohio.edu	Sean	McGann	592-2222	20	Y	A
mcgrath@bobcat.edu	Billie	McGrath	555-6666	3	N	B
wilson@bobcat.edu	Sally	Wilson	555-4444	60	N	B

RESULT

fname	lname	email
Teri	Bucky	bucky@ohio.edu
John	Day	dayj@ohio.edu
Jeremy	Johnson	johnson@bobcat.edu
Thom	Luce	luce@ohio.edu
Sean	McGann	mcgann@ohio.edu
Billie	McGrath	mcgrath@bobcat.edu
Sally	Wilson	wilson@bobcat.edu

In a Select statement, when you use a column list that includes more than one column, you must separate each column name in the list by commas. Some people like to put each column on a separate line and tab over to line up the columns. This method is used simply to improve readability. You can actually put the entire Select statement on a single line, but this situation makes the query much harder to read. Readability becomes more important as your queries become more complex.

As you can see from the result of the query above, the order of the columns in the column list dictates the order in which the columns are shown in the results. The order in which they are shown has no effect on the order in which the columns are actually stored in the table; it simply determines how the data will be displayed.

Sorting with Order By

Typically, the display of data can be improved by showing the results in some logical order. For example, you might want the results in order of the member's last name, which is stored in the lname column. Exhibit 9-9 shows the design of a query with this sorting method.

Exhibit 9-9

Designing a Query with Sorting

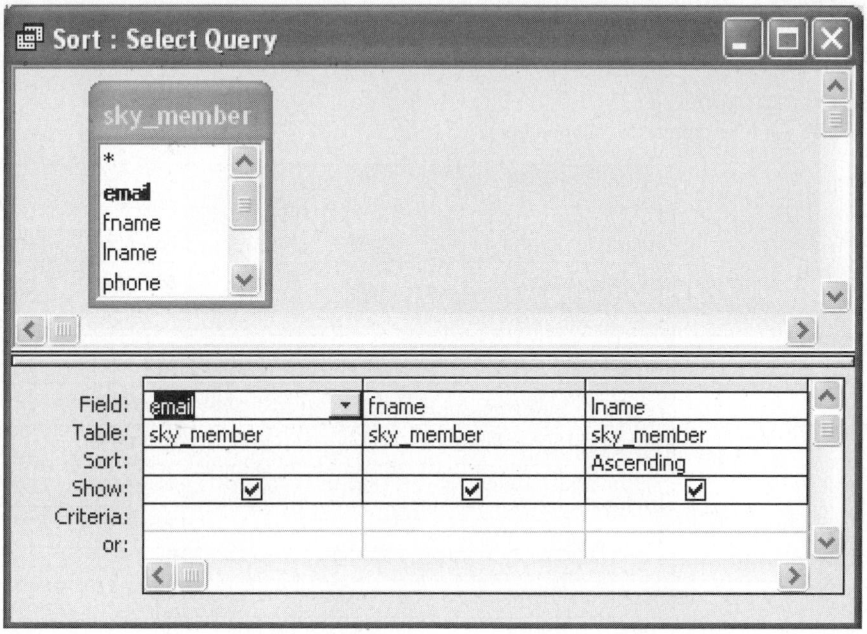

In this query, the columns to be displayed will be email, fname, and lname in that order. To sort the rows based on the data in a particular column, simply select the type of sort from the drop-down box in the panel for that column. An ascending sort orders text data alphabetically and orders numeric data from smallest to largest. A descending sort does the opposite. In SQL, the **order by** clause is used to sort results, as illustrated in the query analysis shown in Exhibit 9-10.

| **Exhibit 9-10** | Select Statement with Order by Clause |

SORTING

List the email, fname, and lname in alphabetical order by lname.

SELECT email
       fname,
       lname
From sky_member
Order by lname;

email	fname	lname	phone	jumps	equip	skill
mcgann@ohio.edu	Sean	McGann	592-2222	20	Y	A
dayj@ohio.edu	John	Day	592-0646	5	Y	B
bucky@ohio.edu	Teri	Bucky	555-5555	22	Y	A
johnson@bobcat.edu	Jeremy	Johnson	555-3333	15	Y	I
luce@ohio.edu	Thom	Luce	592-1111	12	N	I
mcgrath@bobcat.edu	Billie	McGrath	555-6666	3	N	B
wilson@bobcat.edu	Sally	Wilson	555-4444	6	N	B

SELECT email
       fname,
       lname
From sky_member
Order by lname;

email	fname	lname	phone	jumps	equip	skill
mcgann@ohio.edu	Sean	McGann	592-2222	20	Y	A
dayj@ohio.edu	John	Day	592-0646	5	Y	B
bucky@ohio.edu	Teri	Bucky	555-5555	22	Y	A
johnson@bobcat.edu	Jeremy	Johnson	555-3333	15	Y	I
luce@ohio.edu	Thom	Luce	592-1111	12	N	I
mcgrath@bobcat.edu	Billie	McGrath	555-6666	3	N	B
wilson@bobcat.edu	Sally	Wilson	555-4444	6	N	B

RESULT

email	fname	lname
bucky@ohio.edu	Teri	Bucky
dayj@ohio.edu	John	Day
johnson@bobcat.edu	Jeremy	Johnson
luce@ohio.edu	Thom	Luce
mcgann@ohio.edu	Sean	McGann
mcgrath@bobcat.edu	Billie	McGrath
wilson@bobcat.edu	Sally	Wilson

The arrow in the lname column indicates that a sort will occur on the values in that column, by moving the row for Teri Bucky to the top and moving the row for Sean McGann down. Also notice that the order of columns in the column list is independent of the sort order specified in the order by clause (columns used in order by will usually be included in the column list, because it would not make sense to sort by a column that is not displayed). You should also notice that the last names are in "A-to-Z" order, which is called ascending order. Ascending order is the default. If you want the rows to be in descending order (Z to A), you would select the descending option from the drop-down list, or put *desc* after the column name in the SQL Select statement, as shown below:

Select   email,

              fname,

              lname

From   sky_member

Order by   lname desc

Sorting on Multiple Columns

Sometimes a column used for sorting contains duplicate values. In this situation, there is no basis for determining the order of rows containing the same value in the sorted column. In this case, you have the option of including a secondary sort on additional columns; the secondary sort can be used to determine the order of rows with the same value in the column used for the primary sort. Let's look at another example to illustrate how to do this sort. For this example, the skill level of each member will be displayed, followed by his or her number of jumps and last name. The results should be in ascending (alphabetic) order of skill. For any members with the same skill level, their rows should be determined by the number of jumps (fewest to most). Exhibit 9-11 shows the design for this query.

Exhibit 9-11

Design of a Query with Multiple Sort Columns

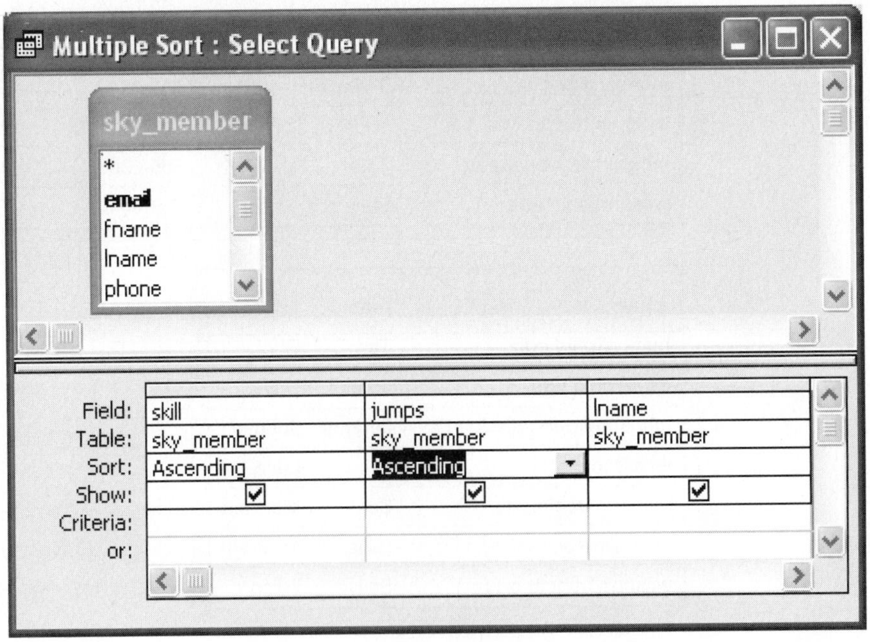

When sorting is specified in multiple columns, the sort order should be selected for the primary sort column (skill, in this case) first, and then for the secondary sort column (jumps, in this case). In SQL, all you have to do is list both sort columns in the order by clause with the primary sort column first, followed by the name of the secondary sort column. The column names must be separated by a comma. Exhibit 9-12 shows the Select statement generated for this query and the analysis.

Exhibit 9-12 | Analysis of Sorting by Multiple Columns

SORTING ON MULTIPLE COLUMNS

List the skill, jumps, and lname in alphabetical order by skill and jumps with skill

SELECT skill,
      jumps,
      lname
From sky_member
Order by skill, jumps;

email	fname	lname	phone	jumps	equip	skill
mcgann@ohio.edu	Sean	McGann	592-2222	20	Y	A
dayj@ohio.edu	John	Day	592-0646	5	Y	B
bucky@ohio.edu	Teri	Bucky	555-5555	22	Y	A
johnson@bobcat.edu	Jeremy	Johnson	555-3333	15	Y	I
luce@ohio.edu	Thom	Luce	592-1111	12	N	I
mcgrath@bobcat.edu	Billie	McGrath	555-6666	3	N	B
wilson@bobcat.edu	Sally	Wilson	555-4444	6	N	B

SELECT skill,
      jumps,
      lname
From sky_member
Order by skill, jumps;

email	fname	lname	phone	jumps	equip	skill
mcgann@ohio.edu	Sean	McGann	592-2222	20 2	Y	A 1
dayj@ohio.edu	John	Day	592-0646	5	Y	B
bucky@ohio.edu	Teri	Bucky	555-5555	22	Y	A
johnson@bobcat.edu	Jeremy	Johnson	555-3333	15	Y	I
luce@ohio.edu	Thom	Luce	592-1111	12	N	I
mcgrath@bobcat.edu	Billie	McGrath	555-6666	3	N	B
wilson@bobcat.edu	Sally	Wilson	555-4444	6	N	B

RESULT

skill	jumps	lname
A	20	McGann
A	22	Bucky
B	3	McGrath
B	5	Day
B	6	Wilson
I	12	Luce
I	15	Johnson

The analysis first indicates that the skill, jumps, and lname columns are included in the query. The arrows in the second panel show that the rows will be first sorted by values in the SKILL table, and then by values in the JUMPS table. In the result panel, you can see that two members have a skill level of A, for advanced. As a result, the first sort on skill level cannot determine which of these two rows should be displayed first. When this situation occurs, the secondary sort is used to determine that McGann should be shown before Bucky, because Bucky has fewer jumps. The same thing happens for the members in skill level B. The primary sort cannot determine the order of the three members in this skill level, so the secondary sort is used to make that determination.

When using multiple columns in sorting, there is no requirement that the sorts be done in ascending or descending order. If you wanted the sort by skill level to be *descending* and the secondary sort on the number of jumps to be in *ascending* order, simply make those selections in the sort lists for those two columns in the query design. In SQL, you would simply insert *desc* after the skill column in the order by clause, as shown below (note that there is *not* a comma between *skill* and *desc*).

Select	skill,
	jumps,
	lname
From	sky_member
Order by	skill desc, jumps

Selecting Rows with Where

Recall from the beginning of the chapter that the selection operation in a relational database is the display of a subset of table rows. To do this operation in SQL, we need to add another element to our simple Select statement. Rows are chosen through conditions specified in a **where clause** in the Select statement. If you wanted to see all columns for rows corresponding to members with fewer than 20 jumps, you would use the Select statement shown below.

Select	lname, jumps
From	sky_member
Where	jumps < 20

A where clause always includes at least one true/false condition, such as "jumps < 20" in the example. If a row meets the condition specified, it is included in the results. Rows that do not meet the condition are not included. Note that you can have more than one condition, but we will get to that later. If you are familiar with a programming language such as Visual Basic or Java, you already know about conditional operators. But just in case you are not, the commonly used operators are shown in Exhibit 9-13. We will add to this list later.

Exhibit 9-13

Conditional
Operators

Operator	Explanation	Example
=	Equal to	equip = 'N'
>	Greater than	jumps > 10
<	Less than	jumps < 20
>=	Greater than or equal to	jumps >= 10
<=	Less than or equal to	jumps <= 20
!=	Not equal to	ability != 'A'

In the query design window, conditions can be created by placing an entry in the Criteria row of the panel for that column. These criteria are then used by Access to generate the correct where condition for the SQL Select statement. Exhibit 9-14 shows the query design for the query described above.

Exhibit 9-14

Entering a Criterion
for a Column

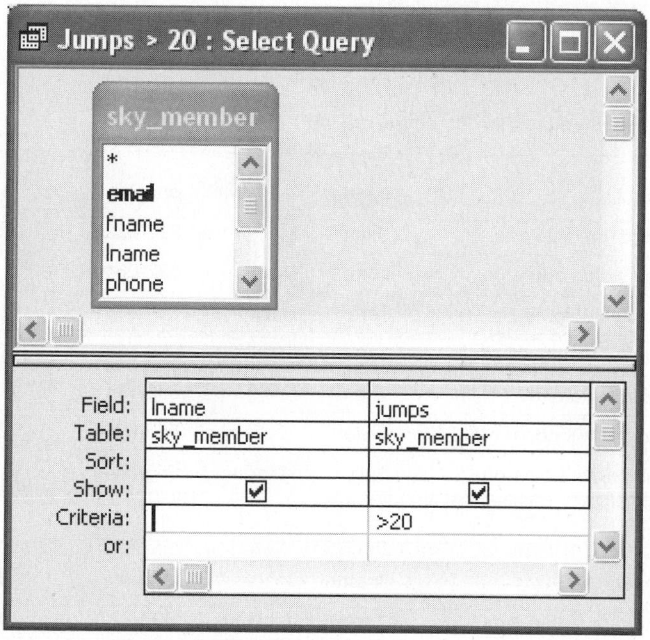

Notice that the column name does not have to be specified in the condition, because the condition is entered into the panel for that column; thus, it is clear to which column the condition will be applied. The analysis for this query is shown in Exhibit 9-15.

Exhibit 9-15   Analysis of Query with a Where Clause

JUMPS > 20
List the lname and jumps for members with more than 20 jumps.

SELECT lname,
        jumps
From sky_member
where jumps > 20;

email	fname	lname	phone	jumps	equip	skill
mcgann@ohio.edu	Sean	McGann	592-2222	20	Y	A
dayj@ohio.edu	John	Day	592-0646	5	Y	B
bucky@ohio.edu	Teri	Bucky	555-5555	22	Y	A
johnson@bobcat.edu	Jeremy	Johnson	555-3333	15	Y	I
luce@ohio.edu	Thom	Luce	592-1111	12	N	I
mcgrath@bobcat.edu	Billie	McGrath	555-6666	3	N	B
wilson@bobcat.edu	Sally	Wilson	555-4444	6	N	B

SELECT lname,
        jumps
From sky_member
where jumps > 20;

email	fname	lname	phone	jumps	equip	skill
mcgann@ohio.edu	Sean	McGann	592-2222	20	Y	A
dayj@ohio.edu	John	Day	592-0646	5	Y	B
bucky@ohio.edu	Teri	Bucky	555-5555	22	Y	A
johnson@bobcat.edu	Jeremy	Johnson	555-3333	15	Y	I
luce@ohio.edu	Thom	Luce	592-1111	12	N	I
mcgrath@bobcat.edu	Billie	McGrath	555-6666	3	N	B
wilson@bobcat.edu	Sally	Wilson	555-4444	6	N	B

RESULT

lname	jumps
Bucky	22

The first panel of the analysis shows the result of including only some of the columns in the original table, as we have seen before. In the second panel, we can see the effect of the where clause on limiting the display to only some of the rows in the table. The final result shows just the name and number of jumps for the one member who has recorded more than 20 jumps.

Where Clauses Involving Text Data

When you want to use columns containing text data in a where clause, you must put any character values used as part of the condition inside quotes. For example, if you wanted to see the first and last names of all members who own their own equipment, you would use the SQL statement shown below.

Select   fname,

                lname

From   sky_member

Where   equip = 'Y'

In the query design view in Access, this query would be created as indicated in Exhibit 9-16.

Exhibit 9-16

Designing a Query
with a Condition
Involving a Text
Column

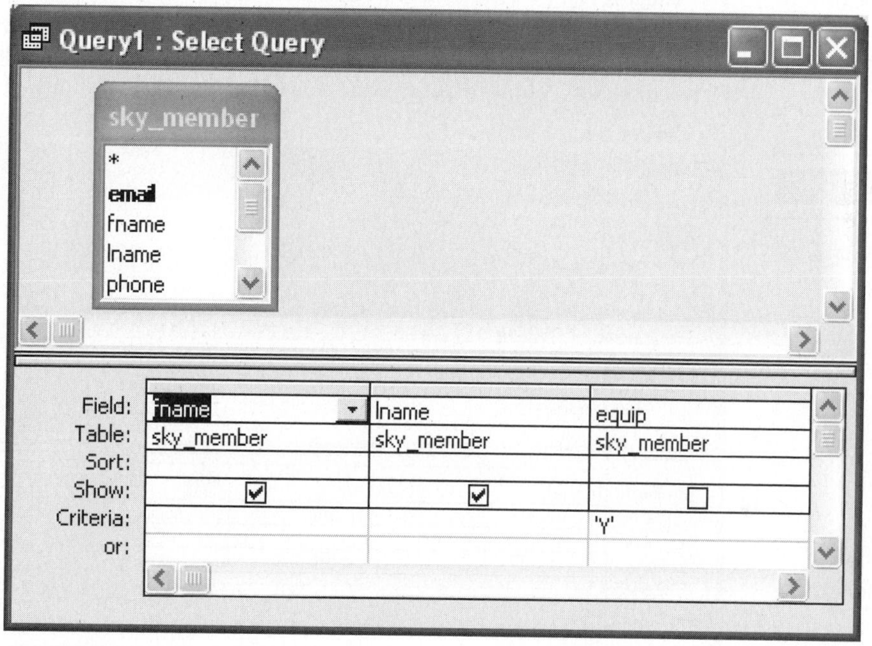

When creating a condition that looks for a particular value in a text column, simply enter that value in the Criteria row of the panel involving that column. In this example, the query is set up to display only the first and last names of the members, but the condition to be used to determine which rows will be displayed involves the equip column. To be able to create this criterion, you must include a panel for the equip column so you will have a place to enter the criterion. This process illustrates the fact that the columns used in a where clause are independent from the columns that will be listed for display. To include a column in the query design but not display that column, you simply uncheck the box in the Show row of the design. In this case, we have a panel for the equip column so that we can enter the criterion, but the Show box in that panel has been unchecked to indicate that the data in that column will not be displayed. To test your understanding, try to create your own analysis for this query.

The LIKE Operator

In SQL there is an additional conditional operator that is useful when dealing with character-based data. The **LIKE operator** allows you to choose rows that share some common characters, but that are not exactly the same. For example, suppose you want to show the first names, last names, and phone numbers of all members who have phone numbers that start with "555." In SQL the query would look like this:

Select   fname,
             lname,
             email,
             phone
From   sky_member
Where   phone like '555*'

The asterisk (*) is used as a wildcard representing any combination of characters (other database software packages sometimes use the percent sign for this purpose). Any row that has a phone value starting with "555" is included in the results, regardless of what or how many characters follow. Exhibit 9-17 shows how this query would be designed.

Exhibit 9-17

Using the LIKE Operator

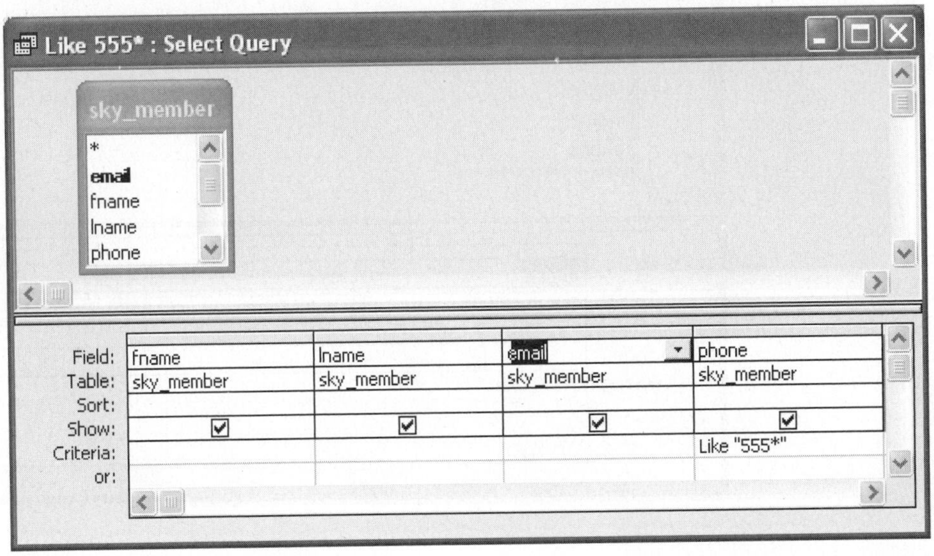

You can also use LIKE to return rows according to characters at the end of a field value. Let's say that you want to execute the same basic query, but this time you want to limit the list to members who have ".edu" email addresses (email addresses that end in "edu"). The SQL statement would be:

Select   fname,
             lname,
             email,
             phone
From   sky_member
Where   email like '*edu'

Complex Where Clauses

Sometimes you need to select rows according to more than one condition. With SQL, you make this selection in a single where clause. Each condition is separated by a logical operator. When conditions are separated by the **AND logical operator,** a row must meet both conditions to be selected. When the conditions are separated by the **OR logical operator,** a row is selected if *either* condition is met.

Let's look at some examples to illustrate how to use each logical condition. For the first example, we want to list the first and last names, number of jumps, and ability for all members who have more than 10 jumps and have intermediate ability. The two conditions we want to satisfy are:

jumps > 10   AND   skill = 'I'

Which rows will be selected using these criteria? Remember that with the AND operator, *both* conditions must be satisfied. Exhibit 9-18 shows how rows will be selected for display.

Exhibit 9-18   Multiple Conditions Linked with an AND

email	fname	lname	phone	jumps	equip	skill	selected?
mcgann@ohio.edu	Sean	McGann	592-2222	20	Y	A	NO
dayj@ohio.edu	John	Day	592-0646	5	Y	B	NO
bucky@ohio.edu	Teri	Bucky	555-5555	22	Y	A	NO
johnson@bobcat.edu	Jeremy	Johnson	555-3333	15	Y	I	YES
luce@ohio.edu	Thom	Luce	592-1111	12	N	I	YES
mcgrath@bobcat.edu	Billie	McGrath	555-6666	3	N	B	NO
wilson@bobcat.edu	Sally	Wilson	555-4444	6	N	B	NO

As the exhibit indicates in the final column, only Johnson and Luce will be selected. Now let's change our condition by substituting an OR logical operator for the AND. This time, we want to list the members who either have more than 14 jumps or are at the intermediate ability. In this case, the two conditions we want to satisfy are:

jumps > 14   OR   skill = 'I'

Can you tell which rows are selected this time? When using the OR operator, any row that meets *either* condition is selected. Exhibit 9-19 shows how rows will be selected for display.

Exhibit 9-19   Multiple Conditions Linked with an OR

email	fname	lname	phone	jumps	equip	skill	selected?
mcgann@ohio.edu	Sean	McGann	592-2222	20	Y	A	YES
dayj@ohio.edu	John	Day	592-0646	5	Y	B	NO
bucky@ohio.edu	Teri	Bucky	555-5555	22	Y	A	YES
johnson@bobcat.edu	Jeremy	Johnson	555-3333	15	Y	I	YES
luce@ohio.edu	Thom	Luce	592-1111	12	N	I	YES
mcgrath@bobcat.edu	Billie	McGrath	555-6666	3	N	B	NO
wilson@bobcat.edu	Sally	Wilson	555-4444	6	N	B	NO

As before, Johnson is selected, because he meets both conditions. McGann and Bucky are also selected because they have more than 15 jumps, even though they do not have the correct skill level. In addition, Luce is selected because he meets the skill condition, even though he does not have more than 14 jumps.

Now we will put each example in the form of a query. An example SQL statement that has two conditions joined with an AND logical operator is shown below.

Select	fname,
	lname,
	jumps,
	skill
From	sky_member
Where	jumps > 10
And	skill = 'T'

Notice that we only have one where clause. That is a rule; you can have only one where clause in any single Select statement. This single where clause combines two conditions with the AND logical operator. Exhibit 9-20 shows the design using an example that uses this AND condition.

Exhibit 9-20

Combining Two
Conditions with
an AND

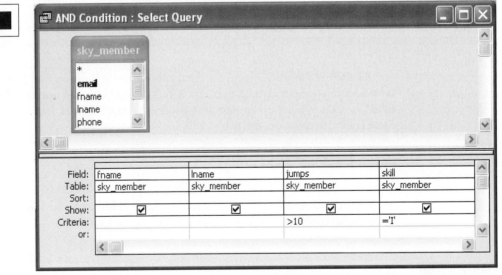

In the query design, two conditions are combined with an AND logical relationship by placing both conditions on the same criteria line. Because the condition under the jumps and skill columns are on the same line, they will be related with an AND relationship. Exhibit 9-21 shows the analysis for this query.

Exhibit 9-21   The Analysis of the Query Using an AND Relationship

JUMP >10 AND SKILL = 'I'

List the fname, lname, jumps, and skill for members with more than 10 jumps and an intermediate skill level.

SELECT fname
        lname,
        jumps,
        skill
From sky_member
where jumps > 10
and skill= 'I';

email	fname	lname	phone	jumps	equip	skill
mcgann@ohio.edu	Sean	McGann	592-2222	20	Y	A
dayj@ohio.edu	John	Day	592-0646	5	Y	B
bucky@ohio.edu	Teri	Bucky	555-5555	22	Y	A
johnson@bobcat.edu	Jeremy	Johnson	555-3333	15	Y	I
luce@ohio.edu	Thom	Luce	592-1111	12	N	I
mcgrath@bobcat.edu	Billie	McGrath	555-6666	3	N	B
wilson@bobcat.edu	Sally	Wilson	555-4444	6	N	B

SELECT fname
        lname,
        jumps,
        skill
From sky_member
where jumps > 10
and skill= 'I';

email	fname	lname	phone	jumps	equip	skill
mcgann@ohio.edu	Sean	McGann	592-2222	20	Y	A
dayj@ohio.edu	John	Day	592-0646	5	Y	B
bucky@ohio.edu	Teri	Bucky	555-5555	22	Y	A
johnson@bobcat.edu	Jeremy	Johnson	555-3333	15	Y	I
luce@ohio.edu	Thom	Luce	592-1111	12	N	I
mcgrath@bobcat.edu	Billie	McGrath	555-6666	3	N	B
wilson@bobcat.edu	Sally	Wilson	555-4444	6	N	B

SELECT fname
        lname,
        jumps,
        skill
From sky_member
where jumps > 10
and skill= 'I';

email	fname	lname	phone	jumps	equip	skill
mcgann@ohio.edu	Sean	McGann	592-2222	20	Y	A
dayj@ohio.edu	John	Day	592-0646	5	Y	B
bucky@ohio.edu	Teri	Bucky	555-5555	22	Y	A
johnson@bobcat.edu	Jeremy	Johnson	555-3333	15	Y	I
luce@ohio.edu	Thom	Luce	592-1111	12	N	I
mcgrath@bobcat.edu	Billie	McGrath	555-6666	3	N	B
wilson@bobcat.edu	Sally	Wilson	555-4444	6	N	B

RESULT

fname	lname	jumps	skill
Jeremy	Johnson	15	I
Thom	Luce	12	I

To illustrate the use of an OR logical operator, consider the SQL statement below that displays members with more than 14 jumps or with an intermediate skill level.

Select	fname,
	lname,
	jumps,
	skill
From	sky_member
Where	jumps > 14
Or	skill = 'I'

In the query design, an OR relationship can be created by using the OR row under the Criteria, as shown in Exhibit 9-22.

Exhibit 9-22

Combining Two
Conditions with
an OR

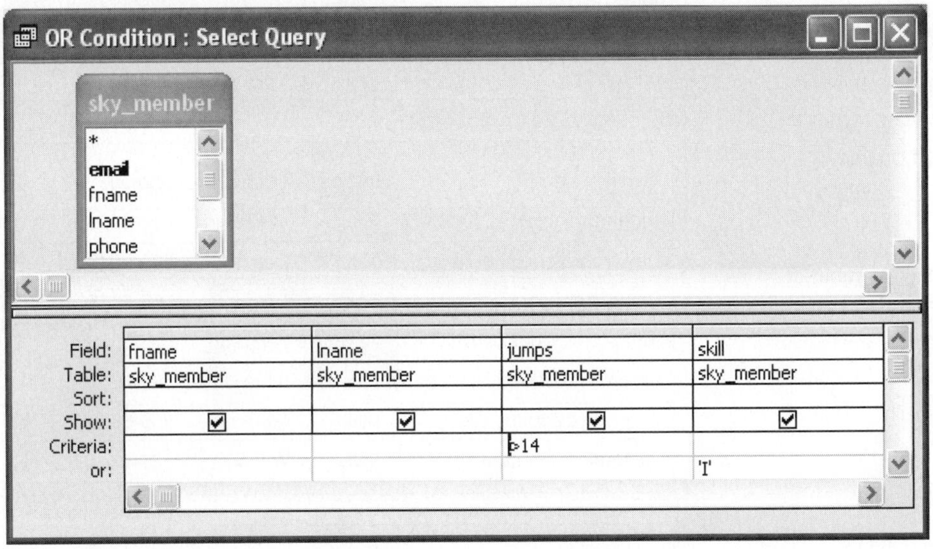

	OR Condition : Select Query

sky_member

*
email
fname
lname
phone

Field:	fname	lname	jumps	skill
Table:	sky_member	sky_member	sky_member	sky_member
Sort:				
Show:	☑	☑	☑	☑
Criteria:			>14	
or:				'I'

In the query design, two conditions are combined with an OR logical relationship by placing one condition on the Criteria line and the other condition on the OR line. Because the condition under the jumps is on the criteria line, and the condition for the skill column is on the OR line, they will be related with an OR relationship. Exhibit 9-23 shows the analysis for this query.

Exhibit 9-23   The Analysis of the Query Using an OR Relationship

JUMP >14 OR SKILL = 'I'
List the fname, lname, jumps, and skill for members with more than 14 jumps or an intermediate skill level.

SELECT fname
    lname,
    jumps,
    skill
From sky_member
where jumps > 14
or skill= 'I';

email	fname	lname	phone	jumps	equip	skill
mcgann@ohio.edu	Sean	McGann	592-2222	20	Y	A
dayj@ohio.edu	John	Day	592-0646	5	Y	B
bucky@ohio.edu	Teri	Bucky	555-5555	22	Y	A
johnson@bobcat.edu	Jeremy	Johnson	555-3333	15	Y	I
luce@ohio.edu	Thom	Luce	592-1111	12	N	I
mcgrath@bobcat.edu	Billie	McGrath	555-6666	3	N	B
wilson@bobcat.edu	Sally	Wilson	555-4444	6	N	B

SELECT fname
    lname,
    jumps,
    skill
From sky_member
where jumps > 14
or skill= 'I';

email	fname	lname	phone	jumps	equip	skill
mcgann@ohio.edu	Sean	McGann	592-2222	20	Y	A
dayj@ohio.edu	John	Day	592-0646	5	Y	B
bucky@ohio.edu	Teri	Bucky	555-5555	22	Y	A
johnson@bobcat.edu	Jeremy	Johnson	555-3333	15	Y	I
luce@ohio.edu	Thom	Luce	592-1111	12	N	I
mcgrath@bobcat.edu	Billie	McGrath	555-6666	3	N	B
wilson@bobcat.edu	Sally	Wilson	555-4444	6	N	B

SELECT fname
    lname,
    jumps,
    skill
From sky_member
where jumps > 14
or skill= 'I';

email	fname	lname	phone	jumps	equip	skill
mcgann@ohio.edu	Sean	McGann	592-2222	20	Y	A
dayj@ohio.edu	John	Day	592-0646	5	Y	B
bucky@ohio.edu	Teri	Bucky	555-5555	22	Y	A
johnson@bobcat.edu	Jeremy	Johnson	555-3333	15	Y	I
luce@ohio.edu	Thom	Luce	592-1111	12	N	I
mcgrath@bobcat.edu	Billie	McGrath	555-6666	3	N	B
wilson@bobcat.edu	Sally	Wilson	555-4444	6	N	B

RESULT

fname	lname	jumps	skill
Sean	McGann	20	A
Teri	Bucky	22	A
Jeremy	Johnson	15	I
Thom	Luce	12	I

You can have a virtually unlimited number of conditions joined with a combination of AND and OR operators in a single where clause. Later in this chapter, we will show you how to use both AND and OR in the same where clause.

Multiple Conditions on the Same Column

You can use AND to separate conditions that deal with the same column. This is one way in which you can select rows based on a range of values. For example, if you want to select rows representing members who have between 10 and 20 jumps, you could use the SQL Select statement shown below.

Select	**fname,**
	lname,
	jumps,
	skill
From	**sky_member**
Where	**jumps > 10**
And	**jumps < 20**

In the query design, the two criteria appear under the same column and are combined with an AND logical relationship, as shown in Exhibit 9-24.

Exhibit 9-24

Using the AND Operator to Select Based on a Range of Values

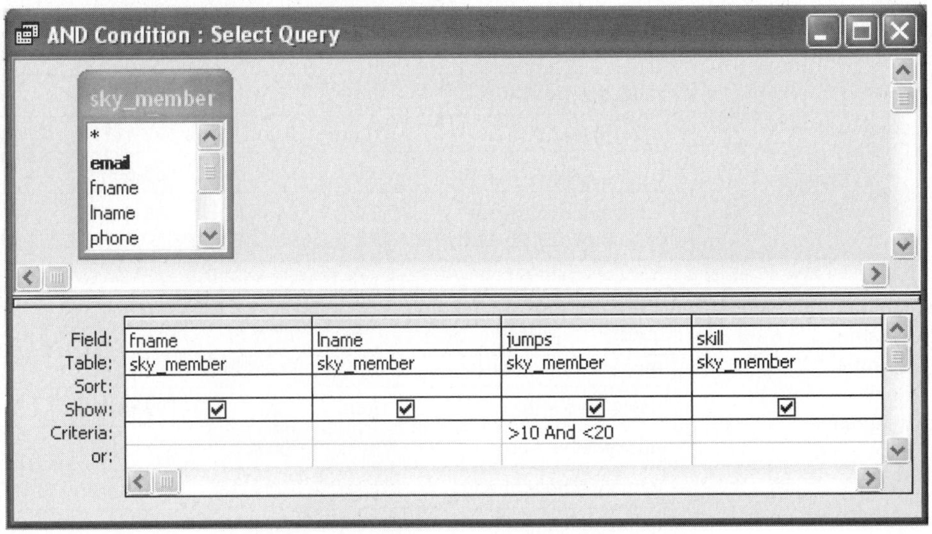

In the analysis for this query shown in Exhibit 9-25, you can see that the first half of the condition (jumps > 10) will select McGann, Bucky, Johnson, and Luce, but then the second half of the condition (jumps < 20) eliminates McGann and Bucky. Thus, the combined condition will result in the display of Johnson and Luce.

Exhibit 9-25	The Analysis of the Query Jumps > 10 and Jumps < 20

JUMPS >10 AND JUMPS < 20

List the fname, lname, jumps, and skill for members with more than 10 jumps but fewer than 20 jumps.

SELECT fname
    lname,
    jumps,
    skill
From sky_member
where jumps > 10
and jumps < 20;

email	fname	lname	phone	jumps	equip	skill
mcgann@ohio.edu	Sean	McGann	592-2222	20	Y	A
dayj@ohio.edu	John	Day	592-0646	5	Y	B
bucky@ohio.edu	Teri	Bucky	555-5555	22	Y	A
johnson@bobcat.edu	Jeremy	Johnson	555-3333	15	Y	I
luce@ohio.edu	Thom	Luce	592-1111	12	N	I
mcgrath@bobcat.edu	Billie	McGrath	555-6666	3	N	B
wilson@bobcat.edu	Sally	Wilson	555-4444	6	N	B

SELECT fname
    lname,
    jumps,
    skill
From sky_member
where jumps > 10
and jumps < 20;

email	fname	lname	phone	jumps	equip	skill
mcgann@ohio.edu	Sean	McGann	592-2222	20	Y	A
dayj@ohio.edu	John	Day	592-0646	5	Y	B
bucky@ohio.edu	Teri	Bucky	555-5555	22	Y	A
johnson@bobcat.edu	Jeremy	Johnson	555-3333	15	Y	I
luce@ohio.edu	Thom	Luce	592-1111	12	N	I
mcgrath@bobcat.edu	Billie	McGrath	555-6666	3	N	B
wilson@bobcat.edu	Sally	Wilson	555-4444	6	N	B

SELECT fname
    lname,
    jumps,
    skill
From sky_member
where jumps > 10
and jumps < 20;

email	fname	lname	phone	jumps	equip	skill
mcgann@ohio.edu	Sean	McGann	592-2222	20	Y	A
dayj@ohio.edu	John	Day	592-0646	5	Y	B
bucky@ohio.edu	Teri	Bucky	555-5555	22	Y	A
johnson@bobcat.edu	Jeremy	Johnson	555-3333	15	Y	I
luce@ohio.edu	Thom	Luce	592-1111	12	N	I
mcgrath@bobcat.edu	Billie	McGrath	555-6666	3	N	B
wilson@bobcat.edu	Sally	Wilson	555-4444	6	N	B

RESULT

fname	lname	jumps	skill
Jeremy	Johnson	15	I
Thom	Luce	12	I

It is also possible to use OR, where each condition includes the same column. You can use this procedure to select rows where a particular column has any one of several values. Suppose you want to list all members who are of beginner (B) or intermediate (I) ability. The SQL Select statement that can be used to produce this list is shown below.

Select	**fname,**
	lname,
	jumps,
	skill
From	**sky_member**
Where	**skill = 'B'**
Or	**skill = 'I'**

This kind of query sometimes causes confusion as to whether you should use AND or OR. When you want to select rows based on multiple values for the same column, using AND can cause problems. If you tried to use AND in the SQL Select statement above, the result would be an empty list. When you think about it, this result makes sense. Using AND requires that *both* conditions be met for a row to be included in the result. We know that each member has one ability level, so it is impossible for any single member to match both conditions. In other words, a particular member could not be both an Intermediate and a Beginner at the same time. Because of this condition, we get an empty list. Exhibit 9-26 shows the design for this query.

Exhibit 9-26

Using OR to Enter Multiple Criteria on the Same Column

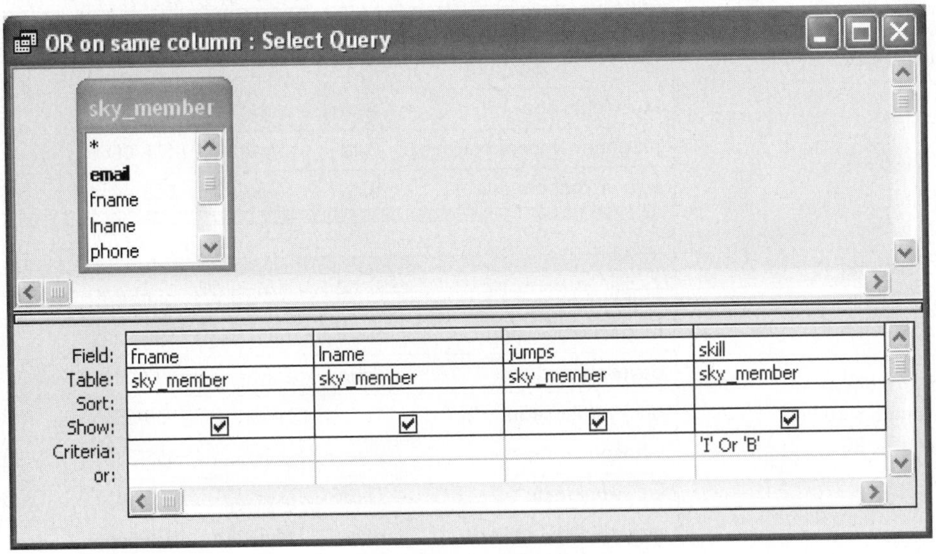

If you find this method confusing, you may wish to use an alternate way to compare a column value to a list. The **IN operator** allows you to select rows based on multiple values for a particular column. Essentially, this operator is the same as having one or more OR conditions. The SQL Select statement using IN rather than OR is shown below.

Select	fname,
	lname,
	jumps,
	skill
From	sky_member
Where	skill in ('B', 'I')

This method is especially useful when you have many values in the value list. If you use OR conditions, you need to use a whole series of ORs to join all the values together. With IN, you simply have to add to the value list (the list of values inside the parentheses). In general, using IN is simpler, and you are less likely to make errors than when entering a series of OR conditions. Exhibit 9-27 shows the design for the query using the IN operator.

Exhibit 9-27

Using the IN Operator

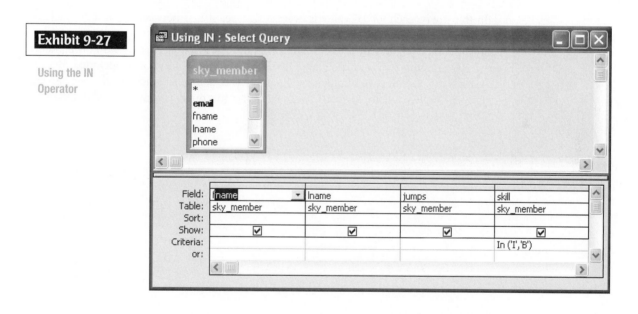

Another useful conditional operator is *BETWEEN*. The **BETWEEN operator** lets you choose rows based on a range of values. Recall our earlier example, which listed members with between 10 and 20 jumps. We could write this query using BETWEEN, as shown in the SQL Select statement below.

Select	fname,
	lname,
	jumps,
	skill
From	sky_member
Where	jumps between 10 and 20

The design for this query is shown in Exhibit 9-28.

Exhibit 9-28

Using the
Between Operator

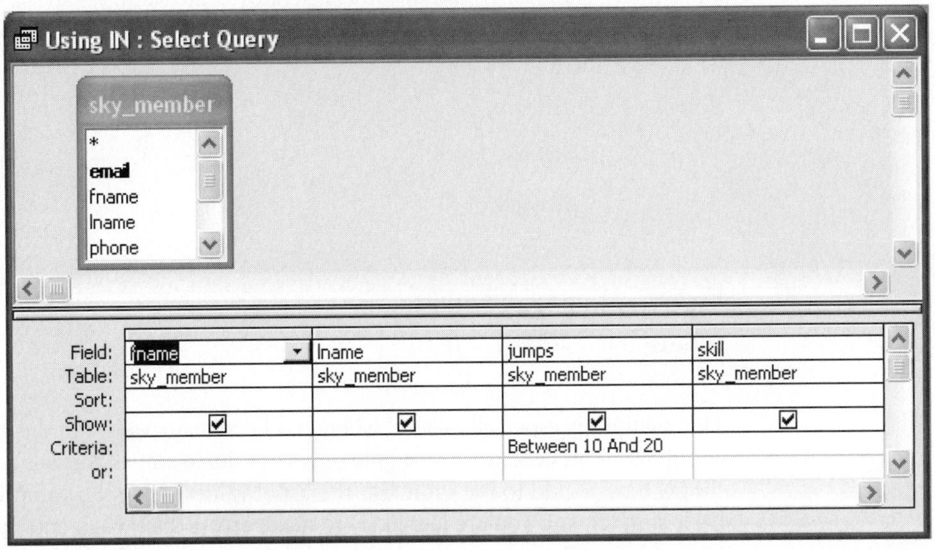

In this query, each jumps value is evaluated to see if it is between 10 and 20, inclusive (including 10 and 20). If so, the row is included in the results. Note that this condition is slightly different from the previous condition of jumps > 10 AND jumps < 20. In the condition using AND, a number of jumps equal to 10 or equal to 20 would not be included. Because BETWEEN includes the two numbers specified in the condition, it is actually the same as writing jumps >= 10 AND jumps <= 20. The analysis for this query is shown in Exhibit 9-29.

Exhibit 9-29   Analysis of the Query Using Between

JUMPS BETWEEN 10 AND 20

List the fname, lname, jumps, and skill for members with jumps between 10 and 20.

SELECT fname
        lname,
        jumps,
        skill
From sky_member
where jumps between
10 and 20;

email	fname	lname	phone	jumps	equip	skill
mcgann@ohio.edu	Sean	McGann	592-2222	20	Y	A
dayj@ohio.edu	John	Day	592-0646	5	Y	B
bucky@ohio.edu	Teri	Bucky	555-5555	22	Y	A
johnson@bobcat.edu	Jeremy	Johnson	555-3333	15	Y	I
luce@ohio.edu	Thom	Luce	592-1111	12	N	I
mcgrath@bobcat.edu	Billie	McGrath	555-6666	3	N	B
wilson@bobcat.edu	Sally	Wilson	555-4444	6	N	B

SELECT fname
        lname,
        jumps,
        skill
From sky_member
where jumps between
10 and 20;

email	fname	lname	phone	jumps	equip	skill
mcgann@ohio.edu	Sean	McGann	592-2222	20	Y	A
dayj@ohio.edu	John	Day	592-0646	5	Y	B
bucky@ohio.edu	Teri	Bucky	555-5555	22	Y	A
johnson@bobcat.edu	Jeremy	Johnson	555-3333	15	Y	I
luce@ohio.edu	Thom	Luce	592-1111	12	N	I
mcgrath@bobcat.edu	Billie	McGrath	555-6666	3	N	B
wilson@bobcat.edu	Sally	Wilson	555-4444	6	N	B

RESULT

fname	lname	jumps	skill
Sean	McGann	20	A
Jeremy	Johnson	15	I
Thon	Luce	12	I

As this analysis shows, the number of jumps for McGann is equal to 20, so it is included in the result; the BETWEEN operator includes any rows with either of the two values specified. In addition to being able to use BETWEEN on numeric data, you can also do alphabetic comparisons by using BETWEEN with character-based data.

The NOT Operator

Any of the operators that we have described can be combined with the **NOT operator** to basically reverse the condition. This reversal is done by preceding the conditional operator with the word *NOT*. Using NOT reverses what would normally happen. The rows that would normally not be chosen *are* chosen with the NOT operator. To illustrate, let's look at the SQL statement that selected rows representing members who are at the beginner or intermediate level. If we precede the IN operator with NOT, we get all members except those at the beginner or intermediate levels, as shown in the SQL Select statement below.

Select	fname,
	lname,
	jumps,
	skill
From	sky_member
Where	skill not in ('B', 'I')

Combining AND and OR

It is also possible to mix AND and OR operators in a single where clause. Unfortunately, this procedure can get a bit tricky. Suppose you want to get a list of all members who have their own equipment and are in either the B or I skill levels. An inexperienced SQL coder might try the SQL Select statement shown below.

Select	fname,
	lname,
	equip,
	skill
From	sky_member
Where	equip = 'Y'
	and skill = 'I'
	or skill = 'B'

In an SQL Select statement, any conditions combined with an AND are evaluated first, and additional conditions combined with an OR are evaluated second. The design for this query is shown in Exhibit 9-30.

Exhibit 9-30

Incorrectly
Combining
AND and OR

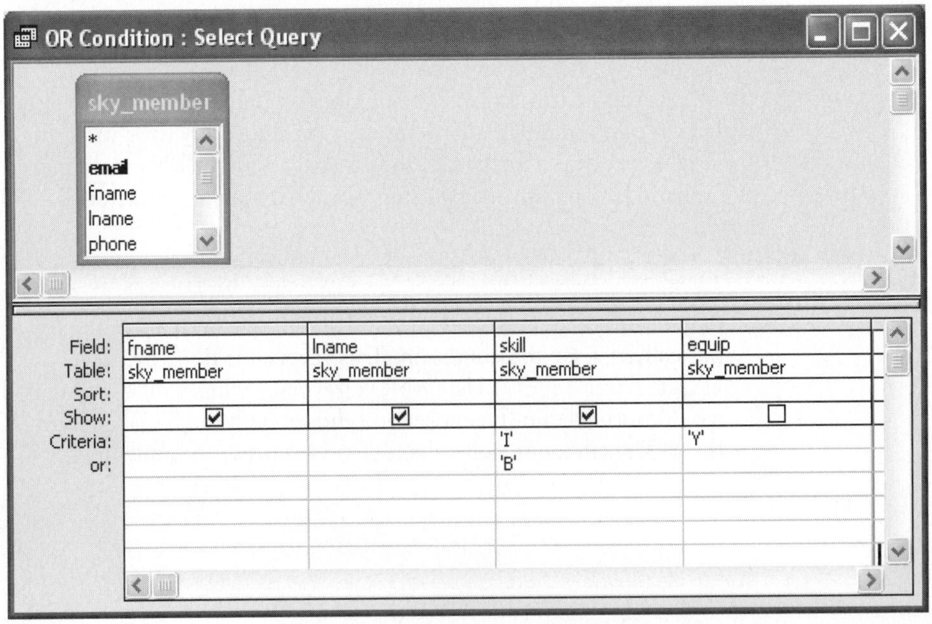

In the query design, the criteria appear on two lines; thus, Access finds all rows that meet the criteria on the first line and then adds rows that meet the criteria on the second line. This query will show intermediate members with equipment, and then any beginners, regardless of whether they have equipment or not, as indicated in the analysis in Exhibit 9-31.

| Exhibit 9-31 | Analysis of the Query Incorrectly Combining AND and OR |

INCORRECT QUERY FOR SKILL = B OR I AND EQUIP = Y

List the fname, lname, equip, and skill for beginning or intermediate members who own their own equipment.

SELECT fname
　　　　lname,
　　　　equip,
　　　　skill
From sky_member
where equip = 'Y'
and skill ='I'
or skill ='B'

email	fname	lname	phone	jumps	equip	skill
mcgann@ohio.edu	Sean	McGann	592-2222	20	Y	A
dayj@ohio.edu	John	Day	592-0646	5	Y	B
bucky@ohio.edu	Teri	Bucky	555-5555	22	Y	A
johnson@bobcat.edu	Jeremy	Johnson	555-3333	15	Y	I
luce@ohio.edu	Thom	Luce	592-1111	12	N	I
mcgrath@bobcat.edu	Billie	McGrath	555-6666	3	N	B
wilson@bobcat.edu	Sally	Wilson	555-4444	6	N	B

SELECT fname
　　　　lname,
　　　　equip,
　　　　skill
From sky_member
where equip = 'Y'
and skill ='I'
or skill ='B'

email	fname	lname	phone	jumps	equip	skill
mcgann@ohio.edu	Sean	McGann	592-2222	20	Y	A
dayj@ohio.edu	John	Day	592-0646	5	Y	B
bucky@ohio.edu	Teri	Bucky	555-5555	22	Y	A
johnson@bobcat.edu	Jeremy	Johnson	555-3333	15	Y	I
luce@ohio.edu	Thom	Luce	592-1111	12	N	I
mcgrath@bobcat.edu	Billie	McGrath	555-6666	3	N	B
wilson@bobcat.edu	Sally	Wilson	555-4444	6	N	B

SELECT fname
　　　　lname,
　　　　equip,
　　　　skill
From sky_member
where equip = 'Y'
and skill ='I'
or skill ='B'

email	fname	lname	phone	jumps	equip	skill
mcgann@ohio.edu	Sean	McGann	592-2222	20	Y	A
dayj@ohio.edu	John	Day	592-0646	5	Y	B
bucky@ohio.edu	Teri	Bucky	555-5555	22	Y	A
johnson@bobcat.edu	Jeremy	Johnson	555-3333	15	Y	I
luce@ohio.edu	Thom	Luce	592-1111	12	N	I
mcgrath@bobcat.edu	Billie	McGrath	555-6666	3	N	B
wilson@bobcat.edu	Sally	Wilson	555-4444	6	N	B

RESULT

fname	lname	equip	skill
John	Day	Y	B
Jeremy	Johnson	Y	I
Billie	McGrath	N	B
Sally	Wilson	N	B

Notice that the results are not what we want. We wanted to list only members who have their own equipment, and the last two rows in our results list members who don't meet this criterion. The reason these rows were included is because of the way SQL groups AND/OR operators: basically, rows that either meet both of the first two criteria (equip = 'Y' and skill = 'I') *or* meet the last criterion (skill = 'B').

Fortunately, there is an easy way to avoid this problem; simply use parentheses to explicitly show how you want the conditions grouped. The correct SQL Select statement is shown below.

Select	fname,
	lname,
	equip,
	skill
From	sky_member
Where	equip = 'Y'
	and (skill = 'I'
	or skill = 'B')

The correct design for this query is shown in Exhibit 9-32.

Exhibit 9-32

Correctly Combining AND and OR

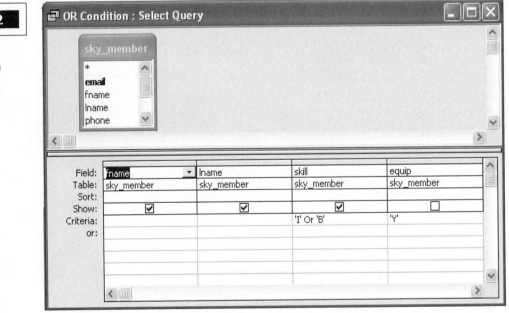

By using the OR operator, all the criteria can be placed on the same line, and the result will display only the rows for Day and Johnson, as shown in the analysis in Exhibit 9-33.

Exhibit 9-33   The Analysis of the Query Correctly Combining AND and OR

CORRECT QUERY FOR SKILL = B OR I AND EQUIP = Y

List the fname, lname, equip, and skill for beginning or intermediate members who own their own equipment.

SELECT fname
      lname,
      equip,
      skill
From sky_member
where equip = 'Y'
and (skill ='I'
or skill ='B');

email	fname	lname	phone	jumps	equip	skill
mcgann@ohio.edu	Sean	McGann	592-2222	20	Y	A
dayj@ohio.edu	John	Day	592-0646	5	Y	B
bucky@ohio.edu	Teri	Bucky	555-5555	22	Y	A
johnson@bobcat.edu	Jeremy	Johnson	555-3333	15	Y	I
luce@ohio.edu	Thom	Luce	592-1111	12	N	I
mcgrath@bobcat.edu	Billie	McGrath	555-6666	3	N	B
wilson@bobcat.edu	Sally	Wilson	555-4444	6	N	B

SELECT fname
      lname,
      jumps,
      skill
From sky_member
where equip = 'Y'
and (skill ='I'
or skill ='B');

email	fname	lname	phone	jumps	equip	skill
mcgann@ohio.edu	Sean	McGann	592-2222	20	Y	A
dayj@ohio.edu	John	Day	592-0646	5	Y	B
bucky@ohio.edu	Teri	Bucky	555-5555	22	Y	A
johnson@bobcat.edu	Jeremy	Johnson	555-3333	15	Y	I
luce@ohio.edu	Thom	Luce	592-1111	12	N	I
mcgrath@bobcat.edu	Billie	McGrath	555-6666	3	N	B
wilson@bobcat.edu	Sally	Wilson	555-4444	6	N	B

SELECT fname
      lname,
      jumps,
      skill
From sky_member
where equip = 'Y'
and (skill ='I'
or skill ='B');

email	fname	lname	phone	jumps	equip	skill
mcgann@ohio.edu	Sean	McGann	592-2222	20	Y	A
dayj@ohio.edu	John	Day	592-0646	5	Y	B
bucky@ohio.edu	Teri	Bucky	555-5555	22	Y	A
johnson@bobcat.edu	Jeremy	Johnson	555-3333	15	Y	I
luce@ohio.edu	Thom	Luce	592-1111	12	N	I
mcgrath@bobcat.edu	Billie	McGrath	555-6666	3	N	B
wilson@bobcat.edu	Sally	Wilson	555-4444	6	N	B

RESULT

fname	lname	equip	skill
John	Day	Y	B
Jeremy	Johnson	Y	I

From this analysis, you can now see that beginner and intermediate members who own equipment are selected. Note that another way to avoid this problem with this particular query is to use the IN operator, rather than the OR.

Aggregate Functions

Access includes many built-in functions. Some of these functions are called **aggregate functions** because they involve groups (aggregations) of rows rather than single rows. Aggregate functions provide summary values in the results list. Typically, the functions take the form:

Function [expression]

Usually, the expression is a column name, although other types of expressions are also valid. Exhibit 9-34 shows some of the more commonly used aggregate functions.

Exhibit 9-34

Commonly Used
Aggregate
Functions

Function	Purpose
Sum	Total of the values in the column for the selected rows
Avg	Arithmetic mean of the values in the column for the selected rows
Count	Number of values in the column for the selected rows
Count(*)	Number of selected rows (including those with nulls)
Max	Highest value in the column for the selected rows
Min	Lowest value in the column for the selected rows

The purpose of most of the functions is straightforward; they do what most people think they would do. For example, if you wanted to get the total number of jumps made by all members, you would use the query shown below.

Select   **Sum(jumps)**

From   **sky_member**

In Access, this query would be designed as shown in Exhibit 9-35.

Exhibit 9-35

A Query that
Sums the Number
of Jumps

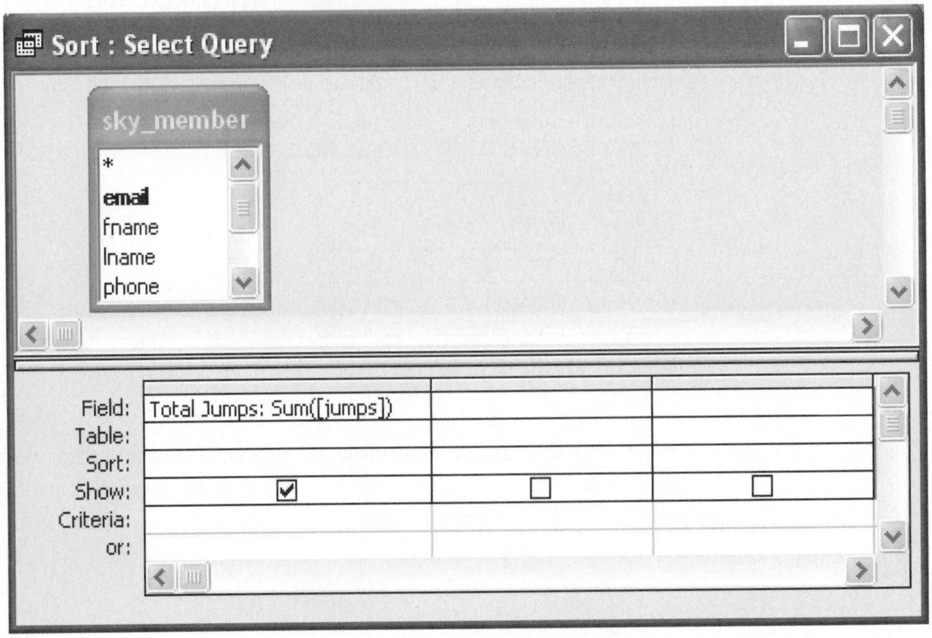

The result of this query is a single number. If the column list of a Select statement includes an aggregate function with no other columns, the result is a single number. We will discuss how to get subaggregations (for example, subtotals) later in this section. The analysis for this query is shown in Exhibit 9-36.

Exhibit 9-36   Analysis of the Query that Sums the Number of Jumps

SUM FUNCTION
List the total number of jumps for all members.

SELECT sum(jumps)
From sky_member;

The query involves only the jumps column.

email	fname	lname	phone	jumps	equip	skill
mcgann@ohio.edu	Sean	McGann	592-2222	20	Y	A
dayj@ohio.edu	John	Day	592-0646	5	Y	B
bucky@ohio.edu	Teri	Bucky	555-5555	22	Y	A
johnson@bobcat.edu	Jeremy	Johnson	555-3333	15	Y	I
luce@ohio.edu	Thom	Luce	592-1111	12	N	I
mcgrath@bobcat.edu	Billie	McGrath	555-6666	3	N	B
wilson@bobcat.edu	Sally	Wilson	555-4444	6	N	B

SELECT sum(jumps)
From sky_member;

email	fname	lname	phone	jumps	equip	skill
mcgann@ohio.edu	Sean	McGann	592-2222	20	Y	A
dayj@ohio.edu	John	Day	592-0646	5	Y	B
bucky@ohio.edu	Teri	Bucky	555-5555	22	Y	A
johnson@bobcat.edu	Jeremy	Johnson	555-3333	15	Y	I
luce@ohio.edu	Thom	Luce	592-1111	12	N	I
mcgrath@bobcat.edu	Billie	McGrath	555-6666	3	N	B
wilson@bobcat.edu	Sally	Wilson	555-4444	6	N	B
				sum( )		

RESULT

Total Jumps
83

In the result of this query, the single value is displayed in a small table, but the column will not be labeled *jumps* because to do so might lead the user to believe he or she is being shown the number of jumps for a particular user. If you look closely at the query design, you will notice that the actual entry for the field is:

Total Jumps: Sum(Jumps)

The label *total jumps* is placed in front of the expression to be used to label the column. This label is separated from the expression by a colon. This query design is implemented in the generated SQL statement using the column naming feature in SQL, by adding the keyword AS following a column name and entering the alternative name to be used when the column is displayed in the result. Thus, the SQL Select statement would become:

Select	Sum(jumps) AS Total Jumps
From	sky_member

This approach of creating a name for a column is useful with expressions but is not limited to this purpose. In fact, you can use this approach to rename any column in a query. Renaming is useful when the names used for columns in the database may be abbreviated, as in the case of the Sky_Member database. For example, the first name column has been called fname in the database, but in a query, a user might like to see this column labeled *first*. This result could be accomplished by simply creating a query and renaming the column as follows:

First: fname

The COUNT Function

The Count function has two variations. You can provide an expression, just as we did with the Sum example. But if the expression is a column name (which is common), and the column contains null (blank) values, you may not get the result you expect. Rows in which the expression column is null are not included in the count. For example, if you had a member for whom the jumps column was left blank, and you used *jumps* as the expression in a Count function, that row would not be counted. You can avoid this problem by using Count(*), as shown below.

Select	Count(*)
From	sky_member

The Count(*) function counts all rows, regardless of any null values.

Using Where with Aggregate Functions

You can also use an aggregate function in a Select statement that includes a where clause. Rows are selected according to the where clause condition(s) before the aggregate function is applied. For example, consider the SQL Select statement below.

Select	Sum(jumps)
From	sky_member
Where	equip = 'Y'

Compare the results in the previous Sum example to those generated by this query, as shown in the analysis in Exhibit 9-37.

Exhibit 9-37 Analysis of the Query that Uses Sum with Where

SUM FUNCTION WITH A WHERE
List the total number of jumps for all members with equipment.

SELECT sum(jumps)
From sky_member
Where equip = 'Y';

The query involves only the jumps column.

email	fname	lname	phone	jumps	equip	skill
mcgann@ohio.edu	Sean	McGann	592-2222	20	Y	A
dayj@ohio.edu	John	Day	592-0646	5	Y	B
bucky@ohio.edu	Teri	Bucky	555-5555	22	Y	A
johnson@bobcat.edu	Jeremy	Johnson	555-3333	15	Y	I
luce@ohio.edu	Thom	Luce	592-1111	12	N	I
mcgrath@bobcat.edu	Billie	McGrath	555-6666	3	N	B
wilson@bobcat.edu	Sally	Wilson	555-4444	6	N	B

SELECT sum(jumps)
From sky_member
Where equip = 'Y';

email	fname	lname	phone	jumps	equip	skill
mcgann@ohio.edu	Sean	McGann	592-2222	20	Y	A
dayj@ohio.edu	John	Day	592-0646	5	Y	B
bucky@ohio.edu	Teri	Bucky	555-5555	22	Y	A
johnson@bobcat.edu	Jeremy	Johnson	555-3333	15	Y	I
luce@ohio.edu	Thom	Luce	592-1111	12	N	I
mcgrath@bobcat.edu	Billie	McGrath	555-6666	3	N	B
wilson@bobcat.edu	Sally	Wilson	555-4444	6	N	B

SELECT sum(jumps)
From sky_member
Where equip = 'Y';

The query involves only the jumps column.

email	fname	lname	phone	jumps	equip	skill
mcgann@ohio.edu	Sean	McGann	592-2222	20	Y	A
dayj@ohio.edu	John	Day	592-0646	5	Y	B
bucky@ohio.edu	Teri	Bucky	555-5555	22	Y	A
johnson@bobcat.edu	Jeremy	Johnson	555-3333	15	Y	I
luce@ohio.edu	Thom	Luce	592-1111	12	N	I
mcgrath@bobcat.edu	Billie	McGrath	555-6666	3	N	B
wilson@bobcat.edu	Sally	Wilson	555-4444	6	N	B
				sum( )		

RESULT

Total Jumps
62

When you compare the results, you will notice that this query reports a lower total number of jumps. The reason is because only those rows where the value of the equip column is "Y" are included in the sum. Complex where clauses can be used in combination with aggregate functions.

Grouping Data in a Query

Now that you have a basic understanding of the options available in the Select statement, this section will look at some of the more advanced options.

Using DISTINCT

Sometimes you do not know how many rows are in a table or how many meet some criteria; what you want to know is how many *different* values are in a particular column of a table. For example, let's say that you want to know how many different skill levels are in the SKY_MEMBER table. You could use the following SQL Select statement:

Select   skill

From   sky_member

This statement would produce the result shown in Exhibit 9-38.

Exhibit 9-38

Selecting Skills

Without Distinct : Select Query

skill
A
B
I
I
A
B
B

Record: 8 of 8

The problem with this result is that you get a skill value for every row in the table, so particular skill values are repeated for each member with the same skill. If you just wanted a list of all possible skills without the duplication, you would use **distinct** to tell SQL that you want to display each value only once. The SQL Select statement to achieve this result would be:

Select   distinct skill

From   sky_member

The distinct option removes the duplicates, as shown in Exhibit 9-39.

Exhibit 9-39

Selecting Skills
Using Distinct

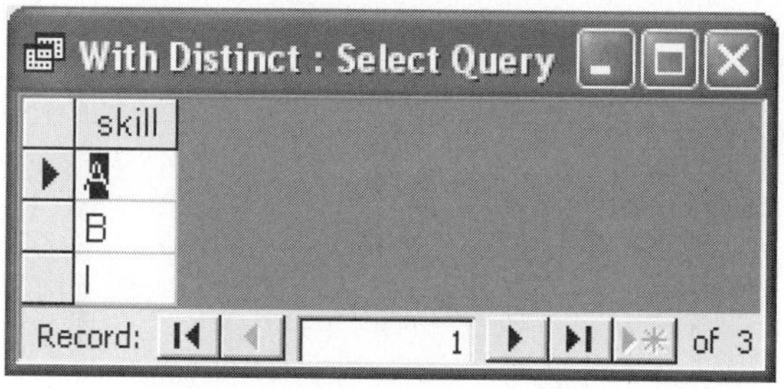

Grouping and Aggregate Functions

SQL also gives you the capability to use aggregate functions to compute subtotals (or subaggregations). In other words, your results can show the result of the function by groups of rows. For example, suppose you want to calculate the average number of jumps for each ability level. To perform this calculation, you need tell SQL how to group the results by the values in a particular column, as shown in the SQL Select statement below.

Select   skill,

            avg(jumps) AS 'AverageJumps'

From   sky_member

Group by   skill

Two aspects of this query are worth noting. First, we included the skill column in the column list, so we can tell which skill group each average goes with. Second, we added the last line, **Group by** Skill, to the query. This line tells SQL how you want to aggregate the rows when computing the average. The single column (or columns) in the column list must match the column(s) in the group by clause. Otherwise, the query produces an error. You will also get an error if you forget to add the group by clause. This is a common mistake. The error message produced is shown in Exhibit 9-40.

Exhibit 9-40

Error Message
Generated with
Incorrectly
Specifying
Grouping

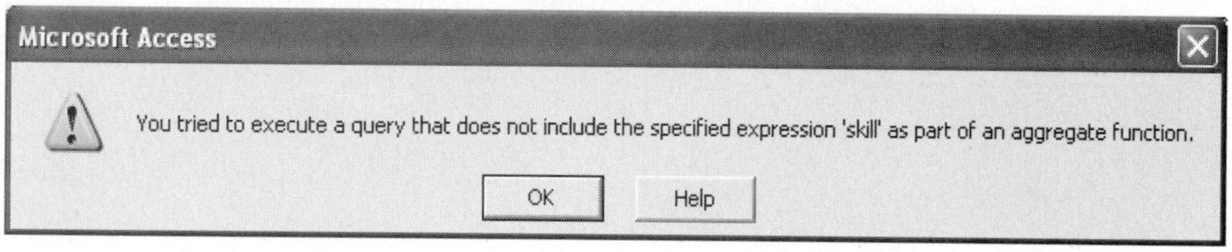

The design for this query is shown in Exhibit 9-41.

In this design, notice the third row in the panels where the grouping is specified on the skill column. This Total row can also be used to indicate aggregate functions. So now, instead of the Avg function being entered in the Field box, it can be entered in the Total box. As with other aggregation functions, the column is named by placing text in front of the column name and separating the two words by a colon. This extra Total row can be added to the design by using the Total option in the View menu. The analysis for the query is shown in Exhibit 9-42.

Exhibit 9-42   The Analysis for the Query Using Group By

GROUP BY

For each skill level, list the average number of jumps by members of that skill level.

SELECT skill,
avg(jumps) as 'AverageJumps'
From sky_member
Group by skill;

email	fname	lname	phone	jumps	equip	skill
mcgann@ohio.edu	Sean	McGann	592-2222	20	Y	A
dayj@ohio.edu	John	Day	592-0646	5	Y	B
bucky@ohio.edu	Teri	Bucky	555-5555	22	Y	A
johnson@bobcat.edu	Jeremy	Johnson	555-3333	15	Y	I
luce@ohio.edu	Thom	Luce	592-1111	12	N	I
mcgrath@bobcat.edu	Billie	McGrath	555-6666	3	N	B
wilson@bobcat.edu	Sally	Wilson	555-4444	6	N	B

SELECT skill,
avg(jumps) as 'AverageJumps'
From sky_member
Group by skill;

email	fname	lname	phone	jumps	equip	skill
mcgann@ohio.edu	Sean	McGann	592-2222	20	Y	A
bucky@ohio.edu	Teri	Bucky	555-5555	22	Y	A
dayj@ohio.edu	John	Day	592-0646	5	Y	B
mcgrath@bobcat.edu	Billie	McGrath	555-6666	3	N	B
wilson@bobcat.edu	Sally	Wilson	555-4444	6	N	B
johnson@bobcat.edu	Jeremy	Johnson	555-3333	15	Y	I
luce@ohio.edu	Thom	Luce	592-1111	12	N	I

SELECT skill,
avg(jumps) as 'AverageJumps'
From sky_member
Group by skill;

email	fname	lname	phone	jumps	equip	skill
mcgann@ohio.edu	Sean	McGann	592-2222	20	Y	A
bucky@ohio.edu	Teri	Bucky	555-5555	22	Y	A
			Avg	21		
dayj@ohio.edu	John	Day	592-0646	5	Y	B
mcgrath@bobcat.edu	Billie	McGrath	555-6666	3	N	B
wilson@bobcat.edu	Sally	Wilson	555-4444	6	N	B
			Avg	4.67		
johnson@bobcat.edu	Jeremy	Johnson	555-3333	15	Y	I
luce@ohio.edu	Thom	Luce	592-1111	12	N	I
			Avg	13.5		

RESULT

Skill	AverageJumps
A	21
B	4.67
I	13.5

From this analysis, you can see that the data is grouped into three groups by skill level. Then for each group, the code for that group is displayed, along with the average of the values in the jump column for all the rows in the group.

Limiting Groups with the Having Clause

Recall that the where clause is used to limit the rows that are included in the results of a query. The **having clause** has a similar purpose, but for aggregations, rather than for single rows. For example, suppose that you want to see a list of any skill groups that have an average number of jumps fewer than 20. Using the proper having clause limits the results to only these groups, as shown in the SQL Select statement below.

Select	skill,
	avg(jumps) AS 'AverageJumps'
From	sky_member
Group by	skill
Having	avg(jumps) < 20

Notice the having clause we added following the group by clause. The having clause is very similar to where in that both use conditional statements to limit results. However, having limits results based on aggregate functions, and where limits results according to single row values. A having clause *always* has an aggregate function as part of its conditional statement. Another thing to remember is that, typically, you need to include a group by clause whenever you include a having clause in a query. The opposite is not true; you can have group by without having.

Entering the having clause in the query design is actually fairly simple. You just enter the criterion in the Criteria row under the aggregate column. When a condition is entered under an aggregate column in the query design, Access automatically assumes that the condition is part of a having clause as opposed to a where clause. Exhibit 9-43 shows the design for this query.

Exhibit 9-43

The Design for the Query Using Having

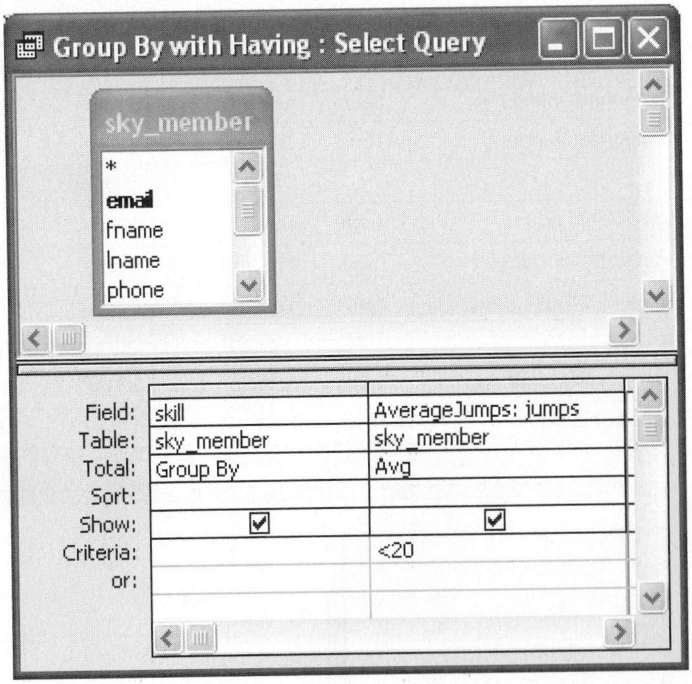

To understand how the having clause works, look at the analysis shown in Exhibit 9-44.

Exhibit 9-44   The Analysis for the Query Using Having

GROUP BY WITH HAVING

List the average number of jumps by members of each skill level having an average number of jumps that is fewer than 20.

SELECT skill,
avg(jumps) as 'AverageJumps'
From sky_member
Group by skill
Having avg(jumps)<20;

email	fname	lname	phone	jumps	equip	skill
mcgann@ohio.edu	Sean	McGann	592-2222	20	Y	A
bucky@ohio.edu	Teri	Bucky	555-5555	22	Y	A
dayj@ohio.edu	John	Day	592-0646	5	Y	B
mcgrath@bobcat.edu	Billie	McGrath	555-6666	3	N	B
wilson@bobcat.edu	Sally	Wilson	555-4444	6	N	B
johnson@bobcat.edu	Jeremy	Johnson	555-3333	15	Y	I
luce@ohio.edu	Thom	Luce	592-1111	12	N	I

SELECT skill,
avg(jumps) as 'AverageJumps'
From sky_member
Group by skill
Having avg(jumps)<20;

email	fname	lname	phone	jumps	equip	skill
mcgann@ohio.edu	Sean	McGann	592-2222	20	Y	A
bucky@ohio.edu	Teri	Bucky	555-5555	22	Y	A
			Avg	21		
dayj@ohio.edu	John	Day	592-0646	5	Y	B
mcgrath@bobcat.edu	Billie	McGrath	555-6666	3	N	B
wilson@bobcat.edu	Sally	Wilson	555-4444	6	N	B
			Avg	4.67		
johnson@bobcat.edu	Jeremy	Johnson	555-3333	15	Y	I
luce@ohio.edu	Thom	Luce	592-1111	12	N	I
			Avg	13.5		

SELECT skill,
avg(jumps) as 'AverageJumps'
From sky_member
Group by skill
Having avg(jumps)<20;

email	fname	lname	phone	jumps	equip	skill
mcgann@ohio.edu	Sean	McGann	592-2222	20	Y	A
bucky@ohio.edu	Teri	Bucky	555-5555	22	Y	A
			Avg	21		
dayj@ohio.edu	John	Day	592-0646	5	Y	B
mcgrath@bobcat.edu	Billie	McGrath	555-6666	3	N	B
wilson@bobcat.edu	Sally	Wilson	555-4444	6	N	B
			Avg	4.67		
johnson@bobcat.edu	Jeremy	Johnson	555-3333	15	Y	I
luce@ohio.edu	Thom	Luce	592-1111	12	N	I
			Avg	13.5		

RESULT

Skill	AverageJumps
B	4.67
I	13.5

As you can see from this analysis, the rows are grouped and the aggregate function is computed. Once the aggregate function is computed for each group, the condition in the having clause is applied to those results to determine if that group should be displayed. In this case, the average for skill group A does not meet the condition, so that group does not appear in the final result.

Combining Having and Where

It is possible to use both having and where in the same query. When you do, SQL applies the where condition(s) to select rows, then it computes the aggregate function based on the rows that meet the condition(s) specified in the where clause. An example will help you understand. Suppose that you want to see the average number of jumps for skill groups whose members average more than 10 jumps. But you want to count only members who have their own equipment; members who do *not* have their own equipment should not be included when the average is calculated. The SQL Select statement for this process is shown below.

Select	skill,
	avg(jumps) AS 'AverageJumps'
From	sky_member
Where	equip = 'Y'
Group by	skill
Having	avg(jumps) > 10

The results of this query are shown in Exhibit 9-45.

Exhibit 9-45

The Results for
the Query Using
Having and Where

Group By with Having and Where : Select Query

skill	AverageJumps
A	21
I	15

Record: I◀ ◀ [1] ▶ ▶I ▶* of 2

As you can see, the results are quite different from the previous query without the where clause. Not only is the beginner skill group (B) average replaced with that of the advanced group (A), but the average for both groups is different. This result is because only rows that have "Y" as the value of the equip column are included when computing the averages. To help you understand this concept, let's take a look at the analysis of the query provided in Exhibit 9-46.

Exhibit 9-46   The Analysis for the Query Using Having and Where

GROUP BY WITH HAVING AND WHERE

List the average number of jumps by members who own equipment in skill levels with an average number of jumps that is greater than 10.

SELECT skill,
avg(jumps) as 'AverageJumps'
From sky_member
Where equip='Y'
Group by skill
Having avg(jumps)<10;

email	fname	lname	phone	jumps	equip	skill
mcgann@ohio.edu	Sean	McGann	592-2222	20	Y	A
dayj@ohio.edu	John	Day	592-0646	5	Y	B
bucky@ohio.edu	Teri	Bucky	555-5555	22	Y	A
johnson@bobcat.edu	Jeremy	Johnson	555-3333	15	Y	I
luce@ohio.edu	Thom	Luce	592-1111	12	N	I
mcgrath@bobcat.edu	Billie	McGrath	555-6666	3	N	B
wilson@bobcat.edu	Sally	Wilson	555-4444	6	N	B

Select skill,
avg(jumps) as 'AverageJumps'
From sky_member
Where equip='Y'
Group by skill
Having avg(jumps)<10;

The Where eliminates some rows from being included in the groups.

email	fname	lname	phone	jumps	equip	skill
mcgann@ohio.edu	Sean	McGann	592-2222	20	Y	A
bucky@ohio.edu	Teri	Bucky	555-5555	22	Y	A
			Avg	21		
dayj@ohio.edu	John	Day	592-0646	5	Y	B
~~mcgrath@bobcat.edu~~	~~Billie~~	~~McGrath~~	~~555-6666~~	~~3~~	~~N~~	~~B~~
~~wilson@bobcat.edu~~	~~Sally~~	~~Wilson~~	~~555-4444~~	~~6~~	~~N~~	~~B~~
			Avg	5		
johnson@bobcat.edu	Jeremy	Johnson	555-3333	15	Y	I
~~luce@ohio.edu~~	~~Thom~~	~~Luce~~	~~592-1111~~	~~12~~	~~N~~	~~I~~
			Avg	15		

SELECT skill,
avg(jumps) as 'AverageJumps'
From sky_member
Where equip='Y'
Group by skill
Having avg(jumps)<10;

email	fname	lname	phone	jumps	equip	skill
mcgann@ohio.edu	Sean	McGann	592-2222	20	Y	A
bucky@ohio.edu	Teri	Bucky	555-5555	22	Y	A
			Avg	21		
dayj@ohio.edu	John	Day	592-0646	5	Y	B
~~mcgrath@bobcat.edu~~	~~Billie~~	~~McGrath~~	~~555-6666~~	~~3~~	~~N~~	~~B~~
~~wilson@bobcat.edu~~	~~Sally~~	~~Wilson~~	~~555-4444~~	~~6~~	~~N~~	~~B~~
			Avg	5		
johnson@bobcat.edu	Jeremy	Johnson	555-3333	15	Y	I
~~luce@ohio.edu~~	~~Thom~~	~~Luce~~	~~592-1111~~	~~12~~	~~N~~	~~I~~
			Avg	15		

RESULT

Skill	AverageJumps
A	21
I	15

The rows that do not satisfy the where condition have a line drawn through them. Then the rows are grouped and the average for the group is computed without using the rows that are crossed out. Then the having condition is applied to these new averages, and the advanced and intermediate groups are selected to be included in the result. The having condition eliminates the beginner group, because its average of 5 is not above 10. Although our example includes only a single condition for the where clause, more complex where clauses with multiple conditions can also be used.

Combining Data from Different Tables

All of the queries we have looked at so far have involved data from a single table. However, meeting some data retrieval requirements requires getting data from multiple tables. Fortunately, SQL gives us a way to perform such data retrievals. Recall that relational databases use matching primary and foreign key values to relate a row in one table to a row in a related table. Understanding this idea is the key to understanding how to retrieve data from multiple tables. Combining data from different tables into a single result set is called performing a join. More specifically, the joins we discuss in this section are called **equi-joins** (or **inner joins**), because they are based on equality between primary and foreign key values. There are other types of joins, but equi-joins are by far the most commonly used.

Because the Sky_Member database we have been using so far has only one table, we need to use another, more complex database to demonstrate how to perform joins. So we will use the Enrollment database, which has five tables. The data model for the Enrollment database is shown in Exhibit 9-47.

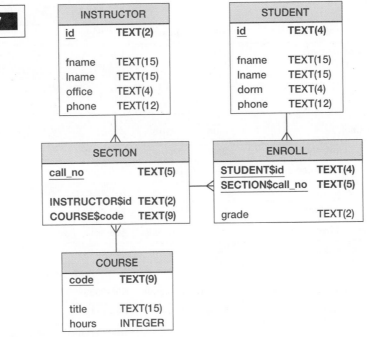

Exhibit 9-47

Enrollment Database Data Model

For our first example, we want to list the call number (call_no), course code, course title, and number of hours for each section. Producing this list requires retrieving data from two tables, SECTION and COURSE. These two tables are connected through the foreign key COURSE$code in the SECTION table, which refers to the primary key *code* in the COURSE table. To perform a join, we specify a where clause whose condition is that the value of the foreign key (COURSE$code) equals the value of the primary key in the related table (code). We also need to include all tables used in the query in the from clause. The SQL Select statement would then be:

Select	call_no,
	code,
	title,
	hours
From	section, course
Where	COURSE$code = code

In Access, the construction of a multitable query is very simple. When the query is created in design mode, you simply add both tables to the design, and Access automatically links the two tables together across the duplicated key. This link is displayed in the graphic model for the query, as shown in Exhibit 9-48.

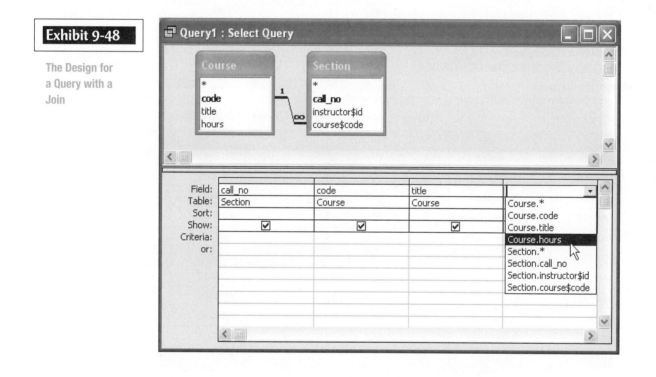

Exhibit 9-48

The Design for a Query with a Join

When multiple tables are included in the query, the drop-down list includes columns from both tables, as shown in the last panel of the query design. When a particular column is selected, the table containing that column is automatically put in for the table. To better understand how joins work, let's work through the join operation manually. The following discussion describes how joins work conceptually. The actual mechanics followed by Access to carry out joins may differ, depending on a number of conditions. Regardless, following the conceptual discussion will help you better understand how to perform joins in SQL.

When a query includes more than one table in the from clause, the first step in evaluating the query is to create a **Cartesian product.** This process involves simply making a temporary table that combines all rows in one table with all rows in another table, as shown in Exhibit 9-49.

Exhibit 9-49   Cartesian Product of Course and Section

Original Tables

COURSE

code	title	hours
MIS380	Database I	4
MIS225	Visual Basic	4
MIS420	Systems II	4

SECTION

call_no	INSTRUCTOR$id	COURSE$code
001	11	MIS380
002	33	MIS380
003	11	MIS225
004	44	MIS420

Cartesian Product

code	title	hours	call_no	INSTRUCTOR$id	COURSE$code
MIS380	Database I	4	001	11	MIS380
MIS380	Database I	4	002	33	MIS380
~~MIS380~~	~~Database I~~	4	~~003~~	~~11~~	~~MIS225~~
~~MIS380~~	~~Database I~~	4	~~004~~	~~44~~	~~MIS420~~
~~MIS225~~	~~Visual Basic~~	4	~~001~~	~~11~~	~~MIS380~~
~~MIS225~~	~~Visual Basic~~	4	~~002~~	~~33~~	~~MIS380~~
MIS225	Visual Basic	4	003	11	MIS225
MIS225	Visual Basic	4	004	44	MIS420
~~MIS420~~	~~Systems II~~	4	~~001~~	~~11~~	~~MIS380~~
~~MIS420~~	~~Systems II~~	4	~~002~~	~~33~~	~~MIS380~~
~~MIS420~~	~~Systems II~~	4	~~003~~	~~11~~	~~MIS225~~
MIS420	Systems II	4	004	44	MIS420

The original tables are shown at the top. The Cartesian product is created by combining each row of the COURSE table with each row of the SECTION table. Multiplying the number of rows in the two tables (3 * 4 in this case) gives us the number of rows in the product (12). The highlighted rows in the product represent rows that satisfy the join condition in the where clause. The rows that do not meet the condition are crossed out.

Count the number of rows that satisfy the condition. Of the 12 rows in the product, only four rows meet the join condition. It is no coincidence that this number matches the number of rows in the SECTION table. When performing joins, you should never have more rows in your result than you have in the largest table involved in the query. In this case, SECTION has the largest number of rows (four), so that is the maximum number of rows we should get in our two-table query. Of course, other conditions could reduce the number of rows in the result. We will look at an example of this situation later. Exhibit 9-50 shows the results of the query.

Exhibit 9-50

The Results of the Join

Join Section and Course : Select Query

call_no	code	title	hours
003	MIS225	Visual Basic	4
001	MIS380	Database I	4
002	MIS380	Database I	4
004	MIS420	Systems II	4

Record: 1 of 4

In Access, the actual syntax for the SQL generated by this query is slightly different from the SQL Select statement shown above. Instead of a where clause, an inner join clause is used in the from clause in which the condition is specified. The actual syntax is:

```
Select    call_no,
          code,
          title,
          hours
From      course Inner Join section
On        code = COURSE$code
```

Other SQL databases may not have the inner join syntax and require the use of the where clause. Regardless of which syntax is used, the critical aspect is the specification of the condition that is used to match rows between the two tables. To further illustrate how joins work let's examine the consequences of *not* including the join condition. The SQL statement below includes two tables, but it does not have a join condition.

```
Select    call_no,
          code,
          title,
          hours
From      section, course
```

The results of this incorrect SQL Select statement are shown in Exhibit 9-51.

Exhibit 9-51

Results from the
Incorrect Join

Join Without the Where : Select Query

call_no	code	title	hours
001	MIS380	Database I	4
001	MIS225	Visual Basic	4
001	MIS420	Systems II	4
002	MIS380	Database I	4
002	MIS225	Visual Basic	4
002	MIS420	Systems II	4
003	MIS380	Database I	4
003	MIS225	Visual Basic	4
003	MIS420	Systems II	4
004	MIS380	Database I	4
004	MIS225	Visual Basic	4
004	MIS420	Systems II	4

Record: I◄ ◄ [1] ► ►I ►* of 12

When you examine the results, you might notice that the results closely resemble the Cartesian product. The only difference is that the query result does not include all columns from both tables. However, there are twelve rows in the results, just as there are twelve rows in the Cartesian product.

When performing multitable queries, it is useful to check the number of rows against the maximum expected. If you have too many rows in your query results, you are missing a join. The results of such an omission are sometimes quite spectacular. For example, if you have two 1,000-row tables in a query and you forget the join condition, the query result will have one million rows!

Combining Joins with Other Where Conditions

When other where conditions are combined with join conditions, it is useful to put the join conditions first, followed by whatever other conditions are required. This is not a rule, but it is helpful in reading and debugging multitable queries. Let's examine an example of adding another condition to a join. The SQL Select statement below produces a list of sections for MIS380.

Select	call_no,
	code,
	title,
	hours
From	section, course
Where	COURSE$code = code
And	code = 'MIS380'

To follow the logic of this query, consider the query analysis shown in Exhibit 9-52.

Exhibit 9-52	**TWO-TABLE JOIN WITH ADDITIONAL CONDITION**
Analysis of a Query with a Join Combined with a Where Condition	List the instructor's fname, lname, and course title for MIS380.

SELECT call_no,
           code,
           title,
           hours
From   section, course
Where   code = 'MIS380'
  And   COURSE$code = code;

COURSE

code	title	hours
MIS380	Database I	4
MIS225	Visual Basic	4
MIS420	Systems II	4

SECTION

call_no	INSTRUCTOR$id	COURSE$code
001	11	MIS380
002	33	MIS380
003	11	MIS225
004	44	MIS420

SELECT call_no,
           code,
           title,
           hours
From   section, course
Where   code = 'MIS380'
  And   COURSE$code = code;

COURSE

code	title	hours
MIS380	Database I	4
MIS225	Visual Basic	4
MIS420	Systems II	4

SECTION

call_no	INSTRUCTOR$id	COURSE$code
001	11	MIS380
002	33	MIS380
003	11	MIS225
004	44	MIS420

RESULT

call_no	code	title	hours
001	MIS380	Database I	4
002	MIS380	Database I	4

In this case, the rows in the COURSE table are limited to MIS380, so this is the only row that will be joined to the rows in the SECTION table. Because there are two rows in the SECTION table involving MIS380, the number of rows in the result is two.

There is no practical limit to the number or type of conditions that can be included with a join. When all of your conditions are combined with AND rather than OR, the queries are typically not difficult to construct (once you understand SQL!). However, combining a join with other conditions separated by OR can be problematic for the same reasons there are problems with combining OR and AND. When combining a join condition with another condition involving an OR in a single where clause, you should use parentheses to prevent the join from being combined with only part of the condition, as shown below.

Select	call_no,
	code,
	title,
	hours
From	section, course
Where	COURSE$code = code
And	(code = 'MIS380'
Or	code = 'MIS420')

In Access, if you use the query designer and allow the SQL to be generated by Access, this situation will not be a problem; the join will be handled with the inner join clause, which will be separate from the where clause, as shown in Exhibit 9-53.

Exhibit 9-53

SQL Generated by Access Combining a Join with an OR Condition

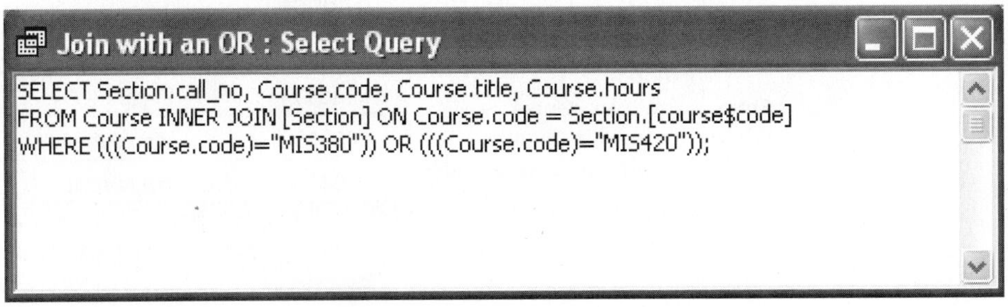

Join with an OR : Select Query

```
SELECT Section.call_no, Course.code, Course.title, Course.hours
FROM Course INNER JOIN [Section] ON Course.code = Section.[course$code]
WHERE (((Course.code)="MIS380")) OR (((Course.code)="MIS420"));
```

Joining More than Two Tables

Sometimes producing the results you want requires data from more than two tables. Fortunately, writing queries that can produce such results is just an extension of what we did for two-table queries. All you have to do is add another condition for each join you want to perform. For example, suppose you wanted a grade list for each section. The list must include the section's call number, the student's id, first name, last name, and the grade; the list should be in order of the call number, then last name, then first name. The first step in writing this query is to understand which tables contain the required data. The Enrollment database data model is provided in Exhibit 9-54. A box is drawn around the required tables.

Exhibit 9-54

Tables Required
for the Grade
Query

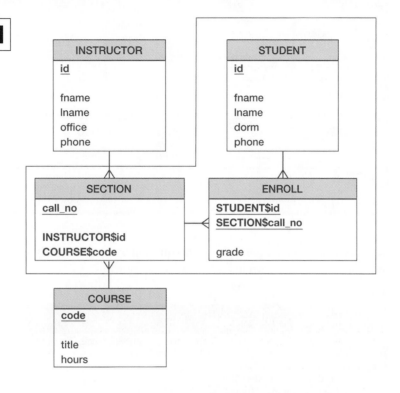

As you can see, we need data from three tables. Combining data from these three tables requires two joins, one joining SECTION and ENROLL and one joining ENROLL and STUDENT. This requirement illustrates an important point. When combining data from multiple tables, *you must have one fewer joins than the number of tables used in the query*. This is an important rule to remember. You can do a quick check of your multitable queries to see if you have the right number of joins. Just count the number of tables in your from clause, subtract one, and that is how many join conditions you must have. The SQL Select statement to produce the grade results is shown below.

```
Select      call_no,

            id,

            fname,

            lname,

            grade
From        section, enroll, student
Where       call_no = SECTION$call_no
And         id = STUDENT$id
Order by    call_no, lname, fname
```

With the query designer in Access, you simply add the tables to the design and select the columns, as shown in Exhibit 9-55.

When Access generates the SQL for this query, it will automatically set up the joins using the inner join clause, as shown in Exhibit 9-56.

```
SELECT Section.call_no, Student.id, Student.fname, Student.lname, Enroll.grade
FROM Student INNER JOIN ([Section] INNER JOIN Enroll
ON Section.call_no = Enroll.[section$call_no])
ON Student.id = Enroll.[student$id]
ORDER BY Section.call_no, Student.fname, Student.lname;
```

As with the where clause, notice that in this query involving three tables, there are two conditions to accomplish the joins.

Adding data from more tables is just more of the same; simply add a join condition for each table added to the from clause. To illustrate this idea, suppose we want to add the instructor's full name, the course code, and the course title to our grade report. This query includes data from all five tables in the database, which means that we need four joins (5 − 1):

- INSTRUCTOR to SECTION
- SECTION to COURSE
- SECTION to ENROLL
- ENROLL to STUDENT

Based on what we have discussed so far, you might try the query shown below.

Select	**call_no,**
	id,
	fname,
	lname,
	grade
From	**instructor, course,**
	section, enroll, student
Where	**id = INSTRUCTOR$id**
And	**code = COURSE$code**
And	**call_no = SECTION$call_no**
And	**id = STUDENT$id**
Order by	**call_no, lname, fname**

Using this SQL statement would generate an error message telling us that Access cannot tell what we mean when we include id in the query. Why is this error happening? The problem results because more than one table in the from clause has a column called *id*, which is included in both the INSTRUCTOR and STUDENT tables. This is known as an *ambiguous column name*. Correcting this problem is rather easy. All you have to do is precede the column name with the table name. The table and column names are separated by a period, as in INSTRUCTOR.id or STUDENT.id. Actually, many people like to put the table name in front of all column names. As you have probably noticed in earlier examples, when you use the query designer to generate the SQL, Access automatically puts the table name in front of all column names.

Thus, if you enter the SQL yourself, you will need to be aware of this requirement to ensure that no columns are ambiguously defined, as shown below.

Select	**call_no,**
	STUDENT.id,
	fname,
	lname,
	grade
From	**instructor, course,**
	section, enroll, student
Where	**INSTRUCTOR.id = INSTRUCTOR$id**
And	**code = COURSE$code**
And	**call_no = SECTION$call_no**
And	**STUDENT.id = STUDENT$id**
Order by	**call_no, lname, fname**

Subqueries

Subqueries are queries contained inside other queries. Problems such as comparing an average value with a group of records can best be solved using a subquery. The **inner subquery** always executes first, and then the results of the inner query are compared with the **outer query.** This is a key to understanding subqueries. Think of the results of the inner query as being fed to the outer query.

To illustrate, we will use the Sky_Member database. Suppose you want to produce a list of all members who have more than the average number of jumps. If you were producing this list manually, the first thing you would do is compute the average. Then you would compare the number of jumps for each member to the average, and write down the information for each member who has more than the average number of jumps. We could do the same thing using two SQL queries. The first one would calculate the average. Then we could take that average and put it into a where clause that selected members with jumps greater than that average. This process would work initially, but as time goes on, members would make more jumps, and the average would change. When this change happens, the query that retrieved members with jumps higher than the average would no longer work. Because SQL can be used to determine the average number of jumps, there should be a way to write a query that determines the average and then selects members whose numbers of jumps exceed that average. This process can be done using the SQL Select statement containing a subquery, as follows:

```
Select      fname,
            lname,
From        sky_member
Where       jumps >
            (Select      avg(jumps)
            From         sky_member)
```

Here, a subquery is used to combine the two queries into a single query. The inner query, which is enclosed in parentheses, calculates the average number of jumps for all members. The result of this inner query is then used as part of the where clause in the outer query that retrieves the members who have jumps greater than the average. The query design for this query is shown in Exhibit 9-57.

Exhibit 9-57

The Design for
the Subquery

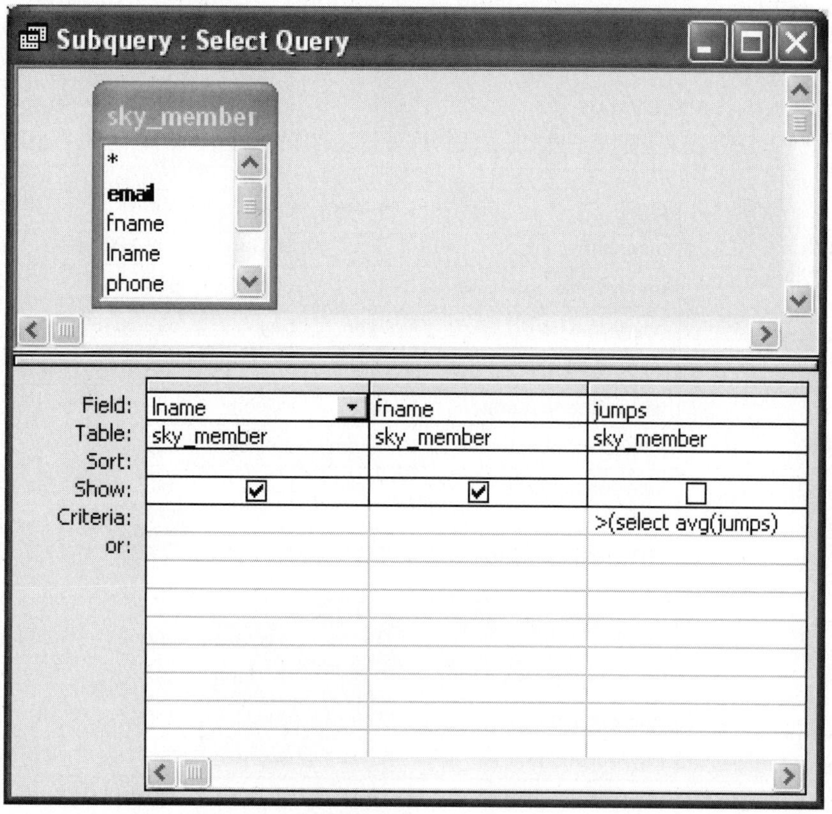

In this design, the where clause is entered under the jumps column as a Select statement. To understand how this query works, consider the analysis shown in Exhibit 9-58.

Exhibit 9-58   The Analysis for the Subquery Returning One Value

SUBQUERY RETURNING A SINGLE VALUE
Show the email address, number of jumps, and skill for all members with more than the average number of jumps.

SELECT fname,
       lname
From sky_member
where jumps >
  (Select avg(jumps)
   From sky_member);

email	fname	lname	phone	jumps	equip	skill
mcgann@ohio.edu	Sean	McGann	592-2222	20	Y	A
bucky@ohio.edu	Teri	Bucky	555-5555	22	Y	A
dayj@ohio.edu	John	Day	592-0646	5	Y	B
mcgrath@bobcat.edu	Billie	McGrath	555-6666	3	N	B
wilson@bobcat.edu	Sally	Wilson	555-4444	6	N	B
johnson@bobcat.edu	Jeremy	Johnson	555-3333	15	Y	I
luce@ohio.edu	Thom	Luce	592-1111	12	N	I
			Avg	11		

SELECT fname,
       lname
From sky_member
where jumps >
  (Select avg(jumps)
   From sky_member);

email	fname	lname	phone	jumps	equip	skill
mcgann@ohio.edu	Sean	McGann	592-2222	20	Y	A
bucky@ohio.edu	Teri	Bucky	555-5555	22	Y	A
dayj@ohio.edu	John	Day	592-0646	5	Y	B
mcgrath@bobcat.edu	Billie	McGrath	555-6666	3	N	B
wilson@bobcat.edu	Sally	Wilson	555-4444	6	N	B
johnson@bobcat.edu	Jeremy	Johnson	555-3333	15	Y	I
luce@ohio.edu	Thom	Luce	592-1111	12	N	I

SELECT fname,
       lname
From sky_member
where jumps >
  (Select avg(jumps)
   From sky_member);

email	fname	lname	phone	jumps	equip	skill
mcgann@ohio.edu	Sean	McGann	592-2222	20	Y	A
bucky@ohio.edu	Teri	Bucky	555-5555	22	Y	A
dayj@ohio.edu	John	Day	592-0646	5	Y	B
mcgrath@bobcat.edu	Billie	McGrath	555-6666	3	N	B
wilson@bobcat.edu	Sally	Wilson	555-4444	6	N	B
johnson@bobcat.edu	Jeremy	Johnson	555-3333	15	Y	I
luce@ohio.edu	Thom	Luce	592-1111	12	N	I
			Avg	11		

RESULT

fname	lname
Sean	McGann
Teri	Bucky
Jeremy	Johnson
Thom	Luce

When constructing a subquery, you should try running the inner query by itself to get a feel for what is going on. If the inner query returns a single value (e.g., select Avg(*x*)), use arithmetic operators (=, <, >, <>, >=, <=) for the comparison in the where clause. If the inner query returns multiple values (e.g., select *x*), use IN or NOT IN for the comparison in the where clause. Other operators can also be used, but many problems can be solved by using IN and NOT IN. Some examples that return more than one value will help you understand subqueries.

In the Enrollment database, suppose you want to list the id, first name, and last name of all students who are *not* enrolled in a course. Recall that we can use the NOT IN comparison operator to choose rows that do *not* match a list of values. By using NOT IN with a subquery, you can easily produce the desired list, as shown below.

Select	id,
	fname,
	lname
From	student
Where	id Not In
	(Select distinct STUDENT$id
	From enroll)

The inner query produces a list of student id values from the ENROLL table. This is a list of all students who *are* enrolled in at least one course. The word *distinct* tells SQL not to repeat any id values, because particular student ids will appear multiple times in the ENROLL table (once for every course in which each student is enrolled). The result of the inner query is used as the value list for the NOT IN function. In the outer query, the requested columns are shown for all rows in STUDENT that do not match one of the values in the NOT IN value list. The design for this query is shown in Exhibit 9-59.

Exhibit 9-59

The Design for the Subquery Returning Multiple Values

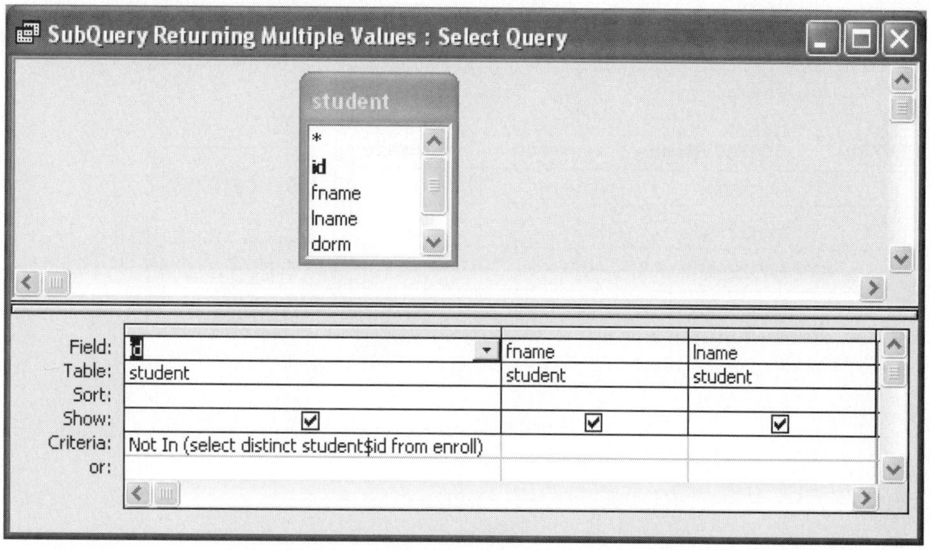

To understand how this subquery works, consider the analysis for this query shown in Exhibit 9-60.

Exhibit 9-60 The Analysis for the Subquery Returning Multiple Values

SUBQUERY RETURNING MULTIPLE VALUES

List the id, fname, and lname for all students *not* enrolled in any course.

```
SELECT    id, fname, lname
From      student
Where     id not in
          (
          Select distinct STUDENT$id
          from enroll
          );
```

STUDENT

id	fname	lname	dorm	phone
1111	Jim	Green	450A	593-2456
2222	Steve	Black	326B	593-4623
3333	Linda	Brown	144A	593-5575
4444	Emma	White	133B	593-4676

ENROLL

STUDENT$id	COURSE$code	semester	grade
1111	MIS380A01	F01	A
2222	MIS225A02	F02	B
3333	MIS225A02	F02	A
1111	MIS420A01	S02	C

STUDENT$id
1111
2222
3333

The subquery result eliminates duplicate student$ids from the Enroll table.

```
SELECT    id, fname, lname
From      student
Where     id not in
          (
          Select distinct STUDENT$id
          from enroll
          );
```

STUDENT

id	fname	lname	dorm	phone
1111	Jim	Green	450A	593-2456
2222	Steve	Black	326B	593-4623
3333	Linda	Brown	144A	593-5575
4444	Emma	White	133B	593-4676

ENROLL

STUDENT$id	COURSE$code	semester	grade
1111	MIS380A01	F01	A
2222	MIS225A02	F02	B
3333	MIS225A02	F02	A
1111	MIS420A01	S02	C

STUDENT$id
1111
2222
3333

Exhibit 9-60 Continued

```
SELECT   id, fname, lname
From     student
Where    id not in
         (
         Select distinct STUDENT$id
         from enroll
         );
```

STUDENT

id	fname	lname	dorm	phone
1111	Jim	Green	450A	593-2456
2222	Steve	Black	326B	593-4623
3333	Linda	Brown	144A	593-5575
4444	Emma	White	133B	593-4676

ENROLL

STUDENT$id	COURSE$code	semester	grade
1111	MIS380A01	F01	A
2222	MIS225A02	F02	B
3333	MIS225A02	F02	A
1111	MIS420A01	S02	C

STUDENT$id
1111
2222
3333

Emma White is the only student in the student list who does not have a matching record in the subquery list.

RESULT

id	fname	lname
4444	Emma	White

SUMMARY

- Three basic retrieval operations for relational databases are selection, projection, and joining.
- These operations are implemented in SQL through the Select statement.
- Each Select statement must have, at a minimum, the word *Select*, a column list, the word *From*, and a table list.
- Using the asterisk (*) as the column list indicates that all columns in the table(s) should be included in the query results.
- The column list may also include an explicit list of column names.
- The order by clause is used to determine the order in which rows appear in the query results.
- The where clause is used to limit the rows included in the query results.
- Each where clause must include one or more conditions.
- Multiple conditions in a where clause are separated by AND and/or OR.
- SQL has a number of aggregate functions, including Count, Sum, and Avg (average), among others.
- The word *distinct* is used to limit results to eliminate duplicate values in query results.
- Group by is used to create subaggregations in query results.
- The having clause specifies one or more conditions involving aggregate functions.
- Data from multiple tables is combined by specifying one or more equality conditions in a where clause. Each of these *join* conditions involves a primary key being equal to a corresponding foreign key.

■ A query should typically have one fewer join conditions than the number of tables included in the from clause.

■ Join conditions can be combined with other conditions.

■ One or more subqueries may be nested within another query.

KEY TERMS

AND logical operator. Operator used in a where clause that allows you to combine two conditions where rows must meet both conditions to be selected.

Aggregate functions. Built-in functions (Sum, Avg, etc.) that can be calculated for groups (aggregations) of rows rather than single rows.

Between operator. Lets you choose rows based on a range of values.

Cartesian product. A temporary table that combines all rows in one table with all rows in another table.

Design view. Interface in Access where you can visually construct the design for a query rather than writing an SQL statement.

Distinct. Option that tells SQL that you want to display each value only once.

Equi-join (or inner joins). Matching rows between tables based on equality between primary and foreign key values.

Group by. Clause that groups rows based on values in a column.

Having clause. Used to select particular groups (aggregations) rather than single rows based on a condition.

IN operator. Allows you to select rows based on multiple values for a particular column. Similar to a series of OR conditions.

Inner subquery. Always executes first, and then the results of this query are used as input to the outer query.

Joining. Relational database operation that combines data from two tables.

LIKE operator. Operator used in a where clause that allows you to choose rows that share some common characters but that are not exactly the same.

NOT operator. Operator used in a where clause that allows you to reverse the condition.

OR logical operator. Operator used in a where clause that allows you to combine two conditions where rows can meet either condition to be selected.

Order by. SQL clause for a Select statement used to sort results.

Outer query. Query containing the inner query and using the results of that inner query as input.

Projection. Relational database operation that retrieves a subset of columns.

Select. SQL statement that is used to implement all three relational database operations.

Selection. Relational database operation that retrieves a subset of rows.

SQL (structured query language). A standard language for creating and using databases.

SQL view. Interface in Access where the SQL statement generated for the query design is displayed.

Subqueries. Queries contained inside other queries.

Where clause. SQL clause for a Select statement used to choose particular rows based on a condition.

EXERCISES

Review

1. Describe the three retrieval operations for relational databases.
2. Describe the simplest form of the Select statement.
3. Describe the basic features of the query design view.
4. Explain what the SQL view can be used to do.
5. How can you display a subset of columns in SQL?
6. How can you sort the results from an SQL statement?
7. How do you perform a descending sort?
8. How do you sort on multiple columns?
9. How do you retrieve only some of the rows from a table?
10. Explain how the LIKE operator is used.
11. How can multiple conditions be included in the same where clause?
12. Explain the difference between the AND and the OR logical operators.
13. What does the NOT operator do?
14. What are aggregate functions?
15. What is the purpose of the group by clause?
16. What does the Distinct option do?
17. How is the having clause used with group by?
18. Explain how a join is accomplished in a Select statement.
19. When you retrieve data from five tables, how many joins will you need? Why?
20. When must you be careful when combining a join with a where condition?
21. Explain what a subquery is.
22. What operators would you normally use when the inner query produces a single value? Multiple values?

Discuss

1. If you wanted to retrieve members whose email address contained "ohio," what where condition would you use?
2. If you wanted to list members who are not from Ohio, what where condition would you use?
3. If you wanted to list members who have their own equipment and a skill level of either B or I, what where condition would you use?
4. Explain how AND and OR conditions interact in a query, and how to use parentheses to ensure the result will be correct.
5. Explain the different effects that where and having can have on a query.

Practice

Exercises 1 through 20 use the Amazon database, which you created in the exercises for Chapter 8. The design of this database is shown in Exhibit 9-61.

Exhibit 9-61   Design for the Amazon Database

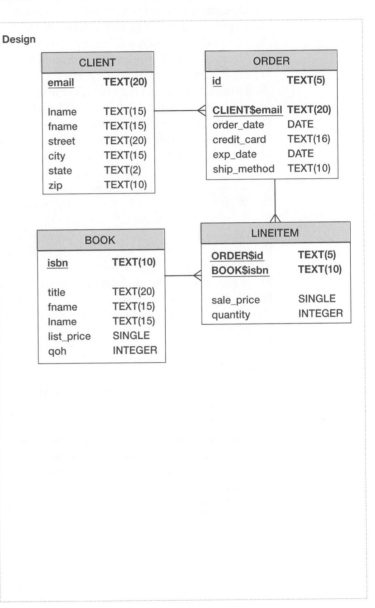

Physical Details

Client : Table

	Field Name	Data Type
🔑	email	Text
	fname	Text
	lname	Text
	street	Text
	city	Text
	state	Text
	zip	Text

Order : Table

	Field Name	Data Type
🔑	id	Text
	client$email	Text
	order_date	Date/Time
	credit_card	Text
	exp_date	Date/Time
	ship_method	Text

Book : Table

	Field Name	Data Type
🔑	isbn	Text
	title	Text
	fname	Text
	lname	Text
	list_price	Number
	qoh	Number

Lineitem : Table

	Field Name	Data Type
🔑	order$id	Text
🔑	book$isbn	Text
	sale_price	Number
	quantity	Number

Design

CLIENT	
email	TEXT(20)
lname	TEXT(15)
fname	TEXT(15)
street	TEXT(20)
city	TEXT(15)
state	TEXT(2)
zip	TEXT(10)

ORDER	
id	TEXT(5)
CLIENT$email	TEXT(20)
order_date	DATE
credit_card	TEXT(16)
exp_date	DATE
ship_method	TEXT(10)

BOOK	
isbn	TEXT(10)
title	TEXT(20)
fname	TEXT(15)
lname	TEXT(15)
list_price	SINGLE
qoh	INTEGER

LINEITEM	
ORDER$id	TEXT(5)
BOOK$isbn	TEXT(10)
sale_price	SINGLE
quantity	INTEGER

Write and execute a query that produces the required results.

1. List all of the data in the CLIENT table in order of email address.
2. List the email address, first name, last name, state, and zip code for all clients. Put the list in order of state, then email address.
3. List the ISBN, title, list price, and quantity on hand for all books. Put the list in *descending* order of quantity on hand.
4. List the email address, first name, last name, city, state, and zip code for all clients in Ohio (OH). Put the list in order of state, then city, then last name.

5. List the ISBN, title, list price, and quantity on hand for all books that have a quantity on hand of 90 or more. Put the list in *descending* order of quantity on hand, then title.

6. List the ISBN, title, list price, and quantity on hand for all books that have a quantity on hand of 90 or more *and* have a list price of more than $12. Put the list in *descending* order of quantity on hand, then title.

7. List the ISBN, title, list price, and quantity on hand for all books that have a quantity on hand of 90 or more *or* have a list price of more than $12. Put the list in *descending* order of quantity on hand, then title.

8. List the email address, first name, and last name for all clients who have "edu" email addresses. Put the list in order of email address.

9. List the ISBN, title, list price and quantity on hand for all books that have a list price between $12 and $20. Put the list in *descending* order of list price.

10. List the total (sum) quantity on hand for all books. Use the column alias "Total On Hand."

11. How many orders were shipped via USPS? Use the column alias "Shipped by USPS."

12. How many *different* shipping methods were used to ship orders?

13. List the order id and total quantity for each order. Put the list in order of total quantity. (Hint: Use the LINEITEM table.)

14. List the order id and total quantity for each order that has a total quantity of four or more. Put the list in order of total quantity. (Hint: Use the LINEITEM table.)

15. List the order id, book ISBN, sale price, quantity, and extended price (sale price multiplied by quantity) for all lineitems. Use the column alias "Total" for the extended price column. Put the list in order of order id.

16. List the order id, order date, client email address, first name, and last name for each order. Put the list in order of email address, then order date.

17. For each order, list the order id, order date, ISBN, title, sale price, and quantity of each book included in the order. Put the list in order of order date, then title. (Hint: You must include the LINEITEM table.)

18. For each order, list the order id, order date, client email address, first name, last name, ISBN, title, sale price, and quantity of each book included in the order. Put the list in order of order id, then title. (Hint: You must include the LINEITEM table.)

19. For each order placed by a customer in Ohio (OH), list the order id, order date, client email address, first name, last name, ISBN, title, sale price, and quantity of each book included in the order. Put the list in order of order date, then title. (Hint: You must include the LINEITEM table.)

20. For each order that includes the books with the ISBNs 014025448X or 0670894370, list the order id, order date, client email address, first name, last name, ISBN, title, sale price, and quantity of each book included in the order. Put the list in order of order date, then title. (Hint: You must include the lineitem table.)

Exercises 21 through 38 use the Hospital database. The design of this database is shown in Exhibit 9-62.

Exhibit 9-62   Design for the Hospital Database

Physical Details

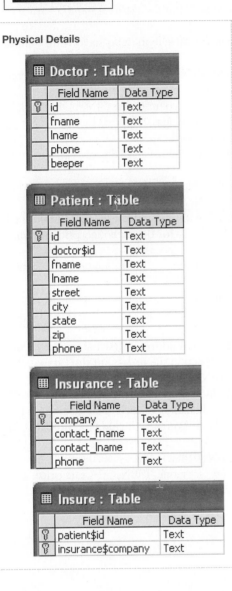

Design

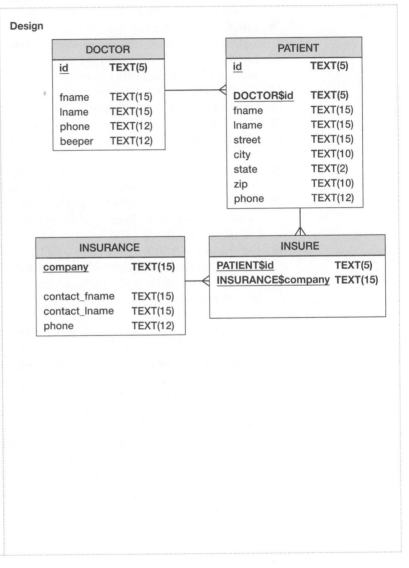

Write and execute a query that produces the required results.

21. List all of the data in the PATIENT table. Put the list in order of state, then last name.

22. List the first name, last name, and beeper number for each doctor. Put the list in order of last name, then first name.

23. List first name, last name, city, state, and zip code of all patients who live in Florida (FL). Put the list in order of city, then last name.

24. List first name, last name, city, state, and zip code of all patients who live in Florida (FL) or Ohio (OH). Put the list in order of city, then last name.

25. List first name, last name, city, state, and zip code of all patients who have a zip code that begins with the numeral 4. Put the list in *descending* order of city, then *ascending* order of last name.

26. List the first name, last name, phone number, and doctor id for all patients who are assigned to doctors with the ids 00001, 00002, or 00004. Put the list in order of doctor id, then last name.

27. List the first name, last name, phone number, and doctor id for all patients who live in Ohio (OH) and are assigned to doctors with the id 00001, 00002, or 00004. Put the list in order of doctor id, then last name.

28. How many *different* doctors have patients assigned to them? (Hint: You must use the PATIENT table.) Use the column alias "Doctors with patients."

29. How many patients live in Florida (FL)? Use the column alias "Patients in Florida."

30. For each state that has more than one patient residing in it, list the state and the number of patients living in the state. Use the column alias "Number of patients." Put the list in *descending* order by number of patients.

31. For each patient, list the patient's first name, last name, and zip code, along with the name of the insurance company used by the patient. Put the list in order of last name.

32. For each patient, list the patient's first name, last name, and zip code, along with the name and phone number of the insurance company used by the patient. Put the list in order of the patient's last name.

33. For each patient insured by Nationwide, list the patient's first name, last name, and zip code. Put the list in order of last name.

34. For each patient living in Ohio (OH) or Kentucky (KY), list the patient's first name, last name, state, and zip code, along with the name and phone number of the insurance company used by the patient. Put the list in order of last name.

35. For each insurance company, list the company name, the contact's first and last names, and the ids, first names, and last names of all patients using that insurance company. Put the list in order of insurance company, then patient last name.

36. For each patient, list the patient's first and last names, the first and last names of the patient's doctor, the patient's insurance company, and the company's phone number. Put the list in order of insurance company, then doctor's last name, then patient's last name.

37. For patients with the id 11111, 33333, or 55555, list the patient's first and last names, the first and last names of the patient's doctor, the patient's insurance company, and the company's phone number. Put the list in order of insurance company, then doctor's last name, then patient's last name.

38. List the id numbers, first names, and last names of all doctors who do *not* have any patients assigned to them. Put the list in order of doctor last name.

Exercises 39 through 46 use the Acme database. The design of this database is shown in Exhibit 9-63.

 Exhibit 9-63   Design for the Acme Database

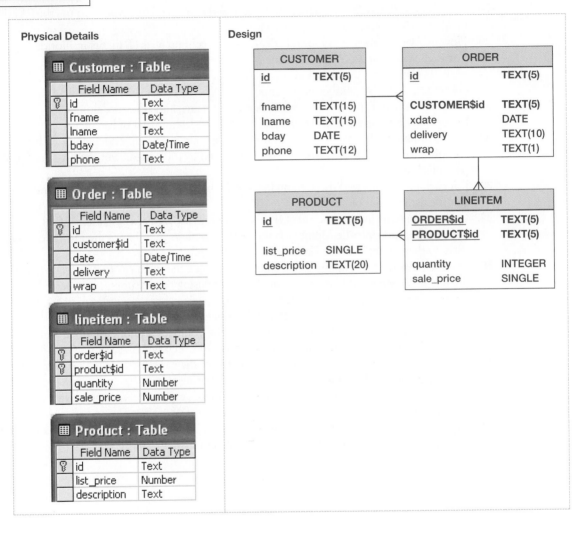

Write and execute a query that produces the required results.

39. How many *different* customers have placed orders?

40. List the first and last names of all customers who have placed more than one order. (Note: This task is quite challenging.)

41. List the product id and number of orders that include the product for all products that have been included on more than one order. Put the list in *descending* order of product id.

42. How many orders have been wrapped?

43. List the first and last name of all customers who have *not* placed orders. Put the list in order of last name.

44. List the id, list price, and description of all products that *are* included in orders. Put the list in descending order of list price.

45. List the id, list price, and description of all products that *are not* included in orders. Put the list in descending order of list price.

46. List the product id, description, and list price for all products that have a list price greater than the average list price for all products. Put the list in order of description.

CHAPTER 10

Creating Databases with Microsoft SQL Server

Introduction

In this chapter, you will learn how to use Microsoft SQL Server to create the databases that were designed in Chapter 3.

Learning Objectives

After completing this chapter, you will be able to:

- Create a database in SQL Server.
- Create one or more tables within the database.
- Define columns and data types for a table.
- Create a primary key for a table.
- Create foreign keys, and use them to establish relationships between tables.
- Display data in a table using Enterprise Manager and Query Analyzer.
- Enter data into a table using Enterprise Manager and Query Analyzer.

Physical Table Design

As you learned in Chapter 3, a conceptual model of a database provides the basic design of the database, including the tables and relationships between those tables. The model also specifies the names for the tables and the columns within those tables, including the specification of primary and foreign keys.

In addition to the general conceptual design, Chapter 3 also specified additional physical details, including data types and widths for each column in the database. Before implementing a database in a particular database management system such as Microsoft SQL Server, you will need to determine the data types available in that system and any restrictions on the widths of columns.

Data Types and Column Widths

Every field in a database table must have a specified data type and column width. In SQL Server, there is a wide range of possible data types, as shown in Exhibit 10-1. Note that there are a few other special data types available, but these data types are not widely used. See the SQL Server documentation for additional details.

Exhibit 10-1

Data Types
Available in
Microsoft SQL
Server

Text	Variable-length, non-Unicode character data. Maximum length of over two billion characters.
Varchar	Variable length, non-Unicode character data. Maximum length of 8,000 characters.
Char	Fixed-length, non-Unicode character data. Maximum length of 8,000 characters.
Ntext	Variable-length, Unicode character data. Maximum length of approximately one billion characters.
Nvarchar	Variable-length, Unicode character data. Maximum length of 4,000 characters.
Nchar	Fixed-length, Unicode character data. Maximum length of 4,000 characters.
Bigint	Integer data ranging from -2^{63} to $(2^{63} - 1)$.
Int	Integer data ranging from -2^{31} to $(2^{31} - 1)$.
Smallint	Integer data ranging from -2^{15} to $(2^{15} - 1)$. ($-32{,}768$ to $32{,}767$)
Tinyint	Integer data ranging from 0 through 255.
Bit	Integer data with the value 0 or 1.
Numeric	Stores a fixed precision and scale number. Ranges from $(-10^{38} + 1)$ to $(10^{38} - 1)$. Equivalent to decimal data type.
Decimal	Stores a fixed precision and scale number. Ranges from $(-10^{38} + 1)$ to $(10^{38} - 1)$. Equivalent to numeric data type.
Float	Floating precision numbers.
Real	Floating precision numbers. Smaller range of values than float.
Datetime	Date and time values ranging from January 1, 1753, through December 31, 9999.
Smalldatetime	Date and time values ranging from January 1, 1900, to June 6, 2079.
Timestamp	Database-wide unique number. Updated whenever a row is updated.
Money	Monetary values ranging from -2^{63} to $(2^{63} - 1)$.
Smallmoney	Monetary values ranging from approximately $-214{,}748$ to $214{,}748$.
Varbinary	Variable-length, binary data. Maximum length of 8,000 bytes.
Binary	Fixed-length, binary data. Maximum length of 8,000 bytes.
Image	Variable-length, binary data. Maximum length of $2^{31} - 1$ bytes (approximately 2.1 billion).

You may have noticed that there are character-oriented data types for Unicode and non-Unicode characters, and you might be wondering what Unicode is. Basically, the idea behind Unicode is to provide a unique number to represent every possible character, regardless of the language. Therefore, Unicode is useful for databases that must store non-English character data. For more information, check out the Unicode Consortium's Web page at **www.unicode.org.**

 ## The Sky_Member Database

We will use the database for the skydiving club to illustrate how a database is created in SQL Server. We will create the one table in the database and populate it with data. Exhibit 10-2 shows the design, physical details, and data for the skydiving club member table. The physical details show how the design of the table will appear in SQL Server when the table is completed. This design includes the name and data type for each column. The design area shows additional details, including the lengths of text columns and specific numeric data types. For example, the jumps column is numeric, because it could be used in a calculation—for example, to determine the average number of jumps for all members. Furthermore, it is an integer numeric data type, because jumps always occur in whole numbers.

In the design area, the primary key (email) is bold and underlined. This designation as the primary key is also indicated under the physical details, with the graphic of a key in front of the column name. As we will see a little later, we will have to change one detail of this design because of a characteristic of SQL Server. Also, notice that we are using generic data type names in the design and physical details. When we actually create the table, we must use SQL Server data types. For example, *text* data types become *nvarchar* when we create the table in SQL Server.

Exhibit 10-2   Design and Data for the Skydiving Club Member Database

Physical Details

Design Table 'tblMember' in 'SkyMember' o...

	Column Name	Data Type	Length	Allow Nulls
🔑	email	nvarchar	20	
	fname	nvarchar	15	
	lname	nvarchar	15	
	phone	nvarchar	12	✓
	jumps	int	4	✓
	equip	nvarchar	1	✓
	skill	nvarchar	1	✓

Design

SKY_MEMBER	
<u>email</u>	**TEXT(20)**
fname	**TEXT(15)**
lname	**TEXT(15)**
phone	**TEXT(12)**
jumps	**INTEGER**
equip	**TEXT(1)**
skill	**TEXT(1)**

Data

email	fname	lname	phone	jumps	equip	skill
bucky@ohio.edu	Teri	Bucky	555-5555	22	Y	A
dayj@ohio.edu	John	Day	529-0646	5	Y	B
johnson@bobcat.edu	Jeremy	Johnson	555-3333	15	Y	I
luce@ohio.edu	Thom	Luce	592-1111	12	N	I
mcgann@ohio.edu	Sean	McGann	592-2222	20	Y	A
mcgrath@bobcat.edu	Billie	McGrath	555-6666	3	N	B
wilson@bobcat.edu	Sally	Wilson	555-4444	6	N	B

Creating an SQL Server Database with a Single Table

One way to create a database in SQL Server is through the **Enterprise Manager.** This program is used to carry out database administration tasks, including creating databases, indexes, and other database objects. Enterprise Manager gives you a relatively easy-to-use, point-and-click interface for carrying out most administrative tasks.

The process of creating a database in SQL Server using Enterprise Manager involves the following steps:

1. Specify the server and database name by:
   - Starting Enterprise Manager, then expanding the server group.
   - Expanding the server that you want to use for the database.
   - Entering the name for the new database.
2. Create a table.
3. Create columns by:
   - Entering a column name.
   - Selecting a data type.
   - Specifying a field size, when applicable.
4. Indicate the primary key.
5. Establish relationships (for multitable databases only).
6. Enter data.

To illustrate this process, these steps (except for step 5) will be used to create the Sky_Member database.

Step 1: Specify the Server and Database Name

To begin creating the database, start Enterprise Manager, then expand the items in the Tree pane until you can see a list of available servers. The screen should look something like Exhibit 10-3. Note that you will have a different list of servers.

Exhibit 10-3

Creating a Database in SQL Server

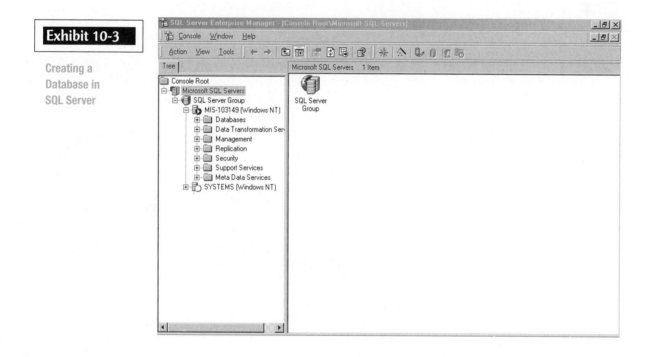

The Microsoft SQL Server interface is a typical Windows application with menus and a shortcut toolbar at the top. To the left is a pane (called the **Tree pane**) that shows the structure of your SQL Server environment. The right-hand pane shows database objects that are associated with whatever item is selected in the Tree pane. For example, in Exhibit 10-3, *Microsoft SQL Servers* is selected in the Tree pane, so the available server groups are shown in the right pane.

To create a new database, right-click the Databases folder in the Tree pane, then select *New database* from the pop-up menu. Exhibit 10-4 shows a screen shot of the pop-up database menu. You can also select the New Database button from the toolbar. The button is circled in Exhibit 10-4. Note that your screen will show a different set of databases in the right pane.

Exhibit 10-4

Creating a New
Database

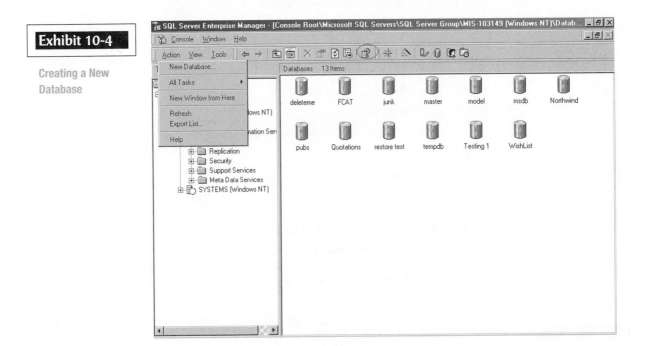

Once you click *New database*, the Database Properties dialog box will appear. Enter the name of the database, which in this case is SkyMember, as shown in Exhibit 10-5. There are some other database properties that can be set in this dialog box, but for our purposes, using the default properties is sufficient.

Step 2: Create a Table

The **database window** displays the various components of an SQL Server database and provides options for creating additional components. These components include:

- Tables: The basic storage units in the database.
- Views: Derived, temporary tables that are based on the basic tables.
- Diagrams: Graphical representations of the database structure (similar to the conceptual model).
- Stored procedures: Procedural programs that are stored as part of the database.
- Rules: Constraints that can be applied to restrict values in a column.
- Defaults: Specifications as to what value is used in a column if no value is specified when inserting data.
- User-defined data types: Data types based on the standard data types, but created by users; used to make sure that all values in a column meet specifications according to data type, column width, and whether null values are allowed.
- User-defined functions: Subroutines that can be used to encapsulate the code for reusability.
- Users: Unique identifiers for each user within a database; permission to access data and perform operations is granted based on the user identification.
- Roles: Collections of users that are granted permissions as a group.

Most of these components are beyond the scope of what we will cover in this text. However, as you become more expert in building SQL Server databases, it is worthwhile to explore these components.

If you expand a database in the Tree pane (the left-hand pane) and then click one of the component types, you will see a list of all components of that type that are included in the database. You can also use the component list to create new components. Simply right-click the Component Type icon, and you will see "New . . . " on the pop-up menu. For example, if you want to create a table, simply right-click the Tables icon, then select New table from the pop-up menu. You can also select the new icon on the toolbar (it looks like a star), or by using the Actions menu, but be sure to first click the proper component in the Tree pane.

Typically, the first components you want to create are the tables. Let's look at how to create a table for the Sky_Member database. Before creating a table, be sure that you have designated the data types and constraints for all columns. Once you tell SQL Server that you want to create a table, you will see the New table window, as shown in Exhibit 10-6.

Exhibit 10-6

Creating a Table
in Design View

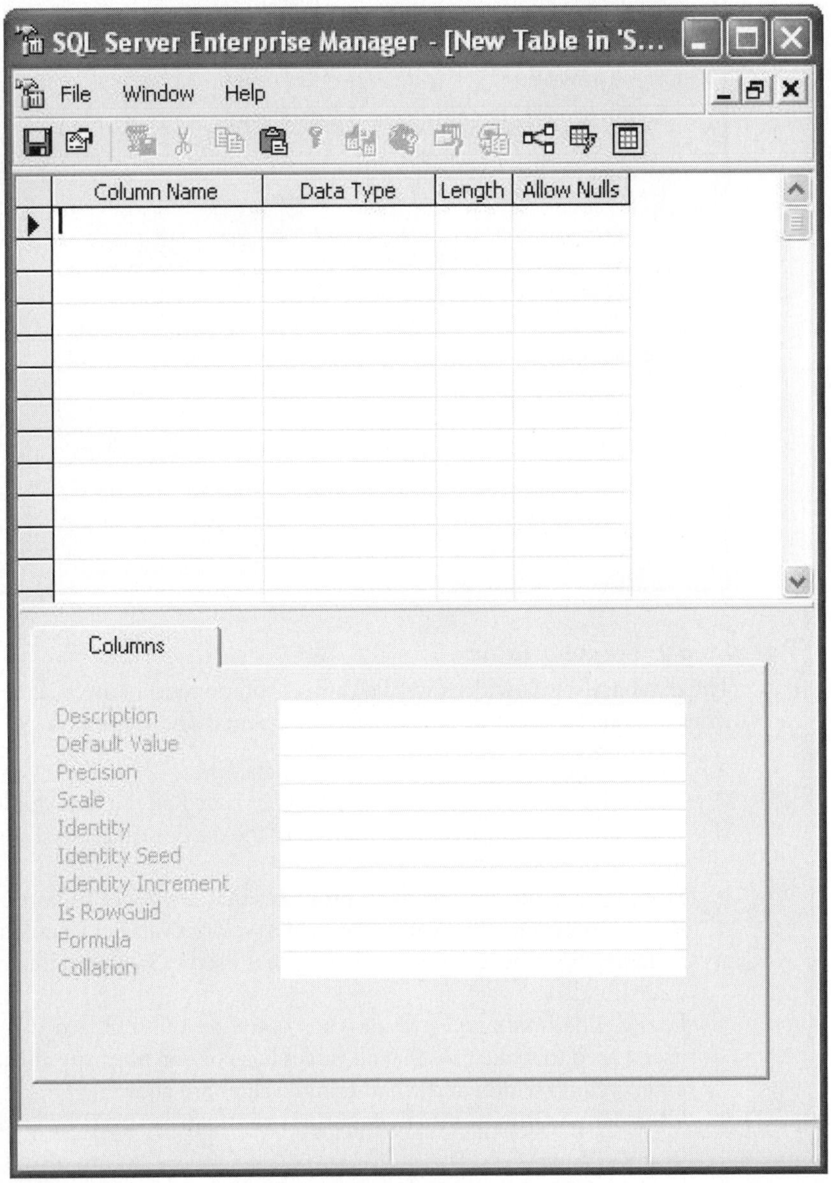

Step 3: Create Columns

Columns are defined by entering the name of the column under the Column Name heading and selecting the data type using the drop-down list. You can also enter the width of the column by entering the appropriate number in the column labeled "Length." Also, you can specify whether null (blank) entries are allowed by checking or unchecking the "Allow Nulls" column. At the bottom of the screen, additional options related to the table columns are available. Let's start with the first column in the SKY_MEMBER table, which is the email column.

In the SKY_MEMBER table, the email column requires a character data type and a maximum field size of 20. We are using the nvarchar data type to allow for special characters. Exhibit 10-7 shows the other columns that make up the SKY_MEMBER table. Notice that the original design of the table had a column called "level." This column name has been changed to "skill" in Exhibit 10-7. We had to make this change because *level* is a *reserved word* in SQL Server. In other words, this word has a particular meaning in SQL Server, and therefore it cannot be used as an object name. All database management systems (DBMSs) have such words, and they vary from one system to another. As you gain knowledge of a particular DBMS, you will learn which words are off limits.

Exhibit 10-7

Creating Columns

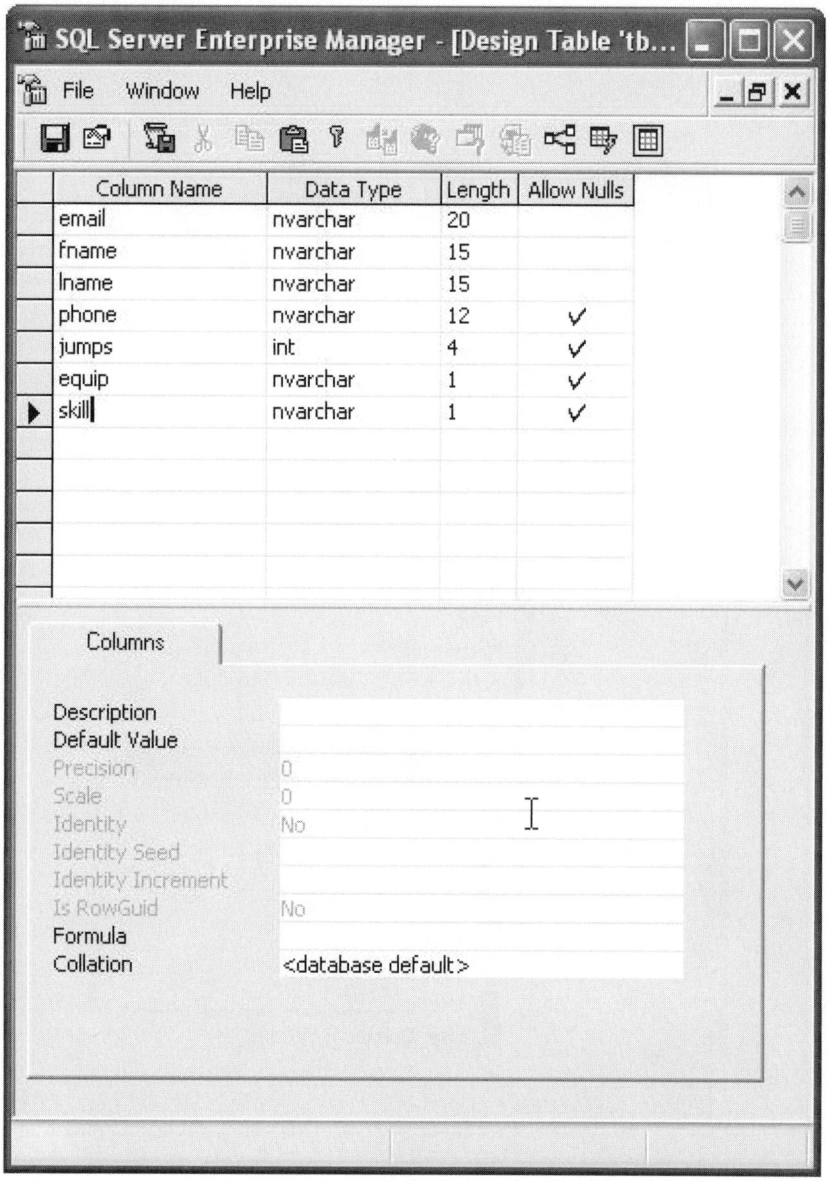

Another useful column setting is the option related to setting up a check constraint for a column. A **check constraint** is a setting for a column where you can specify a condition that data values must conform to when being inserted into the column. In the SKY_MEMBER table, the equip and skill columns have specific data values that need to be stored in them. For example, the equip column is supposed to indicate whether the skydiver has his or her own equipment. The column should either contain a Y for yes or an N for no. In the skill column, the value should be either B for beginner, I for intermediate, or A for advanced. The data allowed in a column can be controlled by setting up a check constraint, which basically allows you to specify criteria that the column values must match. Values that do not match these criteria are not accepted for input.

Once you create all of the columns, you must save the table. Click the Save icon, and name the table tblMember. We like to begin the names of all of the tables we create with "tbl." This lets us quickly know that it is a table that we created (rather than one created by SQL Server for administrative purposes). As you will see later, it also makes it easy to pick out our tables from a large list.

Before specifying a check constraint using Enterprise Manager, you must create a database diagram. A **database diagram** is a view of a database where you can display database tables and create relationships between foreign and primary keys. The creation of this diagram is easy. First, make sure the proper database is shown and expanded in the tree window, then right-click Diagrams and select New Database Diagram, as shown in Exhibit 10-8.

Exhibit 10-8

Creating a New
Database Diagram

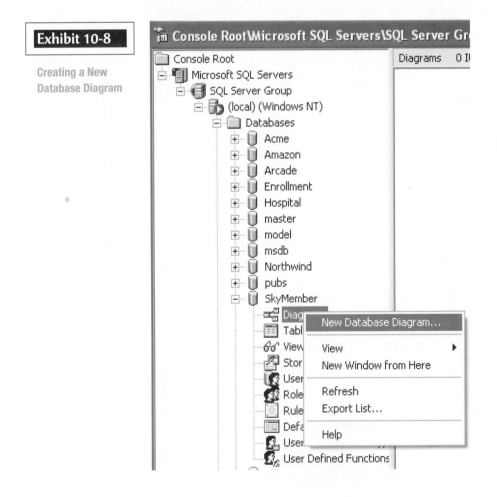

Making this selection will bring up the Create Database Diagram Wizard, which will guide you through the process of creating a new diagram. Be sure to select tblMember as the table you want to show in the diagram. Once the diagram is created, right-click the diagram, select Table View, and then Standard. This process will give you a more informative view of the table. To create a check constraint, right-click the table in the diagram, then select Check Constraints at the bottom of the menu. Doing so will bring up the menu shown in Exhibit 10-9.

Exhibit 10-9

Changing the
Table View

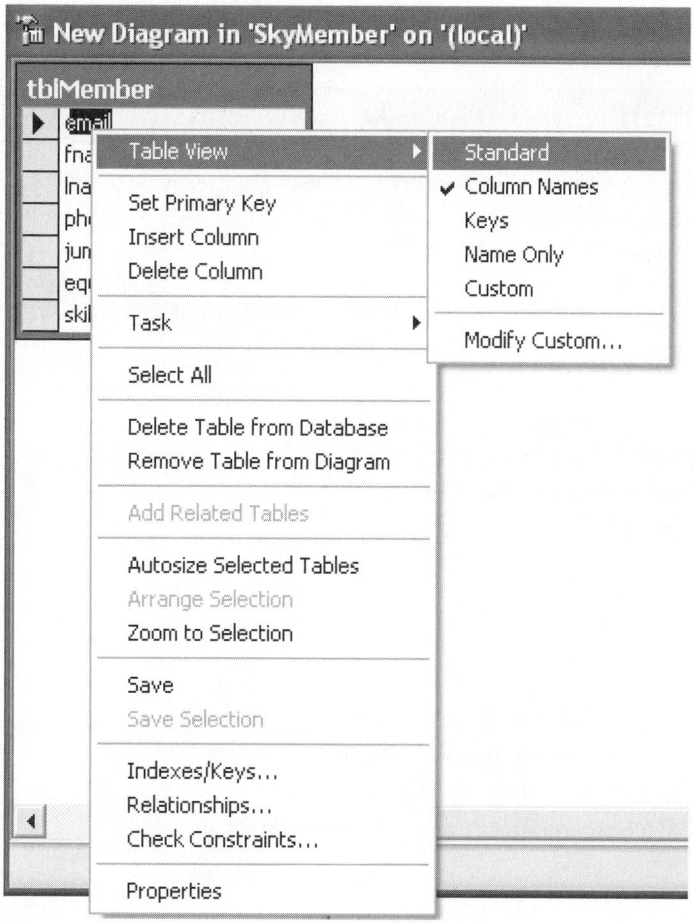

Click New, then enter the constraint expression as shown in Exhibit 10-10. Change the name of the constraint to CK_tblMember_skill, as shown in the exhibit. Once you have performed these tasks, you can click Close. Then when it is time to enter data, only data that meets these criteria may be entered into the skill column. (Do not worry if you do not understand the constraint expression syntax. We will cover this subject in a later chapter.) Another type of database object called *rules* can also be used to restrict allowable column values. However, check constraints are the preferred method. A big reason for this is that there can be only one rule per column, but multiple check constraints can be applied to a single column. At this point, you can close the Properties window, but keep the Diagram window open, because we need it for the next step, specifying the primary key.

Exhibit 10-10

Creating a New
Check Constraint

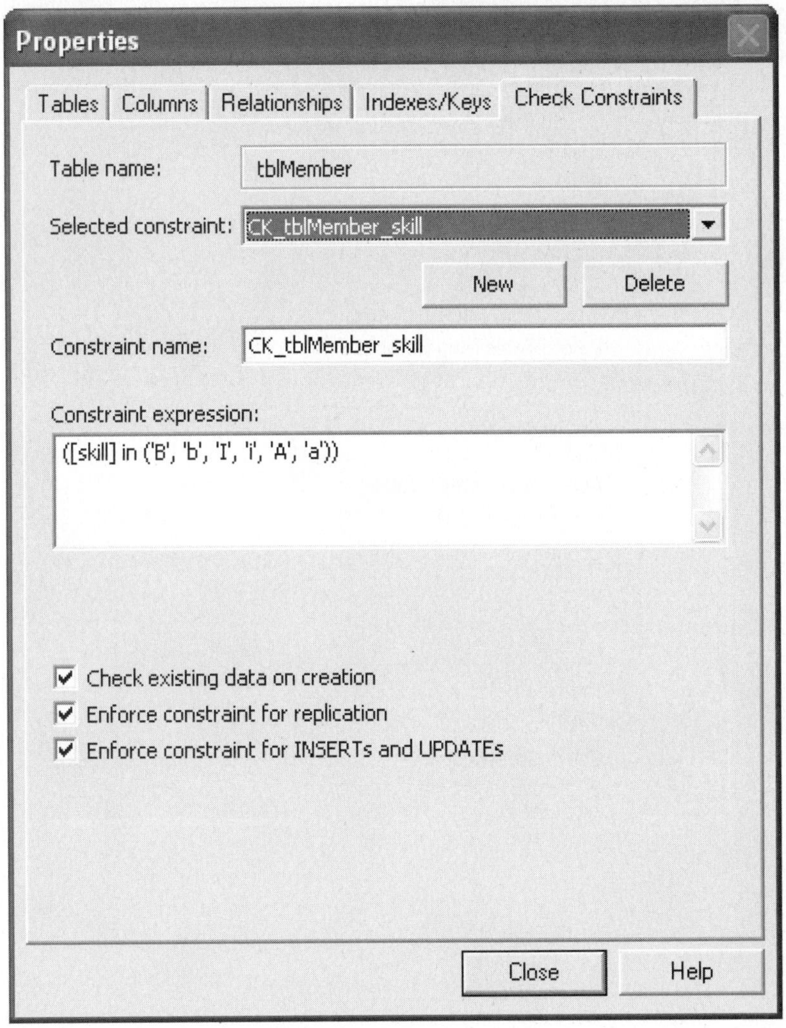

Properties	✕

| Tables | Columns | Relationships | Indexes/Keys | Check Constraints |

Table name: tblMember

Selected constraint: CK_tblMember_skill ▼

New   Delete

Constraint name: CK_tblMember_skill

Constraint expression:

([skill] in ('B', 'b', 'I', 'i', 'A', 'a'))

☑ Check existing data on creation
☑ Enforce constraint for replication
☑ Enforce constraint for INSERTs and UPDATEs

Close   Help

Step 4: Specify the Primary Key

Once the columns are defined, the final task in creating the table is to specify the primary key for the table. We want to set email as the primary key of tblMember. To make this designation, you must right-click the email column in the diagram, then select Set Primary Key, as illustrated in Exhibit 10-11. After you follow these steps, you will see a small key icon to the left of the email column. This key icon indicates that email is the primary key of the table. If you want to create a composite primary key, you must select all of the columns making up the key prior to setting the primary key. We will show you an example of this process later in this chapter.

Exhibit 10-11

Specifying the
Primary Key

Step 5: Entering Data into the Table

At this point, the structure of the table has been saved, and the empty table has been created. To place data into the table, SQL Server provides a **datasheet view** of the table. This view of the table is similar to a spreadsheet and is accessed by opening the table in Enterprise Manager. To open a table, simply select Tables in the tree window, then right-click the proper table (tblMember, in this case), then select Open Table from the menu. If you are dealing with a table with many rows, you may want to select Return Top; otherwise, select Return all rows, as shown in Exhibit 10-12. You may notice that there are many tables listed for our database. These tables were automatically created by SQL Server when we created the database, and they are used for a variety of administrative purposes.

Exhibit 10-12

Opening the MEMBER Table

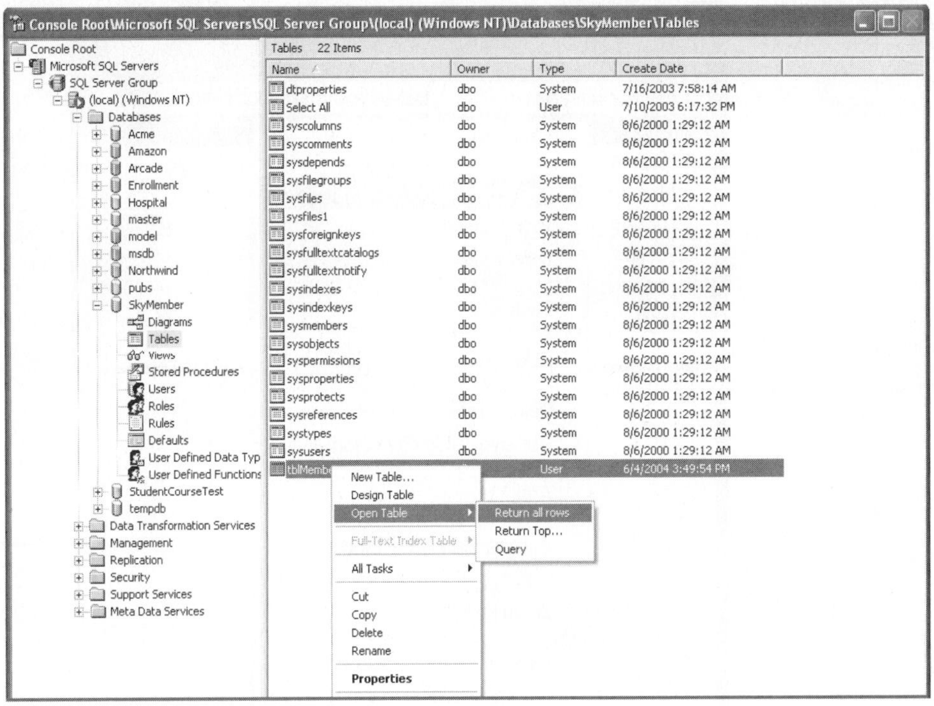

Your table will be empty because you have not yet entered the data into it. Entering data is similar to the way you would enter data into a spreadsheet. Simply enter the data for the first column, then tab to the next column. Once a row of data is completely entered, you simply tab to the next row, and the completed row is saved. Exhibit 10-13 gives the table with some data entered. Enter the data shown into your table.

Exhibit 10-13

The Datasheet View of the SKY_MEMBER Table

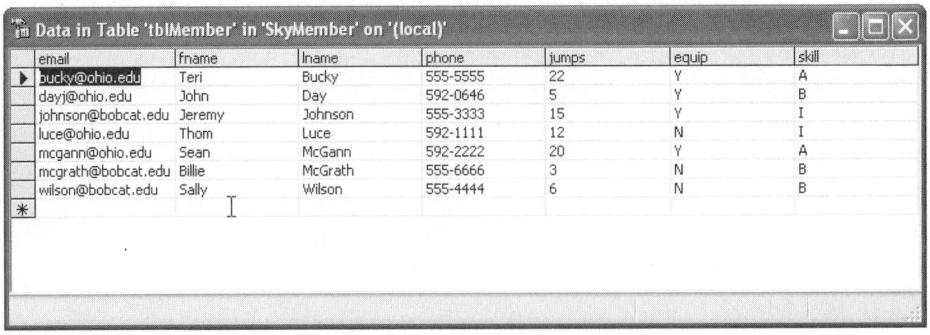
Data in Table 'tblMember' in 'SkyMember' on '(local)'

email	fname	lname	phone	jumps	equip	skill
bucky@ohio.edu	Teri	Bucky	555-5555	22	Y	A
dayj@ohio.edu	John	Day	592-0646	5	Y	B
johnson@bobcat.edu	Jeremy	Johnson	555-3333	15	Y	I
luce@ohio.edu	Thom	Luce	592-1111	12	N	I
mcgann@ohio.edu	Sean	McGann	592-2222	20	Y	A
mcgrath@bobcat.edu	Billie	McGrath	555-6666	3	N	B
wilson@bobcat.edu	Sally	Wilson	555-4444	6	N	B

If you enter a value in the skill column that violates the check constraint for the column, an error message will appear when SQL Server tries to save the row, as shown in Exhibit 10-14.

Exhibit 10-14

The Error
Displayed When
Violating a Check
Constraint

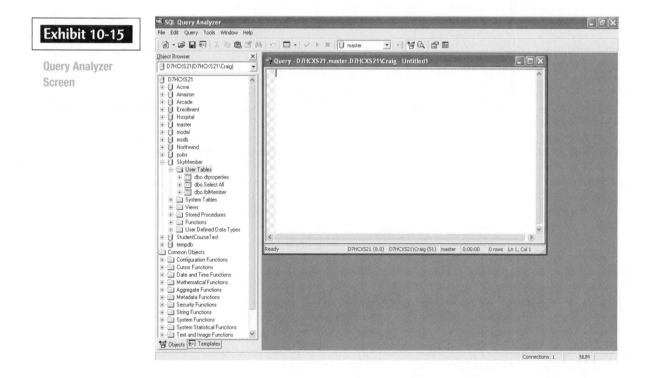

Using Query Analyzer to Insert Data

As we just discussed, you can use Enterprise Manager to display and add data to a table. SQL Server gives you another, similar method for displaying and updating data. You can also use the Query Analyzer for this purpose. We will talk more about the Query Analyzer in a later chapter. For now, we will just examine how to use the program to update data.

As the name implies, the main purpose of the **Query Analyzer** is to process queries to retrieve data from tables. You will use this program extensively in the next chapter. Exhibit 10-15 shows a screen shot from the Query Analyzer.

Exhibit 10-15

Query Analyzer
Screen

If you look on the left, you will see the Object Browser pane. This interface lets you navigate to whatever database object is of interest. We want to examine the Sky_Member database, so expand that database by clicking the plus sign (+) next to it. To show the tblMember table, expand the User Tables folder. Right-click tblMember, and choose Open from the menu. The data will be displayed in a datasheet view, similar to what we saw from Enterprise Manager. This view is shown in Exhibit 10-16. You can add, update, or delete data from this view, just as we could from Enterprise Manager.

Exhibit 10-16

Data Query Window in Query Analyzer

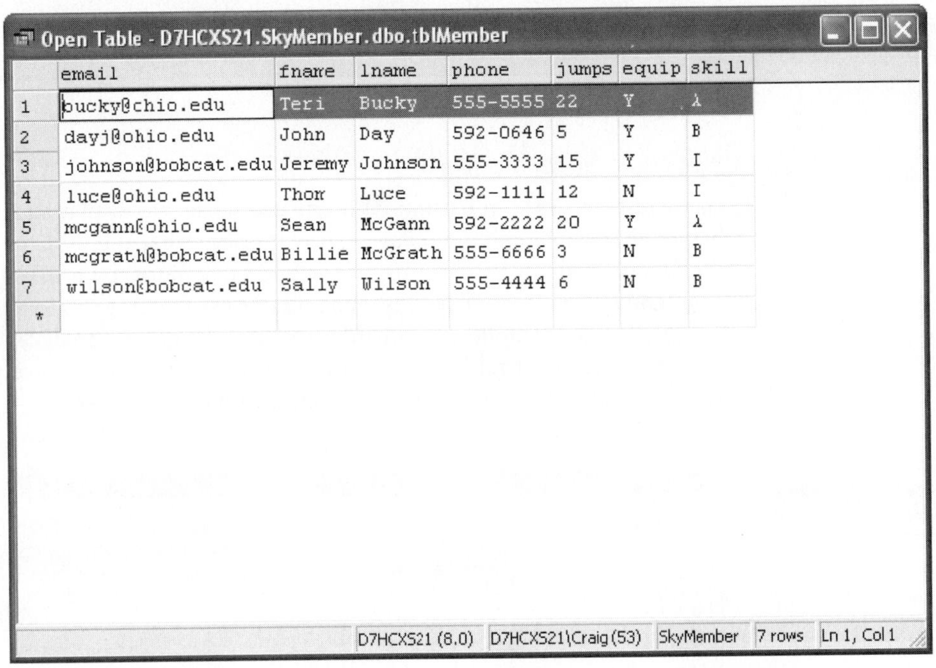

Open Table - D7HCXS21.SkyMember.dbo.tblMember

	email	fname	lname	phone	jumps	equip	skill
1	bucky@chio.edu	Teri	Bucky	555-5555	22	Y	λ
2	dayj@ohio.edu	John	Day	592-0646	5	Y	B
3	johnson@bobcat.edu	Jeremy	Johnson	555-3333	15	Y	I
4	luce@ohio.edu	Thom	Luce	592-1111	12	N	I
5	mcgann@ohio.edu	Sean	McGann	592-2222	20	Y	λ
6	mcgrath@bobcat.edu	Billie	McGrath	555-6666	3	N	B
7	wilson@bobcat.edu	Sally	Wilson	555-4444	6	N	B
*							

D7HCXS21 (8.0)   D7HCXS21\Craig (53)   SkyMember   7 rows   Ln 1, Col 1

We are now finished creating the Sky_Member database. These steps illustrate the basic process of creating a single-table database in SQL Server. Now that you are familiar with the process, we will look at how to create some of the more complex databases from Chapter 3.

The Arcade Database

Exhibit 10-17 shows the design for the Arcade database. There are several differences between this database and the Sky_Member database. The most obvious difference is that this database includes two tables rather than one. In addition, the VISIT table contains columns with a date data type.

To create the relationship between the MEMBER and VISIT tables, the VISIT table contains the foreign key, MEMBER$email, which references its parent table (MEMBER) and corresponding column (email). The foreign key must have the same data type and column width as the primary key that it references. This requirement is very important to remember.

Exhibit 10-17   The Design for the Arcade Database

Physical Details

Design Table 'tblMember' in 'Arcade' on '(local)'

	Column Name	Data Type	Length	Allow Nulls
🔑	email	nvarchar	20	
	password	nvarchar	10	✓
	fname	nvarchar	10	✓
	lname	nvarchar	10	✓
	phone	nvarchar	12	✓

Design Table 'tblVisit' in 'Arcade' on '(local)'

	Column Name	Data Type	Length	Allow Nulls
🔑	id	nvarchar	20	
	member$email	nvarchar	20	✓
	date_time_in	smalldatetime	4	✓
	date_time_out	smalldatetime	4	✓

Design

MEMBER

email	TEXT(20)
password	TEXT(10)
fname	TEXT(10)
lname	TEXT(10)
phone	TEXT(12)

VISIT

id	TEXT(20)
MEMBER$email	TEXT(20)
date_time_in	DATE
date_time_out	DATE

Data

tblMember

email	password	fname	lname	phone
dayj@ohio.edu	rocket	Day	John	529-0646
luce@ohio.edu	bullet	Luce	Thom	592-1111
mcgann@ohio.edu	arrow	McGann	Sean	592-2222

tblVisit

id	MEMBER$email	date_time_in	date_time_out
001	dayj@ohio.edu	6/25/2002 2:00:00 PM	6/25/2002 5:30:00 PM
002	luce@ohio.edu	6/25/2002 6:00:00 PM	6/25/2002 8:00:00 PM
003	mcgann@ohio.edu	6/26/2002 10:00:00 AM	6/26/2002 11:30:00 AM
004	luce@ohio.edu	6/27/2002 9:00:00 AM	6/27/2002 10:00:00 AM
005	mcgann@ohio.edu	6/27/2002 4:00:00 PM	6/27/2002 6:00:00 PM

Create the Database and Tables

To create the Arcade database, start Enterprise Manager. Expand items in the Tree pane until you can see the Databases folder. Then click the Databases folder, and select New Database from the Action menu. You can also right-click the Databases folder and select New Database from the menu. This process brings up the Database Properties window, as illustrated in Exhibit 10-18. Name your new database "Arcade," as shown in the exhibit.

Exhibit 10-18

Creating the
Arcade Database

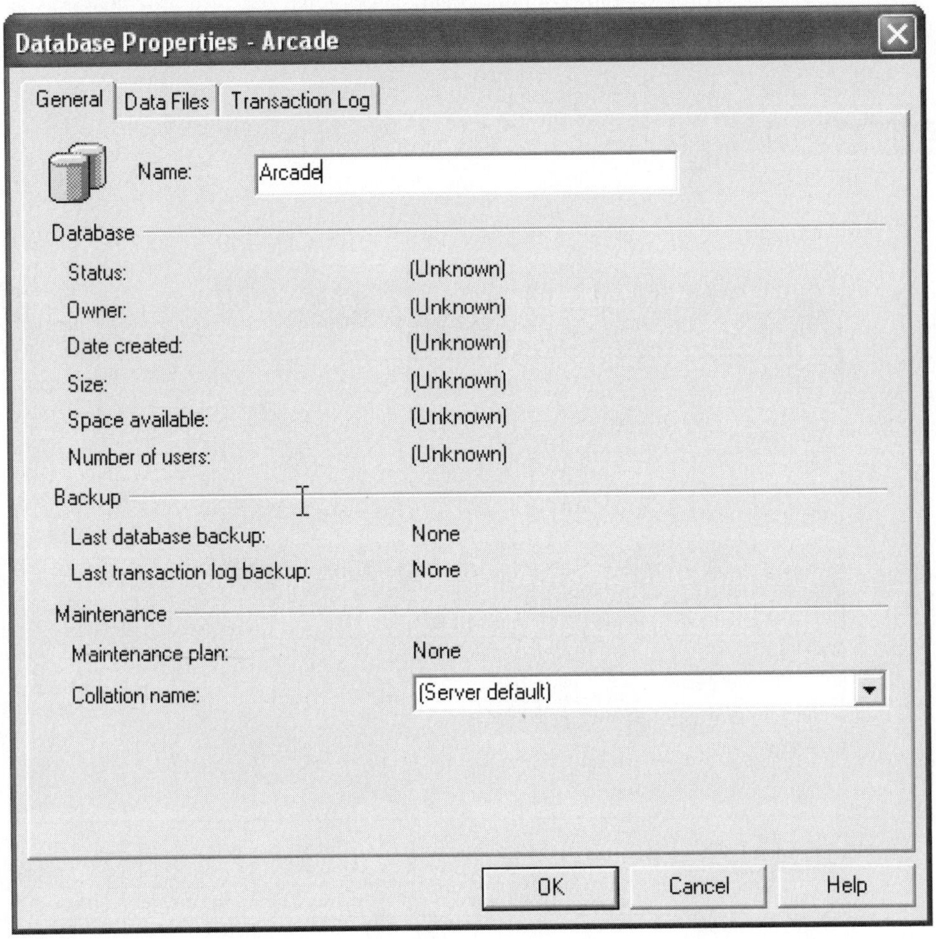

Now expand the Arcade database and create the MEMBER table. To make it easier to find later, and following our naming convention, call the table "tblMember." You can now create a new table and define the columns for the MEMBER table. Make the email column the primary key, and then name the table when it is saved. The completed design for the MEMBER table is shown in Exhibit 10-19.

Design Table 'tblMember' in 'Arcade' on '(local)'

Column Name	Data Type	Length	Allow Nulls
email	nvarchar	20	
password	nvarchar	10	✓
fname	nvarchar	10	✓
lname	nvarchar	10	✓
phone	nvarchar	12	✓

Columns

Description	
Default Value	
Precision	0
Scale	0
Identity	No
Identity Seed	
Identity Increment	
Is RowGuid	No
Formula	
Collation	<database default>

After the MEMBER table is finished, create the VISIT table. Remember to call the table "tblVisit." Set up the columns for the VISIT table as defined above. For the date_time_in and date_time_out columns, select the smalldatetime data type. Do not forget to set id as the primary key. The completed design for the VISIT table is shown in Exhibit 10-20.

Exhibit 10-20

The Design for the VISIT Table (tblVisit)

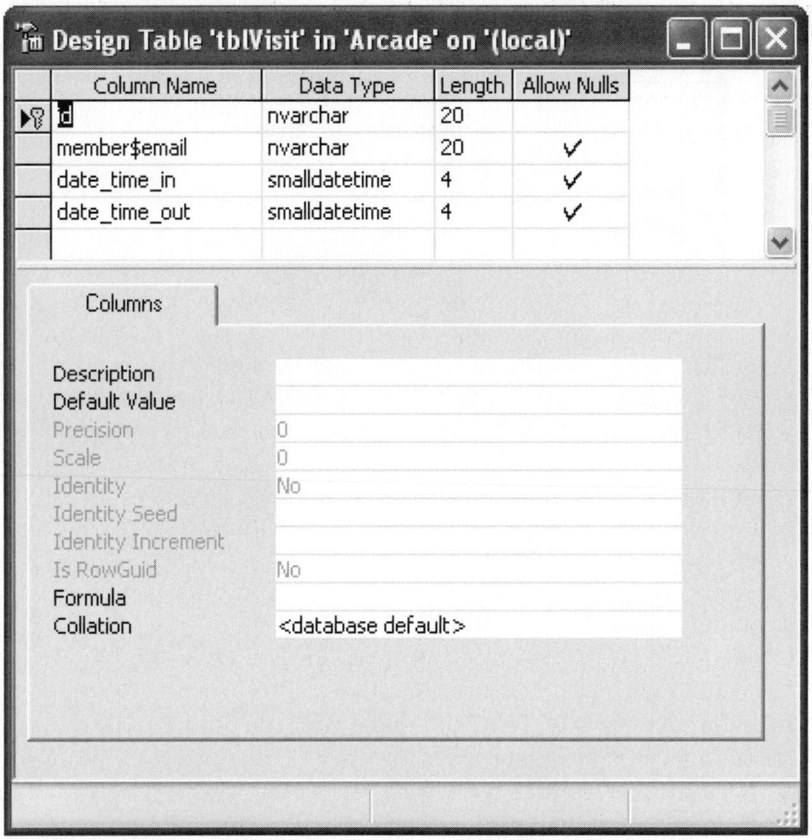

Create the Relationship Between the Tables

Once the tables have been defined, we need to create a relationship to link the foreign key (MEMBER$email) in the tblVisit table to the primary key (email) in the tblMember table. Relationships are created from the table design view. If you closed the design window for the tblVisit table, reopen it. Next, right-click the MEMBER$email column name, then choose Relationships from the menu. (You don't have to click that particular column. Right-clicking any column name will bring up the proper menu.) This process opens the Properties window with the Relationships tab selected, as shown in Exhibit 10-21. Click the New button. Make sure that tblMember is the primary key table and that tblVisit is the foreign key table. Next, you must select the primary key of tblMember (email) from the grid underneath "Primary key table." Then select MEMBER$email from the right-hand side of the grid. This step sets MEMBER$email as a foreign key in tblVisit that references email in tblMember.

Exhibit 10-21

The Show Table
Dialog Box

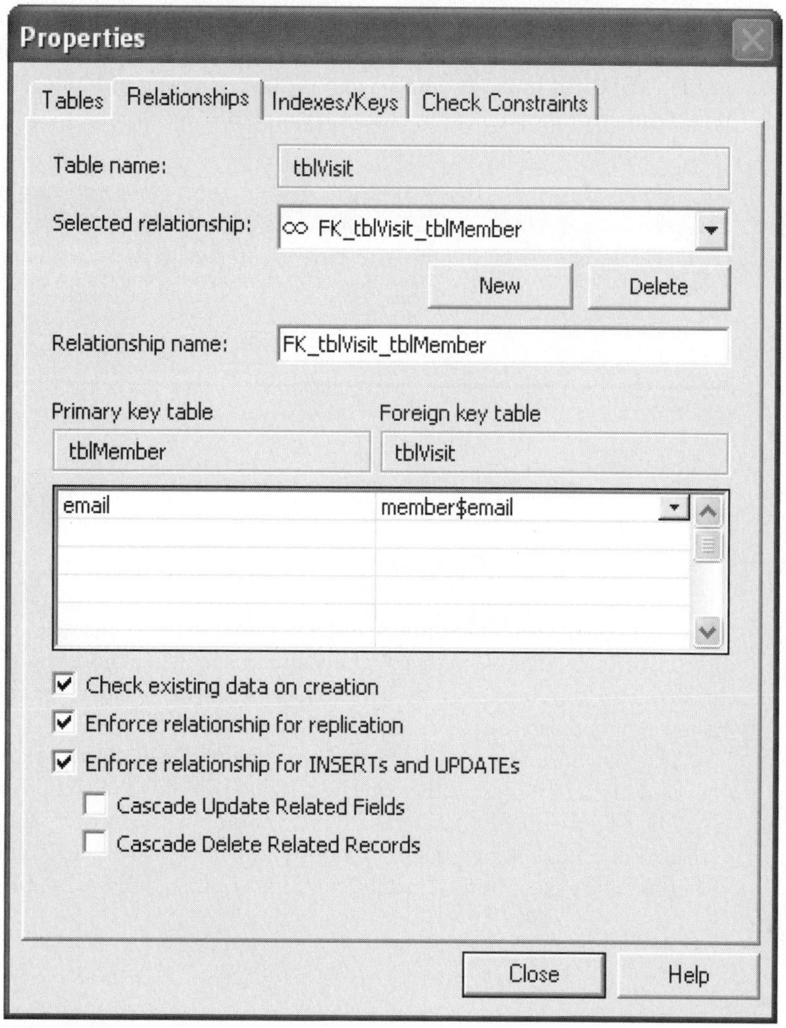

Properties

| Tables | Relationships | Indexes/Keys | Check Constraints |

Table name: tblVisit

Selected relationship: ∞ FK_tblVisit_tblMember   ▼

[New]   [Delete]

Relationship name: FK_tblVisit_tblMember

Primary key table   Foreign key table

tblMember   tblVisit

email	member$email ▼

☑ Check existing data on creation
☑ Enforce relationship for replication
☑ Enforce relationship for INSERTs and UPDATEs
  ☐ Cascade Update Related Fields
  ☐ Cascade Delete Related Records

[Close]   [Help]

Notice that we left two boxes unchecked (Cascade Update and Cascade Delete). These check boxes deal with the issue of what to do with the duplicate values in the foreign key column when changes occur in the primary key column. For example, when an email address is placed in the MEMBER$email column of the VISIT table, it is a duplicate of one of the email addresses in the MEMBER table. If you now try to change the value in the email primary key column, SQL Server will not allow the change because of the duplicate of that key in the VISIT table. The two options in the Properties dialog box related to cascading allow SQL Server to alter the duplicate values in the foreign key column when values in the primary key are updated or deleted. In this case, there is no need to cascade changes in the primary key to the duplicates in the foreign key column.

Entering the Data for the Arcade Database

Once the tables are created and the relationship is established, the data can be entered. In general, data can be placed in tables containing foreign keys only after the data is entered into the tables that they reference. This restriction means that data must be inserted first into the MEMBER table. If not, the data for the VISIT table will be rejected for referential integrity violations—the email address in the MEMBER$email column would reference data that does not yet exist in the MEMBER table.

Once the data is entered in the MEMBER table, referential integrity also means that when values are entered in the MEMBER$email column, they must match the values already in the MEMBER table. If you make a mistake entering a duplicate email address, you will receive an error message, as shown in Exhibit 10-22.

Exhibit 10-22

The Error
Generated When
Violating
Referential
Integrity

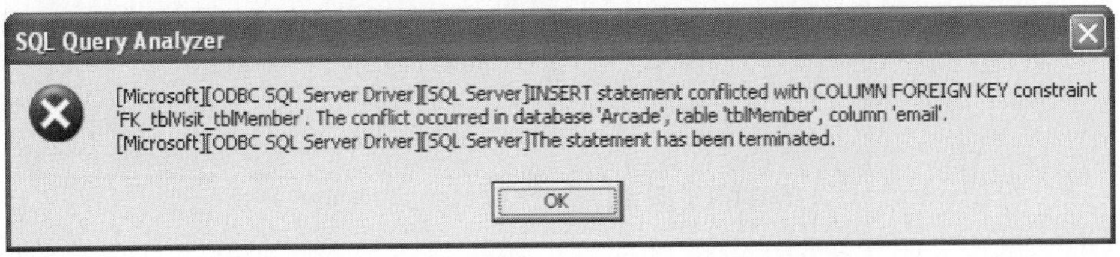

SQL Query Analyzer

[Microsoft][ODBC SQL Server Driver][SQL Server]INSERT statement conflicted with COLUMN FOREIGN KEY constraint 'FK_tblVisit_tblMember'. The conflict occurred in database 'Arcade', table 'tblMember', column 'email'.
[Microsoft][ODBC SQL Server Driver][SQL Server]The statement has been terminated.

[OK]

The Enrollment Database

Now that you have a basic understanding of how to create a single-table database and a database involving two tables with a relationship, let's look at a more complex, multitable database. In Chapter 3, the conceptual design for the Enrollment database was presented. Now let's look at how that database can be created in Microsoft SQL Server.

This database requires the creation of five tables and four relationships. A new feature involved in this database is the concatenated key in the ENROLL table that requires that the STUDENT$id and SECTION$call_no combine to form the primary key of the column. Recall that a concatenated key is simply a primary key that is made up of two or more columns. The design of the Enrollment database is shown in Exhibit 10-23.

Exhibit 10-23   The Design of the Enrollment Database

Physical Details

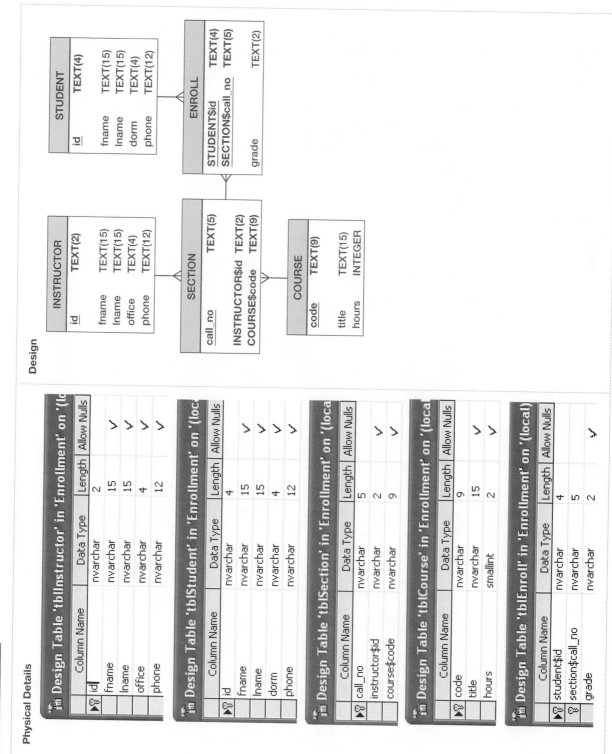

Design

Design Table 'tblInstructor' in 'Enrollment' on '(lo

Column Name	Data Type	Length	Allow Nulls
id	nvarchar	2	
fname	nvarchar	15	✓
lname	nvarchar	15	✓
office	nvarchar	4	✓
phone	nvarchar	12	✓

Design Table 'tblStudent' in 'Enrollment' on '(loc

Column Name	Data Type	Length	Allow Nulls
id	nvarchar	4	
fname	nvarchar	15	✓
lname	nvarchar	15	✓
dorm	nvarchar	4	✓
phone	nvarchar	12	✓

Design Table 'tblSection' in 'Enrollment' on '(loca

Column Name	Data Type	Length	Allow Nulls
call_no	nvarchar	5	
instructor$id	nvarchar	2	✓
course$code	nvarchar	9	✓

Design Table 'tblCourse' in 'Enrollment' on '(loca

Column Name	Data Type	Length	Allow Nulls
code	nvarchar	9	
title	nvarchar	15	✓
hours	smallint	2	✓

Design Table 'tblEnroll' in 'Enrollment' on '(local)

Column Name	Data Type	Length	Allow Nulls
student$id	nvarchar	4	
section$call_no	nvarchar	5	
grade	nvarchar	2	✓

STUDENT

id	TEXT(4)
fname	TEXT(15)
lname	TEXT(15)
dorm	TEXT(4)
phone	TEXT(12)

ENROLL

STUDENT$id	TEXT(4)
SECTION$call_no	TEXT(5)
grade	TEXT(2)

INSTRUCTOR

id	TEXT(2)
fname	TEXT(15)
lname	TEXT(15)
office	TEXT(4)
phone	TEXT(12)

SECTION

call_no	TEXT(5)
INSTRUCTOR$id	TEXT(2)
COURSE$code	TEXT(9)

COURSE

code	TEXT(9)
title	TEXT(15)
hours	INTEGER

(Continued)

Exhibit 10-23

Continued

Data

INSTRUCTOR

id	fname	lname	office	phone
11	Joe	Smith	101	593-2736
22	Sam	Slick	102	594-4657
33	Sally	Sly	115	593-9875
44	Sue	Slim	123	593-4756

COURSE

code	title	hours
MIS380	Database I	4
MIS225	Visual Basic	4
MIS420	System II	4

STUDENT

id	fname	lname	dorm	phone
1111	Jim	Green	450A	593-2456
2222	Steve	Black	326B	594-4623
3333	Linda	Brown	144A	593-5575
4444	Emma	White	133B	593-4676

SECTION

call_no	INSTRUCTOR$id	COURSE$code
001	11	MIS380
002	33	MIS380
003	11	MIS225
004	44	MIS420

ENROLL

STUDENT$id	SECTION$call_no	grade
1111	001	A
2222	001	B
3333	003	A
1111	004	C

Create a new database called "Enroll," and design the five tables as shown in the database design. Remember that you must substitute SQL Server data types for the generic data types shown in the exhibit.

Creating a Concatenated Key

The only aspect of this database that has not been introduced is the need to create a concatenated key in the ENROLL table. In this table, the primary key is the combination of the STUDENT$id and SECTION$call_no. These pairs of student ids and call numbers indicate in which sections a student is enrolled. To create a primary key using multiple columns, simply highlight all the columns when designing the table (use shift-click or control-click to select multiple columns), and set them as the primary key, as shown in Exhibit 10-24.

Exhibit 10-24

Creating a
Concatenated
Primary Key

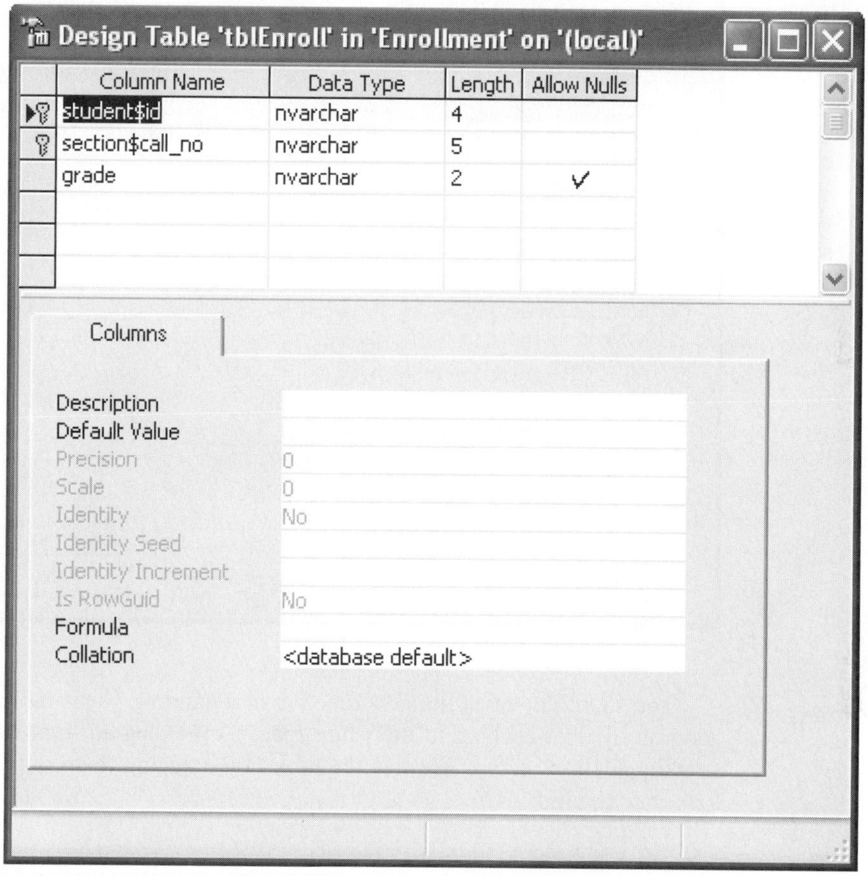

Relationships for the Enroll Database

The other aspect of this database that is a bit different from the previously described Sky_Member and Arcade databases is that the Enroll database requires multiple relationships. There are four foreign keys in this database, and each will require the creation of a relationship linking it to its corresponding primary key. The INSTRUCTOR$id and COURSE$code columns in the SECTION table must be linked to the primary keys in the INSTRUCTOR and COURSE tables, respectively. The STUDENT$id and SECTION$call_no columns in the ENROLL table must be linked to the primary keys in the STUDENT and SECTION tables, respectively.

This time, we are going to build the relationships using a diagram, which is a different method from our earlier example. In our opinion, using a diagram to create a relationship is easier when you have several relationships to create. Start by right-clicking Diagrams in the Tree pane of Enterprise Manager. Next, select New Diagram from the menu. This step will bring up a wizard that will guide you through the process of creating a diagram. Click Next, which takes you to a window where you select the tables to be included in the diagram. Select the five tables you created from the Available Tables list on the left-hand side. You'll probably have to scroll down to find the correct tables. Notice that our tables are grouped together, because all of our tables begin with "tbl." The other tables you see are automatically created by SQL Server. Your wizard should now be similar to the one in Exhibit 10-25. Click Next one more time, verify that you have correct tables selected, and click Finish.

Exhibit 10-25

The Create Database Diagram Wizard

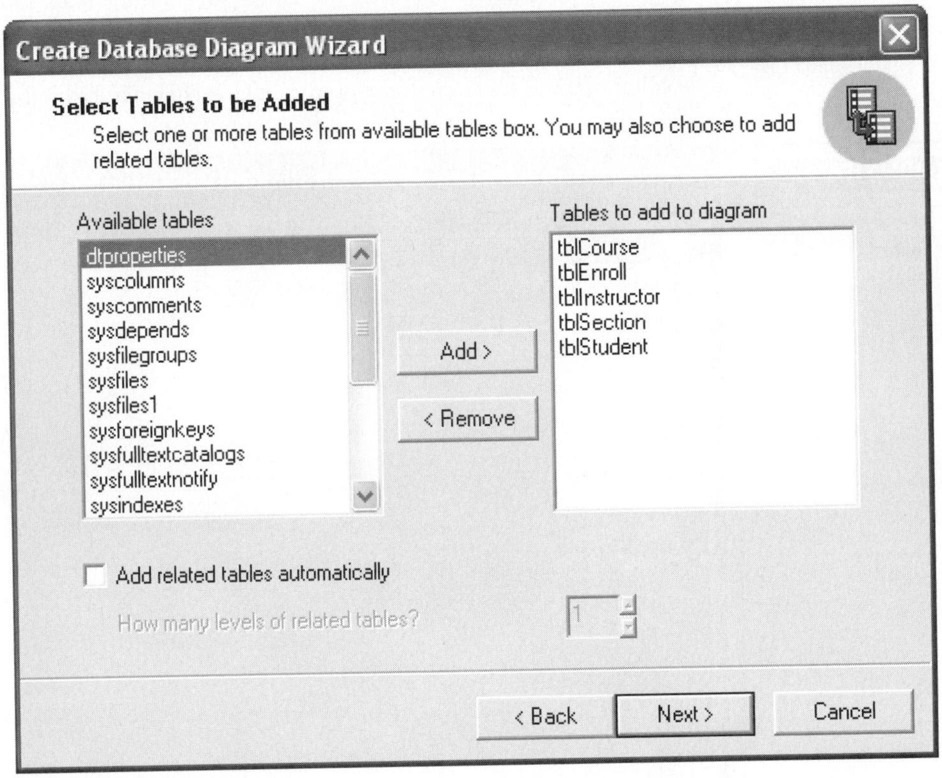

You should now see the new diagram in a window. If the tables are too small, you can zoom in by right-clicking in the white space of the diagram (not on one of the tables) and selecting a 100% zoom. Arrange the tables by dragging them until you get something that looks like Exhibit 10-26.

Exhibit 10-26

Creating a Diagram

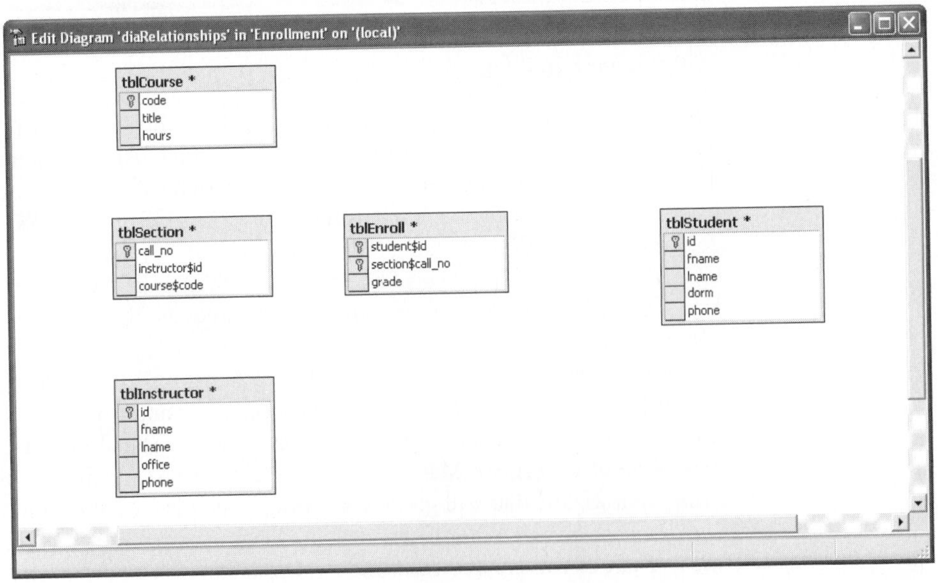

Now you are ready to create the relationships. To create a relationship, first drag from the primary key of the relationship to the foreign key that references it. For example, drag from code in tblCourse to COURSE$code in tblSection. You need to drag from the column next to the column name, not the column name itself. Once you complete the drag operation, a Create Relationship window appears. Make sure that the proper primary and foreign keys and tables are selected. Sometimes the foreign key is not shown or the wrong column is selected, so it is important to make sure this information is correct. Exhibit 10-27 shows the Create Relationship window for the relationship between tblInstructor (primary key) and tblSection (foreign key).

Exhibit 10-27

Creating a
Relationship

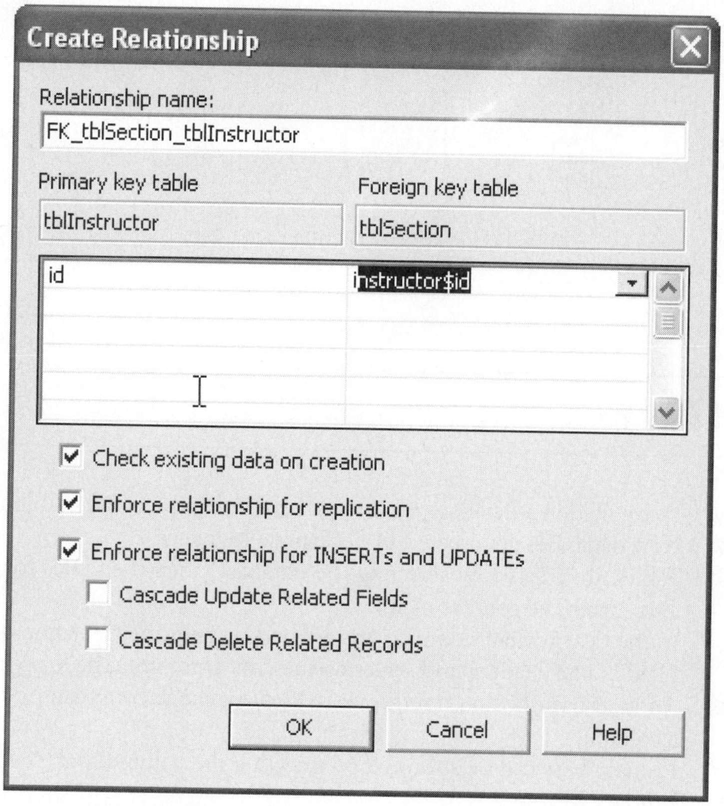

Create Relationship

Relationship name:

FK_tblSection_tblInstructor

Primary key table	Foreign key table
tblInstructor	tblSection

id	instructor$id

☑ Check existing data on creation

☑ Enforce relationship for replication

☑ Enforce relationship for INSERTs and UPDATEs

☐ Cascade Update Related Fields

☐ Cascade Delete Related Records

[OK] [Cancel] [Help]

Continue this process for the rest of the relationships. When you are finished, your diagram should look something like Exhibit 10-28. Save the diagram. Also, be sure to answer "Yes" when asked if you want to save the tables.

Exhibit 10-28

Relationships
for the Enroll
Database

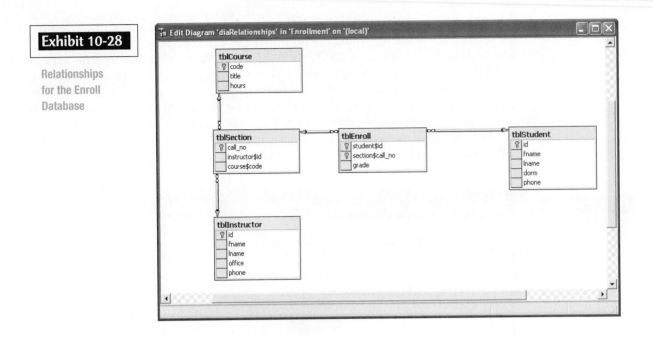

SUMMARY

- Every field in a database table must have a data type and column width.
- New databases are created in Enterprise Manager.
- Tables are created by selecting the database, then the tables folder, then selecting New Table from the context menu.
- In the design view, columns are defined by entering the name of the column under the Field Name heading and selecting the data type using the drop-down list.
- Another useful column setting is to create a check constraint to limit the valid values for a column.
- Primary keys can be specified by selecting the column, right-clicking, then selecting Set Primary Key.
- The table is named when the table design is saved.
- Once the structure of the table is created, the datasheet view can be used to enter data.
- If a validation rule is violated during data entry, a dialog box will appear, indicating the error.
- Either Enterprise Manager or Query Analyzer can be used to display or enter data.
- With a multitable database, the referential integrity between the foreign and primary keys can be created either through the table Properties window or by first creating a diagram, then dragging from the primary key to the foreign key.
- Concatenated primary keys are created by selecting all columns making up the primary key and then selecting Set Primary Key from the context menu.

KEY TERMS

Check constraint. A setting for a column where you can specify conditions to which data values must conform when being inserted into the column.

Database diagram. View of a database where you can display database tables and create relationships between foreign and primary keys.

Database window. Displays the various components of an SQL Server database, and provides options for creating additional components.

Datasheet view. A view of a table in which data can be entered, changed, and displayed.

Enterprise Manager. Program in SQL Server used to carry out database administration tasks, including creating databases, indexes, and other database objects.

Query Analyzer. Component in SQL Server used to process queries to retrieve data from tables.

Tree pane. Area that shows the structure of your SQL Server environment.

EXERCISES

Review

1. What is the Enterprise Manager in SQL Server?
2. What is the Tree pane used for?
3. What are the data types available in SQL Server?
4. What is a reserved word?
5. What is the purpose of a check constraint for a column?
6. How is a primary key specified?
7. What is the datasheet view used for?
8. How is a relationship created in SQL Server?
9. How is a concatenated primary key created?
10. Name two ways in which to establish relationships in SQL Server.

Discuss

1. List and explain the steps for creating a database in SQL Server.
2. What are some of the components of an SQL Server database that appear in the database window?
3. Explain how a check constraint would be used to create a restriction that requires a column to contain either the word *Yes* or the word *No*.
4. Explain how referential integrity is set up in SQL Server.
5. What restrictions does referential integrity place on the way data is entered into tables?

Practice

1. Create the Hospital database using the specifications shown in Exhibit 10-29.

Exhibit 10-29   Design and Data for the Hospital Database

Physical Details

Design Table 'Doctor' in 'Hospital' on '(local)'

Column Name	Data Type	Length	Allow Nulls
id	nvarchar	5	
fname	nvarchar	15	✓
lname	nvarchar	15	✓
phone	nvarchar	12	✓
beeper	nvarchar	12	✓

Design Table 'Patient' in 'Hospital' on '(local)'

Column Name	Data Type	Length	Allow Nulls
id	nvarchar	5	
doctor$id	nvarchar	5	✓
fname	nvarchar	15	✓
lname	nvarchar	15	✓
street	nvarchar	15	✓
city	nvarchar	10	✓
state	nvarchar	2	✓
zip	nvarchar	10	✓
phone	nvarchar	12	✓

Design Table 'Insurance' in 'Hospital' on '(local)'

Column Name	Data Type	Length	Allow Nulls
company	nvarchar	15	
contact_fname	nvarchar	15	✓
contact_lname	nvarchar	15	✓
phone	nvarchar	12	✓

Design Table 'Insure' in 'Hospital' on '(local)'

Column Name	Data Type	Length	Allow Nulls
patient$id	nvarchar	5	
insurance$company	nvarchar	15	✓

Design

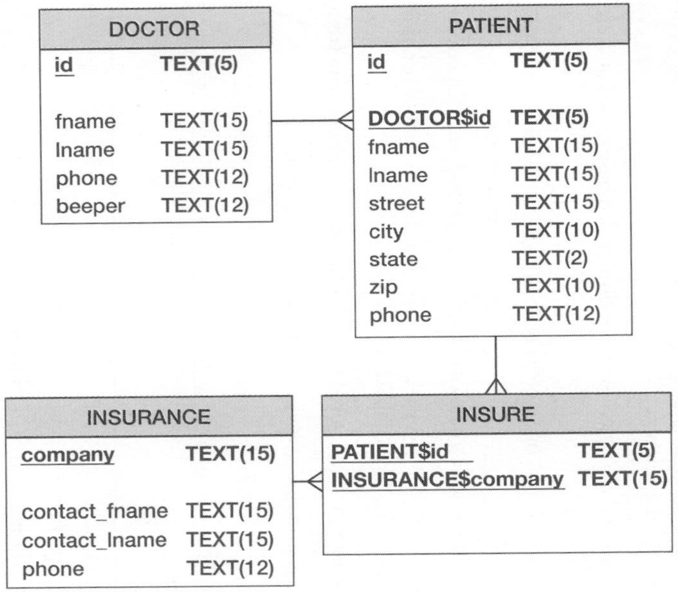

DOCTOR

id	TEXT(5)
fname	TEXT(15)
lname	TEXT(15)
phone	TEXT(12)
beeper	TEXT(12)

PATIENT

id	TEXT(5)
DOCTOR$id	TEXT(5)
fname	TEXT(15)
lname	TEXT(15)
street	TEXT(15)
city	TEXT(10)
state	TEXT(2)
zip	TEXT(10)
phone	TEXT(12)

INSURE

PATIENT$id	TEXT(5)
INSURANCE$company	TEXT(15)

INSURANCE

company	TEXT(15)
contact_fname	TEXT(15)
contact_lname	TEXT(15)
phone	TEXT(12)

Exhibit 10-29

Continued

DOCTOR

id	fname	lname	phone	beeper
00001	Perry	Cox	555-1111	555-1212
00002	Elliot	Reid	555-2222	555-2323
00003	JD	Dorian	555-3333	555-3434
00004	Chris	Turk	555-5555	555-4545
00005	Bob	Kelso	555-6666	555-5656

PATIENT

id	DOCTOR$id	fname	lname	street	city	state	zip	phone
11111	00001	Jim	Perotti	12 Oak St	Shade	OH	45701	555-1234
22222	00001	Glen	Stamler	1 Walnut Ave	Athens	FL	58475	555-2345
33333	00002	Maddy	Gray	45 Maple St	Glouster	KY	73674	555-3456
44444	00003	Blake	Shelton	3 Elm Blvd	Shade	OH	45701	555-4567
55555	00003	EJ	Thornton	92 Ash St	Orlando	FL	85744	555-5678
66666	00004	Dyrk	Ashton	33 Poplar Ave	Columbus	OH	47837	555-6789

INSURANCE

company	contact_fname	contact_lname	phone
Prudential	Jan	Johnson	555-9876
State Farm	Sam	Smith	555-8765
Nationwide	Randy	Buck	555-7654

INSURE

PATIENT$id	INSURANCE$company
11111	Prudential
22222	Prudential
33333	State Farm
44444	Nationwide
55555	Nationwide
66666	State Farm

2. Create the Acme database using the specifications shown in Exhibit 10-30.

Exhibit 10-30   The Acme Database

Physical Details

Design

CUSTOMER

id	TEXT(5)
fname	TEXT(15)
lname	TEXT(15)
bday	DATE
phone	TEXT(12)

ORDER

id	TEXT(5)
CUSTOMER$id	TEXT(5)
xdate	DATE
delivery	TEXT(10)
wrap	TEXT(1)

PRODUCT

id	TEXT(5)
list_price	SINGLE
description	TEXT(20)

LINEITEM

ORDER$id	TEXT(5)
PRODUCT$id	TEXT(15)
quantity	INTEGER
sale_price	SINGLE

Design Table 'Customer' in 'Acme' on '(local)'

Column Name	Data Type	Length	Allow Nulls
id	nvarchar	5	✓
fname	nvarchar	15	✓
lname	nvarchar	15	✓
bday	smalldatetime	4	✓
phone	nvarchar	12	✓

Design Table 'Order' in 'Acme' on '(local)'

Column Name	Data Type	Length	Allow Nulls
id	nvarchar	5	
customer$id	nvarchar	5	✓
[date]	smalldatetime	4	✓
delivery	nvarchar	10	✓
wrap	nvarchar	1	✓

Design Table 'Product' in 'Acme' on '(local)'

Column Name	Data Type	Length	Allow Nulls
id	nvarchar	5	✓
list_price	real	4	✓
description	nvarchar	20	✓

Design Table 'lineitem' in 'Acme' on '(local)'

Column Name	Data Type	Length	Allow Nulls
order$id	nvarchar	5	✓
product$id	nvarchar	5	✓
quantity	smallint	2	✓
sale_price	real	4	✓

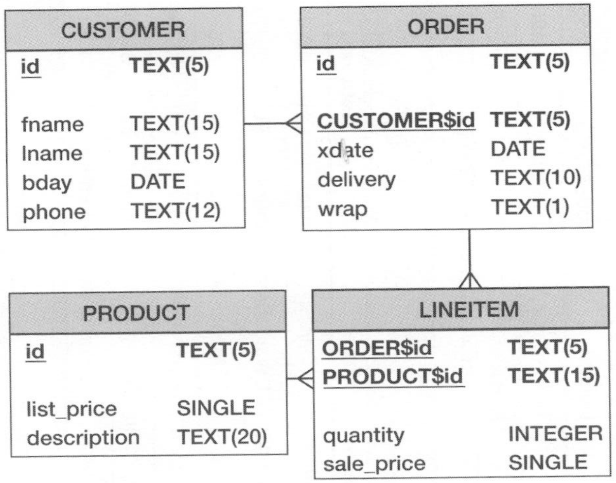

Exhibit 10-30

Continued

CUSTOMER

id	fname	lname	bday	phone
11111	Glen	Stamler	9/13/1974	555-3232
22222	Maddy	Gray	8/05/1984	555-8475
33333	Blake	Shelton	7/25/1975	555-4875
44444	EJ	Thornton	2/04/1988	555-9845

ORDER

id	CUSTOMER$id	date	delivery	wrap
10000	11111	2/04/2003	N	N
10001	22222	2/05/2003	Y	Y
10002	11111	2/05/2003	N	N
10003	33333	2/06/2003	Y	N

PRODUCT

id	list_price	description
00001	15.95	lager
00002	25.24	stout
00003	13.95	light
00004	19.98	pilsner
00005	18.75	microbrew
00006	18.57	ale
00007	15.95	bock
00008	19.95	portor

LINEITEM

ORDER$id	PRODUCT$id	quantity	sale_price
10000	00001	1	15.75
10000	00003	2	13.95
10001	00002	1	23.95
10001	00005	1	18.50
10002	00008	3	21.75
10003	00006	1	18.35
10003	00001	2	15.95
10003	00003	1	12.95
10003	00004	1	19.98

3. Create the Amazon database using the specifications shown in Exhibit 10-31.

Exhibit 10-31

The Amazon Database

Physical Details

Design Table 'Client' in 'Amazon' on '(local)'

Column Name	Data Type	Length	Allow Nulls
email	nvarchar	20	✓
fname	nvarchar	15	✓
lname	nvarchar	15	✓
street	nvarchar	20	✓
city	nvarchar	15	✓
state	nvarchar	2	✓
zip	nvarchar	10	✓

Design Table 'Order' in 'Amazon' on '(local)'

Column Name	Data Type	Length	Allow Nulls
client$email	nvarchar	20	✓
order_date	smalldatetime	4	✓
credit_card	nvarchar	16	✓
exp_date	smalldatetime	4	✓
ship_method	nvarchar	10	✓

Design Table 'Book' in 'Amazon' on '(local)'

Column Name	Data Type	Length	Allow Nulls
isbn	nvarchar	10	
title	nvarchar	20	✓
fname	nvarchar	15	✓
lname	nvarchar	15	✓
list_price	real	4	✓
qoh	smallint	2	✓

Design Table 'Lineitem' in 'Amazon' on '(local)'

Column Name	Data Type	Length	Allow Nulls
order$id	nvarchar	5	✓
book$isbn	nvarchar	10	✓
sale_price	real	4	✓
quantity	smallint	2	✓

Design

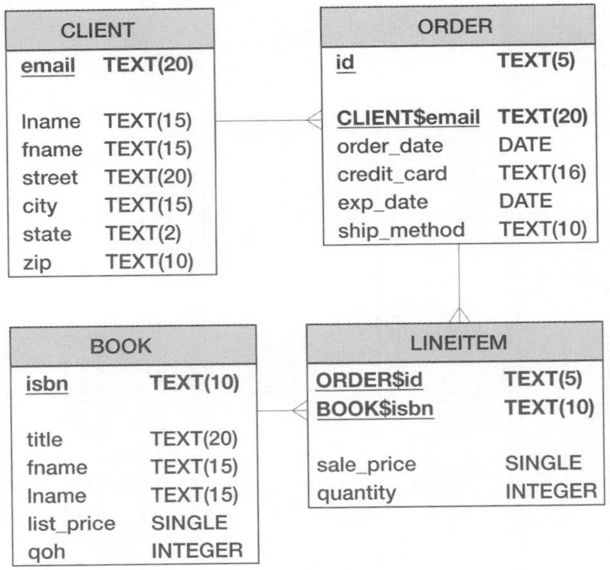

CLIENT

email	TEXT(20)
lname	TEXT(15)
fname	TEXT(15)
street	TEXT(20)
city	TEXT(15)
state	TEXT(2)
zip	TEXT(10)

ORDER

id	TEXT(5)
CLIENT$email	TEXT(20)
order_date	DATE
credit_card	TEXT(16)
exp_date	DATE
ship_method	TEXT(10)

BOOK

isbn	TEXT(10)
title	TEXT(20)
fname	TEXT(15)
lname	TEXT(15)
list_price	SINGLE
qoh	INTEGER

LINEITEM

ORDER$id	TEXT(5)
BOOK$isbn	TEXT(10)
sale_price	SINGLE
quantity	INTEGER

Exhibit 10-31

Continued

CLIENT

email	fname	lname	street	city	state	zip
mtfrost@yahoo.com	Tere	Frost	75 Algaringo	Miami	FL	33134
perotti@ohio.edu	Jim	Perotti	54 Pine Pl.	Athens	OH	45701
thacker@ohio.edu	Rebecca	Thacker	93 Maple Dr.	Athens	OH	45701

BOOK

isbn	title	fname	lname	list_price	qoh
0312099436	Women of the Silk	Gail	Tsukiyama	12.95	150
014025448X	At Home in Mitford	Jan	Karon	12.95	97
0345423097	Joy School	Elizabeth	Berg	11.95	129
0670894370	A Common Life	Jan	Karon	24.95	45

ORDER

id	CLIENT$email	order_date	credit_card	exp_date	ship_method
001	thacker@ohio.edu	11/15/2002	9999888877776666	07/31/2003	FedEx
002	perotti@ohio.edu	11/23/2002	3333444455556666	04/30/2005	USPS
003	thacker@ohio.edu	12/02/2002	4444111122223333	10/31/2004	USPS

LINEITEM

XORDER$id	BOOK$isbn	sale_price	quantity
001	0312099436	10.36	2
001	014025448X	10.36	3
002	0312099436	11.50	1
002	0670894370	17.46	2
003	0670894370	18.00	1

Learning Objectives

After completing this chapter, you will be able to:

- Describe the three basic relational database retrieval operations.
- Use the SQL Select statement to retrieve all data in a table.
- Specify a specific column list in a Select statement.
- Sort the results of a Select statement by one or more columns in ascending or descending order.
- Use one or more conditions in a where clause to limit the rows included in the results of a Select statement.
- Identify and properly use conditional operators in Select statements.
- Properly use AND and OR operators to express multiple conditions in a Select statement.
- Use aggregate functions in Select statements.
- Use group by to create subaggregations in Select statements.
- Use having to limit the results of queries involving aggregate functions.
- Properly use distinct in a Select statement.
- Create join conditions for Select statements that involve multiple tables.
- Use column and table name aliases.
- Use subqueries.

Retrieving Data with SQL Server

Introduction

One of the major advantages of the relational database approach is that it enables very flexible data retrieval. Basically, you can view the data in the database just about any way you desire. The trick is in knowing how to write the code required to retrieve the proper rows and columns. The good news is that for many retrieval operations, the code is quite simple. The bad news is that sometimes the code is very complex. In this chapter, we introduce you to data retrieval using SQL through examples using SQL Server. Although we use SQL Server for our example, the SQL you will learn in this chapter is very transferable to other database management systems.

We begin the chapter by providing an overview of the most basic operations of SQL, and then we provide a number of examples of retrieving data from a single table. After you are familiar with single-table retrieval, we show you how to retrieve data from multiple tables. We encourage you to follow along with our examples and practice problems. To really understand SQL, you have to write a lot of queries. By making errors and figuring out how to fix them, you will gain a deeper understanding of the language.

Basic Retrieval Operations in SQL

There are three core data retrieval operations for relational databases, selection, projection, and joining. (There are additional operations, but these three are the most important for learning SQL.)

- **Selection** retrieves a subset of rows.
- **Projection** retrieves a subset of columns.
- **Joining** combines data from two tables. (You can use more than one join operation to combine data from more than two tables.)

SQL implements all three of these operations through a single statement called the **Select** statement. We know that this idea is a bit confusing at first, but you will get used to it quickly. The most basic form of the Select statement is shown below.

Select   [column list]

From   [table names]

As you can see, an SQL Select statement can be quite simple. The only required elements are (1) the word *Select* followed by a list of columns, and (2) the word *From* followed by the name of the table(s) that hold the requested data. The project operation we described earlier is implemented through the column list in the Select statement.

Let's look at a specific example. Recall that in Chapter 10, we built the Sky_Member database in SQL Server. We will use that database for the examples in this section. The Sky_Member database has only one table, called tblMember. For your reference, the design of the Sky_Member database is shown in Exhibit 11-1.

Exhibit 11-1   Sky_Member Database

Physical Details

Design Table 'tblMember' in 'SkyMember' o...

	Column Name	Data Type	Length	Allow Nulls
	email	nvarchar	20	
	fname	nvarchar	15	
	lname	nvarchar	15	
	phone	nvarchar	12	✓
	jumps	int	4	✓
	equip	nvarchar	1	✓
	skill	nvarchar	1	✓

Design

tblMEMBER	
email	TEXT(20)
fname	TEXT(15)
lname	TEXT(15)
phone	TEXT(12)
jumps	INTEGER
equip	TEXT(1)
skill	TEXT(1)

Data

email	fname	lname	phone	jumps	equip	skill
dayj@ohio.edu	John	Day	529-0646	5	Y	B
luce@ohio.edu	Thom	Luce	592-1111	12	N	I
mcgann@ohio.edu	Sean	McGann	592-2222	20	Y	A

Displaying All Columns and Rows

Suppose you want a complete list of members showing all data about all members. This is the simplest SQL query. (Database people call SQL Select statements *queries*.) Although we could list all of the column names included in the table, we can use a shortcut. If you use an asterisk (*) as the column list in a Select statement, you indicate that you want all columns included in the query results. Exhibit 11-2 shows the Select statement used to retrieve all of the data from the tblMember table.

Exhibit 11-2

Select * Query

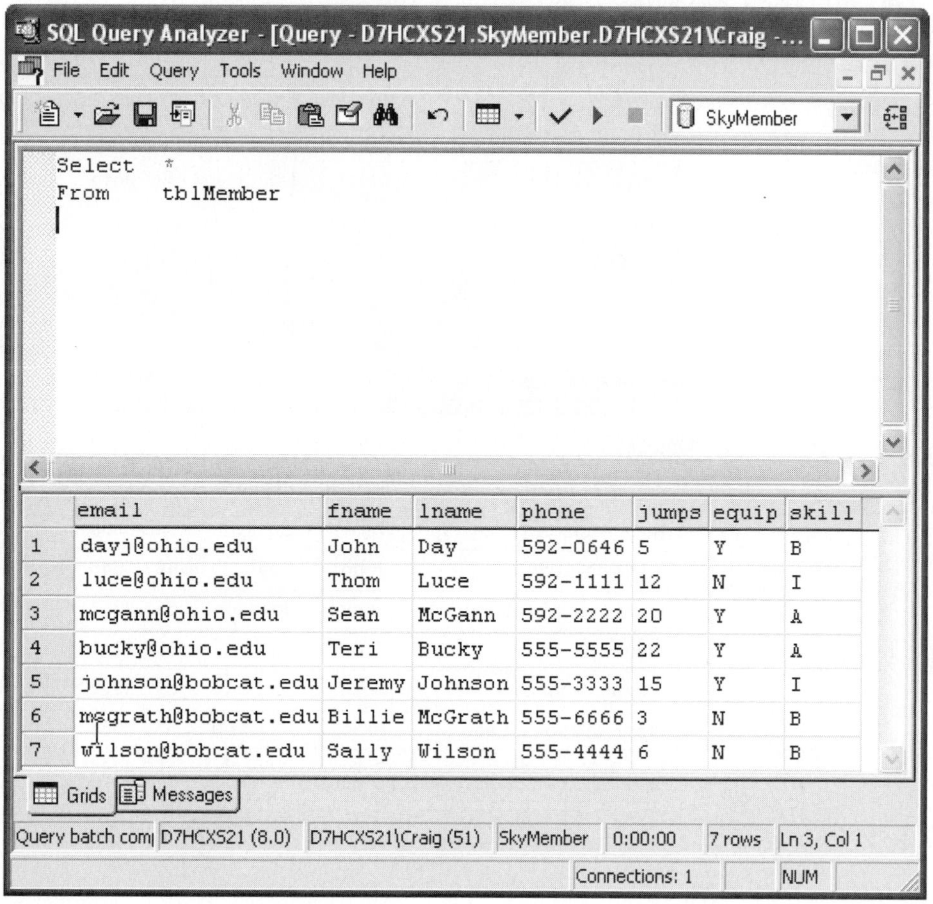
SQL Query Analyzer - [Query - D7HCXS21.SkyMember.D7HCXS21\Craig -...
File Edit Query Tools Window Help
SkyMember
Select *
From tblMember
email fname lname phone jumps equip skill
1 dayj@ohio.edu John Day 592-0646 5 Y B
2 luce@ohio.edu Thom Luce 592-1111 12 N I
3 mcgann@ohio.edu Sean McGann 592-2222 20 Y A
4 bucky@ohio.edu Teri Bucky 555-5555 22 Y A
5 johnson@bobcat.edu Jeremy Johnson 555-3333 15 Y I
6 mcgrath@bobcat.edu Billie McGrath 555-6666 3 N B
7 wilson@bobcat.edu Sally Wilson 555-4444 6 N B
Grids Messages
Query batch com| D7HCXS21 (8.0) D7HCXS21\Craig (51) SkyMember 0:00:00 7 rows Ln 3, Col 1
Connections: 1 NUM

To understand how an SQL statement works, the diagram in Exhibit 11-3 shows a breakdown of each part of the SQL statement and how it relates to the table involved in the query. We will use this type of diagram throughout this chapter when analyzing the SQL statements introduced in each part of the chapter.

Exhibit 11-3   Analysis of the Select Statement Retrieving All Columns and Rows

SELECT ALL ROWS AND COLUMNS
List all information about all members.

SELECT *
From tblmember

The * specifies that all columns appear in the result.

email	fname	lname	phone	jumps	equip	skill
bucky@ohio.edu	Teri	Bucky	555-5555	22	Y	A
dayj@ohio.edu	John	Day	592-0646	5	Y	B
johnson@bobcat.edu	Jeremy	Johnson	555-3333	15	Y	I
luce@ohio.edu	Thom	Luce	592-1111	12	N	I
mcgann@ohio.edu	Sean	McGann	592-2222	20	Y	A
mcgrath@bobcat.edu	Billie	McGrath	555-6666	3	N	B
wilson@bobcat.edu	Sally	Wilson	555-4444	6	N	B

RESULT

email	fname	lname	phone	jumps	equip	skill
bucky@ohio.edu	Teri	Bucky	555-5555	22	Y	A
dayj@ohio.edu	John	Day	592-0646	5	Y	B
johnson@bobcat.edu	Jeremy	Johnson	555-3333	15	Y	I
luce@ohio.edu	Thom	Luce	592-1111	12	N	I
mcgann@ohio.edu	Sean	McGann	592-2222	20	Y	A
mcgrath@bobcat.edu	Billie	McGrath	555-6666	3	N	B
wilson@bobcat.edu	Sally	Wilson	555-4444	6	N	B

In this diagram, the Select statement is shown on the left, with a particular part of the statement in bold type. In the table of data on the right, the aspect of the table affected by the boldfaced portion of the Select statement is indicated with shading.

In the first panel of the diagram, the Select * in the SQL statement is bold, and the diagram indicates the columns that will be selected for the query. In this case, the asterisk causes all of the columns to be selected, so the names of all of the columns have been shaded. The second panel shows the result of the query. In this case, all of the columns and all of the rows will be displayed.

The SQL Server Query Analyzer

Before going any further, it is a good idea to go over SQL Server's Query Analyzer, which is how you run SQL commands in SQL Server. Reviewing the Query Analyzer will help when you try out the examples. The important elements in terms of this chapter are numbered in Exhibit 11-4 and explained below.

1. The database selection list allows you to select the database you want to query. One very common mistake is to *not* select the correct database. Fortunately, this mistake is easily corrected by simply selecting the appropriate database from the list.
2. The *query pane*, which is also known as the *query window*, is where you enter your SQL query. You can copy and paste to or from this window.
3. Once your query is entered, you can run the query by clicking the Execute button.
4. The results of the query display in the *results pane*, which is sometimes called the *results window*. If there are no errors in the query, the record set (query results) will appear. If the query contains an error (or more than one error), an error message(s) will appear.
5. The Clear Window button allows you to quickly clear the contents of the query pane. The effect is the same as highlighting all of the contents and pressing Delete. If you do not clear the query pane before entering an additional query, when you click the Execute button, all queries will run, and multiple sets of results will appear in the results pane.
6. The object browser lets you examine the structure of each database on the server to which you are connected. This tool is particularly handy for looking up table and column names. In Exhibit 11-4, we expanded the tblMember table of the Sky_Member database to show the table's columns. The object browser can be hidden or displayed from the Tools menu.

Exhibit 11-4

SQL Server Query Analyzer

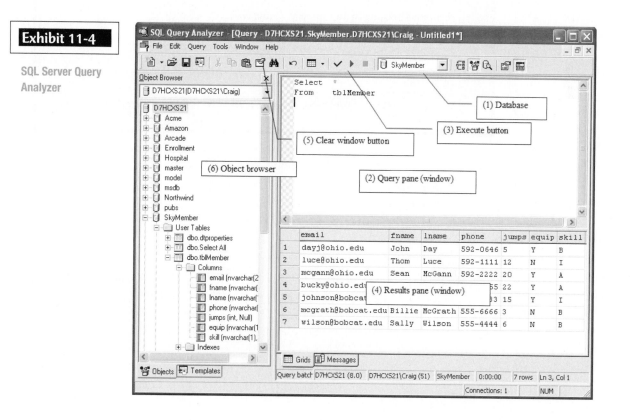

Using a Column List

Now let's say that you do not need all of the columns, and you only want to include the email addresses, first names, and last names of the members, in that order. To accomplish this task, we have to include an explicit column list, as shown in Exhibit 11-5.

Exhibit 11-5

Select Statement
with Explicit
Column List

SQL Query Analyzer - [Query - D7HCXS21.SkyMember.D7HCXS21\Crai...

File   Edit   Query   Tools   Window   Help

SkyMember

```
Select   email,
         fname,
         lname
From     tblMember
```

	email	fname	lname
1	dayj@ohio.edu	John	Day
2	luce@ohio.edu	Thom	Luce
3	mcgann@ohio.edu	Sean	McGann
4	bucky@ohio.edu	Teri	Bucky
5	johnson@bobcat.edu	Jeremy	Johnson
6	mcgrath@bobcat.edu	Billie	McGrath
7	wilson@bobcat.edu	Sally	Wilson

Grids   Messages

Query batch cc   D7HCXS21 (8.0)   D7HCXS21\Craig (51)   SkyMember   0:00:00   7 rows   Ln 5, Col 1

Connections: 1   NUM

When you include a column list that includes more than one column, you have to separate each column name in the list by commas. Some people like to put each column on a separate line and tab over to line up the columns. This process is done simply to improve readability. You can actually put the entire Select statement on a single line, but the query is much harder to read. Readability becomes more important as your queries become more complex. Exhibit 11-6 shows the analysis for this query.

Exhibit 11-6   Analysis of the Select Statement with an Explicit Column List

SELECT SPECIFIC COLUMNS
List email, fname, and lname for all members.

SELECT email,
        fname,
        lname
From tblMember;

email	fname	lname	phone	jumps	equip	skill
dayj@ohio.edu	John	Day	592-0646	5	Y	B
luce@ohio.edu	Thom	Luce	592-1111	12	N	I
mcgann@ohio.edu	Sean	McGann	592-2222	20	Y	A
bucky@ohio.edu	Teri	Bucky	555-5555	22	Y	A
johnson@bobcat.edu	Jeremy	Johnson	555-3333	15	Y	I
mcgrath@bobcat.edu	Billie	McGrath	555-6666	3	N	B
wilson@bobcat.edu	Sally	Wilson	555-4444	6	N	B

RESULT

email	fname	lname
dayj@ohio.edu	John	Day
luce@ohio.edu	Thom	Luce
mcgann@ohio.edu	Sean	McGann
bucky@ohio.edu	Teri	Bucky
johnson@bobcat.edu	Jeremy	Johnson
lmcgrath@bobcat.edu	Billie	McGrath
wilson@bobcat.edu	Sally	Wilson

The order of the columns in the column list dictates the order in which the columns are shown in the results. If you want the order of the columns (from left to right) to be fname, lname, then email, simply put the columns in that order in the Select statement's column list, as shown in Exhibit 11-7.

Exhibit 11-7

Select Statement with fname as the First Column

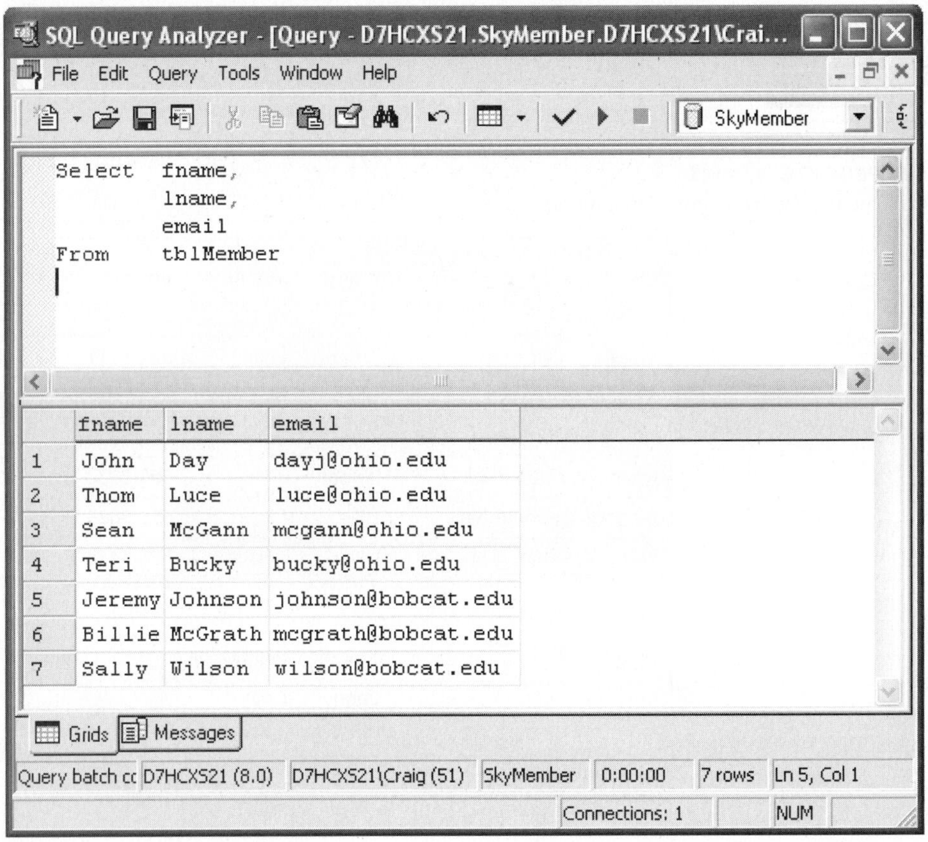

Sorting with Order By

Typically, you want your results to be shown in some logical order. For example, you might want the results in order of the member's email address. In SQL, the **order by** clause is used to sort results, as illustrated in Exhibit 11-8. Exhibit 11-9 shows the analysis for this query.

Exhibit 11-8

Select Statement
with Order by
Clause

```
Select    email,
          fname,
          lname
From      tblMember
Order by  email
```

	email	fname	lname
1	bucky@ohio.edu	Teri	Bucky
2	dayj@ohio.edu	John	Day
3	johnson@bobcat.edu	Jeremy	Johnson
4	luce@ohio.edu	Thom	Luce
5	mcgann@ohio.edu	Sean	McGann
6	mcgrath@bobcat.edu	Billie	McGrath
7	wilson@bobcat.edu	Sally	Wilson

SQL Query Analyzer - [Query - D7HCXS21.SkyMember.D7HCXS21\Crai...

File   Edit   Query   Tools   Window   Help

SkyMember

Grids   Messages

Query batch (D7HCXS21 (8.0)   D7HCXS21\Craig (51)   SkyMember   0:00:00   7 rows   Ln 5, Col 10

Connections: 1   NUM

Exhibit 11-9   Select Statement with Order by Clause

ORDER BY
List in order of email, the email, fname, and lname for all members.

```
SELECT   email,
         fname,
         lname
From     tblMember
Order by email
```

email	fname	lname	phone	jumps	equip	skill
dayj@ohio.edu	John	Day	592-0646	5	Y	B
luce@ohio.edu	Thom	Luce	592-1111	12	N	I
mcgann@ohio.edu	Sean	McGann	592-2222	20	Y	A
bucky@ohio.edu	Teri	Bucky	555-5555	22	Y	A
johnson@bobcat.edu	Jeremy	Johnson	555-3333	15	Y	I
mcgrath@bobcat.edu	Billie	McGrath	555-6666	3	N	B
wilson@bobcat.edu	Sally	Wilson	555-4444	6	N	B

(Continued)

Exhibit 11-9   Continued

ORDER BY
List in order of email, all email, fname, and lname for all members.

SELECT   email,
            fname,
            lname
From   tblMember
Order by email

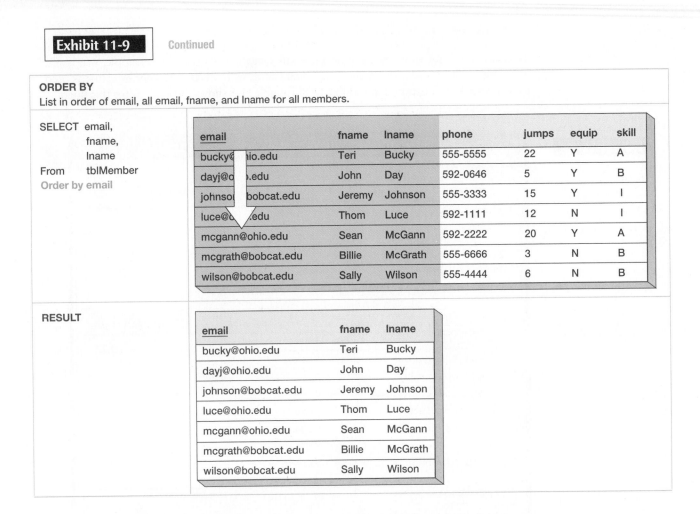

email	fname	lname	phone	jumps	equip	skill
bucky@ohio.edu	Teri	Bucky	555-5555	22	Y	A
dayj@ohio.edu	John	Day	592-0646	5	Y	B
johnson@bobcat.edu	Jeremy	Johnson	555-3333	15	Y	I
luce@ohio.edu	Thom	Luce	592-1111	12	N	I
mcgann@ohio.edu	Sean	McGann	592-2222	20	Y	A
mcgrath@bobcat.edu	Billie	McGrath	555-6666	3	N	B
wilson@bobcat.edu	Sally	Wilson	555-4444	6	N	B

RESULT

email	fname	lname
bucky@ohio.edu	Teri	Bucky
dayj@ohio.edu	John	Day
johnson@bobcat.edu	Jeremy	Johnson
luce@ohio.edu	Thom	Luce
mcgann@ohio.edu	Sean	McGann
mcgrath@bobcat.edu	Billie	McGrath
wilson@bobcat.edu	Sally	Wilson

Notice that the results are now in order of email address. Also notice that the order of columns in the column list is independent of the sort order specified in the order by clause. (Columns used in order by should, of course, be included in the column list. Usually, it would not make sense to sort by a column that is not displayed.) You should also notice that the last names are in A to Z order, which is called *ascending order*. This sort order is the default. If you want the rows to be in *descending order* (Z to A), you put *desc* after the column name. This step is shown in Exhibit 11-10. Although it is the default, you can explicitly specify ascending order by putting *asc* after the column name.

Exhibit 11-10

Sorting in
Descending Order

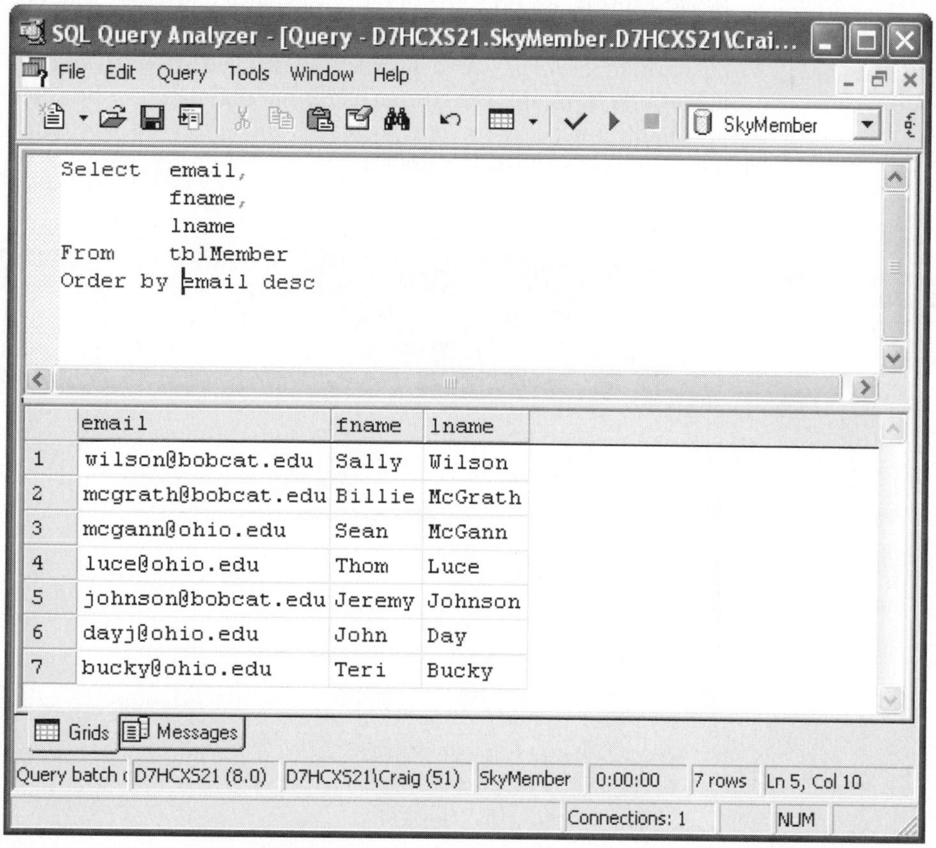

Sorting on Multiple Columns

Sometimes you may want to sort by multiple columns. Let's look at another example to illustrate how to do this sort. For this example, you want to show the skill level of each member, followed by the member's first and last names. The results should be in ascending order of skill level, then by last name in ascending order. For example, all members with one particular skill level are shown before those with the next skill level. Within the list of members with the same skill level, the rows are shown in ascending order by last name. All you have to do is list both sort columns in the order by clause. The column names must be separated by a comma. There is no practical limit to the number of columns you can include in an order by clause. Exhibit 11-11 gives the query used to produce these results.

Exhibit 11-11

Sorting by
Multiple Columns

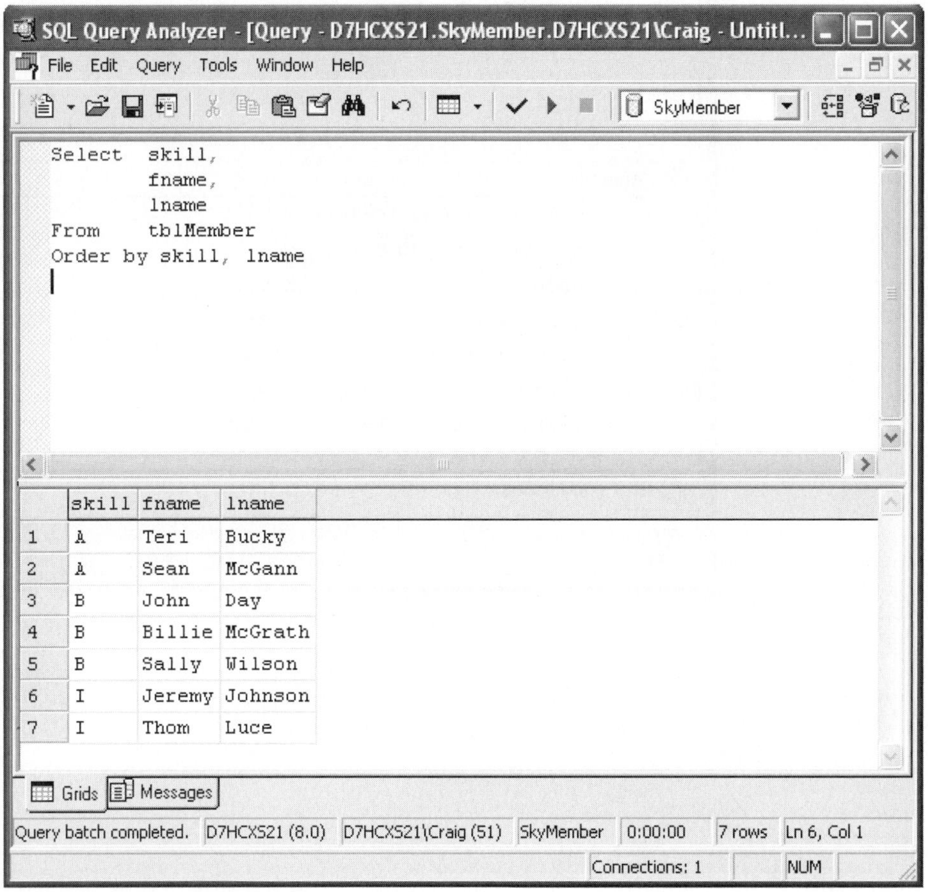

Now the process can get even more complicated. This time you want to list your results in *descending* order of skill level, then in *ascending* order of last name. Actually, this step is easy to do. All we have to do is to make one small change to the last query. Simply insert "desc" after the column name skill. Note that there is *not* a comma between "skill" and "desc." Exhibit 11-12 shows this query and its results.

Exhibit 11-12

Using Desc with
Multiple-Column
Sort

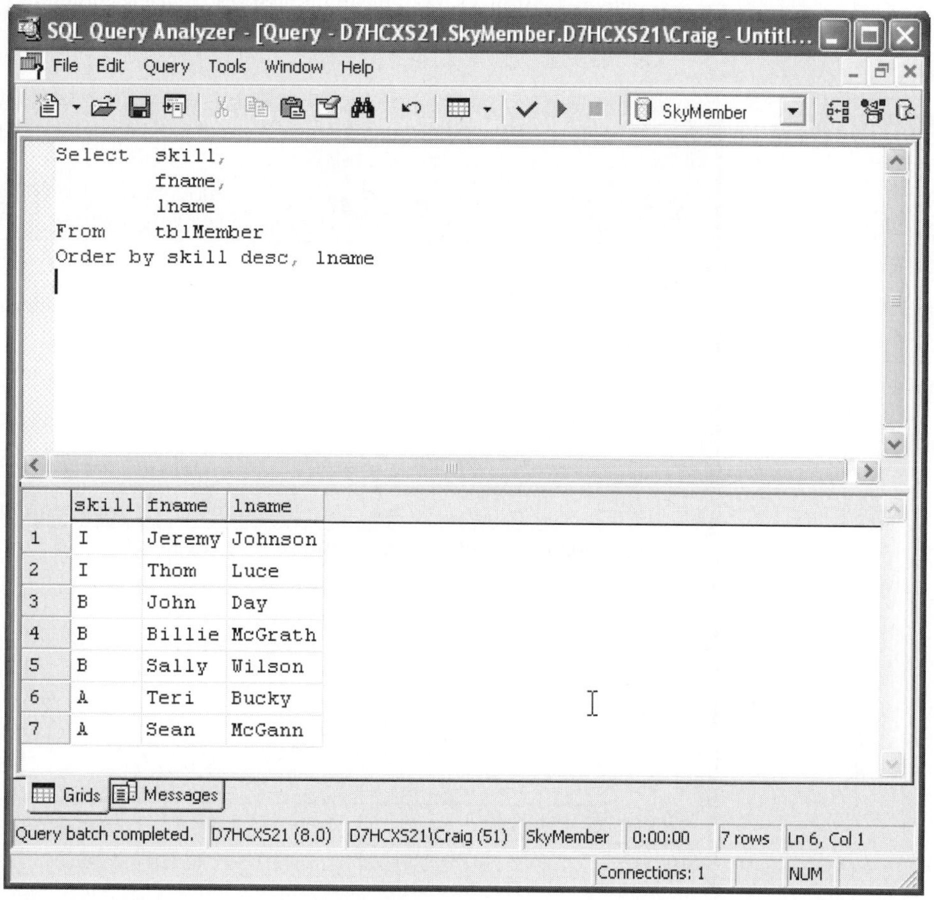

SQL Query Analyzer - [Query - D7HCXS21.SkyMember.D7HCXS21\Craig - Untitl...

File   Edit   Query   Tools   Window   Help

```
Select   skill,
         fname,
         lname
From     tblMember
Order by skill desc, lname
```

	skill	fname	lname
1	I	Jeremy	Johnson
2	I	Thom	Luce
3	B	John	Day
4	B	Billie	McGrath
5	B	Sally	Wilson
6	A	Teri	Bucky
7	A	Sean	McGann

Grids   Messages

Query batch completed.   D7HCXS21 (8.0)   D7HCXS21\Craig (51)   SkyMember   0:00:00   7 rows   Ln 6, Col 1

Connections: 1   NUM

Selecting Rows with Where

Let's take a look at how to limit which rows are included in the results. We will need to add another element to our simple Select statement. Rows are chosen through conditions specified in a **where clause** in the Select statement. (This is the method used to implement the Selection operation discussed at the beginning of the chapter.) If you wanted to see all columns for rows corresponding to members with 20 jumps, you would use the Select statement shown in Exhibit 11-13. The analysis of the query is shown in Exhibit 11-14.

Exhibit 11-13

Select Statement with Where Clause

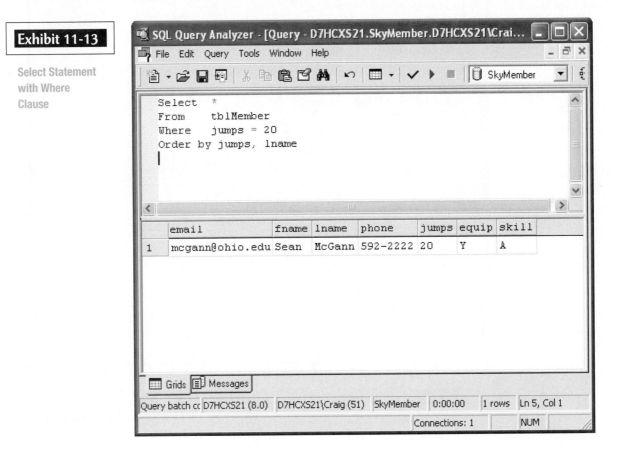

Exhibit 11-14   Analysis of Query with a Where Clause

SELECT SPECIFIC COLUMNS AND ROWS

List the jumps, fname, and lname for all members who have 20 jumps.

SELECT jumps,
        fname,
        lname
From   tblMember
Where jumps = 20

email	fname	lname	phone	jumps	equip	skill
dayj@ohio.edu	John	Day	592-0646	5	Y	B
luce@ohio.edu	Thom	Luce	592-1111	12	N	I
mcgann@ohio.edu	Sean	McGann	592-2222	20	Y	A
bucky@ohio.edu	Teri	Bucky	555-5555	22	Y	A
johnson@bobcat.edu	Jeremy	Johnson	555-3333	15	Y	I
mcgrath@bobcat.edu	Billie	McGrath	555-6666	3	N	B
wilson@bobcat.edu	Sally	Wilson	555-4444	6	N	B

SELECT jumps,
        fname,
        lname
From   tblMember
Where   jumps = 20

Only the rows containing 20 in the jumps column appear in the results.

email	fname	lname	phone	jumps	equip	skill
dayj@ohio.edu	John	Day	592-0646	5	Y	B
luce@ohio.edu	Thom	Luce	592-1111	12	N	I
mcgann@ohio.edu	Sean	McGann	592-2222	20	Y	A
bucky@ohio.edu	Teri	Bucky	555-5555	22	Y	A
johnson@bobcat.edu	Jeremy	Johnson	555-3333	15	Y	I
mcgrath@bobcat.edu	Billie	McGrath	555-6666	3	N	B
wilson@bobcat.edu	Sally	Wilson	555-4444	6	N	B

RESULT

jumps	fname	lname
20	Sean	McGann

A where clause always includes at least one condition, such as "jumps = 20" in the example. If a row meets the condition specified, it is included in the results. Rows that do not meet the condition are not included. Note that you can have more than one condition;

we will get to that situation later. If you are familiar with a programming language such as Visual Basic or Java, you already know about conditional operators. But just in case you are not, the commonly used operators are shown in Exhibit 11-15. We will add to this list later.

Exhibit 11-15

Conditional
Operators

Operator	Explanation	Example
=	Equal to	equip = 'N'
>	Greater than	jumps > 10
<	Less than	jumps < 20
>=	Greater than or equal to	jumps >= 10
<=	Less than or equal to	jumps <= 20
!=	Not equal to	ability != 'A'

Where Clauses Involving Text Data

When you want to use character-based columns in a where clause, you must put the character value inside single quotes. This step is illustrated in the equal to operator in Exhibit 11-15. If you wanted to see the first and last names of all members who own their own equipment, you would use the query in Exhibit 11-16.

Exhibit 11-16

Using Character-
Based Columns in
Where Clause

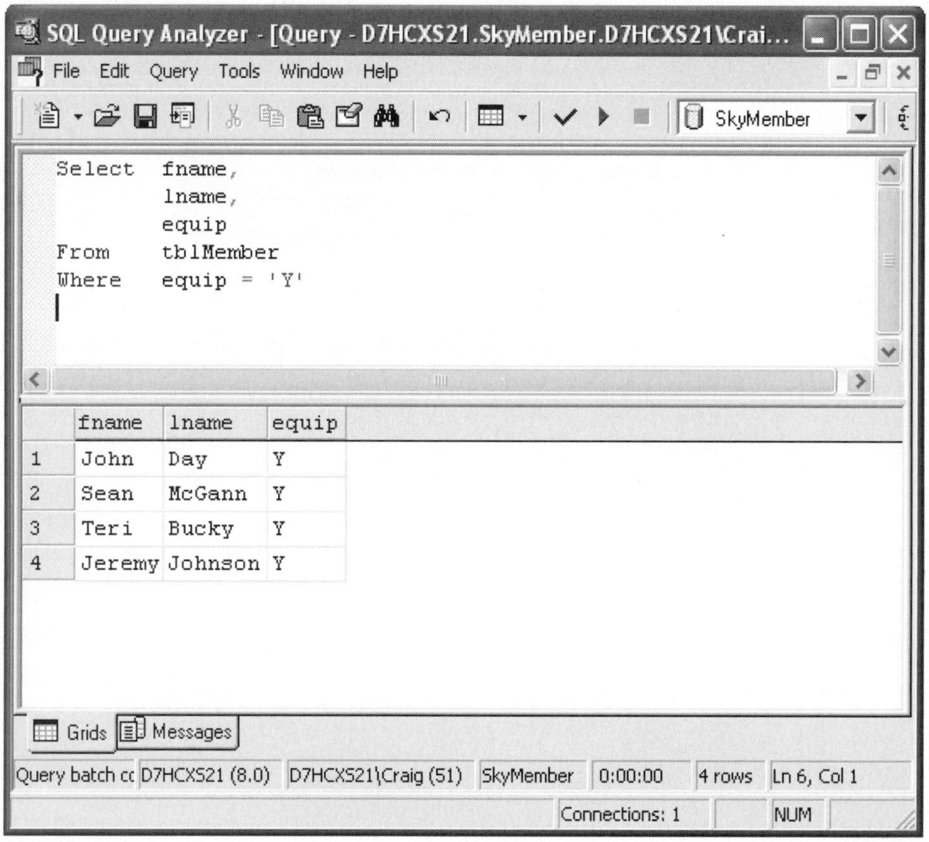

```
Select   fname,
         lname,
         equip
From     tblMember
Where    equip = 'Y'
```

	fname	lname	equip
1	John	Day	Y
2	Sean	McGann	Y
3	Teri	Bucky	Y
4	Jeremy	Johnson	Y

The LIKE operator

There is an additional conditional operator that is useful when dealing with character-based data. The **LIKE operator** allows you to choose rows that share some common characters but that are not exactly the same. For example, suppose you want to show the first and last names, email addresses, and phone numbers of all members who have phone numbers that start with "555." Exhibit 11-17 shows the query that returns the required rows.

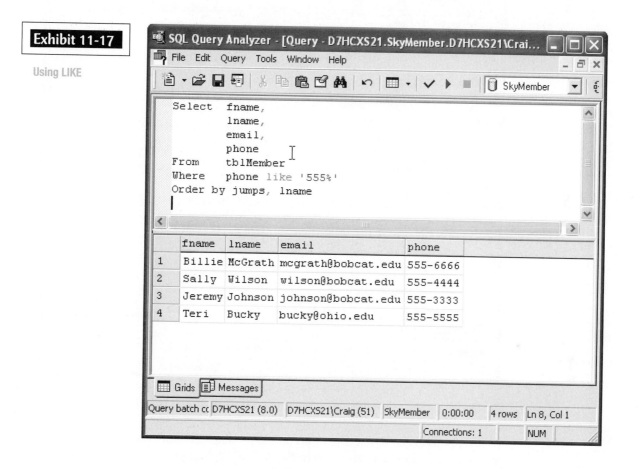

Exhibit 11-17

Using LIKE

The percent sign (%) is used as a wildcard representing any combination of characters. It serves the same function as the asterisk (*) in many operating systems. Any row that has a phone value starting with "555" is included in the results, regardless of what or how many characters follow. You can also use LIKE to return rows according to characters at the end or middle of a field value. Let's say that you want to execute the same basic query, but this time you want to limit the list to members who have "bobcat" email addresses (email addresses that have "bobcat" in them). The proper query is given in Exhibit 11-18.

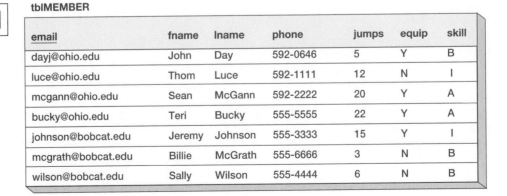

Where Clauses with Multiple Conditions

Sometimes you need to select rows according to more than one condition. With SQL, you make this selection in a single where clause. Each condition is separated by an operator. When conditions are separated by the **AND operator,** a row must meet *both* conditions to be selected. When the conditions are separated by the **OR operator,** a row is selected if *either* condition is met.

Let's look at examples of how to use each condition. Exhibit 11-19 shows data from the tblMember table. This data will help you follow the discussion.

tblMEMBER

email	fname	lname	phone	jumps	equip	skill
dayj@ohio.edu	John	Day	592-0646	5	Y	B
luce@ohio.edu	Thom	Luce	592-1111	12	N	I
mcgann@ohio.edu	Sean	McGann	592-2222	20	Y	A
bucky@ohio.edu	Teri	Bucky	555-5555	22	Y	A
johnson@bobcat.edu	Jeremy	Johnson	555-3333	15	Y	I
mcgrath@bobcat.edu	Billie	McGrath	555-6666	3	N	B
wilson@bobcat.edu	Sally	Wilson	555-4444	6	N	B

For the first example, we want to list the first and last names, number of jumps, and ability for all members who have more than 10 jumps and are at the intermediate skill level. The two conditions we want to satisfy are:

jumps > 10   AND   skill = 'I'

Which rows will be selected using these criteria? Remember that with the AND operator, *both* conditions must be satisfied. So only Thom Luce and Jeremy Johnson will be selected, as illustrated by the shaded rows in Exhibit 11-20.

Exhibit 11-20

Selected Data
Using AND

tblMEMBER

email	fname	lname	phone	jumps	equip	skill
dayj@ohio.edu	John	Day	592-0646	5	Y	B
luce@ohio.edu	Thom	Luce	592-1111	12	N	I
mcgann@ohio.edu	Sean	McGann	592-2222	20	Y	A
bucky@ohio.edu	Teri	Bucky	555-5555	22	Y	A
johnson@bobcat.edu	Jeremy	Johnson	555-3333	15	Y	I
mcgrath@bobcat.edu	Billie	McGrath	555-6666	3	N	B
wilson@bobcat.edu	Sally	Wilson	555-4444	6	N	B

Now let's change our criteria. This time, we want to list the first and last names, number of jumps, and ability for all members who either have more than 10 jumps or are at the intermediate skill level. In this case, the two conditions we want to satisfy are:

jumps > 10   OR   skill = 'I'

Can you tell which rows are selected this time? When using the OR operator, any row that meets *either* condition is selected. As before, Thom Luce and Jeremy Johnson are selected because they meet both conditions. But Sean McGann and Teri Bucky are also selected, because each has more than 10 jumps. It does not matter that neither is at the intermediate skill level. Because they have more than 10 jumps, they are selected regardless of their skill level. Exhibit 11-21 shows the rows selected using OR.

Exhibit 11-21

Selected Data
Using OR

tblMEMBER

email	fname	lname	phone	jumps	equip	skill
dayj@ohio.edu	John	Day	592-0646	5	Y	B
luce@ohio.edu	Thom	Luce	592-1111	12	N	I
mcgann@ohio.edu	Sean	McGann	592-2222	20	Y	A
bucky@ohio.edu	Teri	Bucky	555-5555	22	Y	A
johnson@bobcat.edu	Jeremy	Johnson	555-3333	15	Y	I
mcgrath@bobcat.edu	Billie	McGrath	555-6666	3	N	B
wilson@bobcat.edu	Sally	Wilson	555-4444	6	N	B

Now we will put each example in the form of an SQL query. Exhibit 11-22 shows the first example. We put the list in order of last name. Notice that we have only one where clause. That is a rule; you can have only one where clause in any single Select statement. We used AND to separate the two conditions. Exhibit 11-23 shows the analysis for this query.

Exhibit 11-22

Using the AND Operator

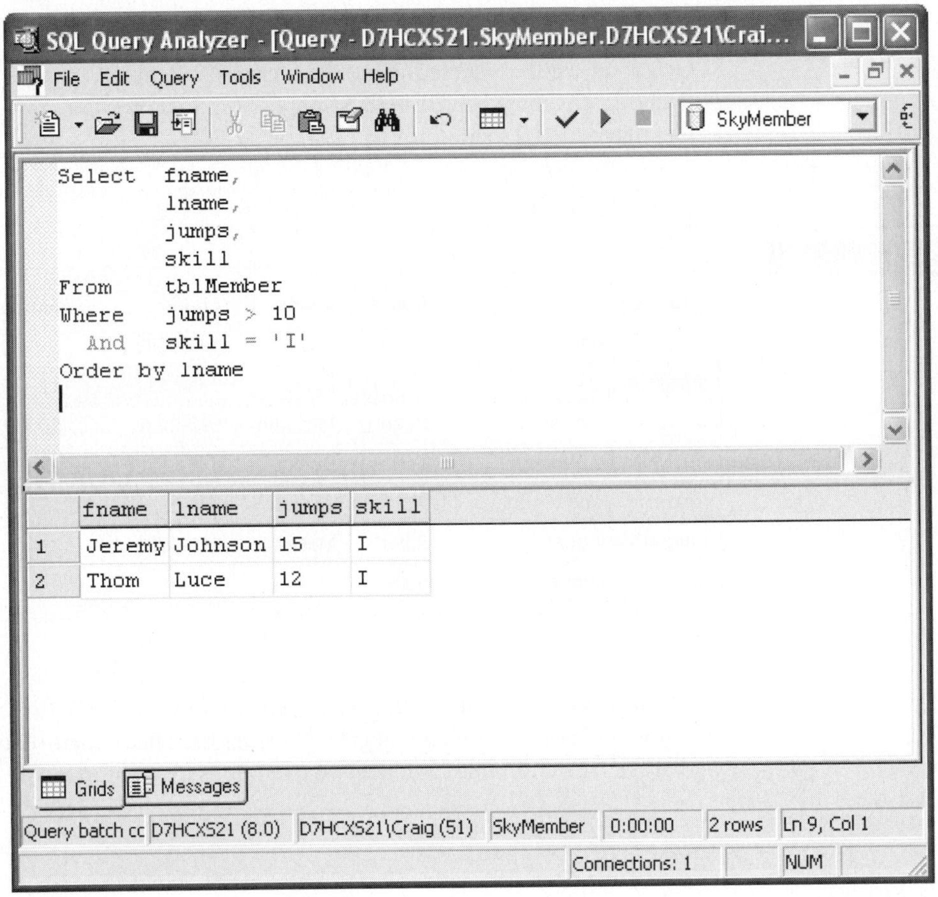
SQL Query Analyzer - [Query - D7HCXS21.SkyMember.D7HCXS21\Crai...
File Edit Query Tools Window Help
SkyMember
Select fname,
lname,
jumps,
skill
From tblMember
Where jumps > 10
And skill = 'I'
Order by lname
fname lname jumps skill
1 Jeremy Johnson 15 I
2 Thom Luce 12 I
Grids
Messages
Query batch cc
D7HCXS21 (8.0)
D7HCXS21\Craig (51)
SkyMember
0:00:00
2 rows
Ln 9, Col 1
Connections: 1
NUM

Exhibit 11-23   Analysis of the Query Using an AND Relationship

SELECT SPECIFIC COLUMS AND ROWS USING AND

List the fname, lname, jumps, and skill of all members who have more than 10 jumps and whose skill level is "I."

SELECT fname,
      lname,
      jumps,
      skill
From   tblMember
Where   jumps > 10
And   skill= 'I'
Order by lname

email	fname	lname	phone	jumps	equip	skill
dayj@ohio.edu	John	Day	592-0646	5	Y	B
luce@ohio.edu	Thom	Luce	592-1111	12	N	I
mcgann@ohio.edu	Sean	McGann	592-2222	20	Y	A
bucky@ohio.edu	Teri	Bucky	555-5555	22	Y	A
johnson@bobcat.edu	Jeremy	Johnson	555-3333	15	Y	I
mcgrath@bobcat.edu	Billie	McGrath	555-6666	3	N	B
wilson@bobcat.edu	Sally	Wilson	555-4444	6	N	B

SELECT fname,
      lname,
      jumps,
      skill
From   tblMember
Where   jumps > 10
And   skill= 'I'
Order by lname

email	fname	lname	phone	jumps	equip	skill
dayj@ohio.edu	John	Day	592-0646	5	Y	B
luce@ohio.edu	Thom	Luce	592-1111	12	N	I
mcgann@ohio.edu	Sean	McGann	592-2222	20	Y	A
bucky@ohio.edu	Teri	Bucky	555-5555	22	Y	A
johnson@bobcat.edu	Jeremy	Johnson	555-3333	15	Y	I
mcgrath@bobcat.edu	Billie	McGrath	555-6666	3	N	B
wilson@bobcat.edu	Sally	Wilson	555-4444	6	N	B

SELECT fname,
      lname,
      jumps,
      skill
From   tblMember
Where   jumps > 10
And   skill= 'I'
Order by lname

email	fname	lname	phone	jumps	equip	skill
dayj@ohio.edu	John	Day	592-0646	5	Y	B
luce@ohio.edu	Thom	Luce	592-1111	12	N	I
mcgann@ohio.edu	Sean	McGann	592-2222	20	Y	A
bucky@ohio.edu	Teri	Bucky	555-5555	22	Y	A
johnson@bobcat.edu	Jeremy	Johnson	555-3333	15	Y	I
mcgrath@bobcat.edu	Billie	McGrath	555-6666	3	N	B
wilson@bobcat.edu	Sally	Wilson	555-4444	6	N	B

RESULT

Results are sorted by lname.

fname	lname	jumps	skill
Jeremy	Johnson	15	I
Thom	Luce	12	I

Exhibit 11-24 gives the query for the second example. You might notice that the only difference between the two queries is that we used the OR operator in the second query. Otherwise, they are the same. You can have a virtually unlimited number of AND and OR operators in a single where clause. Later in this chapter, we will show you how to use both AND and OR in the same where clause. Exhibit 11-25 shows the analysis for this query.

Exhibit 11-24

Using the OR Operator

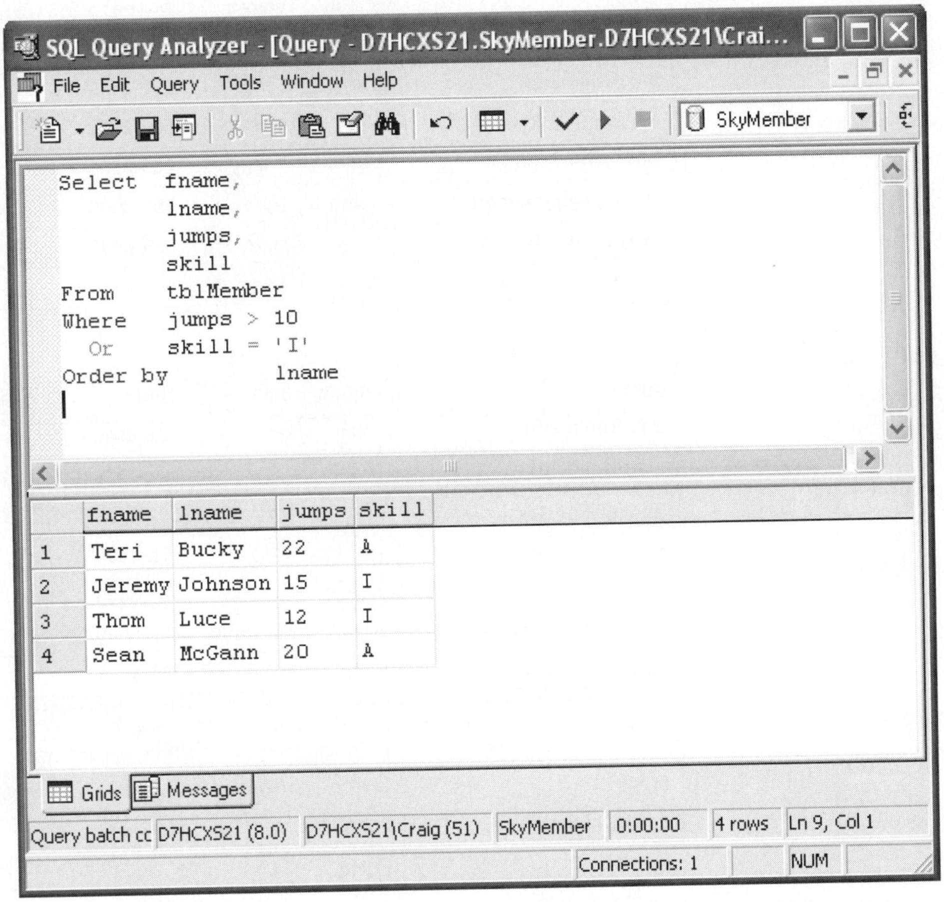
SQL Query Analyzer - [Query - D7HCXS21.SkyMember.D7HCXS21\Crai...
File Edit Query Tools Window Help
SkyMember
Select fname,
lname,
jumps,
skill
From tblMember
Where jumps > 10
Or skill = 'I'
Order by lname
fname lname jumps skill
1 Teri Bucky 22 A
2 Jeremy Johnson 15 I
3 Thom Luce 12 I
4 Sean McGann 20 A
Grids
Messages
Query batch cc
D7HCXS21 (8.0)
D7HCXS21\Craig (51)
SkyMember
0:00:00
4 rows
Ln 9, Col 1
Connections: 1
NUM

Exhibit 11-25 Analysis of the Query Using an OR Relationship

SELECT SPECIFIC COLUMNS AND ROWS USING OR

List the fname, lname, jumps, and skill of all members who have more than 10 jumps *or* whose skill level is "I."

```
SELECT  fname,
        lname,
        jumps,
        skill
From    tblMember
Where   jumps > 10
Or      skill= 'I'
Order by lname
```

email	fname	lname	phone	jumps	equip	skill
dayj@ohio.edu	John	Day	592-0646	5	Y	B
luce@ohio.edu	Thom	Luce	592-1111	12	N	I
mcgann@ohio.edu	Sean	McGann	592-2222	20	Y	A
bucky@ohio.edu	Teri	Bucky	555-5555	22	Y	A
johnson@bobcat.edu	Jeremy	Johnson	555-3333	15	Y	I
mcgrath@bobcat.edu	Billie	McGrath	555-6666	3	N	B
wilson@bobcat.edu	Sally	Wilson	555-4444	6	N	B

```
SELECT  fname,
        lname,
        jumps,
        skill
From    tblMember
Where   jumps > 10
Or      skill= 'I'
Order by lname
```

email	fname	lname	phone	jumps	equip	skill
dayj@ohio.edu	John	Day	592-0646	5	Y	B
luce@ohio.edu	Thom	Luce	592-1111	12	N	I
mcgann@ohio.edu	Sean	McGann	592-2222	20	Y	A
bucky@ohio.edu	Teri	Bucky	555-5555	22	Y	A
johnson@bobcat.edu	Jeremy	Johnson	555-3333	15	Y	I
mcgrath@bobcat.edu	Billie	McGrath	555-6666	3	N	B
wilson@bobcat.edu	Sally	Wilson	555-4444	6	N	B

```
SELECT  fname,
        lname,
        jumps,
        skill
From    tblMember
Where   jumps > 10
Or      skill= 'I'
Order by lname
```

email	fname	lname	phone	jumps	equip	skill
dayj@ohio.edu	John	Day	592-0646	5	Y	B
luce@ohio.edu	Thom	Luce	592-1111	12	N	I
mcgann@ohio.edu	Sean	McGann	592-2222	20	Y	A
bucky@ohio.edu	Teri	Bucky	555-5555	22	Y	A
johnson@bobcat.edu	Jeremy	Johnson	555-3333	15	Y	I
mcgrath@bobcat.edu	Billie	McGrath	555-6666	3	N	B
wilson@bobcat.edu	Sally	Wilson	555-4444	6	N	B

RESULT

Results are sorted by lname.

fname	lname	jumps	skill
Teri	Bucky	22	A
Jeremy	Johnson	15	I
Thom	Luce	12	I
Sean	McGann	20	A

This method is especially useful when you have many values in the value list. If you use OR conditions, you need one fewer ORs than the number of values. With IN, you simply have to add to the value list (the list of values inside the parentheses). In general, using IN is a much better solution than using a series of OR conditions.

Using the BETWEEN Operator

Another useful conditional operator is *BETWEEN*. The **BETWEEN operator** lets you choose rows based on a range of values. Recall our earlier example (Exhibit 11-26), which listed members with between 10 and 20 jumps. We could write this query using BETWEEN, as shown in Exhibit 11-30.

Exhibit 11-30

Using the
BETWEEN
Operator

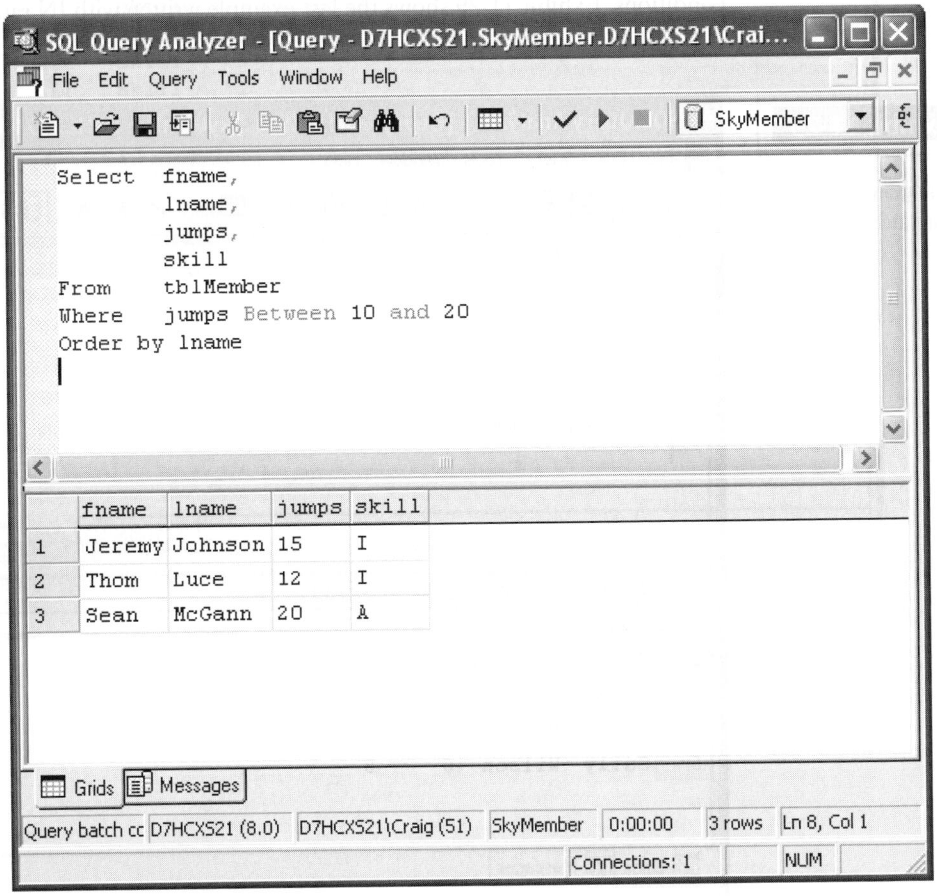

SQL Server compares each jumps value to see if it is between 10 and 20, inclusive (including 10 and 20). If so, the row is included in the results. Note that BETWEEN can be used with character-based data.

The NOT Operator

Any of the operators can be combined with the **NOT operator.** This process is done by preceding the conditional operator with the word *Not* or with the NOT symbol, which is an exclamation point (!). Using NOT reverses what would normally happen. The rows that would normally not be chosen *are* chosen with the NOT operator. To illustrate, let's look at the example from Exhibit 11-29. Recall that this query selected rows representing members who are at the beginner or intermediate level. If we precede the IN operator with NOT, we get all members *except* those in at the beginner or intermediate levels. Exhibit 11-31 shows the query using NOT.

Exhibit 11-31

Using the NOT
Operator with IN

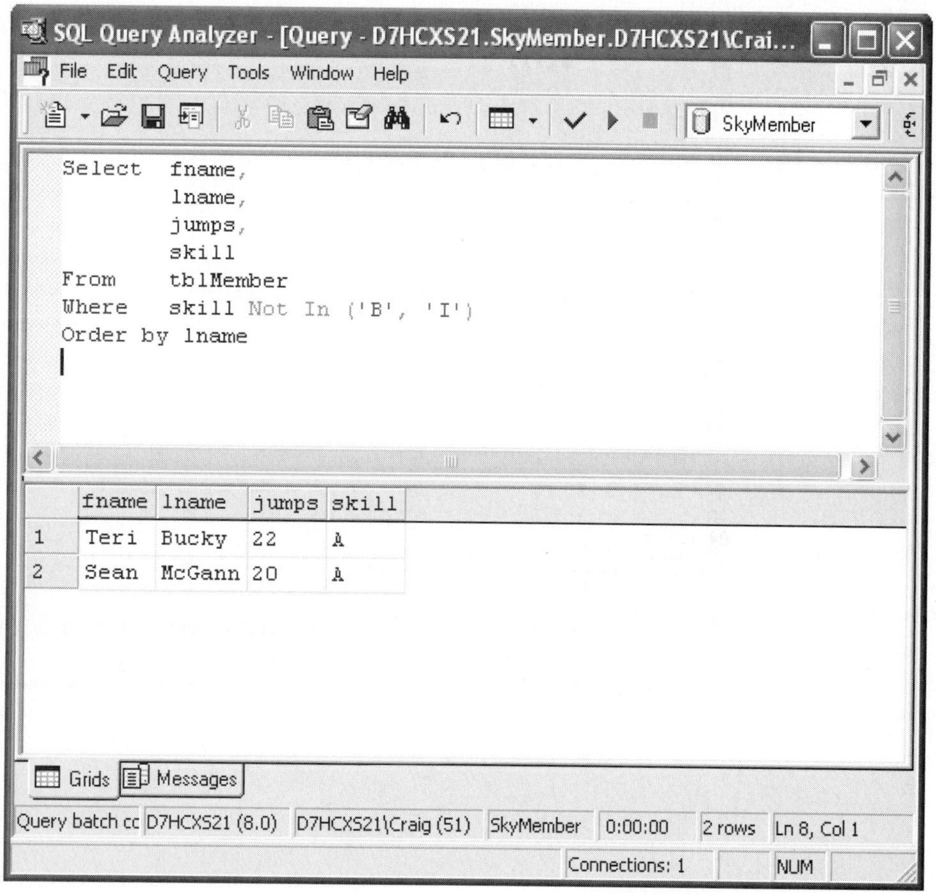

You can also use NOT with mathematical operators, such as equal to or greater than. For example, if you wanted to produce a list of members who are not at the beginner level (B), you could use the query in Exhibit 11-32. When using NOT with a mathematical operator, you must use the exclamation point (!) rather than the word *Not*.

Exhibit 11-32

Using the NOT
Operator (!) with
a Mathematical
Operator

SQL Query Analyzer - [Query - D7HCXS21.SkyMember.D7HCXS21\Crai...

File   Edit   Query   Tools   Window   Help

SkyMember

```
Select    fname,
          lname,
          jumps,
          skill
From      tblMember
Where     skill != 'B'
Order by  lname
```

	fname	lname	jumps	skill
1	Teri	Bucky	22	A
2	Jeremy	Johnson	15	I
3	Thom	Luce	12	I
4	Sean	McGann	20	A

Grids   Messages

Query batch cc | D7HCXS21 (8.0) | D7HCXS21\Craig (51) | SkyMember | 0:00:01 | 4 rows | Ln 8, Col 1

Connections: 1   NUM

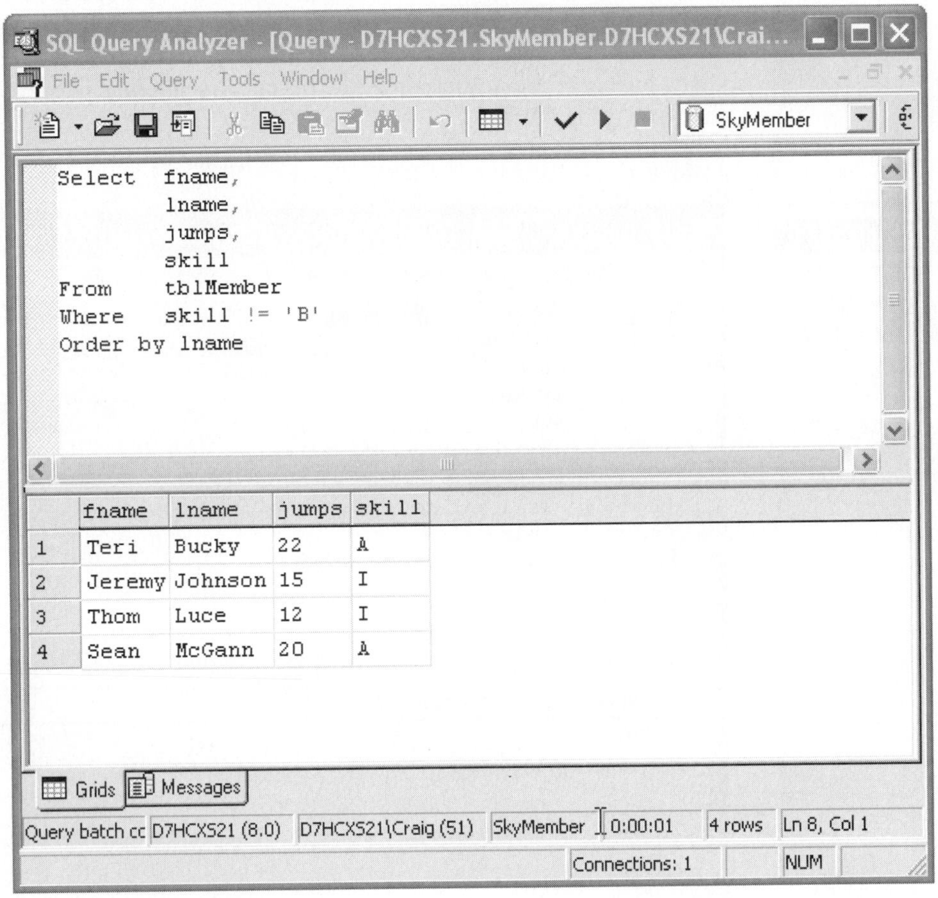

Combining AND and OR

It is also possible to mix AND and OR operators in a single where clause. Unfortunately, this process can get a bit tricky. Suppose you want to get a list of all members who have their own equipment and are in either the B or I skill levels. An inexperienced SQL coder might try the query shown in Exhibit 11-33.

Exhibit 11-33

Incorrectly
Combining
AND and OR

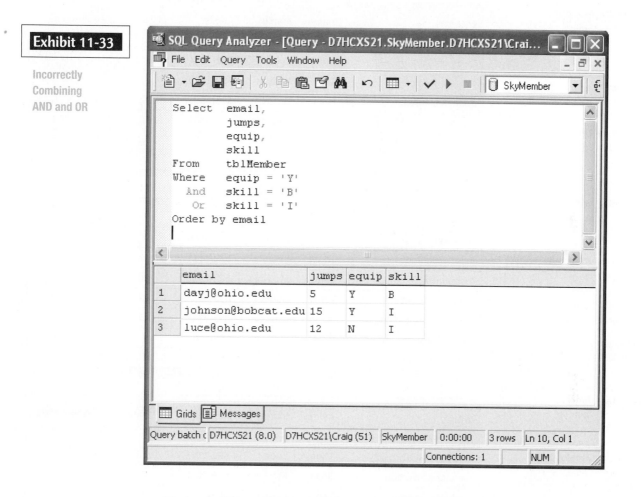

Notice that the results are not what we want. We wanted to list only members who have their own equipment, and the last row in our results lists a member who doesn't meet this criterion. The reason this row was included is because of the way SQL Server groups AND and OR operators. Basically, SQL Server selected rows that either met both of the first two criteria (equip = 'Y' and skill = 'B') *or* meet the last criterion (skill = 'I'). The analysis is shown in Exhibit 11-34.

Exhibit 11-34	Analysis of the Query Incorrectly Combining AND and OR

SELECT SPECIFIC COLUMNS AND ROWS USING AND WITH OR <u>INCORRECTLY</u>

List the email, jumps, skill, and equip for all members who have their own equipment and are at either the B or I skill levels.

SELECT email,
    jumps,
    equip,
    skill
From   tblMember
Where   equip = 'Y'
And   skill = 'B'
Or   skill = 'I'
Order by email

email	fname	lname	phone	jumps	equip	skill
dayj@ohio.edu	John	Day	592-0646	5	Y	B
luce@ohio.edu	Thom	Luce	592-1111	12	N	I
mcgann@ohio.edu	Sean	McGann	592-2222	20	Y	A
bucky@ohio.edu	Teri	Bucky	555-5555	22	Y	A
johnson@bobcat.edu	Jeremy	Johnson	555-3333	15	Y	I
mcgrath@bobcat.edu	Billie	McGrath	555-6666	3	N	B
wilson@bobcat.edu	Sally	Wilson	555-4444	6	N	B

SELECT email,
    jumps,
    equip,
    skill
From   tblMember
Where   equip = 'Y'
And   skill = 'B'
Or   skill = 'I'
Order by email

Row(s) that have equip of Y and skill of B are selected.

email	fname	lname	phone	jumps	equip	skill
dayj@ohio.edu	John	Day	592-0646	5	Y	B
luce@ohio.edu	Thom	Luce	592-1111	12	N	I
mcgann@ohio.edu	Sean	McGann	592-2222	20	Y	A
bucky@ohio.edu	Teri	Bucky	555-5555	22	Y	A
johnson@bobcat.edu	Jeremy	Johnson	555-3333	15	Y	I
mcgrath@bobcat.edu	Billie	McGrath	555-6666	3	N	B
wilson@bobcat.edu	Sally	Wilson	555-4444	6	N	B

SELECT email,
    jumps,
    equip,
    skill
From   tblMember
Where   equip = 'Y'
And   skill = 'B'
Or   skill = 'I'
Order by email

Row(s) that have skill = 'I' are added to the results. This is because of the OR condition.

email	fname	lname	phone	jumps	equip	skill
dayj@ohio.edu	John	Day	592-0646	5	Y	B
luce@ohio.edu	Thom	Luce	592-1111	12	N	I
mcgann@ohio.edu	Sean	McGann	592-2222	20	Y	A
bucky@ohio.edu	Teri	Bucky	555-5555	22	Y	A
johnson@bobcat.edu	Jeremy	Johnson	555-3333	15	Y	I
mcgrath@bobcat.edu	Billie	McGrath	555-6666	3	N	B
wilson@bobcat.edu	Sally	Wilson	555-4444	6	N	B

RESULT

Results are sorted by email.

email	jumps	equip	skill
dayj@ohio.edu	5	Y	B
luce@ohio.edu	12	N	I
johnson@bobcat.edu	15	Y	I

Fortunately, there is an easy way to avoid this problem; simply use parentheses to show explicitly show how you want the conditions grouped. The correct query is shown in Exhibit 11-35. Note that another way to avoid this problem with this particular query is to use the IN operator rather than the OR.

Exhibit 11-35

Correctly
Combining AND
and OR

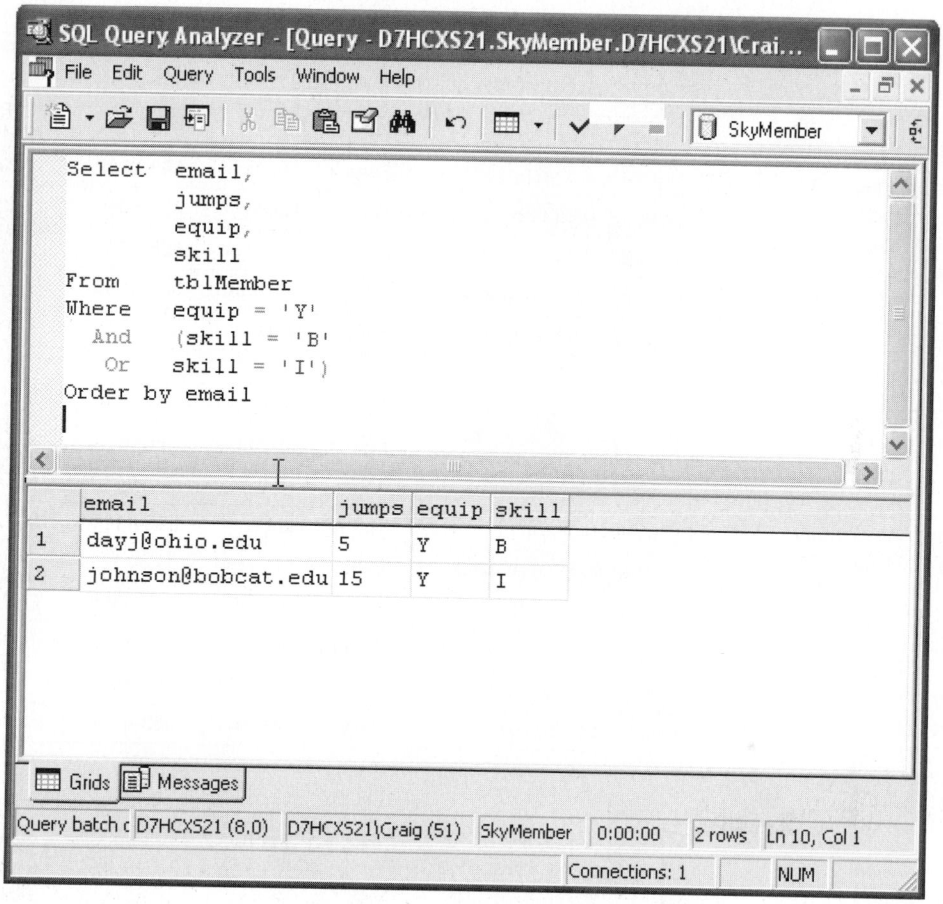

By using the OR operator, all the criteria can be placed on the same line, and the result will display only the rows for Day and Johnson, as shown in the analysis in Exhibit 11-36.

Exhibit 11-36   Analysis of the Query Correctly Combining AND and OR

SELECT SPECIFIC COLUMNS AND ROWS USING AND WITH OR <u>CORRECTLY</u>

List the email, jumps, skill, and equip for all members who have their own equipment and are at either the B or I skill level.

```
SELECT  email,
        jumps,
        equip,
        skill
From    tblMember
Where   equip = 'Y'
And     (skill = 'B'
Or      skill = 'I')
Order by email
```

email	fname	lname	phone	jumps	equip	skill
dayj@ohio.edu	John	Day	592-0646	5	Y	B
luce@ohio.edu	Thom	Luce	592-1111	12	N	I
mcgann@ohio.edu	Sean	McGann	592-2222	20	Y	A
bucky@ohio.edu	Teri	Bucky	555-5555	22	Y	A
johnson@bobcat.edu	Jeremy	Johnson	555-3333	15	Y	I
mcgrath@bobcat.edu	Billie	McGrath	555-6666	3	N	B
wilson@bobcat.edu	Sally	Wilson	555-4444	6	N	B

```
SELECT  email,
        jumps,
        equip,
        skill
From    tblMember
Where   equip = 'Y'
And     (skill = 'B'
Or      skill = 'I')
Order by email
```

Row(s) that have equip of Y are selected.

email	fname	lname	phone	jumps	equip	skill
dayj@ohio.edu	John	Day	592-0646	5	Y	B
luce@ohio.edu	Thom	Luce	592-1111	12	N	I
mcgann@ohio.edu	Sean	McGann	592-2222	20	Y	A
bucky@ohio.edu	Teri	Bucky	555-5555	22	Y	A
johnson@bobcat.edu	Jeremy	Johnson	555-3333	15	Y	I
mcgrath@bobcat.edu	Billie	McGrath	555-6666	3	N	B
wilson@bobcat.edu	Sally	Wilson	555-4444	6	N	B

```
SELECT  email,
        jumps,
        equip,
        skill
From    tblMember
Where   equip = 'Y'
And     (skill = 'B'
Or      skill = 'I')
Order by email
```

Row(s) that have skill = 'B' or 'I' are added to the results because of the OR condition.

email	fname	lname	phone	jumps	equip	skill
dayj@ohio.edu	John	Day	592-0646	5	Y	B
luce@ohio.edu	Thom	Luce	592-1111	12	N	I
mcgann@ohio.edu	Sean	McGann	592-2222	20	Y	A
bucky@ohio.edu	Teri	Bucky	555-5555	22	Y	A
johnson@bobcat.edu	Jeremy	Johnson	555-3333	15	Y	I
mcgrath@bobcat.edu	Billie	McGrath	555-6666	3	N	B
wilson@bobcat.edu	Sally	Wilson	555-4444	6	N	B

RESULT

Results are sorted by email.

email	jumps	equip	skill
dayj@ohio.edu	5	Y	B
johnson@bobcat.edu	15	Y	I

Aggregate Functions

SQL Server includes many built-in functions. Some of these functions are called **aggregate functions** because they involve groups (aggregations) of rows rather than single rows. Aggregate functions provide summary values in the results list. Typically, the functions take the form:

Function [expression]

Typically, the expression is a column name, although other types of expressions are also valid. Exhibit 11-37 shows aggregate functions available in SQL Server.

Exhibit 11-37

Aggregate
Functions in
SQL Server

Function	Purpose
Sum	Total of the values in the expression
Avg	Arithmetic mean of the values in the expression
Count	Number of values in the expression
Count(*)	Number of selected rows (including those with nulls)
Max	Highest value in the expression
Min	Lowest value in the expression

Most of the functions are straightforward; they do what most people think they would do. For example, if you wanted to get the total number of jumps made by all members, you would use the query shown in Exhibit 11-38.

Exhibit 11-38

Using the Sum
Aggregate
Function

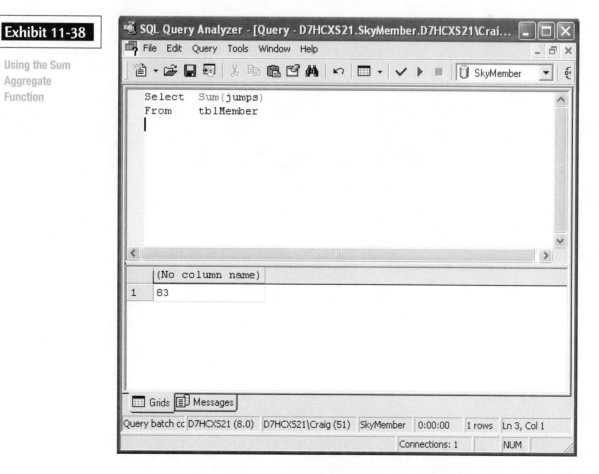

Notice that the result of this query is a single number. If the column list of a Select statement includes an aggregate function with no other columns, the result is a single number. We will discuss how to get subaggregations (for example, subtotals) later in this section. Also, the "No column name" column heading is not very informative. Shortly, we will show you how to give the column a more helpful heading. The analysis for this query is shown in Exhibit 11-39.

Exhibit 11-39   Analysis of the Query That Sums the Number of Jumps

---

SUM FUNCTION

List the total number of jumps made by all members.

sum( )

```
SELECT  sum(jumps)
From    tblMember
```

email	fname	lname	phone	jumps	equip	skill
dayj@ohio.edu	John	Day	592-0646	5	Y	B
luce@ohio.edu	Thom	Luce	592-1111	12	N	I
mcgann@ohio.edu	Sean	McGann	592-2222	20	Y	A
bucky@ohio.edu	Teri	Bucky	555-5555	22	Y	A
johnson@bobcat.edu	Jeremy	Johnson	555-3333	15	Y	I
mcgrath@bobcat.edu	Billie	McGrath	555-6666	3	N	B
wilson@bobcat.edu	Sally	Wilson	555-4444	6	N	B

sum(63)

```
SELECT  sum(jumps)
From    tblMember
```

email	fname	lname	phone	jumps	equip	skill
dayj@ohio.edu	John	Day	592-0646	5	Y	B
luce@ohio.edu	Thom	Luce	592-1111	12	N	I
mcgann@ohio.edu	Sean	McGann	592-2222	20	Y	A
bucky@ohio.edu	Teri	Bucky	555-5555	22	Y	A
johnson@bobcat.edu	Jeremy	Johnson	555-3333	15	Y	I
mcgrath@bobcat.edu	Billie	McGrath	555-6666	3	N	B
wilson@bobcat.edu	Sally	Wilson	555-4444	6	N	B

RESULT

(No column name)
83

The Count function has two variations. You can provide an expression, just as we did with the Sum example. But if the expression is a column name (which is common), and the column contains null values, you may not get the result you expect. Rows in which the expression column is null are not included in the count. For example, if you had a member for whom the jumps column was left blank, and you used *jumps* as the expression in a Count function, that row would not be counted. You can avoid this problem by using Count(*), as shown in Exhibit 11-40. The Count(*) function counts all rows, regardless of any null values.

Exhibit 11-40

Using the Count(*) Aggregate Function

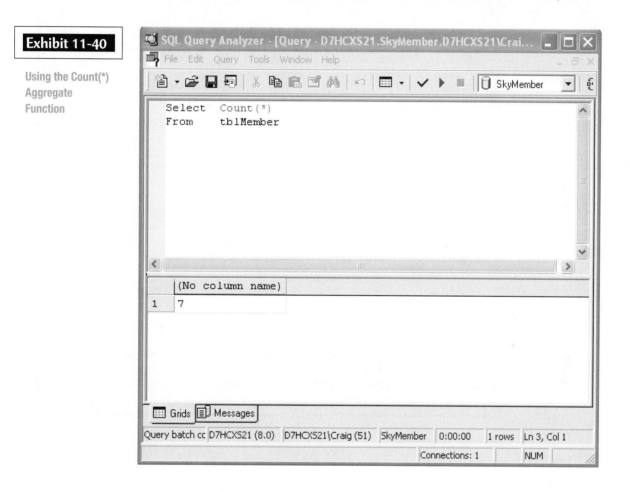

You can use an aggregate function in a Select statement that includes a where clause. Rows are selected according to the where clause condition(s) before the aggregate function is applied. For example, compare the results in Exhibit 11-41 to the result of Exhibit 11-38. The query analysis is shown in Exhibit 11-42.

Exhibit 11-41

Using an Aggregate Function with a Where Clause

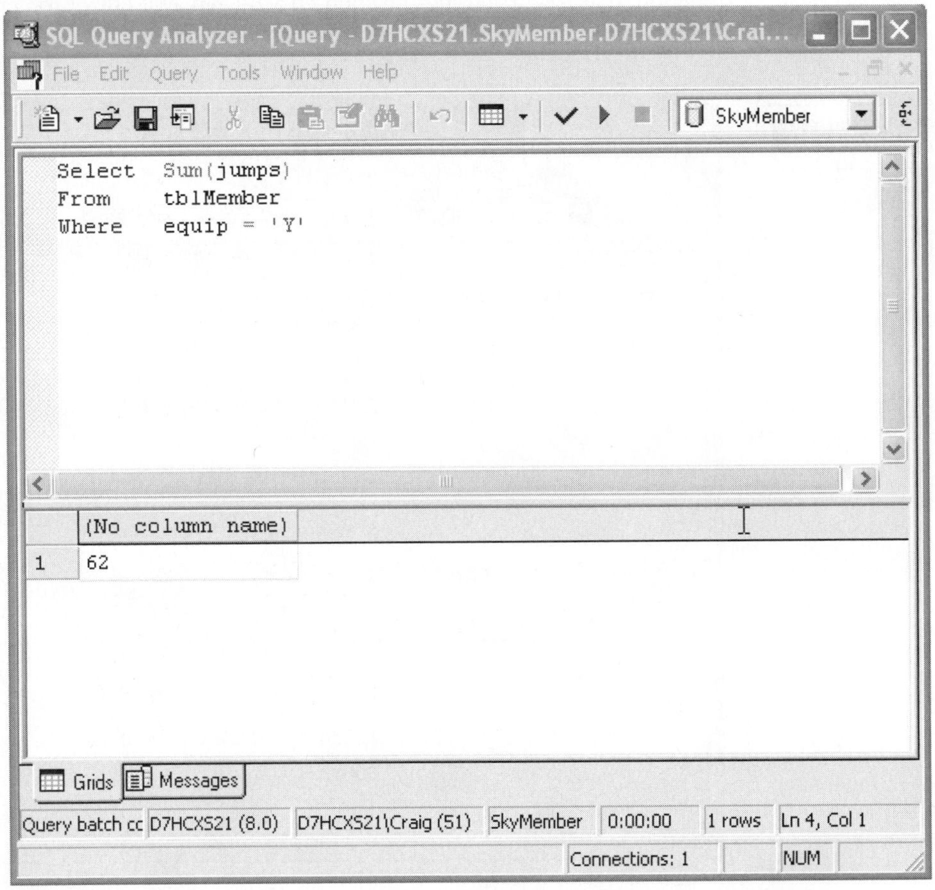

Exhibit 11-42 Analysis of the Query That Sums Jumps for Members with Equipment

SUM FUNCTION	
List the total number of jumps made by all members who have equipment (equip = 'Y').	

SELECT sum(jumps)
From   tblMember
Where   equip = 'Y'

sum( )

email	fname	lname	phone	jumps	equip	skill
dayj@ohio.edu	John	Day	592-0646	5	Y	B
luce@ohio.edu	Thom	Luce	592-1111	12	N	I
mcgann@ohio.edu	Sean	McGann	592-2222	20	Y	A
bucky@ohio.edu	Teri	Bucky	555-5555	22	Y	A
johnson@bobcat.edu	Jeremy	Johnson	555-3333	15	Y	I
mcgrath@bobcat.edu	Billie	McGrath	555-6666	3	N	B
wilson@bobcat.edu	Sally	Wilson	555-4444	6	N	B

SELECT sum(jumps)
From   tblMember
Where   equip = 'Y'

sum(62)

email	fname	lname	phone	jumps	equip	skill
dayj@ohio.edu	John	Day	592-0646	5	Y	B
luce@ohio.edu	Thom	Luce	592-1111	12	N	I
mcgann@ohio.edu	Sean	McGann	592-2222	20	Y	A
bucky@ohio.edu	Teri	Bucky	555-5555	22	Y	A
johnson@bobcat.edu	Jeremy	Johnson	555-3333	15	Y	I
mcgrath@bobcat.edu	Billie	McGrath	555-6666	3	N	B
wilson@bobcat.edu	Sally	Wilson	555-4444	6	N	B

RESULT

(No column name)
62

When you compare the results, you will notice that the second query reports a lower total number of jumps, because only those rows where the value of the equip column is "Y" are included in the sum. Complex where clauses can be used in combination with aggregate functions.

Creating Column Aliases

Take a close look at the results of the aggregate function queries we have done so far. Notice that in the results, the column heading "No column name" is used. This heading is not very informative. To solve this problem, we can assign a column name alias. An alias is simply a substitute name or label for a database object. To assign a column alias, all you need to do is follow the column name (in this case Sum(jumps)) with the word *As*, followed by the alias.

The word *As* can be omitted, but we like to include it. Exhibit 11-43 illustrates the use of a column alias. Notice that the result now has the heading "Total Jumps." Later in this chapter, you will learn how to use table name aliases.

Exhibit 11-43

Using a Column Alias

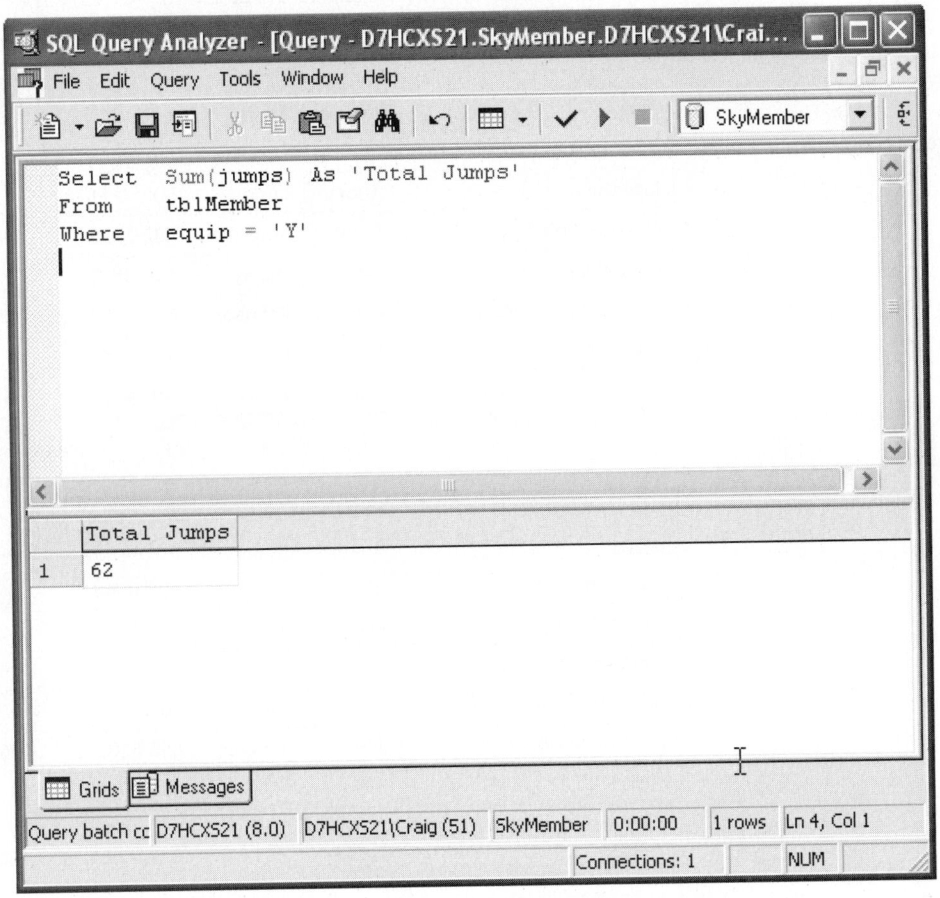

```
Select   Sum(jumps) As 'Total Jumps'
From     tblMember
Where    equip = 'Y'
```

	Total Jumps
1	62

Using DISTINCT

Sometimes you do not want to know how many rows are in a table or meet some criteria; what you want to know is how many different values are in a particular row of a table. For example, let's say that you want to know how many different skill levels are in the table. To answer such a question, you would use **distinct** to tell SQL Server that you want to count only different values. Basically, you want to count only the first occurrence of a value; repeats of a value are not counted. To illustrate, we will write a query that tells us how many different skill levels we have, as shown in Exhibit 11-44.

Exhibit 11-44

Using Distinct

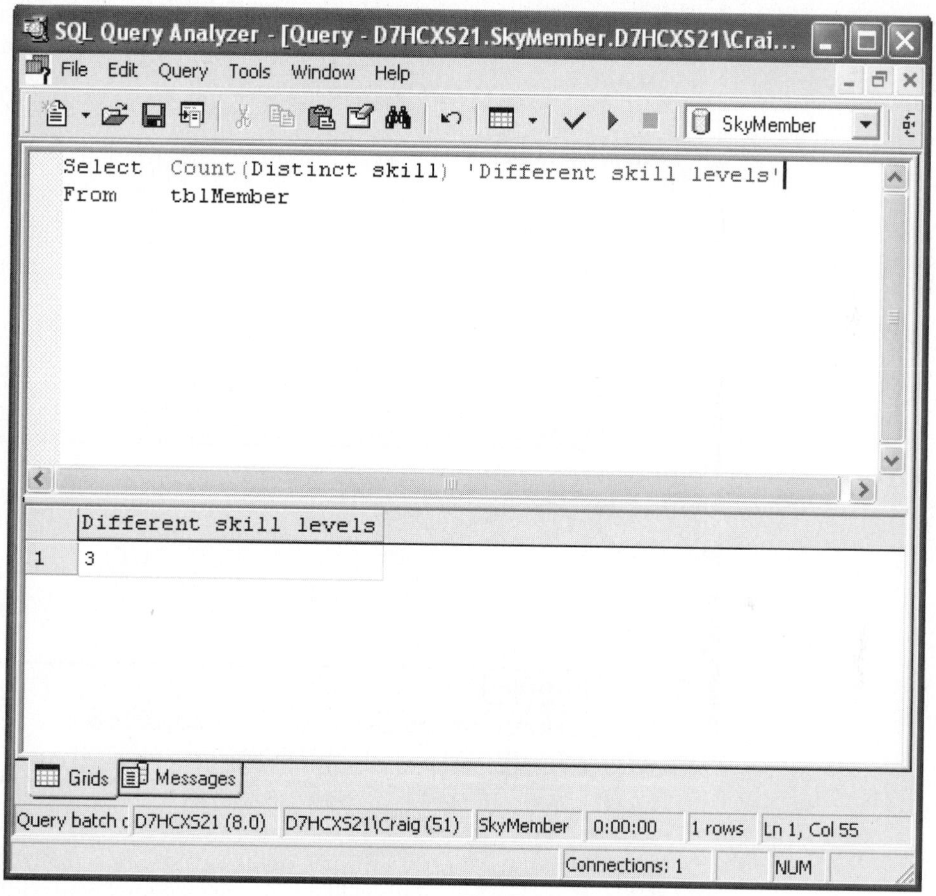

```
Select    Count(Distinct skill) 'Different skill levels'
From      tblMember
```

	Different skill levels
1	3

Creating Subaggregations with Group By

SQL Server also gives you the capability to use aggregate functions to compute subtotals (or subaggregations) using the **Group by** clause. In other words, your results can show the result of the function by groups of rows. For example, suppose you want to calculate the total number of jumps for each skill level. Exhibit 11-45 gives the query that produces this result.

Exhibit 11-45

Using an Aggregate Function with Groups

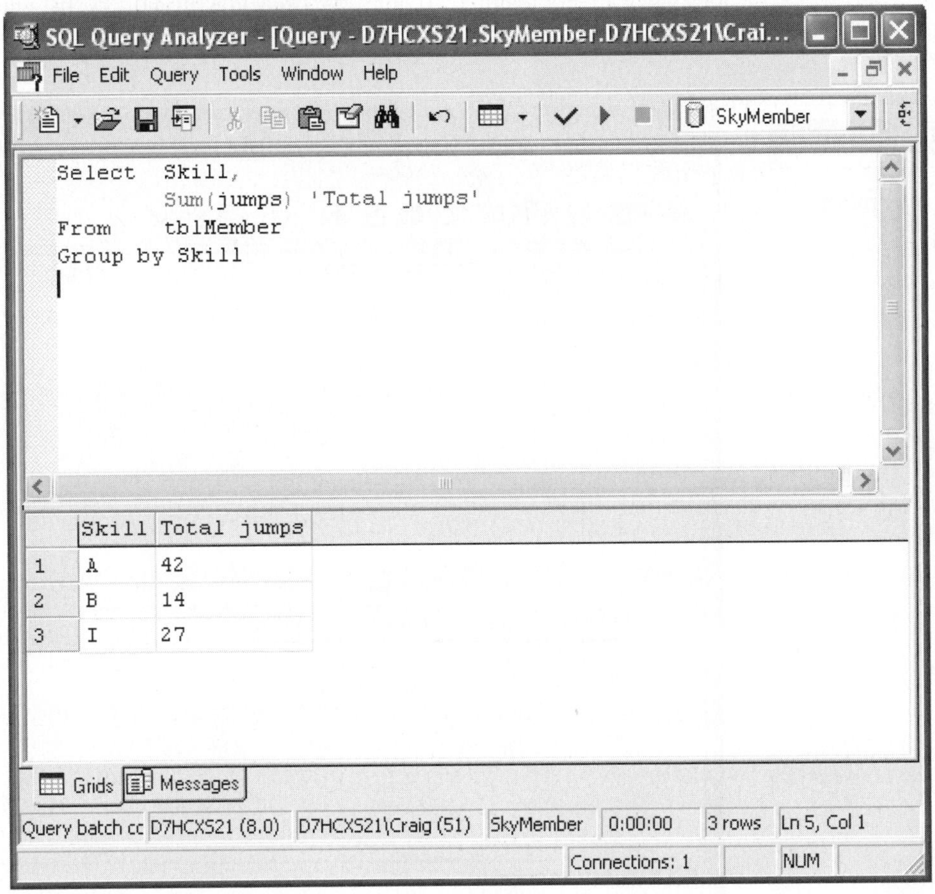

```
Select   Skill,
         Sum(jumps) 'Total jumps'
From     tblMember
Group by Skill
```

	Skill	Total jumps
1	A	42
2	B	14
3	I	27

Two aspects of this query are worth noting. First, we included the column "skill" in the column list, so we can tell which skill group each subtotal goes with. Second, we added the line "Group by Skill" to the query. This line tells SQL Server how you want to aggregate the rows when computing the subtotals. The analysis for this query is shown in Exhibit 11-46.

Exhibit 11-46   Analysis for Query Using an Aggregate Function with Groups

GROUP BY

For each skill level, list the total number of jumps by members of that skill level.

SELECT Skill,
Sum(jumps) 'Total
Jumps'
From tblMember
Group by Skill

*Note that the fname, lname,
and email columns are omitted
to make the table fit in the
available space. This omission
is indicated by the ellipses (...).*

email	...	jumps	equip	skill	Sum(jumps)
dayj@ohio.edu	...	5	Y	B	
luce@ohio.edu	...	12	N	I	
mcgann@ohio.edu	...	20	Y	A	
bucky@ohio.edu	...	22	Y	A	
johnson@bobcat.edu	...	15	Y	I	
mcgrath@bobcat.edu	...	3	N	B	
wilson@bobcat.edu	...	6	N	B	

Select Skill,
Sum(jumps) 'Total
Jumps'
From tblMember
Group by Skill

email	...	jumps	equip	skill	Sum(jumps)
mcgann@ohio.edu	...	20	Y	A	
bucky@ohio.edu	...	22	Y	A	
dayj@ohio.edu	...	5	Y	B	
mcgrath@bobcat.edu	...	3	N	B	
wilson@bobcat.edu	...	6	N	B	
luce@ohio.edu	...	12	N	I	
johnson@bobcat.edu	...	15	Y	I	

Select Skill,
Sum(jumps) 'Total
Jumps'
From tblMember
Group by Skill

email	...	jumps	equip	skill	Sum(jumps)
mcgann@ohio.edu	...	20	Y	A	
bucky@ohio.edu	...	22	Y	A	
					42
dayj@ohio.edu	...	5	Y	B	
mcgrath@bobcat.edu	...	3	N	B	
wilson@bobcat.edu	...	6	N	B	
					14
luce@ohio.edu	...	12	N	I	
johnson@bobcat.edu	...	15	Y	I	
					27

RESULT

Skill	Total jumps
A	42
B	14
I	27

The single column (or columns) in the column list must match the column(s) in the group by clause. Otherwise, the query produces an error. You will also get an error if you forget to add the group by clause. This is a common mistake. The resulting error message is shown in Exhibit 11-47.

Exhibit 11-47

Error Message when Omitting Group by Clause

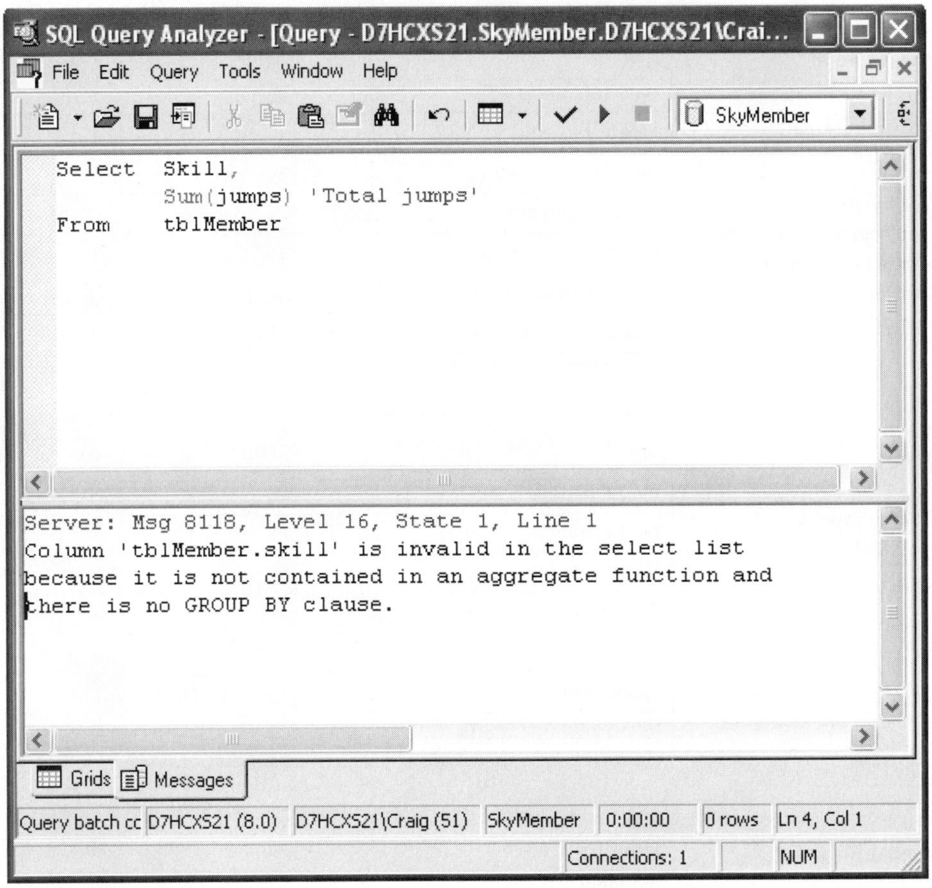

SQL Query Analyzer - [Query - D7HCXS21.SkyMember.D7HCXS21\Crai...

File   Edit   Query   Tools   Window   Help

SkyMember

```
Select    Skill,
          Sum(jumps)  'Total jumps'
From      tblMember
```

```
Server: Msg 8118, Level 16, State 1, Line 1
Column 'tblMember.skill' is invalid in the select list
because it is not contained in an aggregate function and
there is no GROUP BY clause.
```

Grids   Messages

Query batch cc | D7HCXS21 (8.0) | D7HCXS21\Craig (51) | SkyMember | 0:00:00 | 0 rows | Ln 4, Col 1

Connections: 1   NUM

Limiting Groups with the Having Clause

Recall that the where clause is used to limit the rows that are included in the results of a query. The **Having clause** performs a similar purpose, but for aggregations, rather than for single rows. For example, suppose that you want to see a list of any ability groups that have fewer than 25 total jumps. Using the proper having clause limits the results to only these groups. Exhibit 11-48 illustrates the use of having.

Exhibit 11-48

Using Having

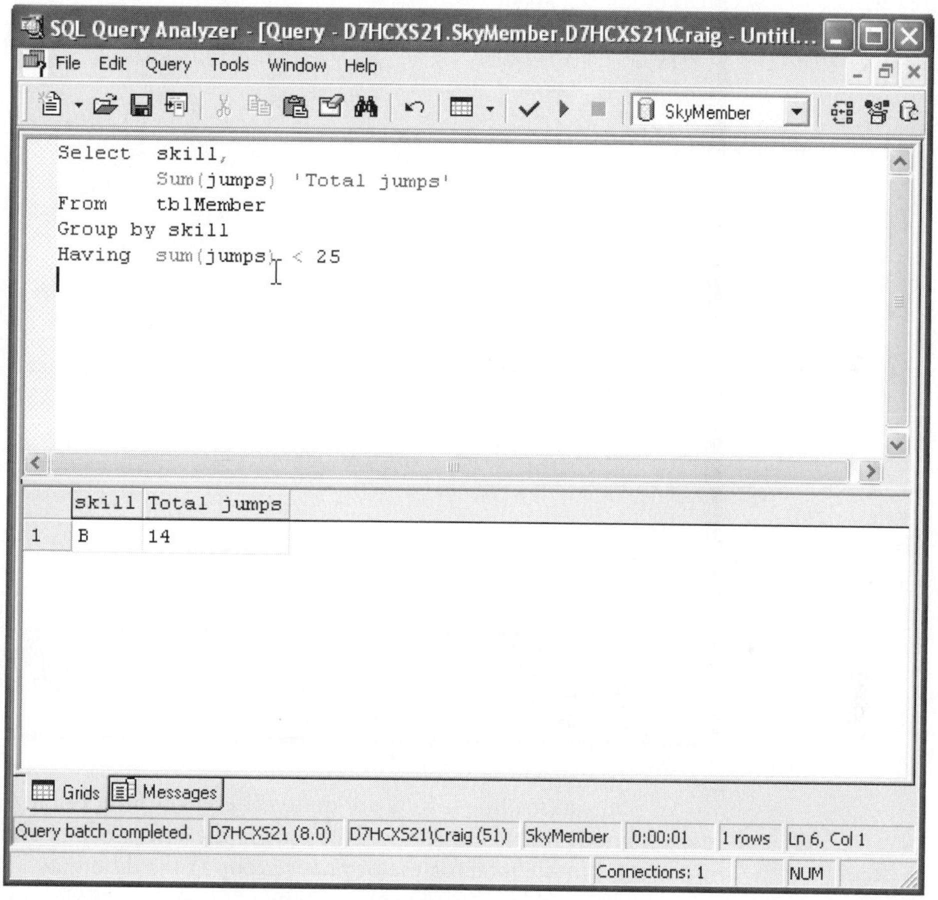

```
Select   skill,
         Sum(jumps)  'Total jumps'
From     tblMember
Group by skill
Having   sum(jumps) < 25
```

	skill	Total jumps
1	B	14

Notice the having clause we added following the group by clause. The having clause is similar to where, in that both use conditional statements to limit results. However, having limits results based on aggregate functions, and where limits results according to single-row values. A having clause should always have an aggregate function as part of its conditional statement. Another thing to remember is that typically, you need to include a group by clause whenever you include a having clause in a query. (The opposite is not true; you can have group by without having.) Although SQL Server will let you use a having clause without a group by clause, the results are very difficult to interpret.

It is possible to use both having and where in the same query. When you do, SQL applies the where condition(s) to select rows, then it computes the aggregate function based on the rows that meet the condition(s) specified in the where clause. Then the having condition is applied to the results. An example will help you understand. Suppose that you want to see the total number of jumps for skill groups whose members have fewer than 25 jumps in total. But you want to count only members who have their own equipment; any members who do *not* have their own equipment should not be included when computing the total. Exhibit 11-49 shows the query used to produce these results.

Exhibit 11-49

Using Where and Having

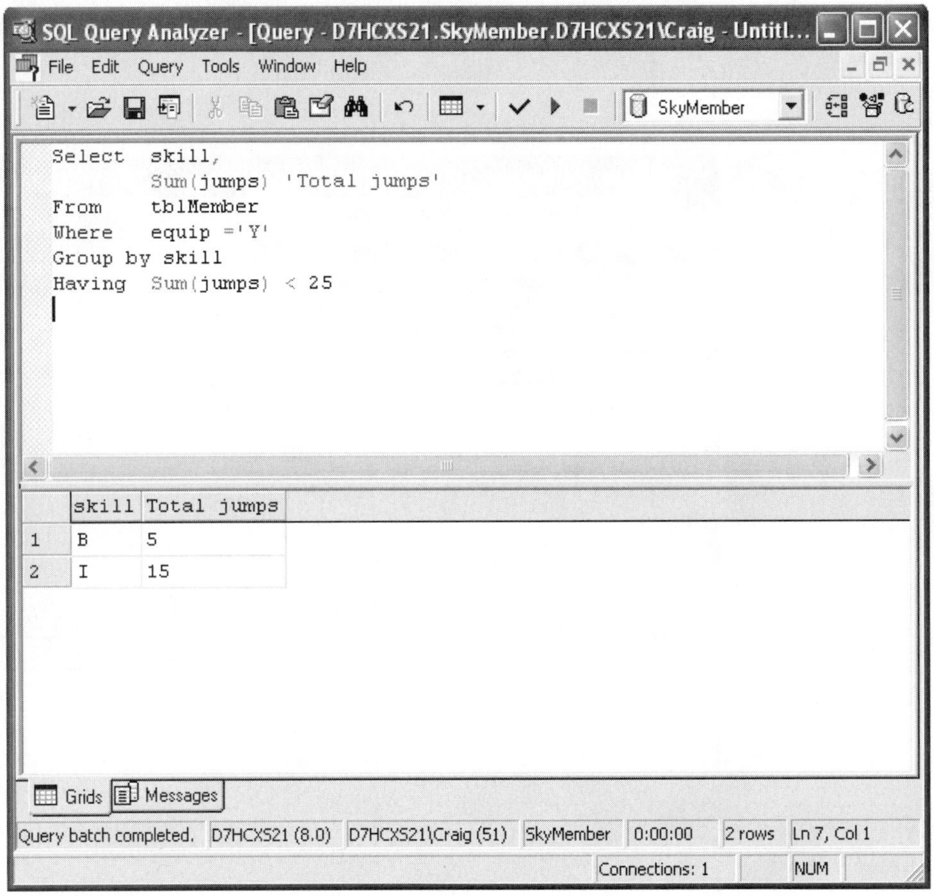

As you can see, the results are quite different from Exhibit 11-48, which is the same query without the where clause. Not only is the intermediate ability group (I) total now appearing, but the total for the beginner group (B) is different. This result is because only rows that have "Y" as the value of the equip column are included when computing the totals. To help you understand this idea, let's take a look at the data from the tblMember table, which is provided in Exhibit 11-50.

Exhibit 11-50

Data from tblMember

email	fname	lname	phone	jumps	equip	skill
bucky@ohio.edu	Teri	Bucky	555-5555	22	Y	A
mcgann@ohio.edu	Sean	McGann	592-2222	20	Y	A
brokaw@oh.edu	John	Brokaw	555-5901	5	Y	B
mcgrath@bobcat.edu	Billie	McGrath	555-6666	3	N	B
wilson@bobcat.edu	Sally	Wilson	555-4444	6	N	B
johnson@bobcat.edu	Jeremy	Johnson	555-3333	15	Y	I
luce@ohio.edu	Thom	Luce	592-1111	12	N	I

The rows that satisfy the where condition are highlighted, and the rows that do not are crossed out. Now let's compute the total number of jumps for each skill group, but we include only the highlighted rows. Exhibit 11-51 shows the sum using all rows, compared to the sum using only the rows that meet the where condition. Notice that when including all rows, the intermediate skill group has a sum (27) that does not meet the having condition. However, when we include only rows meeting the where condition (equip = Y), the sum for the intermediate group now meets the having condition. Therefore, this group is included in the query results. Although our example includes only a single condition for the where clause, complex where clauses with multiple conditions can be used.

Ability Group	All rows	Sum	Rows meeting condition	Sum
A	22+20	42	22+20	42
B	5+3+6	14	5	5
I	15+12	27	15	15

Combining Data from Different Tables

All of the queries we have looked at so far have involved data from a single table. However, meeting some data retrieval requirements requires getting data from multiple tables. Fortunately, SQL gives us a way to perform such data retrievals. Recall that relational databases use matching primary and foreign key values to relate a row in one table to a row in a another table. Understanding this idea is the key to understanding how to retrieve data from multiple tables. Combining data from different tables into a single result set is called a *join*. More specifically, the joins we discuss in this section are called **equi-joins,** because they are based on equality between primary and foreign key values. There are other types of joins, but equi-joins are the type most commonly used.

Because the Sky_Member database we have been using so far has only one table, we need to use another, more complex database to demonstrate how to perform joins. So we will use the Enrollment database, which has five tables. The data model for the Enrollment database is shown in Exhibit 11-52.

Exhibit 11-52

Enrollment
Database Data
Model

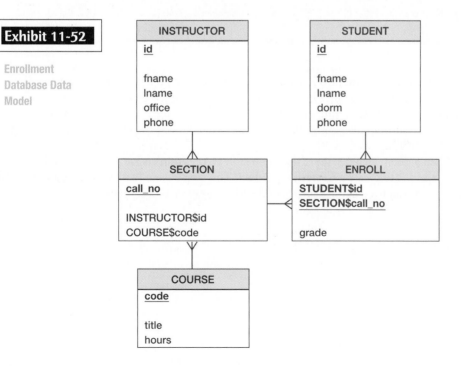

For our first multitable query example, we want to list the call number (call_no), course code, course title, and number of hours for each section. Producing this list requires retrieving data from two tables, SECTION and COURSE. These two tables are connected through the foreign key COURSE$code in the COURSE table, which refers to the primary key code in the COURSE table. To perform a join, we specify a where clause with a condition that the value of the foreign key (COURSE$code) equals the value of the primary key in the related table (code). We also need to include all tables used in the query in the from clause. Exhibit 11-53 shows a query that combines the data as described.

Exhibit 11-53

Joining the
COURSE and
SECTION Tables

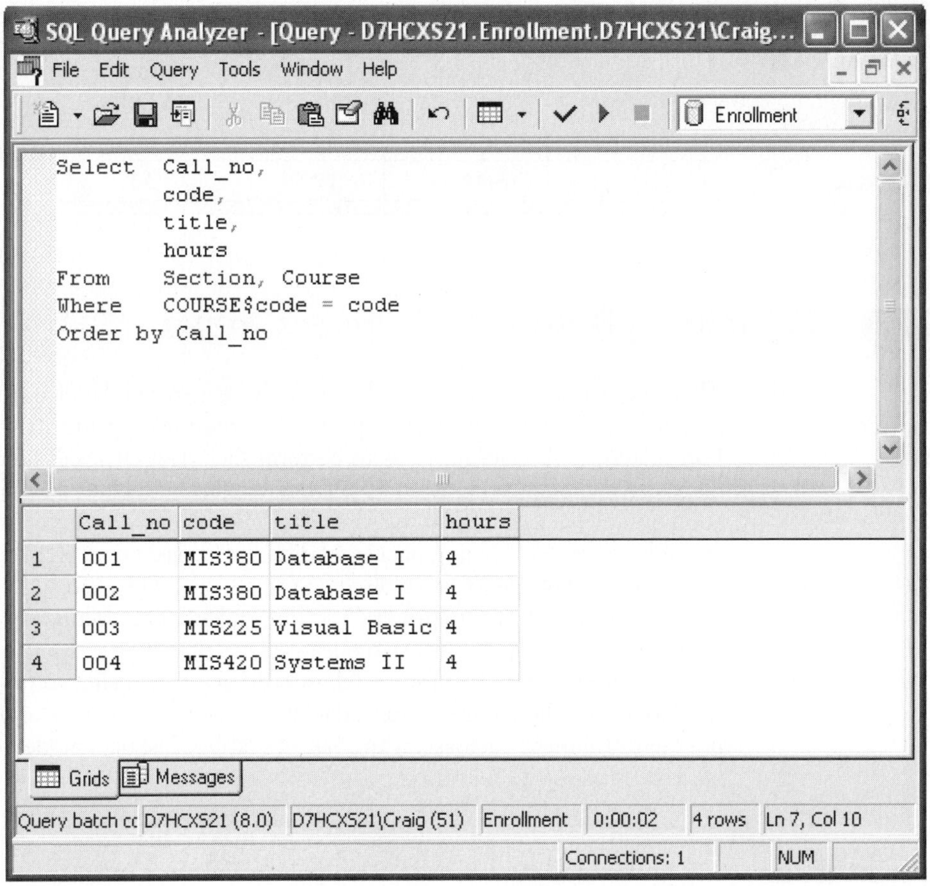

To better understand how joins work, let's work through a join operation manually. The following discussion describes how joins work conceptually. The actual mechanics followed by SQL Server to carry out joins may differ, depending on a number of conditions. Regardless, following the conceptual discussion will help you better understand how to perform joins in SQL.

When a query includes more than one table in the from clause, the first step in evaluating the query is to create a **Cartesian product.** This step is simply making a temporary table that combines all rows in one table paired with all rows in another table.

The Cartesian product that results from the COURSE and SECTION tables is shown in Exhibit 11-54. The original tables are also shown. Notice that we create the product by combining each row of the COURSE table with each row of the SECTION table. Multiplying the number of rows in the two tables (3 * 4, in this case) gives us the number of rows in the product (12). The highlighted rows in the product represent rows that satisfy the join condition in the where clause. The rows that do not meet the condition are crossed out.

Exhibit 11-54

Cartesian Product of COURSE and SECTION

Original Tables

COURSE

code	title	hours
MIS380	Database I	4
MIS225	Visual Basic	4
MIS420	Systems II	4

SECTION

call_no	INSTRUCTOR$id	COURSE$code
001	11	MIS380
002	33	MIS380
003	11	MIS225
004	44	MIS420

Cartesian Product

code	title	hours	call_no	INSTRUCTOR$id	COURSE$code
MIS380	Database I	4	001	11	MIS380
MIS380	Database I	4	002	33	MIS380
~~MIS380~~	~~Database I~~	4	~~003~~	~~11~~	~~MIS225~~
~~MIS380~~	~~Database I~~	4	~~004~~	44	~~MIS420~~
~~MIS225~~	~~Visual Basic~~	4	~~001~~	~~11~~	~~MIS380~~
~~MIS225~~	~~Visual Basic~~	4	~~002~~	~~33~~	~~MIS380~~
MIS225	Visual Basic	4	003	11	MIS225
MIS225	Visual Basic	4	004	44	MIS420
~~MIS420~~	~~Systems II~~	4	~~001~~	~~11~~	~~MIS380~~
~~MIS420~~	~~Systems II~~	4	~~002~~	33	~~MIS380~~
~~MIS420~~	~~Systems II~~	4	~~003~~	~~11~~	~~MIS225~~
MIS420	Systems II	4	004	44	MIS420

Count the number of rows that satisfy the condition. Of the 12 rows in the product, only 4 rows meet the join condition. It is no coincidence that this number matches the number of rows in the Section table. When performing joins, you should never have more rows in your results than you have in the largest table involved in the query. In this case, Section has the largest number of rows (four), so that is the maximum number of rows we should get in our two-table query. Of course, other conditions could reduce the number of rows in the result. We will look at an example of this situation later.

Errors Resulting from Omitting the Join Condition

To further illustrate how joins work, let's examine the consequences of *not* including the join condition. The query in Exhibit 11-55 includes two tables, but it does not have a join condition. When you examine the results, you might notice that they closely resemble the Cartesian product in Exhibit 11-54. The only difference is that the query result does not include all columns from both tables. However, there are 12 rows in the results, just as there are 12 rows in the Cartesian product. There are some special circumstances in which you want to produce a Cartesian product, but typically, this sort of result comes from omitting a join condition.

Exhibit 11-55

Joining the COURSE and SECTION Tables without Join Condition

SQL Query Analyzer - [Query - D7HCXS21.Enrollment.D7HCXS21\Craig - ...]

File   Edit   Query   Tools   Window   Help

```
Select   Call_no,
         code,
         title,
         hours
From     Section, Course
Order by         Call_no
```

	Call_no	code	title	hours
1	001	MIS380	Database I	4
2	001	MIS225	Visual Basic	4
3	001	MIS420	Systems II	4
4	002	MIS420	Systems II	4
5	002	MIS225	Visual Basic	4
6	002	MIS380	Database I	4
7	003	MIS380	Database I	4
8	003	MIS225	Visual Basic	4
9	003	MIS420	Systems II	4
10	004	MIS420	Systems II	4
11	004	MIS225	Visual Basic	4
12	004	MIS380	Database I	4

Grids   Messages

Query batch comj D7HCXS21 (8.0)   D7HCXS21\Craig (51)   Enrollment   0:00:00   12 rows   Ln 7, Col 1
Connections: 1   NUM

When performing multitable queries, we find it useful to check the number of rows against the maximum expected. If you have too many rows in your query results, you are missing a join. The results of such an omission are sometimes quite spectacular. For example, if you have two 1,000-row tables in a query and you forget the join, the query result will have one million rows!

Combining Joins with Other Where Conditions

We can combine other where conditions with join conditions. Sometimes, there are multiple join conditions, as we will see shortly. In these cases, it is a good idea to group the join conditions together. Let's examine an example of adding another condition to a join. The query shown in Exhibit 11-56 produces a list of sections for MIS380. To follow the logic of this query, consider the query analysis shown in Exhibit 11-57.

```
Select    Call_no,
          code,
          title,
          hours
From      Section, Course
Where     Code = 'MIS380'
   And    COURSE$code = code
Order by Call_no
```

	Call_no	code	title	hours
1	001	MIS380	Database I	4
2	002	MIS380	Database I	4

Exhibit 11-57

Analysis of a
Query with a Join
Combined with a
Where Condition

TWO-TABLE JOIN WITH ADDITIONAL CONDITION.
List the call number, course code, title, and hours for all sections of MIS380.

```
SELECT   call_no,
         code,
         title,
         hours
From     section, course
Where    code = 'MIS380'
  And    COURSE$code = code;
Order by call_no
```

COURSE

code	title	hours
MIS380	Database I	4
MIS225	Visual Basic	4
MIS420	Systems II	4

SECTION

call_no	INSTRUCTOR$id	COURSE$code
001	11	MIS380
002	33	MIS380
003	11	MIS225
004	44	MIS420

```
SELECT   call_no,
         code,
         title,
         hours
From     section, course
Where    code = 'MIS380'
  And    COURSE$code = code;
Order by call_no
```

COURSE

code	title	hours
MIS380	Database I	4
MIS225	Visual Basic	4
MIS420	Systems II	4

SECTION

call_no	INSTRUCTOR$id	COURSE$code
001	11	MIS380
002	33	MIS380
003	11	MIS225
004	44	MIS420

Exhibit 11-57

Continued

```
SELECT   call_no,
         code,
         title,
         hours
From     section, course
Where    code = 'MIS380'
   And   COURSE$code = code;
Order by Call_no
```

COURSE

code	title	hours
MIS380	Database I	4
MIS225	Visual Basic	4
MIS420	Systems II	4

SECTION

call_no	INSTRUCTOR$id	COURSE$code
001	11	MIS380
002	33	MIS380
003	11	MIS225
004	44	MIS420

RESULT

The final result is sorted in order of call_no.

call_no	code	title	hours
001	MIS380	Database I	4
002	MIS380	Database I	4

In this case, the rows in the COURSE table are limited to MIS380, so this is the only row that will be joined to the rows in the SECTION table. Because there are two rows in the SECTION table involving MIS380, the number of rows in the result is two.

There is no practical limit to the number or type of conditions that can be included with a join. When we combine other where conditions with join conditions, we find it useful to put the join conditions first, followed by whatever other conditions are required. This is not a rule, but it is helpful in reading and debugging multitable queries. When all of your conditions are combined with AND rather than OR, the queries are typically easy to construct (once you understand SQL!). However, combining a join with other conditions separated by OR can be problematic. To illustrate this idea, we expand the last example to also show sections of MIS420. The query shown in Exhibit 11-58 is an incorrect attempt to produce a list of sections for MIS380 and MIS420.

Exhibit 11-58

Incorrectly Using
OR with a Join
Condition

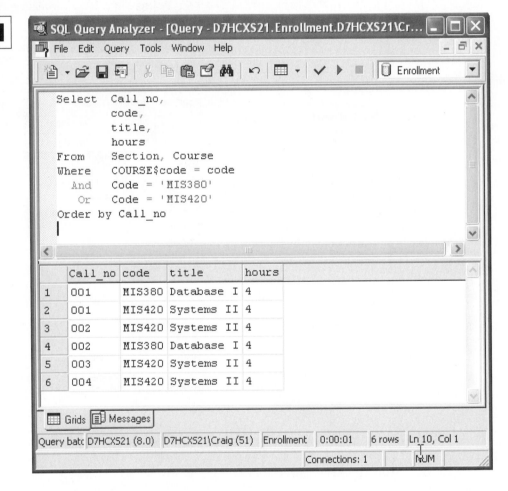

Do you notice anything wrong with the results? The results should have three rows, because there are two sections of MIS380 and one of MIS420. Why does our query result in six rows? The answer has to do with how SQL Server groups the conditions. Basically, the first two conditions are grouped together, and each row is evaluated to see if it meets both of the two conditions (because of the *and*). This step is fine; the trouble comes in with the OR and the Code = 'MIS420' condition. Recall that as long as one condition in an OR combination is true, a row is included in the result. Because of this situation, any row in the Cartesian product that meets both of the first two conditions *or* has a code of "MIS420" is included in the results. The join condition does not matter for rows that have the code "MIS420." The solution to this problem is to be explicit about how you want the conditions grouped by using parentheses, as illustrated in Exhibit 11-59.

Exhibit 11-59

Grouping
Conditions

SQL Query Analyzer - [Query - D7HCXS21.Enrollment.D7HCXS21\Cr...

File   Edit   Query   Tools   Window   Help

Enrollment

```
Select    Call_no,
          code,
          title,
          hours
From      Section, Course
Where     COURSE$code = code
  And     (Code = 'MIS380'
   Or      Code = 'MIS420')
Order by Call_no
```

	Call_no	code	title	hours
1	001	MIS380	Database I	4
2	002	MIS380	Database I	4
3	004	MIS420	Systems II	4

Grids Messages

Query batc D7HCXS21 (8.0) D7HCXS21\Craig (51) Enrollment 0:00:00 3 rows Ln 10, Col 1

Connections: 1   NUM

This time, we get the expected results. Regardless of whether one of the conditions is a join, when you mix ANDs and ORs there is a danger of getting unintended results. Unfortunately, with large databases, you may not recognize that there is a problem. Because of this problem, we always use parentheses to explicitly group conditions in queries that include both AND and OR conditions. We suggest that you do the same.

Joining More than Two Tables

Sometimes producing the results you want requires data from more than two tables. Writing queries that can produce such results is just an extension of what we did for two-table queries. All you have to do is add another condition for each join you want to perform. For example, suppose you wanted a grade list for each section. The list must include the section's call number, the student ids, first names, last names, and the grade, and the list should be in order of the call number, then last name, then first name. The first step in writing this query is to understand which tables contain the required data. The Enrollment database data model is provided in Exhibit 11-60. The required tables are in the box.

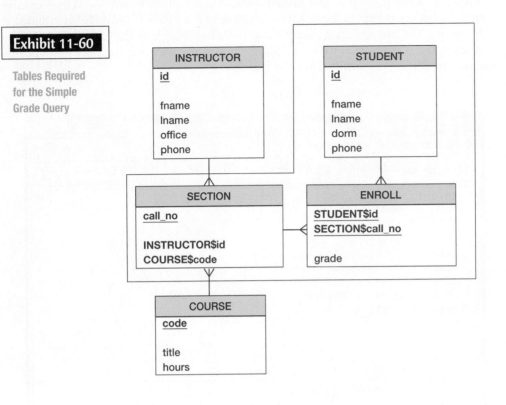

Exhibit 11-60

Tables Required
for the Simple
Grade Query

As you can see, we need data from three tables. Combining data from these three tables requires two joins, one joining SECTION and ENROLL, and one joining ENROLL and STUDENT. This process illustrates an important point. When combining data from multiple tables, *you must have one fewer joins than the number of tables used in the query*. This is an important rule to remember. You can do a quick check of your multitable queries to see if you have the right number of joins. Just count the number of tables in your from clause, subtract one, and that is how many join conditions you must have. Exhibit 11-61 gives the query used to produce the grade results.

Exhibit 11-61

Grade Query

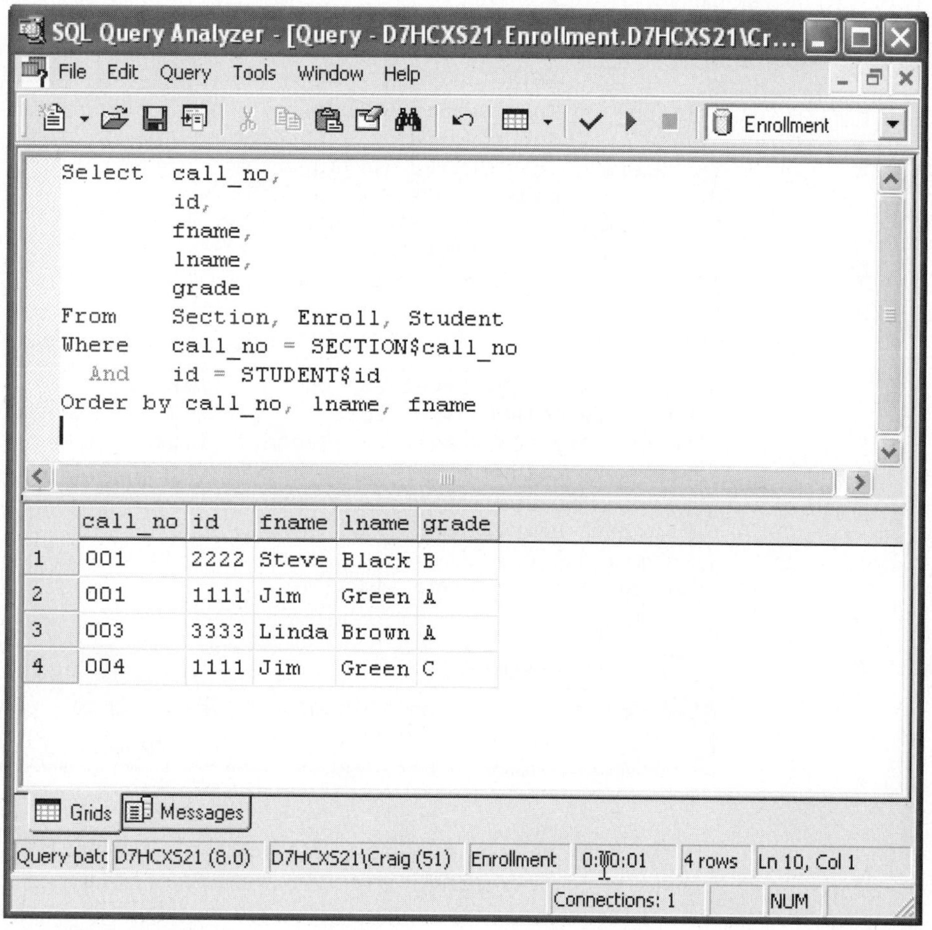

```
Select    call_no,
          id,
          fname,
          lname,
          grade
From      Section, Enroll, Student
Where     call_no = SECTION$call_no
   And    id = STUDENT$id
Order by  call_no, lname, fname
```

	call_no	id	fname	lname	grade
1	001	2222	Steve	Black	B
2	001	1111	Jim	Green	A
3	003	3333	Linda	Brown	A
4	004	1111	Jim	Green	C

Adding data from more tables is more of the same; simply add a join condition for each table added to the from clause. To illustrate this idea, we want to add the instructor's full name, the course code, and the course title to our grade report. This query includes data from all five tables in the database, which means that we need four joins (5 − 1 = 4):

- INSTRUCTOR to SECTION
- SECTION to COURSE
- SECTION to ENROLL
- ENROLL to STUDENT

Based on what we have discussed so far, you might try the query shown in Exhibit 11-62. Unfortunately, this query produces an error, rather than our expected results.

```
SQL Query Analyzer - [Query - D7HCXS21.Enrollment.D7HCXS21\Cr...
File   Edit   Query   Tools   Window   Help

                                                    Enrollment

Select    call_no,
          id,
          fname,
          lname,
          grade
From      Instructor, Course,
          Section, Enroll, Student
Where     id = INSTRUCTOR$id
   And    code = COURSE$code
   And    call_no = SECTION$call_no
   And    id = STUDENT$id
Order by call_no, lname, fname


Server: Msg 209, Level 16, State 1, Line 1
Ambiguous column name 'id'.
Server: Msg 209, Level 16, State 1, Line 1
Ambiguous column name 'fname'.
Server: Msg 209, Level 16, State 1, Line 1
Ambiguous column name 'lname'.
Server: Msg 209, Level 16, State 1, Line 1
Ambiguous column name 'id'.

  Grids   Messages

Query batcl D7HCXS21 (8.0)   D7HCXS21\Craig (51)   Enrollment   0:00:00   0 rows   Ln 13, Col 1
                                                            Connections: 1      NUM
```

The error message is telling us that SQL Server cannot tell what we mean when we include "id" in the query. Why is this message appearing? The problem results because more than one table in the from clause has a column called id, which is included in both the INSTRUCTOR and STUDENT tables. This problem is known as an *ambiguous column name*, and correcting it is rather easy. All you have to do is precede the column name with the table name. The table and column names are separated by a period, as in Instructor.id or

Student.id. Actually, many people like to put the table name in front of all column names. We do not follow this practice personally, but your instructor may feel otherwise. It is a matter of personal (or organizational) preference. Exhibit 11-63 shows the corrected query. You have to be careful to specify the correct table. For example, we want the student's id number, not that of the instructor, to be included in the results. So we used Student.id in the column list.

Exhibit 11-63

Expanded Grade
Query with Error
Corrected

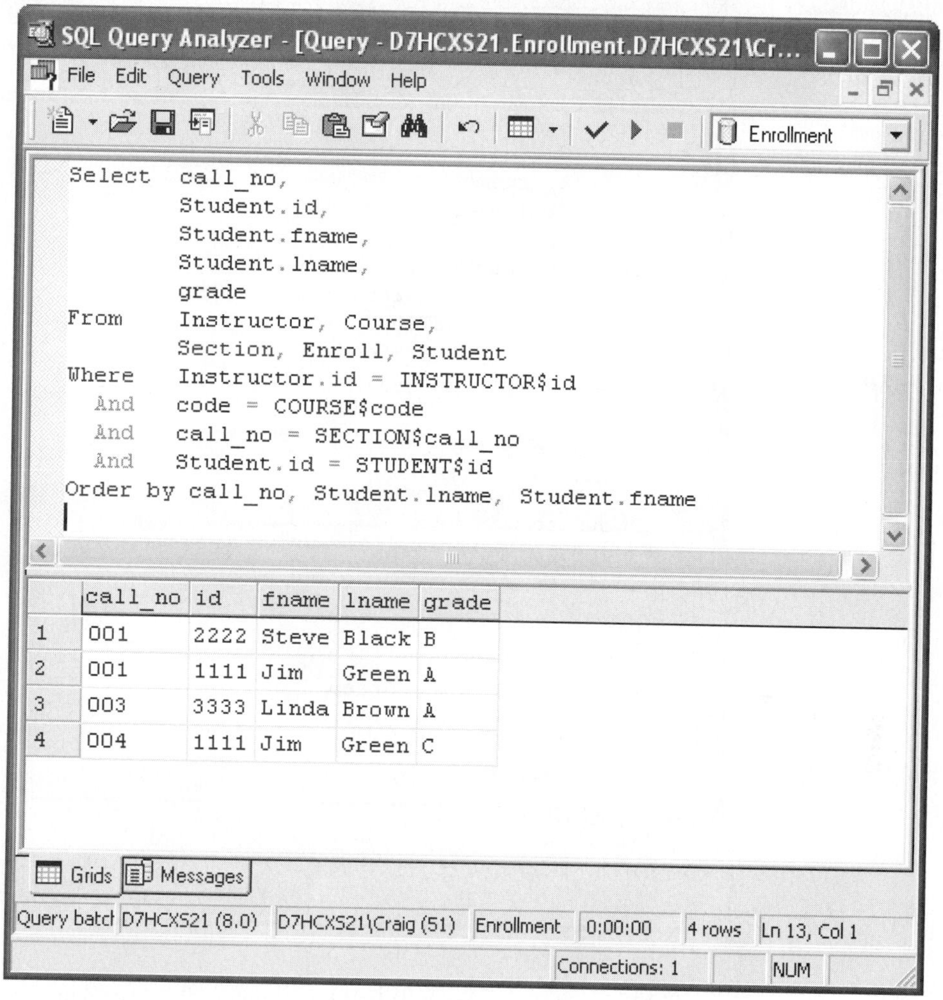

```
SQL Query Analyzer - [Query - D7HCXS21.Enrollment.D7HCXS21\Cr...

File   Edit   Query   Tools   Window   Help

                                                   Enrollment

Select   call_no,
         Student.id,
         Student.fname,
         Student.lname,
         grade
From     Instructor, Course,
         Section, Enroll, Student
Where    Instructor.id = INSTRUCTOR$id
  And    code = COURSE$code
  And    call_no = SECTION$call_no
  And    Student.id = STUDENT$id
Order by call_no, Student.lname, Student.fname
```

	call_no	id	fname	lname	grade
1	001	2222	Steve	Black	B
2	001	1111	Jim	Green	A
3	003	3333	Linda	Brown	A
4	004	1111	Jim	Green	C

```
Grids  Messages

Query batch D7HCXS21 (8.0)  D7HCXS21\Craig (51)  Enrollment  0:00:00  4 rows  Ln 13, Col 1
                                                    Connections: 1        NUM
```

You can use another feature of SQL to save yourself some typing. SQL allows you to specify column and table name aliases. In the case of table names, you typically would use an alias that is shorter than the original table name, a practice which keeps you from having to repeatedly type long table names. An example is given in Exhibit 11-64.

SQL Query Analyzer - [Query - D7HCXS21.Enrollment.D7HCXS21\Cr...

File   Edit   Query   Tools   Window   Help

| Enrollment |

```
Select    call_no,
          St.id,
          St.fname,
          St.lname,
          grade
From      Instructor I, Course C,
          Section Sc, Enroll E, Student St
Where     I.id = INSTRUCTOR$id
  And     code = COURSE$code
  And     call_no = SECTION$call_no
  And     St.id = STUDENT$id
Order by call_no, St.lname, St.fname
```

	call_no	id	fname	lname	grade
1	001	2222	Steve	Black	B
2	001	1111	Jim	Green	A
3	003	3333	Linda	Brown	A
4	004	1111	Jim	Green	C

Grids   Messages

Query batch D7HCXS521 (8.0)   D7HCXS521\Craig (51)   Enrollment   0:00:00   4 rows   Ln 13, Col 1

Connections: 1   NUM

Table name aliases are specified by following the table name with the alias and separating the two with a space. (You can separate the two with the word *As,* but most people omit *As,* which works, as well.) Be sure that you do *not* separate the table name and alias with a comma. Doing so causes SQL Server to think that the alias is an actual table name. We specified aliases for all tables, although we used only two of them (for INSTRUCTOR and STUDENT). We specified these aliases to point out that you need to be careful to not use the same alias for two different tables (as in "S" for STUDENT and SECTION), and to show that you are not limited to a single letter for an alias.

Subqueries

Subqueries are queries contained inside other queries. Problems such as comparing an average value with a group of records can best be solved using a subquery. For most subqueries, the inner subquery executes first, and then the results of the inner query are compared with the outer query. This process is a key to understanding subqueries. Think of the results of the **inner subquery** as being fed to the **outer query.**

When debugging, you should try running the inner query by itself to get a feel for what is going on. If the inner query returns a single value (e.g., select Avg(*x*)), use arithmetic operators (=, <, >, <>, >=, <=) for the comparison. If the inner query returns multiple values (e.g., select *x*) use IN or NOT IN for the comparison. Other operators can also be used, but many problems can be solved by using the operators. Some examples will help you understand subqueries.

For the first example, we will use the Sky_Member database. You want to produce a list of all members who have more than the average number of jumps. If you were producing this list manually, the first thing you would do is to compute the average. Then you would compare the number of jumps for each member to the average, and write down the information for each member who has more than the average number of jumps. We could do the same thing using two SQL queries. The first one would calculate the average. Then we can use that number as part of a where clause in the second query. (Note that we're going to truncate the actual average by dropping off all numbers to the right of the decimal point. SQL Server performs this operation when calculating a function that involves a column that is an integer data type.) These queries are shown in Exhibit 11-65.

Exhibit 11-65

Using Two Queries

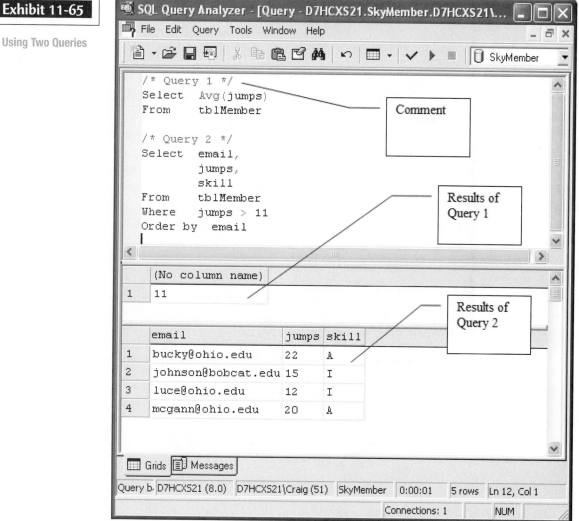

As an aside, there are two additional characteristics of SQL Server that are illustrated in Exhibit 11-65. First, you can execute multiple queries through a single query pane; the output of all queries will then show up in the results pane. The results appear in the order of the queries. Second, you can place comments in a query by placing /* at the beginning and */ at the end of the query. We find this feature quite useful for documenting queries.

We can use a subquery to combine the two queries into a single query. This query is given in Exhibit 11-66. The inner query, which is enclosed in parentheses, calculates the average number of jumps for all members. This result is then used as part of the where clause in the outer query. The complete analysis is shown in Exhibit 11-67.

Exhibit 11-66

Using a Subquery
That Returns a
Single Value

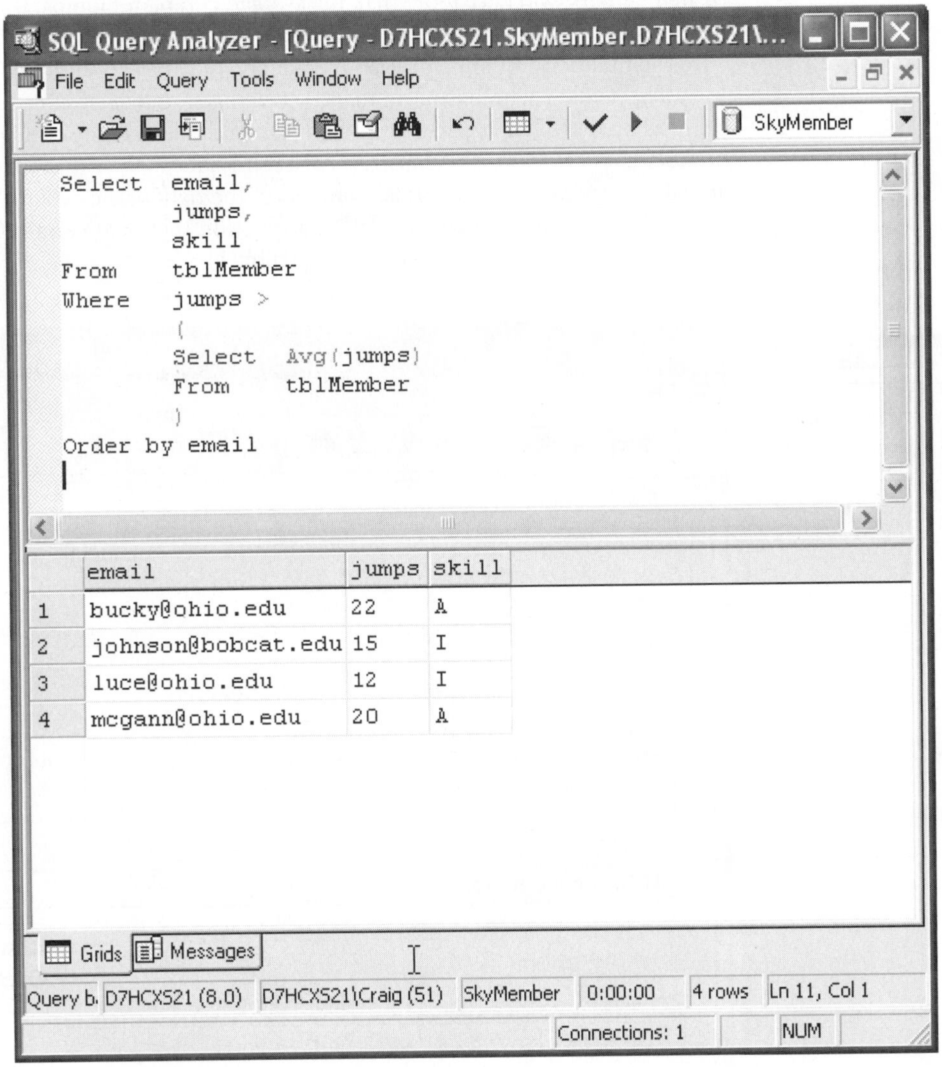

SQL Query Analyzer - [Query - D7HCXS21.SkyMember.D7HCXS21\...

File   Edit   Query   Tools   Window   Help

SkyMember

```
Select   email,
         jumps,
         skill
From     tblMember
Where    jumps >
         (
         Select   Avg(jumps)
         From     tblMember
         )
Order by email
```

	email	jumps	skill
1	bucky@ohio.edu	22	A
2	johnson@bobcat.edu	15	I
3	luce@ohio.edu	12	I
4	mcgann@ohio.edu	20	A

Grids   Messages

Query b. D7HCXS21 (8.0)   D7HCXS21\Craig (51)   SkyMember   0:00:00   4 rows   Ln 11, Col 1

Connections: 1   NUM

Exhibit 11-67   The Analysis for the Subquery Returning One Value

SUBQUERY RETURNING A SINGLE VALUE

Show the email address, number of jumps, and skill for all members with more than the average number of jumps.

SELECT fname,
       lname
From tblMember
where jumps >
   (Select avg(jumps)
    From tblMember)

email	fname	lname	phone	jumps	equip	skill
mcgann@ohio.edu	Sean	McGann	592-2222	20	Y	A
bucky@ohio.edu	Teri	Bucky	555-5555	22	Y	A
dayj@ohio.edu	John	Day	592-0646	5	Y	B
mcgrath@bobcat.edu	Billie	McGrath	555-6666	3	N	B
wilson@bobcat.edu	Sally	Wilson	555-4444	6	N	B
johnson@bobcat.edu	Jeremy	Johnson	555-3333	15	Y	I
luce@ohio.edu	Thom	Luce	592-1111	12	N	I
			Avg	11		

SELECT fname,
       lname
From tblMember
where jumps >
   (Select avg(jumps)
    From tblMember)

email	fname	lname	phone	jumps	equip	skill
mcgann@ohio.edu	Sean	McGann	592-2222	20	Y	A
bucky@ohio.edu	Teri	Bucky	555-5555	22	Y	A
dayj@ohio.edu	John	Day	592-0646	5	Y	B
mcgrath@bobcat.edu	Billie	McGrath	555-6666	3	N	B
wilson@bobcat.edu	Sally	Wilson	555-4444	6	N	B
johnson@bobcat.edu	Jeremy	Johnson	555-3333	15	Y	I

SELECT fname,
       lname
From tblMember
where jumps >
   (Select avg(jumps)
    From tblMember)

email	fname	lname	phone	jumps	equip	skill
mcgann@ohio.edu	Sean	McGann	592-2222	20	Y	A
bucky@ohio.edu	Teri	Bucky	555-5555	22	Y	A
dayj@ohio.edu	John	Day	592-0646	5	Y	B
mcgrath@bobcat.edu	Billie	McGrath	555-6666	3	N	B
wilson@bobcat.edu	Sally	Wilson	555-4444	6	N	B
johnson@bobcat.edu	Jeremy	Johnson	555-3333	15	Y	I
luce@ohio.edu	Thom	Luce	592-1111	12	N	I
			Avg	11		

RESULT

email	skill
mcgann@ohio.edu	A
bucky@ohio.edu	A
johnson@bobcat.edu	I
luce@ohio.edu	I

Now let's look at an example of a subquery that returns more than one value. We will use the Enrollment database in this example. You want to list the ids, first names, and last names of all students who are *not* enrolled in a course. Recall that we can use NOT IN as a comparison operator to choose rows that do *not* match a list of values. Using NOT IN with a subquery, you can easily produce the desired list, as shown in Exhibit 11-68.

Exhibit 11-68

Using NOT IN with a Subquery

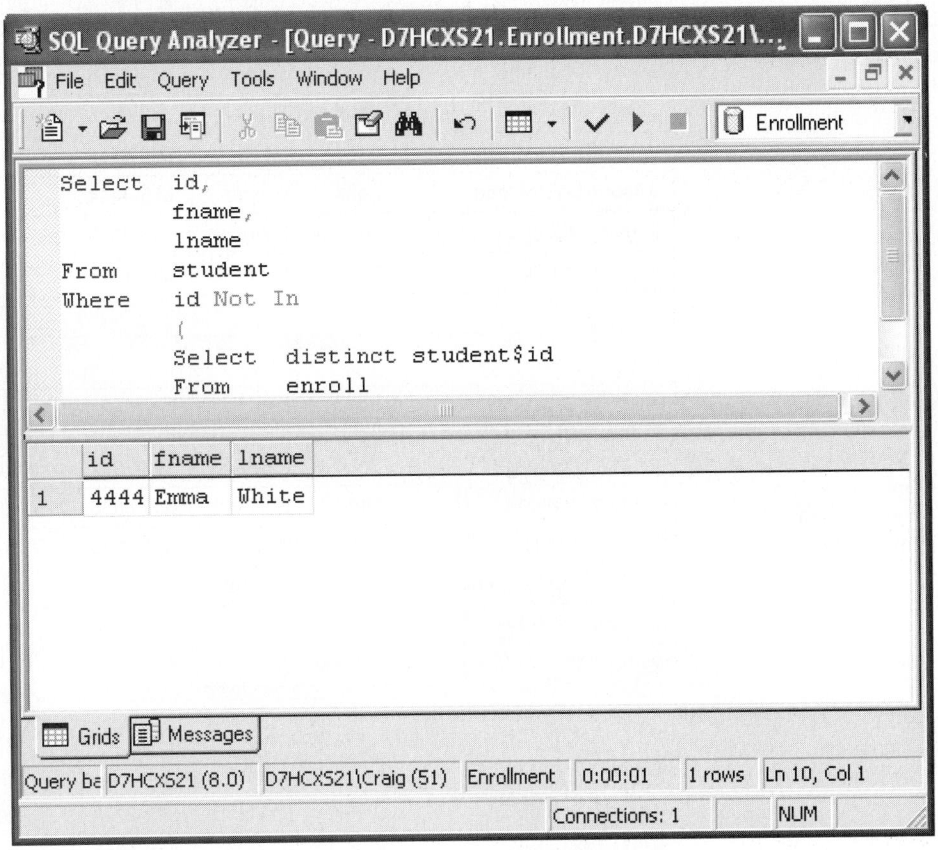
SQL Query Analyzer - [Query - D7HCXS21.Enrollment.D7HCXS21\...
File Edit Query Tools Window Help
Enrollment
Select id,
fname,
lname
From student
Where id Not In
(
Select distinct student$id
From enroll
id fname lname
1 4444 Emma White
Grids
Messages
Query ba D7HCXS21 (8.0)
D7HCXS21\Craig (51)
Enrollment
0:00:01
1 rows
Ln 10, Col 1
Connections: 1
NUM

The inner query produces a list of student id values from the ENROLLMENT table. This is a list of all students who *are* enrolled in at least one course. The word *distinct* tells SQL Server not to repeat any id values. The result of the inner query is used as the value list for the NOT IN function. In the outer query, the requested columns are shown for all rows in STUDENT that do not match one of the values in the NOT IN value list. The complete analysis for this query is shown in Exhibit 11-69.

Exhibit 11-69   The Analysis for the Subquery Returning Multiple Values

---

SUBQUERY RETURNING MULTIPLE VALUES

List the student's id, fname, and lname for all students *not* enrolled in any course.

```
SELECT  id, fname, lname
From    student
Where   id not in
        (
        Select distinct STUDENT$id
        from enroll
        )
```

STUDENT

id	fname	lname	dorm	phone
1111	Jim	Green	450A	593-2456
2222	Steve	Black	326B	593-4623
3333	Linda	Brown	144A	593-5575
4444	Emma	White	133B	593-4676

ENROLL

STUDENT$id	COURSE$code	semester	grade
1111	MIS380A01	F01	A
2222	MIS225A02	F02	B
3333	MIS225A02	F02	A
1111	MIS420A01	S02	C

STUDENT$id
1111
2222
3333

*The subquery is solved by first creating a list of those students who **are** enrolled in a course. The subquery result eliminates duplicate student$ids from the Enroll table.*

```
SELECT  id, fname, lname
From    student
Where   id not in
        (
        Select distinct STUDENT$id
        from enroll
        );
```

STUDENT

id	fname	lname	dorm	phone
1111	Jim	Green	450A	593-2456
2222	Steve	Black	326B	593-4623
3333	Linda	Brown	144A	593-5575
4444	Emma	White	133B	593-4676

ENROLL

STUDENT$id	COURSE$code	semester	grade
1111	MIS380A01	F01	A
2222	MIS225A02	F02	B
3333	MIS225A02	F02	A
1111	MIS420A01	S02	C

STUDENT$id
1111
2222
3333

*This list is then compared with the list of **all** students. Those students in one list but not the other appear in the result.*

(Continued)

Exhibit 11-69   Continued

```
SELECT  id, fname, lname
From    student
Where   id not in
        (
        Select distinct STUDENT$id
        from enroll
        )
```

STUDENT

id	fname	lname	dorm	phone
1111	Jim	Green	450A	593-2456
2222	Steve	Black	326B	593-4623
3333	Linda	Brown	144A	593-5575
4444	Emma	White	133B	593-4676

ENROLL

STUDENT$id	COURSE$code	semester	grade
1111	MIS380A01	F01	A
2222	MIS225A02	F02	B
3333	MIS225A02	F02	A
1111	MIS420A01	S02	C

STUDENT$id
1111
2222
3333

Emma White is the only student in the student list who does not have a matching record in the subquery list.

RESULT

id	fname	lname
4444	Emma	White

▓ SUMMARY

- ▓ Three basic retrieval operations for relational databases are selection, projection and joining.
- ▓ These operations are implemented in SQL through the Select statement.
- ▓ Each Select statement must have, at a minimum, the word *Select*, a column list, the word *From*, and a table list.
- ▓ Using the asterisk (*) as the column list indicates that all columns in the table(s) should be included in the query results.
- ▓ The column list may also include an explicit list of column names.
- ▓ The order by clause is used to determine the order in which rows appear in the query results.
- ▓ The where clause is used to limit the rows included in the query results.
- ▓ Each where clause must include one or more conditions.
- ▓ Multiple conditions in a where clause are separated by AND and/or OR.
- ▓ SQL Server has a number of aggregate functions, including Count, Sum, and Avg (average), among others.
- ▓ *Distinct* is used to limit results to eliminate duplicate values in query results.
- ▓ *Group by* is used to create subaggregations in query results.
- ▓ The having clause specifies one or more conditions involving aggregate functions.
- ▓ Data from multiple tables is combined by specifying one or more equality conditions in a where clause. Each of these join conditions involves a primary key being equal to a corresponding foreign key.
- ▓ A query should typically have one fewer join conditions than the number of tables included in the from clause.
- ▓ Join conditions can be combined with other conditions.
- ▓ One or more subqueries may be nested within another query.

▓ KEY TERMS

Aggregate functions. Built-in functions (Sum, Avg, etc.) that can be calculated for groups (aggregations) of rows, rather than for single rows.

AND operator. Operator used in a where clause that allows you to combine two conditions where rows must meet both conditions to be selected.

Between operator. Lets you choose rows based on a range of values.

Cartesian product. A temporary table that combines all rows in one table with all rows in another table.

Distinct. Option that tells SQL that you want to display each value only once.

Equi-join (or inner joins). Matching rows between tables based on equality between primary and foreign key values.

Group by. Clause that groups rows based on values in a column.

Having clause. Used to select particular groups (aggregations) based on a condition rather than on single rows.

IN operator. Allows you to select rows based on multiple values for a particular column. Similar to a series of OR conditions.

Inner subquery. Always executes first and then the results of this query are used as input to the outer query.

Joining. Relational database operation that combines data from two tables.

LIKE operator. Operator used in a where clause that allows you to choose rows that share some common characters, but are not exactly the same.

NOT operator. Operator used in a where clause that allows you to reverse the condition.

OR operator. Operator used in a where clause that allows you to combine two conditions where rows can meet either condition to be selected.

Order by. SQL clause for a Select statement used to sort results.

Outer query. Query containing the inner query and using the results of that inner query as input.

Projection. Relational database operation that retrieves a subset of columns.

Select. SQL statement that is used to implement all three relational database operations.

Selection. Relational database operation that retrieves a subset of rows.

Subqueries. Queries contained inside other queries.

Where clause. SQL clause for a Select statement used to choose particular rows based on a condition.

EXERCISES

Review

1. Describe the three retrieval operations for relational databases.
2. Describe the simplest form of the Select statement.
3. How can you display a subset of columns in SQL?
4. How can you sort the results from an SQL statement?
5. How do you perform a descending sort?
6. How do you sort on multiple columns?
7. How do you retrieve only some of the rows from a table?
8. Explain how the LIKE operator is used.
9. How can multiple conditions be included in the same where clause?
10. Explain the difference between the AND and OR logical operators.
11. What does the NOT operator do?
12. What are aggregate functions?
13. What is the purpose of the group by clause?
14. What does the Distinct option do?
15. How is the having clause used with group by?
16. Explain how a join is accomplished in a Select statement.
17. When you retrieve data from five tables, how many joins will you need? Why?
18. When must you be careful when combining a join with a where condition?
19. Explain what a subquery is.
20. What operators would you normally use when the inner query produces a single value? Multiple values?

Discuss

1. If you wanted to retrieve members whose email addresses contained "ohio," what where clause would you use?
2. If you wanted to list members who are not from Ohio, what where condition would you use?
3. If you wanted to list members who have their own equipment and with a skill level of either B or I, what where condition would you use?
4. Explain how AND and OR conditions interact in a query, and how to use parentheses to ensure the result will be correct.
5. Explain the different effects that where and having can have on a query.

Practice

Exercises 1 through 20 use the Amazon database, which you created in the exercises for Chapter 10. The design of this database is shown in Exhibit 11-70.

Exhibit 11-70 Amazon Database Design

Design

CLIENT

email	TEXT(20)
lname	TEXT(15)
fname	TEXT(15)
street	TEXT(20)
city	TEXT(15)
state	TEXT(2)
zip	TEXT(10)

ORDERS

id	TEXT(5)
CLIENT$email	TEXT(20)
order_date	DATE
credit_card	TEXT(16)
exp_date	DATE
ship_method	TEXT(10)

BOOK

isbn	TEXT(10)
title	TEXT(20)
fname	TEXT(15)
lname	TEXT(15)
list_price	SINGLE
qoh	INTEGER

LINEITEM

ORDER$id	TEXT(5)
BOOK$isbn	TEXT(10)
sale_price	SINGLE
quantity	INTEGER

Physical Details

Design Table 'Client' in 'Amazon' on '(local)'

Column Name	Data Type	Length	Allow Nulls
email	nvarchar	20	✓
fname	nvarchar	15	✓
lname	nvarchar	15	✓
street	nvarchar	20	✓
city	nvarchar	15	✓
state	nvarchar	2	✓
zip	nvarchar	10	✓

Design Table 'Order' in 'Amazon' on '(local)'

Column Name	Data Type	Length	Allow Nulls
id	nvarchar	5	✓
client$email	nvarchar	20	✓
order_date	smalldatetime	4	✓
credit_card	nvarchar	16	✓
exp_date	smalldatetime	4	✓
ship_method	nvarchar	10	✓

Design Table 'Book' in 'Amazon' on '(local)'

Column Name	Data Type	Length	Allow Nulls
isbn	nvarchar	10	✓
title	nvarchar	20	✓
fname	nvarchar	15	✓
lname	nvarchar	15	✓
list_price	real	4	✓
qoh	smallint	2	✓

Design Table 'Lineitem' in 'Amazon' on '(local)'

Column Name	Data Type	Length	Allow Nulls
order$id	nvarchar	5	✓
book$isbn	nvarchar	10	✓
sale_price	real	4	✓
quantity	smallint	2	✓

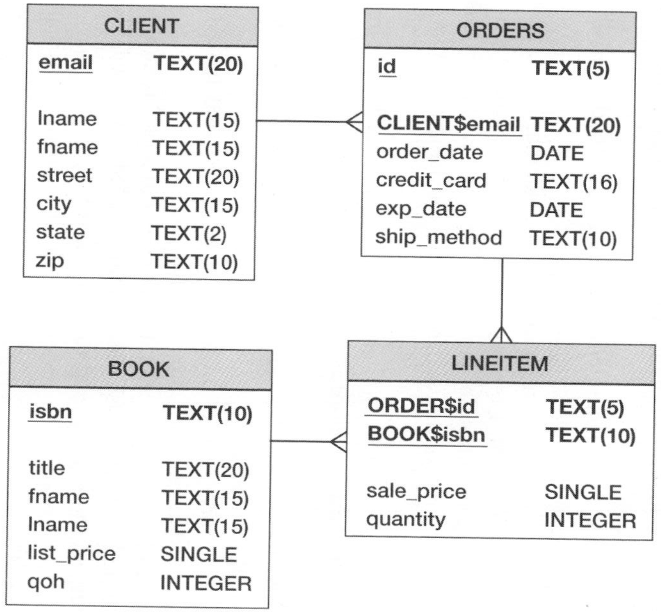

Write and execute a query that produces the required results.

1. List all of the data in the CLIENT table in order of email address.
2. List the e-mail addresses, first names, last names, states, and zip codes for all clients. Put the list in order of state, then e-mail address.
3. List the ISBN, title, list price, and quantity on hand for all books. Put the list in *descending* order of quantity on hand.
4. List the e-mail addresses, first names, last names, cities, states, and zip codes for all clients in Ohio (OH). Put the list in order of state, then city, then last name.
5. List the ISBN, title, list price, and quantity on hand for all books that have a quantity on hand of 90 or more. Put the list in *descending* order of quantity on hand, then title.
6. List the ISBN, title, list price, and quantity on hand for all books that have a quantity on hand of 90 or more *and* have a list price of more than $12. Put the list in *descending* order of quantity on hand, then title.
7. List the ISBN, title, list price, and quantity on hand for all books that have a quantity on hand of 90 or more *or* have a list price of more than $12. Put the list in *descending* order of quantity on hand, then title.
8. List the e-mail addresses, first names, and last names for all clients who have "edu" e-mail addresses. Put the list in order of e-mail address.
9. List the ISBN, title, list price, and quantity on hand for all books that have a list price between $12 and $20. Put the list in *descending* order of list price.
10. List the total (sum) quantity on hand for all books. Use the column alias "Total On Hand."
11. How many orders were shipped via USPS? Use the column alias "Shipped by USPS."
12. How many *different* shipping methods were used to ship orders?
13. List the order id and total quantity for each order. Put the list in order of total quantity. (Hint: Use the LINEITEM table.)
14. List the order id and total quantity for each order that has a total quantity of four or more. Put the list in order of total quantity. (Hint: Use the LINEITEM table.)
15. List the order id, book ISBN, sale price, quantity, and extended price (sale price multiplied by quantity) for all lineitems. Use the column alias "Total" for the extended price column. Put the list in order of order id.
16. List the order id, order date, client e-mail address, first name, and last name for each order. Put the list in order of e-mail address, then order date.
17. For each order, list the order id and order date, along with the ISBN, title, sale price, and quantity of each book included in the order. Put the list in order of order date, then title. (Hint: You must include the LINEITEM table.)
18. For each order, list the order id, order date, client e-mail address, first name, and last name, along with the ISBN, title, sale price, and quantity of each book included in the order. Put the list in order of order id, then title. (Hint: You must include the LINEITEM table.)
19. For each order placed by a customer in Ohio (OH), list the order id, order date, client e-mail address, first name, and last name, along with the ISBN, title, sale price, and quantity of each book included in the order. Put the list in order of order date, then title. (Hint: You must include the LINEITEM table.)
20. For each order that include the books with the ISBN 014025448X or 0670894370, list the order id, order date, client e-mail address, first name, and last name, along with the ISBN, title, sale price, and quantity of each book included in the order. Put the list in order of order date, then title. (Hint: You must include the LINEITEM table.)

Exercises 21 through 38 use the Hospital database. The design of this database is shown in Exhibit 11-71.

Exhibit 11-71   Hospital Database Design

Physical Details

Design Table 'Doctor' in 'Hospital' on '(local)'

Column Name	Data Type	Length	Allow Nulls
id	nvarchar	5	✓
fname	nvarchar	15	✓
lname	nvarchar	15	✓
phone	nvarchar	12	✓
beeper	nvarchar	12	✓

Design Table 'Patient' in 'Hospital' on '(local)'

Column Name	Data Type	Length	Allow Nulls
id	nvarchar	5	✓
doctor$id	nvarchar	5	✓
fname	nvarchar	15	✓
lname	nvarchar	15	✓
street	nvarchar	15	✓
city	nvarchar	10	✓
state	nvarchar	2	✓
zip	nvarchar	10	✓
phone	nvarchar	12	✓

Design Table 'Insurance' in 'Hospital' on '(local)'

Column Name	Data Type	Length	Allow Nulls
company	nvarchar	15	✓
contact_fname	nvarchar	15	✓
contact_lname	nvarchar	15	✓
phone	nvarchar	12	✓

Design Table 'Insure' in 'Hospital' on '(local)'

Column Name	Data Type	Length	Allow Nulls
patient$id	nvarchar	5	✓
insurance$company	nvarchar	15	✓

Design

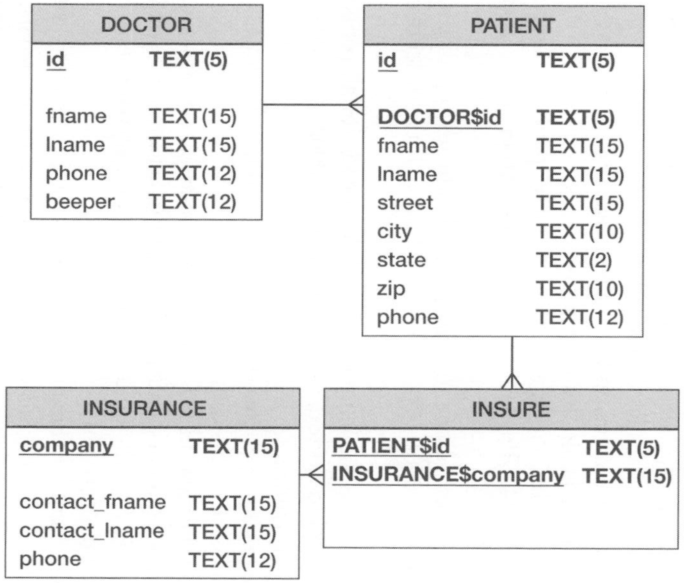

DOCTOR

id	TEXT(5)
fname	TEXT(15)
lname	TEXT(15)
phone	TEXT(12)
beeper	TEXT(12)

PATIENT

id	TEXT(5)
DOCTOR$id	TEXT(5)
fname	TEXT(15)
lname	TEXT(15)
street	TEXT(15)
city	TEXT(10)
state	TEXT(2)
zip	TEXT(10)
phone	TEXT(12)

INSURANCE

company	TEXT(15)
contact_fname	TEXT(15)
contact_lname	TEXT(15)
phone	TEXT(12)

INSURE

PATIENT$id	TEXT(5)
INSURANCE$company	TEXT(15)

Write and execute a query that produces the required results.

21. List all of the data in the PATIENT table. Put the list in order of state, then last name.
22. List the first name, last name, and beeper number for each doctor. Put the list in order of last name, then first name.
23. List first names, last names, cities, states, and zip codes of all patients who live in Florida (FL). Put the list in order of city, then last name.
24. List first names, last names, cities, states, and zip codes of all patients who live in Florida (FL) or Ohio (OH). Put the list in order of city, then last name.
25. List first names, last names, cities, states, and zip codes of all patients who have a zip code that begins with the numeral "4." Put the list in *descending* order of city, then in *ascending* order of last name.
26. List the first names, last names, phone numbers, and doctor ids for all patients who are assigned to doctors with the id 00001, 00002, or 00004. Put the list in order of doctor id, then last name.
27. List the first names, last names, phone numbers, and doctor ids for all patients who live in Ohio (OH) and are assigned to doctors with the id 00001, 00002, or 00004. Put the list in order of doctor id, then last name.
28. How many *different* doctors have patients assigned to them? (Hint: You must use the Patient table.) Use the column alias "Doctors with patients."
29. How many patients live in Florida (FL)? Use the column alias "Patients in Florida."
30. For each state that has more than one patient residing in it, list the state and the number of patients living in the state. Use the column alias "Number of patients." Put the list in *descending* order by number of patients.
31. For each patient, list the patient's first name, last name, and zip code, along with the name of the insurance company used by the patient. Put the list in order of last name.
32. For each patient, list the patient's first name, last name, and zip code, along with the name and phone number of the insurance company used by the patient. Put the list in order of the patient's last name.
33. For each patient insured by Nationwide, list patient's first name, last name, and zip code. Put the list in order of last name.
34. For each patient living in Ohio (OH) or Kentucky (KY), list the patient's first name, last name, state, and zip code, along with the name and phone number of the insurance company used by the patient. Put the list in order of last name.
35. For each insurance company, list the company name, the contact's first and last names, and the ids, first names, and last names of all patients using that insurance company. Put the list in order of insurance company, then patient last name.
36. For each patient, list the patient's first and last names, the first and last names of the patient's doctor, the patient's insurance company, and the company's phone number. Put the list in order of insurance company, then doctor's last name, then patient's last name.
37. For patients with the id 11111, 33333, or 55555, list the patient's first and last names, the first and last names of the patient's doctor, the patient's insurance company, and the company's phone number. Put the list in order of insurance company, then doctor's last name, then patient's last name.
38. List the id numbers, first names, and last names of all doctors who do *not* have any patients assigned to him or her. Put the list in order of doctor last name.

Exercises 39 through 46 use the Acme database. The design of this database is shown in Exhibit 11-72.

Exhibit 11-72   Acme Database Design

Physical Details

Design Table 'Customer' in 'Acme' on '(local)'

Column Name	Data Type	Length	Allow Nulls
id	nvarchar	5	✓
fname	nvarchar	15	✓
lname	nvarchar	15	✓
bday	smalldatetime	4	✓
phone	nvarchar	12	✓

Design Table 'Order' in 'Acme' on '(local)'

Column Name	Data Type	Length	Allow Nulls
id	nvarchar	5	
customer$id	nvarchar	5	✓
[date]	smalldatetime	4	✓
delivery	nvarchar	10	✓
wrap	nvarchar	1	✓

Design Table 'Product' in 'Acme' on '(local)'

Column Name	Data Type	Length	Allow Nulls
id	nvarchar	5	
list_price	real	4	✓
description	nvarchar	20	✓

Design Table 'lineitem' in 'Acme' on '(local)'

Column Name	Data Type	Length	Allow Nulls
order$id	nvarchar	5	✓
product$id	nvarchar	5	✓
quantity	smallint	2	✓
sale_price	real	4	✓

Design

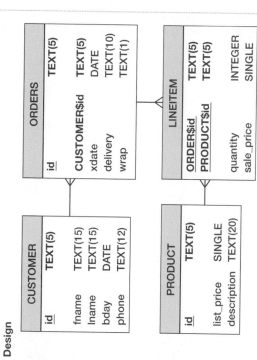

CUSTOMER	
id	TEXT(5)
fname	TEXT(15)
lname	TEXT(15)
bday	DATE
phone	TEXT(12)

PRODUCT	
id	TEXT(5)
list_price	SINGLE
description	TEXT(20)

ORDERS	
id	TEXT(5)
CUSTOMER$id	TEXT(5)
xdate	DATE
delivery	TEXT(10)
wrap	TEXT(1)

LINEITEM	
ORDER$id	TEXT(5)
PRODUCT$id	TEXT(5)
quantity	INTEGER
sale_price	SINGLE

Write and execute a query that produces the required results.

39. How many *different* customers have placed orders?

40. List the first and last names of all customers who have placed more than one order. (Note: This exercise is quite challenging.)

41. List the product id and number of orders that include the product for all products that have been included on more than one order. Put the list in *descending* order of product id.

42. How many orders have been wrapped?

43. List the first and last names of all customers who have *not* placed orders. Put the list in order of last name.

44. List the id, list price, and description of all products that *are* included in orders. Put the list in descending order of list price.

45. List the id, list price, and description of all products that *are not* included in orders. Put the list in descending order of list price.

46. List the product id, description, and list price for all products that have a list price greater than the average list price for all products. Put the list in order of description.

Accessing Databases from Web Applications with Microsoft ASP.NET

Learning Objectives

After completing this chapter, you will be able to:

- Explain the basic architecture of an ASP.NET Web Form application.
- Create an ASP.NET Web Form application.
- Create a data connection to an SQL Server database.
- Create a data connection to an Oracle database.
- Create a data connection to an Access database.
- Create a data source to retrieve all the rows in a table.
- Create a data source to retrieve a subset of rows using a where clause.
- Create and configure a GridView server control.
- Create and configure a Textbox server control.
- Create and configure a Button server control.
- Create and configure a RadioButtonList server control.
- Create and configure a DropDownList server control.

Introduction

In the previous 11 chapters, you have learned how to design and build simple databases. The database management system (Access, SQL Server, or Oracle) has tools that allow you to create and manage database tables and the data stored in them. Once a database has been created, it is possible to access the data through a variety of other applications. One of the most powerful ways to deploy a database is by making it accessible through a Web site. In the next two chapters, you will learn how the Microsoft ASP.NET development environment can be used to build data-driven Web sites that allow users to display and manipulate database data. It will be assumed that you have a basic understanding of how simple Web pages are constructed with HTML.

What Is ASP.NET?

ASP.NET is the Microsoft development environment that allows you to develop Web applications quickly. An **Active Server Page (ASP)** is a Web page that includes programming code to dynamically construct the content of the Web page on the fly in response to user inputs and events related to the page. Perhaps the most powerful way to customize the content of a Web page is to associate the page with a database and to use the information from the database to determine what is displayed on the Web page. Exhibit 12-1 illustrates how an Active Server Page works.

Exhibit 12-1 The Basic Active Server Page Model

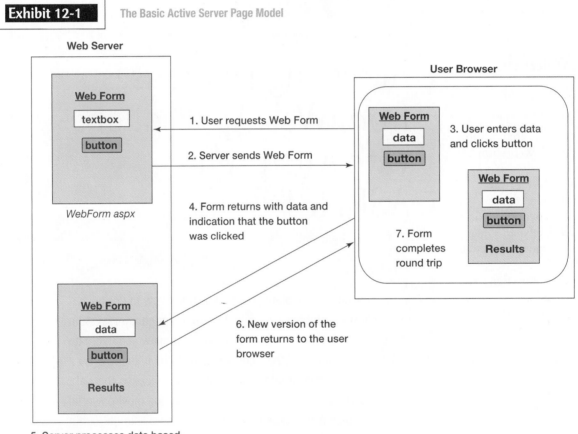

ASP.NET Web Forms

In ASP.NET, the basic component is a **Web Form,** which is essentially a Hypertext Markup Language (HTML) document that includes HTML tags along with server controls. ASP.NET **server controls** include dynamic versions of typical HTML components, including text boxes, tables, bullet lists, radio buttons, and list boxes, as well as unique controls that provide additional functionality far beyond that possible with simple HTML tags. These controls handle functions such as validation, data access, login processing, and navigation.

In ASP.NET, the Web Form is sent back to the server when certain events, like clicking a button, occur. The server then evaluates the events that occurred, reconstructs the page, and sends it back to the browser. Thus, the page essentially makes a *round trip*, with the browser sending the page back to the server and the server processing it and sending it back to the browser. When the Web Form is sent back from the browser, additional information is sent about the events that have taken place on the Web page before the information was sent back to the server. These events could be such things as buttons the user has clicked, textboxes that have been filled in, or selections from drop-down lists, check boxes, or radio buttons. When the page returns to the server, the events are analyzed, and the page is redisplayed with any changes required based on the events that have occurred.

A Web Form is divided into two separate components: the visual component that determines the user interface, and the programming logic that is used to control the behavior of the page and the controls embedded in the page. Each of these components is stored in a separate file on the server, and they combine to produce the page that is ultimately returned to the user's browser, as illustrated in Exhibit 12-2.

Exhibit 12-2   The Active Server Page File Structure

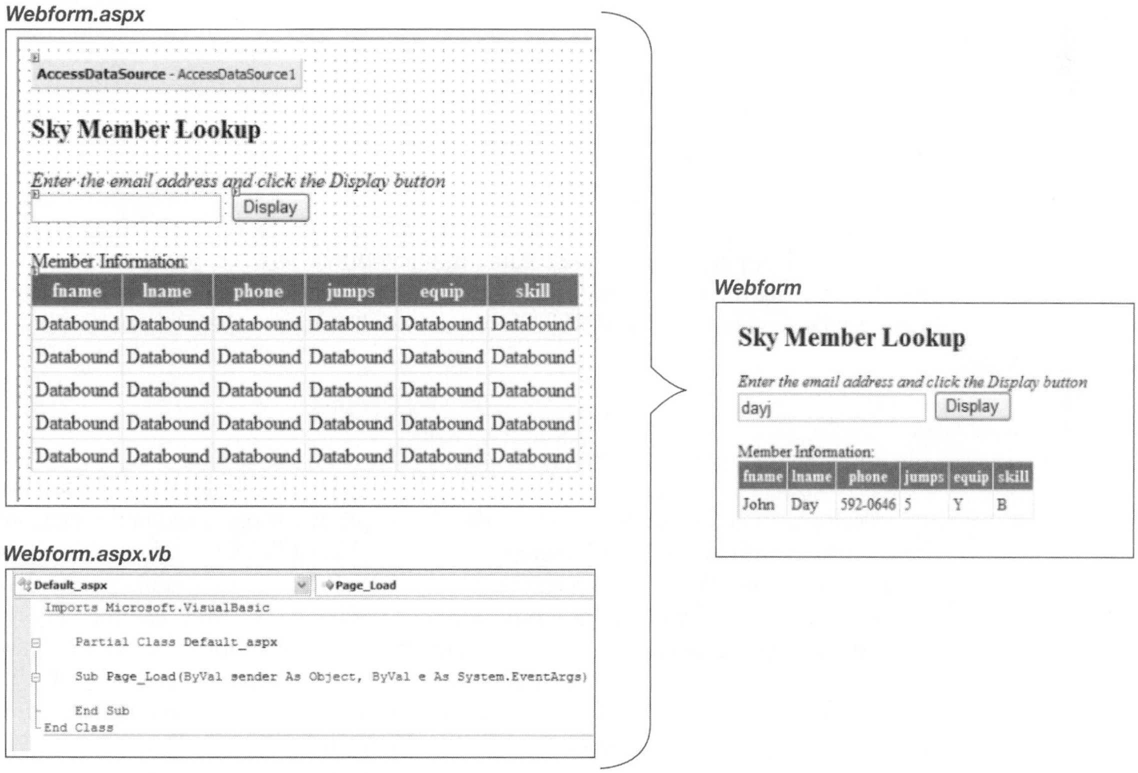

Webform.aspx

Webform.aspx.vb

Webform

 **An Example Web Application**

To illustrate how an ASP.NET Web Form is created, we will go through the process of creating a simple Web page with some text and a button, as illustrated in Exhibit 12-3.

Exhibit 12-3

A Simple Web Page

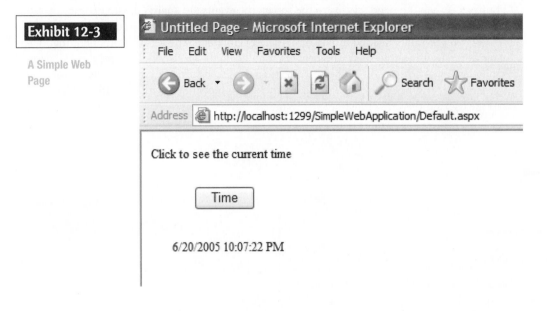

ASP.NET applications can be created in many different ways, but the most powerful tool for creating these applications is Visual Studio. This Microsoft development environment can be used to create ASP.NET Web sites as well as many others types of applications.

An Introduction to Web Developer Express

Microsoft **Web Developer Express** is a complex development environment that includes a variety of powerful tools to assist with the development process. It is a subset of Microsoft's full development environment, Visual Studio. The applications discussed in this chapter can be completed with either Web Developer or the full Visual Studio product. We will focus here on the simpler Web Developer subset because Web Developer enables you to develop the complete range of Web applications. A complete discussion of this environment is well beyond the scope of this book, so we will focus only on those options necessary to illustrate how easy it is to create powerful, database-driven Web applications using ASP.NET.

Web Developer includes all the components needed to build and test applications right on your own computer. In addition to allowing you to create and edit the application locally, you can also use a database on your local computer and test the entire application through the browser on the computer. This way you can prototype an application offline and then deploy it on a Web server later.

When Web Developer is launched, the basic development environment will be displayed in a way similar to what is shown in Exhibit 12-4.

Exhibit 12-4

The Web
Developer
Development
Environment

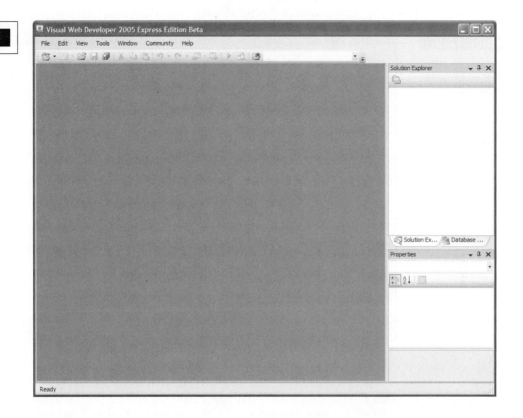

The interface for Web Developer contains many familiar components typical of Windows applications. There is a menu and shortcuts across the top and a status bar across the bottom. In this display, the majority of the screen is blank, because no project is currently active. The panel at the right is the Solution Explorer, which displays the files used in the current project. To learn more about this environment, particularly as it relates to the creation of ASP.NET applications, let's look at how the simple Web application described in the previous section would be created.

Creating a Web Site

All ASP.NET applications are created within a container known as a Web site. A **Web site** is basically a directory in which all the files associated with the Web application are stored. By grouping all the files within this directory, it is easy to pick up the application and move it if necessary. This capability is particularly important when you develop an application on a local computer and then later want to move it to a Web server, as discussed above. Thus, when starting a new Web application, you usually want to create a new Web site and then begin developing pages to be used on that site. To create a new ASP.NET Web site, simply select the File, New Web Site menu option, or use the second option under the first shortcut button at the left. The New Web Site dialog box will be displayed, as shown in Exhibit 12-5.

Exhibit 12-5

The New Web Site
Dialog Box

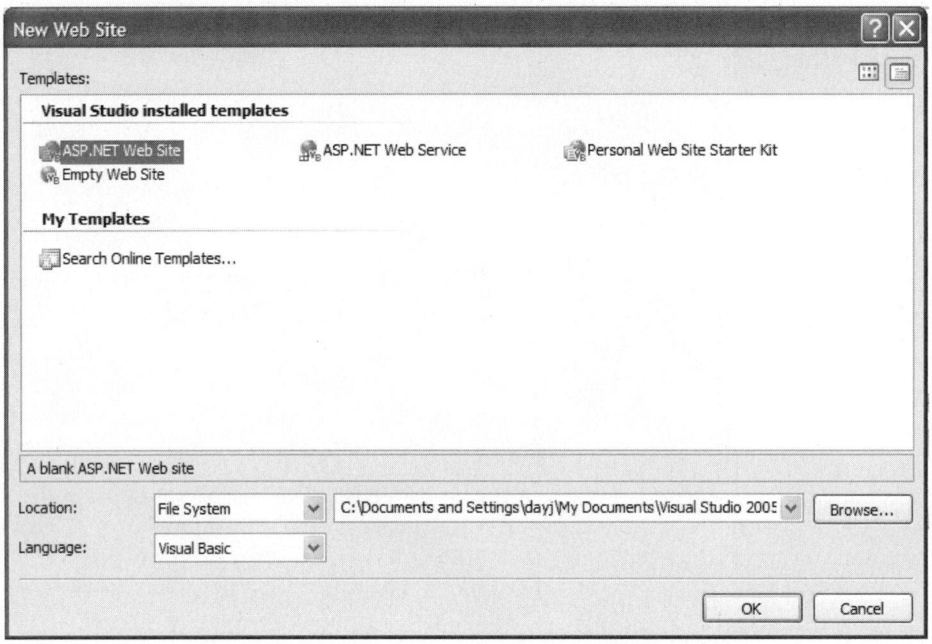

In this dialog box, you have several templates for developing different types of Web sites. For our simple ASP.NET application, we will use the ASP.NET Web Site Template. In the Location box, you will need to specify the location and name of the directory to be created for storing this Web site. If you were developing an application on a Web server, you might have a network drive pointing to the root directory of the Web server where you want to create the application.

When developing applications on your local machine, as is the case in our example, you would specify a location on your local hard drive. By default, Web Developer creates a directory called WebSites on your C drive, and usually this is the location where you want to store all the Web sites that you create locally. The default name for the directory is WebSite#, where the # is a sequential number. To make it easier to distinguish among various Web sites, it is recommended that you change this default to some meaningful name that reflects the purpose of the Web site. In this case, the directory has been named SimpleWebApplication.

When you have selected the correct template and specified the name for the directory, click OK, and Web Developer will create the directory and add the basic files needed for an ASP.NET application. Exhibit 12-6 shows Web Developer as it will appear when you create the application.

Exhibit 12-6

The Initial Display
After Creating the
Application

```
SimpleWebApplication - Visual Web Developer 2005 Express Edition Beta

File  Edit  View  Website  Build  Debug  Tools  Window  Community  Help

Default.aspx                                                              ▼ ×

Client Objects & Events                          ▼  (No Events)              ▼
  1    <%@ Page Language="VB" AutoEventWireup="false" CodeFile="Default.aspx.vb
  2
  3    <!DOCTYPE html PUBLIC "-//W3C//DTD XHTML 1.1//EN" "http://www.w3.org/TR/
  4
  5  ⊟ <html xmlns="http://www.w3.org/1999/xhtml" >
  6  ⊟ <head runat="server">
  7        <title>Untitled Page</title>
  8    </head>
  9  ⊟ <body>
 10 ⊟      <form id="form1" runat="server">
 11 ⊟      <div>
 12
 13 ⊦      </div>
 14 ⊦      </form>
 15 ⊦ </body>
 16 ⊦ </html>
 17

Design   Source         <Page>

Ready                                        Ln 1      Col 3      Ch 3      INS
```

Solution Explorer

C:\...\SimpleWebApplication\
  App_Data
  Default.aspx
    Default.aspx.vb

Solution Ex...   Database ...

Properties

<Page>

Misc
  AspCompat
  Async
  AutoEventWireup false
  Buffer
  ClassName

Misc

As the application is created, you can now see a number of new items displayed in the Web Developer interface. In the main window, the HTML source code for the application is displayed. This code already contains the header information, as well as a form block in which the main code for the application will be displayed.

The Solution Explorer at the right shows that the SimpleWebApplication directory is created and that it already includes a **Default.aspx** file for the user interface component of the application, as well as a corresponding **Default.aspx.vb** file for any Visual Basic programming code that you create for the application. The tab above the main window with the source code is labeled Default.aspx, indicating that you are viewing the contents of the user interface file.

Below the Solution Explorer is the Properties window. This window currently shows the properties of the page itself. As we develop the simple Web application, we will use this window to make changes to the properties of some of the objects.

Design Versus Source View

At the bottom of the main window, there are tabs to view the main page in Design or Source view. At the moment, the source of the page is being displayed. In **Source view,** if you were comfortable with designing Web pages by writing HTML statements, you could proceed by writing HTML statements to design the page. The **Design view,** however, provides an interface that greatly simplifies the design process, particularly with respect to adding server controls and formatting the Web page. Exhibit 12-7 shows the simple Web page after the Design tab at the bottom has been clicked to display the page in Design view.

Exhibit 12-7

The Simple Web
Application in
Design View

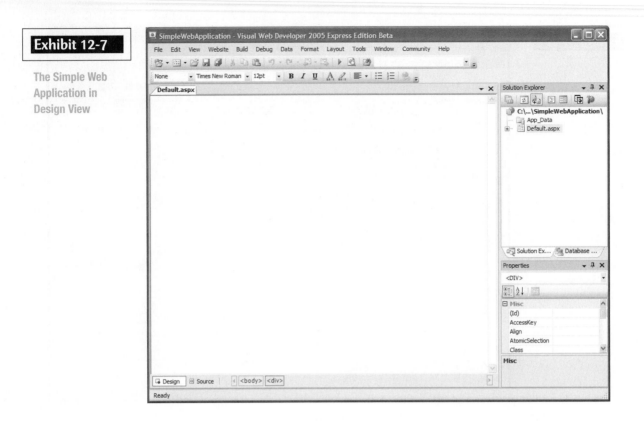

Using the Toolbox to Construct a Page

The simple Web application requires a button and a label to be added to the page. The Toolbox is extremely helpful when adding controls to a page. The Toolbox can be displayed by using the View, Toolbox menu option. This step will display the Toolbox along the left edge of the screen, as shown in Exhibit 12-8.

Exhibit 12-8

Displaying the
Toolbox

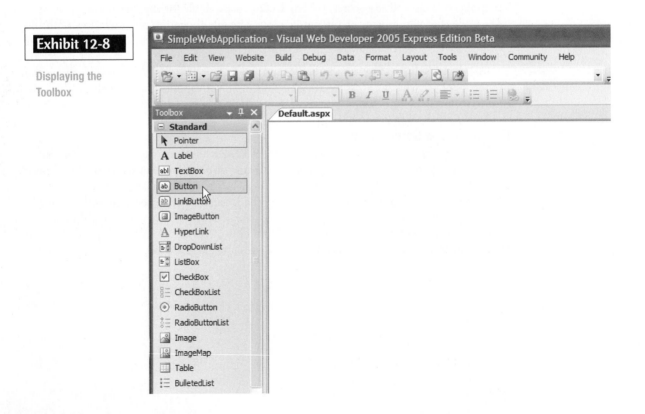

When the Toolbox is displayed, it decreases the amount of the page that is visible. This window, as well as the window for the Solution Explorer and Properties, can be set to be always visible or to autohide by clicking on the little pushpin symbol. In the exhibit above, the pin is pointing down indicating that the window is always visible. If you click the pin, it will turn to the side, and the window will collapse to the left when it is not in use, so that you can see more of the page while you are working on it.

For the simple Web page, click in the white space representing the page, and type the text "Click to see the current time." Then press Enter to add a line break to move to the next line. From the Toolbox, click the Button control and drag it over to the page. This step will add a button to the page. Press Enter again to move down a line, and then drag a Label control from the Toolbox to the page. Click the button and use the Layout, Position, Absolute menu option to allow you to position the button on the page. Then pull the button to the right so it is centered under the text you typed. Do the same thing with the label until the page looks something like Exhibit 12-9.

Exhibit 12-9

The Design for the Simple Web Application

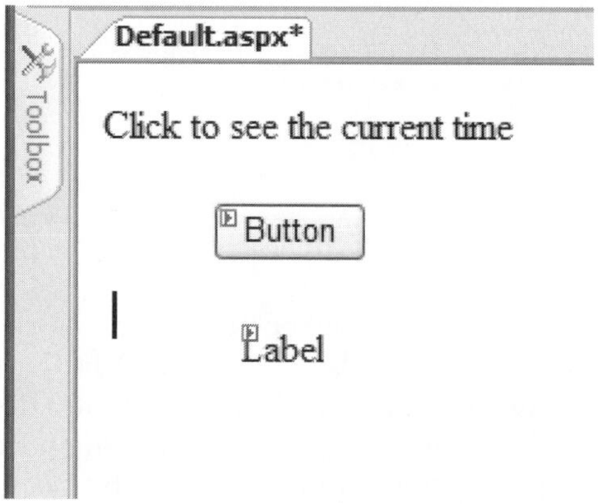

Changing Control Properties

In the simple Web application, the button text has been changed to the word *Time* so the user knows that clicking the button will display the time. This change is made through the properties of the button. Simply click the button in the Design view, and the Property window will display the properties for that server control, as shown in Exhibit 12-10.

Exhibit 12-10

The Properties for the Button

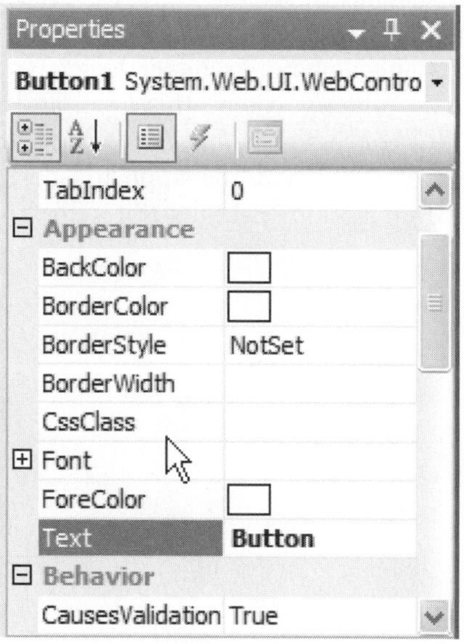

In the Properties window, change the Text property to Time. Similarly, the Text property for the label needs to be empty so that the label will initially not be displayed when the page is first shown. Initially, the Text property for a label server control contains the word *Label*. Click the label control in the Design window, and then delete the contents of the Text property in the Property window.

Entering Code for an Event

Once the layout of the page has been finished, the last task is to create the code for the button that will put the current date and time in the label when the button is clicked. To access the code for a server control, simply double-click that control and the Default.aspx.vb page will be displayed, as shown in Exhibit 12-11.

Exhibit 12-11

The Code for the Button Click Event

```
Default.aspx.vb*   Default.aspx*
(General)                                    (Declarations)
1
2   Partial Class _Default
3       Inherits System.Web.UI.Page
4
5       Protected Sub Button1_Click(ByVal sender As Object, ByVal e As System.EventArgs)
6
7       End Sub
8   End Class
9
```

Note that there are now two tabs at the top of the page, one to display the user interface in Default.aspx and the other to display the code in Default.aspx.vb. These allow you to flip quickly between the two files associated with this application. Note also that when you double-clicked the button, Web Developer made an assumption about the server control event that you wanted to program. In this case, Web Developer assumed that you wanted to write some code to handle the Button1_Click event, which occurs when the user clicks the button called Button1. This is the most common event that occurs with buttons. If you had double-clicked a different type of control like a textbox, a different type of event handler would have been created for the most common event associated with that type of control. You can always manually program other events for that control, but usually the assumption that Web Developer makes about the type of event that needs to be handled is correct.

In this case, we need to add a Visual Basic statement on the line between the Sub and End Sub statements that will put the current time in the text property of the label. To assist you with the creation of Visual Basic statements, Web Developer uses a feature called **Intellisense,** an editor feature that monitors what you type and tries to give you options that relate to the objects you are referencing in the statement. For example, the reference to the text property of the label would be Label1.Text. When you type this label and reach the period, Web Developer knows that you are next going to be typing a property or method for the label, and will produce a list of the properties and methods that apply to labels, so you can simply select it from the list and press the Tab key. Exhibit 12-12 illustrates this feature.

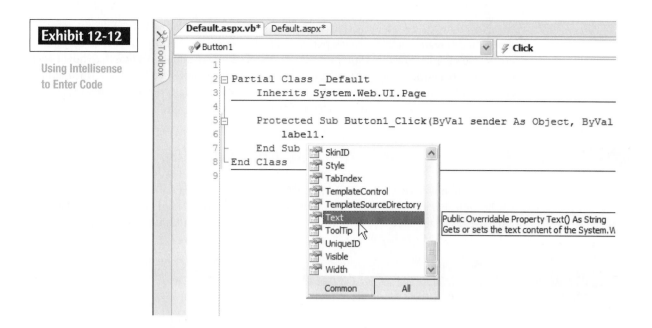

Exhibit 12-12

Using Intellisense
to Enter Code

To complete the code for the button that will put the current date and time into the label, the Visual Basic statement would be Label1.Text = DateTime.Now. Once the code is complete, use the File, Save All menu option to save the user interface (Default.aspx) and code (Default.aspx.vb) files.

Testing the Application

Once the files are saved, you can test the application by displaying the Default.aspx file (click the Default.aspx tab at the top) and using the File, View in Browser menu option. This step will bring the application up in Internet Explorer where the message and button will be displayed. Click the button, and the current date and time should appear in the label, as shown in Exhibit 12-13.

Exhibit 12-13

The Results of
the Simple Web
Application

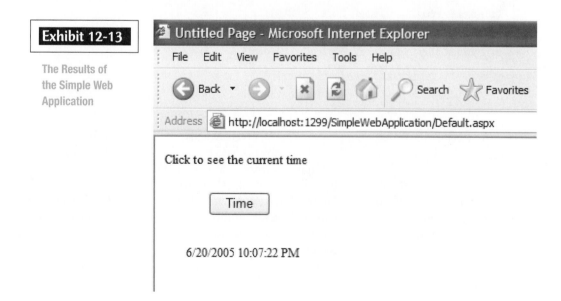

Now that you have a basic understanding of ASP.NET and how ASP.NET Web applications can be created in Web Developer, we will use that understanding to see how easy it is to create Web applications that interact with data stored in a database. To illustrate how easy it can be to create these applications, the remainder of this chapter will walk you through the creation of three applications that retrieve and display data from databases created in Microsoft SQL Server, Microsoft Access, and Oracle.

Example 1: Displaying the Contents of a Table

To illustrate how easy it is to link an ASP.NET Web Form to a database, we will look at an application that simply displays the contents of the MEMBER table from the Sky_Member database. For reference, the completed application is shown in Exhibit 12-14.

Exhibit 12-14

The Application to
Display the
MEMBER Table

Untitled Page - Microsoft Internet Explorer

File   Edit   View   Favorites   Tools   Help

Back   ✕ ⟳ 🏠   Search   ⭐ Favorites

Address   http://localhost:1324/DisplaySkyMembers/Default.aspx

Sky Member Database

List of Current Members

email	fname	lname	phone	jumps	equip	skill
bucky@ohio.edu	Teri	Bucky	555-5555	22	Y	A
dayj@ohio.edu	John	Day	592-0646	5	Y	B
johnson@bobcat.edu	Jeremy	Johnson	555-3333	15	Y	I
luce@ohio.edu	Thom	Luce	592-1111	12	N	I
mcgann@ohio.edu	Sean	McGann	592-2222	20	Y	A
mcgrath@bobcat.edu	Billie	McGrath	555-6666	3	N	B
wilson@bobcat.edu	Sally	Wilson	555-4444	6	N	B

To develop this application, create a new ASP.NET Web site called DisplaySkyMembers. Once the Web site directory and the Default.aspx file have been created, go to the Design view.

To assist with the association of databases with an ASP.NET Web Form, an entire group of server controls is available in the Toolbox under the Data group. For this example, we will display the contents of the Sky_Member database developed in Microsoft SQL Server. The server control used to access a database depends on the type of database to which you are linking. The **SqlDataSource** server control is the one used for either SQL Server or Oracle databases. A separate control (**AccessDataSource**) is used when you are linking to an Access database.

Creating the SqlDataSource Control

For this first example application, the SqlDataSource will be used to access the tblMember table in the SQL Server Sky_Member database. To begin, locate the SqlDataSource server control in the Toolbox, and drag it onto the design for the application as shown in Exhibit 12-15.

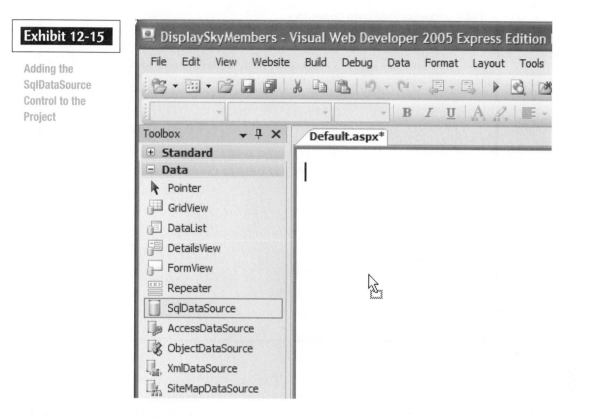

Exhibit 12-15

Adding the SqlDataSource Control to the Project

Complex controls such as this one include an additional feature called **Common Tasks** that gives you quick access to the tasks that typically need to be done to set up a server control. When the SqlDataSource control is dragged to the design page, a box is created. Close examination of this box will reveal that there is a small arrow at the top right. Clicking this arrow will display a menu of common tasks that can be used to configure the control, as shown in Exhibit 12-16.

Exhibit 12-16

Common Tasks for the SqlDataSource Control

The only task currently available for a newly created data source control is to specify the database to which the control should be associated. This task is handled through the Configure Data Source option listed under SqlDataSource Tasks. Selecting this option will bring up the Configure Data Source Wizard that will step you through the process of associating this control with a database. The first step in this wizard is shown in Exhibit 12-17.

Exhibit 12-17

Adding the SqlDataSource Control to the Project

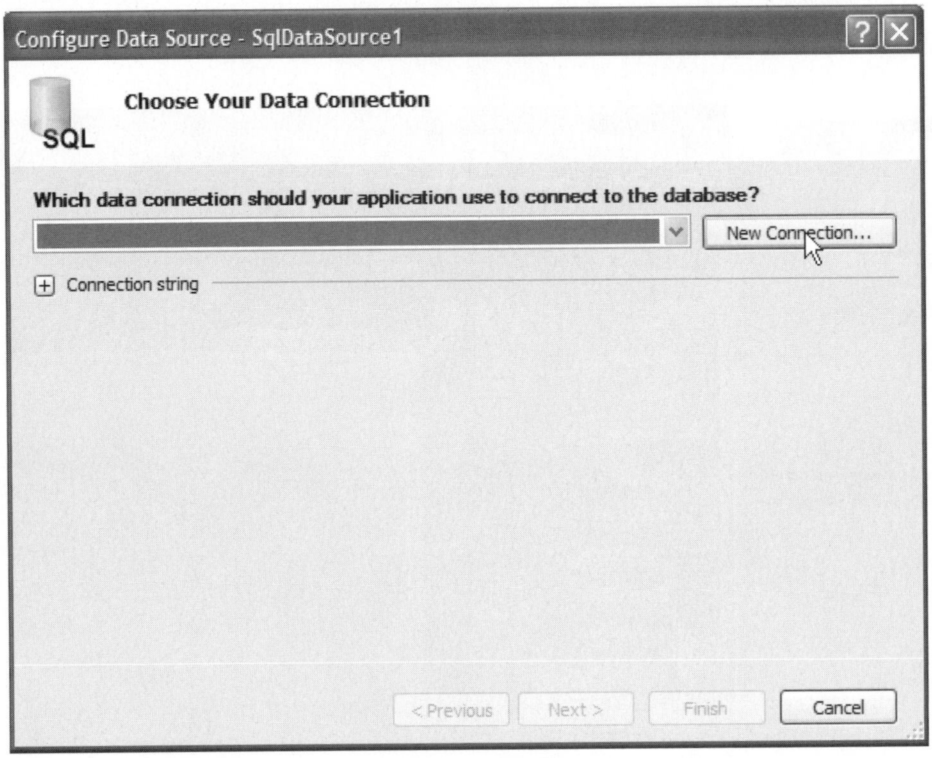

The first step in configuring the SqlDataSource is to determine if you want to use an existing data connection or create a new one. A **data connection** is a link between the ASP.NET application and the database that tells ASP.NET where the database is located.

Selecting the Data Provider

The SqlDataSource control is used to link your Web Form to a variety of databases that use SQL. Exhibit 12-18 shows the sources available.

Exhibit 12-18

Other Data Sources Available for the SqlDataSource Control

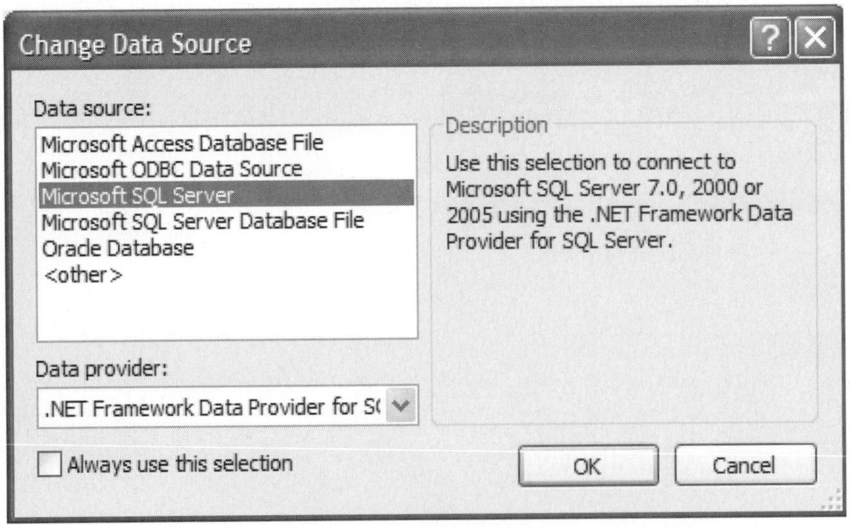

The source needed for this example is Microsoft SQL Server. Note that there is also a data source for Oracle. If this data source is not available in your version, you may need to download and install the free data source for Oracle from the Microsoft Web site. Select the Microsoft SQL Server data source and click OK.

Setting Up a Data Connection

For an SQL Server database, you will need to specify the server where the database is located. You will also need to give a user id and password to gain access to the database. It is possible to run SQL Server on your local machine and create an ASP.NET application that accesses that locally running database. A limited version of SQL Server can be installed as part of the Microsoft Development Environment (MSDE) to give you just the core of SQL Server without having to install the entire product. This is the environment used in this example.

After selecting the data source, a dialog box will appear asking you for the location of the database. This will display the dialog box shown in Exhibit 12-19.

Exhibit 12-19
The Add Connection Dialog Box

Add Connection

Enter information to connect to the selected data source or click "Change" to choose a different data source and/or provider.

Data source:

Microsoft SQL Server (SqlClient) [Change...]

Server name:

localhost [Refresh]

Log on to the server

○ Use Windows Authentication
● Use SQL Server Authentication

User name: sa

Password: ●●●●●●

☐ Save my password

Connect to a database

● Select or enter a database name:

sky_member

○ Attach a database file:

[Browse...]

Logical name:

[Advanced...]

[Test Connection] [OK] [Cancel]

In this dialog box, there are three items that need to be specified. The first is the name of the server where the database is stored. As indicated above, this example will access an SQL Server database running locally under MSDE. When accessing a database on the local computer, the server is called *localhost*. If your database is on a remote server, then you would specify the name of that server.

The second item is to indicate how you will get permission to access that database. In the MSDE version of SQL Server, you specify a password for the system administrator when you set it up. The user id for this account is always sa. If you are connecting to a remote database, you will need a valid user id and password that will allow you to connect to that database.

The final item is to specify the name of the database that is stored on that server. In this case, the Sky_Member database contains the tblMember table that we ultimately want to display on our Web page.

Choosing a Connection for the Data Source

Once you have specified the three items needed for the connection, you can use the Test Connection button to make sure that Web Developer can connect to the database using the information specified. Once the connection is tested, you can click the Next button to move on to the next step, which is shown in Exhibit 12-20.

Exhibit 12-20

Finishing the
Selection of a
Connection

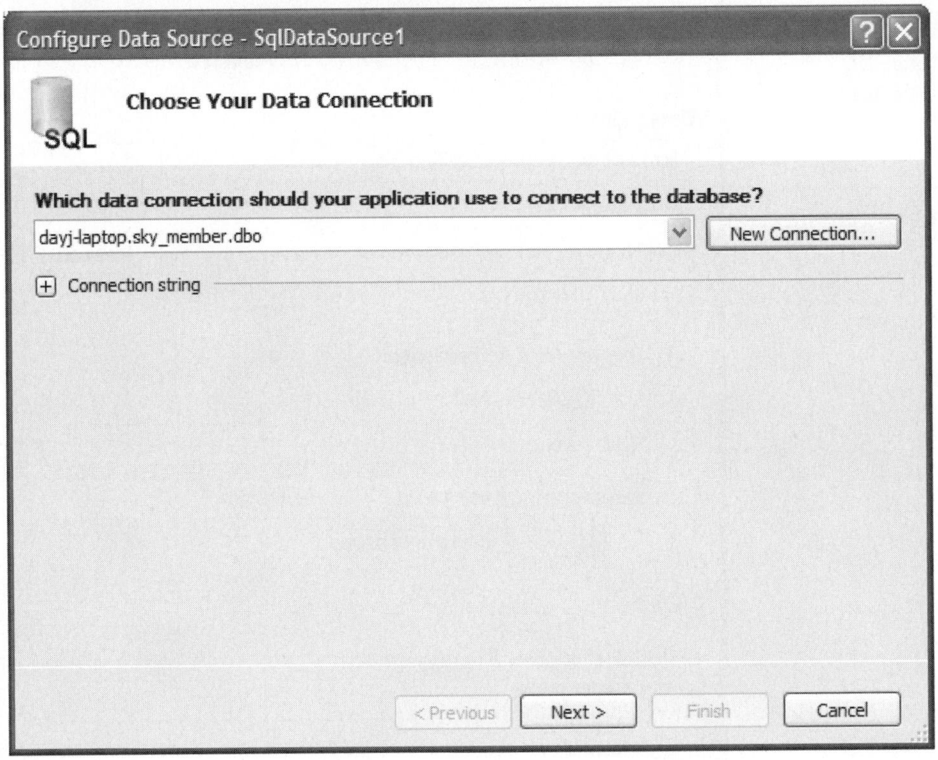

Once you have created the new connection, it will appear in the Choose a Data Connection box. Because this is the only connection we have, it will be the only one available at this point, so simply click the Next button to move on to the next step in the process where you can specify a name for the connection, as shown in Exhibit 12-21.

This step saves the details of the connection in a file in Solution Explorer called Web.config. Saving the details of the connection string in this location makes it easier to make changes to data sources in your application later. As we have done in this example, this connection links the application to a copy of the Sky_Member database running on the local computer. Once the application is finished, you might want to deploy it on your actual Web server where the database is located instead of on your local computer. By naming the connection and storing it in the Web.config file, you can go to this file later and change the details of the connection; the application will then be running against the real database. If you do not save the connection in the Web.config file, the connection details will become embedded in the properties of the Active Server Page. If you have an application that uses several data sources, this situation would complicate the process of deploying the application to the server, because you would have to go into each control and make the change.

By saving the connection in the Web.config file, each server control for a data source just references the name of the connection in the Web.config file. If you change the details of the connection in the Web.config file, every data source that uses that connection is now automatically using the new connection details.

Using a Web.config file is not possible in some environments. This file requires that the application scope be set on the server where the application will run. If this is not possible, then the Web.config file cannot be used and you will not want to save your connection strings in this file.

Configuring the Data Source

In this case, the connection was called SkyMemberConnection. Once the connection is named, click the Next button to go to the next step in the process of configuring the data source, as shown in Exhibit 12-22.

Exhibit 12-22

Finishing the
Selection of a
Connection

Configure Data Source - SqlDataSource1

SQL **Configure the Select Statement**

How would you like to retrieve data from your database?

○ Specify a custom SQL statement or stored procedure
◉ Specify columns from a table or view

Name:

tblmember

Columns:

☑ *	☐ jumps
☐ email	☐ equip
☐ fname	☐ skill
☐ lname	
☐ phone	

☐ Return only unique rows

WHERE...

ORDER BY...

Advanced...

SELECT statement:

SELECT * FROM [tblmember]

< Previous   Next >   Finish   Cancel

Once the connection is saved, the wizard gives you an opportunity to construct a query to determine exactly what data from the connection will be brought into the application. On this screen, you have two options. First, you can use the interface shown to build an SQL statement that will retrieve the data you need. Alternatively, you can write your own SQL statement. For this example, we will use the first option.

In this application, we want to display all the information from the tblMember table in the Sky_Member database. Using the information from the connection, the wizard determines which tables are available in that database and displays them in the drop-down list. In this case, there is only one table, called tblMember. When a table is selected, the Columns: box displays the columns in that table. The seven columns from the tblMember table are displayed, along with an option (*) to select all the columns. Because we want to display the entire contents of the tblMember table, this is the option that was selected.

There are additional options for constructing a where clause and an order by clause. As options are selected, a corresponding Select statement is built at the bottom of the screen. This Select statement will be sent to the database when data is requested through the connection. Once the Select statement is complete, click the Next button to move to the final step, as shown in Exhibit 12-23.

Exhibit 12-23

Testing the Query

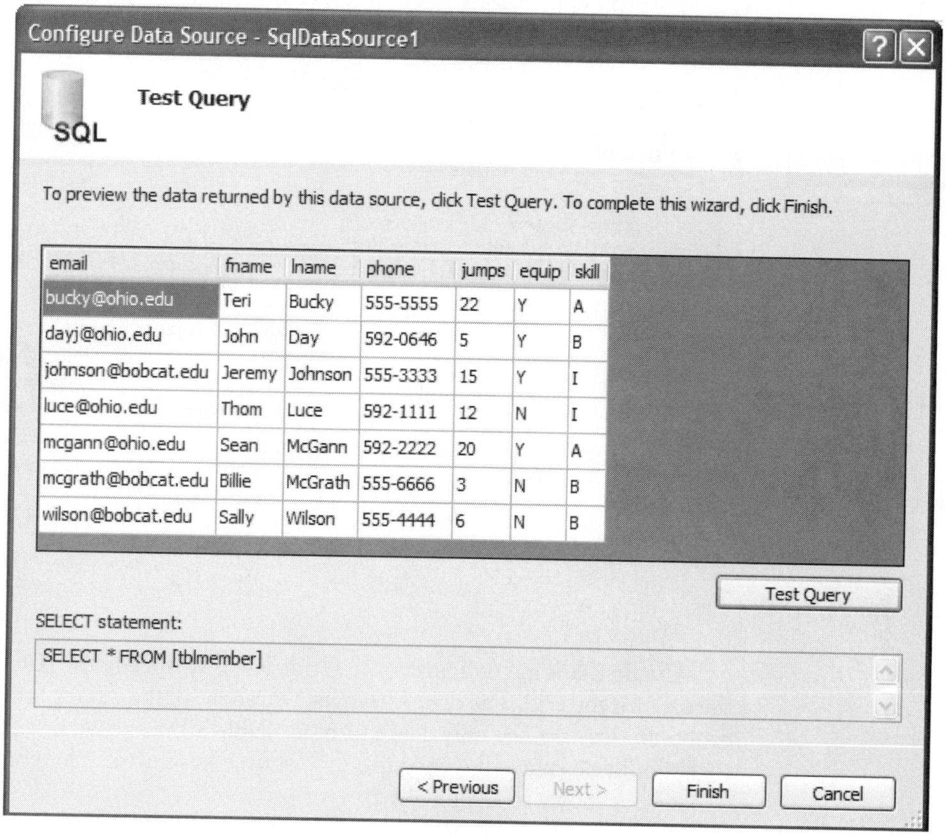

On this screen, you can test the Select statement that was created to see what data will be returned. To do this test, simply click the Test Query button. The resulting data is displayed in the large area on the page, as shown in the exhibit. Once the query for the data source has been successfully tested, click the Finish button to complete the wizard.

This process has resulted in the creation of two major components for the application: a data connection and a data source. As described earlier, a data connection is simply a link from the Web application to the database. A single connection can be used for multiple data sources, as we will see in the third example application in this chapter. The **data source** is basically a query that operates over a connection to retrieve data from the database.

Creating a GridView Control

The data is brought into the application through the data source, but you still need some space on the Web Form to display the data that comes in over the connection. To create this space, we will use another server data control called the GridView. A **GridView** is a server control that can be used to display data in the form of a table. To add the GridView to the form, drag a GridView control from the Toolbox, as shown in Exhibit 12-24.

Exhibit 12-24

The GridView Control

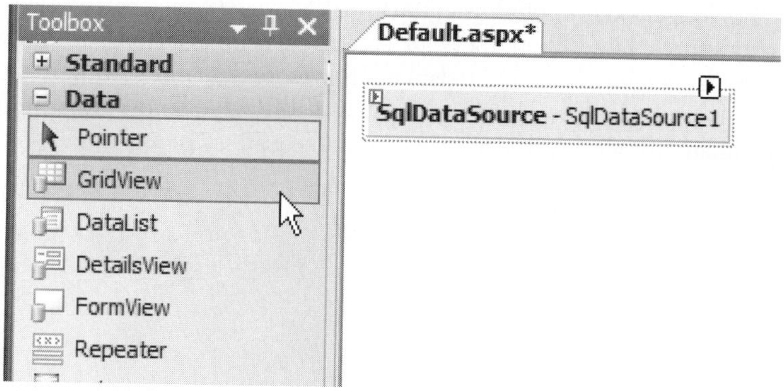

Once the GridView control is added to the Web Form design, you can use the Common Tasks option to set up the GridView, as shown in Exhibit 12-25.

Exhibit 12-25

Common GridView Tasks

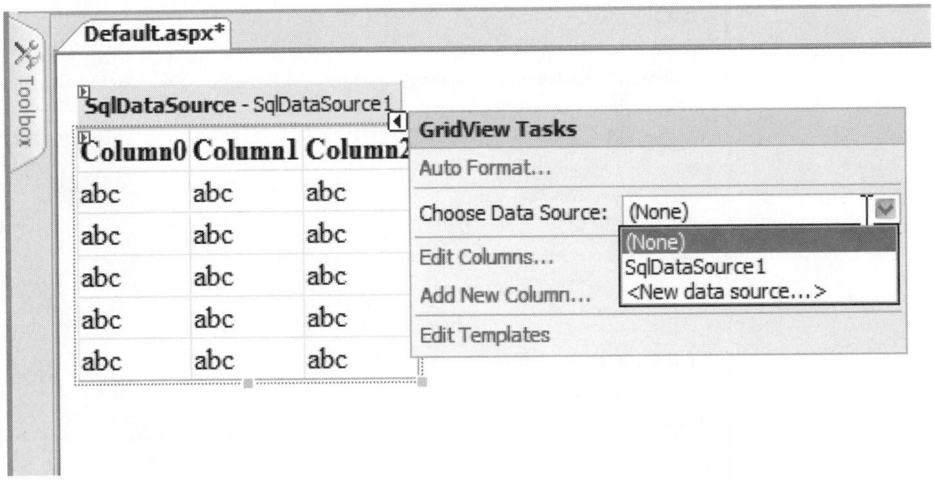

The first task in configuring the GridView is to specify the data source that will supply the data for the grid. The drop-down list will show all the data sources available in the application. In this case, the only data source available is the one we just created, so this is the one that should be selected. Once the data source is selected, the common tasks list will be updated, as shown in Exhibit 12-26.

Exhibit 12-26

The GridView After Selecting the Data Source

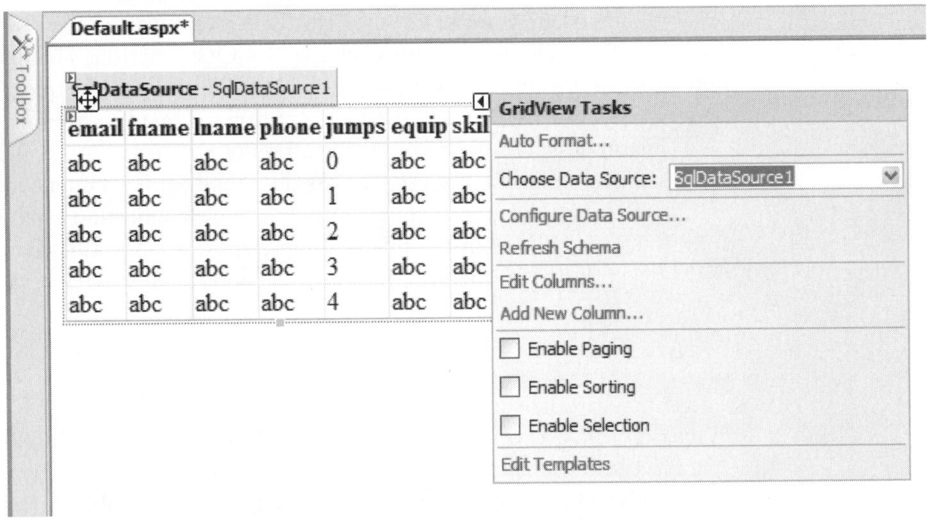

Notice that the columns in the GridView have now changed to reflect the columns in the data source. In addition, there are some new tasks available for the data source. Options for handling paging through the data if it fills more than one screen, for sorting, and for allowing the user to select rows in the grid are available. The Auto Format option provides a series of templates for altering the appearance of the grid, as shown in Exhibit 12-27.

Exhibit 12-27

Auto Format
Options for the
GridView

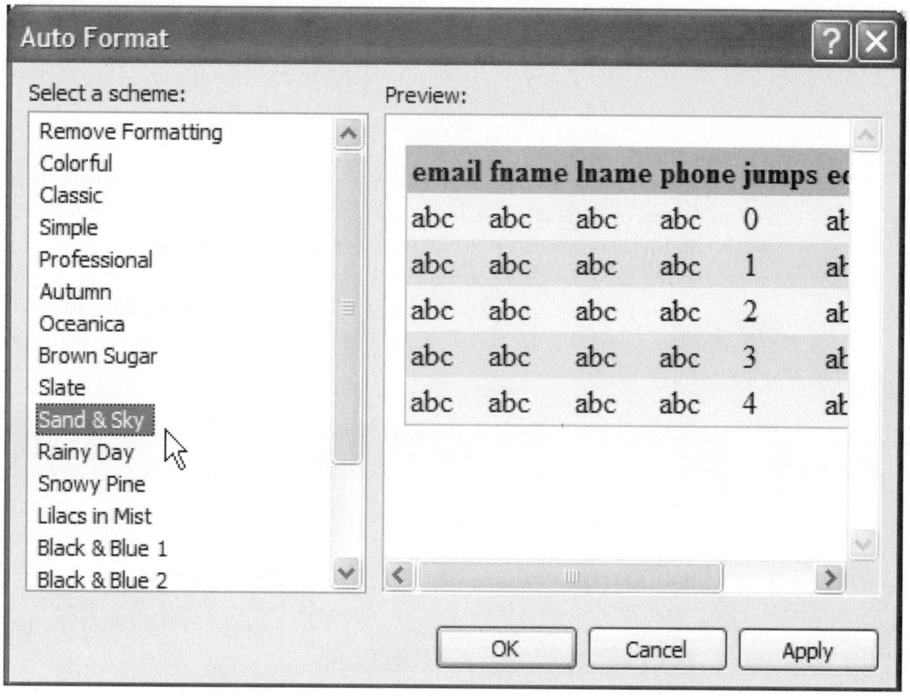

The example application introduced at the beginning of this section uses the Sand & Sky formatting scheme. As you select a scheme, a preview will appear at the right. Select the Sand & Sky scheme, and click the OK button.

Finishing the Application

Use Enter to create some vertical space between the data source control and the GridView control. In this area, enter the text for labeling the Web page. The final design for the page should look something like Exhibit 12-28.

Exhibit 12-28

The Final Design
for the
Application

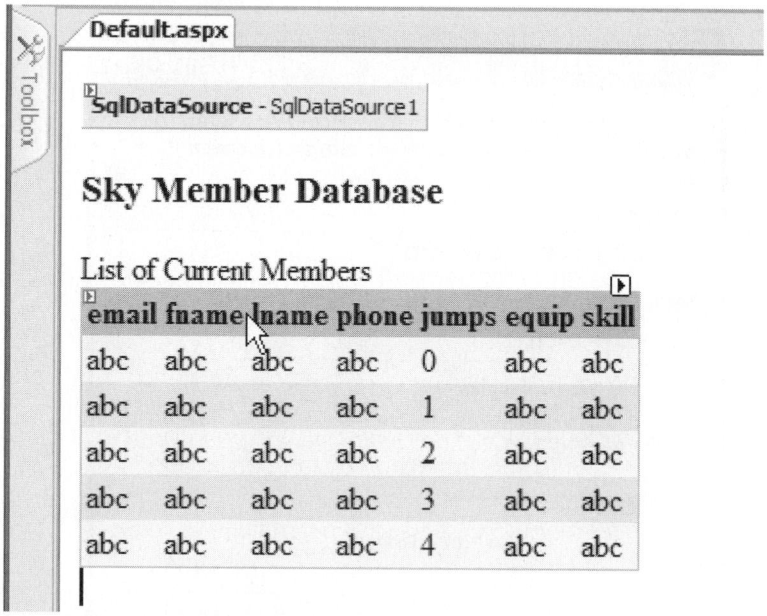

You may have noticed that this application does not require any code in the Default.aspx.vb file. All the functionality is embedded in the server controls themselves.

Once the design for the application is complete, use the File, Save All menu option to save the application and then use the File, View in Browser menu option to test the application.

Setting Up a Connection to an Oracle Database

As indicated earlier, the SqlDataSource server control can be used to access a number of different types of databases, including SQL Server and Oracle. If this example required a connection to an Oracle database, the process would be essentially the same. The only differences would be in the way the data source is configured.

The first difference would be in the selection of the data source to use when creating the data connection. In this case, the data source for Oracle would be selected, as shown in Exhibit 12-29.

Exhibit 12-29

Selecting the Oracle Data Source

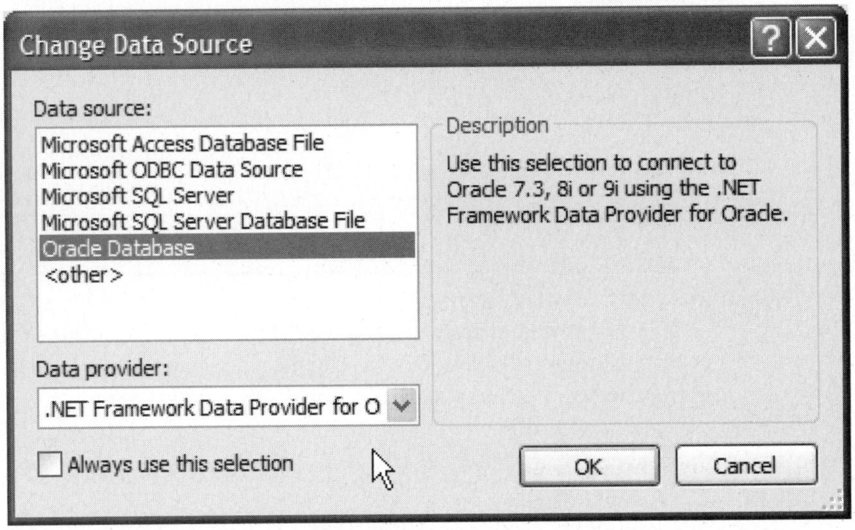

When the Oracle data source is selected, the connection properties will change to reflect the information needed to connect to an Oracle database, as shown in Exhibit 12-30.

Exhibit 12-30

Setting Connection Properties in the Oracle Data Source

For a connection to an Oracle database, you specify the name of the Oracle server and the user id and password to gain access to the database. As before, there is a Test Connection button to make sure the connection is functioning properly. A completed connection to an Oracle database will be listed as shown in Exhibit 12-31.

Exhibit 12-31

Selecting an
Oracle Data
Connection

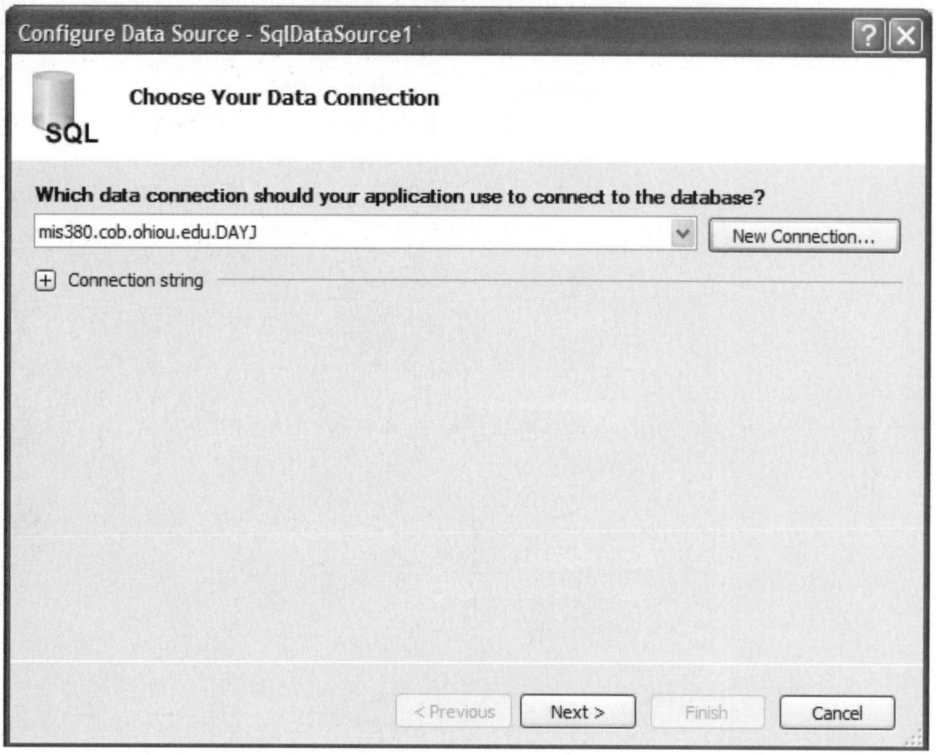

Once the connection for the data source is selected, the specifications for the connection can be saved in the Web.config file, as shown in Exhibit 12-32.

Exhibit 12-32

Saving the Oracle
Connection

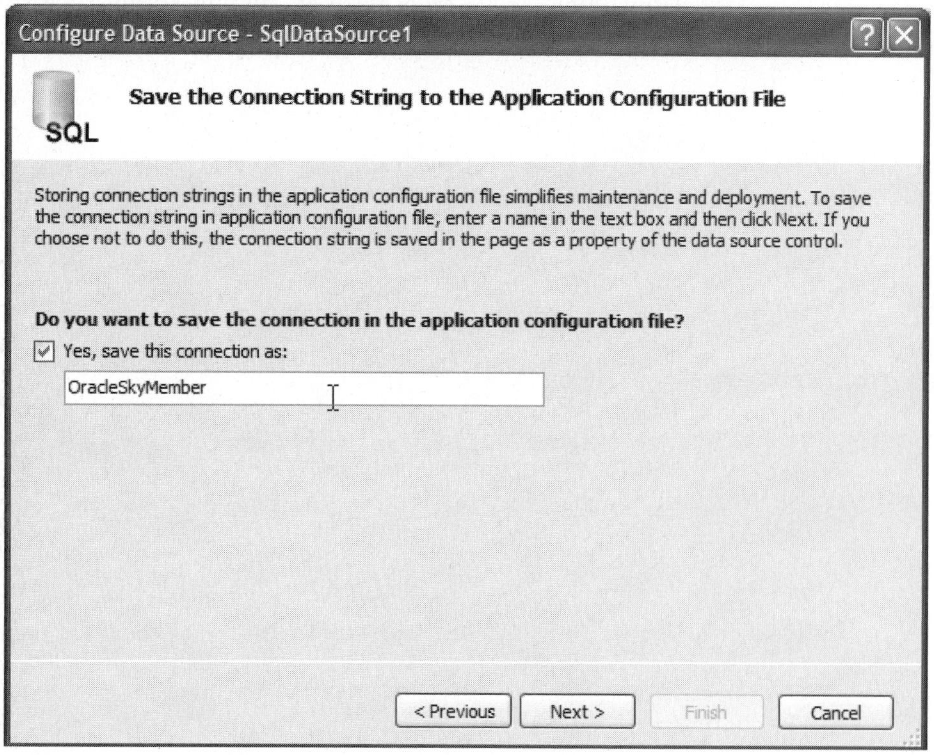

Once the connection is created, the next step is to set up the Select statement for the data source. As with an SQL Server connection, you would select the table from the drop-down list and select the columns to be displayed, as shown in Exhibit 12-33.

Exhibit 12-33

Configuring the
Select Statement

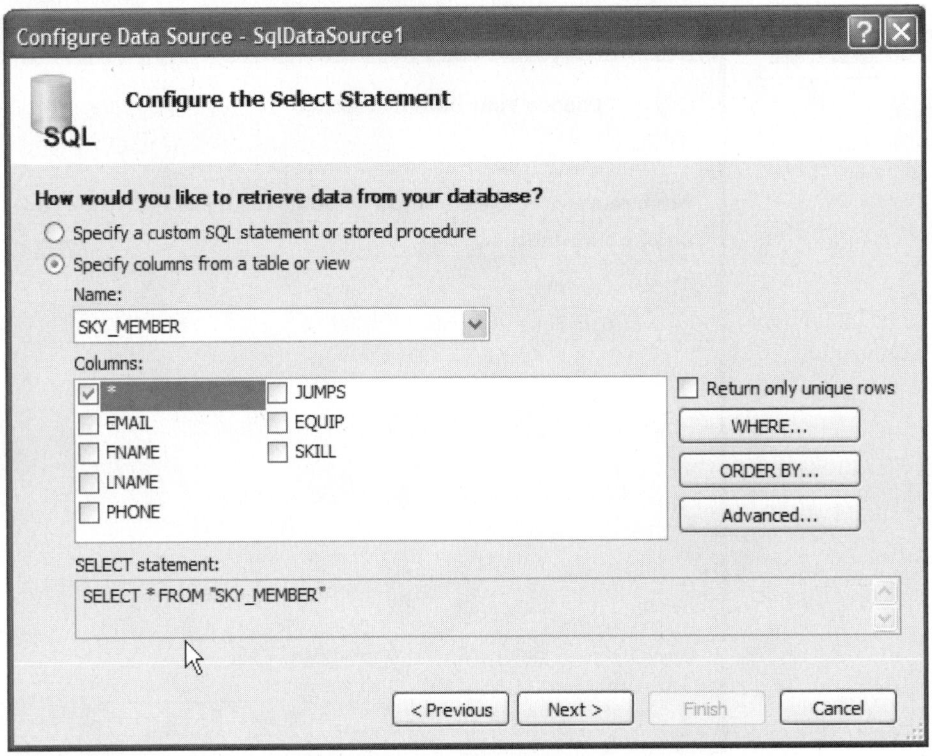

Configure Data Source - SqlDataSource1   [?][X]

SQL   **Configure the Select Statement**

How would you like to retrieve data from your database?

○ Specify a custom SQL statement or stored procedure

⊙ Specify columns from a table or view

Name:

SKY_MEMBER   ∨

Columns:

☑ *   ☐ JUMPS   ☐ Return only unique rows
☐ EMAIL   ☐ EQUIP   [WHERE...]
☐ FNAME   ☐ SKILL
☐ LNAME   [ORDER BY...]
☐ PHONE   [Advanced...]

SELECT statement:

SELECT * FROM "SKY_MEMBER"

                        [< Previous] [Next >] [Finish] [Cancel]

After specifying the SQL statement, you can test the query on the next screen and then complete the process of configuring the data source. The rest of the process of creating the application would be the same as before, with the creation of a GridView control and the specification of the data source associated with that grid.

Example 2: Displaying Single Records from a Table

To illustrate a slightly more complex application, this example will add some user interaction by including a textbox, where the user can specify an email address and have the member with the matching email address displayed. The application will look something like Exhibit 12-34.

Exhibit 12-34

Creating the
Select Statement

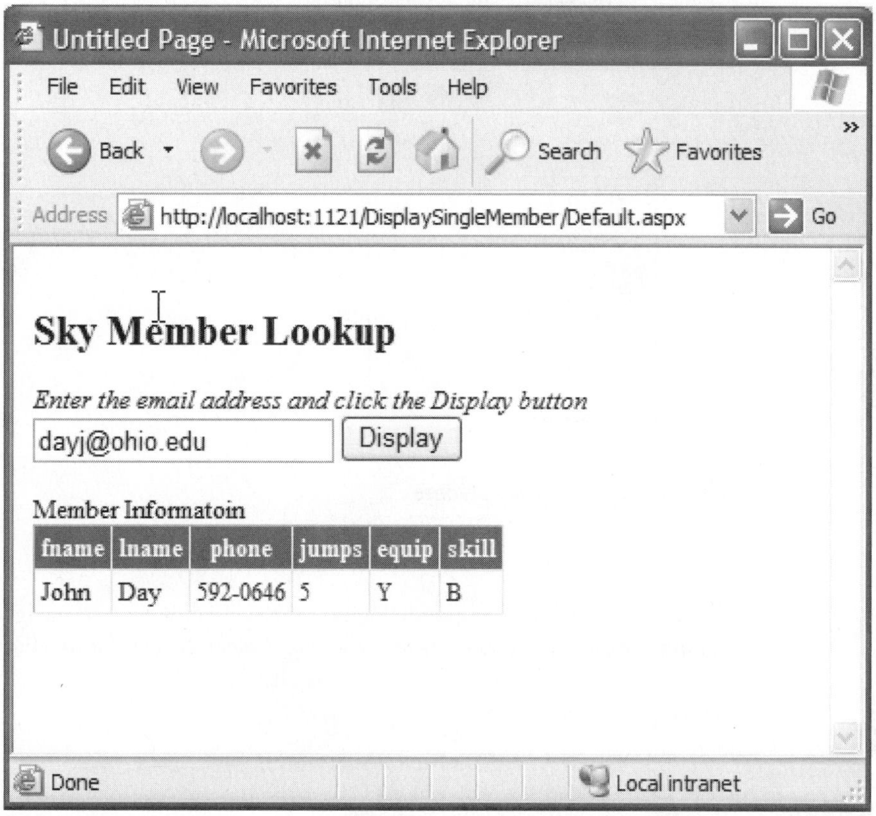

In this example, a user can type an email address into the textbox and click the button to display the information from the database for that member. This process will require that a Select statement with a where clause be used to retrieve the information from the database, and that the value used in that where clause will have to be obtained from the textbox on the form.

Creating the Web Site and Adding the Database

To create this application, open a new Web site called DisplaySingleMember. In addition to learning how to accomplish this application, we will also switch to using an Access database in this example to illustrate how a data source can be linked to an Access database. When you create this Web site, a new folder called DisplaySingleMember will be created in the WebSites folders. To use an Access database, the database file must be located in the Data folder under the Web site directory. Therefore, a copy of the SkyMember.mdb file must be copied to that folder. To add a database to the project, right-click the App_Data folder and select the Add Existing Item option from the menu, as shown in Exhibit 12-35.

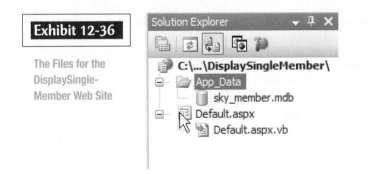

Exhibit 12-35

Adding a
Database to the
Data Folder

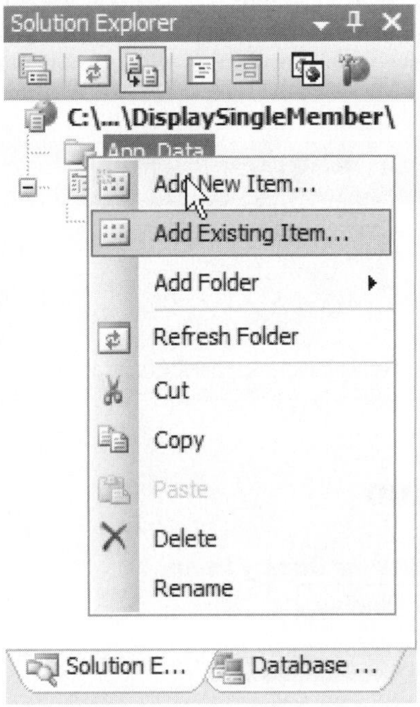

This step will bring up a dialog box that will allow you to navigate to the directory containing the database you want to use in the project. Select the database file and click the Add button, and you should see the database listed in the Data folder in Solution Explorer, as shown in Exhibit 12-36.

Exhibit 12-36

The Files for the
DisplaySingle-
Member Web Site

Adding the Textbox

Before proceeding to create the data source for this application, first go to the design view for the Default.aspx Web Form and drag a TextBox server control to the form, as shown in Exhibit 12-37.

Exhibit 12-37

The TextBox
Server Control

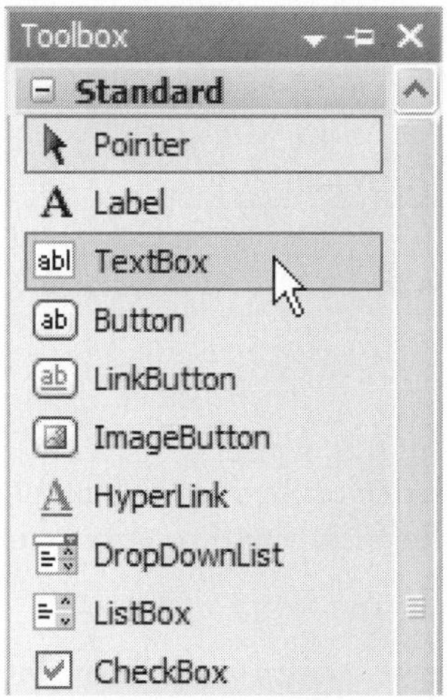

Adding and Configuring the Data Source

The Textbox should be added first because it will be used during the configuration of the data source. Data sources for an Access database are created using the AccessDataSource server control. Drag a copy of this AccessDataSource control onto the form, as illustrated in Exhibit 12-38.

Exhibit 12-38

The AccessData-
Source Server
Control

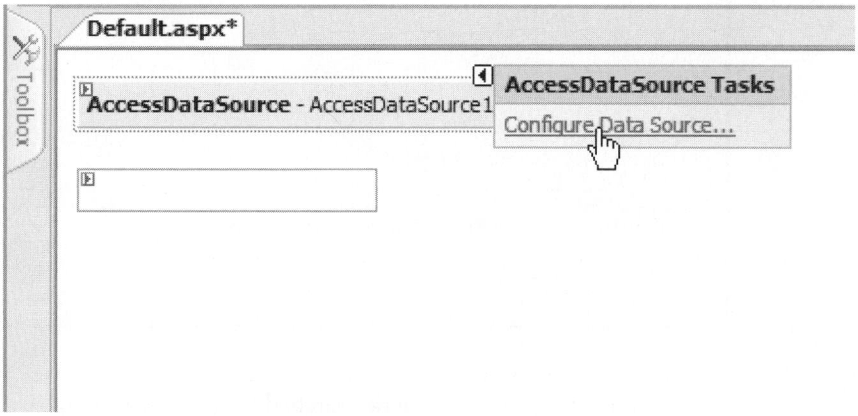

Once the AccessDataSource control is on the form, bring up the common tasks for this server control, and select the Configure Data Source option to start the wizard. Because this control is designed for creating a connection with Access, the steps for configuration are tailored to this type of database. The first step is to show the wizard where the Access database is located, as shown in Exhibit 12-39.

Exhibit 12-39

Selecting the
Access Data

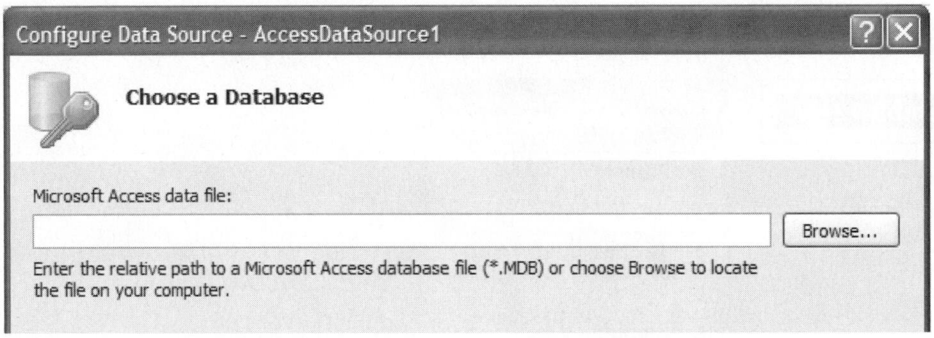

Configure Data Source - AccessDataSource1   [?][X]

Choose a Database

Microsoft Access data file:

[   ]   [Browse...]

Enter the relative path to a Microsoft Access database file (*.MDB) or choose Browse to locate
the file on your computer.

On this screen, you can type in the name of the file containing the Access database or click the Browse button to select the file from the directory structure, as illustrated in Exhibit 12-40.

Exhibit 12-40

The AccessData-
Source Server
Control

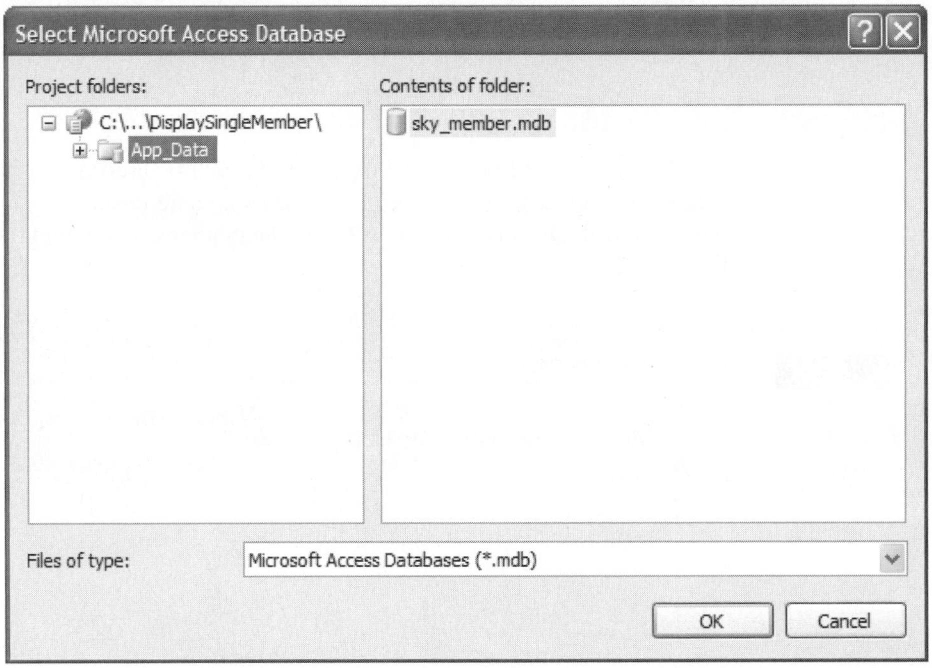

Select Microsoft Access Database   [?][X]

Project folders: Contents of folder:

□ 🖳 C:\...\DisplaySingleMember\   🗋 sky_member.mdb
   ⊞ 🗀 App_Data

Files of type: [Microsoft Access Databases (*.mdb)   ⌄]

                                        [OK]   [Cancel]

The only directory that can be searched for the Access database is the App_Data directory for the Web site. You are limited to this location so that the Web site will remain portable, in case you want to move it to another location after it is developed. By requiring the Access database file to be in this location, if the entire Web site is moved to a server, the entire directory structure, including the database, will be moved, and the application will still be capable of functioning correctly. This is the reason we copied the sky_member.mdb file into the Data directory in the beginning.

To complete this step in the configuration process, select the sky_member.mdb file and click OK to return to the screen for selecting the Data file, as shown in Exhibit 12-41.

Configure Data Source - AccessDataSource1

Choose a Database

Microsoft Access data file:

~/App_Data/sky_member.mdb   Browse...

Enter the relative path to a Microsoft Access database file (*.MDB) or choose Browse to locate
the file on your computer.

Note that the location of the database now appears in the Microsoft Access Data File box. Also note that the location begins with a tilde (~). This symbol means that the database is listed as being in the Data directory of whatever directory contains the Web site. This symbol prevents the complete location from being coded into the application; thus, you can copy the Web site to another location like a server, and it will still function.

You may have noticed that setting up the interaction with an Access database is different than doing so with SQL Server or Oracle. With Access, the database is a local file contained in the directory along with the Web site itself. With SQL Server and Oracle, you have to create a data connection that specifies how to connect to a remotely located database. With Access, there is no need for a data connection, because the database file is always located in the same place as the Web application itself.

Creating the Query for the Data Source

Once the location of the Access data file is filled in, click the Next button to move on to the next step in the process of configuring the data source, as shown in Exhibit 12-42.

Configure Data Source - AccessDataSource1

Configure the Select Statement

How would you like to retrieve data from your database?

○ Specify a custom SQL statement or stored procedure
◉ Specify columns from a table or view

Name:

sky_member

Columns:

☐ *	☑ jumps	☐ Return only unique rows
☐ email	☑ equip	WHERE...
☑ fname	☑ skill	ORDER BY...
☑ lname		Advanced...
☑ phone		

SELECT statement:

SELECT [fname], [lname], [phone], [jumps], [equip], [skill] FROM [sky_member]

< Previous   Next >   Finish   Cancel

As with the other data sources, the next step is to build the Select statement that will retrieve the data from the database. First, select the table from the drop-down list so the columns will be displayed. In this case, the Sky_Member database only contains one table.

In this application, you may have noticed that the email address was not included in the grid. The user supplies this information, so it was not repeated in the display. Thus, in the exhibit above, you will see that the email column is not included in the data.

Setting Up the Where Clause for the Query

This application requires an additional where clause on the Select statement to locate the member with the email address that matches the address in the textbox. To create a where clause for the data source query, simply click the WHERE button, and the Add WHERE Clause dialog box in Exhibit 12-43 will be displayed.

Exhibit 12-43

The Add WHERE Clause Dialog Box

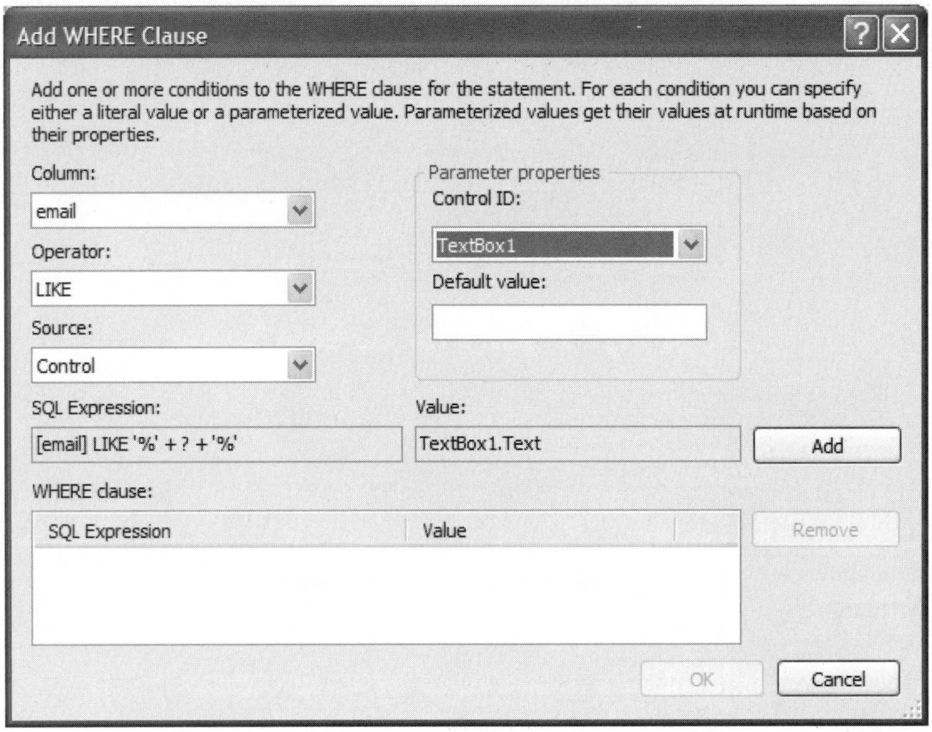

In this dialog box, you build the where clause by making a series of selections. First, select email as the column on which to base the condition for the where clause. Then select an operator for the condition. Because we are matching text, use the LIKE operator. Next, you need to specify the source that will contain the information to be compared with the email column. In this case, the information will come from another control on the form, so the Control option was selected. Once Control is selected as the source, the Parameter Properties box will be displayed. In this box, you can specify which control will contain the email address. The only control on the form at this point is the TextBox1 text box. This is the reason that we created the textbox before configuring the data source. If the textbox did not exist yet, it would not be available to use as part of the where clause.

Once all the selections have been made to build the where clause, you need to click the Add button to have the condition displayed in the SQL Expression box at the bottom. Once the expression appears there, click the OK button to return to the screen where the Select statement is being built. On that screen, click the Next button to finish the specification of the query and move on to the Test Query screen, as shown in Exhibit 12-44.

Configure Data Source - AccessDataSource1

Test Query

To preview the data returned by this data source, click Test Query. To complete this wizard, click Finish.

fname	lname	phone	jumps	equip	skill
John	Day	592-0646	5	Y	B

Test Query

SELECT statement:

SELECT [fname], [lname], [phone], [jumps], [equip], [skill] FROM [sky_member] WHERE ([email] LIKE '%' + ? + '%')

< Previous   Next >   Finish   Cancel

When you click the Test Query button, a dialog box will be displayed with the columns that include conditions and a box in which you can enter a test value. Once you enter the value, the query is tested, and the results are displayed as illustrated above.

Adding the GridView

Now that the data source has been added and configured, the next step is to create the GridView to display the member information that is retrieved from the database. Drag a GridView server control to the form and use the Common Tasks menu to specify AccessDataSource1 as the data source for the GridView, as shown in Exhibit 12-45.

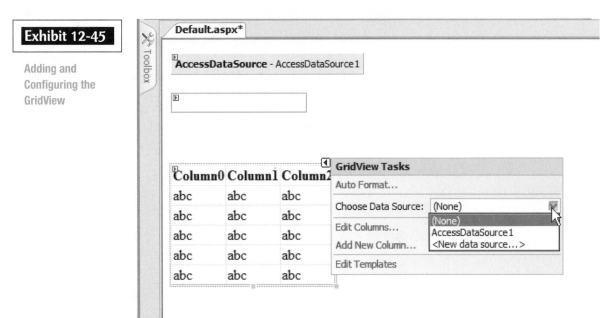

Default.aspx*

AccessDataSource - AccessDataSource1

Column0	Column1	Column2
abc	abc	abc
abc	abc	abc
abc	abc	abc
abc	abc	abc
abc	abc	abc

GridView Tasks

Auto Format...

Choose Data Source: (None)

Edit Columns...

Add New Column...

Edit Templates

(None)
AccessDataSource1
<New data source...>

Finishing the Application

To complete the application, a button must be added, as well as the explanatory text that will be displayed for the user. When you add the button control, change the Text property to the word *Display*. Use the Auto Format option on the common GridView tasks menu to apply the Snowy Pine format scheme to the GridView. Add some vertical space between the controls so you can enter the text, as shown in Exhibit 12-46.

Because the TextBox is integrated into the AccessDataSource and the AccessDataSource is linked to the GridView, there is no code required to get them to work together. All that needs to happen is for the user to fill in the textbox and then cause the page to make a round trip to the server and back. When the form goes back to the server, the server controls are evaluated, and the data in the textbox will be used in the Select statement for the data source. If a matching row can be found, the GridView is automatically filled in when the page is returned to the browser. If no matching row is found, the GridView is not displayed.

Once the design is completed, use the File, Save All menu option to save the design, and then use File, View in Browser to test the application. Because the where clause uses the

LIKE operator, you only need to enter part of the email address in the textbox to retrieve the matching user, as shown in Exhibit 12-47.

Exhibit 12-47

The Finished
Application

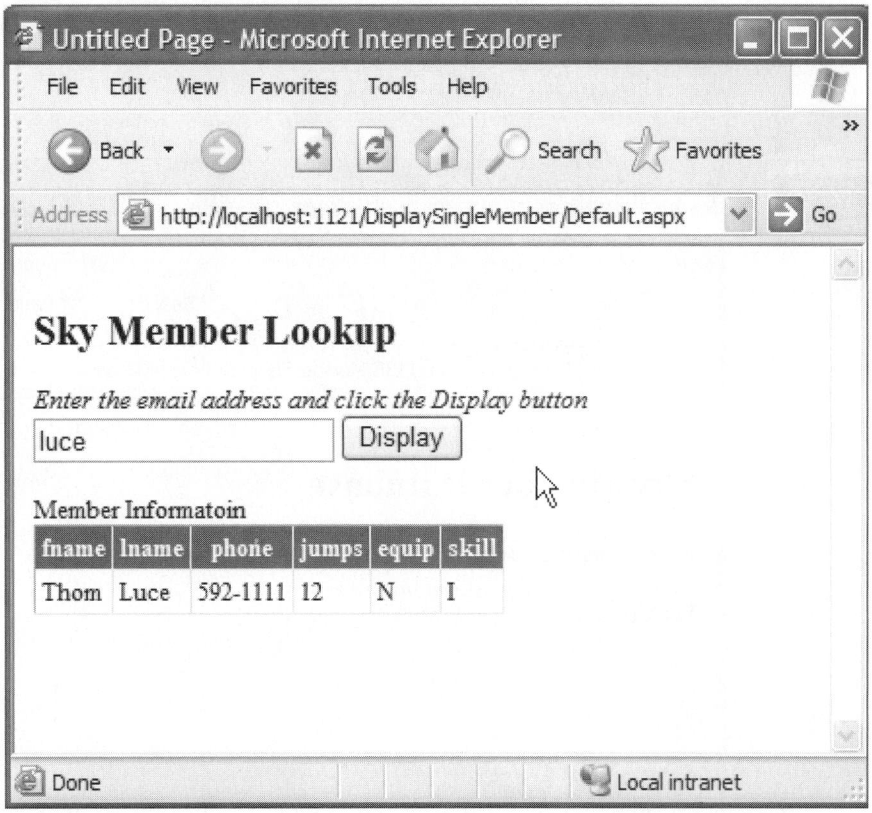

Example 3: Retrieving Data with Multiple Conditions

To illustrate some additional controls and a more complex use of multiple data sources through a single data connection, this example will allow a user to display members by indicating whether they have their own equipment and by selecting a skill level. Exhibit 12-48 shows the completed application.

Exhibit 12-48

The Results
Displayed

For this application, create a new Web site called MemberEquip-Skill and add an AccessDataSource server control. This data source will ultimately be related to the GridView at the bottom that displays the members fitting the user's criteria.

This Web Form will use a drop-down list and a radio button list to give the user choices for the possible values that can be selected for the equip and skill columns in the MEMBER table. These controls will be tied back to the table to determine the legitimate values that can be displayed to the user. These controls need to be created before creating the data sources that support them. Thus, the next step is to drag a RadioButtonList and a DropDownList control to the design of the form, as shown in Exhibit 12-49.

Default.aspx*

AccessDataSource - AccessDataSource1

○ [RadioButton1]

Unbound ▾

Once these two controls are created, right-click on the App_Data folder and choose the Add Existing Item option. Navigate to the sky_member.mdb file and add it to the directory. Next, click the AccessDataSource control, and use the Configure Data Source option in the AccessDataSource Tasks menu to choose the database file you just added to the App_Data folder.

Once the basic connection to the MEMBER table is created, you can go on and create the query for the data source. This query should select all the columns from the table. To incorporate the choices the user makes in the radio button list and drop-down list, we will use the where clause to set up conditions to match the selections the user makes to the data in the corresponding columns in the table. For example, the first part of the where clause should match the equip column with the RadioButtonList1 control, as shown in Exhibit 12-50.

Add WHERE Clause   ? ✕

Add one or more conditions to the WHERE clause for the statement. For each condition you can specify either a literal value or a parameterized value. Parameterized values get their values at runtime based on their properties.

Column: Parameter properties
equip   ▾   Control ID:
                                              RadioButtonList1   ▾
Operator: Default value:
=   ▾
                                              [   ]
Source:
Control   ▾

SQL Expression: Value:
[equip] = ?   RadioButtonList1.SelectedValue   Add

WHERE clause:

SQL Expression	Value

                                                               Remove

                                                         OK   Cancel

Once this condition is created, use the Add button to put the condition in the SQL Expression box at the bottom. Then build a second condition that equates the skill column with the contents of the DropDownList1 control, as shown in Exhibit 12-51.

Exhibit 12-51

Setting up the Condition for the Drop-Down List

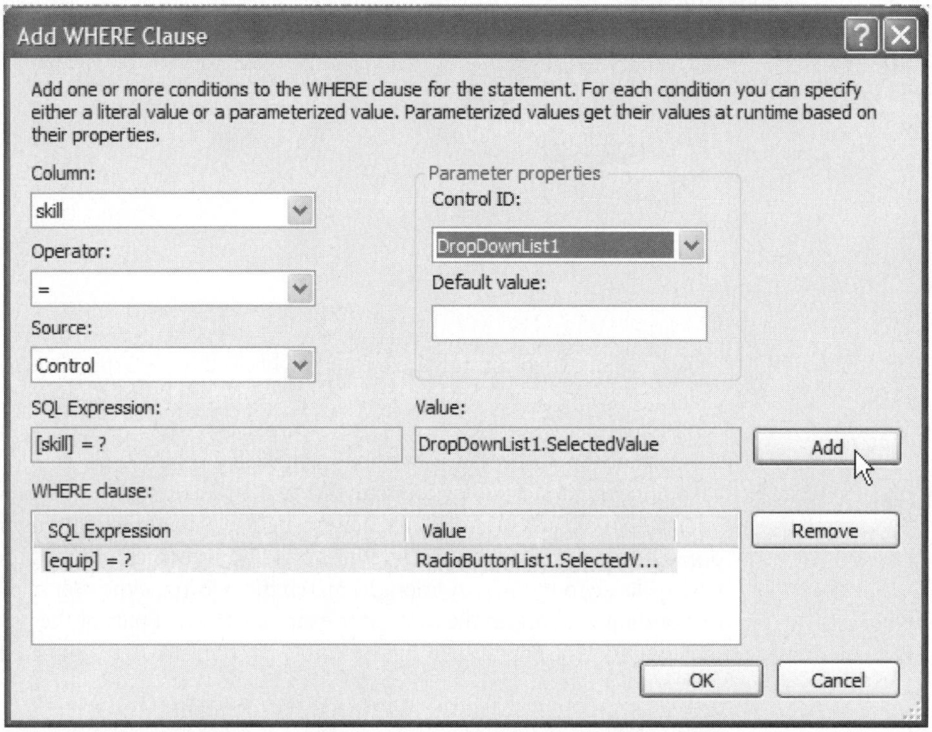

Add WHERE Clause

Add one or more conditions to the WHERE clause for the statement. For each condition you can specify either a literal value or a parameterized value. Parameterized values get their values at runtime based on their properties.

Column:
skill

Operator:
=

Source:
Control

SQL Expression:
[skill] = ?

WHERE clause:

SQL Expression	Value
[equip] = ?	RadioButtonList1.SelectedV...

Parameter properties
Control ID:
DropDownList1

Default value:

Value:
DropDownList1.SelectedValue

Add

Remove

OK   Cancel

Once the second condition is specified, click the Add button again so that both conditions are in the SQL Expression box, and then click OK to complete the query, as shown in Exhibit 12-52.

Exhibit 12-52

Finishing the Query for the Drop-Down List

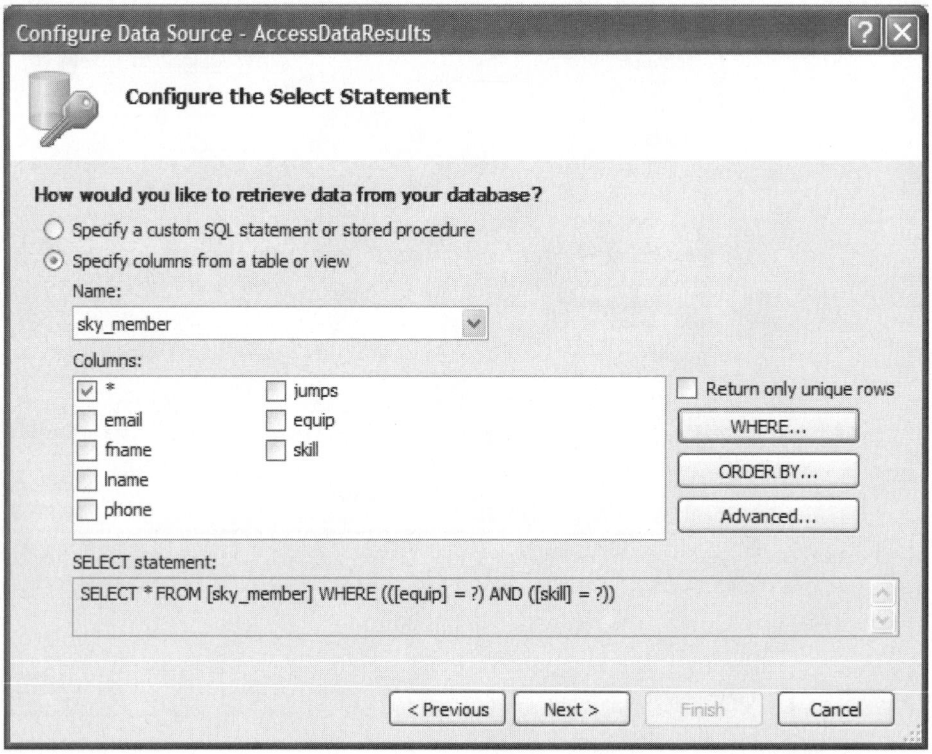

Configure Data Source - AccessDataResults

Configure the Select Statement

How would you like to retrieve data from your database?

○ Specify a custom SQL statement or stored procedure
◉ Specify columns from a table or view

Name:
sky_member

Columns:

☑ *   ☐ jumps
☐ email   ☐ equip
☐ fname   ☐ skill
☐ lname
☐ phone

☐ Return only unique rows

WHERE...

ORDER BY...

Advanced...

SELECT statement:

SELECT * FROM [sky_member] WHERE (([equip] = ?) AND ([skill] = ?))

< Previous   Next >   Finish   Cancel

Click the Next button to get to the Test Query screen. Click the Test Query button to test the query. This step will bring up a Parameter Values Editor, where you can put in some test values for the equip and skill columns. Enter the values shown in Exhibit 12-53.

Exhibit 12-53

Testing the Query

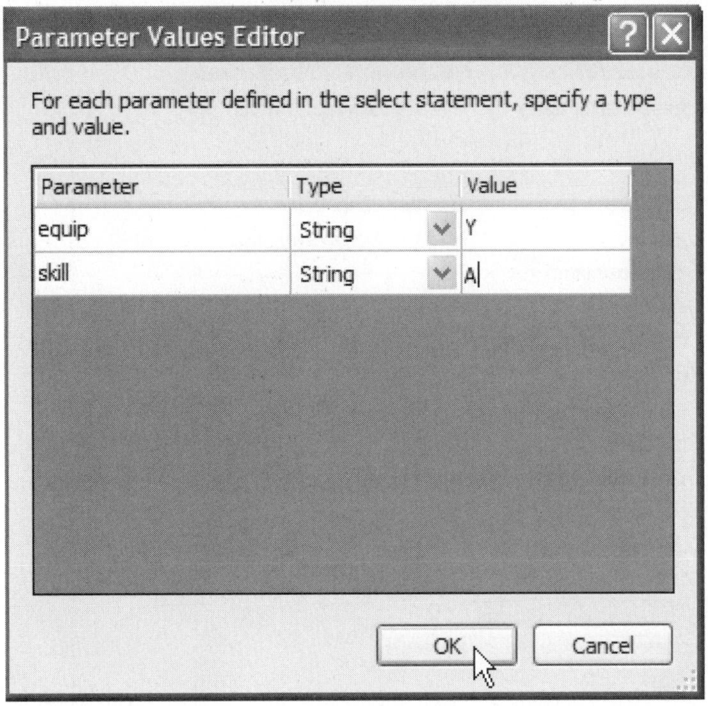

Parameter Values Editor

For each parameter defined in the select statement, specify a type and value.

Parameter	Type	Value
equip	String	Y
skill	String	A

OK   Cancel

Once the values are entered, click the OK button to test the query, as shown in Exhibit 12-54.

Exhibit 12-54

The Results of the Test

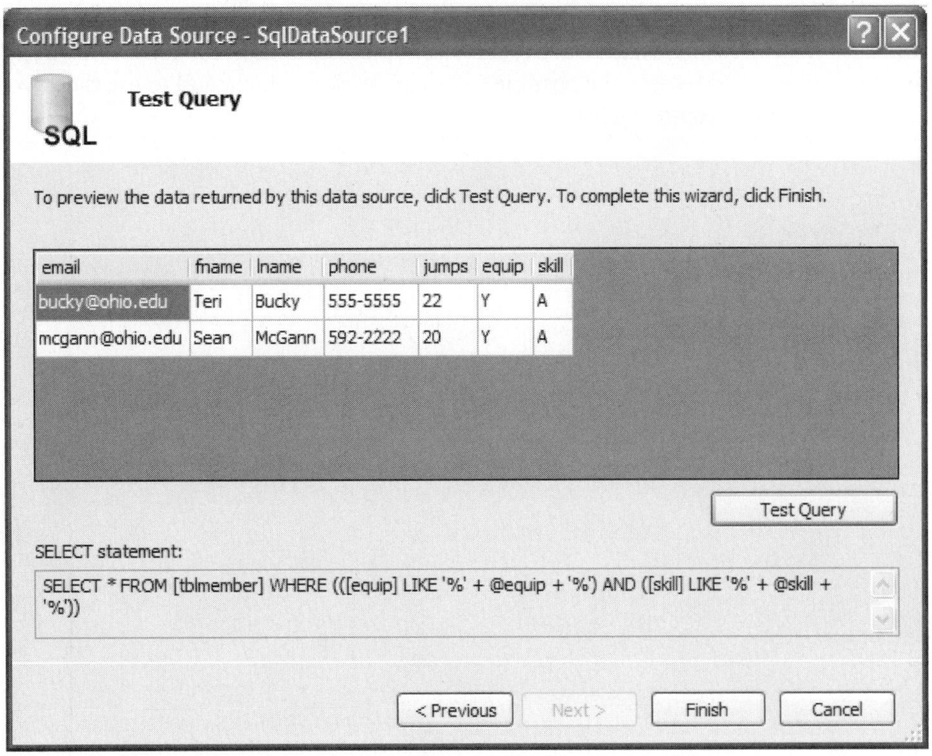

Configure Data Source - SqlDataSource1

Test Query
SQL

To preview the data returned by this data source, click Test Query. To complete this wizard, click Finish.

email	fname	lname	phone	jumps	equip	skill
bucky@ohio.edu	Teri	Bucky	555-5555	22	Y	A
mcgann@ohio.edu	Sean	McGann	592-2222	20	Y	A

Test Query

SELECT statement:

SELECT * FROM [tblmember] WHERE (([equip] LIKE '%' + @equip + '%') AND ([skill] LIKE '%' + @skill + '%'))

< Previous   Next >   Finish   Cancel

Because there will eventually be three data sources on this form, the name of each data source should be changed to more easily distinguish them. Click the AccessDataSource control and go to the Properties window. Change the id property to AccessDataResults to indicate that the data source will be for the results of the query, as shown in Exhibit 12-55.

Properties	▾ 🔲 ✕
AccessDataResults System.Web.UI.WebControls.. ▾	
ConflictDetection	OverwriteChanges
DataFile	**~/App_Data/sky_me**
DeleteCommandType	Text
DeleteQuery	(Query)
FilterExpression	
FilterParameters	(Collection)
InsertCommandType	Text
InsertQuery	(Query)
OldValuesParameterForm	original_{0}
SelectCommandType	Text
SelectQuery	(Query)
SortParameterName	
UpdateCommandType	Text
UpdateQuery	(Query)
⊟ Misc	
(ID)	**AccessDataResults**

Once this first data source has been configured, add two additional Access data sources to the form. One of these data sources will be used to retrieve the possible values in the equip column and to use them to set up the options in the radio button list. The other will be used to retrieve the possible values in the skill column and to use them to set up the options in the drop-down list.

Start by configuring one of the two new data sources using the Configure Data Source option in the AccessDataSource Tasks menu. When the wizard launches, use the Browse button to locate and select the database file in the App_Data directory, as shown in Exhibit 12-56.

Exhibit 12-56

Configuring the
Second Data
Source

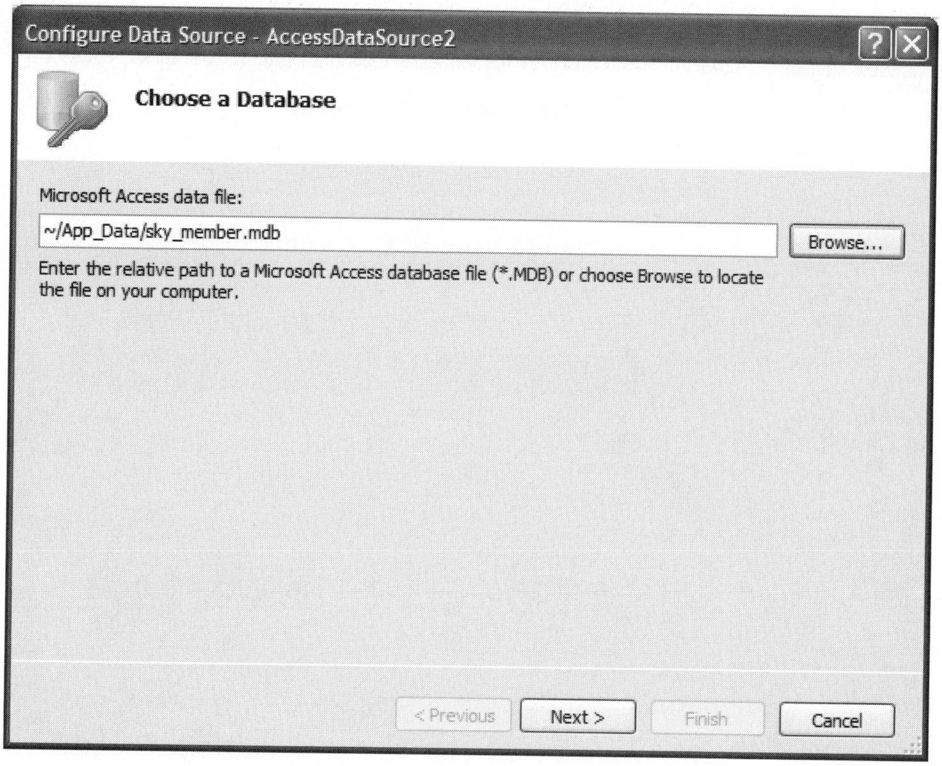

Configure Data Source - AccessDataSource2

Choose a Database

Microsoft Access data file:

~/App_Data/sky_member.mdb

Browse...

Enter the relative path to a Microsoft Access database file (*.MDB) or choose Browse to locate the file on your computer.

< Previous   Next >   Finish   Cancel

Once you select the database, click the Next button to go on and configure the query for the data store.

For the data source associated with the radio button list, we want to produce a list of all the possible values that appear in the equip column of the table. In the database, this column contains either a Y or an N. Therefore, we want to construct a query that will retrieve these two values so they can be used to populate the radio button list. This way, the user will see a radio button list with two options, Y or N.

If the query is set up to retrieve the data from the equip column, you will get back a series of Ys and Ns—one from each row of the table. Because we just need to know the possible values that appear in the equip column, we can use the Distinct option on the Select statement to eliminate all the duplicates retrieved from the table. To do this step, simply select the equip column from the table, and check the box for the Return only unique rows option as shown in Exhibit 12-57.

Exhibit 12-57

The Query for
Selecting the
Possible Values in
the Equip Column

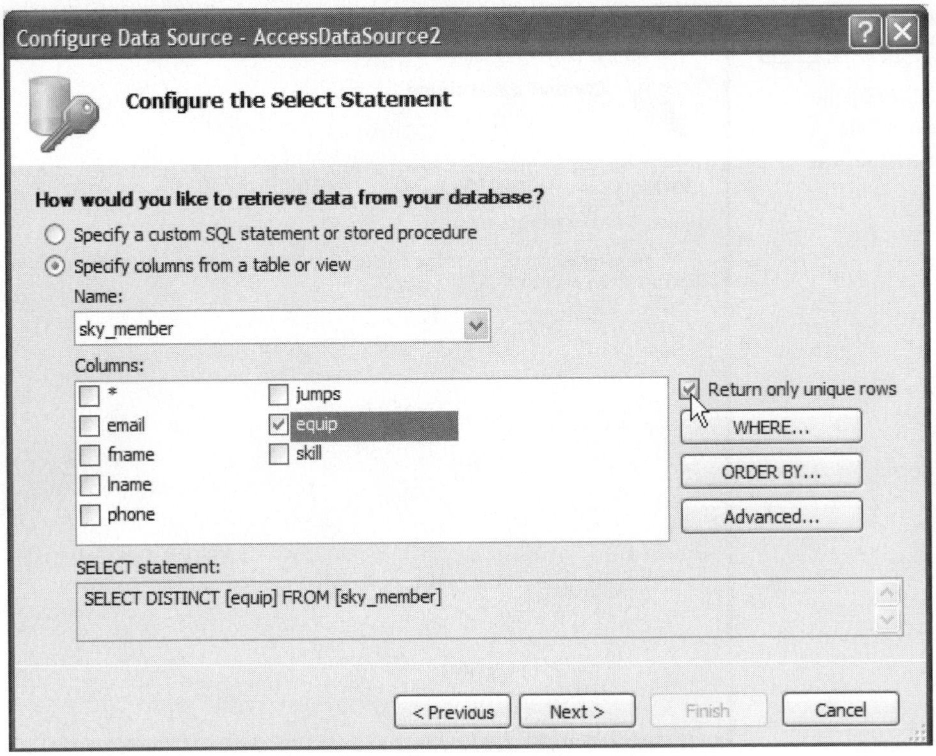

Once this query is completed, test it to make sure it retrieves just two values—Y and N. When the configuration of the data source is finished, change the id property to AccessDataEquipOptions.

The remaining data source should be similarly configured. First, select the database in the App_Data directory, and then build a query that selects the distinct values from the skill column in the MEMBER table, as shown in Exhibit 12-58.

Exhibit 12-58

The Query for
Selecting the
Possible Values in
the Skill Column

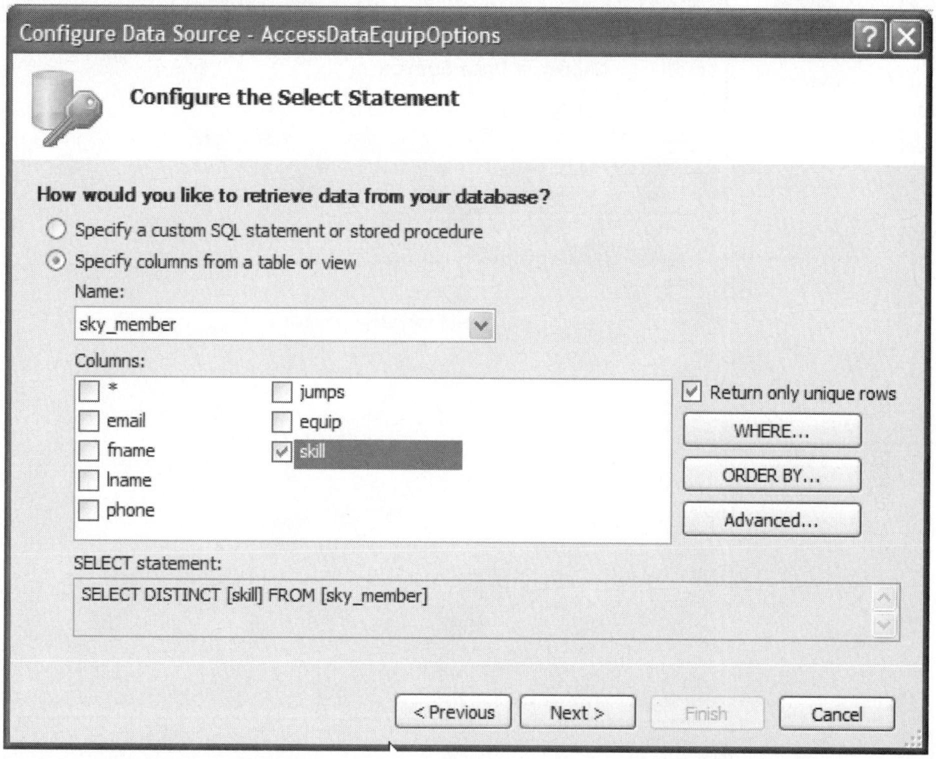

Once the data source is configured, change the id property to SqlDataSkillOptions.

Now that the two data sources for retrieving the values from the equip and skill columns are configured, the next step is to set up the drop-down list control so it will show the values from the skill column, and the radio button list so it will show the values from the equip column. First, click the RadioButtonList control you had previously added, and display the RadioButtonList Tasks menu, as shown in Exhibit 12-59.

Exhibit 12-59

The RadioButton-
List Tasks

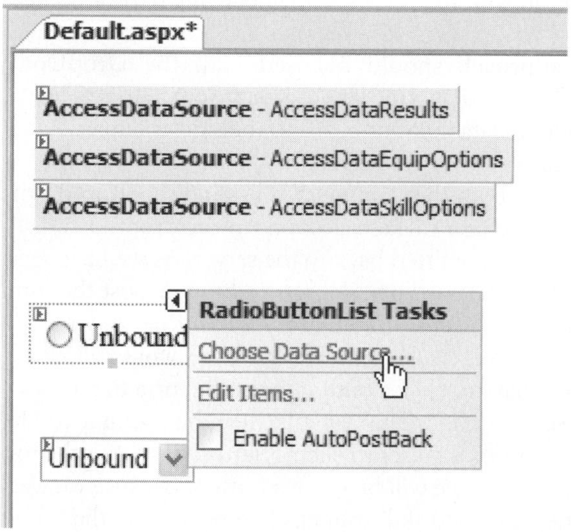

From this menu, select the Choose Data Source option to associate the drop-down list with the AccessDataEquipOptions data source that we created above, as shown in Exhibit 12-60.

Data Source Configuration Wizard

Choose a Data Source

Select a data source:

AccessDataEquipOptions

Select a data field to display in the RadioButtonList:

equip

Select a data field for the value of the RadioButtonList:

equip

Refresh Schema

OK   Cancel

To associate the AccessDataEquipOptions data source with the radio button list, simply select it from the list of data sources. Once the data source is selected, the columns from that data source will appear in the other two drop-down lists. In this case, there is only one column in the data source, so the equip column will appear in both boxes. The first box determines which columns will supply the values that will appear on the screen next to each radio button in the list. The bottom box is the column that determines the value that will be sent back with the form when the user selects that button in the list. In this case, the equip column contains either a Y or an N. When the user selects one of these options, we want the Y or N to be sent in with the form so it will become part of the query you built for the first data store.

The same approach should be used with the DropDownList control. Use the DropDownList Tasks to get to the Choose Data Source task. The data source for this control should be the AccessDataSkillOptions, and the skill column will be the column for both the display and values of the drop-down list.

On the tasks for both the radio button list and the drop-down list is the option Enable AutoPostBack. As the user makes selections in the drop-down list or clicks a radio button, the form does not get submitted back to the server. As we have seen in the previous application, a button is typically used on a form to submit or post the form back to the server. The AutoPostBack property sets a radio button list or drop-down list to post back to the server whenever the user makes a selection. This function would allow you to create a form where the user would not have to click a button to get the form to go back to the server and process the inputs the user has made. This capability can be useful if you have an application where you do not want to force the user to click a button to submit the form.

For this application, we will be using a button, because we want the user to make selections for both the equip and skill columns before sending the form back to the server to see if a member with that combination can be found.

Now that the main controls and data sources are configured, we are ready to add a button to submit the form, a GridView to display the results, and some text to help the user understand how to use the form. These items are shown in Exhibit 12-61.

Exhibit 12-61

The Completed
Design

Drag a button to the form and set the Text property to the word *Display*, as shown. The GridView data source should be the AccessDataResults data source, and the Rainy Day format scheme should be used. Use Enter to insert the vertical space between objects so the text can be added as shown.

Save the project, and then use the File, View in Browser menu option to test the application, as shown in Exhibit 12-62.

Exhibit 12-62

Testing the
Application

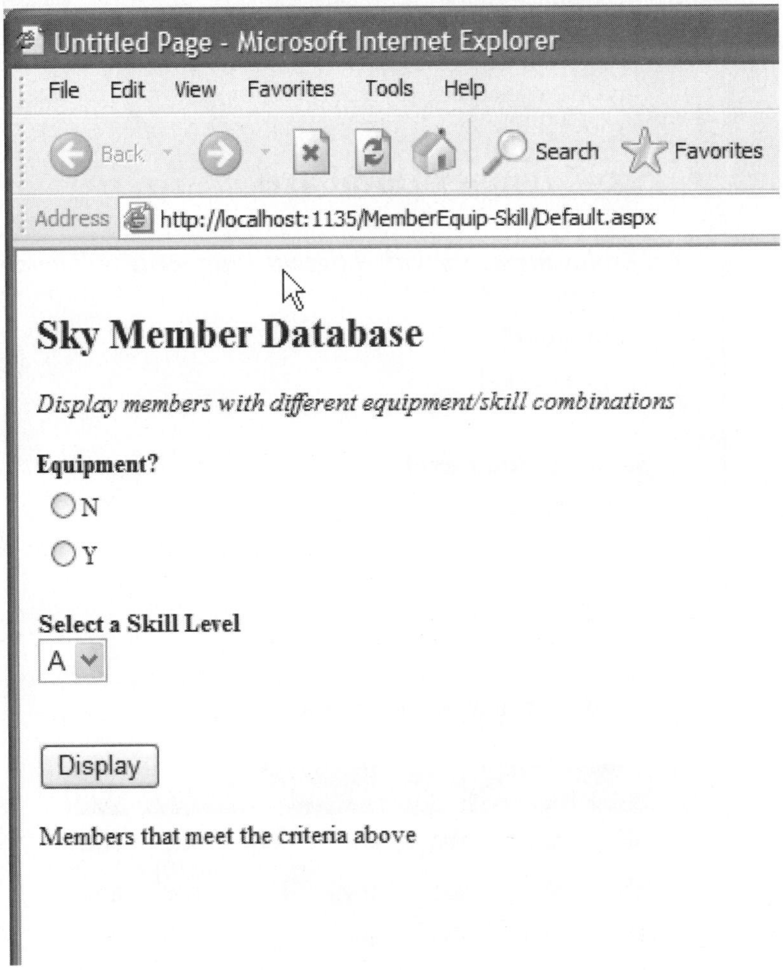

To retrieve members, the user must make a selection in the radio button list and the drop-down list, or the button will not submit the form back to the server. It is possible that the user will select an equip and skill combination that does not exist in any of the rows of the MEMBER table. In that case, the button will submit the form back to the server; however, there will be no results in the Select statement, so nothing will be displayed. If the user selects a combination that does exist in the table, the Select statement will fill the GridView when the form is posted back to the server by clicking the button. Once the data is filled in, the form with the data is returned to the browser displaying the data as the round trip is completed.

SUMMARY

- The Microsoft ASP.NET development environment can be used to build data-driven Web sites that allow users to display and manipulate database data.
- An Active Server Page (ASP) is a Web page that includes programming code to dynamically construct the content of the Web page on the fly, in response to user inputs and events related to the page.
- In ASP.NET, the basic component is a Web Form, which is essentially an HTML document that includes basic static HTML tags along with server controls.
- The page essentially makes a round trip; the browser sends the page back to the server, and the server processes it and sends it back to the browser.
- A Web Form is divided into two separate components: the visual component that determines the user interface, and the programming logic that is used to control the behavior of the page and the controls embedded in the page.
- In addition to the standard HTML tags, an Active Server Page includes unique tags that represent the ASP server controls included in the page.
- The Web pages sent to the browser are still simple, static Web pages, but they are dynamically generated at the server such that the page that is sent back changes based on the events that occur prior to the page being sent back to the server.
- Web Developer allows you to develop a wide range of Web applications, including Web applications for mobile devices.
- All ASP.NET applications are created within a container known as a Web site. A Web site is basically a directory in which all the files associated with the Web application are stored.
- The design view provides an interface that greatly simplifies the design process, particularly with respect to adding server controls and formatting the Web page.
- There are two tabs at the top of the page, one to display the user interface in Default.aspx and the other to display the code in Default.aspx.vb. These tabs allow you to flip quickly between the two files associated with the application.
- When you double-click a control, an event handler is created for the most common event associated with that type of control.
- Web Developer uses a feature called Intellisense, an editor feature that monitors what you type and tries to give you options that relate to the objects you are referencing in the statement.
- To assist with the association of databases with an ASP.NET Web Form, an entire group of server controls is available in the Toolbox under the Data group.
- The SqlDataSource server control is the one used for either SQL Server or Oracle databases. A separate control (AccessDataSource) is used when you are linking to an Access database.
- Complex controls such as data sources include an additional feature called Tasks that gives you quick access to the tasks that typically need to be done to set up a server control.
- A data connection is a link between the ASP.NET application and the database that tells ASP.NET where the database is located.
- Once the connection is created, the next step is to set up the Select statement for the data source.
- Once the connection is saved, the wizard gives you an opportunity to construct a query to determine exactly what data from the connection will be brought into the application.
- The data brought into the application through the data source can be displayed with the server data control called the GridView.
- Once the design for the application is complete, use the File, Save All menu option to save the application, and then use the File, View in Browser menu option to test the application.

■ To use an Access database, the database file must be located in the Data folder under the Web site directory. Therefore, a copy of the database file must be copied to that folder by right-clicking the Data folder and selecting the Add Existing Item option.

■ In Access, the database is a local file contained in the directory with the Web site itself. In SQL Server and Oracle, you have to create a data connection that specifies how to connect to a remotely located database.

■ The where clause of a data source query can be linked to a control on the form such that the information in that control could be used to determine what data is returned.

■ Drop-down list and radio button list controls can also be associated with a data source by having the data source provide the options that appear in these controls.

■ The AutoPostBack property sets a radio button list or drop-down list to post back to the server whenever the user makes a selection. This procedure would allow you to create a form where the user would not have to click a button to get the form to go back to the server and process any data entered by the user.

KEY TERMS

AccessDataSource. Server control used when you are linking to an Access database.

Active Server Page (ASP). A Web page that includes programming code to dynamically construct the content of the Web page on the fly, in response to user inputs and events related to the page.

ASP.NET. The Microsoft development environment that allows you to quickly develop Web applications.

Common Tasks. Give you quick access to the tasks that typically need to be done to set up a server control.

Data connection. A link between the ASP.NET application and the database that tells ASP.NET where the database is located.

Data source. Basically, a query that operates over a connection to retrieve data from the database.

Default.aspx. File for the user interface component of the application.

Default.aspx.vb. File for any Visual Basic programming code that you create for the application.

Design view. Provides an interface that greatly simplifies the design process, particularly with respect to adding server controls and formatting the Web page.

GridView. A server control that can be used to display data in the form of a table.

Intellisense. An editor feature that monitors what you type and tries to give you options that relate to the objects you are referencing in the statement.

Server controls. Dynamic versions of typical HTML components, including textboxes, tables, bullet lists, radio buttons, and list boxes, as well as unique controls that provide additional functionality far beyond that possible with simple HTML tags. These controls handle functions such as validation, data access, login processing, and navigation.

Source view. Provides an interface for writing HTML statements to design an Active Server page.

SqlDataSource. Server control used for either SqlServer or Oracle databases.

Web Developer. A complex development environment that includes a variety of powerful tools to create a wide range of Web application projects.

Web Form. An HTML document that includes basic static HTML tags and server controls.

Web site. Basically, a directory in which all the files associated with the Web application are stored.

EXERCISES

Review

1. What is a Web Form in ASP.NET?
2. What are the two components of a Web Form that combine to create the Web page that is sent back to the browser?
3. Explain how the tags for server controls differ from those of a standard HTML tag.
4. Explain the purpose of the Default.aspx and Default.aspx.vb files.
5. Explain the difference between the source and design views of the application.
6. How do you change the properties of a control?
7. What is Intellisense?
8. What is the SqlDataSource control used for?
9. What server control is used with an Access database?
10. Explain how the Common Tasks feature works.
11. What is a data connection?
12. How is the query for a data source specified?
13. Explain what a GridView control is used for and how it is configured.
14. How does connecting to an Oracle database differ from connecting to an SQL Server database?
15. Explain the configuration of a data source for an Access database.
16. How is an Access database added to the Data directory for the project, and what is the advantage of adding it to this location?

Discuss

1. Explain how an Active Server Page makes a round trip from the browser to the server and back to the browser.
2. What is a Web site in Web Developer, and how is it related to changing the location of an ASP.NET application?
3. Why is it useful to save a data connection in the Web.config file?
4. Explain how a server control can be used as part of a where clause to determine the rows that will be returned by the data source.
5. Explain how a data source can be used to populate the values displayed in a radio button list or a drop-down list.
6. What is the purpose of the AutoPostBack property of a radio button or drop-down list?

Practice

For the applications below, use the databases you created in Oracle, Access, or SQL Server in previous chapters. If your databases were created in Access, use the AccessDataSource server control; otherwise, use the SqlDataSource control.

Enrollment Database

1. Create an ASP.NET Web application to display the contents of the Course table that looks like Exhibit 12-63.

Exhibit 12-63

Application for
Exercise 1

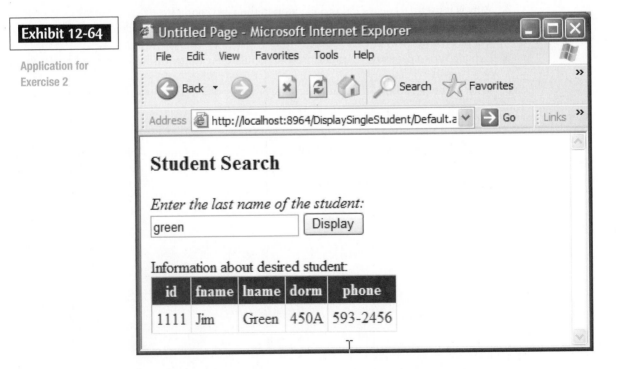

2. Create an ASP.NET Web application to allow the user to enter a student's last name in a textbox and have that student's information displayed. The design should look like Exhibit 12-64.

Exhibit 12-64

Application for
Exercise 2

In this application, create a where clause using the LIKE operator that links the query to the entry the user makes in the textbox and displays the information for that student when the button is clicked.

Hospital Database

3. Create an ASP.NET Web application to display the contents of the Doctor table that looks like Exhibit 12-65.

Exhibit 12-65

Application for
Exercise 3

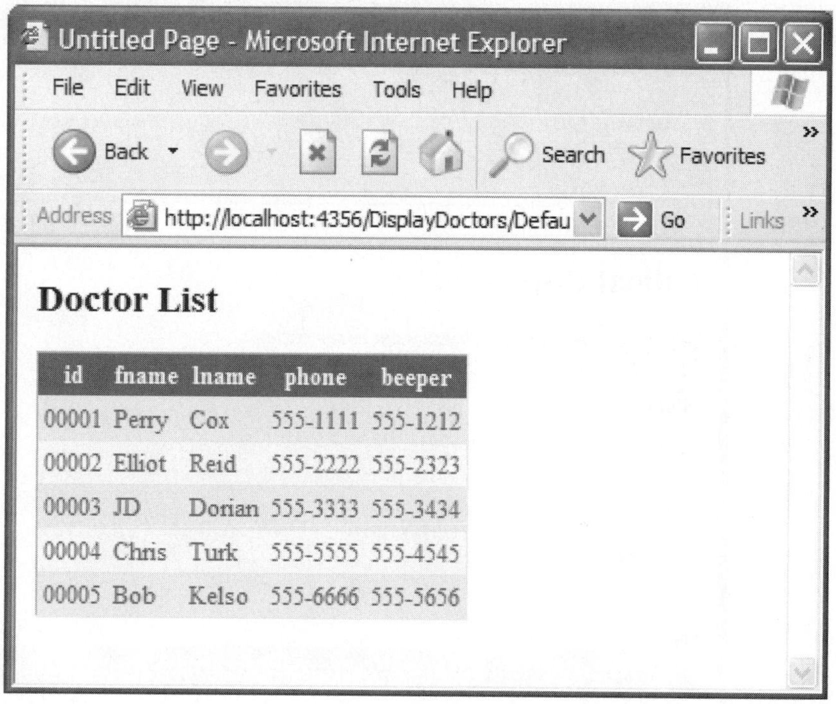

Untitled Page - Microsoft Internet Explorer

File   Edit   View   Favorites   Tools   Help

Back   •   ✕ ↻ 🏠   Search   ⭐ Favorites   »

Address http://localhost:4356/DisplayDoctors/Defau → Go   Links »

Doctor List

id	fname	lname	phone	beeper
00001	Perry	Cox	555-1111	555-1212
00002	Elliot	Reid	555-2222	555-2323
00003	JD	Dorian	555-3333	555-3434
00004	Chris	Turk	555-5555	555-4545
00005	Bob	Kelso	555-6666	555-5656

4. Create an ASP.NET Web application that displays a radio button list of the states of patients and allows the user to select a state and have patients in those states displayed. The design should look like Exhibit 12-66.

Exhibit 12-66

Application for
Exercise 4

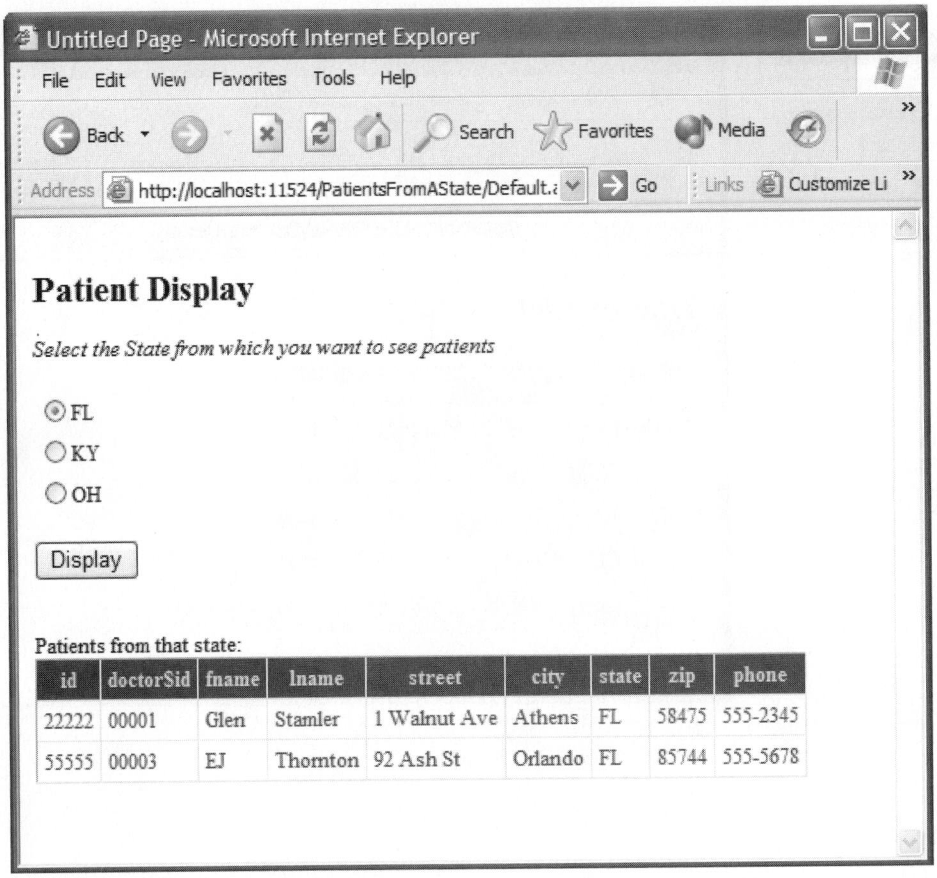

This application will require two data sources. One should display the results in the GridView and be linked to the selection the user makes in the radio button list. The second data source should be used to supply the values to the radio button list by retrieving the distinct values from the state column of the Patient table.

Acme Database

5. Create an ASP.NET Web application to display the contents of the Product table that looks like Exhibit 12-67.

Exhibit 12-67

Application for
Exercise 5

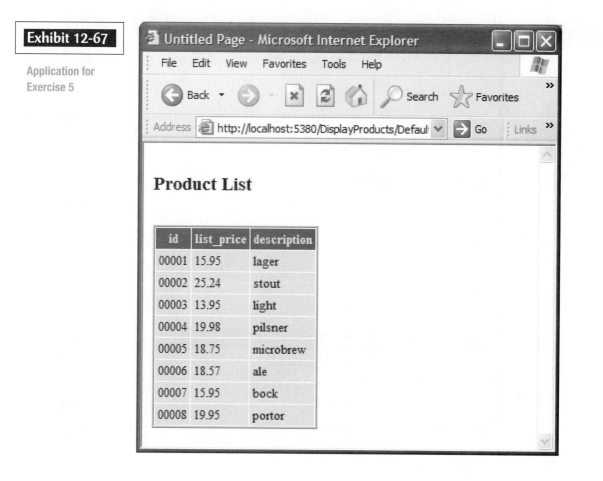

6. Create an ASP.NET Web application to display a drop-down list of the customer ids in the Order table and to enable the user to select a customer number and have orders for that customer displayed. The design should look like Exhibit 12-68.

This application will require two data sources. One should display the results in the GridView and be linked to the selection the user makes in the drop-down list. The second data source should be used to supply the values to the drop-down list by retrieving the distinct values from the CUSTOMER$id column of the Order table.

Amazon Database

7. Create an ASP.NET Web application to display the contents of the Client table that looks like Exhibit 12-69.

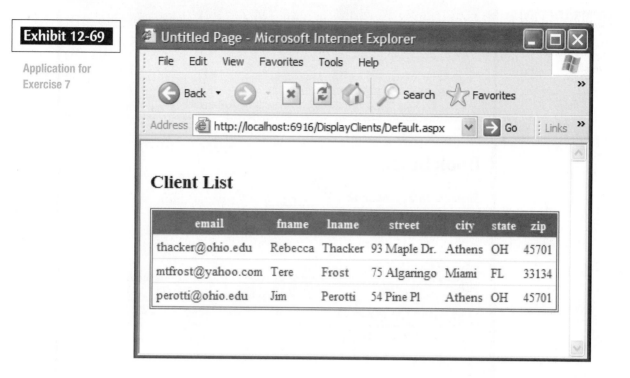

Client List

email	fname	lname	street	city	state	zip
thacker@ohio.edu	Rebecca	Thacker	93 Maple Dr.	Athens	OH	45701
mtfrost@yahoo.com	Tere	Frost	75 Algaringo	Miami	FL	33134
perotti@ohio.edu	Jim	Perotti	54 Pine Pl	Athens	OH	45701

8. Create an ASP.NET Web application to allow the user to enter a title of a book and to have that book's information displayed. The design should look like Exhibit 12-70.

In this application, create a where clause using the LIKE operator that links the query to the entry the user makes in the textbox and displays the information for that book when the button is clicked.

Maintaining Databases from Web Applications with Microsoft ASP.NET

Introduction

In this chapter, we will extend the discussion of Web applications to show how data in a database can be changed through a Web page.

Learning Objectives

After completing this chapter, you will be able to:

- Create and configure a DetailsView control.
- Set up a DetailsView control to allow for inserting new rows.
- Set up a DetailsView control to allow for updating rows.
- Set up a DetailsView control to allow for deleting rows.
- Set up a GridView control to allow for updating rows.
- Set up a GridView control to allow for deleting rows.

The DetailsView Server Control

To illustrate how an ASP.NET page can be used to make changes to data in a database, we will use a new server control called the **DetailsView.** This control is similar to a GridView, in that it can be used to display rows from a database. The main difference is that a DetailsView control displays a single row, whereas a GridView control displays multiple rows. Exhibit 13-1 shows an application that uses the DetailsView control.

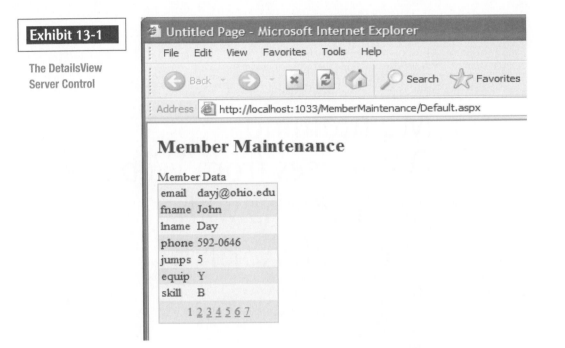

The numbers across the bottom of this control allow you to navigate through the records in the table. In this example, the MEMBER table has seven rows, and the numbers at the bottom are links to the other rows in the table.

 ## Creating a Member Maintenance Web Application

To illustrate how a DetailsView server control can be used to manipulate the data stored in a database, we will create an application that can be used to view and change the data in the Sky_Member database.

To begin, first create a new Web site called MemberMaintenance. When the Web site files are displayed in the Solution Explorer, right-click the App_Data folder, and choose the option for adding an existing item. Browse to the location of your Sky_Member Access database (sky_member.mdb file) and add that database to the solution.

In the Design view, add an AccessDataSource control and a DetailsView control from the Data group in the toolbox. After adding these controls, your design should look something like Exhibit 13-2.

Exhibit 13-2

The Design with
the Data Source
and DetailsView
Controls

Exhibit 13-2

The Design with
the Data Source
and DetailsView
Controls

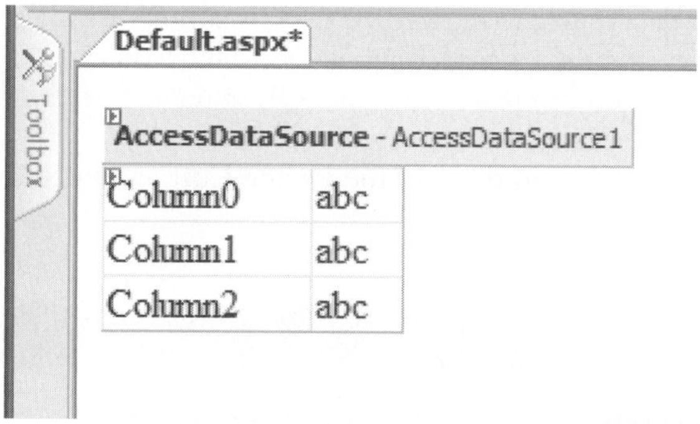

Configuring the Data Source

The first step in this design will be to set up the data source to display the rows from the SKY_MEMBER table. Once that process is working, we will move on to adding the ability to change the data that is displayed.

Activate the AccessDataSource Tasks pop-up menu by clicking the icon in the top left corner of the data source. There are two ways to configure the Select statement as well as the insert, update, and delete statements that will be needed to change the data that is displayed.

In the Configure Data Source dialog box, these two options are represented by the two radio buttons. In the previous chapter, you used the second option when setting up the Select statements. The first option can be used to construct a custom Select statement and also to construct insert, update, and delete statements. The second option includes an option to automatically generate standard insert, update, and delete statements. To better understand such generated statements, we will first use the first option to construct the select, insert, update, and delete statements and then come back and look at the alternative of having these statements automatically generated.

To see how to construct custom select, insert, update, and delete statements, select the first option for specifying a custom SQL statement, as illustrated in Exhibit 13-3.

Exhibit 13-3

Configuring the
Data Source

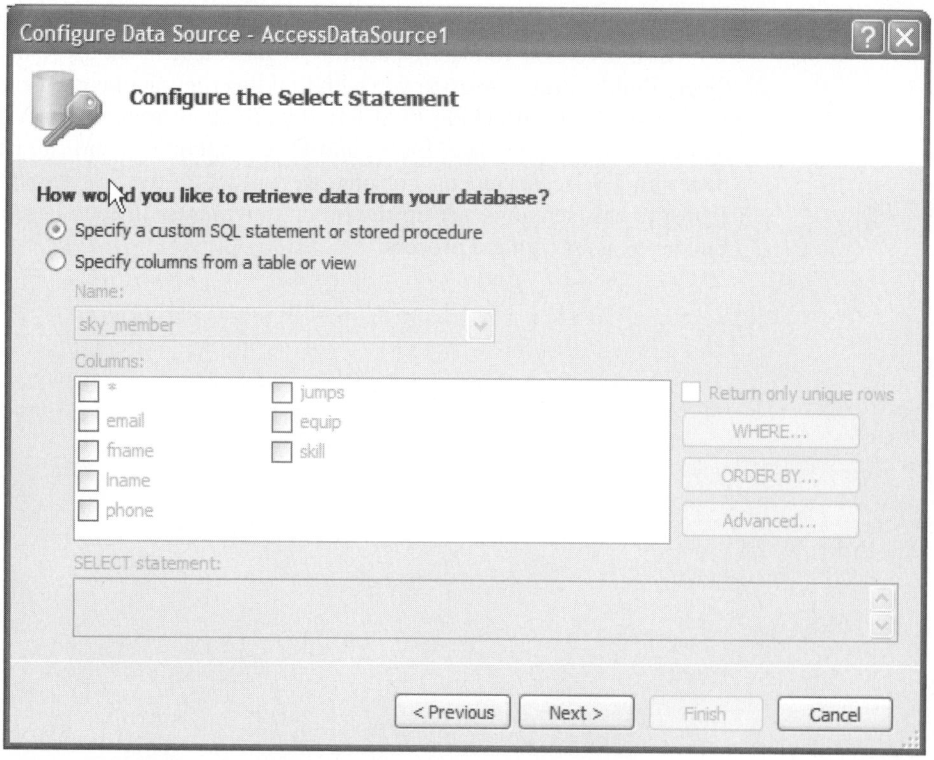

To set up the data source to retrieve the data from the MEMBER table, we could still use this option. However, the steps for setting up the ability to alter the data in the table requires that you understand how to create a custom SQL statement, so this option will also be used for generating the Select statement to display all the rows.

Selecting this first option displays the Define Custom Statements screen, as shown in Exhibit 13-4.

Exhibit 13-4

The Define Custom
Statements Screen

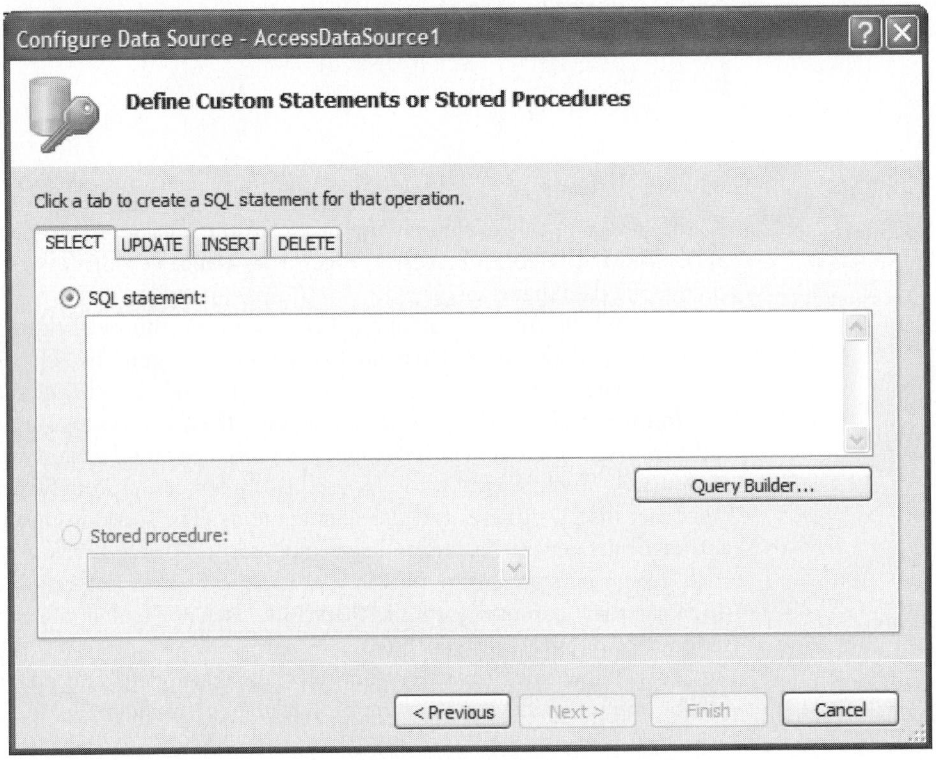

On this screen, you can type an SQL statement in the large box, or you can click the Query Builder button to assist you with building the statement. Also note the four tabs at the top for SELECT, UPDATE, INSERT, and DELETE statements. A data source can be configured to perform Update, Insert, and Delete operations and can be configured to retrieve data with a Select statement. For now, we will set up the Select statement, and later, we will return to this screen to set up the other statements. In each case, we will use the Query Builder to assist with the process.

When you click the Query Builder button, the tables in the database will be displayed, and you can select the one you want to use in the query. In this case, the Sky_Member database has only one table, called SKY_MEMBER. Select this table and click the Add button and then the Close button to bring that table into the Query Builder, as shown in Exhibit 13-5.

In the Query Builder, you can use the check boxes in the top panel to select the columns to be included in the data source. In this case, we want to display all the information in the SKY_MEMBER table, because the box at the top was checked to display all the columns.

This process will add the columns in the table in the middle and build the Select statement in the third panel. This step is all that is needed for a simple Select statement that displays all the information in the table. The purpose of the table in the middle panel will be discussed later, when we set up the data source to manipulate the data in the table. For now, simply click the OK button to finish this query. Then click Next to move to the step to test the query. Test the query and then click the Finish button to finish configuring the data source.

Configuring the DetailsView Control

Once the data source is configured, the next step will be to configure the DetailsView server control. Under the DetailsView Tasks pop-up menu, select AccessDataSource as the data source for the DetailsView control. Use the Auto Format option to select the Sand & Sky formatting scheme. To display the links to the rows in the table at the bottom of DetailsView, click the Enable Paging check box, as shown in Exhibit 13-6.

Exhibit 13-6

Configuring the
DetailsView
Control

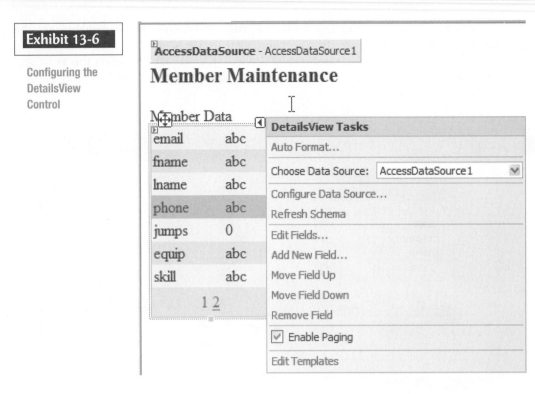

After saving this application, use the File, View in Browser option to test the application. The page displayed should look like Exhibit 13-7.

Exhibit 13-7

The Completed
Member
Maintenance
Application

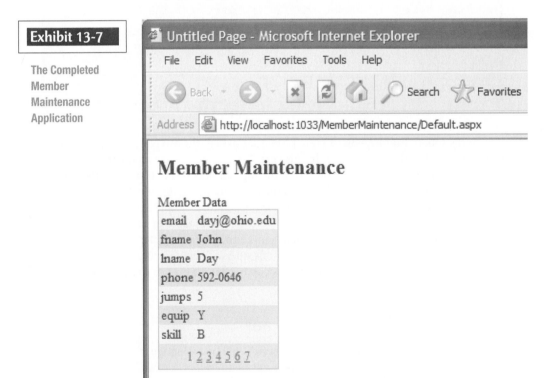

Adding the Ability to Insert New Rows

Now that the basic application to display rows from the SKY_MEMBER table is completed, the next step is to begin adding the ability to make changes to the data in the table. The first change will be to add the ability to insert new rows into the table through an Insert statement associated with the data source. The key to this process is to create an Insert statement in the data source that is associated with the columns in the DetailsView control.

Altering the DetailsView Control

The first step is to alter the properties of the DetailsView control to display a link for initiating the insertion of a new row. Click the DetailsView control, and find the AutoGenerateInsertButton property in the Behavior property group. Change this property from the default of False to True, as shown in Exhibit 13-8.

Exhibit 13-8

Changing the
AutoGenerate-
InsertButton
Property

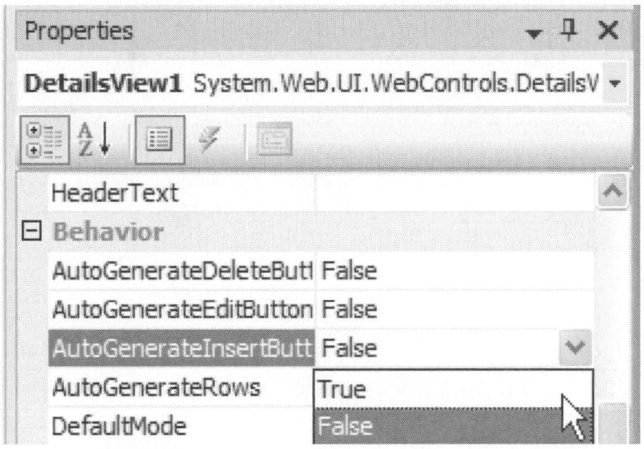

This step will add a New link at the bottom of the DetailsView control that allows the user to click on the link and have a blank row open up in the control. Exhibit 13-9 shows how the New link is added at the bottom of the DetailsView control when the AutoGenerateInsertButton property is changed to True.

Exhibit 13-9

The DetailsView
Control with the
New Link Added

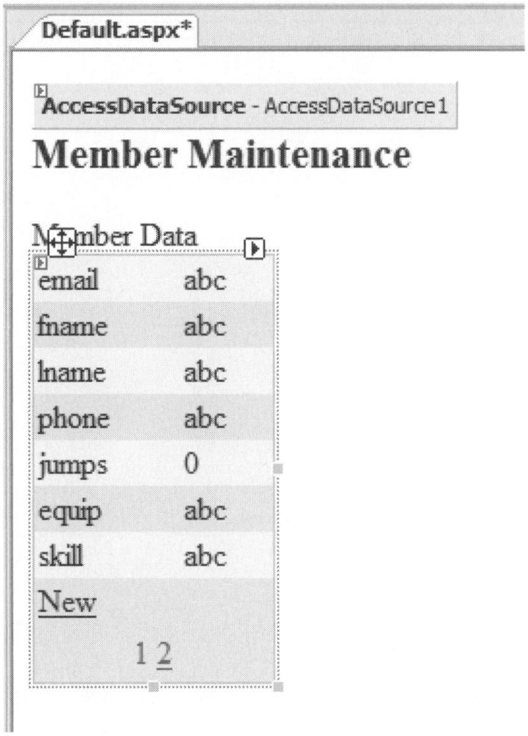

Altering the Data Source

Once the DetailsView control is set up to allow for inserting, the data source needs to be altered to create the Insert statement that will be used when a row is added. Use the AccessDataSource Tasks menu to configure the data source. Select the Specify Custom SQL Statement option. On the Define Custom Statements screen, click the INSERT tab at the top, as shown in Exhibit 13-10.

Exhibit 13-10

Creating an Insert Statement in the INSERT Tab

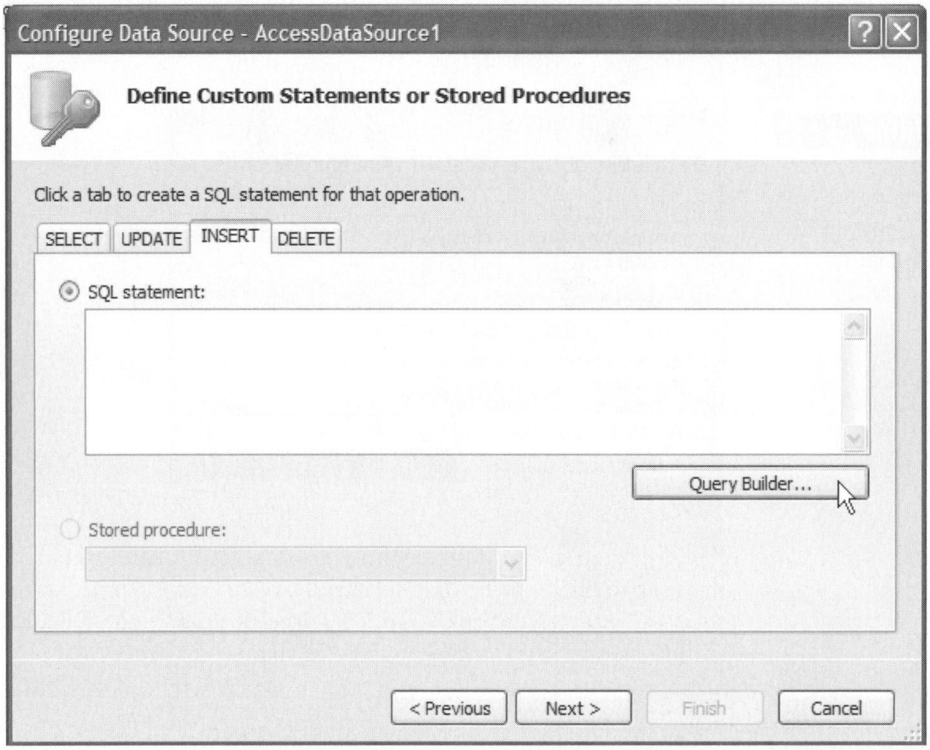

As we did with the Select statement, use the Query Builder to assist with the construction of the Insert statement. When the Query Builder starts, select the SKY_MEMBER table as the table on which to base the Insert statement. This step will add the table columns to the Query Builder and start a skeleton of the Insert statement at the bottom, as shown in Exhibit 13-11.

Exhibit 13-11

Building the Insert Statement

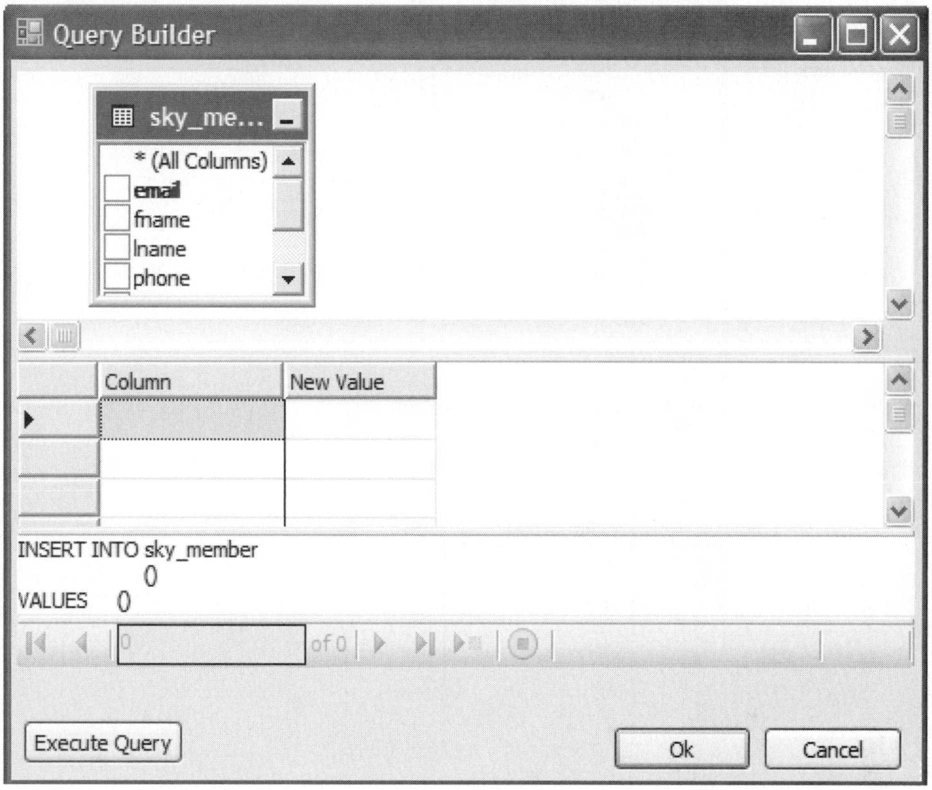

Because the Insert statement will add a row to the table, all the columns in the table should be checked off. Thus, each column will be added in the center panel. All the columns will then be added to the Insert statement at the bottom, as shown in Exhibit 13-12.

Exhibit 13-12

Adding the Columns to the Insert Statement

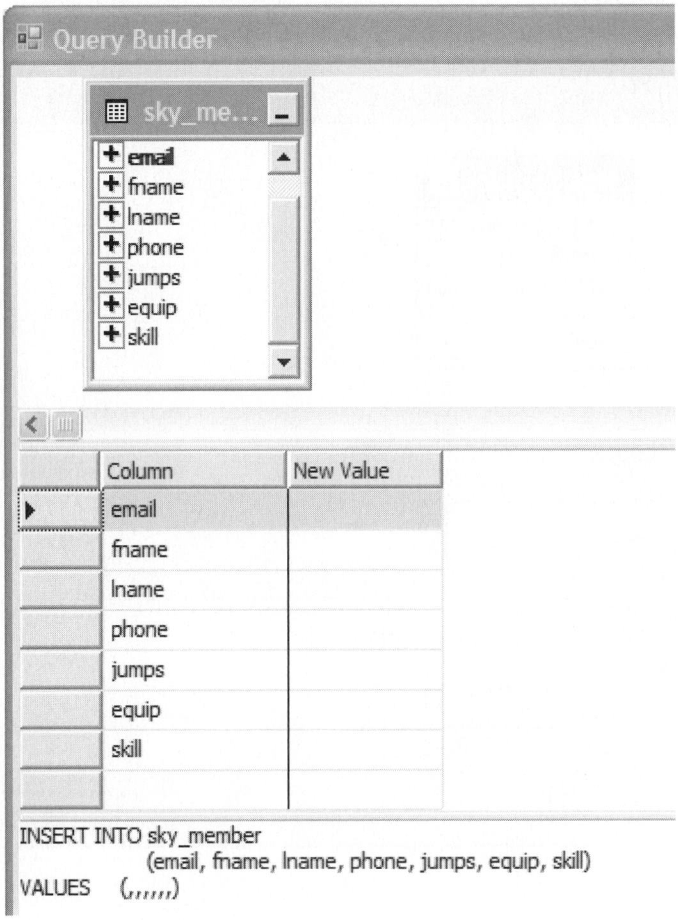
Query Builder
sky_me...
email
fname
lname
phone
jumps
equip
skill
Column
New Value
email
fname
lname
phone
jumps
equip
skill
INSERT INTO sky_member
(email, fname, lname, phone, jumps, equip, skill)
VALUES (,,,,,,)

In the center, notice that each column is listed under the Column heading. The column at the right lets you specify the new values to be inserted. These values would go in the list following the VALUES keyword in the Insert statement. You could put actual values in this New Value column, but doing so would create an insert statement capable only of inserting the same row each time. Instead, we need to tell the application that the values for the Insert statement will be coming from the DetailsView control. The DetailsView control has a series of values with the same names as the columns from the table. To reference these items on the form, put a question mark under the New Value column, as shown in Exhibit 13-13.

Exhibit 13-13

Completing the
Insert Statement

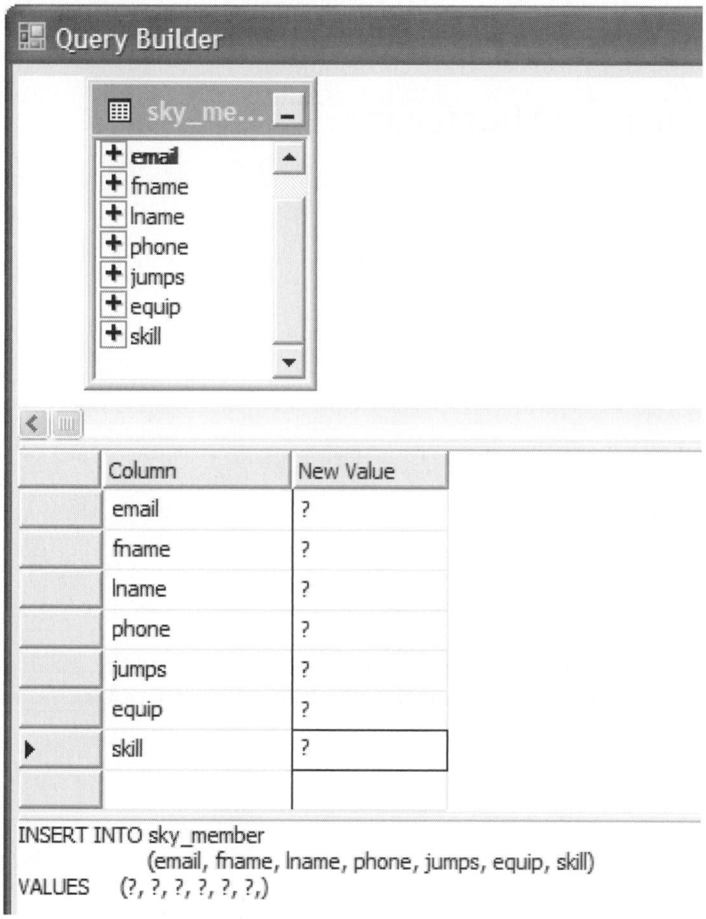

Notice in the exhibit above that as each entry is made in the New Value column, the entries in that column are used to fill in the list of values following the VALUES keyword in the Insert statement at the bottom. Once the Insert statement is complete, click the Next button and then the Finish button to finish.

Testing the Insertion of a New Row

Save the application again, and view it in the browser, as shown in Exhibit 13-14.

Exhibit 13-14

The Member
Maintenance
Application with
Inserting

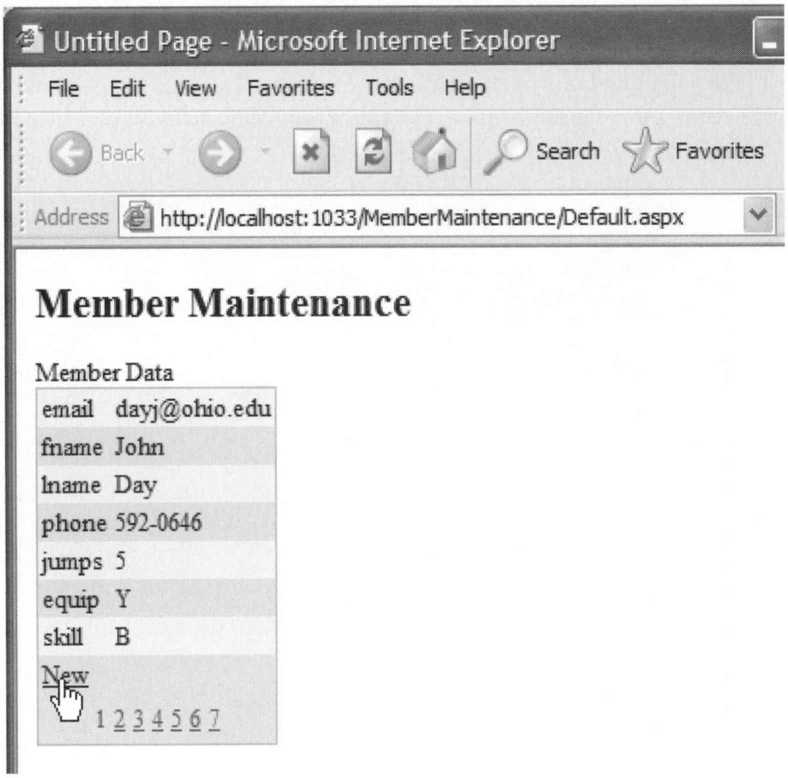

When the application is displayed, the New link will be available at the bottom. Clicking this link will open up a new row in the DetailsView control, as shown in Exhibit 13-15.

You can enter data for each column and use the Insert link at the bottom to have the new row inserted into the table. There is also a Cancel link, to abandon the process of adding the new row. Once you enter the new row and click the Insert link, the DetailsView will again display the rows in the table, as shown in Exhibit 13-16.

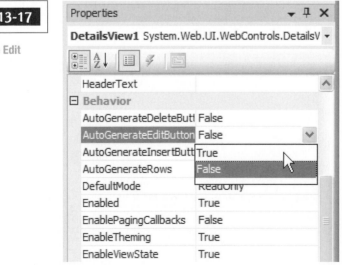

Member Maintenance

Member Data

email	dayj@ohio.edu
fname	John
lname	Day
phone	592-0646
jumps	5
equip	Y
skill	B
New	

1 2 3 4 5 6 7 8

In this exhibit, notice that there are now links to eight rows in the table, rather than seven, as previously shown. The eighth row is the one that was just added.

Adding the Ability to Update Rows

The next change to the application will be to add the ability to make updates to the data displayed in the DetailsView control. As with inserting, the first step is to alter the properties to display a new link, to allow updating to occur through the control. In this case, you need to change the AutoGenerateEditButton property to True as shown in Exhibit 13-17.

Properties	▾ ⏸ ✕
DetailsView1 System.Web.UI.WebControls.DetailsV ▾	

HeaderText	
⊟ **Behavior**	
AutoGenerateDeleteButt	False
AutoGenerateEditButton	False ▾
AutoGenerateInsertButt	True
AutoGenerateRows	False
DefaultMode	ReadOnly
Enabled	True
EnablePagingCallbacks	False
EnableTheming	True
EnableViewState	True

This step will add a link called Edit to the bottom of the DetailsView control, next to the New link added before.

Setting Up the Update Statement

Configure the data source again, and go to the UPDATE tab in the Custom SQL Statement screen. Use the Query Builder button to start the Query Builder, and add the SKY_MEMBER table to the query.

The construction of the Update statement is similar to that of the Insert statement. First, add all the columns, except the email column, to the query. Because this column is the primary key of the table, we will set it up so this value cannot be updated. Then in the New Value column, add a reference to the items in the DetailsView control by putting in a question mark. For each of these columns, also check the Set box so that the columns will appear in the Set clause of the update statement. Finally, add the email column but do not check the box in the Set column and do not place a value in the New Value column. Instead, put an equal sign followed by a question mark in the Filter column, as shown in Exhibit 13-18.

Exhibit 13-18

Setting Up the
Update Statement

	Column	Table	Set	New Value	Filter	Or...
▶	fname	sky_member	☑	?		
	lname	sky_member	☑	?		
	phone	sky_member	☑	?		
	jumps	sky_member	☑	?		
	equip	sky_member	☑	?		
	skill	sky_member	☑	?		
	email	sky_member	☐		= ?	

```
UPDATE   sky_member
SET      fname = ?, lname = ?, phone = ?, jumps = ?, equip = ?, skill = ?
WHERE    (email = ?)
```

To prevent the email column from being changed, the new value is left empty and the Set box is not checked. This leaves the email column out of the set clause in the update statement. The filter is used to set up the where clause so that the row to be updated is the one with the same email address as is currently being displayed. To accomplish this task, the email address currently being displayed in the DetailsView control is used to locate the row to be updated by entering "=?" in the Filter column. Making this entry in the Filter column causes the where clause to be added to the Update statement at the bottom.

The completed Update statement at the bottom shows that all columns except the email column will be set equal to the values currently being displayed in the DetailsView control. This update will occur in the row in the table with an email address that matches the email address currently being displayed in the DetailsView control.

Testing the Update Statement

Once the data source is configured to include the Update statement, save the application and view it in the browser. It should look something like Exhibit 13-19.

When the user clicks the Edit button, the DetailsView control changes, and text boxes are opened for all of the columns except the email column. The current values are displayed in the textboxes, and the user can make any changes desired, as shown in Exhibit 13-20.

Once the user changes any of the values in the textboxes, the Update link can be clicked. The new values will thus be sent back to the database to replace the matching values in the same row in the database.

Adding the Ability to Delete Rows

The final type of change that can be made to a row in the database is the ability to delete rows. As with the ability to insert and update, you need to make changes to both the DetailsView control and the data source to add the ability to delete rows.

To configure the DetailsView control to allow deleting, change the AutoGenerate-DeleteButton property to True, as shown in Exhibit 13-21.

Once the AutoGenerateDeleteButton property is changed, a Delete link will be added to the bottom of the control, along with the Edit and New buttons added previously.

Setting Up the Delete Statement

For the data source, select the Configure Data Source option from the AccessDataSource pop-up menu. Go to the DELETE tab on the Define Custom Statements screen, and use the Query Builder to build the Delete statement. As with typical delete statements, you will need a where clause to limit the delete to the specific row desired, as illustrated in Exhibit 13-22.

Exhibit 13-22

Setting Up the Delete Statement

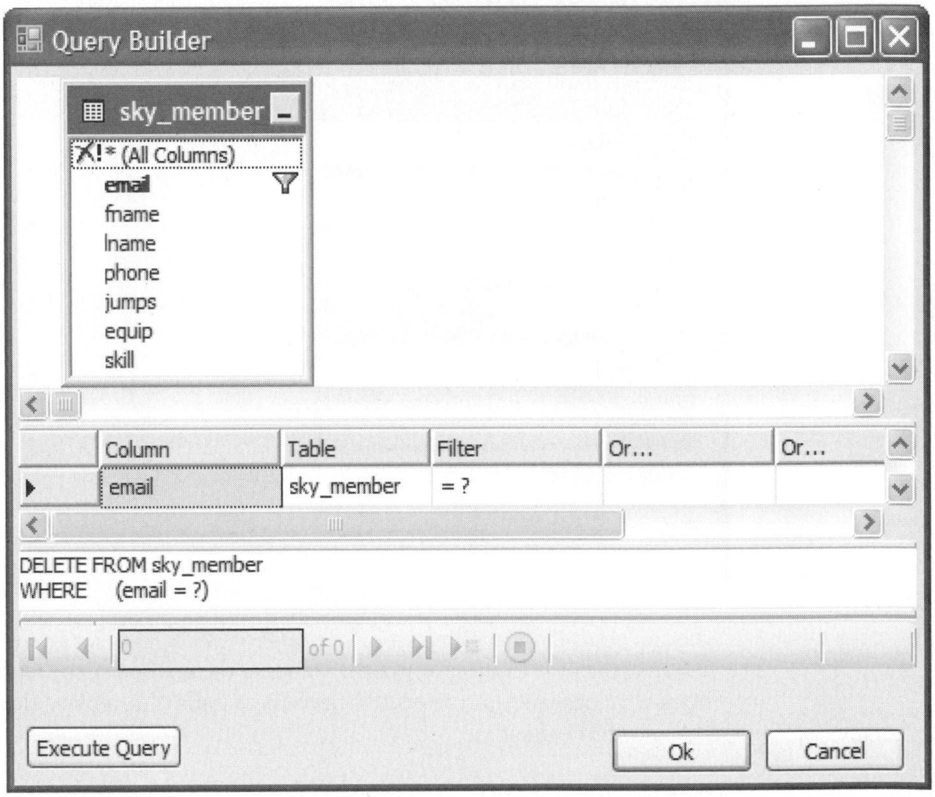

In the Query Builder, add the SKY_MEMBER table and select the email column in the first box under the Column heading so it can be used as the basis of the where clause. In the Filter column, enter "=?" to have the delete affect the row in the table with an email address that equals the value from the email item in the DetailsView control. At the bottom, a where clause will be added with that condition.

Testing the Delete Statement

Once the Delete statement is complete, save the application and view it in the browser, as shown in Exhibit 13-23.

Exhibit 13-23

Testing the Delete
Statement

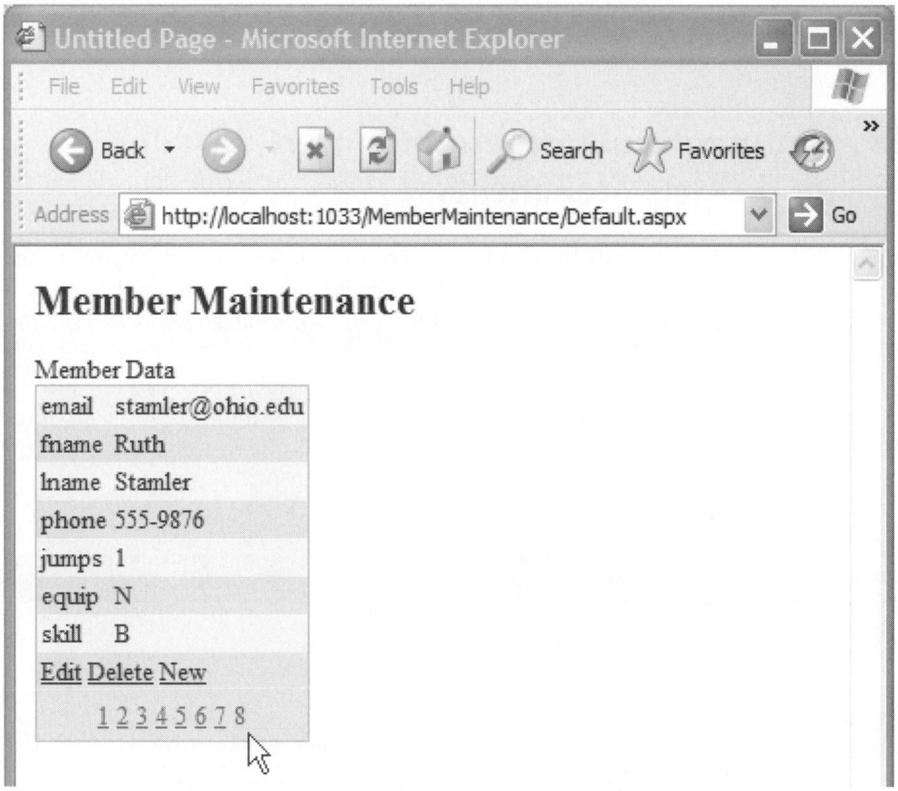

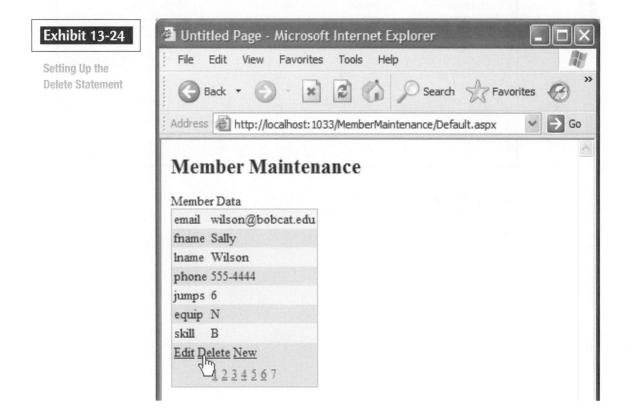

To delete a row, click the number of the row you want to delete, so that row will be displayed in the DetailsView control. Once the row is displayed, click the Delete button to remove the row. Exhibit 13-24 shows the result of deleting the eighth row.

Exhibit 13-24

Setting Up the
Delete Statement

After the eighth row is removed, the seventh row is displayed, and the numbers at the bottom indicate that there are now seven rows left in the table.

Automatically Generating Insert, Update, and Delete Statements

You have just learned how insert, update, and delete statements are constructed to interact with a data source on an Active Server Page. With this knowledge, you can construct complex variations of these statements to fit custom applications as well as simple standard applications like the one just discussed.

There is an alternative method for using the second option for specifying columns from a table or view on the screen to configure the Select statement for a data source configuring a basic insert, update, and delete statement for a data source, as shown in Exhibit 13-25.

Exhibit 13-25

Design Using the
Advanced Option
to Configure a
Data Source

Configure Data Source - AccessDataSource1

Configure the Select Statement

How would you like to retrieve data from your database?

○ Specify a custom SQL statement or stored procedure

◉ Specify columns from a table or view

Name:

| sky_member | ⌄ |

Columns:

☑ *	☐ jumps
☐ email	☐ equip
☐ fname	☐ skill
☐ lname	
☐ phone	

☐ Return only unique rows

WHERE...

ORDER BY...

Advanced...

SELECT statement:

SELECT * FROM [sky_member]

[< Previous] [Next >] [Finish] [Cancel]

This option allows you to construct the Select statement by checking off the columns to be retrieved. To set up the basic insert, update, and delete statements, click the Advanced button. This will display the screen shown in Exhibit 13-26.

Exhibit 13-26

Advanced SQL
Generation
Options

Advanced SQL Generation Options

Additional INSERT, UPDATE, and DELETE statements can be generated to update the data source.

☑ **Generate INSERT, UPDATE, and DELETE statements**

Generates INSERT, UPDATE, and DELETE statements based on your SELECT statement. You must have a primary key field selected for this option to be enabled.

☑ **Use optimistic concurrency**

Modifies UPDATE and DELETE statements to detect whether the database has changed since the record was loaded into the DataSet. This helps prevent concurrency conflicts.

OK   Cancel

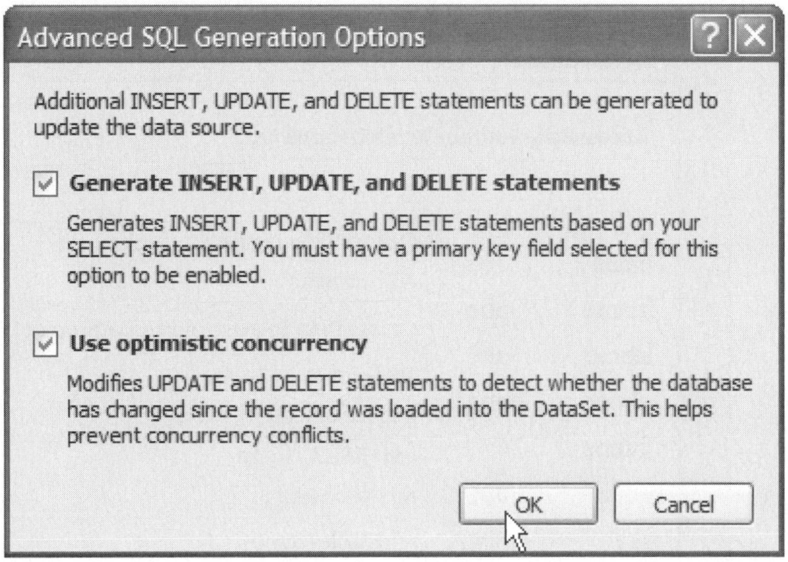

On this screen, you can use the first check box to have the insert, update, and delete statements created based on the Select statement created on the previous screen. Notice in the description of this option that the table must have a primary key column to be able to use this option.

Once the first check box is selected, the second option becomes available. This option deals with concurrency control in a multiuser database. When a row is retrieved from the database for changing or deleting, it is possible that another user might also retrieve the same row and make changes to it before you have time to complete your change. This concurrency conflict could lead to a problem if your change overwrites the change made by the previous user. This option makes the application check the database prior to saving your changes to make sure somebody else has not made a change since you retrieved the row.

Once these two options are selected and you click the OK button, the insert, update, and delete statements are generated and available in the data source. Once this data source is associated with a control such as the DetailsView, additional options will be available in the tasks for that control that allow you to access the additional options in the data source, as shown in Exhibit 13-27.

Exhibit 13-27

Using the Generated Insert, Update, and Delete Statements in the DetailsView Control

Default.aspx*

Toolbox

AccessDataSource - AccessDataSource1

email	abc
fname	abc
lname	abc
phone	abc
jumps	0
equip	abc
skill	abc

Edit Delete New

1 2

DetailsView Tasks

Auto Format...

Choose Data Source: AccessDataSource1 ▾

Configure Data Source...

Refresh Schema

Edit Fields...

Add New Field...

☑ Enable Paging

☑ Enable Inserting

☑ Enable Editing

☑ Enable Deleting

Edit Templates

Notice that the DetailsView Tasks now include new options for enabling inserting, editing, and deleting. These options can be checked to add the links in the DetailsView control without having to modify the properties of the control, as was done in the previous application.

The generated insert, update, and delete statements are the same as the basic statements we created manually in the previous example. Thus, for simple applications that involve basic modifications to a single table, automatically generating these statement is the best option. For more complex applications that involve multiple tables or instances where only part of a table is modified, you will have to create these statements manually. Therefore, it is important that you understand both methods of constructing insert, update, and delete statements.

Creating a Member Maintenance Application with a GridView

Just as the DetailsView control can be used to make changes to the data in a database, the GridView control can also be used to make some of the same types of changes. Recall that the GridView control is used to display multiple rows from a data source. The GridView control can be set up to both update and delete rows from a data source. It cannot be used to insert new rows.

To illustrate how a GridView control can be used to update and delete rows, create a new Web site called MemberMaintenanceGridVew. On the design view of the application, add an AccessDataSource control and a GridView control along with the headings as shown in Exhibit 13-28.

Exhibit 13-28

Design for
the Member
Maintenance Site

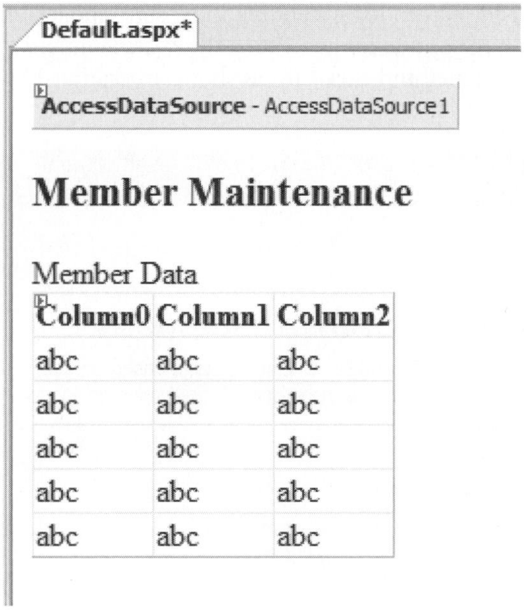

Default.aspx*

AccessDataSource - AccessDataSource1

Member Maintenance

Member Data

Column0	Column1	Column2
abc	abc	abc
abc	abc	abc
abc	abc	abc
abc	abc	abc
abc	abc	abc

Setting Up the Data Source

Once the basic application is created, add the sky_member.mdb file to the App_Data folder
and configure the data source to use that database. For the Select statement, use the second
option to specify columns from a table or view and then click the Advanced button shown in
Exhibit 13-29.

Exhibit 13-29

Configuring the
Data Source

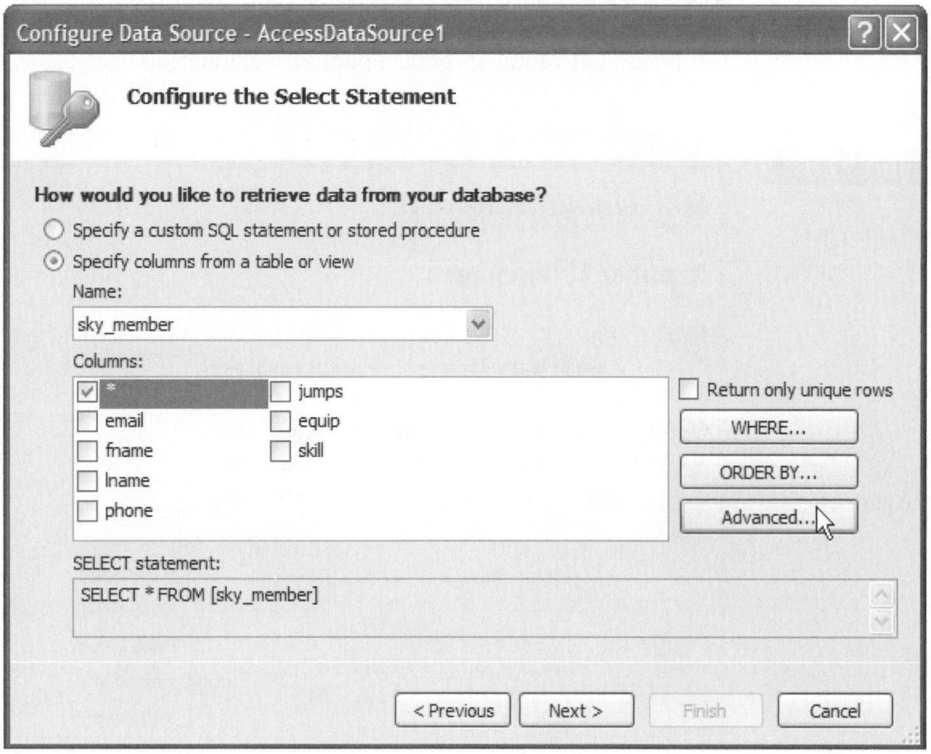

Configure Data Source - AccessDataSource1

Configure the Select Statement

How would you like to retrieve data from your database?

○ Specify a custom SQL statement or stored procedure

◉ Specify columns from a table or view

Name:

sky_member

Columns:

☑ *   ☐ jumps   ☐ Return only unique rows
☐ email   ☐ equip   WHERE...
☐ fname   ☐ skill   ORDER BY...
☐ lname   Advanced...
☐ phone

SELECT statement:

SELECT * FROM [sky_member]

< Previous   Next >   Finish   Cancel

This will display the screen for generating the insert, update, and delete statements for the data source. Select the option for generating the statements and then select the option for using optimistic concurrency and click OK, as shown in Exhibit 13-30.

Exhibit 13-30

Generating the Insert, Update, and Delete Statements

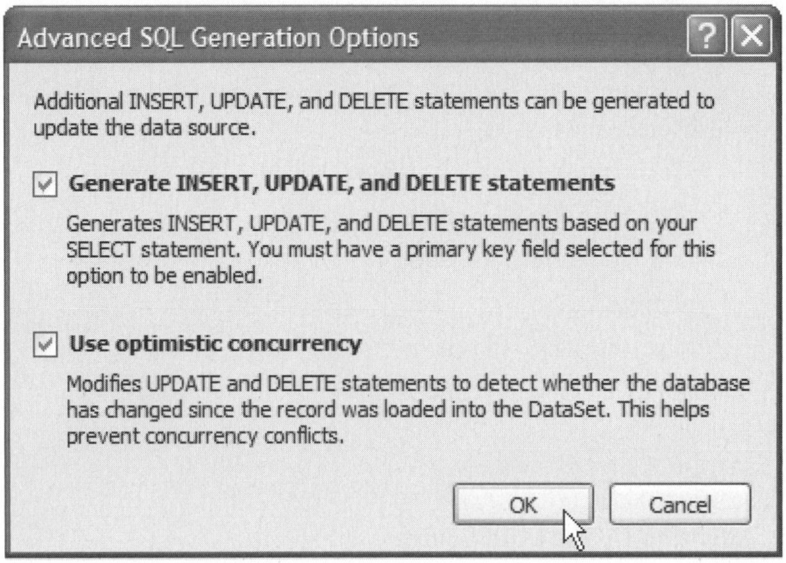

Once the statements are generated, click Next to move to the final screen, test the query, and click the Finish button to complete the configuration of the data source.

Setting Up the GridView Control

Now that the data source is configured, the next step is to select the data source for the GridView control and select the options for editing and deleting, as shown in Exhibit 13-31.

Exhibit 13-31

Configuring the GridView Control

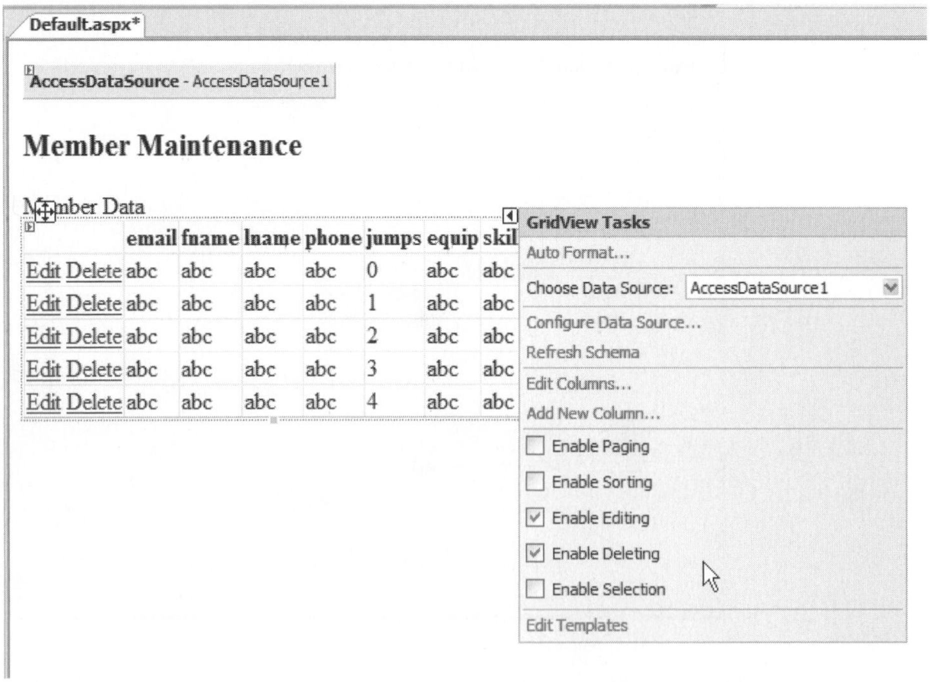

As we did with the DetailsView control, the options for editing and deleting data have been selected. These add the Edit and Delete links in front of the rows as shown. As discussed in the beginning of this application, inserting is not allowed through a GridView control, so there is no option to select for that operation. Thus, although an insert statement is generated for the data source, it will not be used.

Testing the Application

Once the GridView control is configured, save the application and view it in the browser. Edit and Delete links will appear at the beginning of each row. When the user clicks one of the Edit links, the values in that row will be opened in text boxes. The Edit link will be replaced with an Update link and a Cancel link, to allow the user to either complete the update or abandon it, as shown in Exhibit 13-32.

Exhibit 13-32

Updated Data in a GridView

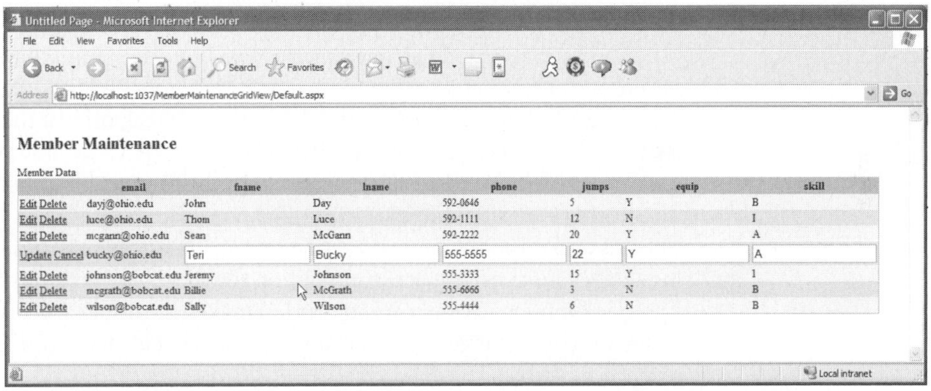

To delete a row, the user simply clicks the Delete link at the beginning of the row, and that row will be deleted. The rows will be redisplayed with the deleted row removed.

SUMMARY

- The DetailsView control can be used to display single rows from a database.
- When configuring a data source with a custom SQL statement, there are four tabs at the top for creating SELECT, UPDATE, INSERT, and DELETE statements.
- To display the links to the rows in the table at the bottom of the DetailsView, click the Enable Paging check box.
- To add the ability to add new rows to the table through the DetailsView control, you need to create an Insert statement in the data source that is associated with the columns in the DetailsView control.
- The first step is to alter the properties of the DetailsView control to display a link for initiating the insertion of a new row, setting the AutoGenerateInsertButton property to True.
- The next step is to configure the data source to create the Insert statement through the Query Builder.
- The values in the insert statement should be question marks to indicate that they are the values that come from the items in the DetailsView control.
- When the application is displayed, the New link will be available at the bottom. Clicking this link will open up a new row in the DetailsView control.

■ You can enter data for each column and use the Insert link at the bottom to have the new row inserted into the table. There is also a Cancel link, to abandon the process of adding the new row.

■ To allow updating to occur through the DetailsView control, change the AutoGenerate-EditButton property to True.

■ Then construct an Update statement in the data source. The Set clause in the update statement should refer to the values in the DetailsView control, which are question marks. This procedure would be done for all columns except the primary key.

■ The final part of the Update statement is to set up a filter that creates the condition that is used in the where clause. This condition should set the primary key column in the database equal to the corresponding column in the DetailsView control by entering =? as the filter for the primary key column.

■ When the user clicks the Edit button, the DetailsView control changes, and textboxes are opened for all the columns except the email column. The current values are displayed in the textboxes, and the user can make any changes desired and click the Update link.

■ To configure the DetailsView control to allow deleting, change the AutoGenerate-DeleteButton property to True.

■ To set up a Delete statement in the data source, check off just the primary key column so it can be used as the basis of the where clause. In the Filter column, enter a condition for the primary key column that sets it equal to the same column in the DetailsView control by entering =? as the filter.

■ There is an alternative method for configuring a basic insert, update, and delete statement for a data source using the second option for specifying columns from a table or view.

■ The Use Optimistic Concurrency option makes the application check the database prior to saving your changes to make sure somebody else has not made a change since you retrieved the row.

■ The GridView control can be set up to both update and delete rows from a data source. It cannot be used to insert new rows.

■ The data source would be configured to add update and delete statements in the same way as with the DetailsView control.

KEY TERMS

DetailsView. A control similar to a GridView in that it can be used to display rows from a database. The main difference is that a DetailsView control displays a single row whereas a GridView control displays multiple rows.

EXERCISES

Review

1. Describe the DetailsView control.
2. What does the Enable Paging option do in a DetailsView control?
3. What property do you change in a DetailsView control to allow updating?
4. What property do you change in a DetailsView control to allow inserting?
5. What property do you change in a DetailsView control to allow deleting?
6. Can you perform inserting with a GridView control?
7. When you precede the name of a column with a question mark (?), what does that mean?
8. How is a where clause set up in the Query Generator?
9. In an Update statement, which column is usually set up so it cannot be changed?
10. Which column is usually the only one included in the query for a Delete statement?

Discuss

1. Compare the DetailsView control to the GridView control.
2. Explain how you prevent the primary key column from being updated through the DetailsView control.
3. Explain how an Insert statement can be set up in the Query Builder when configuring a data source.
4. Explain how an Update statement can be set up in the Query Builder when configuring a data source.
5. Explain how a Delete statement can be set up in the Query Builder when configuring a data source.

Practice

For the applications below, use the databases you created in Oracle, Access, or SQL Server in previous chapters. If your databases were created in Access, use the AccessDataSource server control; otherwise, use the SqlDataSource control.

Enrollment Database

1. Create an ASP.NET Web application called CourseMaintenance to allow a user to view and change the contents of the Course table that looks like Exhibit 13-33.

Exhibit 13-33

Application for Exercise 1

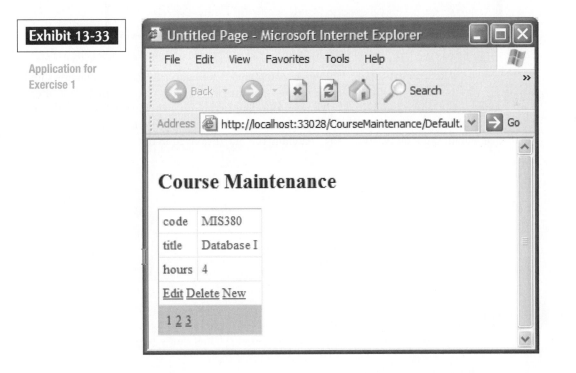

The DetailsView control should allow inserting, updating, and deleting. The Insert statement should include all three columns from the table. The Update statement should allow the user to change all the columns except the primary key column. Include a filter to generate the where clause that will limit the update to the row matching the one displayed in the DetailsView control. For the Delete statement, set up a filter to generate the where clause that will limit the delete to the row matching the one displayed in the DetailsView control.

2. Create an ASP.NET Web application called StudentMaintenance to allow the user to display, edit, and delete information about multiple students. The design should look like Exhibit 13-34.

The GridView control should allow updating and deleting. The Update statement should allow the user to change all the columns except the primary key column. Include a filter to generate the where clause that will limit the update to the row matching the one displayed in the GridView control. For the Delete statement, set up a filter to generate the where clause that will limit the delete to the row matching the one displayed in the GridView control.

Hospital Database

3. Create an ASP.NET Web application called DoctorMaintenance to allow a user to view and change the contents of the Doctor table that looks like Exhibit 13-35.

Exhibit 13-35

Application for Exercise 3

The DetailsView control should allow inserting, updating, and deleting. The Insert statement should include all three columns from the table. The Update statement should allow the user to change all the columns except the primary key column. Include a filter to generate the where clause that will limit the update to the row matching the one displayed in the DetailsView control. For the Delete statement, set up a filter to generate the where clause that will limit the delete to the row matching the one displayed in the DetailsView control.

4. Create an ASP.NET Web application called PatientMaintenance to allow the user to display, edit, and delete information about multiple patients. The design should look like Exhibit 13-36.

The GridView control should allow updating and deleting. The Update statement should allow the user to change all the columns except the primary key column. Include a filter to generate the where clause that will limit the update to the row matching the one displayed in the GridView control. For the Delete statement, set up a filter to generate the where clause that will limit the delete to the row matching the one displayed in the GridView control.

Acme Database

5. Create an ASP.NET Web application called ProductMaintenance to allow a user to view and change the contents of the Product table that looks like Exhibit 13-37.

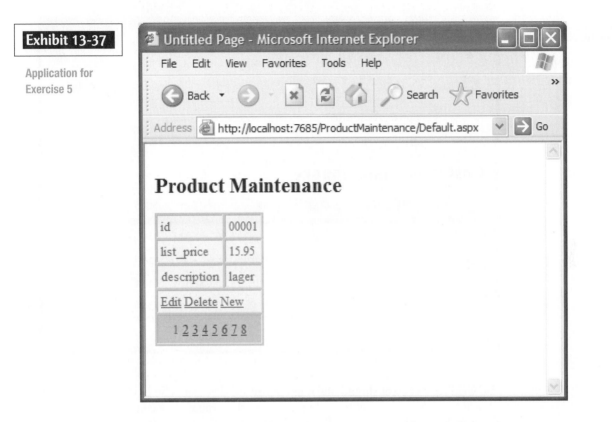

The DetailsView control should allow inserting, updating, and deleting. The Insert statement should include all three columns from the table. The Update statement should allow the user to change all the columns except the primary key column. Include a filter to generate the where clause that will limit the update to the row matching the one displayed in the DetailsView control. For the Delete statement, set up a filter to generate the where clause that will limit the delete to the row matching the one displayed in the DetailsView control.

6. Create an ASP.NET Web application called CustomerMaintenance to allow the user to display, edit, and delete information about multiple customers. The design should look like Exhibit 13-38.

The GridView control should allow updating and deleting. The Update statement should allow the user to change all the columns except the primary key column. Include a filter to generate the where clause that will limit the update to the row matching the one displayed in the GridView control. For the Delete statement, set up a filter to generate the where clause that will limit the delete to the row matching the one displayed in the GridView control.

Amazon Database

7. Create an ASP.NET Web application called BookMaintenance to allow a user to view and change the contents of the Book table that looks like Exhibit 13-39.

The DetailsView control should allow inserting, updating, and deleting. The Insert statement should include all three columns from the table. The Update statement should allow the user to change all the columns except the primary key column. Include a filter to generate the where clause that will limit the update to the row matching the one displayed in the DetailsView control. For the Delete statement, set up a filter to generate the where clause that will limit the delete to the row matching the one displayed in the DetailsView control.

8. Create an ASP.NET Web application called ClientMaintenance to allow the user to display, edit, and delete information about multiple clients. The design should look like Exhibit 13-40.

Exhibit 13-40

Application for
Exercise 8

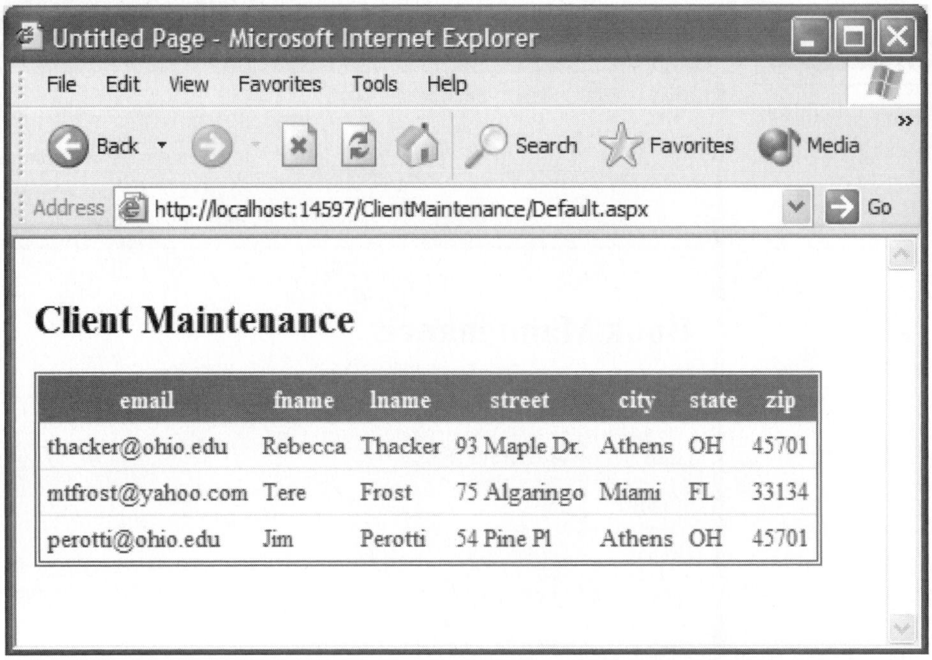

The GridView control should allow updating and deleting. The Update statement should allow the user to change all the columns except the primary key column. Include a filter to generate the where clause that will limit the update to the row matching the one displayed in the GridView control. For the Delete statement, set up a filter to generate the where clause that will limit the delete to the row matching the one displayed in the GridView control.

1NF. Normal form specifying that all fields must contain single values only.

2NF. Normal form specifying that part of the primary key may not determine a non-key field all by itself.

3NF. Normal form specifying that a non-key field may not determine another non-key field.

4NF. Normal form specifying that, in an all-key table, part of the key may determine multiple values of at most one other field.

AccessDataSource. Server control used when you are linking to an Access database.

Active Server Page (ASP). A Web page that includes programming code to dynamically construct the content of the Web page on the fly, in response to user inputs and events related to the page.

Aggregate functions. Built-in functions (Sum, Avg, etc.) that can be calculated for groups (aggregations) of rows rather than single rows.

AND operator. Operator used in a where clause that allows you to combine two conditions where rows must meet both conditions to be selected.

ASP.NET. The Microsoft development environment that allows you to quickly develop Web applications.

Associative table. (1) A new table created to implement a many-to-many relationship. It literally associates records between its two parent tables. (2) A child of two parent tables that are in a many-to-many relationship.

Attribute. A property of an entity or a relationship. For example, employee id is an attribute of the employee entity.

Base tables. The core set of tables in a database.

BCNF. Normal form specifying that every determinant is a key.

Between operator. Lets you choose rows based on a range of values.

Business logic. Rules that govern an organization's processes.

Cardinality. The technical term used to describe the number of records in the relationship.

Cartesian product. A temporary "table" that combines all rows in one table with all rows in another table.

Check constraint. A setting for a column where you can specify conditions to which data values must conform to when being inserted into the column.

Client/server architecture. A computing arrangement where tasks are divided between clients, which handle presentation (interface) tasks and make requests from servers, which then respond to those requests.

Commit. Structured query language statement used to save all the changes made during the current session.

Common Tasks. Give you quick access to the tasks that typically need to be done to set up a server control.

Conceptual model. A generic description of the data that is not tied to any specific database software product.

Create table. Structured query language statement used to create a table.

Data connection. A link between the ASP.NET application and the database that tells ASP.NET where the database is located.

Data item. A single piece of data.

Data source. Basically, a query that operates over a connection to retrieve data from the database.

Data type. The kind of information that may be stored in an attribute.

Database. An organized collection of data.

Database administrator (DBA). The person who runs the database.

Database diagram. View of a database where you can display database tables and create relationships between foreign and primary keys.

Database management system. Collection of programs that help store, manage, and use the collections of data.

Database window. (1) Interface in Access in which all the components of a database (tables, queries, forms, reports, etc.) can be created and displayed. (2) Displays the various components of an SQL Server database, and provides options for creating additional components.

Datasheet view. A view of a table in which data can be entered, changed, and displayed.

Default.aspx. File for the user interface component of the application.

Default.aspx.vb. File for any Visual Basic programming code that you create for the application.

Dependent table (weak entity). A child table that requires a parent table for identification.

Describe table. Command used to display the column and field names for an existing database.

Design view. (1) Provides an interface that greatly simplifies the design process, particularly with respect to adding server controls and formatting the Web page. (2) Interface in Access where you can visually construct the design for a query rather than writing an SQL statement.

DetailsView. A control similar to a GridView in that it can be used to display rows from a database. The main difference is that a DetailsView control displays a single row whereas a GridView control displays multiple rows.

Determinant. A field, or group of fields, that determines the value of another field.

Disjoint rule. This term simply means that an instance of the supertype may belong to *at most* one subtype category.

Distinct. Option that tells SQL that you want to display each value only once.

Domain. A set of values.

Drop table. Structured query language statement used to remove a table from the database.

Enterprise Manager. Program in SQL Server used to carry out database administration tasks, including creating databases, indexes, and other database objects.

Entity. (1) A person, place, or thing that is being modeled. For example, employees and work locations are both entities. Entities are represented by rectangles. (2) Something about which we want to store data.

Entity integrity. Requires that the designer specify a primary key at the time that the table is created.

Entity relationship diagram (ERD). A diagram containing entities, relationships, and cardinality constraints.

Equi-join (or inner joins). Matching rows between tables based on equality between primary and foreign key values.

Expression Builder. An Access component where a validation rule can be specified.

Field. A single piece of data.

First normal form (1NF). A table in which each field in that table contains single values only.

Foreign keys. Duplicate primary key fields that link the related records between parent and child tables.

Generalization/specialization (supertype/subtype) hierarchy. A structure that consists of a general entity that includes all common attributes along with specialized entities that have the attributes common only to certain instances of the entity.

GridView. A server control that can be used to display data in the form of a table.

Group by. Select statement clause that groups rows based on values in a column.

Having clause. Used to select particular groups (aggregations), rather than single rows, based on a condition.

IN operator. Allows you to select rows based on multiple values for a particular column. Similar to a series of OR conditions.

Inheritance. This term means that any instance of a subtype entity inherits all properties of the supertype, including its attributes and any relationships in which the supertype is involved.

Inner query. Part of the subquery that always executes first, and then the results of this query are used as input to the outer query.

Insert. Structured query language statement used to add a row of data to a table.

Intellisense. An editor feature that monitors what you type and tries to give you options that relate to the objects you are referencing in the statement.

Joining. Relational database operation that combines data from two tables.

Key. A field or set of fields that uniquely identifies a record.

LIKE operator. Operator used in a where clause that allows you to choose rows that share some common characters but are not exactly the same.

Many-to-many relationship. Rows in one table are associated with many rows in the second table, and a row in the second table is associated with many rows in the first table.

Multivalued dependency (MVD). Multivalued dependencies exist only in all-key tables. For one subset of the key, there are multiple instances of another subset of the key. For example, one employee (identified by employee id) may speak multiple languages.

Normal form (NF). Normal forms are rules that allow designers to check for and eliminate data redundancy.

NOT operator. Operator used in a where clause that allows you to reverse the condition.

One-to-many relationship. A row in one table is matched to multiple rows in the second table, and a row in the second table is matched back to one row in the first table.

OR logical operator. Operator used in a where clause that allows you to combine two conditions where rows can meet either condition to be selected.

Order by. SQL clause for a Select statement used to sort results.

Outer query. Query containing the inner query and using the results of that inner query as input.

Overlap rule. This term means that a supertype instance may belong to more than one subtype category.

Partial specialization. When there are some instances of the supertype that do not belong in any of the subtype categories.

Primary key. (1) A field or group of fields whose values uniquely identify each record in a table. (2) The key used to uniquely identify a record in a table.

Primary key button. Toolbar button that can be used to indicate that a column should be treated as a primary key for the table.

Projection. Relational database operation that retrieves a subset of columns.

Query. (1) An SQL Select statement, (2) A component of an Access database that is used to display data.

Query Analyzer. Component in SQL Server used to process queries to retrieve data from tables.

Record. A collection of related data items that are specific to an instance of an entity.

Recursive relationship. Relationship that associates two instances of the same entity (also known as unary relationship).

Referential integrity. Requires that foreign key values must match existing primary key values in the table to which they refer.

Relational database. A database that organizes data into overlapping tables.

Relational database management system (RDBMS). A software application used to implement a relational database.

Relationship. A logical connection between records from two or more tables. All relationships can be categorized as one-to-one, one-to-many, or many-to-many.

Relationships view. View of a database where you can display database tables and create relationships between foreign and primary keys.

Reserved words. Words that cannot be used to name database elements such as tables and columns.

Rollback. Structured query language command used to undo changes made since the last commit.

Script. A series of SQL commands that can be saved and executed in iSQL*Plus.

Select. SQL statement that is used to implement all three relational database operations.

Select * from table. Select is the SQL command used to display data in a database. The * option indicates that all fields should be displayed.

Select table_name from user_tables. Structured query language command used to show all the tables you have created using your Oracle account.

Selection. Relational database operation that retrieves a subset of rows.

Server controls. Dynamic versions of typical HTML components, including textboxes, tables, bullet lists, radio buttons, and list boxes, as well as unique controls that provide additional functionality far beyond that possible with simple HTML tags. These controls handle functions such as validation, data access, login processing, and navigation.

Set echo on. Turns on the display of all information processed in the script when it is executed.

Source view. Provides an interface for writing HTML statements to design an Active Server page.

SQL (structured query language). A standard language for creating and using databases.

SQL view. Interface in Access where the SQL statement generated for the query design is displayed.

SqlDataSource. Server control used for either SQL Server or Oracle databases.

Subqueries. Queries contained inside other queries.

Subtype entity. Specialized entities that have the attributes common only to certain instances of the entity in a supertype/subtype hierarchy.

Supertype entity. The general entity that includes all common attributes in a supertype/subtype hierarchy.

Three-tier architecture. A computing architecture that consists of clients; application servers, which enable business logic; and data servers, which provide data to the application servers.

Total specialization. When all instances of the supertype must belong to at least one subtype category.

Tree pane. Area that shows the structure of your SQL Server environment.

Validation rule. A setting for a column where you can specify a condition that data values must conform to when being inserted into the column.

View. A subset derived from the base tables. Views enable the DBA to restrict the portion of the database visible to each user.

Web Developer. A complex development environment that includes a variety of powerful tools to create a wide range of Web application projects.

Web Form. An HTML document that includes basic static HTML tags and server controls.

Web site. Basically, a directory in which all the files associated with the Web application are stored.

Where clause. SQL clause for a Select statement used to choose particular rows based on a condition.

Workspace. The interface in Oracle iSQL*Plus for typing all SQL commands and viewing their results.